The Timeless Texture

of

The Book of Revelation

WHAT PEOPLE ARE SAYING ABOUT THIS BOOK

The average Christian who reads the book of Revelation often finds it difficult to keep in mind the structure of the whole book. There is a range of discourses to consider for the interpretation and meaning of individual passages. Stephen's comprehensive study provides the kind of in-depth view that will encourage the lay person, as well as the specialist, to better understand this seemingly difficult book.

His work is an excellent tool that combines a linguistic analysis of the discourses in Revelation with a precise theological exegesis. It also demonstrates the wide-ranging semantic structure inherent in the book. Stephen presents Jesus as the main topic of the book, and the revelation of the mysteries in the book are about Him, as he makes plain throughout this study.

There are excellent charts and cross-references throughout. I would recommend it for any person who wishes to study the book of Revelation in depth.

Karl J. Franklin, PhD, DHL. *Fellow at the Pike Center for Integrated Scholarship. Translator for two New Testaments, Linguistics Consultant, and Co-Founder of GIAL (now Dallas International University).*

This is a thorough and well-documented study of the book of Revelation. The charts and other supplemental material were very helpful. I highly recommend this book for laypersons and pastors alike. It will deepen your understanding of the end times and will provide encouragement for followers of Christ, as you more fully see God's timeless plans for humanity.

Stephen Campbell, BA, JD. *Attorney and Life-long Bible Student.*

As someone who has been preaching from Revelation for over 50 years, I have always been drawn to its importance, and to its relevance for a mature level of Christian discipleship.

So I welcome Stephen's book, as it gives an analysis of the whole of Revelation, which demonstrates its unity, which I have found refreshingly different. It is academically weighty, but the layout is clear, which will make it very helpful for those who want to look at it again, and preach on its total, timeless message. Most important is the emphasis that Revelation is about Jesus and the need to constantly focus on Him.

Rev. Jeremy Anderson, BSc, BCTS. *A seasoned minister of God's Word, having served for five decades in five different dioceses of the Church of England.*

A comprehensive reference book - the truths trapped inside are worth releasing.

Charles Palmquist *who was devouring Revelation at the age of 17, has been fascinated by the mysteries in this book ever since, and is still panning for gold as he is preparing to write his own book about his discoveries.*

The Book of Revelation is one of the Bible's most complex texts, but Stephen leads us with great skill down an unusual path to help us better understand exactly what the author intends to say.

So, this book, with the help of 70 charts, takes us on a meticulous journey of analyzing the complete linguistic structure of the book of Revelation. As a result the author teases out mysteries and treasures often missed in traditional commentaries.

The interesting conclusion is that Revelation is not a fearsome tome of judgments, condemnation, and wrath, but a revelation of Hope. The subject is Jesus the Saviour, in His various forms of Lion, Lamb, King, Bridegroom, and He is the timeless Ruler over all things through whom God's plan of Judgment and Salvation is initiated and enacted. He it is who ensures the complete elimination of evil, and the establishment of a solid present hope and of a glorious future destination for His followers

The call to all is to Repent. The choice is imperative. Then, hang in there, keep close, trust the invested blood of the Lamb to fulfill His promise and establish His victory in this Global War. "The King is coming!". And so, with the sound of the trumpets still ringing in our ears, a new indescribable cycle begins. Omega returns to Alpha for one last time.

Joye Knauf Alit *A life-long follower of the Lamb, pioneer missionary, intercessor extraordinaire, international author and teacher, and founder of Jubilate Ministries.*

Any future work on Revelation will need to take account of what is in this book.

The Timeless Texture

of

The Book of Revelation

A Holistic Discourse Analysis

Stephen J. Schooling

SEVEN STARS
PUBLICATIONS

Your Word shows me the way to go,
and reveals the path in front of me.
Psalm 119:105

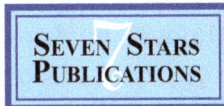

The Timeless Texture of the Book of Revelation
A Holistic Discourse Analysis

Published by : Seven Stars Publications, Queensland, Australia.

National Library of Australia Cataloguing-in-Publication Entry :

Creator: Schooling, Stephen J., 1951- ; Author.
Title: **The Timeless Texture of the Book of Revelation**
A Holistic Discourse Analysis

ISBN: 978-1-7641747-0-1 (hardcover)
ISBN: 978-1-7641747-1-8 (e-book)
ISBN: 978-1-7641747-2-5 (abridged edition)

Subjects:
Language and Linguistics
Philosophy and Religion

Other Subjects Included in the Discussion:
The Book of Revelation
Discourse Analysis
Jesus the Messiah
Biblical Studies
How to Live in Difficult Times
The Structure of Hebrew Writings
Mysteries
The Church
Eschatology
The End Times
Postmillenialism
Biblical Prophecy
The New Creation
Covenant Theology
Repentance and Perseverance

Cover, Photographs and Other Credits
Copy Editor : Joanna Schooling
Layout Advisor : Joanna Schooling
Cover Design : Andrea Schooling
Author's Photograph : Andrea Schooling

The Seven Stars : Andrea Schooling
The Rider on the White Horse : Andrea Schooling
Hebrew Textiles : AI produced from input by the author
The Robin Needlework : Lois Coulson and the author
The Kadavumbhagam Ernakulam Malabar Jewish Synagogue :
Robin Klein, CC BY-SA 4.0
The Arrival of Jews in Cochin, India : work of art, public domain
The Lion and the Lamb : Lyn Graham and the author
The Menorah : AI produced from input by the author
The Scrolls :AI produced from input by the author
The Way Forward : AI produced from input by the author
St. George and the dragon, by Alexander von Bensa,
work of art, artist died 1902, public domain
All other photographs and graphics : the author

All English translations of biblical texts have been provided by the author.

Inquiries :
All inquiries, including copyright inquiries, review copy inquiries, book order inquiries and any feed-back, questions, or comments for the author :
seven_stars_publications@protonmail.com

I

acknowledge with much appreciation,
the contribution made to the final stage of this thirty year project,
by the following people.

*T*hank *Y*ou

Janice,
Joanna,
Andrea,
Joye,
Karl,
Jeremy,
Doug,
Steve,
Charles

and, above all,

The One

without whose help nothing would be possible.

This
Book
of
Mysteries
is
Unreservedly Dedicated to
the
One
who
has
the
7
stars
held
in
His
Right Hand

JC

PREFACE TO THIS 2025 EDITION

The roots of the study which will be presented in the following pages go back to the 1980's. The research for it was accomplished during the 1990's and the original edition was produced in 2004. This was a dissertation presented to Trinity College, which is part of the University of Bristol in the UK, for the degree of Doctor of Philosophy in Biblical Studies.

When the research for this study was undertaken, the branch of linguistics which has become known as Discourse Analysis was still in its infancy. It had different proponents who developed different methods which took the discipline in different directions. So now, some thirty years later, it is perhaps time to review the progress which has been made, and to assess the fruitfulness and usefulness of the different methods. At the same time, it would be appropriate to consider also, what unexpected insights have been discovered as a result of these attempts to view the Bible as a linguistic artifact first and foremost, considering only the data provided by the author himself

The starting point was ground-breaking instruction received from Robert Longacre, John and Kathleen Callow and others. This was followed by a lengthy trial of their methodologies on the shorter books of The Song of Solomon and the Minor Prophets, before venturing into the lengthier linguistic mine field of the book of Revelation. Those early studies were undertaken in order to teach classes in Bethel Bible Institute, Bethesda Bible College and the Crossroads Bible Institute in New Caledonia. This anecdotal material turns out, in the end, to be of considerable significance. This is because a considerable awareness of Hebrew discourse characteristics was developed as a result of those wide ranging investigations on a variety of styles by different authors.

In the first instance then, this study demonstrates that this particular approach to Discourse Analysis is extremely fruitful in providing insights into a complex discourse like the book of Revelation. These insights are far-ranging, and the results which have been produced can justifiably claim to be complete, coherent and comprehensive. This is because it uncovered structures and arrangements which had not been previously recognized, and also managed to resolve all the known difficulties and anomalies concerning which, no meaningful consensus had previously been reached.

To my knowledge even twenty years later, this achievement has not yet been replicated. Nonetheless, I extend my apologies to any analysts out there whose work I have not yet managed to find.

This is one of the reasons then, that the work has finally been accomplished to make this analysis of the structure of Revelation more readily available to those interested in such things. As a result, it is our hope that it will bring greater insight into, and better understanding of this important book. The advantage of a methodological study like this one, which is based on clear principles, is that it is repeatable. This means that it is possible to re-visit the same data using the same methodology. In this way consensus can be built up and this present work can be improved if needs be.

However, there is another reason. Even though this study was based on the Greek text of Revelation, once it was complete, and especially with hindsight, it was noticeable that it was very Hebraic in nature. This was an unexpected insight which was made possible because of the work done previously, in applying the same Discourse Analysis methods to texts from the Old Testament, as mentioned above.

Consequently, it was at the same time a surprise, but yet not a surprise, to discover some time later that Hebrew versions of Revelation not only existed, but that the linguistic evidence suggested that at least one of them was quite probably the original version. This then would totally explain the Hebraic flavor of the Greek version. This is because, at the higher levels of a discourse, which were the subject of this analysis of Revelation, these features transfer over quite naturally into a translation. So the same features are present in the Greek, and also in the English, but it is quite possible to overlook their significance, if the analyst is not aware of them and is not particularly looking for them.

One of the corollary insights provoked by the Hebraic format of Revelation's structure is that it is cyclic and not linear, which means in turn that it is timeless in nature, and not limited to one period of time, whether past or future. In any case, the insights gained from a study such as this one are also timeless, to the extent that they come close to discerning the truth of the matter in view. Then, since truth is timeless and never goes out of date, any such presentation of truth remains timeless and of value to any reader, regardless of how much time may have elapsed between the beginning of the process and its end.

This then is another reason why it was considered appropriate to make an updated version of this research available to a wider audience. So the goals of this present version have been expanded. Once the technical analysis of the book has been completed, we will take a little time at the end to explore in more detail some of the implications of the Hebraic aspects of this book.

In these present times the message of Revelation continues to intrigue, but also to baffle, our modern day readers who face an increasing range of challenges in the world around them. It is to be hoped then that these timeless truths will contribute considerably to a greater level of faith in a great God, and a greater level of hope that His plans for good will indeed be accomplished. From that foundation may there be developed also an increased level of strength to endure hardship, and a positive perseverance which presses on to victory.

These reflections are presented then to you, the reader, with this express wish and prayer that you will be blessed and encouraged by this journey of discovery, which we will take together through this amazing book.

Here's wishing you every blessing on this journey.

Stephen Schooling
Brisbane, 2025

TABLE OF CONTENTS

APPENDIX 2

CHAPTER 3

APPENDIX 3

Ancillary Information Pertaining to the Analysis of the Seven Cycles 168

CHAPTER 4

Topics, Themes and Interludes 190

APPENDIX 4

Ancillary Information Pertaining to the Analysis of the Interludes 238

CHAPTER 5

The Seven Cycles Revisited 245

APPENDIX 5

Ancillary Information Pertaining to the Analysis of the Seven Cycles 320

CHAPTER 6

Prominence: the Mountains and Valleys of Text 337

APPENDIX 6

CHAPTER 7a

The Proof of the Analysis: 421
The Harmony of the Macro Structure, the Topic and the Sub-Topics

CHAPTER 7b

The Proof of the Analysis: 481
The Harmony of the Macro Structure and the Micro Structure

CHAPTER 8

Table of Charts

***Apply** yourself to studying*
all of God's Word.
***Aim** to be well qualified, so that*
you may stand before Him,
completely unashamed.
***Aspire** to know how to cut through*
to the heart of the matter,
when it comes to
deciding what is true,
and what is not.

(A dynamic, expanded translation of 2 Timothy 2:15-16a)

A STUDY GUIDE

This book is intentionally very complete and covers a lot of ground. One reason is because it aims to cater for the interests of a wide range of readers. For this reason, it may well not be a book which you would want to read from cover to cover, to begin with at least. Instead, you may just prefer to search in it for the precise details which are of interest to you. For this reason, this Study Guide has been prepared in order to help you to quickly find the information which is the most useful to you.

1. Bible Translators and Commentators

Chapters 1-6 will be of the most interest to you, since all the detail of the structure of the book, along with its supporting argumentation, will be found here. The description which you will find acknowledges and builds on what has gone before. Yet at the same time it breaks new ground by suggesting proposals for resolving the outstanding issues, and by describing features, which have not previously been recognized.

Chapters 7-8 will also be of secondary interest because they deal with many lower level features and provide the proof of the preceding analysis. They also deal in more depth with the topic of the book as well as its purpose. In particular, a full description of the Hebraic characteristics of the structure of the book will be found at Chapter 8.1.

In addition, all the Appendices provide extra technical detail, which is designed just for you. This includes extensive interaction with previous generations of commentators, which shows how this work both builds on, and improves, the insights which they contributed in their day.

2. Pastors, Preachers and Bible Teachers

For you, I would like to draw your attention to all the Charts which you will find scattered throughout this book. Most of these provide an outline which can be used to kick start a sermon or a classroom session. By using these charts as a starting point, it would be possible to preach through the whole of Revelation without leaving anything important out.

Since one of the goals of this book is to remind us that Revelation is timeless and, therefore, relevant to every generation of Christians, then these charts are a significant way of helping us all achieve that goal.

You might like to follow this up by consulting Chapters 7-8 which provide extensive supplementary information concerning the topic and the sub-topics of the book. Chapter 5 explains the elegant parallel arrangement of the book, and Chapter 6 will help you find the most important parts of its timeless message.

In addition, you will also find a lot of information in these latter chapters, which highlights why, and how, the message of Revelation is edifying for Christians of all ages and all generations, especially those going through difficult times.

3. Serious Bible Students of Any Age

For you, it will depend on your interests. If you are interested in structures and outlines, then Chapters 1-6, along with all their charts, will be the place to start. If you are interested in the topic of the book and its themes, then Chapter 4 is the place to start, supplemented by Chapter 7.

To kick start your studies, you may want to look straight away at the charts which contain the outline of the book as a whole. A simplified version to start with, will be found in Chart 1, and complete versions will be found in Charts 47a and b. These important charts are bolded in the Table of Charts.

If you would like to know what the metaphorical meaning of the Seals, Trumpets and Bowls is, then take a look at Chapter 5.6

4. Disciples of Jesus

For those of you who are most concerned about finding out more about Jesus, and the amazing things which Revelation has to say about Him, then start with Chapters 6.8 and 8.6.

For an extensive description of Jesus the Messiah, and what He can mean for you, please take an unhurried journey through the sub-topics of the book which concern Him, as described in Chapter 7.3, and 7.4.

For more detailed instruction on how to be best aligned with His plans for your life, and with His ways of working, have a good look at the Seven Letters, as described in Chapter 7.5 and 7.6. To find out about God's plan for the followers of the Lamb, have a good look as well at Chapter 5.5 through to Chapter 5.7

5. Hebrew and Old Testament Specialists

There is something for everyone in this book, even for the OT specialists. This is because one of the keys to understanding Revelation is in understanding that it is a Hebraic work, which was possibly first written in Hebrew.

The fine detail of the Hebrew nature of the structure of the book is described in the technical analysis of the book, which is to be found in

Chapters 1-6. Following that, some of the implications of the Hebraic aspects of this book, will be developed in Chapter 8. In particular, a full description of the Hebraic discourse features can be found in Chapter 8.1.

Most of the structural charts to be found throughout, also illustrate many facets of the linguistic organization which are typical of the Hebrew language.

6. Christians Going Through Hard Times

The book of Revelation is not all doom and gloom as some have been led to believe. On the contrary, it has a very positive message about the calling and destiny of Christians throughout all the ages. It does not sanitize the difficulties of life, but it explains why this has to happen, in order to comfort and encourage us.

Then, in addition, it shows us how to learn to be an overcomer in, and through, those difficulties. The best place to look for this kind of information is in Chapters 4 and 7, and especially 7.4 through 7.6.

Chapter 6.4.1 explains why bad things may still happen to good people. Complementary to that, Chapter 6.4.2 through to 6.4.6 sets out in some detail the overall purpose of the visions which John received.

This will help you see what God's plan is, and how He intends for the hard times to help you grow strong in the seasons of life. There are also some helpful hints as to how that can be put into practice.

7. For Everyone

As we have said before, there is something for everyone to be found in this book. It is probable that anyone who has tried to read or study the book of Revelation before, will automatically want to get some insights into the complexities of its structural outline.

If you are impatient to learn more about how the author himself intentionally organized his book, then you will find a simplified overview of its structure at the end of Chapter 1, in Chart 1.

If you want to see all the detail, and how it all so elegantly fits together, then you will find this at the beginning of Chapter 7, in Charts 47a and 47b, which, in this present version of the analysis, have been considerably expanded, and made easier to read.

For the convenience of everyone, the most important charts are shown in bold print in the Table of Charts which begins on page x above.

A WORD OF WISDOM

The central idea of this volume is the insistence that the structure of a part of a text needs to be explained in light of the structure of the whole. This thesis needs to be repeated anew to every generation of linguistics students as a warning against analytic nearsightedness – the fixation on particular parts of a text without regard to the whole. Holistic Discourse Analysis is not a plea to abandon the analysis of lower levels of grammar, but to enrich the study of them by putting them in broader perspective.

Robert E. Longacre and Shin Ja J. Hwang
(2012)

CHAPTER 1

Introductory Issues - What is This Book All About?

1.1 Introduction : Clearing the Way

The book of Revelation is perhaps the most fascinating and yet the most frustrating book in the whole Bible. Generations of scholars have been drawn to plumb its depths and yet none have completely done it justice and many have given up hope of fully coming to terms with the complexity of the structure which underlies it.

Charles 1920,xiii considered that the teaching of the book was an ‘unintelligible mystery’ due to the rearrangement of the text imposed by a later editor. Twenty years later Lenski 1943,24-5 declared ‘we frankly give up the attempt to divide this book in an ordinary way’. Then, some fifty years later again, Bauckham 1993,1 summarized his findings by stating that ‘the major literary study of Revelation which will do justice to it has yet to be written’.

So how then does one react to such categorical assessments of the situation? The answer, I think, can be derived from the book itself, namely, by putting into practice the two primary commands which are presented in the opening chapters: these are the exhortations to repent and to persevere!

> **QUOTE**
>
> **The diverse proposals are a maze of interpretive confusion**
>
> **Beale 1999,108**

Since this book is being written by a Bible translator to help today’s translators and other interested parties, let’s take a moment to do some translation. The word ‘repent’ is not a word which is commonly used in everyday speech any more. So what would be a better, more up-to-date equivalent? Traditionally, it is often explained as being a change of mind, based on the Greek, but actually its roots go back at least to the Hebrew. The Hebrews were more holistic in their outlook and for them to repent was a visceral process, which affected, and involved, every part of their being. So on that basis, we suggest that a better, twenty-first century translation would be ***‘to change your worldview’.*** The importance of this brief aside will become clear shortly, and will become even clearer as we progress through this study of Revelation.

So then, let’s make an effort to adjust our worldview to what the authors of this book want to communicate to us. After that, let’s keep on persevering as well.

Having accomplished that little, practical exercise we can now go back to considering the implications of the statements presented at the beginning. The authors of the above quotations assume that books of this nature can normally be assessed, analyzed and appreciated. Therefore, by the same token this one is a bit unusual in that respect. This implies, in turn, that traditional methods previously used in biblical studies, have not yet been sufficiently relevant to crack the code of Revelation. It implies also that the analysts, who have approached this book from their point of view, have clearly not made a connection with the author of the book, and so have been unable to perceive it from his point of view.

Despite the rather negative ethos of the statements, these assumptions nonetheless point us, who are following on behind, in a positive direction. There is no doubt that historically speaking, generations of scholars have provided the Body of Christ with a huge corpus of insights into the various books of the Bible, including Revelation itself.

So there is an existing foundation of work which can be fruitfully built upon, if we are willing to honestly face the past and also to look with confidence into the future. If we can courageously consider the pieces of the puzzle which are still missing, then it may be possible to address those outstanding issues in a more complete and coherent fashion.

From a linguistic point of view, any discourse, however long and complex that it may be, must, of necessity, have a coherent underlying structure, otherwise it could not exist. If then, we exercise our faith in order to believe ahead of time that the structure exists, then the process of discovery can continue. For, clearly, the ones who seek by faith will eventually find what they are looking for. This is the advantage of a linguistic approach to a complex book such as this one.

Before developing that thought any further let's consider briefly the other assumptions implied by the statements which we are considering. What is often overlooked in biblical studies is that studying the books of the Bible is a cross-cultural enterprise. Everybody, whoever they may be, has a worldview derived from the culture they grew up in. This is inevitable and unavoidable. As a consequence, we all approach any enterprise which we undertake, from the perspective imposed upon us by our native **worldview.**

However, in biblical studies our goal is to try and understand a text written by a person emanating from a completely different culture, and influenced by a completely different worldview. This means that a distinct and conscious effort needs to be made to appreciate and accommodate the author's worldview, and by the same token, to refrain from imposing our worldview on his discourse. This has not always been accomplished in the past so there is room for improvement in this domain as well.

Finally, in this review of assumptions there is the question of authorship and the context of the book. It is assumed by most commentators that the apostle John is the author of the book, and this present study also often refers to him as such. It has always been recognized that Jesus is involved in the authorship especially when the Prologue is under the microscope, but it is rarely fully recognized that He is the rightful author of the book from start to finish, and that John was only the delivery boy.

DEFINITION

A person's ***worldview*** is produced by everything which has affected and shaped their life. It is the combined effect of the influence exerted on them by their up-bringing, education, belief systems, cultural norms, expectations, geographic location, personal experiences and so on.

Everyone has a worldview although most people, who have not been significantly impacted by a different culture, are usually unaware of it. Yet our worldview determines to a large extent how we view life, how we relate to people, how we understand what read, and how we interpret what we experience and what other people say to us.

Both of them were Hebrews by human birth and by culture, and this in and of itself, requires any subsequent reader to recognize that Revelation was therefore, of necessity, written from the viewpoint of a Hebraic worldview. This fact remains true regardless of whether the book was originally written in Greek or originally written in Hebrew, for an author's worldview will always show through, even in a work written in a different language. But what is more important, is that the context of other things that the author, Jesus, said and had recorded for posterity, ought to be included in the discussion, for when this is done it is usually very insightful and fruitful.

So, as it happens, there are some things which Jesus said while on earth, as recorded in Matthew 13:9-17, which are repeated in very similar forms in his speeches in Revelation. The first is the well-known phrase: 'he who has ears to hear let him hear'. This phrase is only used once in this particular discourse as recorded in the Gospels, which is significant, but it is repeated seven times in Revelation with the only differences being the plural or singular form of the noun 'ears', and the tense of the verb 'to hear'. It thus forms a lexical chain – or, in more accurate terms, a lexical thread – which runs through the book.

The second is the blessing Jesus pronounced in verse 16 on those who had ears to hear, which is very similar to one of the seven blessings in Revelation. But most important of all, is the word translated 'mysteries' or 'secrets' in verse 11, which, again, only occurs once in this explanatory discussion with the disciples, as recorded in the synoptic Gospels. The context is very precise: the secret mysteries concern the Kingdom of God and Jesus explains that it is only given to certain people to understand them, which is why He taught using parables.

This context turns out to be very important for a proper understanding of Revelation because the word ***'secret mysteries'*** not only re-occurs in the book but also forms another word chain. The whole book, in effect, is all about these secrets concerning the Kingdom of God or, in other words, the reign of God over the earth through the Lamb and His followers, just as Matthew 13 was. Furthermore, the whole of the book is also couched in symbolic language and pictures based on concepts which earth-bound human beings could understand, just as Jesus' parables were. This is no surprise because it is the same speaker and teacher with the same goals in view.

It becomes clear then, in the light of the explanation given by Jesus Himself in Matthew, that not everyone can understand these secrets. In order to do so one must align oneself with the attitude of the disciples of the Gospels, and to have the same relationship with Jesus as they did. This overlooked piece of the puzzle may explain why some people do not seem to get a grip on Revelation. By the same token, coming to terms with these proprietary conditions concerning the Kingdom and its King, may be a key, which will unlock its secrets for those who have ears to hear, a receptive heart, and a preexisting willingness to put the King's instructions into practice.

This brief survey of the assumptions underlying the challenge of understanding this book and of delineating its outline, reveals that Revelation has a certain texture which has to be grappled with, if this challenge is to be taken on successfully. The word 'texture' implies already that its composition is complex and has many aspects or threads, and this is certainly the case for Revelation. But in order to clear the way and to give us something to aim for, we are proposing here to describe this texture primarily as being timeless. Timeless, because this discussion reminds us that the book is about the Kingdom of God and its King. Both this entity and this person are, by their very nature, timeless. If that is the case, then everything about its message should be timeless as well, and therefore, relevant to every generation of reader/listeners.

It is a challenge, but certainly worth a try. If the truths which we will discover are timeless and, therefore, of crucial relevance and importance for everyone of us, then surely it is worth the effort to take up this challenge. So, on my side, I will do my best to explain what I have understood about these mysteries and how they have been communicated, but it will be the task of every reader to open their ears and to align their hearts to fully receive this message from the Timeless King.

The purpose of this study, therefore, is firstly to examine the organization of this complex book from a linguistic point of view. The goal will be to discern the structural devices which the author of Revelation used to guide his audience through the maze of parables, visions, numbers and symbols to an understanding of the message he wished to communicate to them. This task, since it is complex and foundational to everything else, will occupy our attention for most of the time throughout the next few chapters. However, later on, we will come round full circle to this topic of Jesus the King and the timeless nature of His Kingdom.

The ultimate purpose of the book is to help its readers make good decisions so that they can benefit from the blessings of this Kingdom. Consequently, any discussion of its message should attempt to accomplish this goal as well, otherwise it would be missing the point. So an attempt will be made to earth the theory in the practical implications, and to demonstrate how the organization of the book must, of necessity, influence an understanding of its message. The purpose of building a house is not just to create a structure, but so that people can live in it. The purpose of applying linguistic principles to elucidate the structure of a discourse, as we shall be doing here, is so that people can benefit by better understanding its message.

1.2 Methodology : How Do We Go About It ?

Such a study has become more feasible in recent decades due to the emergence of the discipline of linguistics at the beginning of the twentieth century. This development, in turn, gave birth to the sub-discipline of Discourse Analysis (also known as Text-Linguistics) in the last quarter of the century. However, in more recent times another term has been coined by Robert Longacre 2012 in his most recent book entitled ***Holistic Discourse Analysis.*** This is because the discipline of Discourse Analysis has developed in different directions and the term no longer means exactly the same thing to everybody.

This present study then is, more specifically, a ***holistic*** study of the book of Revelation. In common with most other views of discourse analysis, this approach views text primarily as a linguistic phenomenon and analyzes it using linguistic tools and assumptions. These tools and assumptions were originally developed as a result of studying a wide variety of the world's languages and were only subsequently applied to biblical texts.

However, there is one basic assumption that the proponents of holistic discourse analysis hold to above all else. This is that any discourse, whether it be orally or textually transmitted, should be studied in its entirety and in the form received from its author. In addition, they consider that the data should be interpreted within its context and be allowed to speak for itself without having inappropriate worldviews, or preconceived systems of interpretation, imposed upon it. Thirdly, this approach assumes that all complete discourses have a structure, that this structure can be discovered by appropriate analysis, and that an awareness of the structure contributes directly to an appropriate understanding of the message.

The analysis of the organization of Revelation which will be presented in this study was developed on the basis of the above assumptions and by using several different linguistic tools. In practice, the tools which proved to be the most useful were those which focus primarily on the semantic structure of the text (i.e. the meaning-based relationships between propositions and groups of propositions, Callow 1998) and those which focus on parallel structures (i.e. a holistic viewpoint which discerns relationships between parts of the text which may in fact be discontinuous, Parunak 1981 and 1983). This approach to analysis is practical in nature rather than theoretical, that is, it is not focused exclusively on one particular theory. Its value was independently confirmed by Parunak's own experience (Parunak 1992). He also found that an eclectic approach to methodology was the most fruitful and he also found that the two methods cited above are two of the three which were the most useful for him.

These two approaches were guided and informed by some universal principles which will be outlined below.

This methodology has certain advantages over its predecessors at both the conceptual and the practical level. At the conceptual level Revelation is firstly a written representation of a particular language and, as such, it is a linguistic phenomenon built up incrementally out of phonemes, graphemes, morphemes, lexemes and units of the higher orders of discourse. It is only subsequently that it can be considered to be, for example, a literary, a rhetorical, or a theological phenomenon. Consequently, this methodology puts the priority on studying the book, in the first instance, as a linguistic entity using linguistic presuppositions, hypotheses and tools as its essential components. At the same time it does not discount the value of other methods of study, but it does assume that the other methods of study should be applied at a later stage and should take account of the insights previously provided by the process of linguistic analysis. This avoids the methodological danger of imposing a viewpoint derived from other sources on something which is, in its essence, a linguistic entity, thereby running the risks of both deforming the structure and of misunderstanding the content of the original message.

This separation of analysis from interpretation and application was rigorously applied to this study. Consequently, the first seven chapters of this book will only develop the analytical issues, with almost no further comment. The question of how the results of the analysis should influence our subsequent interpretation was developed as a separate phase, some time later. The results of this phase of reflection will be found in Chapter 8.

On a practical level, the linguistic methodology has the advantage of being repeatable, refutable and improvable. Since the raw material is the text as it stands, any other analyst can work with the same data. Since the linguistic tools have been described in various places, as noted in Appendix A1, and are applicable in principle to any language, they are recoverable and testable on the same or different data. This means that any hypotheses presented can be reviewed and refined.

The Greek text used as a basis for this study was the 27th edition of the Nestlé-Aland text edited by Aland et al. 1993. The English glosses are personal translations. Both for practical reasons, and also as an experiment to see what could be accomplished by using a purely linguistic methodology, the evidence for the analysis (apart from some external, supporting influences which are mentioned in section 1.3.3 below) was drawn entirely from within the Greek text cited above. To accommodate a broad readership, the Greek alphabet will not be used when the Greek text is cited, but a transliteration of the words in the Roman alphabet.

1.3 Getting to Grips with Technical Terms and Concepts

Like any discipline, linguistics functions on the basis of a number of universal concepts which eventually became so widely accepted that they function as presuppositions. The universals underlying this study are primarily those systematized by K. Pike and listed in Pike and Pike 1982,1-5. A number of these, which are particularly relevant to understanding the explanations presented in the following chapters, will be reviewed below.

1.3.1 The Concept of Hierarchy

The concept of ***hierarchy*** formalizes the insight that languages operate at several levels at the same time. It is because of this inherent, multi-level complexity that language is such a flexible and dynamic tool of communication. However, for the same reason, it is difficult to analyze and to explain exactly how it works. The way forward is to separate out the levels

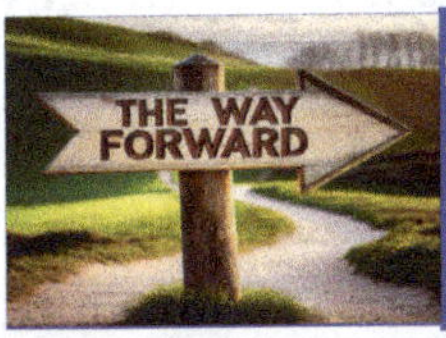

SEPARATE out the levels in the hierarchy and STUDY them separately.

in the hierarchy and to study them individually before trying to understand how they relate to each other.

Having said that, however, the relationship between the different levels can already be stated in general terms, because the linguistic units which belong together on one level, usually function as constituents of the next higher level in the hierarchy. For example, in the case of Revelation, the highest possible level in the hierarchy is the book as a whole. Following a principle of well-formed discourses, the book is organized in its most basic form, into three main parts, namely a beginning (setting/introduction), a middle (body) and an end (conclusion). To say that a discourse has a beginning, middle and an end is so obvious as to be a truism. However, it is often wise to start by stating the obvious so that the less obvious observations can be built onto a solid foundation. The Introduction and the Conclusion of Revelation at the book level, have traditionally been called the Prologue and Epilogue, and so these terms will be retained in the more specific discussion to facilitate communication. Chapter and verse references will not be given in this section, but will be found in the following chapters.

The body, being the most complex of these three units, is, in its turn, composed of a series of units which, in the case of this study, will be called ***Cycles.*** This term was chosen with care in order that it may have some descriptive value and thereby facilitate better communication. It is intentionally based on the use of this term within the discipline of literary criticism. In this case, it refers to a series of distinct literary works (or discourses) which have similar form and content and are considered to form a distinct grouping of discourses. In the case of play cycles, the constituent dramas were usually performed in a series, and taken as a group communicated a message more vast and complex than any one of the dramas taken alone. In addition, the term intentionally implies that these units are cyclic in nature as they combine both elements of repetition and elements of linear progression. Taken as a group they create a spiral progression from near the beginning of the book through to the end.

It is recognized that this preview of the Cycles assumes a lot concerning the ultimate conclusions, which may be open to debate, but the purpose here is simply to prepare the way for the future argumentation. It can also be noted that the most recent of all commentaries at the time of the original writing up of this research, Beale 1999,141, comes down heavily in favor of recapitulation as an organizing principle of the book.

The cycles in their turn are composed of paragraphs and groups of paragraphs. For the sake of simplicity however, the constituents of the cycles will be called sections in this study. Since each cycle is dominated by a particular motif (e.g. letters, seals, trumpets etc.) it is also convenient to identify the section under consideration in terms of its place in the series of seven (e.g. the first letter, the second seal etc.).

Finally, the concept of hierarchy gives rise to the concept of ***embedding.*** In other words, patterns which occur at one level of the hierarchy in any given text may reoccur on a different scale at other levels. So, for example, a book as a whole may be a narrative, but embedded narratives may also occur as constituents of the lower levels of the discourse.

The concept of hierarchy is important for a study of Revelation because it contributes to a better appreciation of the function of ***the Narrative Framework*** in the book as a whole. This important feature will be discussed in detail in due course, and a discussion of its various features will be found in Chapter 2.

1.3.2 Units and Patterns

An insight into language which is widely accepted is that discourses are composed of constituent units. In this study the terms '***unit***' and '***sub-unit***' will be used generically to designate various components of the structure according to the context.

It is this linguistic assumption which lies behind the creation of an outline of a biblical book. However, another linguistic assumption, which is not so widely recognized, is that these units are also intentionally placed together in groups and relate to one another in patterns. Consequently, as well as discerning unit boundaries it is also possible to discern groupings of units and describe their relationship to one another, and a balance has to be maintained between these two processes.

DEFINITION

A Template

is a particular use of words or a particular pattern of paragraphs, which create an expectation in the reader's mind concerning what may follow on later in the discourse. An expectation may be derived from general knowledge. So, when John talks about writing to the 'churches', the reader will automatically assume that he is writing to people, even though the people are not specifically mentioned. The number 'seven' is rooted more specifically in Hebraic culture and creates an expectation that the author is talking about something which is complete. A series of seven letters, followed by a series of seven seals, and then by seven trumpets, creates the expectation that more such groups may follow. Such a template is specific to its own particular discourse.

Templates are also known as ***expectation patterns.***

It must be understood that patterns definitely need to be established at the beginning of a discourse. This intentional organization on the part of an author creates a kind of ***template*** which enables the reader to know what to expect in the text which follows.

However, at the same time, it also needs to be said that, once established, patterns are not fixed features of the discourse. On the contrary, they are fluid and can be changed, or intentionally left incomplete, to produce a variation on a theme. Therefore, even the absence of a particular pattern, in a context where it might otherwise be expected, can be interpreted as an intentional organizational feature.

This phenomenon of establishing a pattern and then repeating it with variations or as an incomplete pattern is a universal which goes beyond language. It is a dominant feature in music and also occurs in other artistic disciplines. It can also be remarked that a non-response in the context of a conversation is a type of response, just as a non-decision in the context of an authority structure, is also a type of decision. See Callow 1998,329 for a selection of examples of 'meanings...expressed by a zero in a known pattern' at the clause level.

DEFINITION

Etic data is raw data which can be drawn randomly from any appropriate source. So, in Phon-**etics,** the sounds (phones) being studied may be drawn from any language in the world

Emic data is the same kind of data but drawn only from a particular closed system. So, in Phon-**emics,** only the sounds which are used to distinguish different words in a given language are studied.

A fundamental theoretical issue which has guided Pike's insights into language and all those who have followed him, are the related concepts of ***'etic'*** and ***'emic'***. In general terms, data viewed etically is data viewed from the outside and is described in terms of its external characteristics. Data viewed emically is data viewed from within a particular system, and is described according to the constraints imposed on it by its position and function within that system.

A goods train could be taken as an example. To a casual observer standing on a bridge, the train is apparently a random string of wagons. It can be observed that some of these wagons are the same, or of a similar type, whereas others are different and possibly unique. These wagons can also be counted and their order described. This is an 'etic' and relatively superficial view of the train. What the train manager knows, however, is that the presence, placement, and ordering of the wagons are not at all random. The grouping of the wagons is determined by their destination, and the number and type of wagons used is determined by the merchandise ordered by the clients for that particular trip. This additional awareness of the overall plan and internal organization of the train permits the observer to have a more 'emic' view of its structure.

This means that when analyzing a discourse, it is not sufficient to create a string, or a list, of its constituent units as this would just be an etic view of the data. The concept of a pattern also needs to make a contribution. The patterns being used by an author in any particular discourse need to guide the analyst's understanding of the various units and their role in the overall system. This will produce a more systematized, or emic, description of the structure. It is this emic nature of a discourse which produces its particular texture. This texture which is specific to the discourse in question, influences an understanding of the whole discourse, and cannot be disassociated from it.

Finally, before leaving the question of units and patterns it should be noticed that individual units have to be connected together in order to form patterns. It is only a small step from here to remark that those connections can be made in a variety of ways, ranging from very loose to very tight connections. This is important for an understanding of the structure of Revelation because at some strategic points, the major units of the book are so tightly connected that they could be described as having overlap joints. This phenomenon creates difficulties when division into units alone is in view, but the problem can be overcome when the same data is seen in the context of the cohesion, created when units are viewed as functioning in an emic pattern.

1.3.3 Cultures and Contexts

Another of Pike's universals is that 'speech does not occur in a cultural or conceptual vacuum, but is relative to...***a universe of discourse***' (Pike and Pike 1982,5, their emphasis). This universe of discourse can be a specific one, relevant only to the book as a total unit, or it can be a literary universe composed of a collection of works, or it can be the referential universe, within the context of which, the book was created. A universe of discourse is very similar in concept to a worldview which has been defined previously.

The similarity is that it comprises everything which may influence in some way the person who is relating to it. It could be the author of a book such as this one, or conversely it could be the reader who is learning about and imbibing the influences of this universe of discourse as described by the author. The main difference is that the universe of discourse embodied in a particular book may be a totally imaginary and unreal universe.

Whereas a worldview is created by real-life experiences which are external, for the most part, to the person concerned and, therefore, are not imaginary.

The setting of *The Lion, the Witch and the Wardrobe* by C.S. Lewis 1950, is an example of an imaginary universe of discourse. This universe was created solely out of Lewis' imagination. But in order to appreciate the book and understand its message, a reader must be willing to enter into that universe and accept it for what it is. The book is only comprehensible within the context of its own particular universe, Narnia. However, in order to be even more fully appreciated, the book needs also to be understood in the context of the other books in the series, which are also based in the same universe of discourse

Internally within Revelation itself, John makes reference to two different universes. The first is the physical one in which he found himself on Patmos, and from where he sent a written account of his visions to the Christians living in Asia Minor. The second is a heavenly one, peopled by angels and beasts, and where he experienced some radically different situations. In addition, Revelation contains allusions to the Hebrew Scriptures - the modern-day Old Testament (OT) - and as a consequence, these constitute an external literary universe of discourse to which the book belongs.

The book was also written in the context of the Middle-Eastern culture of the first century of the Christian era and was originally read and pondered by people of that period. Although a text will not inevitably reflect all the characteristics of its surrounding culture, since it may intentionally be a 'counter-culture' work, nonetheless, most texts are strongly influenced by the different universes to which they belong.

An underlying assumption of this study then, is that a text does not exist in a vacuum, but exists within, and will always be influenced by, the context of the surrounding culture. Consequently, some of those external influences were used to confirm the validity of the analysis which was emerging simply from internal linguistic evidence. This is because a universe of discourse inevitably has a major influence on any discourse and these influences, where discernible, need to be taken into account. The author's universe of discourse will always have an impact on his writings and so the reader must be willing to let those same influences constrain his understanding of what he is receiving from the author. To refuse to do so, or to fail to do so, will almost inevitably result in misunderstandings of considerable magnitude. The more there is a difference between the author's universe of discourse, or worldview, and the reader's, the more likely there are to be misunderstandings.

So, as the analysis progressed, it was assumed that the text of Revelation would have been read by some people since it was a discourse in written form. Yet at the same time, it was also assumed that most other people would only have heard it as it was read aloud. This is why in the following chapters reference is made to both readers and hearers when alluding to the original recipients, the actual usage being contextually constrained.

Secondly, evidence is accruing that both the Middle-Eastern cultural universe in general, and the biblical literary culture in particular, had a predilection for organizing discourses according to ***parallel and concentric patterns*** of various kinds. This is because the culture was still an oral culture as far as the majority of the population was concerned. This widespread practice of oral communication – even if it was the orality of reading aloud a written text – would have had an enormous influence on the worldview of the people of that time period. Consequently, it would have influenced the universe of discourse which lay behind the writing and reading of the book of Revelation. In particular, it would have produced a systematic use of repetition and parallelism since this is typical of oral cultures.

A recent article by Bergli 2023 describes how parallel patterns of all kinds were typical of the oral Quechua discourses which she studied. This continues to confirm what is now becoming more widely understood, that repetition, with its consequent parallelism, is a hallmark of oral-based cultures in all parts of the world. This was the case in the past, just as it still is today, wherever such cultures or sub-cultures still exist.

An appreciation of this cultural background, definitely helped to guide the course of this analysis. As a consequence, it will be seen throughout the following chapters that an awareness of balanced, parallel – that is to say, non-linear – textual organization, is very helpful in coming to terms with the complexities of Revelation's structure.

Harvey 1998,97-8 rightly remarks that controls are needed to ensure that any parallel structures which may be proposed, are not arbitrary. He suggests the following three guiding principles:

1. There should be examples not only of conceptual parallelism but also of verbal and grammatical parallelism between elements in the two 'halves' of the proposed structure.
2. Verbal parallelism should involve central/dominant terminology and words/ideas not regularly found elsewhere within the proposed structure.
3. The central element should have some degree of significance within the structure. (Principle 3 is not relevant to structures with an even number of constituents.)

These propositions can be accepted with the following provisos.

Although care is needed, parallelism based purely on concepts should not be ruled out entirely. This is because concepts are the basis of all communication and the key to all comprehensibility.

INFORMATION

To recognize that **concepts** lie behind all words in the surface structure is an important insight into the nature of language. Evidence for this insight is that transmitted messages are rarely passed on verbatim but are usually summaries or paraphrases. In translation, nothing of the surface structure of the original message is transmitted, and yet communication is possible to the extent that the underlying concepts are correctly transmitted.

Callow 1998,49-95 lucidly devotes two chapters to this issue.

Discourse of any kind cannot exist without the embodiment and transmission of concepts. As a consequence, an analyst cannot legitimately eliminate from consideration such an important part of the author's repertoire of communication tools. However, it is always true, as Harvey (op.cit.) and Blomberg 1989,7 are at pains to point out, that any argument is more compelling to the extent that more items of clear evidence are adduced to support it.

The second proviso is that under the general rubric 'grammar' (principle 1 above), discourse grammar must also be included, because any repetition of structural form may be interpreted as evidence for parallelism. In any case, as principle 2 indicates, all parallelism should be based on dominant features and not on peripheral ones.

DEFINITION
A Chiasm
is a parallel structure with an uneven number of components, of the type : A.B.C.B'A'

In this study the traditional term ***'chiasm'*** will be reserved for all the parallel structures which have an unequal number of constituents of the type ABCB'A', at whatever level in the hiearchy they appear. The term ***'concentric'*** will be used generically to refer to all such structures, whether they have an odd number of constituents (as in a chiasm), or an even number (as in symmetrical ABB'A' type structures). The advantage of using the same term for the same phenomenon at all levels is that it reveals an underlying emic principle of organization.

A further general principle which is effective in constraining the positing of parallels is that of ***balance.*** In practice it has been observed that units which are in parallel to each other normally operate at the same level of the discourse hierarchy, and for the same reason would tend to be of similar size. Therefore, a single paragraph is unlikely to be in parallel with a whole cycle and a single word is unlikely to be in parallel with a group of paragraphs.

As with all general principles, the above discussion is relevant to text which is not modified by any special discourse features which tend to override and even disrupt the normal flow. As has been noted previously, even though authors will establish general patterns, or ***templates,*** in their discourse, they may also disrupt these patterns to obtain special effects. The usual purpose of these effects is to draw special attention to, or to downgrade the importance of the unit(s) in question.

In the case of Revelation, the structure is finely balanced. There are no obvious flaws, but a complete and complex tapestry is created with variety of form and symmetry of shape.

1.3.4 Interludes and Overlays

Not only may structural patterns be disrupted, but they can also be somewhat disguised because language is multi-dimensional and, as a consequence, several things may be happening at once, which renders any analysis more difficult. However, an understanding of the principle that such things can occur is a useful prerequisite for coping with both complexity and ambiguity.

At a very significant level of the book, at the level of the cycles, the regular structural pattern in Revelation is broken up by units of text which will be called ***interludes.***

> **DEFINITION**
> ***An Interlude***
> is a block of text which abruptly disrupts the flow of the preceding text, in order to develop a different theme, without any overt connection, grammatical or otherwise.

This term was also chosen with care since it intentionally implies a moment of dramatic pause in the development of the logical flow of the discourse. Thus by the use of this word it is being pointed out that the occurrences of these features in Revelation are intentional rather than being an arbitrary disruption, a later addition, or even a mistake, as may be implied by other terms. It can be foreseen then, that one of the functions of the interludes is to provide this dramatic pause.

However, this is not their only function since they also carry as a group the development of one of the main themes of the book. This means that, having more than one function, they are in effect an example of a ***linguistic overlay.*** The term 'overlay' is used in the same sense as

Callow 1998,253 who uses it to refer to two (or more) parameters which are so closely intertwined that 'they necessarily overlap'.

There are two kinds of overlap which are possible. The first involves a single unit which has a double function. Examples in Revelation are where a unit, functioning as a conclusion to one cycle, functions, at the same time, as an introduction to the following cycle. This phenomenon consequently creates an overlap between the two cycles. This kind of overlay will be generally referred to as an ***overlap*** for obvious reasons.

Nonetheless, this same phenomenon can also occur on a much larger scale and affect several, even non-contiguous, units functioning at the same level of the hierarchy. The technical term for this dynamic, wave-like effect which can be observed in language is a ***prosody.*** Palmer 1970 and Schooling 1992,128-44 provide examples and references to prosodies in phonology, the domain where the term was first coined. Callow 1998,161-4 et al. explains how prosodies operate in the domain of discourse analysis.

The interludes in their second function as a group are an example of this form of overlay. This is because they superimpose on the central cycles a contrastive topic and theme of equal, if not greater, importance than those which are the most immediately obvious. The term 'overlay' is helpful because it is analogous with a series of transparencies placed on an overhead projector. Each transparency is separate and can be analyzed in isolation, and this is especially useful if the detailed organization of the whole needs to be understood. However, each transparency is only relevant and fully meaningful when it is placed in relation to its fellows, and the combined effect is appreciated as a complete pattern.

DEFINITION

A Prosody

is a linguistic feature of any kind which influences long portions of text but only appears at a few strategic points in the surface structure.

An example in this book is the word ***'revelation'*** in Greek, which only occurs once at the very beginning of the book but never again throughout. Yet the ***whole book*** is about this revelation which was given to John. This one, single word, has an influence on, and constrains the interpretation of, the whole book. Thus, it is a prosody.

1.3.5 A Dynamic Overview

Pike's final universal (Pike and Pike 1982,5) concern the all important issue of ***perspective*** which concerns how an observer perceives the object of study.

According to Pike it is possible to study the world in general, or language in particular, from a static perspective which sees things in terms of particles, or in linguistic terms, ***units.***

On the other hand, it is possible to view the same entities from a dynamic perspective which sees things in terms of moving waves. In linguistic terms this involves analyzing a text in terms of its ***overlays*** or ***prosodies***.

Finally, it is possible to look again from a relational perspective, and view the same data as a field, or ***a network of relationships.*** A discourse viewed from this perspective sees the units in terms of the relationships which they have with other units in their context. In the case of Revelation the networks of relationships often create balanced, symmetrical or concentric patterns.

Each of these perspectives has its own particular usefulness and contributes complementary insights into the organization of a complex discourse such as Revelation.

1.4 A Summary of the Methods and Goals

A guiding principle of the following analysis then, is to look at the structure of Revelation in terms of its levels of hierarchy and its different strata of overlay in turn. Each will be viewed in terms of its units, and patterns of units, within the relational cohesion provided by their context. Having done all that, however, the main aim, from the linguistic point of view, will be to gain an insight into the structure of the book as a whole. We will accomplish this by trying to appreciate the combined result of all the multiple effects which the author has used to create his work of art.

This work of art, however, was designed to communicate an important message which is a revelation concerning the secret mysteries woven around the person of Jesus, the King. Therefore, our task will not be complete until we have made an effort to consider how the technical aspects of the organization of this book were intended to influence our understanding of the total message. This impact of the structure of the book on the message of the book has been overlooked up until now, and so this important aspect of the overall task will be addressed in the final chapters.

1.4.1 Acknowledging Those Who Have Gone Before

There is no question that a large number of commentaries and other studies have been produced on this book, and this continues to be the case. There is also no question that the book of Revelation has been a challenge for the commentators of all the preceding centuries, with the result that there are many different viewpoints.

Nonetheless, a global review of the existing analyses of its structure indicated that a limited number of patterns emerge from the wealth of material which could potentially be examined. For those interested in this topic the full review can be found in Schooling 2004,18, but for our purposes here, we will limit ourselves to a brief summary of the most important points and a list of the matters arising which need further elucidation.

1.4.2 The Synergy of the Generations

The study, of which the findings will be presented in the following pages, was intentionally and purposefully undertaken as a piece of primary research. In other words, the commentaries, which will be referred to below, were not consulted beforehand, but only afterwards. The reason for this was to make every attempt to ensure that the study was not biased by preexisting viewpoints. It was not the purpose to champion a particular eschatological viewpoint, nor to follow a particular school of thought, but to seek after the truth of the matter. The over-riding aim was to ensure that the result would be derived solely from the linguistic evidence to be found in the book itself, and nothing more than that.

Nonetheless, it is appropriate to give credit where credit is due and to recognize the contribution made by those who have gone before.

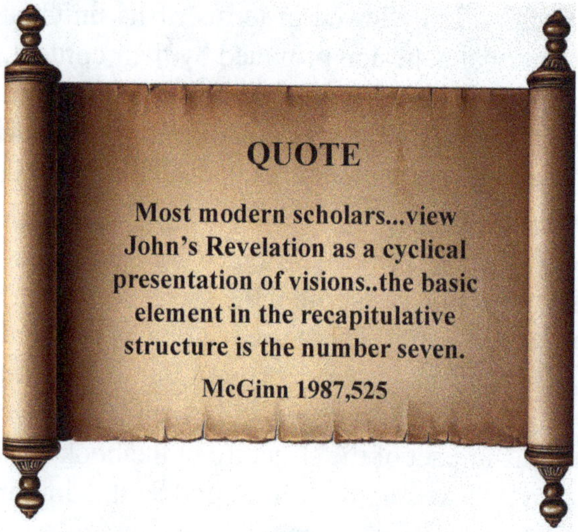
QUOTE
Most modern scholars...view John's Revelation as a cyclical presentation of visions..the basic element in the recapitulative structure is the number seven.
McGinn 1987,525

Unfortunately, if we are very honest about this, the overall impression is that most writers on this subject seem to have been doing what was right in their own eyes. There is very little evidence of cooperation or of trying to better understand the truth woven into this discourse by consciously building, in a positive and progressive manner, on what had gone before.

Having said that, as the various generations succeeded each other, it can be discerned that the weight of the textual evidence did indeed gradually impinge on them, so that there was a progression in their insights. So it is then, that in more recent decades a growing number of commentators allowed the weight of evidence woven into the fabric of the text to influence their explanations about the book.

Consequently, repetition and a consequent cyclic pattern began increasingly to be adopted as a basic starting point. This is because the parallel arrangement of the seven letters, seals, trumpets and bowls, were so obviously structurally present in the text, that their importance could hardly be overlooked any more.

Some of these scholars pressed on further down this path of discovery. A certain number suggested that there may be seven groups of parallel units in the book, and some even ventured to suggest that each of these seven units were composed of seven sub-units.

Others dimly discerned the presence of the Narrative Framework, the overlap links and the interludes, as well as the cyclical nature of the book. In a more recent review of the situation Kuykendall 2017 confirms that it is precisely these same features which have accrued around them a certain amount of partial consensus, but no more than that.

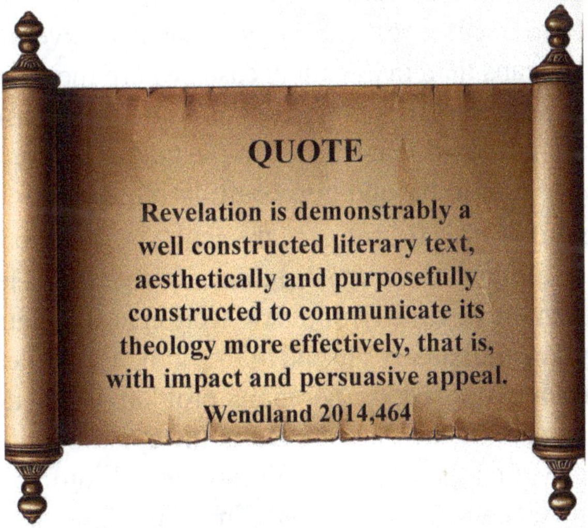
QUOTE
Revelation is demonstrably a well constructed literary text, aesthetically and purposefully constructed to communicate its theology more effectively, that is, with impact and persuasive appeal.
Wendland 2014,464

This indicates that no further progress has been made on this matter since Bauckham's time in 1993. However, as promising as these insights would seem to be, closer inspection reveals that their proposals were very limited in their scope, and were far from taking account of all the evidence which the two co-authors had left for us to discover.

This is not intended to be negative, but rather a dispassionate appraisal of the situation. This is because these people were pioneers in this field. As pioneers, they dimly saw in which direction the path was leading, but they were by no means able to fully map out the route for others to easily follow. So, even though this present study was conducted independently of those previous findings, nonetheless, at this later stage it is appropriate to acknowledge their ground-breaking contribution.

What has since been discovered independently confirms these contributions and highlights these hypotheses. The purpose now is to endeavor to consciously build on the foundation previously laid. This will be accomplished by elaborating and elucidating the subtle intricacies and delicate nuances, which had not previously been discovered in the texture of this book.

The aim then, is to consciously try and build a consensus of opinion, by recognizing what has gone before, but at the same time pressing on in faith, and with determination, beyond what has gone before. This can best be accomplished by addressing in a positive manner the issues which have been overlooked up until now.

1.4.3 Issues Needing Further Attention

The first issue which needs to be addressed is that of methodology. Clearly a number of different methods have been used by the commentators referred to above. However, in no case are these methods easily recoverable and therefore repeatable. This means that, in the many cases where the structure is not self-evident, it is, in effect, personal opinion or theological persuasion, which is the deciding factor. This means that it is no simple matter to refute constructively a particular proposal or to try and purposefully build a consensus.

The second issue is the scope of the analysis. A number of the analyses referred to above divide the text into different size sections. Thus, for example, it is easy to discern the beginning of a new section at Revelation 4:1, but then this section may run until nearly the end of the book. Regardless of the method used and the outline proposed, the perennial problem is that this approach can only account for part of the data. There is always a significant amount of residual material which cannot be neatly integrated into such a plan. Some of the insights revealed by these analyses may be legitimate and helpful, but the goal of integrating all the data in a coherent and elegant manner under the covering of a single structural hypothesis, has not yet been attained.

The third issue is that of prominence, or of the relative importance, of different blocks of text. The outlines proposed by the commentators referred to above are almost all linear and one-dimensional in their approach. This means that there is no clear indication, if any, as to which parts of the book are the most important. For all that can be deduced, they may all have the same value, which is not normal for any text, and certainly not one of this complexity. It is true that sometimes indentation is used to make the outline of the book easier to read, but for the most part, no conscious attention seems to be given to this issue.

Consequently, it is by no means clear that there is any true correlation between the degree of indentation in the outline and the degree of prominence attributed to the passage concerned. The only exceptions to this generalization are the cases where the structure is organized as a chiasm, since this organization is considered by its proponents to automatically indicate that the central section is the most prominent part.

The fourth issue is the explanatory power of the structural hypothesis. The weakness of the existing proposals is that, for the most part, they concentrate almost entirely on dividing the text into units while leaving to one side its cohesion and coherence. However, a text has meaning and communicative usefulness only to the extent that a reader perceives it as a coherent whole. Consequently, an analysis which only contributes to an understanding of a text as a collection of units without contributing to an understanding of it as a complete, coherent unit of communication, only goes part of the way towards a full explanation. A useful hypothesis needs to take account of all that the author did, and to make an attempt to explain why he may have done it that way.

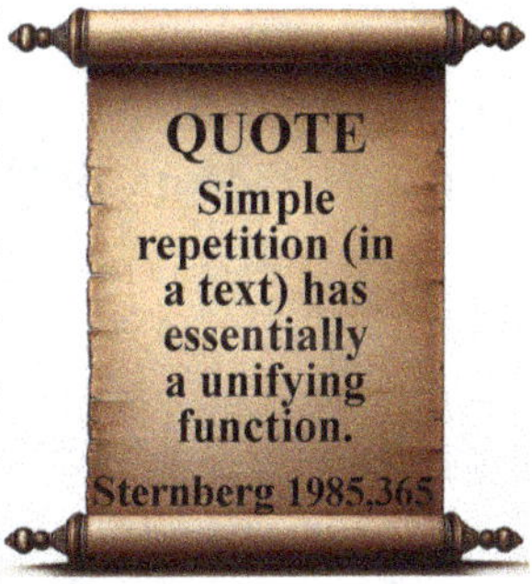
QUOTE
Simple repetition (in a text) has essentially a unifying function.
Sternberg 1985.365

The occurrence of repetition which many commentators cite as evidence for making a division in the text is, contrary to their opinion, almost certainly evidence for cohesion rather than for division. As a general rule, repetition must logically be interpreted as an indicator of cohesion since one is establishing a relationship on the basis of sameness. The confusion arises because repetition, and thus cohesiveness, is evidence for parallelism, which can sometimes be cited as evidence for establishing two different units when for example the parallelism occurs at the beginning or the end of two or more different units.

However, the point which needs to be made clear is that it is the occurrence of ***parallelism*** which can be a reason for division, and not simply the occurrence of repetition. Conversely, some of the analysts recognized that the repeated occurrence of a particular word or phrase is not an indicator of division in the text. However, at the same time they overlooked the possibility that it may be a structural marker indicating cohesion.

Once again this problem is mitigated in the cases where some degree of parallelism is recognized. In recognizing parallelism, an analyst has already gone beyond the surface structure of the text. In effect, he has recognized that the parallel units have an element of sameness, but also an element of difference sufficient to warrant division into different units. It is this kind of insight which leads to synthesis, and perhaps even synergy, which in turn contributes explanatory power to a hypothesis.

The fifth issue is the contribution which the discipline of linguistics can make to biblical studies. It is true that linguistics, and more particularly discourse analysis, are recent developments, but perhaps it is time to heed the call of people like Reed 1996 for greater interaction between the disciplines of linguistics and biblical studies. A text is first and foremost a linguistic phenomenon and, in the first instance, it should be studied as such. Until this is done correctly and consistently, commentaries on books like Revelation will continue to suffer from deficiencies which may detract from their interpretive usefulness.

A key issue in linguistics is understanding the distinction between 'etic' and 'emic' descriptions, which technical terms have been defined previously in Section 1.3.2 above. A basic inadequacy of the structural hypotheses so far proposed for Revelation are that they are primarily etic in nature. Until this issue is addressed, the goal of reaching a consensus on the structure of the book which is within striking distance of being definitive, will remain unattainable.

An illustration of this concept can be drawn from ordinary life. So, for example, a person who is the driver of a vehicle may be very well able to put it to use with great skill. However, if he needed to know how the vehicle functions, then it would be best for him to call upon a mechanic, whose job it is to understand such internal workings.

Likewise, a commentator may be skilled in appropriating the richness of the message which is embodied in a text. But, by the same token, to have a good understanding of the internal mechanics of a text, it may also be appropriate to take account of the insights gained from a specific study of these internal workings. In such a case, it is the prior, and more fundamental skill of a linguist which is required.

Just as it is impossible to measure a sphere with a straight edge, so it is unreasonable to try and get the measure of a text with anything other than linguistic tools.

As long as the underlying emic patterns are overlooked, any genuine insights into the foundational textual organization, and thence the message of the book, will tend to be inconsistent and incomplete. As mentioned above, a number of commentators have correctly observed discourse features of Revelation such as interludes and overlapping connections between different units of text. However, not all the different types of interlude were documented, units of text which are quite different were all included under the rubric 'interlude', and no helpful explanation of their function was given.

Likewise, with the overlapping connections, sometimes not all of them were noticed and sometimes this analysis was imposed on a part of the text where it was not warranted. As a consequence, a description of the complete emic pattern of interludes, or of overlap connections, was not presented and so, as a second consequence, how the total pattern fits into the plan of the book and contributes to its message could not be appreciated.

A sixth issue is the issue of worldview. Even though the discussion of this issue has been left to last in this list, it is probably the most important of them all. This is because a worldview is foundational to everything and, therefore, has an influence on all the issues previously mentioned. It is so important that it has already been referred to at the beginning of this chapter, and it will be referred to again before the end of this journey together.

It is of interest to note that in the course of my own personal journey with this book, which has lasted several decades, I have had several 'revelations'. To do it justice, such a project takes time, for as one set of truths sink in, they prepare the way for another set to sink in at a later time. There are so many nuances and aspects of truth embedded in the texture of this book, that you cannot claim to be serious about understanding it, unless you are prepared to devote considerable time to this quest for truth.

DEFINITION

A Text

From the Latin *textus* 'something which is woven'.

Being the past participle of the verb *textere,* which means anything like this: 'to weave, to join, to fit together, to braid, to interweave, to construct, to thread, to embroider, to fabricate, to construct, or to build'.

www.etymonline.com

So it was then, quite recently, in other words, late on in the project, that I had a revelation about the word ***'text'***. Now, it has to be admitted that English is my mother-tongue language, and that I had also studied Latin for many years, even if it was a long time ago, yet I did not know this fact. So, even though I know both English and Latin very well, it was Agot Bergli 2023 who opened the door for me to realize for the first time, what the word 'text' really meant in its original usage.

In its origins the word 'text' had to do with the art and industry of weaving. It was all about weaving threads in patterns through the parallel strands of the warp and the woof. As it can often be with revelations, such insights, by definition, include some new information, as in this case. But at the same time, the dynamism of a revelation is that it confirms ideas, which you already intuited, and had even pondered and wondered about, for many years. This was also true in this case, and the implications were very far-reaching.

In the course of grappling with the complexities of Revelation and with the challenge of explaining those complexities to others, I had myself, latched onto the word 'tapestry', as a good illustration. This happened on a number of occasions, as can be seen at various places throughout this treatise. I had observed that the book which I was studying, was composed of threads which appeared and then disappeared, only to appear again later on. Consequently, it is a misunderstanding and a misnomer to talk of lexical 'chains' – even as I have already done from habit earlier in this chapter – because they are not connected together like a chain. Instead they appear and disappear like the threads in the texture of woven cloth.

INFORMATION

An ancient metaphor: a thought is a thread and the raconteur is a spinner of yarns - but the storyteller, the poet, is a weaver. The scribes made this old and audible abstraction into a new and visible fact. After long practice, their work took on such an even, flexible texture, that they called the written page a *textus* which means 'cloth'.

Bringhurst 2002

Even though threads, as they show through the surface structure of the discourse, can be said to be individual 'things' or units, once they are woven together they form a completely new, and rather different, item. It is so different that it even has a different name, for the threads have now become 'fabric' or 'cloth'. Generically, it is a ***text***-ile, with a ***text***-ure!

This is how I observed Revelation to be. It was composed of threads which were woven together rather than units connected together like a chain. This is true to such an extent in some places, that it is impossible to separate the discourse into distinct parts. To try and do so would be like tearing a woven fabric into pieces, thereby destroying its coherence and its value.

The further back you go in history, the more likely that the connection between written text and woven *textus* would have been obvious. Even today, the echoes of the ancient metaphor still ring clearly through the cloisters of the English language as exemplified by the explanation in the information box above. Although it may not be provable at this distance in time, it is a reasonable supposition to think that the ancient Hebrews would still have viewed language, and the creation of a discourse, whether oral or written, in those same pictorial terms. This is a reasonable supposition because the textual arts and story telling are still closely related to the art of textile weaving among the Quechuans of South America even today, as recounted by Bergli 2023, as cited above.

It is all a question of perspective. If you look at this woven art-work of a robin as a whole, and as the artist intended you to view it, the picture, and the intended message is totally clear. Even the details are clear. It is true that the joins between the different parts of the picture are blurred, but that is normal for the texture of material which is woven together. Nonetheless, the overall picture is clear.

A needlework expert may wish to inspect the reverse side to see it from a technician's perspective, and that is fine if that is the purpose. However, viewing the picture from the reverse side, unit-based, perspective, does not at all provide an accurate impression of what was intended by the artist. Some parts of it are somewhat clear, but the details are a complete muddle and cannot be correctly deciphered at all.

The Unit-Based Perspective:
A Jumbled Muddle of Threads

The Holistic Perspective:
A Clear Coherent Image

This is why, over the course of time, I became convinced that in the past we had been too preoccupied with dividing a text such as Revelation into small units. As a consequence, it seemed to me, that we were running the risk that we could no longer see the larger design of the picture for focusing too intently on the threads. This is also why, at various times and in various places, I have tried to convince anyone who would listen, that we should try and get a better balance in our approach to dealing with biblical texts.

The ancient authors seemed to be more preoccupied with cohesion, that is with weaving their discourse together into a coherent whole. It seemed obvious, therefore, that anyone coming along centuries later as an analyst, ought to try and have the same focus rather than doing the opposite and trying at all costs to divide the fabric of the text into smaller units. These concerns have already filtered out in the course of the discussion of the preceding issues in the paragraphs above, and will continue to do so, as we proceed.

At root, this is a worldview issue as was stated at the outset of this discussion. As one dispassionately reviews what has been written about Revelation in the past, it is clear that there is a linear mindset with the preoccupation of imposing a straight-edge type structure on the book. This preoccupation, which, I dare say, could almost be called an obsession, is based on the assumption that the structure must be something like beads on a string, and that it is the analyst's job to locate and describe those beads. But we have to wonder whether this is the correct template which is being used, or is it an inappropriate one.

The question of which template to use is a worldview problem. The Greek-based, western worldview assumes that life is composed of straight lines and therefore, quid pro quo, when one reads a book such as Revelation that is what one can expect to find. This is what can be observed when reading through the commentaries – at least those emanating from a westernized worldview.

Anyone of us who has spent any amount of time in a non-western culture will probably understand immediately what is being said here. Significant contact with another culture automatically calls into question many, if not all, of the assumptions we inherited from our native worldview.

Just because life was like that back home, does not mean to say that it is like that elsewhere, because it is not. In particular, one of the most immediately noticeable things is that people constantly and casually repeat themselves – including whole stories – and they think nothing of it. Since one's worldview affects the whole of life, it may be that our clothing reflects the texture of our worldview in some way as well.

Hebrew Textiles with Parallel Designs and Circular Motifs

Westerners seem to have an on-going love-affair with straight lines, with getting to the destination as fast as possible, and being the first past the winning post. But in other cultures it is not like that.

Time goes more slowly according to the seasonal cycles, so that there is more time for relationships and inter-action. This includes telling the story twice and going back to pick up where I left off, if needs be. In reality, there is no need at all to always progress in a straight line and get to the end as fast as possible. In fact, it is perhaps more pleasant, and more intuitively satisfactory, to do it a different way.

But in any case, the point here is that this book, which we are about to look at in detail, clearly was produced from within a very different culture. A culture where weaving, repetition, parallels and circles, or cycles, were all considered a normal part of life.

This then is the issue and the challenge for those seekers after truth who want to get the most out of this enigmatic, yet enthralling, book. We, the ones who are following on behind, are the ones who have to make the effort to adapt our worldview and perspective, to be aligned with those of the authors. The texture of Hebraic text is full of curves and contours. It is up to us to bend our minds around the contours of those curves in our attempt to appreciate its meaning.

1.5 A Final Word : Tying the Threads Together

A basic contention and motivation underlying this present study then, is that there is only one way by which justice can be done to the complexity and richness of the textual organization of the book of Revelation. It can only be done to the extent that the basic claim that a text is primarily a linguistic phenomenon, is taken seriously. This means approaching the text, in the first instance, from a linguistic point of view, using linguistic tools, based on linguistic presuppositions.

Even so, for the whole task to be complete, a stage of theological reflection is also necessary for such a book. Since it is recognized that the theological stage of research can, and should, have its place, these issues will addressed, at least in preliminary form, in the final chapter. But this will only be done after the technical work of analysis has been completed. This is because it is reasonable to suppose that the theological reflection will be greatly enhanced by being based on a reliable linguistic foundation.

The aim of this study then, is to understand and describe the structure of the book of Revelation as a linguistic entity. It was initiated as an enterprise of faith since the text itself was allowed to guide the process of research without having any fixed idea in advance of where the process would lead.

It is true that some interpretation is necessary when working with a text, since it is only possible in theory to make a distinction between form and meaning. However, every effort was made to limit this interpretation to the linguistic level of determining the function of a unit within the context of the total structure of the units under consideration at any one time. Discussion of semantic issues, such as symbolism, consciously sought only to make appeal to linguistic principles of general applicability.

INFORMATION

For the technically minded among you, please take note of the following information. Extra technical information regarding the contribution made previously by Bible commentators, as mentioned in this chapter, can be found in Schooling 2004, as well as in the Appendices which are located at the end of each chapter of this book. The same is true for extra technical information regarding the linguistic analysis which is being presented here.

The focus then, is to produce an analysis which, like any good hypothesis, has good explanatory power. It aims to take account of the maximum amount of data in the most coherent and comprehensive manner possible, and to present an outline of the book which is both as simple and as elegant as possible. The objective is to provide an insight into the internal architecture of the book on the basis of the linguistic evidence available in the text, and to make an attempt to explain why the author may have presented the text in this particular way, as Reed 1996 suggested.

To use a different analogy, Revelation as a whole book can be viewed as a multimedia presentation. Apart from its introductory and closing segments it is composed of seven autonomous presentations of approximately equal length and communicative effect. Each one has its own range of simultaneous actions, sounds and visual effects. Each has its own beginning and end and can be viewed in isolation, but at the same time to obtain the full effect, the visitor to this extraordinary cosmic show needs to take in each of the presentations in turn, and then to come full circle to the point of entry.

As with all artistic enterprises, the production can simply be viewed and appreciated in terms of its total effect and that is all. For those who are more curious however, it is possible to discover how the producer conjured up some of those dramatic effects. In order to satisfy that desire, it is necessary to draw back the curtains, and dismantle the partitions, in order to discover the projectors, the smoke machines and the loudspeakers which are all programmed to work in harmony with one another, to transmit the desired communication package to the public's senses.

Here then, in order to whet your appetite, is a sneak preview of those seven presentations or cycles.

Chart 1.

A Simplified Plan of The Body of the Book of Revelation

A. 1:9-3:22 **CYCLE 1 The Seven Letters: The Church on Earth**

B. 4:1-8:6** **CYCLE 2 The Seven Seals : Revelation of Judgment**

C. 8:1-11:19** **CYCLE 3 The Seven Trumpets: Warning of Judgment**

D. 11:15-16:1** **CYCLE 4 The Seven Signs: Explanation of Judgment**

C' 15:1-16:21** **CYCLE 5 The Seven Bowls: Consummation of Judgment**

B' 16:17-19:21 **CYCLE 6 The Seven Proclamations: Certainty of Judgment**

A' 20:1-22:7** **CYCLE 7 The Seven New Things: The Church in Heaven**

(** The texts marked by ** are connected to the following unit by an overlap link. See Section 1.3.5 above for a brief preview of this feature.)

What is to follow is a journey of discovery which endeavors to take a peep behind the scenes of this magnificent presentation to see how it all works. If the journey is in any way successful, it is to be hoped that having taken the book apart, it will be possible to put it back together again with an increased insight into the mystery of these visions. With this increased insight, perhaps it will be possible to better appreciate the whole as a synergistic combination of its parts, and to better appreciate the artistry and the aim of the message, which is contained within its pages.

You can imagine it as a road trip if you like, but personally, I prefer the idea of a slow cruise down a big river. It is not a straight line but has plenty of curves and contours and constantly changing scenery: mountains and valleys in the distance, and large islands which you come across quite unexpectedly. But, with the same, they are gone, and the same large expanses of water re-appear. Having cleared the way to some extent, let's get on board and start our journey. Above all, take your time, drink in the scenery, and don't be in too much of a hurry to get to the other end.

FOLLOW THE TRAIL ALONG THE NARRATIVE FRAMEWORK...

APPENDIX 1

PREFACE

The Appendices in this book are specifically provided for the more technically minded reader. The purpose is to provide extra technical information, which is easily accessible, for those readers who need it, or who wish to expand their horizons a bit further.

This appendix is designed to complete and to complement the general review of the methodology used in this study, which was previously provided in the main text of the first Chapter. It will be particularly helpful to Bible translators or linguists who wish to either emulate this methodology in some detail, or who wish to put it to the test and perhaps even improve it.

It provides a detailed description of the process used, presented in a step by step manner. Particularly important are the references provided for each step. These references indicate where the particular aspects of the methods have been previously described and delineated.

This, in turn, permits the reader to do more research and gain more insight into the various aspects of the methodology, as desired or needed.

As will be seen, there are many references because, as explained previously, an eclectic approach is, by far, the most pragmatic and effective way forward. Rigidly following one particular theoretical view point or theory-driven method, boxes in the analyst, stifles creativity, and needlessly puts out of reach methods which could have been useful.

The rule of thumb is: use whichever method is suitable and effective for you, as the analyst, and for the language, or the particular discourse, which you are studying.

All other readers are invited to move on straight away to Chapter 2. Except, if you are anxious to start investigating the cycles then feel free to move on to Chapter 3.

APPENDIX 1
A Description of the Process of Analysis

A1.1 Overview

This process assumes the study of a whole, predefined discourse, such as a whole book of the Bible. The first phase of the method consisted of reading the text in its entirety several times in order to gain a general overview of its organization and content. Where the genre of the book is known, and previous genre studies have established some general principles of possible structure, these may be considered as possible guidelines. This was not possible with the present analysis.

A1.2 Division into Units

Method

The method consists of observation of features in the text which are the same or different. Similar features were interpreted as being evidence that the blocks of text concerned should be grouped together on the basis of internal cohesion, and different features were interpreted as evidence that the blocks may be considered to be different units. Where there is good evidence for maintaining cohesion and also good evidence for proposing a division into separate units, clearly the evidence has to be weighed and a decision made. Such analytical difficulties were used as signposts. This is because such ambiguities may indicate that some other linguistic feature is co-occurring at the same point in the text.

This phenomenon of co-occurrence may be the reason for the linguistic signals being more difficult than usual to interpret, and discovery of the less apparent features of the text can often lead to a deeper understanding and to a more refined analysis. In situations such as this, where the best analysis was not immediately obvious, structural patterns which were clearly present elsewhere in the text were allowed to influence the decisions in the more ambiguous cases. As Callow 1998,150 says 'the significance of any given part can only be understood in the light of the whole: a top-down approach is essential'. In all cases, the analytical decisions sought to take account of the most available data in the most coherent manner possible. Evidence to support some of the decisions presented in the analysis may be found in Appendix A2. This indicates how these decisions were reached.

Criteria

The criteria are the similarities or differences in any type of linguistic feature including for example, phonological, lexical, semantic, grammatical/ syntactic, structural, participants, topic/theme, situation and discourse type.

Clear indicators of unit boundaries provided by the author himself were also taken into account. These included orienters (or signposts) where appropriate, and the obvious beginning or end of a clear grouping such as a series of seven.

As the study progressed it became more and more clear that cohesion needed to predominate over division into units. As a consequence, especially where the division into units was difficult, linguistic segments were grouped together on the basis of internal cohesion and completeness regardless of the consequences. This meant in the first pass through that the ending of one unit did not necessarily match with the beginning of the next. This problem was ignored temporarily until a fuller understanding of what was happening became evident.

It was in this way that the overlap links were discovered. Once the overlap feature was established and defined, then it became possible to posit the difference between the units concerned and confirm that there really were a series of different units. However, at the same time it became necessary to state clearly that there were two distinct units but that they were connected by an overlap. This concept was previewed in Chapter 1 and will be discussed further in Chapter 3. In a similar way, the position and the purpose of the series of interludes also became clearer with this approach.

References

The publications which provide information concerning this part of the process include Bergli 2023, Callow 1974 and 1998, Dooley and Levinsohn 2001/2023, Dorsey 1999, Larson 1984, Levinsohn 1992/2024, 2020, 2023a and 2023b, Longacre 1983a, 1999, 2003, 2020, Longacre and Hwang 2012, and Parunak 1981.

A1.3 Establish a Template

If an author is going to go to all the trouble to create a complex discourse, it is only because he believes that he has an important message to communicate to a certain audience. In that case he is going to take great pains to ensure that his audience can discern and receive his message in an appropriate way. This means, in turn, that he will signal to his audience both by clear direct means, and also by more subtle, covert means, how they should follow his threads. One of the main ways in which he will do this, is by indicating what template or grid they should use in order to best understand his thoughts. Sometimes that will be a universal grid based on an existing worldview, or it may be discourse specific.

It is important, therefore, to establish – or develop a working hypothesis concerning – what that template may be.

Method

Sometimes the genre of a discourse will immediately provide a template which is considered 'normal' for such a discourse. This is an expectation based on existing universal or cultural knowledge. Since Revelation is such a complex book, and since (as far as I know) no definitive template has been developed for prophetic books, this was not possible in this case. Nonetheless, since it should not be overlooked that it is a letter (or an epistle in biblical studies terms), this created the expectation that there would be some hortatory material. This, in turn, helped to ensure that the volitional import thread was discovered and delineated.

However, in such complex cases, where there is a mixture of genres, it is to be expected that the author will provide a discourse specific template near the beginning of his work. This is certainly the case with this book.

The template pattern which is the most obvious for Revelation is the recurrent series of sevens, such as the seven letters, seals, trumpets and bowls. This is where a little bit of linguistically based know-how goes a long way. Since this pattern was so obviously placed in the text in such a way that it could not be missed, the linguistic expectation was that this was a deliberate ploy on the part of the author, and that, therefore, it was a template. Once this was recognized and applied to other parts of the text, which were not as clearly delineated, it was a simple matter to find the seven signs and the seven proclamations. Cycle 7 was a different story which will be explained in more detail later on.

In any case, the rule of thumb for the analysis of any discourse is to start with the easy parts first. Then using what you have learned with those easy parts, explore the possibilities to see how they lead you to understand the more difficult parts.

If in doubt, start by perusing the topic of the book and the sub-topics which are set up at the beginning, since these are threads which are bound to weave their way all through the book. Consequently, any expectations which they create may well help to understand later parts of the message. For example, in the case of Revelation, we learn at the beginning that it is all about Jesus, and that He is involved in speaking and instructing the churches. Since this is the case, from previous knowledge about Him, it can be expected that He will speak in parables, with stories, metaphors and dynamic imagery.

Similarly, we are told that it contains a supernatural 'revelation', or 'apocalypse'. This also implies that what will follow will contain unusual descriptions of other-worldly personages and events, which must, of necessity be interpreted accordingly. This would have been obvious and common knowledge to the first reader/hearers, and so, for the most part, did not require very much supplementary explanation.

Criteria

The criteria remain the same. It is constantly a case of looking for the things which are the same compared to the things which are different. Any patterns, especially repeated patterns, which are the same, but therefore, different from what surrounds them, are what we are looking for. Such patterns, which can be found at the beginning of a discourse, are likely to be some form of template.

References

The publications which provide information concerning this part of the process include Bergli 2023, Callow 1998, Dooley and Levinsohn 2023, Levinsohn 1992/2024, Longacre 2003, 2020, Longacre and Hwang 2012 and Schooling 2024a.

A1.4 Relationships Between Units

Three types of relationship were considered. Firstly, the linear relationships between contiguous units such as the setting, the body and the conclusion of a discourse. Secondly, there were the relationships between non-contiguous units of text when they combine together in parallel and concentric structures. Thirdly, there were prosodic-type relationships, when non-contiguous units develop the same topics, themes or motifs without necessarily forming clear, parallel structures.

Method

The method consists of observing and charting the various types of relationships which are possible and which are relevant to the text in view:

1) Grammatical relationships. This concerns the surface structure issues of conjunctions and other connectives which occur in the text.

2) Semantic (logical) relationships. This concerns the relationships between units when viewed as propositions. These relationships concern the content and meaning contained in the text such as the relationship between a proposition (or group of propositions) which express a reason (for an action or event), and another proposition (or group) which express the related result.

3) Functional relationships. This concerns the relationships which are primarily structural in nature rather than semantic, as for example, the relationship between an orienter and the text which it introduces.

4) Concentric relationships. This concerns the relationship between units which are not necessarily contiguous, but are considered to be in relationship to one another on the basis of the occurrence of parallelism.

Another aspect of relationships between units which needed to be accounted for is their multi-dimensional nature. Thus, for example, the constituent units of a discourse relate in a horizontal way in the first instance with other units of a similar type, which are functioning at the same level of the linguistic hierarchy. However, any given unit also relates vertically to those units which function just above it, and just below it, in the hierarchy.

In Revelation, the seven cycles were considered to relate to each other horizontally as discourse units of the same type. However, each cycle was also considered to relate vertically upwards to the book viewed as a total unit, and downwards to its main constituent sub-units. These would be the cycle setting, the cycle body, usually comprised of seven sub-units and an interlude, in some cases. When taking account of these relationships, it was also necessary to take account of the linguistic phenomena of embedding and skewing. Embedding occurs when a particular discourse type occurs on a smaller scale at a lower level of the hierarchy than usual. Skewing occurs when the author assigns a function to a linguistic unit which is not its usual one as explained in Longacre 1983a,10-13.

Criteria

The criteria for establishing linguistic relationships are any possibility of establishing a logical relationship between different units on the basis of the form, the content or the function of the units concerned. See the references for extensive illustrations of the possibilities. The criteria for establishing symmetric relations and prosodies are the same as those listed in A1.2 above.

References

The publications which provide information concerning this part of the process include Alter 1985, Beekman et al. 2017, Beekman and Callow 1974, Callow 1998, Dorsey 1999, Grimes 1975, Harvey 1998, Heckert 1996, Larson 1984, Levinsohn 1992/2024, Longacre 1976, 1980 and 1983a, Longacre and Hwang 2012, Lund 1970, Palmer 1970, Parunak 1981, 1983a and 1983b, E.Pike 1967, K.Pike 1959, Schooling 1992, 2017, 2024a, 2024b and 2025, Terry 1995, Wendland 1998 and 2014.

A1.5 Prominence Features

All meaningful discourses must indicate to the reader which parts of the discourse are more important for understanding the message correctly than others. There are very many ways by which an author can accomplish this task. This is why it is useful to read up about what others have found in the past. This can be complemented by keeping an eye open for anything which is unusual or difficult to process on first encountering it, and thereby learning from practical experience.

Method

The method consists of observing and charting those linguistic features which indicate that some units are more important for the communication of the overall message than others. Callow 1998,156 distinguishes between natural prominence which is derived from the basic semantic relationship which exists between the units concerned, and special prominence which is observable when units are specially marked by the author for prominence. Longacre's method is to look at the discourse in terms of its plot development and uses the term peak for the most important part of the text being analyzed. Usually this coincides with Callow's special prominence.

Criteria

The linguistic features which may be used to mark prominence as a general rule are those which stand out as being different from the context and the standard patterns (templates) previously established by the author. Any device which serves to draw particular attention to a part of the text may well be a prominence feature. These can include, for example, the following: unusual, intense, emotive lexical items or collocations, imperatives, direct speech, repetition, rhetorical questions, change in the word order, change in habitual verb form, change of pace, skewing, embedding, concentration of participants, special particles or words, change of text type, a unit being noticeably longer or shorter than others occurring at the same level and so on.

References

The publications which provide information concerning this part of the process include K.Callow 1974 and 1998, Dorsey 1999, Larson 1984, Longacre 1983a and 1985, and Terry 1995. Longacre and Hwang 2012 use the term 'salience'.

A1.6 Multiple Processing

A book cannot be analyzed by simply applying a single process in isolation on a once-only basis. The process outlined above was applied to the different levels of the hierarchy and on several occasions to the same expanses of text. In practice a 'top-down, bottom-up' approach (Dooley and Levinsohn 2001,51-2) is what is the most effective.

Method

The process began by looking at the discourse as a whole and seeing what that revealed about its parts. Then, in the light of the insights gained, it was possible to look back up at the whole from the perspective of (some) of its constituent parts. This more detailed study in turn illuminated the understanding of the whole. Once again, the process was reversed, using the understanding gained of the whole discourse to further analyze and understand the organization and the function of other lower level constituent parts. This process was repeated until the whole discourse had been elucidated.

Since human communication is such a complex process there are sometimes residual parts of the text which seem to defy analysis. Experience has demonstrated that multiple processing is the best way of reducing the number of these residual items to a minimum. In theory, all parts of a text ought to be amenable to some level of analysis and description, even if ambiguity is an inevitable part of life and may even have been placed intentionally in the text by the author.

In the cases where the ambiguity would seem to be intentional, it was considered appropriate to include all the possible meanings as relevant and having a contribution to make. This rule of thumb was also invoked even when the ambiguity was inevitable, because the word or grammatical form was, at root, ambiguous and nothing could be done about that. An important example of this is the ambiguous genitive to be found at Chapter 1 verse 1, where the literal translation of the Greek is 'a revelation of Jesus Christ'. This could mean that it was information given, or revealed, *by* Jesus, or that it was a revelation *about* Jesus. In such a case, both meanings were taken to be relevant and part of the overall message.

On a practical note, it is advantageous to begin with those parts of the text (usually the introductions and/or settings) where the author himself lays out his plan and purpose. Having come to terms with the parts of the discourse which are more clearly laid out, it is much easier then to move on to those parts which are perhaps purposely, for reasons of prominence or suspense, less clearly laid out. The process of looking for analogies was very helpful at this stage. In any case, before proposals concerning prominence can be posited, the more obvious, standard structural patterns of the discourse had to be found first.

This process involved developing hypotheses of what the structural architecture may be, based on the first information to be discovered. These hypotheses were then gradually refined and tested as more and more data was dealt with, until all the data had been appropriately accounted for. At each pass through the data, more evidence was accumulated which led to the rejection of the weaker hypotheses and the development of the hypotheses which withstood the test of detailed scrutiny. This is important for, clearly, the more evidence which can be adduced to support any particular structural hypothesis, the more reliable that hypothesis is likely to be.

Criteria

The aim is to account for every part of the discourse with no residual pieces left over, or deleted for convenience. The function of every part needs to be described and its place in its context, both the local context and the context of the whole book needs to be adequately accounted for. The connections and relationships should not be forced, nor skewed, by the analyst to fit his desired structural plan. The units which function together on the same level of the hierarchy should be of approximately the same size. The only exceptions would be those cases where there are compelling reasons, like prominence, for positing a deviation from the normal pattern.

To the extent that the structural hypothesis being developed does not fit these criteria, then the process of analysis should continue until all the outstanding issues have been dealt with.

References

The publications which provide information concerning this part of the process include Brown and Yule 1983, Callow 1998, Callow and Callow 1992, Dooley and Levinsohn 2001 (2023), Longacre 1999, 2020, Longacre and Hwang 1994, Pike and Pike 1982, Reed 1996, Sternberg 1985.

A1.7 Charting

Discourses such as Revelation are, by their very nature, complex in terms of the message being communicated, and also in terms of the choice of linguistic features used to transmit them. As a result there are often several things going on at once. As mentioned before, it is best to keep it simple and try and analyze one feature at a time. Now, it can also be said, that it greatly helps to visualize what is going on by creating a visual display of some kind. This method has been used and recommended by many analysts and in generic terms is called charting.

Method

The basic rule of thumb is to use whatever kind of charting method that best suits your needs. In previous decades this would have been done on paper but nowadays many charts can be produced on the computer.

Different kinds of charts can be developed for different purposes. In one case the purpose may be to track the occurrence of particular linguistic features throughout part or all of the discourse.

In other cases, it may be to make a comparison to see where the same things are happening in different places. Conversely, it may be a contrastive chart to show where different things are happening and are contrastive to what is happening elsewhere. They are all tools, so whatever is useful can be used freely throughout the process of analysis.

At each stage a chart of the results of the analysis was also produced. The aim was to produce a kind of organigram which reproduces, in visual form, the structure of the whole book. This continued to be expanded, corrected and enhanced as the analysis proceeded towards its end goal. The extent to which this can be done without doing an injustice to the text, is an indicator that the hypotheses illustrated on the flow chart of the whole book, have some objective reality in the discourse, and that the analysis is maturing.

Criteria

Since charts are tools which have no direct impact on the final analysis, there are no strict criteria for developing them or using them. The main criteria is that they should be practical, easy to produce and use, and accomplish a clear task in the process. If they are reproduced in the final description, then it is obvious that they should be easy to understand. They should bring clarity and insight to the reader, and not confusion.

References

The publications which provide information concerning this part of the process include Bergli 2023, Callow 1998, Dawson 1994, Dooley and Levisohn 2001 /2023, Levisohn 2023a and 2023b, Longacre 1990, Longacre and Hwang 1994 and 2012, and Pike and Pike 1982.

These publications for the most part concentrate on narrative genre discourses, which are predominantly linear in format, and other linear non-narrative formats. Unless care is used these can be misleading when dealing with non-linear formats, as in the case of Revelation. Examples are given throughout this present publication of ways of charting non-linear format text.

A1.8 Description

The ultimate goal was to produce a description of the analysis which others can study and as appropriate, learn from, refine and improve. Once again, to the extent that an analysis can be clearly described, it is to the same extent that it will become obvious (or otherwise) that the analyst has gained a clear insight into the issues at stake.

It should be obvious that there is no set method for producing a description of a discourse. It will all depend on the complexity of the discourse, the creativity of the writer and consideration for the target audience. However, if it fails to communicate its message in a reasonably coherent manner, then it will have failed in its task and will not qualify as a well-formed discourse!

A1.9 Alternative Methods

Language is such a rich and flexible medium that, by the same token, there is no fixed method by which one can or should study it. On the contrary, there are doubtless as many procedural variations as there are analysts. However, if there is to be serious progress in the study of discourse, then the methods used need to be testable and re-usable by others if needs be. They must also take account of the various aspects of language mentioned above, which have been found by researchers throughout the world to be fundamental to the use and organization of any language.

At the date of the first version of this book, only a few analytical methods had been made accessible in published form. Callow 1998 is, in effect, a description of an analytical method and all the Semantic Structural Analyses produced by the Summer Institute of Linguistics are illustrations of the same method. See, for example, Sherman and Tuggy 1994, and Persson 2016.

Terry 1995,14-15 and 37-38, gives a brief outline of his methodology, Wendland 1998,195-224 provides a complete ten step method with an illustration, while Dorsey 1999,21-44 explains in some detail his methodology and provides many examples. Various methodologies are referred to in Porter and Carson 1995, Porter and Reed 1999, and Reed 1996. Examples of several different analyses of the same text are presented in Mann and Thompson 1992.

Other books which can be used as manuals have been produced or updated in recent years. The best of these would be Beekman and Callow 2017, Levinsohn 2023a and 2023b, Longacre and Hwang 2012. However, none of these manuals cover all the possibilities in a complete manner, for this would be a difficult task. So, for example, Levinsohn 2023b only devotes a very small sub-section to the topic of chiastic and parallel structures. Therefore, it is not wise to follow just one manual, for an eclectic approach is best, selecting the advice which is the most pertinent to the discourse being analyzed.

Recent examples of analyses which attempt to provide a holistic analysis of a complete biblical book can be found in Scacewater 2020 and Schooling 2017, 2024a and 2024b. References to older ones can be found in the bibliographies of Schooling 2004.

A1.10 A Final Caveat

The more refined level of interpretation which concerns itself with the theological import of the text was avoided, and no appeal was made to any particular theological school of thought during the process of analysis. Indeed, the structure of the book is, in and of itself, a major area of research and so it is worthy of time and effort to explore this domain in detail beyond what has been accomplished previously. The final chapter nonetheless, will, after the fact, attempt to draw out some of the theological implications of the structural conclusions which will be proposed. But fully developing the question of whether the structural insights may serve to refute or confirm any particular theological positions will have to be left for another time and place.

Every word of Scripture was breathed out
from the very mouth of God.
Each one, therefore, is useful for
learning something new,
for bringing error into line,
for correcting incomplete thinking
and
for helping everyone
to grow into their God-given destiny.
The purpose in all this is,
that we may all accomplish the tasks
which have been prepared for us.

(A dynamic, expanded translation of 2 Timothy 3:16)

WRESTLING WITH WORLDVIEWS (1)

In the beginning, when I first began to write the very first version of this book, I had very clear ideas about how it should unfold. It was to be linear and chronological. It had to proceed in a straight line and deal with each part of Revelation in order, starting at the beginning and ending at the end. Of course, there should be no repetition to speak of, because that would be bad style.

This is how it had to be, because it had always been like that. That is what I had been taught. That is what I expected from the books which I had read, particularly biblical commentaries, and that is what my examiners expected of me in my turn. It was my worldview, and that left me no other viable option to consider.

However… I very soon hit a problem. It was a practical problem and a big one. There was too much information in each section of Revelation to fit practically into one chapter of a dissertation. I did not realize it at the time but only much later, that it is very difficult to produce a coherent, linear explanation of a book which is not structured linearly !! It is that simple.

The reality, as I was being forced to discover, is that Revelation is not linear. Its structure is composed of thread-like, parallel layers weaving horizontally through the book, influencing many different parts of it. With a linear explanation you would have to explain them multiple times, each time they appear, along with all the other features which appear in that particular section of the book. All this was a complex logistical problem which needed resolving.

The solution was to separate out the different threads and treat them one at a time. The complementary solution was that, for each chapter of explanation being written, focus on one or two issues at a time and leave the others ones until later.

That solution forced a review of my planned outline and a shuffling around of the chapters. Consequently, there was some inevitable repetition (oh horrors !) but the end result turned out to be something like a chiasm. That was quite an extraordinary coincidence! But it was actually a very satisfactory solution on a practical level and, most remarkable of all, it was emotionally satisfying as well !

CHAPTER 2
Unraveling the Narrative Framework
2.1 Introduction

One of the distinctive features of the linguistic approach to analyzing a text is its hierarchical view of language. This theoretical insight enables the analyst at the outset of the process to distinguish constituent units of the text which are operating at different levels of the linguistic hierarchy, rather than just viewing the text as a mass of undifferentiated detail.

This possibility simplifies the task of describing the structure of a complex text like Revelation. The purpose of this chapter is to distinguish the Narrative Framework of the book, from the rest of the book, and to describe its form and function. A general overview of the Narrative Framework will be presented first. This will be followed by a more detailed presentation of its constituent parts in the second half of the chapter.

This is not an entirely new insight since a number of commentators have noticed the narrative aspects of Revelation, as mentioned briefly in Chapter 1. As pioneers often do, they became aware of aspects of their subject which their predecessors had overlooked. But at the same time, they only developed a limited understanding of what they saw, and were not able to incorporate that understanding, in any significant way, into their structural analysis of the book.

> **DEFINITION**
>
> ***The Narrative Framework***
>
> is the textual thread in which John appears directly in the discourse in his role as the narrator. This thread runs through the entire book from beginning to end. As such, it provides the principal structural backbone to which all the other components are attached. By this means, it provides the most basic level of cohesion which knits the entire book into a coherent whole. Consequently, the book is not composed of a random collection of disparate units, but is a complete discourse, which should be studied and interpreted as such.

Those who come behind the pioneers, therefore, may not be the first to observe a particular phenomenon, but with the advance in technology in the interval, they may be better placed to more fully comprehend, and describe, what was only dimly perceived before. In this case, the advance in linguistic technology in recent years makes it possible to take account more fully of the textual features which are being subsumed here, under the term **the Narrative Framework.**

The first step beyond the pioneer stage which can be proposed then, is to provide a definition of the Narrative Framework material so that it can be objectively recognized wherever it occurs in the text. The principal part of the definition is that the Narrative Framework is composed of those sections of text which are characterized by the appearance of the narrator, John.

In 1:4-5 both John and Jesus are introduced in parallel as joint authors of the book. As well as being a co-author, Jesus also appears directly in many of the visions, even though He is usually not identified by His personal name. However, it is the presence of John, the narrator, participating in the story which he is narrating, which is the only obligatory criterion for deciding if a particular text forms part of the Narrative Framework. Optionally, Jesus, as co-author, can be considered to be part of the Narrative Framework when He intervenes under His personal name and directly addresses the readers. So, for example, He appears as 'Jesus', in 22:16, and is speaking directly to the recipients of the letter. So this occurrence, along with the more ambiguous first person speeches in 22:12-15 and 22:18-20a, are interpreted as being part of the narration process.

This is not intended to imply that every sub-unit of a Narrative Framework constituent must obligatorily refer to the narrator's participation. What it does imply is that for any section of text which, for various reasons, is considered to be a single unit, it is considered to be part of the Narrative Framework if the participation of the narrator is a major feature of that section. Other complementary features of the framework are the predominance of the aorist aspect and of first person singular forms of the verb, accompanied in some places by the first person singular pronouns (subject and/or object). The aorist aspect is typical of narrative text and consequently occurs elsewhere in the book, but primarily in narratives which are embedded at lower levels of the hierarchy.

2.2 The Components of the Narrative Framework

2.2.1 The Major Components

Using the above criteria, major components of the Narrative Framework can be located at 1:1-11 which introduces the book, 10:1-11:2 which forms a central interlude, and 22:6-21 which brings the book to a close. Traditionally, the opening has been called the Prologue and the closing has been called the Epilogue, so these terms will be retained in the following discussion. These components have been called major components because they are units which can stand alone. Even though their boundaries are not totally unambiguous, there is a consensus among commentators that the passages cited above are distinct units in the structure of the book. More detailed information on these boundary issues is provided in the Appendix to this chapter, and in subsequent discussion which will be found below.

As their names imply, the Prologue is a unit whose primary function is to provide an introduction, or setting, to the book as a whole, while the Epilogue serves to bring the whole book to closure. The central unit is called an 'interlude' for several reasons. Firstly, this passage occurs within the boundaries of the series of the seven trumpets, the first of which occurs at 8:7 and the last at 11:15, and thereby creates a pause in the natural flow of events.

Secondly, the content of the vision itself contributes directly to the idea of an interlude in the progression of the book. In the first part of the vision (10:1-4) John is told to stop writing, even though his previous instructions had been to write down all that he saw and heard. His own personal involvement (10:9-11) gives the clear impression that he experienced a definite pause in the total event of viewing and writing down the visions which he received. In addition, the central sub-unit (10:5-7) is an announcement anticipating the seventh trumpet.

This is therefore functioning as an orienter to prepare the way for something more important. As a consequence, it also creates a break in the progression of the main events, which, at this point in the book, is the sounding of the seven trumpets. Thirdly, there are other units at other places in the analysis which are called 'interludes', as will be seen in Chapter 4 below. It is considered that all these units, in their different contexts, have a similar function. Consequently, the analysis is rendered more transparent if the same label is used for all such units.

The central interlude is attached by an overlap link (11:1-2) to the unit which follows. This feature will be discussed below.

2.2.2 The Minor Components

Other elements of the Narrative Framework occur at 1:17-20, 4:1, 5:4-5, 7:13-17, 14:13, 17:1-18, 19:9-10 and 21:5-10. These elements are called minor components firstly, because they are not units which stand alone with clear-cut boundaries, but are integrated, for the most part, with their immediate context. The second reason for treating them as minor components is because the participation of John in these passages is more incidental than in the major components.

Apart from the overt presence of John, these components have another similarity which supports the proposal that they function together to provide a supporting framework for the rest of the text. The feature in common is the presence of some form of instruction to John. Seven of the eight have direct commands and 7:13-14 has instruction in the form of a question and answer, the former of which, in any case, could be interpreted as a mitigated command (Tell me who these are ...). The passage 17:1-18 also has a question and answer (17:7-18) as well as a command (17:1). In all these cases, extra information is provided which stands apart from, and provides supporting explanation or commentary concerning the surrounding visionary material.

2.2.3 The Narrative Orienters

The narrator's presence is maintained throughout the text by means of the narrative orienters. The most common of these is the phrase *kai eidon*, 'and I saw/looked'. Other less common ones are the phrase '(and) I heard' (e.g. 5:13, 6:1, 16:5, 21:3); 'and was seen', which is the passive form of the verb 'to see', where the grammatical first person agent is elided but is, nonetheless, implicit at the semantic level (11:19, 12:1 and 3). In addition to these conjunctive forms, there is the command, 'Write!', when it is directed towards John (e.g. 2:1 and 3:14).

DEFINITION

An Orienter

is a linguistic term meaning a signpost, for it orients the reader in a certain direction. The narrative orienters specifically cause the reader to look ahead, with the expectation that the next segment of John's visionary experience will now come into view. In this way the whole vision is seen to be sewn together with no gaps.

The word *eidon* 'I saw', occurs about 76 times in the whole of the New Testament, but of these, about 42 occurrences are in Revelation alone. This gives an indicator of how important this word is for the book's organization. For more technical discussion of the function of *kai eidon* see Schooling 2004, chapter 3, section 1.2, and note 6 in loc, and Schooling 2025.

This phrase, and the others like it, are an overt reminder that the text is being narrated. However, unlike the major and minor components described above, the narrator at these points is simply telling his story and is not otherwise directly participating in the action or the dialogue which he is describing.

The function of these words is to provide a regular orientation on the lower levels of the discourse, whereby the reader and those who are listening to the reading, are kept in constant touch with the narrator and are guided along a clear path as they view the various visions through his eyes. The structural observation that these orienters often (but not always) occur near unit boundaries have led some commentators to use them as the basis for dividing the text into constituent units. However, on the basis of the above understanding of their function, the preferred analytical interpretation in this study, is that the narrative orienters are linguistic features which contribute to the internal cohesion of the book as a whole. Thus, the orienters, along with the other narrative components, combine together to create a coherent framework for the whole book. By this means the hearer is kept regularly and specifically in touch with the narrator, as he proceeds to describe his experiences in a vastly different world.

2.3 The Narrative Framework Viewed as a Whole

2.3.1 Concentricity as Style

It has been observed above that the Narrative Framework can be viewed as composed of three sets of components. They all reveal the presence of the narrator, but they differ from each other to the extent in which the narrator actively participates in his narrative. It can now be observed that when viewed as a whole, the Narrative Framework is organized in a concentric manner. In the following chart each of the major and minor components are presented.

Each component presents an aspect of John's personal participation in his own narrative and the chart assumes this as it has been mentioned above. The purpose of the chart is to illustrate the overall concentric organization and to display the instructions (bolded in the chart) which occur in each component. The chart also displays the other repetitions which indicate that the various passages belong together and were apparently intended, therefore, to be construed as being in parallel with one another.

It is self-evident that the Prologue and the Epilogue demarcate the beginning and the end of the book and are, therefore, functionally in parallel with one another. Moreover, it can be noted that they contain a large number of significant lexical parallels. Some of the lexical and semantic parallels appear in Charts 2a and 2b. Those shown in the charts are limited to the ones which are considered to be unique to the passages concerned, for there are other parallels not listed which also link these passages together, but which link them, at the same time, to other parts of the book.

> **QUOTE**
> **Revelation 1:1-3 & 22:6-7 obviously function as a frame or inclusio for the entire book.**
> **Aune 1997,1188**

These parallels, which co-occur along with the presence of the narrative material described above, provide substantial support for the proposal that the Prologue and the Epilogue are also structurally in parallel. More information on this is presented in section 2.5.1 and Chart 3 below.

However, the fact that the Narrative Interlude is also in parallel with the Prologue and the Epilogue has been overlooked up until now. It is in parallel in the first instance, because it is a homogenous unit devoted entirely to the recounting of a vision in which John is personally involved. This general narrative material is complemented by the specific repetition of a series of important imperatives. Thus, at 1:10 John is instructed to write down what he saw. But then at 10:4 he is told to 'seal up' and 'not write'

Chart 2a.
The Concentric Organization of the Narrative Framework
An Overview

A. PROLOGUE 1:1-11 The Introduction to the Whole Book

KEY WORDS, PHRASES & CONCEPTS:
God gave a revelation or mystery, John, Jesus Christ, the Alpha and the Omega, a loud voice (from Heaven); his servant, words of prophecy written down, Write in a book! the time is near, a blessing, God's/Jesus' angel, Look, He is coming.

B. THE NARRATIVE INTERLUDE 10:1-11:2
An Interlude for the Whole Book

KEY WORDS, PHRASES & CONCEPTS:
The mystery of God, John (implicit), Jesus Christ, is implicitly present because of the reference to the voice from Heaven which John heard previously, his servants the prophets, metaphorical words in the little book, seal up, and do not write it down, you must prophesy again, another angel.

A'. EPILOGUE 22:6-2 The Conclusion to the Whole Book

KEY WORDS, PHRASES & CONCEPTS:
God will add/God will take away, John, Jesus (Christ), the Alpha and the Omega, his servants (the prophets..), the words of this prophecy (x3)/(written) in this book (x5), must happen soon, a blessing, Jesus' angel, Look, I am coming soon.

the particular things which the seven thunders revealed, only to be instructed once more at 22:10, to 'not seal' the words which he has written down. This final command is further reinforced by the warning in 22:18-19 not to add to or subtract anything from the book.

The interlude passage creates a hinge in this series where it is made clear that to seal the prophecy has the same essential meaning in this context as the command to not write. This is because, in either case, the words are not available to be read and understood. Thus, it is clear that the command to write in 1:11 has the same essential meaning as the command to not seal in 22:10, since in both cases the words are available to be read. The combination of the narrative material then, and these instructions to John, create a parallelism which makes it possible to posit an ABA' chiastic relationship between the Prologue, the Central Interlude and the Epilogue.

These parallel relationships are set out in more graphic form in Chart 2a above, and also in Chart 2b which follows.

The parallelism and the overall concentricity is, in fact, more complex than the summary given in Chart 2a, because it is completed by the minor components of the framework, four of which come before the interlude and four more after it, as shown in Chart 2b. Each minor component is not specifically in parallel with every other component. But this is by no means necessary to indicate an overall organizational plan, for there are enough specific parallels to indicate a comprehensive network of relationships between all these different passages. This suggests in turn, that the similarities are not coincidental. As the details are observed, it becomes patently clear that there is some sense in which all these passages are intended to function together. Since they function together, they obviously create a framework which spans the whole book, and which integrates into a coherent whole all the disparate visions, which constitute the informational content of the book.

Obviously, one example of a series of parallels does not establish a definitive pattern. However, the purpose in presenting this view of the Narrative Framework is to clear the ground in a number of ways. Firstly, it is helpful to make a basic distinction between the Narrative Framework material which occurs at different points throughout the book, and the rest of the visionary content. But then, it is also helpful to discern the precedent which is being established here, that parallelism with some elements of concentricity can be observed in the book at the highest level of the linguistic hierarchy, on the basis of good evidence. It is only a precedent for the moment, but it will be seen later that there are enough other examples at all levels of the hierarchy, to suggest that this combination of parallelism and concentricity is a characteristic of the book as a whole.

Chart 2b. The Detail of The Concentric Organization of the Narrative Framework

A. PROLOGUE 1:1-11

Jesus & John Introduce the whole book of prophecy

God gave a revelation of Jesus Christ, through Jesus and John in order to **show his servants** the things which must happen soon, and He revealed it by sending his angel. John passed on the word of God and what was revealed about Jesus, according to all that he saw.

God said: **Blessed** is the one reading the words of the prophecy and keeping the things written in it, because the time is near. He said that Jesus is **coming soon** and that He is the Alpha and the Omega, the one who was and **is to come.**

John said: I was in the spirit... and I heard behind me a voice like a trumpet which said: Whatever you see, **WRITE in a book,** and send it to the seven churches.

The Minor Components Part 1

1:17-20	I fell at his feet (the one with the voice like a trumpet). Do not be afraid... **WRITE t**herefore the things which you saw, the things which are and the things which are about to happen after these things.
4:1	The voice which I heard at first like a trumpet said to me: **COME UP** here and I will show you the things which must happen after these things. Immediately, I was in the spirit.
5:4-5	One of the elders said to me: **Do not weep**
7:13-17	One of the elders said to me: (**Tell me:**) Who are these dressed in white?

B. THE NARRATIVE INTERLUDE 10:1-11:2

John is Rested to be Recommissioned in his Prophetic Ministry

I heard a voice from Heaven saying, **SEAL** the things spoken...and **DO NOT WRITE** them, but at the time when the seventh angel sounds his trumpet, ***the mystery of God*** which He announced to **his servants** the prophets will be accomplished.

The voice which I heard from Heaven said to me: **Go, take the book... Take and eat it...** and they said to me, you must prophesy some more. **Get up and measure..**

The Minor Components Part 2

14:13	**WRITE**: **Blessed** are the dead in the Lord from now on, that they may *rest* from their labors...
17:1-18	One of the seven bowl angels came and said to me: **COME**, I will show you the judgment of the great harlot... Babylon the great... and I saw a woman. He carried me away... in the spirit
19:9-10	(The bowl angel) says: **WRITE: Blessed...** These words of God are true. I fell at his feet to worship him, and he says to me, **Don't do that... worship God.**
21:5-10	The one sitting on the throne said: **WRITE:** These words are reliable and true... I am the Alpha and the Omega. I give to the one who is thirsty the water of life to drink freely. But the murderers, immoral, sorcerers, and all liars... One of the seven bowl angels said to me: **COME (UP)**, I will show you the wife of the lamb, and he carried me away in the spirit...to a very high mountain and showed me... the holy Jerusalem.

A' EPILOGUE 22:6-21

Jesus & John Conclude the whole book of prophecy

These words are reliable and true, and the God of the spirits of the prophets sent his angel to **show his servants** the things which must happen soon.

Blessed is the one keeping the words of the prophecy...

I fell to worship at the feet of the angel, and he says to me:

Don't do that...worship God

I am **coming soon** (x2). I am the Alpha and Omega.

DO NOT SEAL the words of the prophecy... for the time is near.

The sorcerers, the immoral, murderers, idolaters, and all who love to be liars... Let the one who is thirsty take freely the water of life.

2.3.2 The Function of the Narrative Framework

> It should be noted that some messages have a superstructure which...stands outside the message proper. Books have forewords and introductions; letters have salutations and greetings. These set the message in the larger... context and relate both the message itself and the message sender to the addressee, but they do not form an integral part of the message.

This quotation from Callow 1998,164 neatly summarizes the principal functions of the Narrative Framework and provides a general foundation for the following discussion. What needs to be stated in addition, is that the Narrative Framework of Revelation is a complex infrastructure. It has several components, which between them, contribute several supportive functions to the book as a whole.

Message Support

As indicated above, messages do not stand alone but generally have to be supported in some way, and this is particularly true of long messages. As a general rule, a message may need support material which facilitates three aspects of the communication process, namely, *comprehension*, *accuracy* and *acceptability*.

Comprehension is particularly facilitated by recalling to the hearer's mind a relevant, preexisting conceptual network, which will enable him to correctly interpret the information which is embodied in the message itself. In general terms, this is accomplished by indicating what kind of message is in view, what the geographical and social situation may be, who is the author of the message and who are the intended recipients.

This kind of support material occurs primarily in the Prologue of Revelation, as, for example, 1:1-2, 3, 4, 9-11.

Even if situational support often occurs at the beginning of a message in anticipation of what is to come, there is nothing to prevent it coming after the fact, in confirmation of what has already been communicated. Thus, the Epilogue repeats some of the support material previously provided by the Prologue.

Another kind of support which both the Prologue and the Epilogue provide are allusions to the Hebrew Scriptures. From a message support point of view it can be deduced that, by this means, the author intended to trigger existing knowledge of this wider literary context in the minds of his hearers. By this means he indicated to them that the main content of the book should be understood within the context of this network of existing information.

Comprehension is also facilitated by explanation, particularly when there is a change of situation or when an author judges that the recipients may not have an adequate, conceptual network to suitably understand what needs to be communicated. There is a change of situation at 4:1, when John is transported in the spirit from Patmos to the heavenly throne room. This is not just an ordinary change of situation but is also a change from one referential world to a completely different one. Therefore, it is clearly important for the hearers to be given the opportunity to adjust to the fact that, from here on, a different world is the context within which the message needs to be interpreted.

Another place where explanatory information is provided is in Chapter 17. Even though the principal topic, Babylon, is conceptually integrated with the preceding and succeeding context (see 16:19 and 18:2), the unit, as a whole, is nonetheless, part of the Narrative Framework (see 17:1, 6-7,15-16 and 19). It is clear that it has a supporting role because it could be removed in its entirety without materially altering the overall message. The chapter explains who, or what, Babylon is, and this extra supporting material, without being a necessary part of the whole, nonetheless does facilitate the comprehension of what follows. Other explanations which are also part of the Narrative Framework occur at 1:20, 5:4-5 and 7:13-17.

Authors may also indicate to their readers to what extent they can count on the **accuracy** of what is being communicated and may actively encourage them to accept the message and respond positively to it. The support which refers to accuracy occurs in 1:2, 5 ('the one who bore witness', and 'the witness',) and 22:6, and the support which promotes the **acceptability** of the message are the blessings and warnings found in 1:3, 22:7 and 22:18-19.

The Narrative Interlude (10:1-11:2) may also be considered as contributing to the support feature of acceptability. This is because John is presented as having a personal experience which may serve as an example to the hearer. By this means the reader is encouraged, at least implicitly, to embrace willingly a similar sort of bitter-sweet reaction which he may experience in reading John's prophecy. John is apparently someone who is known and trusted by the intended audience. Consequently, the reason for including this personal example and involvement in his visionary experience, may be that of authenticating and making more acceptable the more 'bitter' aspects of his message.

Message Signposts

Signposts are 'tracking devices' which mark 'progression' (Callow 1998,163) and they guide the reader or hearer through the discourse in a convenient way. These features of the text 'contribute no fresh referential material to the message; they stand aside from it as a sort of commentary to assist the recipient' (ibid.,164). Revelation has an obvious set of such signposts in the form of the repeated phrase, 'and I saw' (and similar phrases), which are part of the Narrative Framework and which occur throughout the book. These phrases contribute nothing to the content of the book but contribute to the general supporting framework within which the visions being described should be understood and interpreted.

The coherence of the Narrative Framework as a whole is due to the presence of these 'tracking devices' which logically link together the disparate parts even though they are not contiguous. In fact, one reason why the framework is called a *Narrative* Framework is because it is characterized by a sequential chronological development. This is typical of narratives in general, as Longacre 1976,197-201 and 1983a,2-10, and Callow 1998,21 have previously explained. But the point here is that this sequential development is due, in particular, to the presence of the message signposts.

However, the Narrative Framework does not exist in isolation, but it co-exists with the rest of the text. The message signposts, in particular, are those parts of the framework which link it inextricably with every other part of the visionary content. These signposts, therefore, do not just link together the parts of the Narrative Framework but also provide a sequential and chronological development for the book, which is easy to follow. Without these, the visionary content would have no internal chronological tracking device, and it would be more difficult for the hearer to discern the thread which connects the different visions together.

In fact, this is an important point about narrative in general: because the chronological sequence is the easiest to understand and to follow, this is undoubtedly a major reason why it is such a common text-type. By contrast, the development of other text-types, which do not have an inherent chronological sequence, is more difficult to present clearly and more demanding of the hearer's comprehension skills. It is for this reason, according to Callow 1998,163-4, that signpost-type tracking devices occur the most often in 'logical ... or persuasive messages, since these lack the references to time and location that mark progression in time-based messages'.

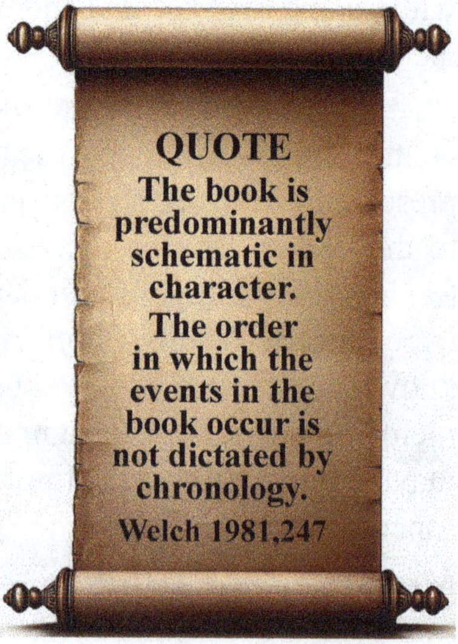
QUOTE
The book is predominantly schematic in character.
The order in which the events in the book occur is not dictated by chronology.
Welch 1981,247

It can be seen then, that the Narrative Framework is not just a useful coincidence, but provides an essential cohesive element which is also necessary for a discourse of this nature. This is because the main referential content of Revelation is not developed according to a time-based structure, but is rather a persuasive (hortatory) message with logical (expository) components.

Other kinds of message signposts occur elsewhere in the text which are not part of the Narrative Framework. However, these signposts do not have the same function as the Narrative Framework signposts. As has been explained, these particular ones exist to provide a sequential tracking system. The other signposts will be discussed in Chapter 6.

Message Prosodies

Prosodies are features of a message which cannot be easily defined in terms of units. This is because, even though they may appear as units in the surface structure, they always 'pervade extended parts of the message' (Callow 1998,161).

> As she explains: '**A prosody** is operative in a unit, not as a smaller sub-unit building up its structure, but as relevant throughout. Thus, if a chapter in a story describes what happened when the hero ran away to sea, then the location "at sea" is relevant to the whole of that chapter. The writer does not need to mention it in every sentence, but it is something that is true of each sentence'. Conversely, 'it is possible...for an established prosody to be realized repeatedly in the surface structure'.

Like other supportive material prosodies operate on a different plane to the content which may surround them. As such, they may relate to more extended sections of text than just the propositions which occur in their immediate context in the surface structure. We are talking here then, about elements of text, which have no obvious role or relationship in their immediate context. Consequently, they do not contribute significantly to the development of the referential content of the message, but they, nonetheless, reoccur like threads in a tapestry. Due to the fact that they reappear sporadically, they may be considered to be prosodies.

According to Callow (ibid.,171), some prosodies, such as those of viewpoint or referential situation, must obligatorily occur in all texts, whereas many others are optional. The Narrative Framework provides a number of these prosodies and thereby contributes cohesion to the book.

The most obvious example of a prosody is that the book is an account of John's experience. In it he tells his story, which provides the basic referential situation, and the story as a whole is narrated from his viewpoint.

This is not overtly stated in every paragraph, but it is nonetheless something which is true of every single proposition in the book. This remains true even if the narrator is relating the activity or speech of another participant. It is made overtly obvious at various points, starting with the Prologue and ending with the Epilogue, with its presence being maintained throughout by the narrative orienters.

There are many examples of this linguistic phenomenon in Revelation some of which also begin in the Prologue, and end in the Epilogue, suggesting that they are also features which intentionally exert an influence on the whole book. One such book level prosody is the series of seven blessings, the first and last of which occur at 1:3 and 22:7 respectively. This series can be analyzed as a prosody because it occurs intermittently throughout the book. In addition, none of the blessings is closely attached to their immediate context. All of them could be removed, and it would not change the informational content of the book at all. Likewise, they could be placed elsewhere in the text, and still contribute almost as effectively as they do in their actual positions. To that extent they stand 'aside from the hierarchical structure of units within units' (ibid.,181).

A further point to be noticed is that four of the seven blessings occur within the confines of parts of the Narrative Framework (1:3, 14:13, 19:9 and 22:7). This observation supports the idea that this feature is part of the support material of the book, just as the Narrative Framework is. The function is to foreground in the hearers' mind at the outset, the whole broad concept of 'blessing' and the possibility of being blessed. This possibility is confirmed at the end, with various reminders interspersed throughout. The blessings in Revelation are hortatory communications, inviting people to a particular course of action, and so this prosody establishes the fact that exhortation is a feature of the whole book as well.

Another book level prosody, whose function is less obvious, is the declaration concerning the Alpha and the Omega, which occurs three times in the book at 1:8, 21:6 and 22:13. If the synonymous parallels, 'He who is, was and is to come' (1:8), 'the first and the last' (1:17, 2:8, 22:13), and 'the beginning and the end' (21:6 and 22:13), are taken into account, there are nine occurrences. Undoubtedly, what is true for one is true for all of them. This has the effect of foregrounding the immense concept of the sovereignty of the Godhead, integrated also with the concept of the totality of time, perhaps even implying timeless eternity to a finite mind. Regardless of the extent to which anyone can comprehend these concepts, nonetheless, they pervade the whole book by means of this prosody.

2.3.3 An Overview of the Functions of the Narrative Framework

It can be seen then, that the Narrative Framework has a variety of functions, which all contribute in some way to creating a supporting backbone for the whole book. Even though this supporting structure is an essential component of the book, nonetheless, it fades into the background in the context of the more dramatic visionary content which constitutes the rest of the discourse. This insight may help explain why the Narrative Framework, as a total linguistic entity, has apparently been overlooked until now. Nonetheless, once the role of this material is more clearly understood, backgrounded though it may seem to be, it helps prepare the way for a clearer insight into the rest of the text. Having distinguished this set of markers, it makes it considerably easier to discern the boundaries and the function of the visionary components, which contain the significant content of the book at the informational level.

2.4 The Influence of the Narrative Framework on the Chronology of the Book

Chronology is a particular problem for Revelation more than for most books. The very terms (preterist, futurist etc.) which have been traditionally used to label the different interpretive viewpoints indicate that differing views of chronology lie behind the discussion. The main structural issue in the debate is whether the book is ordered according to a linear chronology, or whether it is recapitulative in nature.

The term 'recapitulative' has raised unnecessary issues because some have argued that it implies that any element which recapitulates a previous element, must be identical with it. All literature, music, art and even life itself, is characterized by the repetition of certain elements. It is rare that such repetition is absolutely identical. On the contrary, a basic aim of art is to find creative ways of expressing the same things in different forms, by different media, and with subtle and beautiful variations. To argue that the author of Revelation, or of any other book, must, if he wishes to repeat himself, do so in an exactly identical way, is forcing the issue to an unhelpful extreme. The whole issue of how the analysis in this study of the structure may eventually influence decisions concerning the recapitulative nature of the book, will be explored in Chapter 8.

It is beyond the scope of this study to do justice to this complex issue. Nonetheless, some brief remarks will be made just to indicate the importance of coming to terms with the presence of the Narrative Framework, and its implications for the interpretation of the book.

The key issues are firstly, that the book describes events in two different referential worlds and consequently, it cannot be assumed that what is true for one of these worlds is automatically true for the other. In particular, it cannot be assumed that the system of chronology, which operates in the physical, earthly world, is the same as that in the spiritual, heavenly one.

Secondly, the linguistic shape of the book as a whole, is created by the set of textual units which is being called the Narrative Framework. As its name suggests these texts give the impression that the book is some kind of narrative with a particular chronological sequence, even though the main purpose of the book is not just to tell a story. It is helpful therefore, not to assume that the book is a true narrative, but to make a distinction between the narrative components and the components containing the visionary content.

Thirdly, even if the system of chronology is the same in all cases, a narrator is free to tell his story according to a chronology which is independent of the referential world in which his story is set. Therefore, it cannot be assumed without justification, that the chronology of the story, as expressed in this case by the Narrative Framework, is the same as the chronology of the events described in the story.

Once again then, it can be seen that the Narrative Framework is not just a secondary linguistic convention, for the chronology which it provides pervades the whole book, and gives an impression of linear sequence. However, before issues of interpretation are addressed, it is important to discern that this apparent chronological sequence is a characteristic of the Narrative Framework in the first instance. Even though this observation is correct, this does not automatically mean that it is also a characteristic of the events represented by the visions themselves. For those interested in this topic, a more detailed discussion is provided in Appendix 2, at the end of this chapter.

2.5 The Internal Organization of the Narrative Framework Components

This section presents a brief description of the proposed analysis of the internal structure of the components of the Narrative Framework. The evidence for the boundaries of the Prologue and the Epilogue is presented in section 2.5.3 below, which describes the overlap links. If required, more detailed argumentation to justify the division into units may be found in Appendix 2 at the end of this chapter.

2.5.1 The Prologue and Epilogue

The discussion in this section is supported and illustrated by Charts 3 and 4, which will be found on the next four pages. The explanation of the charts will be continued and completed on the pages following after Chart 4.

NOTES FOR CHART 3

This chart illustrates the existence of parallelism between the Prologue and the Epilogue by providing conceptual resumes of the pertinent content. Concepts expressed with different words, and more precise explanations of the underlying referents, are indicated in parentheses

The bolding of some entries is to facilitate reading, and to highlight important parallels.

The genitive 'of Jesus' in 1:1 is ambiguous. It can mean 'belonging to' or 'concerning'. In such cases both options are possible meanings, and are consequently included in the Chart. This comment is also relevant to Chart 4.

The Greek verb *blépo* 'to see', is only used referring to John in 1:11, 12 and 22:8 (twice), and a group of four parallel occurrences in Chapter 6, making a total of eight occurrences of this verb. In all the rest of the book the verb **eidéo* is used with reference to John seeing something. (The reconstructed proto-form **eidéo* is used here since it retains more transparently the linguistic origins of *eidon*.)

For more detailed discussion of the issues implicit in 1:11-12 as regards the transition between the end of the Prologue and the beginning of Cycle 1, see Appendix 2 at the end of this chapter.

Here are a list of the references in the Old Testament which are alluded to in the Prologue and the Epilogue.

For the Prologue, 1:5-7 makes allusion to Psalm 89:27 and 37 (cf. Isaiah 55:4), to the general concepts of kings and priests, and to Daniel 7:13, Isaiah 53:5 and Zechariah12:10.

For the Epilogue, 22:14-15 makes allusion to Genesis 2:9 and 3:22-4, Exodus 19:10-11, Isaiah 26:2, 62:10, Deuteronomy 18:9-13, 27:15-26, 28:1-6 and 30:15-20.

Beale 1999,1131 and 1138 thinks that 1:4, 8 and 22:11 and 13, are also direct allusions to the Hebrew Scriptures of the Old Testament.

Chart 3a.
The Internal Structure of the Prologue

THE PROLOGUE 1:1-11

Unit 1. 1:1-2
God gave a revelation to/concerning Jesus Christ To His servants about **what must happen soon.** He sent His **angel** to his servant John who faithfully **wrote** the words from God and **the testimony** of Jesus Christ - all that he saw.

Unit 2. 1:3
Those who read and hear the words of the prophecy and **obey what is written** in it will be **blessed,** because it **will happen soon.**

Unit 3. 1:4-5a
John addresses greetings of grace and peace **to the seven churches** in Asia from **(the eternal one)** and from Jesus Christ, who **testifies** faithfully.

Unit 4. 1:5b-6
Ascription of glory/**worship** to Jesus who set his people free from their sins by his blood, to be kings and priests. This is an allusion to what He has accomplished for his followers.

Unit 5. 1:7
Behold, (Jesus) is coming... in the context of a series of allusions to the Hebrew Scriptures.

Unit 6. 1:8
God is **the Alpha and the Omega... (the Eternal one)** who is, was, and **is coming**

Unit 7. 1:9-11
John suffered on Patmos because of his faithfulness to the word of God and to the **testimony** of Jesus. All that he saw ***(blépo),*** he was to **write** in a book and send to **the seven churches** in Asia.

Chart 3b.
The Internal Structure of the Epilogue

THE EPILOGUE 22:6-21

Unit 1. 22:6-7a
The Lord, the God of the prophets sent his **angel** to inform his servants about what **must happen soon.**
These words have been faithfully transmitted.
Jesus is coming soon

Unit 2. 22:7b
Those who **obey the words** of the prophecy **(written)** in this book will be **blessed**.

Unit 3. 22:8-11
John **testifies** that he is the one hearing and seeing ***(blépo)*** all these things.
When he heard and saw, he fell to **worship** the angel who showed him these things.
But the angel is a fellow-servant of the prophets and of those who **obey the words** of this book. John should **not seal** up the words of the prophecy because it **will happen soon.**

Unit 4. 22:12-13
Jesus is coming soon.
He is **the Alpha and the Omega, (the eternal)** in the context of allusions to what He will yet accomplish for his followers.

Unit 5. 22:14-15
Those who fully purify themselves are **blessed,** in the context of allusions to the Hebrew Scriptures.

Unit 6. 22:16-20
Jesus sent his angel to testify of these things in the churches. Those who hear should say 'Come'. Jesus **testifies** to those who hear the words of the prophecy of this book. He who **testifies** to these things says: **Yes, I am coming soon.**

Unit 7. 22:21
(A final **blessing** is addressed to the readers/hearers of the book **i.e. the churches:**)
The grace of the Lord Jesus be with you all.

Chart 4a.
The Function of The Constituents of The Prologue

THE PROLOGUE 1:1-11

Unit 1. 1:1-2
Situates the source of message as being God Himself, the highest possible authority. It specifies the general topic as being a revelation about Jesus Christ (in genitive in Greek). It specifies the method of transmission. It states that John acted as a witness.

FUNCTION: Establishes veracity and acceptability.

Unit 2. 1:3
Promise of blessing to those who respond positively to the message.

FUNCTION: Positive motivation to act, plus implied need to act quickly.

Unit 3. 1:4-5a
Establishes the eternity, and reliability of the supernatural source of the message, plus the benevolent intentions of the divine source(s).

FUNCTION: Establishes veracity and acceptability.

Unit 4. 1:5b-6x
Ascription of Glory to Jesus: this is an implicit invitation to the hearer to do the same. Statement of benefit for those who are Christ's.

FUNCTION: Provides positive motivations and invites positive response.

Unit 5. 1:7
Foregrounds the Old Testament as an appropriate frame of reference.

FUNCTION: Establishes veracity and acceptability. Positive & negative reinforcement.

Unit 6. 1:8
Establishes the divinity and eternity of the ultimate source of the message.

FUNCTION: Establishes veracity and acceptability.

Unit 7. 1:9-11
Establishes John as a reliable authority and the spiritual nature of the message. The message was written down.

FUNCTION: veracity and acceptability.

Chart 4b.
The Function of The Constituents of The Epilogue

THE EPILOGUE 22:6-21

Unit 1. 22:6-7a
Situates the source of message as being God Himself, the highest possible authority. It specifies the method of transmission. It specifically claims that the words are reliable. With emphasis it says that Jesus is coming soon.

FUNCTION: Establishes veracity and acceptability plus the implied need to act quickly.

Unit 2. 22:7b
Promise of blessing to those who respond positively to the message.

FUNCTION: Positive motivation to act.

Unit 3. 22:8-11
Establishes the divinity and reliability of the source by confirming the method of transmission. Instruction concerning personal behavior (v.11).

FUNCTION: Establishes veracity and acceptability plus instruction concerning behavior, plus need to act quickly ('for the time is near').

Unit 4. 22:12-13
Imminence. 'Behold, I am coming soon'. Divinity and eternity of source.
Promise of reward.

FUNCTION: Establishes veracity and acceptability; provides positive motivation; need to act quickly.

Unit 5. 22:14-15
Foregrounds the Old Testament as an appropriate frame of reference.
Promises and warnings.

FUNCTION: Veracity and acceptability, positive and negative reinforcement.

Unit 6. 22:16-20
Establishes Jesus as co-witness and transmitter of the message, and that He is coming soon. Promises and warnings. Invitation to respond positively.

FUNCTION: Establishes veracity and acceptability, positive and negative reinforcement.

Unit 7. 22:21
Prayer for positive help.

FUNCTION: Request for help.

As has been mentioned previously in section 2.3.1 above, the Prologue and the Epilogue are structurally in parallel, and function in complementarity to each other, as opening and closing brackets to the book. Additional evidence for the structural parallelism is the fact that the Prologue and the Epilogue can be analyzed as being composed of seven sub-units, which are similar in content and function.

These sub-units are presented side by side in Chart 3. It can be seen by comparing the two columns, that a considerable amount of similar material occurs in both of them, thereby confirming their parallel organization. In some cases (e.g. unit 2), two entire sub-units are in direct parallel, but this is not consistently so. Nonetheless, there is enough evidence to establish that the Prologue and the Epilogue, as complete entities, can be viewed as a matching pair.

By reading down the columns, other parallels can be observed, which confirm the internal coherence of the Prologue and Epilogue which, at the outset, was principally based on the overt presence of John in the text. The most striking of these internal parallels is the threefold repetition in the Epilogue of 'I am coming soon' (22:7,12,20).

In addition, each of these occurrences, is marked for special prominence by *idou,* 'behold', or by *nai*, 'yes'. Apart from these occurrences this phrase only occurs in this form in one other place in the book, which is at 3:11. In this latter case, *idou* does not occur in the Aland text but it does occur in the Textus Receptus version. The combination of the verb 'to come', in various forms, and the adverb 'soon', occurs seven times in the whole book which creates another seven-fold lexical thread. For more detailed discussion of the use of *idou* 'behold' and *nai* 'yes', please see Appendix 2, sections 2.2.1 and 2.2.2, at the end of this chapter.

For the most part, the sub-units of the Prologue and the Epilogue are grouped together with no overt grammatical connection, otherwise known as **asyndeton**. See Chapter 3.2 for a fuller definition of this technical term. Nonetheless, they do, in fact, belong together by virtue of their similarity of function, and this similarity in turn provides another semantic link between the two larger units. Both units provide support for the main message of the book, by establishing basic book level prosodies, in the case of the Prologue, and by bringing them to completion in the case of the Epilogue (see section 2.3.2 above).

These prosodies provide a basic situation and orientation, which influences everything in between. In the case of Revelation, a significant function of the introductory and concluding units is to support the veracity and the acceptability of the intervening message, as is illustrated by Chart 4. In addition, the Prologue and Epilogue sub-units provide behavior influencing material, such as invitations to certain kinds of action (e.g. 22:17), promises of positive results if the message is heeded, and warnings of negative results if it is not (e.g. 22:14-5).

> **DEFINITION**
>
> ***Volitional Import***
>
> is a term used in the study of meanings (semantics) which describes a discourse in which the author tries to influence the volition of the reader. In other words, the goal of the discourse is to persuade the reader to follow a certain course of action.
>
> It is one of three kinds of import which a text can have (the others being informational and expressive) as described by Callow 1998:97-125.
>
> Callow 1974:13 originally used the term 'hortatory text type' for this kind of discourse, as did other linguists such as Larson 1984, Nida 1984, Beekman et al. 1981 and Longacre 1983a. The term 'volitional import' is, therefore, a more recent and more refined insight into semantics.
>
> See Chapter 6 for a more detailed discussion of this concept.

All these factors taken together reveal that the Prologue and Epilogue combine to provide a framework which establishes that the whole book is dominated by a volitional import. In other words, it is a hortatory kind of text whose main aim is to influence the behavior of its hearers in a particular way. Superficially, the vast majority of the content of the book appears to be discourse with an informational import (i.e. whose main aim is to impart information). However, there are enough other indicators provided by the author in different places, which will confirm in due course what is being revealed by this study of the Prologue and Epilogue. That is, that the main aim of the book as a whole, is to influence behavior rather than just to provide information

2.5.2 The Narrative Interlude 10:1-11:2

This unit can be analyzed in two complementary ways depending on which participant is used as the main criterion to guide the process. Because of the presence of John, this unit is seen primarily as functioning as part of the Narrative Framework as has already been stated.

For your convenience then, these two complementary analyses are laid out next to each other on the following page in Charts 5a and 5b.

Viewed then, from the narrator's standpoint, it can be divided into a three part chiastic structure, which is laid out in Chart 5a below, where it can be seen that John is in focus.

Chart 5a.
The Structure of the Narrative Interlude
(First possible version 10:1-11:2)

A. John is ordered to stop his prophetic activity 10:1-4

B. John is ordered to take and eat the little scroll and is re-commissioned in his prophetic activity 10:5-11

A' John is ordered to recommence his prophetic activity 11:1-2

This analysis requires the inclusion of the segment 11:1-2 because John is personally implicated in these verses, thereby creating a parallel with John's involvement in his own story as recounted in10:1-4.

Chart 5b.
The Structure of the Narrative Interlude
(Second possible version 10:1-11)

A. Introduction of the Angel & his first Intervention ('he cried'), together with the Voice from Heaven 10:1-4

B. Principal Declaration of the Angel ('he swore') 10:5-7

A' Concluding Intervention of the Angel ('he says') together with the Voice from Heaven 10:8-11

A second analysis is possible based on the participation of the angel and the result is also a three part chiasm, as is presented in Chart 5b.

This analysis demonstrates that 10:1-11 can stand alone as an autonomous unit distinct from the unit 11:1-13. This apparent analytical discrepancy can be resolved by positing an overlap link at 11:1-2 as will be described below. The advantage of the two complementary analyses is that they both independently point to a section beginning at 10:5 as being the most important since it is in the middle of a chiasm. See Chapter 6 on prominence for more discussion of such issues.

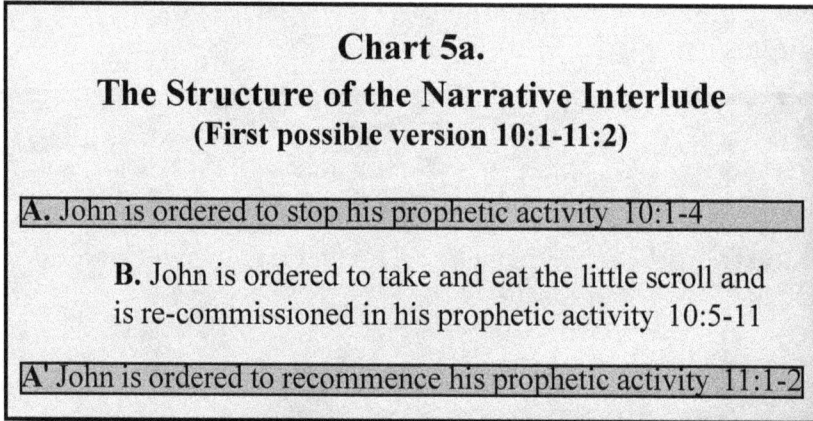

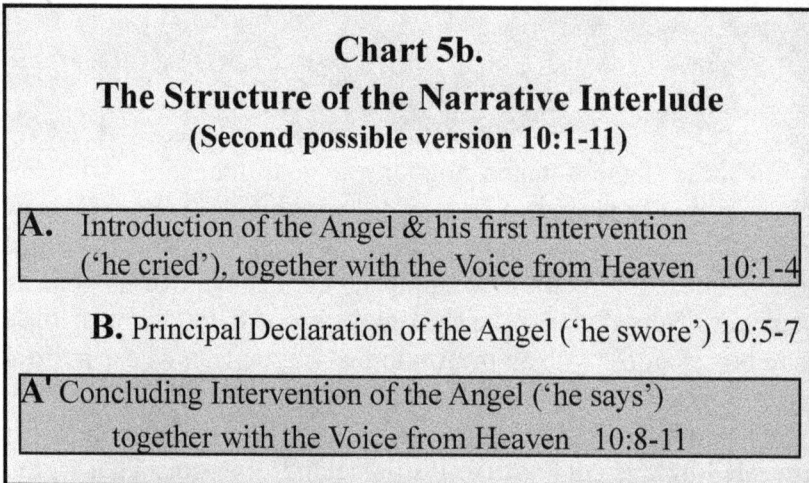

Both analyses also confirm that this unit has a supporting role in the discourse as a whole, as do all the components of the Narrative Framework. The unit does not contribute anything to the informational content of the visions, but it provides a signpost pointing towards the seventh trumpet (10:7), and more information concerning John's personal experience (10:4 and 10:8-11:2). The latter is also contributing to the volitional (hortatory) import of the book. As Callow 1998,136 remarks 'it is informational messages...which are most likely to carry a covert import in addition to the obvious one. ... An example...is the parable'.

It is considered in this case, that the story about John is superficially an informational message, but that it is also a hortatory message of the parable type. This is because the most obvious reason why this part of John's story should be told, is because it serves as an example to his hearers. As Beale 1999,549 explains, 'the interpretive link between chapters 10 and 11 will reveal that what is true of John as a prophet and of his reigning through suffering, is true of all Christians in general'.

2.5.3 The Overlap Links

There is no significant disagreement over the contention that Revelation is introduced by a Prologue and is concluded by an Epilogue, nor even that Chapter 10 is an autonomous unit. The differences of opinion which exist concern the precise point at which these units are attached to the contiguous units. The Prologue has been variously analyzed as 1:1-3, 1:1-8 or 1:1-20, while the Epilogue has been analyzed as 22:10-21, 22:8-21 and 22:7-21, with the majority opinion being in favor of 22:6-21. Lambrecht 1980,78-9 and Beale 1999,110 provide a good general discussion of the issues concerning the Prologue and the Epilogue, while Aune 1998,555 provides discussion on the issues surrounding Chapters 10 and 11.

DEFINITION

An Overlap Link

is that situation in a discourse where one semantic unit functions at the same time, as both the Conclusion to the preceding unit, and also as the Introduction to the following unit.

There are many examples of this feature in Revelation, as will be seen in the course of the following chapters.

Revelation is characterized by the fact that major units are joined together by overlapping links, where one or more sub-units of text serve as both the conclusion of one unit and the beginning of the next, at the same time. This insight into the organization of the text helps to resolve the difficulties, which have previously been encountered, in determining the precise boundaries between sections of text which, on other grounds, are generally considered to be distinct.

The most satisfactory solutions for the Prologue and Epilogue are as follows. As previously indicated, the Prologue ends at 1:11 because this is where there is a coincidence of four distinct features of the text. It is the ending of a major component of the Narrative Framework, since it is a passage in which John's involvement is a significant characteristic. It is the end of a series of seven distinct sub-units connected by asyndeton (i.e. the absence of an overt connection), and this is confirmed by the fact that paragraphs are regularly linked by *kai*, 'and', from 1:12 onwards. These seven sub-units all contribute to situate the book as a whole, and/or contribute to the volitional import of the book. In contrast to this, the first section of visionary content begins at 1:12.

DEFINITION

A Tail-Head Link

is a situation in a discourse where a particular linguistic or semantic feature occurs at the end of one unit and then is repeated at the beginning of the next. Although for other reasons the two units are considered to be distinct, nonetheless, this kind of repetition builds a bridge-like connection between the two units.

In the first instance this kind of repetition is clearly a marker of cohesion. Nonetheless, in situations like this, it can also be posited as confirmatory evidence that a boundary between two units exists at this point in the text.

Finally, 1:12 is also the place where the lexical item used for the verb, 'to see', changes from *blépo* back to **eidéo*. In fact, the presence of John and the verb *blépo* in both 1:10-11 and 1:12, create **a tail-head link.** This repetition therefore, does not contradict, but rather confirms the proposal that a major unit boundary falls between 1:11 and 1:12. If supplementary detail is required, the first sentence of 1:12 is further discussed in Appendix 2, section 2.2.3.

Even though the setting material of 1:9-11 is relevant to the whole book, at the same time it is clear, as the consensus of opinion confirms, that it also specifically serves as the introduction to the first vision (1:12-16). This is validated by the fact that this passage is a homogenous whole, since it can be analyzed as having a concentric structure as shown in Chart 6.

The result is that there are two distinct units of text 1:1-11 and 1:9-20, both of which are complete and could stand alone. However, in reality they are placed together in such a way that the conclusion of the first also acts as the introduction for the second. Consequently, 1:9-11 is best interpreted as an overlap link with a double function.

Chart 6.

The Structure of Revelation 1:9-20

A. Introductory elements including John, the recipient of the vision, the seven churches, and the command 'to write' 1:9-11

B. The content of the vision 1:12-16

A' Concluding elements including John, the command 'to write', and supplementary explanation concerning the seven churches 1:17-20

The Epilogue, being in parallel with the Prologue can be analyzed in an analogous manner, with the exception that the overlap link attaches to the beginning rather than the end of the unit. Thus, as was noted above, 22:6-7 can be readily construed as referring in the first instance to the immediately preceding section on the grounds of the parallel between 'he showed...', and 'he said...' (22:1 and 6), and that the natural antecedent of 'these words' (22:6), is what immediately precedes. At the same time, the parallels between 22:6-7 and the Prologue are undeniable. So this observation supports the previously presented analysis, that the Epilogue also begins here and continues on for the space of seven distinct sub-units. These are also connected for the most part by asyndeton, and contribute to issues of situation and volitional import, the same as the Prologue.

The overlap link therefore, is composed of 22:6-7 as a minimum, although its second boundary is not as clear as for the Prologue. The preferred analysis is that the overlap ends at the end of 22:7. This is firstly, because the *kai*, 'and', at 22:8, logically can really only connect back to the Prologue (1:9-11) and not to any other intervening text. Secondly, because the verb tenses for 'hearing', 'seeing', and, especially, 'he says to me', in 22:8,9 and 10, switch to the present tense, and thirdly, because the verb *blépo*, 'to see', is used once again (22:8), in contrast to the verb **eidéo*, as it was in the Prologue.

Giblin 1991,17-8, Bauckham 1993,5 and Aune 1998,1203 have also noticed that 22:6-9 serve both as the conclusion to the preceding section and the beginning of the Epilogue, and Beale 1999,114 and 1123 makes the same observation about 22:6. Longenecker 2001,111 states 'that the author had a penchant for overlapping techniques is clear from any analysis of Revelation that moves past a rudimentary level'.

What has been called an overlap link in this discussion is similar to the feature which Parunak 1983a,540-6 called a hinge. His study indicated that this phenomenon not only occurs in biblical discourses, but in many other languages as well. Similar overlapping connections between units of discourse have also been found by Heimerdinger 1999,62 in the OT, by Levinsohn 1992,192 in Acts, by Reed 1993,241 in 1 Timothy, and Sherman and Tuggy 1994,29 in 1 John. Longenecker 2001,105 claims that such overlapping techniques were widely used by 'respected rhetoricians of the ancient world'. More examples and discussion of this phenomenon will be presented in the following chapters which concern the five central Cycles.

In the case of the Narrative Interlude, 11:1-2 is the overlap link between it and the following section. This is because it belongs with the preceding text by virtue of John's presence, and with the following text by virtue of the reference to 'the city', and the time period of forty-two months (which is in parallel with the 1260 days of 11:3 and 'the city', in 11:8 and 13). In addition,11:1-2 contributes to the balance of the total structure as can be seen in the chart which follows.

Chart 7.

The Structure of the Trumpets Interlude 11:1-13

A. Introduction 11:1-2

B. The miraculous ministry of the two witnesses 11:3-6

C. The earthly destiny of the two witnesses 11:7-10

B' The miraculous confirmation of the ministry of the two witnesses 11:11-12

A' Conclusion 11:13

It can be noted also that sections B,C, B' and A' all begin with a specific time reference. In conjunction with that, the central section C also has a time reference embedded in the middle, in addition to the one at the beginning. Section A has a time reference at the end. This grouping of these features is remarkable because Revelation otherwise has very few such specific time references. This then, is another piece of evidence which confirms that this is a clear, coherent grouping of sub-units, which is different to those that surround them.

In this particular case, it would probably be best to consider the overlap of 11:1-2 as primarily a literary device designed to link the two units together, rather than as a unit contributing primarily to the information flow of the text. This is because John, having been commanded to recommence his prophetic activity in 11:1, just fades from the scene with no explanation, no overt closure, and no report of the results of his measuring activity.

With reference to the above overlap links then, several conclusions can be drawn with some confidence.

- Firstly, in each case it is clear that the texts concerned divide into two separate units, each with their own structure and their own function.
- Secondly, although the units can be distinguished, the boundary between them cannot be clearly defined, since there is some measure of ambiguity.
- Thirdly, the most justice is done to the data by proposing that, one or more sub-units have the double function of being a conclusion to the first unit, and also an introduction to the second, at the same time.

This solution is particularly satisfactory, because it provides a theoretical justification for the impressionistic nature of the boundary between the units. It also makes the analysis of each unit more satisfactory, and, in some cases, more balanced, by permitting the overlap unit to contribute to the structure of both the units, rather than arbitrarily assigning it to just one of them. Finally, when two units are joined in such an organic way, it creates a strong element of cohesion, which causes the message to flow along from one unit to another in a seemingly seamless way.

More discussion of overlap links in the five central cycles and their function will be presented in Chapter 3.

2.5.4 The Minor Components of the Narrative Framework

The internal structure of the minor components cannot be analyzed in the same way as the major components, since for the most part, they are integrated into the surrounding text and cannot be separated out as a distinct unit. What is interesting to note is that most of them are integrated with a setting of another major unit. A setting is, by definition, introductory, or support, material and the Narrative Framework is also support material. So it is understandable that text material with similar discourse functions should combine together and reinforce each other. The settings will be defined and discussed in the following chapter.

As a reminder, the minor elements of the Narrative Framework occur at 1:17-20, 4:1, 5:4-5, 7:13-17, then again at 14:13, 17:1-18, 19:9-10 and

21:5-10, in two sets of four. For a visual representation of this organization, please look back at Chart 2b.

Thus it is, that 1:17-20 forms a closure to the setting of the first Cycle of visions (the seven letters), and both 4:1 and 5:4-5 contribute to the setting for the visions which follow. Although it could be defined as a separate unit, 17:1-18, nonetheless, contributes directly to the setting of the Cycle concerning Babylon, by providing additional explanatory material.

Three other minor components 7:13-17, 14:13 and 19:9-10 are attached to interludes, which will be defined and described in Chapter 4. The first one is an explanation, which is also support material, while the second two incorporate blessings, which are contributing to the volitional import of the book in the same way as the Prologue and the Epilogue. The only one which is different is 21:5-10, which is embedded in the middle of the seventh Cycle, but since this Cycle is different in many ways (as will be seen later), this is not surprising. The fact that it is a unique use of part of the Narrative Framework may suggest that, in this case, it is contributing to the prominence of the cycle.

2.6 Concluding Remarks on the Narrative Framework

It is the linguistic principle that language in general and, therefore, specific discourses in particular, are organized in a hierarchical manner, which has guided the discussion in this chapter. An awareness of this principle has opened up the possibility of viewing Revelation as a whole, at the highest possible level, before getting taken up, and perhaps sidetracked, by the detail of the visions themselves.

Once this is attempted, it is not difficult to see that the book, as a whole, is not composed entirely of heavenly visions. As a result of our observations, it can be seen that the visions are surrounded, supported and completed, by the presence of an infrastructure which is being called the Narrative Framework. This is a thread-like component, which interweaves its way throughout the whole book, and thereby provides a supporting backbone for the other primary parts of the discourse.

Since both the Narrative Framework, and the visions themselves, are constituents of the book as a whole, they do not occur as a single block of text in one place. On the contrary, they need to permeate the whole book in order to fulfill their role. But, since, in any discourse only one package of information can be presented at a time, there has to be an element of alternation if there is more than one type of information to be presented. Thus it is, that the book begins and ends with elements of the Narrative Framework, but in between, there is a distinct process of alternation as this introductory material gives place to the first part of John's visions, which are presented next. These visions are then followed by other elements of the Narrative Framework, followed, in turn, by more visionary content, and so on, right to the end.

Even though it has many parts, Revelation consists, at the highest level, of a single narrative which tells the story of a man called John who received a series of heavenly visions. Reading a book of this complexity, especially as it explores the unfamiliar territory of other-worldly visions, may be likened to undertaking a rather complex journey to a previously unknown destination. The destination, in this case, is the goal of trying to understand accurately the experience which John described, and the message which he intended to communicate by means of this particular discourse.

To help the hearers find their way to the intended destination, the Narrative Framework is provided to serve as a guide. The Prologue is the starting point which provides information on the general direction, and what may be expected on the journey. The Epilogue indicates that the end has been reached, and provides more information which confirms, after the fact, aspects of the discourse which were previewed in the Prologue.

About halfway through, a way-station is provided in the form of the Narrative Interlude which provides both the narrator and the listeners with the opportunity to take a pause, and be refreshed, in order to persevere to the end of the journey. In between these major points on the journey, lesser signposts are provided in the form of the minor components, which remind the hearers of the kind of path on which they are traveling. These keep the hearers going in the right direction, and they provide additional explanation at strategic points. Not least in importance is that these way-side markers regularly remind them that, ultimately, the author wants them to make some important decisions as a result of reading this message.

Then, in addition, the pathway is constantly illuminated by the occurrence of the various narrative orienters, which may be likened perhaps to the white lines on the road, which give a sense of direction even when everything else may be foggy. All these different components have the same basic function and are designed to complement each other as a single package. Their aim is to guide the hearers along a logical pathway towards an optimal understanding of the message.

The Narrative Framework then, provides a skeleton for the discourse as a whole, to which the disparate visions can be attached in a convenient and coherent way. Since narratives are always organized according to some kind of chronology, the framework also provides the discourse with an element of sequential development. This is very useful for it aids the human mind in its task of receiving, assimilating, and categorizing, a large quantity of new information. This is particularly important when it is remembered that the content of John's visions concern a different referential world, whose system of chronology is at best unknown, and perhaps completely different from the one which pertains to this world. It is this framework which gives a sense of chronological sequence to the book. But at the same time, it needs to be stated clearly that the book as a whole is not a true narrative, and is not organized according to a chronological schema.

An awareness of this first level of discourse organization then, greatly simplifies the task of successfully analyzing the remaining content of the book. This is because significant parts of it, which obviously do not contribute directly to the main message, have been previously categorized and assigned an appropriate place in the author's overall plan.

It should be remembered then, that, unlike many other stories, the story, or narrative part of Revelation is not told for its own sake. It is only intended to be a skeleton which provides sequence, and a measure of support, for another kind of discourse which is contained within it.

To that extent, the Narrative Framework is not the part of the book which immediately attracts the interest of the reader, and possibly that is the reason why, thus far, it seems to have been overlooked by analysts and commentators alike. However, now that it has been delineated, and it is possible to discern the general flow of the book as a whole, it is appropriate to consider the lower levels of the hierarchy, namely, the details of the content of the individual visions which occur in the body of the book.

INTRODUCING THE SEVEN CYCLES

APPENDIX 2

PREFACE

This Appendix has been placed here to provide extra technical information relating to the analysis of the Narrative Framework for those who wish to explore these matters further. There is no need to read this Appendix if this extra information is not required, for the technical information already given in the main text is sufficient for the general purpose of understanding the structural organization of the book. The Appendix just broadens out what has already been explained and makes more specific connections with the methodology used, and the commentators who have gone before.

The extra contents are as follows :

1) Precise information to explain and support the division into units which was described in Chapter 2.

2) A more highly developed argumentation concerning the chronology issues contained in the book.

3) Some technical discussions and remarks concerning various grammatical issues, including the connectives and the overlap links.

4) A review of remarks by previous commentators concerning the Narrative Framework.

All other readers are invited to move on straight away to Chapter 3, where we will start explaining and describing the seven cycles, which make up the main part of the book. .

APPENDIX 2
Ancillary Information Pertaining to the Analysis of the Narrative Framework

A2.1 Evidence for the Division into Units

A2.1.1 A General Explanation

Language is structured on the basis of two opposing, yet complementary tendencies. On the one hand, it is composed of discrete units which can be analyzed and distinguished from each other, but, on the other hand, distinct units which share certain similarities naturally group together in order to form larger, more complex units. As a result of these naturally occurring linguistic phenomena, a larger text can be divided into units at the points where the effects of these two tendencies most clearly coincide. That is, a significant juncture can be posited where the tendencies for units to cohere together is pulling in two opposite directions thereby creating a separation. Where this separation is confirmed by evidence for positing two distinct units, a division can be established. In addition, all units have a function in the overall structure, and where different functions can be discerned, this provides additional support for the proposed division into distinct units.

As a general principle, evidence derived from features drawn from the higher levels of the hierarchy carries more weight than that drawn from the lower levels. In addition, marked features, where relevant to the division into units, carry more weight than unmarked features.

In this Appendix evidence will be provided in summary form, to indicate on what basis the text was divided into units for this study. In order to keep the material manageable, the information will be provided in abbreviated form, and not all the sub-units will be presented. However, a sample of the more difficult cases will be provided in order to show what is possible.

The main aim at this stage is to demonstrate that text can be divided into units on the basis of linguistic evidence, and that this evidence can be made available for perusal by other analysts. What this means is that the on-going debate concerning the analysis of a particular text can consciously work towards a definite consensus as the evidence itself is appraised, and the decisions approved, or modified, as the case may be, until most parties are satisfied with the outcome. In the case of continued ambiguity, a final value judgment can at least be made on the basis of consciously preferring some parts of the evidence over others, while still recognizing that alternative interpretations of the data are viable options for those who may prefer them.

The abbreviations used in the presentation of the data are as follows:

D = Differences permitting a division into distinct units. Normally reference is made to the division at the beginning of the unit and also to that at the end of the unit.

IC = Internal Coherence requiring that similar units be grouped together on account of their internal similarity.

F = Function of the unit.

A2.1.2 The Narrative Framework As a Whole

D: Composed of all those units where the narrator(s), John (and Jesus), is (are) actively involved, or in some way overtly present in the surface of the text. The content of these units is also composed of text which is primarily volitional (hortatory) in nature. There are major units, minor units and short phrases (like 'and I saw') which contribute to the Narrative Framework.

IC: The internal coherence of this framework is dependent on the narrative characteristics of the text concerned, with a primary participant situated in particular places and a chronological development, and also the volitional import of the texts concerned. The major units, the Prologue, the Narrative Interlude and the Epilogue create a three-part ABA' linguistic structure.

F: Provides a coherent framework anchored in the referential world known to the addressees, within which other-worldly visions can be recounted and potentially understood. It provides both a setting and introduction to the book as a whole (the Prologue) and a conclusion (the Epilogue). However, the Prologue is more than just a low level setting, since it also clearly establishes the objective of the book as being volitional in nature (i.e. intending to influence the behavior of the readers). In addition, the Central Interlude provides an example of how they should respond to the content of the book. The predominance of volitional import type text is interpreted as marking the Narrative Framework for special prominence. This means that whereas a normal setting and framework of this nature would usually be interpreted as being less important than the body of the book which contains the informational content, in this case the Narrative Framework overall is interpreted as being more important than the body, or at least equally important.

It should be noted that as a general rule, conclusions are naturally prominent in many kinds of text, but especially those where the major units are in a coordinated relationship as is the case for Revelation.

A2.1.3 The Prologue 1:1-11

D: Beginning of the book, no preceding text. End of Narrative Framework text, overlap with following unit which begins vision content, and which starts using *kai* 'and' as the usual higher level connective.

IC: Composed of units which all contribute support material to the book as a whole and which have no overt connection (asyndeton). Most of these units contribute to establishing various aspects of the volitional import (hortatory text-type) of the book. Overt presence of John the narrator, and reference to Jesus as co-narrator.

F: Establishes the initial narrative anchor point and as such constitutes the introduction to the book as a whole.

Unit 1 1:1-2

D: No preceding text.

IC: Statement concerning the nature of the book: its topic, origins and transmission.

F: Establishes the general situation. Introduction to the Prologue.

Unit 2 1:3

D: New text type (blessing)

IC: A blessing - first of seven such blessings.

F: Foregrounds a hortatory conceptual network. Initiates a book level prosody.

Unit 3 1:4-5a

D: Different text type. Different topic, participants, grammar and lexical items.

IC: Typical constituents of an epistolary introduction.

Repetition of *apo...kai apo* 'from…and from…'

F: Epistolary introduction.

Unit 4 1:5b-6

D: New text type. New addressee. New topic. Ends with 'Amen'.

IC: Doxology (ascription of glory to the Son of God with reasons).

F: Could be viewed as an aside with no specific function relating to its context. However, its probable function is to foreground an awareness that the whole text is dominated and impregnated by the divine presence of the Godhead. It also specifically foregrounds previously known information concerning the results of Christ's death for His followers. It foregrounds volitional import by implicitly inviting the readers to participate in the ascription of praise. Note the presence of 'amen' which implies a participatory role for the hearers. It introduces the sub-theme of worship.

Unit 5 1:7

D: Different text type. Different topic. Follows an 'amen' and ends with an 'amen'. *idou* 'behold', at beginning of a sentence/ paragraph.

IC: A statement concerning Jesus Christ (implicit) containing allusions to the OT.

F: Continues to foreground Jesus Christ as a principal personage (same as units 1,3 and 4), and specifically foregrounds the Old Testament as an appropriate interpretive network.

Unit 6 1:8

D: Different text type. Different topic and grammatical form. Follows an 'amen'.

IC: A single statement concerning a single personage.

F: Foregrounds the importance of the Godhead and in particular His eternal nature and His omnipotence. Initiates a book level prosody which is completed in the Epilogue.

Unit 7 1:9-11

D: Repetition of *ego* 'I' referring to a different personage. Different text type and topic. End of Narrative Framework followed by first segment of visionary content. Tail-head link, being a double reference to John in connection with the verb *blépo* 'to see'.

IC: Presence of John and same topic throughout. Repetition of 'I came to be in...' in 1:9-10.

F: Overlap link. End (seventh unit) of the Prologue and also first unit of the following section.

A2.1.4 The Epilogue 22:6-21

D: Return to Narrative Framework type text with volitional import. End of book, no following text. Parallelism with Prologue.

IC: Overt Presence of John. Reoccurrence and repetition of the prosody indicating that Jesus is coming soon (verses 7,12,17 and 20). Reoccurrence of primary linkage of the discourse units by asyndeton. Presence of seven sub-units which contribute directly to the volitional import of the book.

F: End point of the Narrative Framework and as such constitutes the conclusion for the book as a whole.

Unit 1 22:6-7a

D: Return to Narrative Framework type text. The text changes from being visionary content to being commentary on the visionary content, from conveying informational import to conveying volitional import.

IC: Verse 6 is a single sentence addressing a single topic. Verse 7a is part of a book level prosody and, as such, has no close structural connection with its immediate context. It is nonetheless considered to be grammatically connected to verse 6 because of the presence of *kai* 'and'. Alternatively, the *kai* connects it back to the last preceding appearance of the prosody at 16:15.

F: Concluding commentary on previous visionary content. Part of overlap link which creates a transition to the Epilogue. Introductory unit of the Epilogue.

Unit 2 22:7b

D: Different text type (blessing) and different topic.

IC: A single sentence and a single topic.

F: Contributes to a book level prosody (the seven blessings).

Unit 3 22:8-11

D: Different text type and topic (first person narrative). Different principal personage. Presence of initial *kai* 'and', which does not link back to immediately preceding text but either to 22:6 or more likely right back to the Prologue. (See discussion of connectives at A2.2.4 below)

IC: Dialogue linked internally by *kai.* It is not obvious whether verse 11 belongs with verse 10 or should be considered a separate unit since it is introduced by asyndeton. The present analysis is preferred because the third person form seems to accord better with a continuation of the previous speech rather than as an introduction to the following first person speech. The mitigated imperatives and the consequent hortatory nature of the text also accord better with what precedes than with what follows. The presence of asyndeton can be accounted for on the basis that it is a continuation of a direct speech beginning in verse 10. If verse 11 were to stand alone it is difficult to adduce any evidence to support this and to attribute a significant separate function to such a unit.

F: Brings to a conclusion the description of John's personal situation and involvement in the transmission process. Concludes the worship motif. Contributes to and brings to conclusion the hortatory material characterized by second and third person type imperatives aiming at the personal behavior of the reader.

Unit 4 22:12-13

D: Different text type, topic, speaker and grammatical form. Introduced by *idou* 'behold' alone.

IC: First person speech throughout.

F: Part of the prominent material of the Epilogue. Concludes book level prosodies ('Alpha and Omega', 'I am coming quickly'). Contributes to the hortatory nature of the Epilogue. Completes the reward motif.

Unit 5 22:14-15

D: Different text type, topic (blessing) and grammatical form.

IC: Same topic and form (blessing and cursing). Most of the seven blessings are simply a blessing. This one is different in that it adds a complementary cursing reminiscent of the paired blessings and cursings in Deuteronomy. Both parts allude to the Old Testament.

F: The last in the series of seven blessings. The addition of the cursing may make this the most prominent in the series. The final hortatory material aiming at the personal behavior of the reader.

Unit 6 22:16-20

D: Different text type, topic and grammatical structure (first person declarations with responses). Repetition of *ego* 'I' referring to a different personage.

IC: A single dialogue with two statements and two sets of responses creating a balanced parallel structure (ABA' B') unified by the concept of 'witness'. Inclusio type repetition of 'Jesus' in verses 16 and 20. Verse 17 is attached to verse 16 because of the presence of *kai* 'and'.

F: Concluding statement or revelation specifically from Jesus. Final exhortation concerning the reader's attitude towards the words of the prophecy. Final references to the motifs of the plagues, the tree of life and the holy city. Conclusion of the 'come' prosody.

Unit 7 22:21

D: New text type and topic (prayer of blessing). Different principal speaker (John).

IC: Single sentence and topic. Typical epistolary closure.

F: Conclusion to Epilogue and the whole book viewed as a letter.

A2.1.5 The Narrative Interlude 10:1-11:2

D: A new main participant 10:1. It is not the seventh trumpet as would be expected from the numerical sequencing. A different main speaker is overtly marked as from 11:3. Reappearance of John. 11:1-2 is interpreted as an overlap link with 11:1-13.

IC: Symmetrical ABA' structure involving new main participant (angel) ending at 10:11 with his involvement in 11:1 being ambiguous. Symmetrical ABA' structure based on John's involvement which runs from 10:1 to 11:2.

F: An interlude for the whole book. The major central component of the Narrative Framework. A signpost pointing towards the seventh trumpet. John's personal example contributes to the volitional import of the book.

Unit 1 10:1-4

D: A new main participant ('another angel') and his first utterance. The first command ('seal') to John in a new series.

IC: A single main participant and event. 10:4 is included because of coherence created by the repetition of the seven thunders.

F: Introductory unit of a coherent series. Sets the scene for the larger unit. First command to John which has significance at the higher level of the Narrative Framework (Prologue-Narrative Interlude-Epilogue).

Unit 2 10:5-11 (Alternative Analysis of Unit 2: 10:5-7)

D: Same participants as unit 1 but a different event.

IC: Primary coherence provided by the involvement of John in a single event. Coherence between 10:5-7 and 10:8-11 is provided by the fact that vv.5-7 are a setting for what follows and the repetition of the lexical items concerning the concept of prophecy in verses 7 and 11.

F: Central unit in a series of three and probably the most important because of the chiastic structure of the whole and because of its greater length.

Unit 3 11:1-2 (Alternative Analysis of Unit 3: 10:8-11)

D: A new event involving John.
IC: John's continuing presence.
F: Concluding unit in a series of three, but also functioning as an overlap link and as the introduction to the next main unit 11:1-13.

A2.2 Other Interesting Features of the Narrative Framework

A2.2.1 Prominence Features in the Prologue

The Greek word *idou* 'behold' occurs thirty times (including occurrences in the Textus Receptus) in Revelation, spread evenly throughout the book. This, in and of itself, indicates that it must have a significant role in the overall organization of the discourse.

The first time *idou* appears is in the Prologue in 1:7, where it introduces the Old Testament prophecy about Jesus coming in the clouds. This is particularly significant, since it is the first use of the word in the book. As a consequence, if the rule of the importance of the first mention of a feature is applied, then a good understanding of its function here should stand the analyst in good stead for the rest of the book. This is why it is important to take the time to have a good look at features like this, insignificant though they may seem to be, because they are a kind of mini-template which can help interpret more ambiguous occurrences elsewhere.

In addition, this occurrence is the first time it is used at the beginning of a sentence, but that is not all, because it also stands at the beginning of a full paragraph. This is quite clear in this instance (as templates tend to be) because it immediately follows a paragraph ending with an 'Amen!'. So there is no dispute that it is indeed the beginning of a complete paragraph. Then, to confirm this insight still more, this same paragraph (1:7), also ends with another 'Amen!' So, right at the beginning then, we find a clearly demarcated paragraph introduced by this word.

So now let's not forget to consider its meaning before getting caught up in the technical details. Obviously, it means 'Look!', being regularly translated as 'Behold', or 'Lo!'. Straight away, then, it can be seen that this word has no informational content to contribute to the discourse. It is clearly a 'signpost' word which is literally, and specifically, directing the readers' attention away from itself, or even away from what has gone before, to something else. (See Reed 1995,90).

So then, the basic, looming question, which needs to be asked and answered, is this: '**What** exactly is this signpost word pointing at ?' Van Otterloo 1988,40 (cf. Wendland 1992,107) considers that the primary function of *idou* is to introduce important personages. This observation immediately shows us how important it is to look closely at features such as these (especially a first occurrence) and to be as rigorous and as rapier-like as possible in our remarks.

So, in this case, the sign-post leaves us, mouth agape, with more questions than answers. This is because, if its function is to introduce important personages, then where is the personage ? He is nowhere to be seen, since he has been completely grammatically elided. Consequently, the *idou* is left rather forlornly propped up against a verb (which is not a personage), which only has an implied third person case marking. Otherwise, there is no other distinctive personage in the whole of the paragraph.

The implied personage in question is Jesus, and undoubtedly He is important, but He is not being introduced here. This is because He was introduced at great length throughout 1:1-6, and his appearance, at that point, was not highlighted by *idou.* So at the very first inspection, then, this hypothesis does not hold water.

In addition, this proposal does not correlate with the important occurrence at 4:1. This is another major beginning, like Chapter 1, where new information is being introduced. However, even with a good imagination it is not possible to perceive that the *idou*, which is present there, is introducing a personage either.

It is much more likely that its generic usage is that of a prominence marker, which can imply different meanings in different contexts. These meanings and contexts would depend also on which level of the linguistic hierarchy the marker is functioning. This would explain why it can be attached to many different linguistic units, whether it be a person, a verb (as in 1:7) or an inanimate object like a door, as in 4:1.

There are four possibilities for explaining its appearance in 1:7:

1) It marks the verb 'he comes' simply at the clause level, thereby drawing attention to the (future) coming of Jesus on the clouds.
2) It marks the verse as a unit of the Prologue, hence indicating that it is the most prominent unit in the Prologue.

3) It marks the phrase beginning 'he comes...' as the first occurrence of a book level prosody which is taken up again, particularly in the Epilogue ('Behold I am coming soon' 22:7).
4) A combination of the above three possibilities.

At the lexical level it marks the verb 'he comes' as being particularly important. If we stop there, it does not really make much sense as to why this one word should be marked as particularly important, especially since the whole of Chapter 1 is full of important words. The only reason why an individual word could be that important is if it starts an important, book-level, lexical thread (or prosody). This interpretation aligns it with option 3), making it thereby a very pertinent possibility.

At the sub-unit, or paragraph, level, its presence here would be to mark that sub-unit as being the most important within the larger section which surrounds it, which, in this case, is the Prologue. This is of interest when it is considered that there is no clear natural prominence in the Prologue, to indicate which part of it should be considered the most important.

Within the context of the Prologue as a whole, it draws attention to the fact that it is Jesus Christ who is coming, so in that case it is drawing attention to an important participant of the discourse as a whole. It is also drawing attention to the fact that He is (or, is due to be) coming again on the clouds, and that therefore, this coming should be understood within the context of the OT prophecies, and of what His disciples were told in Acts 1:11.

As a book level feature it seems to indicate that all this information should be kept in view as a key cluster of concepts which will reoccur and, in effect, permeate the whole book. This possibility is very pertinent to an introductory set of units, situated at the beginning of a discourse. If this is correct, then it leads to the understanding that these concepts may be intended as an important interpretive key for the content of the book. Then, in addition to that, they may be intended to be viewed as a major motivating factor within the context of the volitional import of the book.

So then, in general terms, *idou* is interpreted as being a marker of special prominence in this study. This means that it can appear with, and be applied to, different components of the discourse, and also that it can operate at different levels of the hierarchy.

Specifically, with regard to its use in 1:7, my preference is for Option 4). In cases of ambiguity like this, where several different interpretations are viable and reasonable, then the best way-forward is to take account of, and benefit from, all the possible interpretations.

A2.2.2 Prominence Features in the Prologue and the Epilogue Together
In the previous section we discussed the first occurrence of *idou* 'and', in conjunction with, 'he is coming', referring to Christ, which appears at 1:7. In addition to that occurrence, it is very significant to note that *idou* occurs another four times in conjunction with a phrase referring to Christ coming. All of these together are:

- Behold, he is coming with the clouds 1:7
- Behold, I am coming soon in 3:11 (Textus Receptus),
- Behold, I am coming as a thief in 16:15
- Behold, I am coming soon in 22:7 and
- Behold, I am coming soon in 22:12

These are the only cases in the whole book where a grammatically identical phrase, or a conceptually identical phrase is used with *idou*. The first one in 1:7 is the first use of *idou* in the book and the last two at 22:7 and 12 are the last two uses of *idou*. In addition, there is at least one other occurrence in the middle of the book. To say that there is a pattern here, would be an understatement, because if all the occurrences are counted, there are five of them, which is the number of grace.

However, that is not all, for the phrase 'I am coming soon' occurs one more time, right at the end of the book in 22:20, and on this occasion, it is also marked for prominence. On this occasion it is not marked by *idou,* but by *nai* 'yes'. This is also very interesting because if we take the phrase, 'Behold, I am coming as a thief', as being conceptually synonymous with the phrase, 'Behold, I am coming soon', then we end up again with five occurrences of this particular phrase.

But that is still not all. The Nestlé version of the Greek text has *nai* in 22:20, but the Textus Receptus has it twice. All of the occurrences of *nai* in Revelation are as follows:

- It occurs in 1:7, along with *idou*, so that this verse has two prominence features and not just one. In addition, it has an 'Amen' at the end, which is really serving as a prominence feature as well. So, therefore, there are three special prominence features in one paragraph in this verse.
- It then occurs on two more occasions in the middle of the book at 14:13 and 16:7, once associated with the Spirit, and once associated with the Lord God Almighty.
- Finally, as previously noted, it occurs twice in 22:20, if the Textus Receptus reading is included. So counting them all together, there are five occurrences of *nai* in the whole book.

This means that *nai* occurs together with *idou* in 1:7, and for both of them this is their first occurrence in the book, and both of them are reinforcing the concept of Jesus coming again in the clouds. Then *nai* occurs twice in other contexts to do with the Godhead in the middle of the book, whereas *idou* occurs twice more in the context of Jesus coming again.

Finally, their last two occurrences at the end of the book are both also associated with the concept of Jesus coming again. These 'coincidences' are quite remarkable, and common sense suggests that these are intentional features, which the author has deliberately woven into the texture of his text.

In passing, and for completeness, it can be noted that 'Amen!' functioning as a prominence marker (it also occurs once as a noun at 3:14) occurs nine times in the book. It occurs twice in close proximity to 1:7: once immediately preceding it (the first occurrence) and once at the end. As if that is not enough, it also occurs twice again right at the end of the book: once directly after the last repeat of 'I am coming soon' and once more, a few words later, as the very last word of the book in the Textus Receptus.

The first conclusion, which we can deduce then from these observations, is that this concept cluster concerning Christ's coming again is intended to be prominent in the Epilogue. But as we have seen, a similar concept was marked by three different prominence markers in the Prologue as well. These features all taken together therefore, suggest secondly, that this concept is intended to be retained as being important for the whole book.

However, since the reference to Christ's (imminent) coming again is particularly prominent in the conclusion, this phrase could be defined then, as the true 'After Word' of the whole book. This is not the first time this has been proposed since the message is so well communicated, that this idea is intuitively obvious to many, if not most, readers. However, what is happening here in this discussion, is that we are demonstrating that this intuition is correct. This is because we have shown in an objective manner, with visible linguistic evidence, that the author has indeed gone out of his way to lodge these precise thoughts indelibly in the readers' awareness and memory. It seems as if he has done a remarkably good job.

A2.2.3 The Overlap Connection between the Prologue and the Following Setting

Over the years there has been a considerable lack of consensus over where the Prologue ends exactly, and numerous possibilities have been suggested. So is it possible to improve that consensus and at the very least narrow down the options to those which have the best linguistic support from the text itself

The answer is probably yes, because previous analysts and commentators have not observed the overlap link which occurs here for the first time, and which then continues to be a regular feature throughout the rest of the book. In addition, neither have they taken into account the series of settings which occur in the book as a regular, systematic feature. This oversight is particularly problematic because settings are an extremely well-known feature of literature of all kinds. This is because no coherent, well-formed, discourse can exist without a setting, or an introduction of some kind. There is no rule that a discourse must have only one setting, but on the contrary, an author is free to provide as many settings as he thinks fit. As many as are necessary to make his message as relevant, as comprehensible, and as coherent as possible, in order for his readers to fully understand what he is trying to tell them.

So the Prologue is indeed, an introduction, or a setting, for the book as whole. But in this case, John has also provided a series of lower-level settings, spaced regularly throughout the whole book, and the first one starts at 1:12. See Chapter 3 for more information on the settings and particularly this setting to Cycle 1.

In the main text of Chapter 2 above, it has been suggested that the Prologue is to be found between 1:1 and 1:11. The main reason for this is because all these verses are clearly part of the Narrative Framework, and the analysis produces seven coherent units with no overt connection (asyndeton) between them. From verse 12 onwards, the tone changes, for it becomes visionary material rather than Narrative Framework material, and all the sections start to be systematically linked together by the conjunction *kai* 'and'.

However, the obvious difficulty with this proposal is that John's overt presence continues on into the first part of 1:12. One solution would be to consider it as part of the Narrative Framework and, therefore, as attached to verse 11. If it were attached to verse 11 and the end of the overlap link made to fall in the middle of verse 12, it would make no difference to the overall analysis.

However, it was decided to make the division at the end of verse 11 for the following reasons:

1) Overlap links by definition are transitional in nature and their borders cannot always be defined with neat precision.

2) Verse 12 has considerable internal cohesion and is not amenable to division. The natural pulling apart between two segments bound together by internal cohesion occurs at the end of verse 11.

3) In verse 12 there is the description of John's first action within the context of his following vision, which is in direct contrast to his previous actions, which were in the context of his normal physical experience. In this first instance therefore, this action is considered to be integrated into the visionary content, rather than into the preceding component of Narrative Framework. This is similar to the way in which the minor Narrative Framework components are considered to be inextricably integrated into their immediate context.

4) In addition, this action ('turning to see') is a necessary orientation for the description of what he actually saw, which is unambiguously part of the visionary content. The second part of the description of his action occurs together in a single grammatical clause with the content of what he saw This means that the two parts cannot be separated. This means in turn, that this grammatical integration implies that the same measure of integration should be carried over into any subsequent interpretation of the meaning or of the function of the unit in question

5) The first occurrence of *kai...eidon* 'and… I saw' is in this verse. Although this phrase is part of the Narrative Framework, it is a special component which is directly integrated into the visionary content and cannot be separated from it. It is therefore different from the Narrative Framework which occurs in verse 11. The first occurrence of a special feature is likely to be specially marked (similar argument to that of numbers 3) and 4) above). The lengthy orientation involving the repetition of the verb 'to turn' clearly builds up to, and draws special attention to, the key verb 'I saw'. Consequently, this orientation of verse 12a is analyzed as belonging with *kai eidon* and, therefore, as belonging with the immediately following visionary content.

6) There is a switch here between *blépo* 'I see' and **eidéo* 'I see'. The two occurrences of *blépo* in verses 11 and 12, along with the repetition of John's participation in these same two verses, can be interpreted as a tail-head link. This feature is very common in Hebraïc style discourses such as this and occurs elsewhere in Revelation, as, for example, at the beginning of Chapter 13. Therefore, this viewpoint serves to confirm that the natural linguistic division between discrete units, occurs between these two verses.

7) The use of the connective *kai* as the primary means of linking sentences and higher level units begins in this verse. The *kai* at the beginning of verse 12 introduces a new paragraph. It is therefore interpreted as connecting two paragraphs as distinct units (1:9-11 and 1:12-16), which are the first two paragraph level units of the setting of Cycle 1 (1:9-20). If this understanding of the function of *kai* is accepted, it is not possible to interpret

it as connecting the beginning of verse 12 with the end of verse 11 at the sentence level. See below for further discussion of this issue.

A2.2.4 The Connectives Used in Revelation

There are only two grammatical conjunctions which are used in Revelation. These are asyndeton, which is the absence of a grammatical marker, and *kai*, which is traditionally translated as 'and'.

Asyndeton is characteristic of the Prologue where it is interpreted as linking together a series of different sub-topics which will all be developed in different ways throughout the book. It is also characteristic of the latter part of the Epilogue, where it is interpreted as being an intentional reminder that the Epilogue should be understood as being in direct parallel with the Prologue. In any case, most, if not all, the sub-topics initiated in the Prologue are brought to closure, one after another, in the Epilogue. This may be another reason why this feature re-occurs in the Epilogue.

The use of *kai* is characteristic of all the rest of the book, where it occurs innumerable times in all sorts of contexts. Possibly because of its ubiquitous presence, it turned out that this feature was never a decisive issue in the analysis of the macro structure of the book. It is for this reason therefore, that it is not discussed in the main text of this book. The aim here then, is to make some reference to it for the sake of completeness, and to point forward to more discussion of this topic which will be developed elsewhere.

One of the problems inherent in the task of taking account of *kai* is that previous authors have only investigated its occurrence in narrative-type texts which are linear in nature. The characteristic of Revelation is that it is not a true narrative and is cyclic rather than linear in nature.

What was observed, however, in the course of this research is that the use of *kai* in a long, complex discourse of this nature is much broader in scope than in other contexts. At the most basic level, it has always been understood that *kai* connects words and sentences together. At this level it is perceived as a word which has the function of joining together discrete, pre-existing units, like beads on a piece of string, or like links in a chain. For this reason over time it has come therefore, to be used as a short-cut for dividing a text into its composite units. In addition, by default, it is assumed that conjunctions such as *kai* join together units which must, of necessity, be directly contiguous.

This default viewpoint overlooks the fact that this word has always been called a conjunction, which implies that it conjoins two parts of the discourse, and therefore, has the function of linking them together into a coherent whole. In other words, somewhere along the line it was viewed as a cohesive device and not a separator.

So it was that, in the course of this study of Revelation, it became obvious that *kai* was also being used to link together – or thread together, if you prefer – units of text which were bigger than the sentence. It was not difficult to see that whole paragraphs were being sewn together as well. In this case the two paragraphs, as units, would be contiguous, but you could no longer say that the last words of the first paragraph were being directly, and specifically attached to the first words of the second paragraph. No, it was the paragraph, *as a unit,* which was being attached, joined, linked, threaded on to the following paragraph, as a unit.

Then to make it more challenging and interesting, why should this system of threading stop with the paragraph? After the paragraph, came the cycles, and it was clear that they were being placed in an additive, or conjunctive relationship as well. But the relationship was between what and what? The only logical answer to this question was that one cycle as a unit, was being sewn together with another cycle, as a unit. This was so even though the beginning of the previous cycle was now at a distance of several dozen paragraphs from the beginning of the second.

When you attempt to operate at these higher levels of the hierarchy in this way, the traditional concept of a conjunction with its implication of joining (or separating, depending on your viewpoint) two discrete units, begins to become cumbersome and hard to handle.

In order to alleviate these practical difficulties, a working hypothesis was developed which posited *kai* as a topic marker. Its function would be to indicate to the reader that more information on the same topic would follow in the next section of the discourse. In opposition to this, asyndeton, in the case of Revelation, and *dé* 'but', in the case of other Greek texts, would indicate the start of a new topic.

It seems quite possible that in the era of a totally oral/aural culture, this clear marking of the development of the thread of a particular topic, would have been a useful, if not an essential, linguistic feature. Then, with the passage of time, as the culture became more book-based, with writing coming to the fore, these topic markers then began to be viewed differently, and, perhaps, even changed their function. The only way to confirm this hypothesis would be to investigate this issue in cultures which are still currently oral in nature. However, since I, personally, have no means of doing this, my proposal will have to remain a hypothesis for now.

This is just a brief summary of this rather complex subject. A more detailed discussion of these issues can be found in Schooling 2025.

A2.3 The Influence of the Narrative Framework on the Chronology of the Book

Chronology is a particular problem for Revelation more than for most books. The very terms (preterist, futurist etc.) which have been traditionally used to label the different interpretive viewpoints indicate that differing views of chronology lie behind the discussion. The main structural issue in the debate is whether the book is ordered according to a linear chronology or whether it is recapitulative in nature.

This issue can be clarified by appeal to two related linguistic concepts, that of the referential hierarchy and that of the narrative text-type. Language does not exist in a vacuum but is a phenomenon of human behavior to the extent that there is a need to communicate about something. The 'something' which is conceptualized and then talked about is usually something which exists outside of the speaker in a 'real' world of some kind. This external world is what is referred to when communication is undertaken and is called the referential world of the speaker or the referential hierarchy. It is called a hierarchy because the world of things and events is considered to be organized in a hierarchical form in a way analogous with the organization of the phonological hierarchy or the grammatical hierarchy. See Pike and Pike 1982,7.

In the majority of cases, this referential world is the physical world of things and events which are experienced through the physical senses, and which is the usual context for human activity.

Because the physical world is so all-pervasive of human experience it can be taken for granted and, for this reason, it is possible to overlook the fact that it is not the only referential world which is relevant to human communication. Because it is possible to conceptualize anything which can happen in the real world, it is therefore possible to 'envisage' things and events which have not actually existed or happened in the real world. It is also possible to 'imagine' a completely different referential world which has a different set of characteristics and rules of behavior. Although this phenomenon rarely occurs in daily life, it often occurs in literature both written and oral. See Callow 1998,65-7 for definition and discussion of the terms 'envisaging' and 'imagining'.

Revelation is an unusual book for the very reason that it requires the reader to take account of two different referential worlds within the scope of the same text. The first world to be introduced is the usual referential world of normal, human experience. John himself, the island of Patmos and the seven churches in Asia Minor all belonged to that world. It is one of the functions of the Narrative Framework to set the book in the context of this world, to describe relevant aspects of this world and to keep the reader in constant touch with this world. John needed to root his book specifically in the real world with which his readers were familiar, and this included establishing himself as a known and reliable witness (cf. 1:1,9 and 22:8), in order that they may be convinced enough to believe him when he goes on to describe another world, which was undoubtedly less familiar to them.

This other world is the heavenly referential world which John sees (1:12) and even visits (4:1), a world which is peopled by angels and dragons, and where great distances can apparently be traveled in no time at all (17:3 and 21:10). In our modern day culture, for example, fairy stories are based in an imaginary world as are literary classics like C.S.Lewis' *Chronicles of Narnia* or J.R.Tolkien's *Lord of the Rings*.

It is of little importance for questions of analysis whether the world John experienced in his visions is another real, existing world, or whether it is just a world of symbols which he only experienced in his imagination. What is important is to recognize that the book refers to two different referential worlds, and that both of these worlds have to be understood and interpreted in terms of their own particular characteristics. It is not, therefore, legitimate to transfer the characteristics of one world and apply them to the other world, without consciously justifying this process.

Having established the earthly setting of the book at the outset, the author by means of subsequent parts of the Narrative Framework creates a bridge between the familiar world and the unfamiliar one. However, the fact that the two worlds are linked and that there is interaction between the two, should not cloud this basic fact that the author, and thence the reader, is dealing with two different worlds.

The characteristic of referential worlds, which is under discussion here, is the issue of chronology. So, having established the fact that two different worlds 'exist' in the same text, it also needs to be clearly stated that both these worlds, normally speaking, should have a system of chronology. But, and this is the crucial issue to bring out into open discussion, it cannot be assumed that the two systems of chronology are identical. In fact, nothing can be assumed about any similarities or differences, except on the basis of relevant information provided, in the first instance, by the author himself.

The basic framework of Revelation has been called a Narrative Framework, because it has the usual characteristics of a narrative text type. In particular, narratives are organized according to a chronological structure and, unless the author wants to create a special effect, which he is obliged to indicate clearly, in order to avoid being misunderstood, that chronology will be presented in a linear fashion. In the case of Revelation, a man called John witnessed a series of visions which he wrote down, presumably according to the chronological order in which he viewed them. The chronology then, which provides cohesion for the book, is a characteristic of the Narrative

Framework. As such, it is the chronology of the physical world which is being expressed and not that of the heavenly world, whatever that system of chronology may be. Even though some parts of the visionary content of the book, which are based in the heavenly referential world, contain some narrative text, it is still being narrated by John from his standpoint of a human being who is observing the heavenly world as a temporary visitor, and according to his system of chronology.

In contrast to this explanation, Aune 1997,xciii believes that the order of the visions is such as it is 'because (the author) intends the visions themselves to constitute *a single chronological narrative of the eschatological events that will soon begin to unfold'* (his italics). However, he does not provide any data or argument to support this opinion.

A key verse for the chronology of the book is 1:19, for it is on the basis of this verse that some commentators divide the book into three parts, and claim that each part refers to succeeding periods of earthly history. However, this interpretation assumes more than this verse alone can support, because it rides roughshod over a straightforward understanding of its surface grammar. In terms of basic linguistic analysis, phrases like 'the things which you saw, (the things) which are, and (the things) which are about to occur after these things' in 1:19, can only refer, in the first instance, to the things which John saw in his visions and which are being referred to from within the context of the Narrative Framework.

Likewise, any chronology implicit in such phrases can only refer to the chronology of the Narrative Framework, which is the order in which he observed the visions in the 'real' time of the earthly world, which is the referential context of this framework. If the things which John saw, do, in fact, have relevance to some future period of the history of the physical world, then this has to be extrapolated on the basis of other evidence. It is not legitimate to pass from the immediate referents of the words in 1:19, to some future time and place in world history, without justifying the intervening process.

This is particularly true because the actual content of the visions is portrayed from the viewpoint of a different referential world, and no specific information is available concerning its chronological organization. It may have the same chronology as the physical world, a totally unrelated and skewed chronology (as in *The Chronicles of Narnia*), or no time (as we know it) at all. To argue that 1:19 serves as a model for imposing a particular chronologically-based structure on the content of the visions in the book, would involve assuming that both worlds have the same chronological organization, without justifying that assumption.

Another issue which needs to be clarified is that even though the presence of the Narrative Framework, and other embedded narratives, give the impression that the book is some kind of other-worldly story, this is nonetheless only an impression. In reality, the book as a complex whole, is an extended exposition which has a hortatory aim. When they stand alone, expository and hortatory texts are not linked together on the basis of chronological development, but rather on the basis of logical or thematic development. In fact, Longacre 1983a,9 remarks specifically that 'expository discourse tends to have linkage through... parallelism of content'.

The point is that Revelation is a complex book, and even though that creates special challenges for the analyst, it is not a reason for failing to take account of the complexities. The complexity in view here is that it is composed of different types of text, which have their own particular characteristics but which, nonetheless, support and complement each other.

At one level it can be analyzed as a series of blocks of text which are narrative in nature and which comprise the Narrative Framework. This complete set of passages gives the book its overall narrative shape and provide it with an element of chronological linearity. However, this chronology refers to John's personal experience and is rooted in the referential reality of his human experience in his physical world.

On the other hand, this framework is intricately interwoven with blocks of text which are different in nature, as they provide the main, message-bearing content, which is a combination of expository and hortatory types of discourse. These units of text are not specifically linked together among themselves by a linear, time-based development, but by themes which are developed in a parallel, cyclic fashion.

The situation is further complicated by the fact that narratives can also be found embedded within the visionary content material, as noted above. But this fact should not be allowed to cloud the simplicity of the basic distinction between the Narrative Framework, and the content of that framework, which is being presented.

The issue of the Narrative Framework as a distinct component in the structure of the book is also an example of another underlying linguistic issue, namely that the 'grammatical structure and the referential structure may be varied independently of each other' (Pike and Pike 1982,7). As the Pikes explain it, 'the **telling** order of a story has to do with the grammatical structure, whereas the **happening** or chronological order, has to do with the referential structure' (ibid.,7, their emphasis).

In Revelation the Narrative Framework provides the telling order of one particular story of a man called John, who received and recounted a series of visions in a particular order. However, the content of the visions, what John actually saw, is composed of events which took place in a particular referential world. In fact, to complicate matters, as has been mentioned above, what he saw concerned two different referential worlds, the earthly and the heavenly.

However, the issue at stake is that it cannot be assumed that the order of events as they happened (or will happen) in the context of the viewpoint of the heavenly world, is identical with the order in which John recounted the story of what he saw. This is because there is no universal principle requiring a one-to-one relationship between the grammatical (telling) structure and the referential (happening) structure. Narration of a story demands a definite sequential linearity, since only one event can be recounted at a time, but at the same time it is self-evident that different events can take place simultaneously (for example) within the reality of any particular referential world.

Similarly, events in the referential world can be far removed in time from the time of the narration, or they can happen many times even though their occurrence was only narrated once. Likewise, they could feasibly take place in a chronological system which is not the same as the one operative in the earthly referential world.

In this brief discussion it has not been possible to resolve all the questions concerning chronology in Revelation, especially the interpretative ones. However, it has been possible to clear the ground more fully at the linguistic level. The key issues are firstly, that the book describes events in two different referential worlds and, as a consequence, it cannot be assumed that what is true for one of these worlds is automatically true for the other. In particular, it cannot be assumed that the system of chronology which operates in the physical, earthly world is the same as that in the spiritual, heavenly one.

Secondly, the linguistic shape of the book as a whole, is created by the set of textual units which is being called the Narrative Framework. As its name suggests, these texts give the impression that the book is some kind of narrative with a particular chronological sequence, even though the main purpose of the book is not just to tell a story. It is helpful, therefore, not to assume that the book is a true narrative, but to make a distinction between the narrative components and the components containing the visionary content.

Thirdly, even if the system of chronology is the same in all cases, a narrator is free to tell his story according to a chronology which is independent of the referential world in which his story is set. Therefore, it cannot be assumed without justification that the chronology of the story, as expressed in this case by the Narrative Framework, is the same as the chronology of the events described in the story.

Once underlying linguistic issues such as these have been clarified, it is possible to maintain a more conscious control of the assumptions which influence any subsequent analysis of a text, and the interpretation of its message. This, in turn, makes it possible to more readily discern the linguistic signposts which the author will undoubtedly have placed in his text to guide the reader to the intended semantic destination, rather than drawing hasty conclusions which are not supported by the data in the text.

A2.4 A Review of Other Opinions on the Narrative Aspects of Revelation

A2.4.1 The Narrative Framework

Considerable research was undertaken in the 1970's to clarify the nature of the genre 'apocalypse' and this resulted in a definition of the genre published in Collins 1979. In this article Collins states 'there is always a Narrative Framework' (ibid.,9), but how this specifically applies to Revelation is beyond the scope of his article. The coining of the term 'Narrative Framework' by Collins and in this present work happened separately, which suggests that there is an underlying linguistic reality inherent in the text which has been independently perceived by different observers.

Barr 1984,46 in providing a brief summary of the content of the book observes that 'the unity of the work is achieved in several ways' one of which is 'a common setting'. Barr's setting is the same as what is traditionally described as the Prologue and the Epilogue. He then goes on to say that 'this common setting constitutes a frame (from which) John directly addresses the reader/hearers'. He does not specifically relate this 'frame' to the narrative aspects of the work because he views the frame as creating 'the fiction of a letter'.

However, he does go on to append the insightful observation that the frame 'bridges the gap between the normal world and the fictive world', which is the heavenly world into which John journeys in his vision. (See also Barr 1986,249.) Nonetheless, he does not develop these insights any more than that.

Boring 1989,29 seems to be following his predecessors for he expresses himself in this way: 'the general compositional scheme followed by John is clear, for it is a narrative presentation of the broad apocalyptic pattern found in many other documents'. He then goes on (ibid.,37) to cite the definition quoted by Collins as referred to above.

Although in the context of this discussion Boring presents an outline of the book (ibid.,30-1), the concept of 'a narrative presentation' does not contribute to his analysis in any way. There is only a brief reference to the opening and the closing of the book, since, like Barr, he also prefers to treat the text primarily as 'a letter' (ibid.,30) rather than as a narrative. Similarly, Aune 1987,xcii-iii recognized that John as the narrator 'is present as a character in the story but only in a secondary role...'. It is perhaps for this reason, that he only views this phenomenon as 'secondary', that he does not incorporate this insight into his analysis.

More recently than these earlier commentators, Longenecker 2001,105-6, developed an approach which seems to have been influenced by modern linguistic discoveries as well as research into ancient rhetorical devices. He attributes 'part of (Revelation's) artistic impressiveness' to 'the striking infrastructure that undergirds its narrative development'.

Unfortunately, however, his interest is limited to one small section of text and his discussion, therefore, only concerns secondary structural issues. As a consequence, his dramatic statements concerning 'the striking infrastructure' do not actually lead to a deeper understanding of the complexities of the book as a whole.

More recently still, Garcìa Ureña 2014,322 has indicated that when 'the narrator interrupts the story to express his own feelings, report an issue, or even question the listener/reader', then this is characteristic of a discourse intended for oral transmission as in the case of Revelation.

As far as can be ascertained then, these general statements are as far as research has so far progressed with regard to an understanding of the scope and the function of the Narrative Framework in Revelation as a whole.

A2.4.2 The Narrative Interlude and the Minor Components

At the time at which this research was undertaken there was even less information available concerning the other parts of the Narrative Framework. As regards the Narrative Interlude, Beale 1999,520-21, viewed 10:1-11 and 11:1-13 together as 'a parenthetical literary delay'. He also used the term 'interlude', as does Boring 1989,139 who, in addition, noted that 11:1-2 'fits somewhat awkwardly into his vision' (op. cit. 143). Barr 1986,248 refers to Chapter 10 as 'an intercalation between the sixth and seventh trumpets' which term also implies a break or a pause in this sequence.

Some of the writers dimly perceived some of the overlap links, including the one between the Narrative Interlude and the Trumpets Interlude, as was mentioned in the main text of Chapter 2 above.

Longenecker 2001 also argues that there is an overlapping connection at the beginning of the Epilogue but he proposes that it continues through to 22:9, primarily on the grounds that 22:8-9 is in parallel to 19:9b-10 and that both passages are closure units (ibid.,106). It is true that they occur near the end of major units but in fact they are not simple conclusions in isolation but participate in a complex series of conclusions (see also Chapter 5 on this topic).

What Longenecker overlooks is the fact that these passages are part of the Narrative Framework and, as such, both are in parallel to the first occasion when John fell at the feet of someone in 1:17. So then, 22:8-9 is a conclusion, but it is a conclusion to the sub-theme of worship which began in the

Narrative Framework (1:17 preceded by 1:5b-6 which also evokes the theme of worship). Therefore, it is more appropriate to assign such a conclusion to the Epilogue per se, which is part of the Narrative Framework. This is more satisfactory than assigning it to the overlap link which has the double function of being the closure to Cycle 7 as well as being part of the Epilogue.

Furthermore, Longenecker does not support his claim that 'the chain-link construction...is the dominant structural feature of (the) transitional verses 22:6b-9a' (ibid.,116). Neither does he justify dividing up sentences to suit his analysis (ibid.,117) rather than respecting the natural division into sub-units (including whole sentences) which the author provides. Overall then, even though it is recognized that 22:8-9 is a closure unit and participates in the complex series of closures which are to be found in 22:6-21, it was considered more appropriate to assign it to the body of the Epilogue rather than include it as one of the overlap link sub-units. More detailed discussion of the various overlap links will be found in Chapter 3.

However, nobody seemed to perceive the thread of the minor components of the Narrative Framework, which link all the various parts together. Many spent time on discussing Chapter 17, since this is clearly an anomaly which needs to be addressed. So for example, Beale 1999,109 says that 'there is radical disagreement about the literary outline of chs.17-22', which sums up the situation quite succinctly.

Collins 1984,117 views this passage (Chapter 17) as an appendix implying also that it is extra material not totally necessary for the main thrust of the message. However, for her, the passage runs from 17:1 to 19:10. Beale 1999,847 also views Chapter 17 as an explanatory aside. He believes that it is 'a large interpretive review of the sixth and seventh bowls... Furthermore, ch.17 emphasizes what leads up to and causes the demise of Babylon'.

As can be seen, he and others did not observe that one of the defining characteristics of Chapter 17 is the fact that John participates in the vision. As a consequence, no iota of consideration that this was an element of narrative intruding into a vision, entered the discussion.

Unlike the other minor components, this section is remarkable in that it is much longer and has well defined boundaries, as well as having a narrative component. Nonetheless, the separating out of this passage as part of the Narrative Framework, as has been proposed in this study, is an innovation, which creates a more consistent analysis. This in turn, permits a better explanation for the function of this passage.

Finally then, just a brief supplementary note on the **Narrative Orienters,** that is to say, the phrases like 'and I saw'. These features were previously discussed in the main text at section 2.2.3. In that discussion it was suggested that these features are contributing to the cohesion of the discourse, even though they often occur at, or near, the beginning of units.

In support of that proposal it can be noted that other writers have made similar proposals for other books of the New Testament which lend support to this idea. In my own research I found this to be true for Matthew, as documented in Schooling 1985. The purpose of this research was to investigate some other surface structure features in Greek, like time references, which also occur on some occasions near unit boundaries. The intention at the outset was to confirm that they could be used with confidence as markers of unit boundaries. However, the research actually led in practice to the opposite conclusion. In the end, my primary conclusion was that their principal function was to promote and enhance the cohesion of the discourse as a whole. The purpose of this, in turn, was to facilitate the overall flow of the author's communicative thrust. See also Levinsohn 1992,49- 51 and 192 for supporting argumentation.

Sherman and Tuggy 1994,8 make reference to the use of the verb form, 'I write', in 1 John, which is almost identical in form and function to the narrative orienters in Revelation. They also reject the analysis of this kind of orienter as being a marker of unit boundaries. However, at the same time they overlook the possibility of its cohesive function. In their case, they favored a function which strengthens the relationship between the writer and his readers. However, this insight is most interesting. This is because it turns out to be the same as one of the other functions proposed for the orienters in Revelation, which is the function of promoting the acceptability of the message. For more on the importance of this relationship, and for an explanation of the notion of acceptability, see the discussion of **Message Support** in section 2.3.2 of the main text above.

Then there is Pattemore 2020, which is the most recent analysis of the book of Revelation as a whole, which I could find. It claims to be a Discourse Analysis of the book and is included in a collection which is full of linguistics-based DA's. However, the logical connection between his approach and what most people understand linguistics to be, is singularly opaque. So I include it here because he does refer to John as being the narrator of the book, and this is about the only reference to a linguistic element of the book which had been raised and discussed by our predecessors.

For the rest, he does not address at all the issues arising out of the work accomplished by previous commentators and analysts, as were summarized in Chapter 1 of this book above. Furthermore, his analysis does not contribute any new or helpful insights to the on-going discussion of the organization and message of this important book.

For these reasons, therefore, I have formed the impression that no significant progress has been made on these macro structure issues in the past twenty years.

Nonetheless, for the sake of completeness, I will just make a brief reference to two more recent positive contributions to the discussion. The first is Morales 2007. This is a more recent study than most of those cited above, and takes the view that the whole book of Revelation is a narrative and, therefore, has a plot structure typical of narratives. It is a very creditable attempt to put foundational Discourse Analysis principles into operation, but, at the same time, his attempt does not go far enough. This is because it does not take account of all the data (i.e. the whole of 1:1-22:21), and does not find many other linguistic features which are present in the text, in addition to the ones which he discusses. Furthermore, he only deals with mid to lower levels of the hierarchy, and so does not capture the shape of the book as a complete discourse.

The second is Brogden 2020 and 2022 who deserves a special mention. This work does not claim to be a discourse analysis at all, and approaches the book of Revelation from a different starting point. Nonetheless, the author perceives that Revelation is a kind of story rather than a prophecy about the end times, as is generally understood. He sees that the book is Christ-centered, because it is a story all about Jesus, which coincides completely with the ultimate conclusion which this present analysis of the book eventually reached. This accurate insight into the true focus of the book, was quite unique in all the commentaries which I consulted. So for this reason he deserves unique remarks and recommendation.

So, we have done our homework then, as regards those who have gone before us - and my apologies to anyone out there who has had a break-through and I have not heard about it. Now let's move on with confidence and faith that there are still new things to be learned, if appropriate methods are applied to a linguistic artifact such as this.

The galvanizing motivation, is that we need to do better than our predecessors from now on, even as we try and build on what they have accomplished. The bottom line is that only a thorough-going linguistics-based approach – guided by the same Holy Spirit who inspired the writing of the book in the first place – is capable of doing the job.

STUDY THE EVIDENCE
AND
THINK BIG !

LIKE FATHER LIKE SON

Before I started work on this study of Revelation, I practiced dissecting discourses and ferreting around with features of language, by doing some analyses of the Minor Prophets of the Old Testament, which were originally written in Hebrew.

The first thing which I noticed was the constant use of repetition in various forms and at different levels of the linguistic hierarchy. Repetitions were everywhere and far more prevalent than you would find in texts originally written in English or French.

Secondly I noticed a consequence of this repetition: the various themes and concepts kept appearing and disappearing, only to reappear a bit later on. As a westerner, this was, at first, very confusing and made it very difficult to discern what the book was all about and where it was going. Quite literally, it seemed to be going around in circles and it made it very difficult, if not impossible, to easily discern a linear thread. Eventually I realized that the reason for this confusion was because I was looking for the wrong thing, or, that I was looking for the right thing but in the wrong place.

Each coherent discourse does go somewhere and takes the reader to a destination, which is not the same as the starting out point. But in Hebrew discourses, writers do this by repeating themselves in subtly disparate ways. By going over the same ground several times but with great artistic skill, the author weaves together intricate and elegant patterns.

So it was that in the course of time, I was trying my ideas out with Hosea. At first, I left it to one side because it was too difficult! But, nonetheless, I came back to it later, and tried again. If you have ever tried to read Hosea, and especially if you have tried to make an outline for it, you will know that it is very difficult. The first three chapters are easy enough because they tell the story of Hosea and of his marriage to Gomer. But the rest of it, well, it is a good example of the morass of tangled threads which do not seem to tell any straight-forward story at all, which I was describing previously.

To cut a long story short, this is where the concept of a template came to my rescue. If the first three chapters are easy to figure out, I reasoned, maybe the author has put some keys in here to unlock the rest of the book. This turned out to be the case

Apart from setting the topic of the book, which is infidelity in a sacred relationship, which is already a good start, it also provided some structural clues. The main structural clue was that there are seven imperatives in this short, introductory section of Hosea 1-3. This was worthy of note because imperatives are usually quite rare in most kinds of discourse, and so, to have so many in such a short span of text was particularly unusual. Then there were seven of them, which suggests that this was intentional on the part of the author.

So then, on exploring the rest of the book, it was found that, once again, there were just seven imperatives spread through the whole of Chapters 4-14. Was this a coincidence or not ? Only time will tell if this is the solution to the Hosea enigma, but, at least, with these seven imperatives, I had some objective linguistic data to work with. The result of using this template was much more promising than any other system of analysis that I had tried or that I had found in other commentaries.

Rule of thumb. Look for a template, because it might just do the trick ! What you find at the beginning of the book (the father of the story), just might lead you to find something similar (the son) in the rest of it.

CHAPTER 3

Seven Cycles of Seven

3.1 Introduction

The book of Revelation is a remarkably well-constructed literary piece, containing a multiplicity of neatly intertwining patterns.
Strand 1987,107.

This opinion of Strand's is representative of many like him who have been impressed by the structural complexity of this book. However, if the challenge of analyzing such a complex text is to be fruitfully taken up, it is necessary to disentangle its constituent parts in order to discover and delineate the most significant ones. In Chapter 2 this process was begun as the Narrative Framework was identified and described. What remains after the Narrative Framework has been dealt with may be called the body of the book (1:9-22:7), and it corresponds with the content of the series of visions which John received. In this chapter an attempt will be made to identify the primary components of this visionary content of the book. The more complex details will be elucidated in the following chapters.

3.1.1 A Review of the Issues which Need Addressing

A brief review was provided in Chapter 1 which summarized, in general terms, the findings of previous authors on the subject of the internal organization of Revelation. These can be recapitulated as follows. A minority amongst them had explored the possibility of there being a basic seven-fold structure, while some others had dimly discerned the presence of some of the interludes, some of the settings and some of the overlap links. Each one did the best they could to describe their perceptions, but there was no one analyst or commentator, who perceived all these structural issues at the same time, and managed to integrate them into a coherent whole.

In order to build on this foundation therefore, and to go further, we will home in on the more specific elements which need clarification, in order to do justice to the body of the book. This will be the topic of this chapter from here onwards. But for anyone interested in pursuing these preliminary remarks a bit further, a more detailed review of the literature on these topics is provided in the Appendix following this chapter.

The history of research summarized above is doubtless typical of many such processes, as the boundaries of knowledge slowly expand and the new insights are gradually accepted by the majority. However, the disadvantages of such early stages of research are twofold. Firstly, only some of the issues are somewhat dimly discerned, and secondly, in concentrating on the smaller elements of information, researchers tend to overlook the larger picture.

In the case of Revelation, the discoveries noted above are helpful and have contributed to a growing consensus on several important issues, and yet there are many issues which still remain unresolved.

Firstly, the exact position of the boundaries of some of the textual units at various levels remain uncertain. Consequently, these boundaries need to be defined and described with more rigor and precision.

A second related point is that more balance is needed in applying a range of complementary principles to the task of text analysis. In the past, commentators seem to have concentrated almost exclusively on trying to divide the text into units, and once this has been accomplished, they move on immediately to the tasks of interpretation and exposition. However, there is a lot more to text analysis than just dividing the discourse into units. Even this latter task is best accomplished by both looking for evidence for divisions between textual units, while at the same time, looking for indicators of cohesion which bind the different parts of the text together. It is in maintaining a balance between these two complementary phenomena that the ultimate goal of a systematic outline of the book is best achieved.

> **QUOTE**
>
> **The author of Revelation does not divide the text into separate sections... but joins units together by interweaving them...It is therefore more crucial to find out the joints of the structure which interlace the different parts than to discover 'dividing marks'.**
>
> **Fiorenza 1977,362**

This specific issue is particularly relevant to Revelation since it is a book which seems to have an above average number of markers of cohesion, relative to the number of unambiguous division markers. Consequently, ignoring issues of cohesion can be a considerable impediment to the task of producing a viable analysis of this book.

Thirdly, when special features like interludes are posited, there is a lack of rigor in defining them. It is necessary to ensure that all units bearing the same label really do resemble each other, and really do function in a similar way.

Fourthly, there is often a failure to distinguish primary structural features which contribute to an understanding of the book at the macro level, and secondary features, which only elucidate the structure at subordinate levels. In such cases, the structural insights may well be valid, but confusion arises from a failure to correctly discern their place, and their role, relative to other features in the overall plan.

Fifthly, one of the indicators that an analysis is reaching maturity, is that there are no significant units which are left unaccounted for. Usually, authors say what they mean to say, and so each part of their book has a contribution to make to the overall message. Pauses, or even incoherence, can have their planned place in a text, but their intended role should be discernible within the overall context. It is the task of the analyst to listen carefully to what the author has to say, and how he expresses himself, and then try and understand how *all* the pieces fit together.

Finally, any valid structural hypothesis ought to support and contribute to the stated aims of the book, and should certainly not be running counter to those aims. For example, it has already been established that the Narrative Framework indicates that the overall aim was to influence the behavior of the hearers, who were, initially, the Christians of the first century. Since this is the case, any subsequent analysis ought to confirm and support that aim. Analyses which emphasize other issues, to the detriment of this central purpose, will always tend to be found wanting, and will not attract the support which they may otherwise deserve.

As it turns out, the results of the linguistic analysis which will be presented below, and in the following chapters, will serve to confirm the most useful insights of earlier scholarship. However, it will also aim to be more rigorous in its use of definitions and other analytical tools. By this means it is to be hoped that many of the unresolved issues will be clarified, if not fully resolved. As a consequence of this process then, it is our goal to produce a more complete, and a more elegant appreciation of this enigmatic, and yet enduring, piece of biblical literature, which has fascinated and provoked the imagination of its readers for centuries.

3.1.2 An Overview of the Seven Cycles of Seven

The Prologue, the Epilogue and the longer components of the narrative framework have been previously discussed, and so can now be temporarily left to one side. The text which remains constitutes the body of the book, and can be divided neatly into seven cycles. Each cycle has a setting, and a body which is dominated by a seven-fold motif of some kind, and some of them also have an interlude. The term ‘cycle’ is used because it intentionally indicates that there is a large degree of repetition and parallelism in each of the cycles and that, as a consequence, they all contribute in some unique and semi-autonomous way to the same principal topic of the book.

An overview of the outline of the seven cycles is presented in Chart 8. This is just an overview of the basic features. The more complex issues will be discussed later and the outline refined as a consequence. For a more complete outline see Chapter 1, Chart 1.

Chart 8.
An Overview of the Seven Cycles

Cycle			
Cycle 1 1:9-3:22	**The Seven Letters**		
	Setting 1:9-20	Body 2:1-3:22	
Cycle 2 4:1-8:6**	**The Seven Seals**		
	Setting 4:1-5:14	Body 6:1-8:6	Interlude 7:1-17
Cycle 3 8:1-11:19**	**The Seven Trumpets**		
	Setting 8:1-6	Body 8:7-11:9 (Excluding 10:1-11)	Interlude 11:1-14
Cycle 4 11:15-16:1**	**The Seven Signs**		
	Setting 11:15-19	Body 12:1-16:1	Interlude 14:1-5
Cycle 5 15:1-16:21**	**The Seven Bowls**		
	Setting 15:1-16:1	Body 16:2-21	No Interlude
Cycle 6 16:17-19:21	**The Seven Proclamations**		
	Setting 16:17-21 (+ Special Development 17:1-18)	Body 18:1-19:21	Interlude 19:1-8
Cycle 7 20:1-22:7**	**The Seven Characteristics of the New Creation**		
	Setting 20:1-15	Body 21:1-22:5	Conclusion 22:6-7

(**A double asterisk indicates that an overlap link connects the unit so marked with the following unit)

In order to qualify as a cycle then, the passage in question must be of such a nature that it could feasibly stand alone as a coherent whole, with its own internal structure, including a beginning, a body, and an end. It should also be balanced in terms of length, function, relative prominence and content, with respect to the other cycles. Endowed with these features, it should make its own unique contribution to the main topic of the book.

The topic of the book in its most basic form is taken from Revelation 1:1, where John states clearly what the book is about, by providing the hearers with an introductory sentence which could almost be a title. In the Greek version we are told that it is, 'a **revelation** of Jesus Christ, given to him by God'.

The genitive in the Greek (*of* Jesus Christ) is ambiguous because it could mean '*belonging to* Jesus' or '*concerning* Jesus'. From an analytical point of view this is considered to be an asset rather than a problem. An ambiguity such as this provides more than one possibility for the development of the meaning. This provides an extra dimension to the message and a greater depth of understanding. It is considered that in a case like this, such an ambiguity may have been intentional. The topic has to be *about* Jesus, because the whole of the rest of the book constantly portrays Him as the central pivot, around which all the action revolves.

In the Hebrew version this title, and therefore, the inherent topic, is not identical. The first words are 'These are **the secret mysteries** given by God to, or, concerning, Jesus the Messiah' Nonetheless, the genitive (or the dative, as the case may be) is also ambiguous, the same as in the Greek. Since Hebrew has much greater latent semantic potential than the Greek, this is not surprising. For more information concerning the Hebrew version of Revelation, please see Chapter 8.

Other elements concerning the topic of the book are scattered throughout the book. See, for example, verses like 1:7-8; 10:6-7; 15:1 and 21:5-6. If these are also taken into account, a more developed form of the topic is possible. It could be rendered something like this: 'God has a plan for this world, which has been kept secret until now, but is now being revealed and will be brought to completion. This plan is centered on Jesus Christ and will bring blessing on everyone who receives it'. For more discussion on the topic of the book please see Chapters 4 and 7.

3.2 The Letters Cycle 1:9-3:22

This cycle is relatively easy to describe since it is the one which is the most obviously delineated by the author himself. The body of the cycle clearly begins at 2:1 where the first message begins, and ends at 3:22 where the last one ends. Even though the word for a letter is never used, nonetheless the context communicates clearly that the series of seven messages is dominated and unified by this over-riding motif, as has been recognized by generations of scholars.

It has also been recognized that the vision described at 1:9-20 provides a setting for the series of seven letters which follows. This is made explicitly clear by the author himself, in that he provides direct grammatical, lexical, and topical links between the setting and each of the seven letters. The personage who is (re-)introduced in 1:9-20 is the one who explicitly dictates each of the seven letters. One or more elements of the description of this person, as found in 1:12-16, is repeated in each of Letters 1-6, and the topic of a written message which is initiated in 1:10, is carried through each part of the body. The descriptive details for Letter 7 'the faithful and true witness', and 'the chief ruler' (3:14), refer back to 1:5 in the Prologue. This observation supports the proposal which will be made later, that the Prologue and the setting to Cycle 1 are actually functioning together, as an introduction to the whole book.

The setting therefore, presents a heavenly personage who is generally accepted to be the risen Christ. He is glorious, victorious, is fully master of the situation, and clearly has all the authority necessary to speak to the churches as He does. By direct contrast, the letters themselves reveal human communities whose imperfections are multiple, and whose need for change is therefore evident. This antithesis contributes directly to the overall thrust of the cycle, since the implication is clear that, because Christ is risen and victorious, the people who constitute the churches can also aspire to complete victory exactly like Him (cf.3:21).

The setting is no mere embellishment, but guides and informs an understanding of all the units in the body of the cycle because the relationship of each unit of the body is directly back to the setting. This is because each one is dictated by the person described in the setting. This link with the setting is clearly marked by the introductory command 'to write', and also by the following words 'These things says the one...'. In addition, it may be deduced from the context that *kai* 'and', at the beginning of letters 2-7 links back to 2:1, rather than to the end of the preceding letter.

DEFINITION

Asyndeton

is derived directly from a Greek word which means 'not bound together'. For text analysis this means that there is no conjunction present to connect the two contiguous units together.

This is a new feature because the first letter (2:1) is not connected in the same way to the preceding setting. In this case there is no overt grammatical connection, which is technically known as **asyndeton.** This creates a parallel organizational arrangement between each of the sub-units of the body, relative to the setting, rather than a linear one. Theoretically, each part of the body could stand alone, but in reality they are grouped together because referentially, they were produced by the same person within the same time frame. In addition, conceptually, they are united by a single motif, that of a letter. In fact, there is such a similarity of form and content between all the letters, that this also creates an internal structural and semantic parallelism. The internal structure of the first cycle, therefore, may be presented diagrammatically in the following way:

Chart 9.
The Structure of Cycle 1 - The Seven Letters

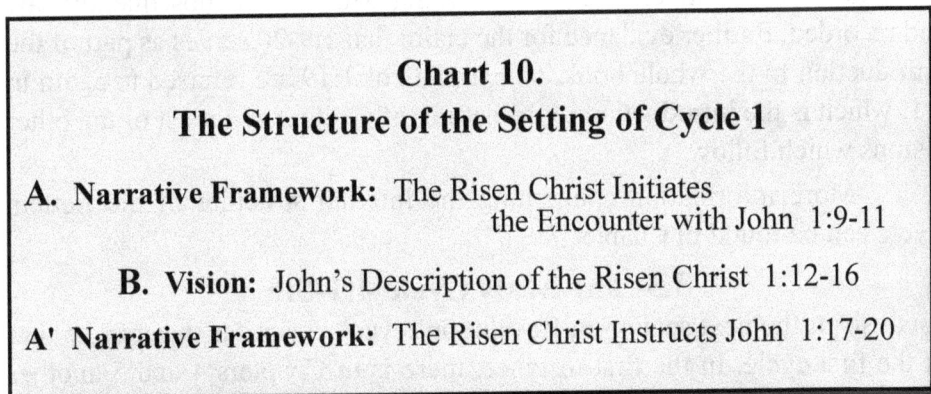

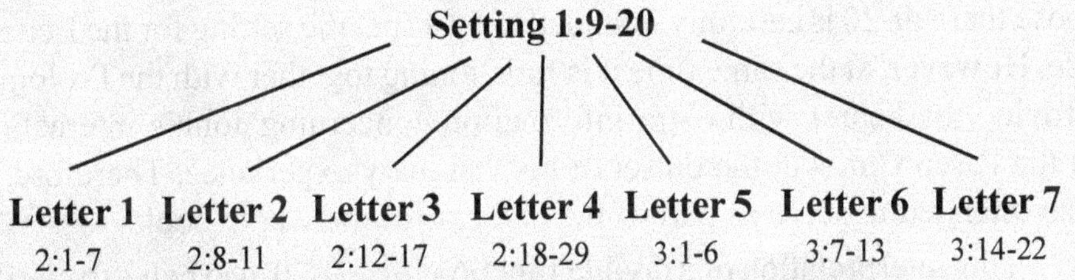

The internal organization of the setting is a simple ABA' chiastic structure, and so its boundaries and internal coherence are not difficult to discern. See Chart 10 below for a visual representation of the chiastic structure of this setting.

Chart 10.
The Structure of the Setting of Cycle 1

A. Narrative Framework: The Risen Christ Initiates the Encounter with John 1:9-11

B. Vision: John's Description of the Risen Christ 1:12-16

A' Narrative Framework: The Risen Christ Instructs John 1:17-20

However, even though the structure of the setting is easy to discern, its function is more complex. This is firstly, because the setting is closely attached to the Prologue by an overlap link (1:9-11) which makes this sub-unit part of the Narrative Framework. Then, secondly, because the last sub-unit (1:17-20) of the setting also contains elements of the Narrative Framework.

(See Chapter 2.5.3 above). Nonetheless, 1:9-20 is a complete unit, being unified by references to the central personage, the presence of John, and the process of writing down what John sees and hears. Consequently, it can only be divided into sub-units.

The complexity is due to the ambiguity engendered by the intertwining of two kinds of text. It is not self-evident whether 1:9-20 is part of the Prologue and should, therefore, be interpreted as having the same function as the latter, or whether it is just the setting for what follows, for the reasons previously delineated. The best solution in cases like this is to embrace the reality of the ambiguity, and to profit from all the information which it supplies or implies.

Consequently, the preferred interpretation of the evidence is to propose that 1:9-20 is certainly intended to be a specific setting for the Letters Cycle. However, at the same time it is functioning together with the Prologue to provide the hearer with extra information concerning John's interaction with the Risen Christ at the outset of his visionary experience. Therefore, it is also intended to serve as part of the context for the whole book.

This interpretation of a double function for 1:9-20 also helps to clarify the role of 1:19. Leaving aside the debate which this verse has engendered (see Appendix A2.3), it is clear from the basic semantic content that the instruction contained in this verse is intended to be all encompassing in some way. As a consequence, 1:19 by virtue of its place in the wider section of 1:9-20, provides a clear indicator that this whole unit implicitly does not just apply to the seven letters, but to everything which John subsequently saw and recorded. Further evidence for the claim that 1:9-20 serves as part of the introduction to the whole book, is that parts of 1:19 are referred to again in 4:1, which is the introduction to the setting of Cycle 2 and most of the other visions which follow.

More information concerning the internal structure of the Letters Cycle can be found in Chapter 7.

3.3 The Seals Cycle 4:1-8:6

Analysis of the next section of Revelation reveals a similar structure to that of the first cycle. In the first instance, there is in Chapters 4 and 5 another description of a heavenly situation with all its beauty and perfection, which is similar to the setting of Cycle 1. It is similar in terms of general ethos, but also in the principal detail, because the main participant continues to be Christ; the only difference being that He appears this time in the form of a Lamb. The other major difference between these two settings is that this setting is much longer than the previous one. Even though Chapters 4 and 5 are similar in many ways, they have different participants and different topics, and so could be treated as two separate units.

Following on from this is a cycle body (6:1-8:6), which is composed primarily of seven similar, but distinct units, unified by the same motif. In this case, it is the concept of the opening of a seal. This series of seven, like its counterpart in Cycle 1, is concerned primarily with the problems and the imperfections of the situation on the earth and is, therefore, in contrast to the setting. Like the seven letters, the seven seals are not linked to each other, but rather, they are all specifically linked back to the person presented in their setting. So it is then, that each seal unit begins with the phrase 'when he opened...'.

However, the body is significantly different from its counterpart in Cycle 1 in that a large amount of contrastive material is placed between Seals 6 and 7 (7:1-17). This material is different because it interrupts the sequence of the seven seals motif, and also because its topic, that of the special privileges of the people of God, is different from what precedes and from what follows.

This section, and others like it, will be called an interlude for two principal reasons. Firstly, it is a unit of text which is different from its immediate context. As such, it clearly breaks up, and creates a pause in, a series of units (in this case the seven seals) which otherwise belong together.

Secondly, the content projects a definite sense of hopeful anticipation, in contrast to the destruction and despair of the immediately preceding context. These factors imply that the author intended to change the tone and the pace of his discourse, and to provide complementary information. However, and this is important to note, this information is neither extraneous nor superfluous, but contributes directly to the development of the author's overall purpose.

Despite these differences, this interlude nonetheless, belongs in the Seals Cycle because there are a number of semantic features which link it with the rest of the body. There is a clear lexical link between the first part of the interlude and the series of seals in that the verb 'to seal', which reflects the same root in the Greek as the noun, is used at least five times.

Reference is made to 'the one sitting on the throne' and 'the Lamb' at 6:16 near the end of Seal 6, but then a similar doublet occurs at 7:10 in the interlude. These two concepts occur again in close proximity at 7:15 and 17, and reference is also made to 'the throne' of God and to 'the Lamb' at 7:9.

In conclusion, two further points can be made. Firstly, both the setting and the interlude are interwoven with minor elements of the Narrative

Framework (4:1, 5:4-5 and 7:13-17). Secondly, the opening of the seventh seal which occurs at 8:1, leads straight into the setting for the Seven Trumpets. This is interpreted as an overlap link with the following cycle.

3.4 The Trumpets Cycle 8:1-11:19 & the Bowls Cycle 15:1-16:21

For the sake of economy the Trumpets Cycle and the Bowls Cycle will be discussed together since they have similar structures and clearly continue the pattern established in the first two cycles.

The first trumpet is sounded in 8:7 and the series of seven continues until the seventh trumpet is sounded at 11:15. This means that 8:1-6 should be the setting of the cycle, and the evidence available indicates that this is the case. For example, it is clearly located in the same heavenly situation as that of Cycle 2, and describes events taking place in that location. So, for example, there are references to 'in heaven', 'before God', 'before the throne' and 'the prayers of the saints', in 8:1,2,3 and 4, which parallel similar references in 4:1,2,5 and 5:8.

Textually, 8:1-6 is a unit which cannot be broken into separate units, since it has a symmetric structure based on lexical and semantic parallelism, as indicated in Chart 11 below.

Chart 11.
The Structure of the Setting of the Trumpets Cycle 8:1-6

A. Silence in Heaven: Introduction of the 7 angels with their 7 trumpets 8:1-2

  B. Another angel stands on the altar with a censer 8:3a

    C. Incense with the prayers of the saints is offered before the throne 8:3b

    C' Incense with the prayers of the saints goes up before God 8:4

  B' The same angel takes fire from the altar and fills the censer 8:5a

A' Noises (on the earth): The 7 angels get ready with their 7 trumpets 8:5b-6

This confirms the presence of an overlap joint beginning at 8:1, as was mentioned above. This setting clearly prefigures the motif which unites the following body, in that the seven trumpet angels are introduced in 8:2 with parallel repetition in 8:6. This observation permits the establishment of a further parallel patterning between the settings of the different cycles. This is because this same kind of prefiguring of the septenary motif also occurs in the setting of Cycle 1 at 1:11, and of Cycle 2 at 5:1-5.

The Bowls Cycle confirms the pattern which is continuing to emerge. The body of the cycle consists of seven units united by the bowls motif, beginning at 16:2 and ending at 16:17. The preceding passage (15:1-16:1) has all the marks of being the expected setting. It is situated in heaven (15:1,5) with clear parallel references to both the setting of Cycle 1 and Cycle 2.

So it is that the reference to 'a glassy sea', is parallel to 4:6, a song to/about the Lamb parallels 5:8-12, the juxtaposition of king/kingdom and the nations is parallel to 5:9-10. Universal worship is paralleled in 5:13, harps and bowls are paralleled at 5:8, the four living creatures are parallel to Chapters 4 and 5, and a loud voice is parallel to both 1:10 (and thence 4:1) and 5:2. The concept of overcoming is parallel to the body of Cycle 1, although not the setting, except that 1:5 refers to Jesus as being 'the firstborn from the dead' and 'the ruler'.

The setting is a complete unit since it also has a concentric structure with a number of clear internal parallels. The most striking of these parallels is the five-fold reference to the seven angels with their seven plagues, or bowls, as can be seen in Chart 12 below. This is a reinforced version of the same pattern as in Cycles 1-3 in which the septenary motif is prefigured in the setting.

Chart 12.

The Structure of the Setting of the Bowls Cycle 15:1-16:1

A. A great and wonderful sign is seen in Heaven: 7 angels with the 7 last plagues which will complete God's anger 15:1

B. On the glassy sea: those who overcome the beast stand and sing before God: Great and wonderful are the works of God Almighty, who will not fear and glorify His name ? 15:2-4

A' The sanctuary in Heaven releases the 7 angels who are given the bowls of the anger of God – the sanctuary is so filled with smoke that no one can enter until the completion of the 7 plagues 15:5-8
(there are 3 references to the 7 angels)

Coda: A loud voice gives instructions to the 7 angels 16:1

Features of the setting are also taken up in all of the bowl units except the sixth, which again demonstrates that the septenary units relate primarily back to their setting and not to each other. This is also true for the Trumpets Cycle. Each of the first four trumpets presents material which is in a specific-generic relationship to the end of the setting, and Trumpet 6 also has a clear parallel link with its setting.

The concepts in the setting for the seven bowls cycle reappear in the following way:

- Bowl 1: the beast and its image
- Bowl 2: the sea;
- Bowl 3: God Almighty, righteous and true
- Bowl 4: great, name of God, glorify
- Bowl 5: the beast
- Bowl 6: the beast
- Bowl 7: the loud voice from the sanctuary.

The end of the Trumpets setting describes in generic terms the results of the angel throwing his censer on the earth. The first four trumpets describe specific things which are thrown onto the earth (or into the domain of the earthly creation – Trumpet 4) and the specific results which ensue (8:7-12). Trumpet 5 has no clear link to its setting but links back to material in Cycle 2 (the sealing of the 144,000, and thence probably to Seal 5). Trumpet 6 links to its setting (via the concept of the altar) and to Bowl 6 (Euphrates), and Trumpet 7 links back to the setting material in Chapter 4.

The Trumpets Cycle has an interlude, (11:1-13) occurring at the expected place between the sixth and seventh trumpets. However, it is attached to Chapter 10, which has been previously analyzed as being the interlude of the Narrative Framework. As a result, this connection creates a double unit with complementary functions, even though the content of each part is different.

In confirmation of this proposal, it can be noted that there are other such lengthy double units in Revelation. For example, 7:1-17, which is also an interlude, Chapters 4-5, 16:17-17:18 and a smaller one at 14:14-20. Thus it can be seen, that it would seem as if this may be another intentional feature of the book, which also emphasizes cohesion relative to division into units. The Narrative Interlude and its connection by an overlap link with the Trumpet's interlude (10:1-11:13) was discussed in Chapter 2. Their combined function will be taken up in Chapter 6, and the significance of Chapters 4-5 will be developed in Chapter 5.

The interlude is conceptually and lexically linked to the rest of the cycle, just as the other interludes are linked to their respective cycles. So, for example, the concept of intercession occurs in 8:4-5,and 11:5-6, and the word 'fire', occurs in the same verses as well as in 8:7 and 9:17-18. The concept of protection occurs at 9:4 and 11:5, the passage from lack of repentance to fear of God occurs at 9:20, 11:10 and 11:13, and water being turned to blood is referred to at 8:8 and 11:6.

On the other hand, the Bowls Cycle does not have an interlude like the preceding cycles. Nonetheless, a short unit (16:15) which is clearly different from its context does occur, and has to be accounted for. It occurs embedded near the end of Bowl 6 rather than between the last two bowl units and, being a blessing, is a volitional import text rather than informational import. It does not provide a major pause in the flow of thought, has no parallel links with the rest of the cycle, and does not contribute to the salvation theme (see Chapter 4 for discussion of the Salvation Theme). Consequently, it does not match the definition of the other interludes and therefore, is not assigned to this category. Its function will be accounted for in subsequent chapters.

The Trumpets Cycle has one unique feature in that it has a series of three short units, which are clearly related to one another, but yet are distinct from their immediate context. These occur at 8:13, 9:12 and 11:14 and are usually called the Three Woes. Like 16:15, these are a special feature and will be discussed in Chapter 6.

In conclusion, it can be stated that these two cycles have a basic structure which resembles the ones previously discussed. They have a setting, and a body with seven sections united under a single motif, and one of them has an interlude. There are also clear links between the setting and the body of each cycle.

3.5 The Signs Cycle 11:15-16:1 and the Proclamations Cycle 16:17-19:21

The previous discussion has accounted for the four septenaries which are generally acknowledged. So now it remains to present textual data which supports the proposal that there are other septenaries, which are not numbered in the same way. Clearly, what an author has already written will influence in some way what follows. This is why it is considered reasonable to allow an appreciation of the clear seven-fold patterns to influence our understanding of other parts of the text.

In support of this reasoning Dooley and Levinsohn 2001,106-7 remark that 'stories in oral traditions often show characteristic PATTERNS OF REPETITION'. These patterns of repetition 'can be thought of as furnishing a kind of **template** or outline. When a hearer recognizes one in a text, he or she quickly uses it in a top-down fashion, to structure...subsequent material'. Furthermore, they say (ibid.,90) that 'when semantic relations are not coded explicitly and completely, clues are often furnished which help narrow down the range of possible interpretations'. One of these clues they call 'expectation structures', which is when the author gives certain information which causes the hearer to make an astute guess (or 'projection') concerning what may follow.

> Certain types of discourse organization seem designed to generate such projections (e.g; repetition...)... Many expectation structures have their source both in the culture and in the text. Whatever their source, though, they are powerful devices which aid the hearer in arriving at a mental representation and maintaining interest in the text (ibid.,52) .

So, the case in point here, is that the repetition of clear seven-fold structures can be interpreted as 'a clue'. This 'narrows down the range of possible interpretations' for the material which is 'not coded explicitly'.

QUOTE
Once the analyst has found the template (or has a working hypothesis about it), it makes it easier to apply the template to other parts of the discourse, which are less clear, and by this means to look for structures which may be there but are a bit hidden.
Schooling 2024a,5.

With the issue of repetition in mind then, this section will concentrate on establishing the similarities between the two cycles under discussion, and between them and the other cycles. Even though some reference to the differences is inevitable, detailed discussion, and an assessment of their significance, will be reserved for later.

3.5.1 The Setting of the Signs Cycle 11:15-19

The first similarity which can be noticed for both the Signs and the Proclamations Cycles is that they are composed of a setting and a body, and in both cases, the setting is linked to the previous cycle by an overlap joint. The setting for the Signs Cycle is 11:15-19. This begins with the blowing of the seventh trumpet, and ends just before the presentation of the first sign at 12:1. Since it is a chiasm, it cannot be broken down into separate parts, but must be treated as a single unit (see Chart 13). This example of cohesion leads to the interpretation once more of an overlap link, whereby 11:15-19 functions both as a closure to the Trumpets Cycle and as a setting for the Signs Cycle, at the same time. The situation described in this passage is clearly the throne-room of heaven, the same as for the other central cycles.

Chart 13.

The Structure of the Setting of the Signs Cycle 11:15-11:19

A. Introductory event in Heaven which is the last main event of the previous Cycle. The result: loud noises in Heaven, i.e. 'loud voices' 11:15a

B. Direct Speech: Generic statement about the Reign of Christ 11:15b

C. A Response: Worship 11:16

B' Direct Speech: Specific statements about the Reign of God Almighty 11:17-18

A' Concluding event in Heaven which prepares the way for the first main event of the next Cycle. The result: loud noises in Heaven including voices 11:19

This setting, unlike the others, does not directly introduce the following seven-fold motif. However, there is a unique lexical connection between them, and it does introduce the two most significant sub-themes of the cycle. So it is then, that it is stated that something 'was seen'. This is unusual, for it is the passive form of the verb 'to see', and this form occurs only in 11:19 and 12:1 and 3, that is to say, in the setting and the body of this cycle. This feature will be referred to again in Chapter 6 in the discussion on prominence.

The center, and the most important part, of the setting (11:16) is concerned with the sub-theme of worship, and the second sub-theme is that of reigning (sections B and B'). The specific aspects of reigning which are portrayed in 11:18 are the accomplishment of a plan, which will bring judgment upon the nations and reward to the saints.

The sub-theme of worship is specifically taken up again in Sign 3 (13:1-10), Sign 4 (13:11-18) and Sign 5 (14:6-12), and is implicit in the Interlude (14:1-5). The sub-theme of reigning to impose judgment is taken up directly in Sign 5 (14:6-12) and in Sign 6 (14:14-20), and it is taken up contrastively in the description of the activities of the dragon and the two beasts from 12:17 through to13:18.

The fact that the word for 'a sign', is not specifically used in the setting, and that not all the seven signs are specifically mentioned and numbered, may be due to the fact that John arranges his material so that this word occurs as a lexical thread just seven times in the book as a whole. It may also be that John intended this cycle to be different and so he used various means to make this clear. See Chapter 6 in particular, where it will be explained why certain constituents are noticeably different, as compared to other similar, or contiguous, units.

3.5.2 The Body of the Signs Cycle 12:1-16:1

Even though it is not clearly foreshadowed in the setting, the sevenfold motif of Cycle 4 is, nonetheless, marked for special attention by the author at the outset, and that motif is the concept of a sign.

Inspection of the text demonstrates that the word 'sign' is linguistically marked in a number of ways. In its first occurrence (12:1), it is fronted, and it is marked by a strong adjective 'great'. In addition, it is clearly topicalized by the use of the passive form of the verb, which eliminates the usual first person pronoun suffix which occurs frequently elsewhere. As if that were not enough, the word is repeated soon afterwards (12:3) and is again marked by the use of the passive form of the verb 'to see'. The repetition of this unusual form of the verb links it specifically with the setting of the cycle. At the same time this repeated use of 'sign' is clearly linked back to its previous use by the word 'another'. It is then further marked by the repetition of the phrase 'in heaven', and by the use of the word 'behold', at the point of definition.

This amount of marking in such a small space is unusual and clearly indicates that John is intentionally drawing attention to what he is saying. The last sign (15:1) is also marked by the words 'another', 'in heaven', and by the doublet 'great and wonderful'.

As noted above, it is true that John, in this case, does not use the word 'sign' on each occasion. Nonetheless, it is self-evident that at least he marks the first, second and the last occurrences (12:1,3 and 15:1), which serve to indicate his general intention.

The other thing which he clearly indicates is that the signs are to be interpreted as representing personages, since the first two signs are clearly interpreted as being 'a woman' (12:1), and 'a dragon' (12:3). Then to complete the series, the last one is also equated with a group of personages, the bowl angels.

The first and the last signs also show that the personage in view in the text as the embodiment of the sign, can be two or more personages of the same type, closely grouped together. Thus, the first sign is a woman but she is closely linked with a child who is implicit in 12:2, but explicit in 12:4-5, and the last sign is clearly a group of angels (15:1). The dragon (second sign) is also associated with other personages who are not in focus to the same extent (12:7-9), but who are just part of his story.

These observations immediately demonstrate that there is a certain amount of fluidity in the organization of the text, because characters come and go in a story, and also interact with each other. In the cycles previously discussed this was not the case, because the motifs were embodied primarily by events, and were thereby limited to a specific block of text which dealt with that event. However, the deduction that all of John's other motifs must also be represented by blocks of text, which can be delineated and separated one from another, is not valid. His motifs are actually embodied by events or personages, and so the surface structure representation of his message is of secondary importance. This, therefore, should not become an impediment to discerning what he is actually doing.

For this reason then, the fact that the first two signs are intermingled in the text (the woman occurs at 12:1,4 and again at 12:13-17) is of no consequence from a linguistic point of view. This certainly does not nullify the claim that the body of this cycle is constructed on the basis of a sevenfold manifestation of a single motif, as are the other cycles.

To understand this difference better it is helpful to realize that language is at one level a manifestation of physical reality, either in the form of speech, or in the form of words on a page. As such, the same reality can be viewed and represented either as a series of particles, or as a wave, or as a field. Cycles 1-3 represent their particular motif in terms of a series of distinct particles, like beads on a string. However, Cycle 4 represents its motif rather in terms of a field, like points on the same sheet of paper. These concepts, borrowed from physics, were first applied to linguistics by K. Pike (1959), as was indicated in Chapter 1 section 1.3.5.

Since John has demonstrated how his sign motif is embodied and has interpreted the first two, it is possible to pursue his logic and discover the other signs which he has placed in his text. This is possible, even though the word 'sign', does not overtly occur, just as it was possible in the first cycle, even though the word 'letter' did not even occur at all.

So it is then, that John indicates that the story of the dragon's encounter with the woman and her child comes to an end at 12:17. As from 13:1 there is a change of situation, of primary participant and of topic, which are the basic linguistic signals that a new semantic unit has begun. In addition, there is a tail-head link based on the word, 'sea', between 12:18 and 13:1 which is also an indicator of a transition from one linguistic unit to another. At this point of linguistic juncture, a new personage is introduced, namely, the beast from the sea. According to the pattern of expectation which John has already set up, this next new, major personage should be the next sign.

This beast's story is told and then another beast is introduced at 13:11. This new personage is differentiated from the previous one by the word 'another', as was also the case at 12:3, and by the fact that it is a beast which comes up out of the earth. This then, is the fourth sign.

Next, at 14:1 there is another new situation, a new primary participant and a new topic, the new participant being marked for prominence by the word 'behold'. However, in this case, the unit breaks the thematic continuity of the series of signs so far introduced. The latter have developed the judgment theme, with references to the concepts of war, woe, judgment, defeat, deception and persecution, and their general focus has been events on the earth or concerning the earth. The unit beginning at 14:1, however, is situated in the throne-room of heaven once more and develops the salvation theme.

Following the same logic and using the same linguistic criteria, it can be established that new units with new primary participants begin at 14:6 and at 14:14. The angels who appear in 14:15,17 and 18 cannot be considered new primary participants. They are obviously secondary participants because they interact with the primary participant introduced at 14:14, and participate in his story. Likewise, the angels at 14:8 and 9 are not new primary participants. The passage cannot be broken up linguistically (it is a chiasm) and each participant contributes to the same topic and theme. In this case, the sign could be considered to be the angels as a group, the same as the last sign at 15:1.

The first of these units (14:6) is marked by the word 'another', and the second (14:14) by 'behold'. If the final sign at 15:1 is included, this produces a list of eight possible signs. It would be normal to expect an interlude, but in this case there is nothing resembling an interlude in the usual position just before the seventh unit. The passage in question (14:14-20), even though it begins somewhere in the heavenlies (vv.14-15), is clearly concerned with judgment on the earth.

However, the passage at 14:1-5 has all the hallmarks of being an interlude. It breaks up without warning a series of units which developed the judgment theme, and switches the hearer back to the heavenly setting and the Salvation Theme. It is also marked by 'behold'.

The only difference is its position between the fourth and fifth signs, instead of between the sixth and seventh members of the motif series, as would have been expected on the basis of the precedents of the previous cycles. This means that it has been fronted, and this prominences feature along with the presence of 'behold', suggests that it is being marked for special prominence. See Chapter 6 for a full discussion of the issues concerning prominence.

If this passage is taken as the interlude for the cycle, then the result of the analysis of the Signs Cycle is that there is a setting (11:15-19), a body and an interlude. The body is unified by a single motif (a sign), which is presented seven times in the form of seven principal personages, or groups of personages in the case of the first, fifth and seventh signs (12:1-15:1). The interlude, in this case, appears between the fourth and fifth signs (14:1-5), but it fits neatly into the same schema as the signs, in that it is dominated by an important personage, namely, the Lamb, in this case.

Because of the lack of an overt numbering system, the consensus concerning the seven signs has been slower in developing than for the numbered cycles. However, in reality it is not the evidence which is lacking, it is just that John did not use the same system in this section, even though it has the same basic structure as the previous cycles.

In addition, it can be noted that each of the sign units (Signs 1 and 2 form a single linguistic unit) and the interlude are structurally coherent, in that they all exhibit an internal chiastic structure. This is the first time that this has happened in the book, so this is an unusual system of organization, which is unlike the organization of the seven seals and seven trumpets. These chiasms confirm that the divisions between the units do fall at the points proposed, because of the internal coherence of the concentric structures.

Furthermore, each sign sub-unit, and the interlude, end with a coda. This is also a new, unusual feature. Codas also occur later on in the book, which shows that it is a particular feature of the book as a whole, but this is the only place where they occur systematically attached to each sub-unit of a whole cycle. These two common elements of the chiastic internal structure and of the coda, suggest that they are sub-units functioning together as part of a larger whole. This in turn, confirms the internal coherence of the Signs Cycle as whole, in case there was any doubt about the matter. See the following Appendix for more details of the internal structure of the Signs Cycle, including its sub-units, and Appendix 4 for the interlude.

A coda is a small unit relative to its context, which stands outside a structural unit, and provides a final conclusion to it. It 'is a final non-event section "that makes a meta-comment on the story, gives a summary, or gives some post-resolution information...". A coda can also furnish explanations after the fact...; it can draw an application (moral) or give a final word of evaluation' (Dooley and Levinsohn 2001,106, quoting Brewer 1985,183).

The codas in the Signs Cycle will be briefly elucidated, small though they may be, because codas occur at some strategic points in the structure of Revelation, and, therefore, contribute significantly to the macro structure. These codas occur at 12:17c (Signs 1 and 2); 13:9-10; 13:18; 14:4-5 (interlude); 14:12-13; 14:20 and 16:1. The reasons why the Signs Cycle is particularly important are discussed in Chapter 6. Another important coda occurs at the end of Cycle 7 and is discussed in Chapter 5.5.

DEFINITION

A Coda

is a small unit, relative to its context, which stands outside of, and provides a final conclusion to, a larger structural unit. It is a term which has been borrowed from the domain of music.

The clearest of these codas is at 13:9-10. The clue is the repetition (with slight variation) of the general exhortation 'he who has an ear to hear, let him hear', which occurs seven times in the Letters Cycle but nowhere else in the whole of the book. This first sentence, and the last one in the group 'here is...', are in the third person indefinite form. They are positive exhortations addressed directly to the hearers, over the heads as it were, of the participants of the embedded narrative which comprises the immediate context.

The middle part of the coda (13:10a-b) is only slightly different. It is also a third person indefinite form, and is, at the same time, a commentary on what was described in the immediately preceding narrative (cf. 13:7), and a double warning. A warning is a negative exhortation which can either be understood as an encouragement to persevere, which is likely here in the light of the immediately following exhortation to endure, or as an encouragement to avoid a hidden danger. In either case, the hortatory intent is not difficult to discern.

Another coda occurs at the end of the fourth sign (13:18). It is introduced in the same fashion as the last exhortation in 13:10, with the words 'here is'. It is also couched in the third person form and is a combination of a commentary on what precedes, and a positive exhortation to the hearer.

A third coda occurs at 14:12-13. Verse 12 is an exhortation which is almost identical to the one in 13:10c. In this case the commentary which goes with it serves to reinforce the exhortation itself, rather than relating to the immediate context. Verse 13 is part of the Narrative Framework but its semantic content contributes directly to the exhortation of verse 12. The underlying hortatory intent, which is presented in the form of a blessing, is also in the third person.

In effect, all the sub-units of the Signs Cycle would appear to have this coda, although some of the other examples are not as obvious as those presented above. However, when the group is studied as a whole, and the principle of analogy is applied, it can be seen that each of the sections does have an unusual ending, for which the best interpretation is that of an intentional pattern of codas. In all cases, the units preceding the codas are structurally and conceptually complete, and so the codas are an additional conclusion. But it is equally true that the context makes it clear that each coda belongs with, and should be understood in the light of, the preceding unit.

The presence of the codas then, serves as additional confirmation that this cycle is composed of a series of units containing seven signs, plus an interlude, as has been presented above. At the same time, the Signs Cycle is set apart from the previous ones by reason of its extra structural details.

3.5.3 The Setting of the Proclamations Cycle 16:17-21 and 17:1-18

The setting of the Proclamations Cycle is also located in the throne-room first described in Cycle 2. In addition, the general motif of the following body (statements about the destruction of the great city Babylon) is prefigured in the setting (16:20), which is the case for most of the previous settings. The setting of this cycle appears to be particularly long, but strictly speaking, it only extends from 16:17 to 16:21, with the extra length being generated by a portion of the Narrative Framework (17:1-18).

In this segment, John receives a special explanation concerning Babylon, just as he had received an explanation concerning the people in white robes in 7:13-17. Even though this is the first time we have encountered such a phenomenon so far in the course of this study, this is nothing unusual from a linguistics point of view. According to Callow 1998,293-4 'explanations... characteristically occur in spoken messages...(or) in written materials...if the readers are known to be unfamiliar with the topic under consideration'. Since Babylon, as described in 17:1-18, is likely to be an unfamiliar topic, this would be the reason why the narrator considered that some extra explanation was required at this point. Just as I have included an extensive explanation of codas in the preceding paragraphs.

It is not unusual for settings to be linked with parts of the Narrative Framework, for such was the case for Cycles 1 and 2. However, in this case, the Narrative Framework section also contributes a great deal of information which is relevant to the following visions. Presumably, both John as narrator, and his hearers, needed this in order to fully appreciate what was to follow. This is one of the unique features of this cycle which will be taken up in the chapter on prominence.

Chart 14.
The Structure of the Setting of the Proclamations Cycle 16:17-21

A. The last Plague (Bowl 7) is poured out:
The result is loud noises in heaven, a voice says: 'It is done', and a great earthquake (with emphasis on its great magnitude) 16:17-18

B. Babylon is remembered before God and is destroyed 16:19

A' The last part of the Plague:
The result is the equivalent of a universal earthquake and a great hail (with emphasis on the magnitude of the plague) 16:20-21

Chart 14 illustrates the internal cohesion of the basic setting which is similar in type, content and size to the previous settings as will be explained below. By analogy therefore, it is this section of text which is interpreted as being the basic setting which is in parallel with the other settings. This setting then, together with the following component of the Narrative Framework, is interpreted as another example of a complex bipartite unit, of which there are several in Revelation. The result is two quite distinct units which, nonetheless, function together to accomplish the same primary objective, as was previously explained at section 3.4 above.

3.5.4 The Body of the Proclamations Cycle 18:1-19:21

It has been argued above, that the last of the seven bowls is also a new setting in a pattern similar to that of the seventh unit in each of Cycles 2-4. Because of the chiastic structure of 16:17-21, it can be deduced that Babylon is prominent, since this occurs in the middle of the structure. This is confirmed by the fact that an explanation concerning Babylon becomes the topic of the long section of Narrative Framework which follows (17:1-18). Further evidence which supports this deduction is that Babylon was referred to without further comment in the fifth sign (14:8). It is normal in a discourse that if a topic is introduced in one place in the book, but is not discussed in detail at that point, then it will be developed elsewhere. This is what is happening here in this cycle.

Further confirmation still for this line of reasoning is that, regardless of which structural analysis is eventually preferred, there is no question that the judgment of Babylon continues to be the most highly developed topic in the whole of the section 18:1-19:10.

The body of this cycle then, is considered to begin at 18:1 in the first instance because the preceding Narrative Framework section clearly ends at 17:18. The function of the phrase 'after these things' is ambiguous in the book as a whole, and so is not used as evidence for a new unit. However, the presence of 'another', does generally indicate a new unit, although not always a major unit. What has to begin as a working hypothesis is then confirmed by the discovery of the sevenfold motif which does begin, in fact, at 18:1, as previously proposed.

The Sevenfold Motif

There is unanimity among commentators that the system of sevenfold motifs typical of earlier parts of the book, is no longer overtly marked from this point on. However, as has been previously argued, it is reasonable to suppose that John made this structural feature obvious because he intended it to be noticed, and having thus marked it several times he did not need to do so every time.

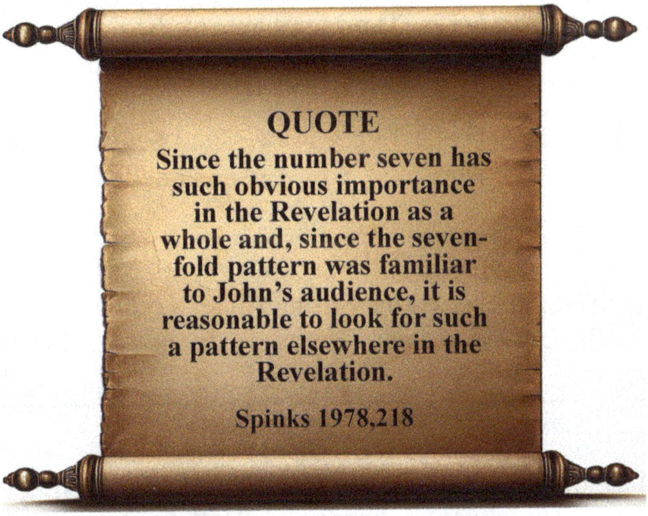
QUOTE
Since the number seven has such obvious importance in the Revelation as a whole and, since the sevenfold pattern was familiar to John's audience, it is reasonable to look for such a pattern elsewhere in the Revelation.
Spinks 1978,218

This is an example of an expectation being generated both by general knowledge of the culture, and by indicators in the text, as mentioned previously in the quotation from Dooley and Levinsohn 2001, in section 3.5.

Such a search will be rewarded, or otherwise, by the text itself, because, if the sevenfold pattern is present, it should be objectively apparent, and if it is not, that will also be apparent. The pertinent data which reveals a sevenfold structure is summarized in Chart 15. In order to keep things simple, just the minimum essential data is provided in the chart to establish that there is a clear system of parallel patterning in the text.

More detailed inspection of the text will show that there is more evidence for parallelism present than is shown in the chart. These details will be presented in the text which follows.

Chart 15.
The Structure of the Body of the Proclamations Cycle
18:1-19:21

Proclamation 1. 18:1-3 Another Angel… out of Heaven **saying:**
'Fallen, fallen is Babylon the Great … **because**

Proclamation 2. 18:4-8 Another Voice out of Heaven **saying:**
'Come out of her… because; Give back to her… **because…**'

Proclamation 3. 18:9-10 The Kings of the Earth… **saying:**
'Woe, woe… **because** in one day…'

Proclamation 4. 18:11-17a The Merchants of the Earth **saying:**
'Woe, woe… **because** in one hour…'

Proclamation 5. 18:17b-19 Every Pilot… and Sailor **saying:**
'Woe, woe… **because** in one hour…'

(Book level prominence feature 18:20)

Proclamation 6. 18:21-24 One Strong Angel **saying:**
'By no means shall… any longer… (six times)… **because…**'

INTERLUDE 19:1-8
The loud Voice of a Great Crowd in heaven **saying:**
Hallelujah … **because**… Hallelujah !

(Book level prominence feature 19:9-10,
being part of the Narrative Framework,
and 19:11-21 being a conclusion to the whole of Cycles 2-6.)

Proclamation 7. 19:17-18 (being part of 19:11-21)
One Angel **saying:** 'Come, Assemble... in order that...

Inspection of the data indicates that the motif which unites the units presented below, is that of a proclamation. The first indicator is the fact that the beginning of every single proclamation itself is introduced by the word 'saying', which is, of course, the present participle of the verb 'to say', followed by direct speech (18:2,4,10,16,18, 21and 19:17).

The word 'proclamation' itself is not used, just as the word 'letter' was not used in Cycle 1, nonetheless, the concept is certainly present. Just as happened at the beginning of the Signs Cycle, John draws attention to this predominant concept on its very first usage. Thus, at 18:2 a series of strong lexical items points to the occurrence of the first proclamation. The lexical items are those which describe the angel in terms of its great authority and glory, followed by the very strong verb 'he cried out', and the ringing phrase 'in a loud voice' (18:1-2a).

The Oral/Aural Context

In case this first occurrence was missed, John takes pains also to underline the speaking verbs used in the other proclamations as well. The strong verb 'he cried out', is used again in the fifth proclamation (twice), and the seventh (once); doublets of the verbs 'weep', and 'wail', or 'sorrow', are used in Proclamations 3, 4 and 5; and the phrase 'in a loud (great) voice', is used again in Proclamation 7, in direct parallel to the previous occurrence of this phrase in Proclamation 1, as well as in the interlude. In more general terms, it can be observed that between 18:1 and 19:10, which coincides with the main body of this cycle and its interlude, all the events described are oral, or aural, events, with various verbs of speaking being used throughout. This is unusual because in the rest of the book it is nonetheless true, that references to the visual aspects of John's experience predominate almost exclusively.

> **QUOTE**
>
> **These textual units 'are more distinguished by ear than by eye, as was generally the case before'.**
>
> **Wendland 1990,383**

However, the details of this phenomenon are fascinating, for there are also two passages in the book where there is a mixture of visual and aural clues. The first of these begins at 16:17 and ends at 18:1 and this coincides with the setting to this cycle. Then a second mixture of aural and visual clues occurs again in the section 19:11-21, which coincides with the text which contains the final proclamation.

This observation then, serves to confirm the proposal that the motif of oral/aural events is clearly introduced in the setting of this cycle in a transitional manner, becomes dominant in the body of the cycle, and then transitions out again in the conclusion to the cycle. It is of note that in the previous unnumbered cycle, the Signs Cycle, the usual visual orienter 'and I saw', is also replaced by other orienters for a significant length of text near the beginning of the cycle. This feature will be discussed in Chapter 6.

The Seven Proclamations in Detail

Perusal of each of the first six proclamations show that they all bear witness to the fall of Babylon, viewed, with one exception, as a past event. In the seventh, the reference to Babylon is implicit rather than explicit, since the same basic event of her fall is proclaimed but in different terms. There are also some other important features of the structure of each of the first six proclamations, which demonstrate their similarity and, hence, their parallel organization.

Each proclamation includes a significant repetition of some kind, whether it be grammatical or lexical, in the basic statement of the proclamation. This is followed by a reason clause which is usually introduced by the word 'because', but secondarily also by 'in order that'. Once again the first unit sets the pattern by the repetition of the same verb 'it has fallen'. This repetition occurs as the first words of the direct speech, and with the attributed prominence due to fronting, it is clearly intended to be noticed.

The second proclamation is an exception to the primary pattern because it is addressed to the people of God, and continues the hortatory thread of the book. As such, it views the judgment of Babylon as still future.

However, in line with the remarks already made, the second proclamation has two imperatives 'come out', and 'give back', which latter is in turn repeated. This second level of repetition is manifest firstly by the doublet phrase, 'double to her the double of her works', and secondly by the unadorned verb 'to give'. Each of the primary verbs (after all the repetition is completed) is then followed by its own reason clause. The third, fourth and fifth proclamations repeat the word 'woe', followed in the reason clause by the phrase, 'because in one day, or, hour...', and the sixth has a six-fold repetition of the phrase 'by no means...any longer'. The seventh has a double, synonymous imperative 'come', and 'assemble'.

As regards Proclamation 7, it can be seen from Chart 12 above, that it is embedded in the section 19:11-21, which is a complex conclusion with a double function. There are multiple parallel relationships between 19:11-21 and preceding passages, which is consonant with the fact that this is a concluding passage as will be seen in Chapter 5.4. However, the most striking parallels for the seventh proclamation (19:17-18) and its introductory context (19:16), are with passages concerning Babylon. Thus, the superlative title

'King of kings and Lord of lords' of 19:16, recalls the declaration of victory over the kings and the beast in 17:14.

However, this is in the middle of a passage of which the primary topic is Babylon, and the final word of this exposition is that Babylon is the mistress of the kings of the earth (17:18). Furthermore, most of the proclamations concerning the fall of Babylon are spoken by kings (18:9) and other groups of people, and all these people are paralleled by the generic list in 19:17. So it is that when the kings and all the people of the earth are defeated, as in the seventh proclamation, then, so is Babylon.

Evidence for Parallelism

As with the previous septenary motifs, the evidence for linkage and parallelism between the six principal proclamation units, is not lacking. Each of the proclamations is the utterance of a particular personage or a group. These personages are divided into two evenly organized groups. The first two are an angel, or some other heavenly voice, and both are accompanied by the word 'another', and the last two are also angels. In their case, they are specifically demarcated as 'one angel' (18:21 and 19:17), and these are the only two places in the whole book where this precise phraseology is used. This is the first group whose base is in heaven.

The second group (Proclamations 3 to 5), are based on the earth and are therefore, groups of humans. In addition, two of these human groups, the kings and the merchants, are introduced in the first proclamation at 18:3, while the merchants reappear in the sixth proclamation (18:23), and the kings in the seventh (19:18).

These three groups of participants are also linked together by the fact that they specifically stand at a distance, and for two of them (the kings and the merchants) the hearer is told that they keep away for fear of the torment (18:10,15), whereas for another two (the kings and the sailors), they both saw the smoke of the burning of the city (18:9 and 18).

In 19:18 the merchants are not specifically present but are obviously included in the generic terms, because the whole point of their presence in the passage at all is because they were influential ambassadors for the city of Babylon (see 18:23). The importance of the sailors is that they were in symbiotic relationship with the merchants. Without the sailors the merchants would never have become rich, and vice versa.

Another interesting detail is that the verb 'to stand' in these three verses, is consecutively in the present, future and past tenses in 18:10,15 and 17. In this way, all the possible perspectives from a temporal point of view, past, present and future, are included.

The Concentric Pattern

When looked at from this perspective of the witnesses, both heavenly and earthly, who testify to the fall of Babylon, the seven proclamations are organized in a concentric pattern with the merchants' section being the central one. Chart 16 provides a visual representation of this pattern.

Chart 16.
The Concentric Pattern of the Proclamations Cycle
18:1-19:18

A. Proclamation 1. 18:1-3 Another Angel out of Heaven

B. Proclamation 2. 18:4-8 Another Voice out of Heaven

C. Proclamation 3. 18:9-10 The Kings of the Earth

D. Proclamation 4. 18:11-17a The Merchants of the Earth

C' Proclamation 5. 18:17b-19 All Sailors who Work on the Sea

B' Proclamation 6. 18:21-24 One Strong Angel…

A' Proclamation 7. 19:17-18 One Angel…

This observation is further highlighted by the fact that this unit is by far the longest due to an extensive description which precedes the proclamation.

Closer observation shows that most of this long passage (18:11-14) is in fact an extra reason clause (v.11b-13) introduced, in line with nearly all the other proclamations, by 'because', which confirms that this extra material is intentional and not extraneous. The extra length, the extra reason clause, and its central position in a concentric structure, suggest that this unit is the most prominent of the series.

Other Features of the Cycle

It should be noted that 18:20 is slightly different from its context in that it is a direct, second person exhortation, which promotes a positive outlook rather than a negative one. There are two possible analyses, neither of which affect the overall structure of the cycle in any significant way.

It can be understood as simply part of the fifth proclamation, functioning as a coda to the unit as was found in the Signs Cycle. Otherwise, the preferred interpretation is that it is a book level feature which contributes to the hortatory intent of the book. As the book draws to a close, extra material of this nature would be expected, as the author consciously makes clear the overall purpose of the book. That the verse belongs in its place is made clear since it participates in the interweaving of themes, and lexical and grammatical parallels, which are consonant with its context.

So it can be observed that it is clearly in direct speech form. Although not immediately preceded by the verb 'to say', (because it is not one of the seven proclamations), it is introduced by asyndeton which is normal for direct speech. The basic structure is an imperative followed by a reason clause introduced by 'because', which is the same as the structure of the other proclamations. The reference to the saints and the prophets is echoed in verse 24, and the general address to the population of heaven is echoed in the following interlude, as is the concept of God intervening in judgment in order to vindicate his people.

The interlude occurs in its usual place after the sixth proclamation (19:1-8). It has all the usual characteristics of an interlude and more. It is situated in the throne-room of heaven and concerns the praise and worship addressed to God. It thereby breaks up the Judgment Theme which has been dominant in the preceding proclamations, and inserts a segment on the Salvation Theme.

In addition it needs to be stated clearly that it obviously fits in the exact place where it is located. This is because it has all the structural hallmarks of the rest of the cycle; that is to say it starts off with a loud noise of voices from Heaven, the same as Proclamations 1 and 2. The following speech is introduced by the present participle of the verb 'to say', the same as all the other proclamations. The first word of the speech is a strong declaration ('Hallelujah!') which is semantically the same as an imperative, and which is then repeated a second time towards the end. Then finally, this first declaration is followed by 'because' with a following reason clause, the same as all the proclamations. See Chart 15 above for a brief outline of the content of the interlude.

As a result of all these interwoven details there is no possibility of dismissing these verses as being extraneous interpolations, or anything of the sort. On the contrary, it is obvious that these verses were intentionally put in this exact place by the author and that, therefore, they have a significant contribution to make to the whole discourse. These issues will be developed further in Chapter 4, where their significance should become apparent.

Concluding Remarks

As can be seen from the preceding paragraphs, there is a lot of detail to be accounted for in the Proclamations Cycle. I trust therefore, that the explanations have not been so dense as to be totally incomprehensible, but that, in fact, you have been able to grasp a general idea of the ethos of this part of the book.

I have, nonetheless, included these details for two reasons. In the first place, it is important for us all to recognize that the book of Revelation is artistically created by means of a complex network of intricately interwoven words, ideas and concepts. It is not a case of a truck-load of random words being tipped onto the page, and left to jostle for position and preeminence without any authorial oversight.

The proof of the pudding is in its eating, as they say, and the proof of a compelling and consistent discourse like this, is in the details of its wordplay and parallelism. The text will withstand close inspection. As a result you will find that, even though there is a lot of detail in these proclamations, nonetheless all the details fit together neatly, and without any contradiction. They complement and support each other in a variety of ways, such that it can be seen that they are all there for a purpose, and each one is playing its part.

The second purpose is to provide sufficient data to be of interest and of help to the more technically minded reader, especially for those who may have started out being rather skeptical of the analysis which is being presented here. Our starting point for any analysis must be the data. So the data is there, in your Greek New Testament, if you have one, and then laid out and explained in these pages. If we let the data speak for themselves, then it is clear that there are seven sections in this passage which can legitimately be called proclamations, or some such thing. They are all structured and organized in the same way, and are completed by an interlude, which is different in content and theme, but is the same at the level of the structure. Any alternative analysis must, of necessity, take account of all the same data in a similar, or more coherent manner, to be worthy of any serious attention.

3.5.5 The Seventh Proclamation 19:17-18

Most of the evidence for proposing that this section is the seventh proclamation and, therefore, that it belongs with the rest of the cycle has already been presented.

So, in summary then, there is an angelic personage who fits into a concentric structure, and is linked to the previous angel by the unique use of the word 'one'. He makes a proclamation in a loud voice. This proclamation is dominated by a doublet of imperatives followed by a subordinate clause introduced by ‘in order that’. There is conceptual linkage to the rest of the cycle including the nearby Narrative Framework through the words ‘kings’, and ‘supper’.

To reinforce this internal coherence another similarity can now be noticed. The imperative doublet, ‘come/assemble’, is followed by a purpose clause marked by ‘in order that’. Grammatically and conceptually this parallels the first imperative in the second proclamation (18:4) although with an antithetical sense. In Proclamation 2 at18:4, God’s people are urged to come *away* from Babylon in order that they *not* share in the fate of that city, whereas in Proclamation 7 the birds are urged to come *together* in order *to* share in God’s provision at his feast resulting from His judgment of Babylon.

Even though there are enough similarities to warrant a clear connection with the rest of the cycle, nonetheless the seventh proclamation is different from the other ones. The most striking difference is that it is cut off from the rest of its cycle by intervening text (19:11-16), and so this has to be accounted for, before a final decision can be made about 19:17-18.

Firstly, 19:11-16 is quite different from the preceding proclamations interlude, and even the nearby Narrative Framework. It is also quite different from the following seventh proclamation. For example, there is no direct speech, no messages in doublet form, no present participle of ‘to say’, and no reason clauses. It does not continue the same topic, and has only weak lexical links with its immediate context. In addition, the visual orienter ‘and I saw’ reoccurs in 19:11, after being replaced by aural orienters in the previous body of the cycle.

This means that it is not possible to consider it either as a coda to the interlude, which already has one in effect, since the Narrative Framework section (19:9-10) already follows it. Nor is it reasonable to interpret it as a long introduction to the seventh proclamation.

Secondly, the whole of 19:11-21 would appear to be a complete unit. This is because 19:11-16 belongs together with 19:19-21 because of the threefold reference to the one sitting on the white horse (19:11,19 and 21). If this whole passage is analyzed in terms of its linear narrative development, 19:11-16 provides a descriptive introduction, while 19:19-21 provides the events which are the climax, and the denouement, of this embedded narrative.

From within this paradigm, 19:17-18 is little more than an aside which, along with its parallel reference in 19:21b, contributes nothing to the central action; this action being the war between Christ and his armies, and the beast and his armies. Rather, it just serves as an embellishment of, or a commentary on, the main action. From this point of view, 19:17-18 could be removed from the text and not be missed. This confirms that it can be viewed as a separate unit, whose primary function is something other than contributing to the narrative flow of its immediate context.

However, at the same time, there are many parallels in the passage and when this paradigm, based on parallelism, is applied, it can be viewed as a chiasm as demonstrated in Chart 17. In the sub-titles of the chart, implied information is enclosed in brackets. The words and phrases which are in a smaller font, and are also enclosed in brackets, indicate the primary lexical parallels which support the chiastic analysis.

Chart 17.
The Parallel Structure of 19:11-21

A. The victorious Christ (who is the Lamb who was sacrificed/killed)
('the one sitting on a horse'// vv.19,21; 'name written...His name', 'garment'// v.16) 19:11-13

B. The heavenly armies follow Christ to victory over the nations
('armies' and 'His (Christ's) army'// v.19; 'a sword...from His mouth' // v.21 'to strike the nations... King of kings'// v.19) 19:14-16

C. Proclamation 7: The Invitation to God's Feast 19:17-18
('assemble'// v.19; 'kings'// v.19; 'birds... flesh/bodies'// v.21)

B' The earthly armies assemble to make war with Christ and His army 19:19

A' Christ is victorious over the beast (who was previously killed, yet lives) and its cohorts ('the rest'//'the kings'... etc., vv. 18 and 19) 19:20-21

A major parallel which is implicit rather than explicit is that between Christ (19:11-15) and the beast (19:19-20). The beast is fully described in 13:1-10, where it is described as being one that was killed/sacrificed (13:3) and, in the same context, reference is also made to the Lamb who was killed/sacrificed (13:8). This point of comparison is alluded to in 19:13 in the phrase 'a robe dipped in blood'.

The beast's main characteristic is that it speaks against God (cf. 'a mouth speaking...blasphemies'(x 2), 'to blaspheme his (God's) name' (13:5-6)). This is contrastively parallel to 19:13 where it is stated that Christ's name is the Word of God.

A second characteristic of the beast is that it makes war very powerfully against God's people (13:4,7). This is repeated in 19:19, and the contrastive parallel is to be found in Christ and his armies (presumably God's people - cf. 'white linen' (19:14)) in 19:14-15.

Considered from this point of view therefore, Proclamation 7, which is contained in verses 17-18, is inextricably linked with the whole of 19:11-21, as can be seen in Chart 17. This is not only due to the relatively minor relationship with verse 19 and the more significant one with verse 21 (by the repetition of 'birds', and associated concepts), but particularly, because it is at the center of a chiasm.

This makes it the most important part of this passage, and, therefore, an essential component of the whole. It is not just tagged on as an afterthought, but is clearly built into the whole, from the start, as the centerpiece of the whole section. Consequently, what has been labeled the seventh proclamation is clearly embedded in the middle of another unit and cannot be separated from it.

From a hypothetical point of view this is not a problem. Embedding of one unit in another and creating complex units which have more than one function at the same time, are normal occurrences in both oral and written discourses. Furthermore, such complex units (e.g. the previous seventh units which are overlap links) have already been noticed in Revelation so this is not a new issue.

What is being proposed, then, to explain this phenomenon, is as follows. This cycle does indeed consist of a setting, followed by a body composed of seven units constructed in a similar fashion around the motif of a proclamation, which are complemented by a similarly constructed interlude.

The seventh proclamation is different from the others and to that extent shares a common denominator with the other seventh units of Cycles 2-5. In this case, seen from a linear point of view, the seventh proclamation completes the series of seven and shares the defining features, which put it on a par with its predecessors. In addition, seen from this point of view it does not have a crucial function in its immediate context, but could be analyzed as an extraneous aside.

However, reconsidered from within a parallel structure paradigm, this same unit of text can be analyzed as being the most important unit in its context and, therefore, far from being redundant, is essential for the structural integrity of the whole. This means that it has two concurrent functions. Firstly, it is the closure to the series of seven proclamations, and secondly it shares in the function of the text (19:11-21) where it is embedded, and this function will depend on the analysis of this surrounding text. Since this text needs to be analyzed in the context of a view of Cycles 2-6 as a total linguistic unit, further discussion will be postponed until that task can be adequately handled in Chapter 5.

3.6 The Relationships Between the Cycles

> Human language uses many devices to join successive segments of text into larger units. (There are some) techniques... in which transition and unification, rather than delimitation, seem to be the primary effects. Parunak 1983a,526-7.

Reference has already been made to the overlap links which bind together major components of the book of Revelation. This is also a significant feature of Cycles 2-6, which set them apart as a group from Cycles 1 and 7. The kind of transition involved is similar to the one called 'a hinge' by Parunak (op.cit.,540-6) which, in his case, is 'a transitional unit of text, independent to some degree from the larger units on either side, which has affinities with each of them...' (ibid.,540). The overlap links encountered in Revelation, however, are different in that the units concerned are not autonomous. Rather, they are integral parts of the larger units on either side, and belong to the internal structure of each of them, at the same time. The result of this double role of the transitional unit is that the two larger units actually overlap each other, hence the descriptive term which has been coined. When several units are joined together in this way, as is the case in Revelation, the result is striking, as it creates a large block of text, which is joined together in such a way that it cannot be separated into units without breaking apart, as it were, the internal structure of some or all of the units concerned. Yet, at the same time, it is clear to even a casual observer, that such a long stretch of text (i.e. running from 4:1 to 19:21) is, nonetheless, composed of a number of different parts.

INFORMATION

The study of relationships which may exist between the larger components of a discourse is a discipline which is still in its infancy. Furthermore, it is becoming clear that such relationships which exist in Revelation are complex and multi-stranded. Consequently, the present discussion can only claim to be an introduction to this subject which, it is to be hoped, will be taken further in the future. A further consequence is that the role of the connective *kai* 'and', will not be discussed here. This is a subject which needs more research, but the insights and hypotheses which have been developed so far are presented in the discussion on connectives in Appendix A2.2.4

In order to better understand this linguistic phenomenon, it is helpful to use the analogy of a telescope. It is self-evident that a telescope is composed of several different parts, all of which are connected in series and cannot be separated without destroying the telescope as a functioning instrument. In addition, all the primary parts have the same shape, the same internal structure and function (except for the parts at each end) and are similar in size.

It is almost exactly the same for Cycles 2 to 6 of Revelation: each cycle is approximately the same size, has a similar function relative to the whole, and, above all, has the same basic shape or internal structure. The differences of detail in the structure which do occur, are directly related to the differences in function which make the cycles complementary to each other, rather than identical clones. The differences occur because there has to be a beginning and end part, as in the telescope. However, a text of this nature, being more complex in concept than a telescope, also has variations in other places since it is governed by the laws of linguistics, rather than the laws of physics.

The connections and similarities will be highlighted below and the differences and their significance will be discussed in subsequent chapters.

3.6.1 The Overlap Links Between Cycles 2-6

The units of text which comprise the overlap links are presented in Chart 18 for ease of reference. The parallel lexical items are in a smaller font.

These seventh units are, of course, also the settings to the cycles which follow, and so their structure, in slightly different form, has already been presented in Charts 11-14. The sub-titles provided in the chart are intended to make explicit the key issues which indicate that the unit in question is both a seventh in a series, and also a setting for what follows. The information in parentheses provides the textual evidence both for the internal parallelism of each unit, and also for the parallelism, and thus the inherent connection, which exists with what follows.

The first unit presented (8:1-6) may be taken as an example, since what is true of this unit is true, with only slight variations, for all the others. The first point is that in the first verse of this unit, it is explicitly stated that it is the seventh seal. The only exception in the other units is in 15:1, where the word ‘a sign’, reoccurs although it is not stated that it is the seventh.

This means that there is no question that the beginning of the unit clearly belongs to, and brings to closure, the preceding series of seven. The second point is that the unit unambiguously introduces the angels who are going to sound the following series of trumpets (8:2 and 6), which begins immediately after this introduction at 8:7.

Thirdly, the symmetric structure of the unit is such that it cannot be reasonably broken down into autonomous sub-units. The only other way to account for such detailed repetition would be to propose a tail-head link, where the details at the end of one unit are taken up again at the beginning of the next. However, this would involve creating a major break between 8:3 and 8:4, which is hardly plausible given the significant unity of 8:1-6 in terms of logical flow, narrative structure and thematic cohesion.

Chart 18.
The Overlap Links Between Cycles 2-6

The Seventh Seal 8:1-6

A. The 7th Seal 8:1-2 (There occurred silence in Heaven, the 7 Angels with their 7 Trumpets)
  B. Temple/Throne Room Furniture 8:3a (Another angel, altar, censer)
    C. Action of the Angel 8:3b (Incense, prayers of the saints, before the throne)
    C' Action of the Angel 8:4 (Incense, prayers of the saints, before God)
  B' Temple/Throne Room Furniture 8:5a (The angel, altar, censer)
A' Preparation for the 1st Trumpet 8:5b-6 (There occurred noises on the earth, an earthquake, and the 7 angels get ready with their 7 Trumpets)

The Seventh Trumpet 11:15-19

A. The 7th Trumpet 11:15a (There occurred loud noises in Heaven, i.e. 'loud voices')
  B. Direct Speech: 11:15b (Generic statement concerning the Reign of Christ)
    C. Temple/Throne Room Worship 11:16
  B' Direct Speech: 11:17-18 (Specific statements concerning the Reign of God Almighty)
A' Revelation of/from Temple/Throne Room in Preparation for the 1st Sign 11:19 (was seen..., there occurred loud noises in Heaven including voices)

The Seventh Sign 15:1-16:1

A. The 7th Sign 15:1-2 (7 Angels with the 7 Last Plagues which will complete God's Anger)
  B. Temple/Throne Room Worship 15:3-4
A' Revelation of/from Temple/Throne Room in Preparation for the 1st Bowl 15:5-8 (The 7 Angels who are given the Bowls of the Anger of God, completion of the 7 Plagues)
    Coda. Final Instructions to the 7 Angels 16:1

The Seventh Bowl 16:17-21

A. The 7th Bowl 16:17-18 (There occurred, loud noises in Heaven, a voice from the Temple/ Throne Room) saying, 'It Is Done', a great earthquake, special emphasis on the magnitude of the plague, people on earth)
  B. Babylon is remembered before God and is destroyed 16:19 (great city)
A' The Last Part of the Plague 16:20-21 (the equivalent of a universal earthquake and a great hail with special emphasis on the magnitude of the plague, out of Heaven upon people (on earth), they speak to/blaspheme God). Followed exceptionally by a Narrative Framework section 17:1-18, and then immediately by the 1st Proclamation.

Note the clear parallelism between 'there occurred', and silence in 8:1, as opposed to 'there occurred', and noises in 8:5-6. A lot of debate has been generated concerning the theological import of the silence (cf. Beale 1999,445-54). However, before that debate can be enjoined, account has to be taken, in the first instance, of the dramatic contrast which is created, simply by evoking the concept of silence in 8:1, in a position of parallelism with expressions which create an impression of a wild cacophony of noise and uncontrolled activity in 8:5.

Nonetheless, in spite of this internal cohesion, many commentators have proposed a break between 8:1 and 8:2. A notable example is Beale himself (op.cit.,136,454, 460-4) who admits that this division has 'an apparent awkwardness'. He goes on to say that this analysis 'allows vv. 2-5 to act as a parenthetical transition both concluding the seals and introducing the trumpets'. However, this brings him right around to saying the same thing as has been proposed in the text above, and yet this latter analysis has none of Beale's awkwardness, but takes account of all the data in the most elegant, complete, and coherent way possible.

So then, this proposed division between 8:1 and 8:2 is only plausible if the unit is treated alone and out of the context of the rest of the book. However, no text exists in a vacuum and this is an example of where an understanding of the larger linguistic systems functioning in a book like Revelation, need to be taken into account. It is essential that they be observed first of all, and then they can be both appreciated, and allowed to influence the micro analysis of texts such as this one. It is particularly important to do this in cases like this, where the most elegant analysis may not be immediately obvious.

In this case, 8:1-6 is just one of a series of texts which function as settings to major components of the book. They are unified by their reference back to the major throne-room setting in Chapters 4 and 5, which acts as a backdrop to everything which happens in Cycles 2-6, and even, arguably, to everything which happens in the whole book. They are also unified by the fact that they all have an internal concentric structure. This higher level evidence then, is the deciding factor in difficult cases such as this. The consequence of this process is that it is possible to establish an analogy with other similar units with the same function. From there it is a small and logical step to propose that 8:1-6 should be treated as a coherent whole. Just like the other overlap links, it has a double role, that of conclusion to the Seals Cycle, and also that of setting to the Trumpets Cycle, at the same time.

The same basic argumentation is true for the other units in Chart 18, where the evidence for the parallelism is also presented, with the exception of the seventh bowl. This latter is different from the others in that the direct connection with what follows is not as clear-cut as with the other overlap links. This is mainly due to the presence of Chapter 17, which is inserted between the setting and the first proclamation, which starts at 18:1.

Nonetheless, the lexical and thematic evidence is clear. Babylon is established as being the most important topic of the setting by virtue of being at the center of a chiasm (16:19; see Chart 14 above) and this continues as the dominant topic right throughout Chapters 17 and 18 without interruption. The reference at 16:19 then, serves as an introductory reference to the next main topic of discussion, as would be expected in a setting, followed, in this case, by further introductory description and explanation in Chapter 17.

However, it also needs to be noticed that this reference in 16:19 is not the first reference to Babylon, as it is previewed in 14:8, which is the first reference of six in the book. However, this phenomenon is typical of all the main personages in the book. Jesus is previewed at 1:1 before being fully introduced at 1:9-20. Satan is previewed in Cycle 1 (2:9,13,24 and 3:9) long before his main introduction at 12:3. The new Jerusalem is previewed at 3:12 but is only fully introduced at 21:2, while the beasts are introduced in Chapter 13 but are previewed at 11:7.

Furthermore, the reference to Babylon being remembered before God in 16:19 is directly in the context of a forceful proclamation in 16:17, and the obvious logic of the passage is that the judgment of Babylon is a direct consequence of this proclamation. Therefore, even though the term 'proclamation' is not used, the reporting of an actual proclamation which has direct consequences for Babylon, forms approximately ninety percent of the content of the setting.

In fact, it could be said that this is the initial proclamation, which is the first cause for all the others in the body of the cycle. Finally, the setting is lexically linked to the body by the phrase (with reference to Babylon) 'the great city', occurring at 16:19, in the Narrative Framework section at 17:18, and then several times in Chapter 18, beginning implicitly at 18:2 and explicitly at 18:10.

Perusal of the evidence demonstrates that all the settings prefigure, in some way, the main issues which will be developed in the body of the cycle. In the case of the setting of the Signs Cycle, the link is more allusive but becomes clearer on closer inspection. There is no overt reference to signs in the setting, but conceptually it indicates that God and his Christ have taken up their reign to judge the nations, who have been 'full of wrath', and to 'destroy those who destroy the earth' (11:15, 17-18). Then, in the following series of signs, it is disclosed how Satan tries to stir up the nations to rebellion and in the process causes the destruction of the earth (12:17, 13:4-7, 13-17; 14:9-11), and then how God has a plan to bring an end to this period of trial and turmoil (14:1-6 and 14:14-20).

Longenecker 2001,14-15 has also independently discussed the transitions at 8:1-6 and 15:1-4 and has proposed that these are examples of a 'chain-link construction' of the type Ab/aB. However, he overlooked the analogous transitions at 11:15-19 and 16:17-21, and the fact that 15:1-16:1 is a complete unit.

Longenecker has provided a significant service in demonstrating that such linkage was not only common, but was apparently obligatory, for good style in ancient discourses. Citing his ancient sources, Lucian of Samasota (ibid.,111) in this case, Longenecker indicates that, when an author/speaker brings together different parts of his message, the end of one must be tightly interwoven with the beginning of the next.

Longenecker 2001,111 himself observes that this kind of 'transitional overlap...might appear somewhat untidy to modern eyes since it threatens to disrupt the linear progression of logical thought'. Nonetheless, his discovery of this ancient practice confirms that the proposal that there are overlapping links in Revelation is not misplaced.

However, the weakness of Longenecker's analysis of these two texts is that he tries to impose a single AbaB formula (his version of the notation) on both of his examples, and it is not satisfactory in this case. This is because, as Parunak 1983a demonstrates, once a basic linguistic principle like this one for overlapping connections has been established, the number of variations of the basic form which are possible, is only limited by the extent of human creativity.

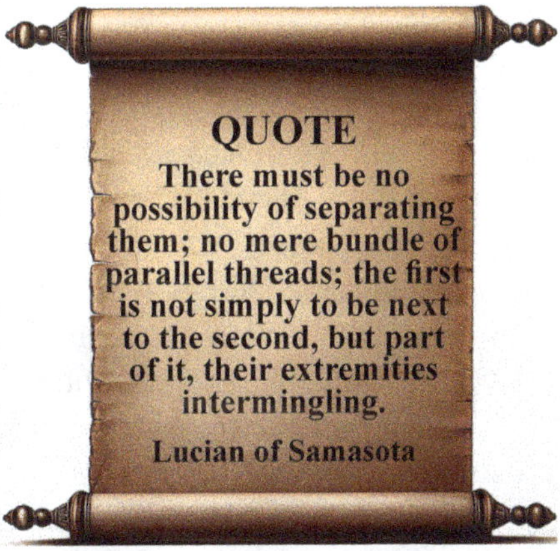
QUOTE
There must be no possibility of separating them; no mere bundle of parallel threads; the first is not simply to be next to the second, but part of it, their extremities intermingling.
Lucian of Samasota

Longenecker's analysis then, is weakened because he is not able to demonstrate that 8:1-6 and 15:1-4 are examples of this specific type of Ab/aB connection. In addition, he himself quotes Quintilian (op.cit.,112), in this case, who says that 'artistic structure must be ... varied', but on this occasion he failed to apply the very principle which he had quoted about the necessity of variation in a discourse.

This is quite a technical point, so let's just look at one example in detail so that we can nonetheless, understand the important underlying principle, which governs the joining together of ancient texts. One example is sufficient, because what is true of one of these examples, is true for all of them. The example then, is the overlap link between the Signs Cycle and the Bowls Cycle which occurs at 15:1-16:1, according to the analysis presented in the previous paragraphs.

Longenecker's formula (ibid.,116), based on the letters A,B, a, and b, as indicated in the text above, is to be interpreted as follows. This has to be done, bearing in mind that he does not perceive the organization of the text in the same way as has been presented in the present analysis. His notation Ab/aB, for this intermingled, overlap link, therefore, is to be interpreted as follows.

A is 12:1-14:20. This represents a major unit of text which, for him, is the same as the Signs Cycle.

b is 15:1. This represents a minor portion of text which, for him, is typical of, and belongs with, the following major unit of text which is represented by the letter **B.**

B is 15:5-16:21, representing a major unit of text which, for him, is the same as the Bowls Cycle.

a is 15:2-4. This represents a minor portion of text which, for him, is typical of, and belongs with, the previous major unit of text which is represented by the letter **A.**

INFORMATION

The AbaB notation used by Longenecker is derived from Parunak 1983a, where the capitals 'A' and 'B' represent significant portions of text which are clearly distinct from each other, and the lower case 'a' and 'b' represent material which clearly belongs with the section represented by the matching capital. In Parunak's notation a slash '/' is included to mark the division between the two major units. The transition of the type Ac/cB is what is known in modern linguistic parlance as a 'tail-head link'. In this kind of link, the letter 'c' represents low-level material which is not particularly representative of either major unit, but is present in the text mainly to provide a transition between them. An example of such a tail-head link occurs in Revelation in 12:18 and 13:1. A true example of an Ab/aB connection does, in fact, occur between Cycle 1 and Cycle 2 and this will be discussed shortly. Another, more complex, example of this kind of connection links together Cycle 6 and Cycle 7, and this one will be discussed in Chapter 5, sub-section 4.

So then, as a reminder, Longenecker says that an example of an Ab/aB connection can be found in 15:1-4. He says that '15:2-4 form the conclusion to the narrative in chapters 12-14. The conflict of those chapters reaches its apex in the song of triumphant praise in 15:3b-4' (ibid.,115-16).

However, he overlooks the fact that within the broader context of Cycles 2-6 this 'song of triumphant praise' is part of a unit which is reactivating a whole series of setting material whose roots go back to Chapter 4. Not only do the roots go back further than Chapter 12, but the thematic thread also continues on beyond 15:4.

This is because the key content of the song includes a reference to the Lord God Almighty whose ways are righteous and true (15:3b), and this information is repeated almost word for word in the third bowl unit at 16:7.

Since this latter verse is a comment and contributes no essential content to the third bowl, it would appear that its primary structural function is to create a parallel link with 15:3b. All this means that 15:1-4 is not self-evidently an 'a' unit which is particularly characteristic of his section 'A', which is 12:1-14:20.

In addition, he claims that 15:1 ('b' in his notation) is an introduction to what follows, but he overlooks the fact that it also refers to a sign which, in the broader scheme of organization, is explicitly the last of a series of three, and, implicitly, the last of seven. This means that 15:1 is not self-evidently a 'b' unit either. So, Longenecker has correctly observed the interwoven nature of the connection, but has not quite taken account of all the data. A better interpretation of the data is that the sub-units 15:1 and 15:3b-4 are not just part of an introduction or a conclusion, but that each of them are part of both an introduction, and a conclusion, at the same time.

Another oversight is that the AbaB formula should contain an indicator of a major division in the middle (and therefore should be written Ab/aB), and this division should occur after 15:1. Even though a major division can be imposed on the text at this point, it would destroy the internal integrity of the section 15:1-16:1 and ignore the parallel structure which unifies it. The best solution therefore, which takes account of all the data and not just part of it, appears to be the proposal previously made, that 15:1-16:1 (and likewise 8:1-6) is an example of an overlap link.

It can be seen from the above discussion then, that the linguistic evidence supports the proposition that the units which join together Cycles 2-6 are complete units. They are complete units because they have an internal integrity, such that they cannot be reasonably broken down into smaller autonomous units. Consequently, each unit is interpreted as being a conclusion to the cycle which precedes, but also in its entirety, a setting for the cycle which follows. This is why they have been called overlap links.

3.6.2 The Parallelism Between Cycles 2-6

The most striking parallelism which arises from the discussion so far, is the parallel structure shared by all these cycles, in that each have a setting, and a body organized according to a seven-fold motif, and that four of the five also have an interlude. In addition, where it is possible, namely for Cycles 2-5 only, the conclusion of each cycle is an overlap link joining it inextricably to the following cycle.

Reference has already been made above to the similarities between the settings. In brief, they all have references rooted in the initial large setting of Chapters 4 and 5, which alludes to the heavenly Throne Room and its furniture, upon which the organization of the Israelite Tabernacle and Temple were based. Furthermore, they all have references to extraordinary events, either positive, negative, or implicitly both, which emanate from the Throne Room in Heaven. Just as the Holy of Holies was God's Throne Room on earth, so to speak, it was still only an imperfect copy of the real thing. In John's case he had the privilege of visiting the real Throne Room, which is the true center of the universe, and so everything which he recounts in his book flows out from there.

These supernatural events, which are perceived by the narrator either aurally or visually, are directly related to the events taking place in the Throne Room. Thus, there is the loud acclamation in song and spoken worship in 5:11-12, 11:16 and 15:2-4, and conversely, there is a striking silence in 8:1, followed by the explosive noises of shouts, thunder, lightning, accompanied by hail and earthquakes in 8:5 (cf.v.7), 11:15,19; and 16:17,18,21. The Bowls Cycle setting (15:8) also portrays the phenomenon of the unapproachable smoke of the glory of God.

QUOTE

The bowls are generally parallel thematically and temporally to the trumpets (and ultimately to the seals), which is borne out by their similarity.

Beale 1998,203-4

Furthermore, except for Cycle 4, which is different from the others in a number of ways, each of the seven-fold sub-units relate directly back to their respective settings, rather than back to the preceding sub-unit.

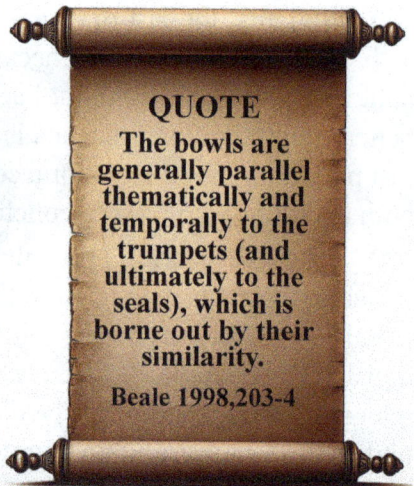

This is an example of another kind of repetition. On this occasion, this is a repetition of a particular structural organization which the author has previously used, for this linking of each sub-unit back to its settings was previously observed in Cycle 1. From a linguistic point of view, this is not a novelty. As Callow 1998,291 explains at some length, settings are obligatory components of discourses. Then, once the basic setting has been established, either at the beginning of the whole discourse, or at the beginning of a major section, it can be optionally 'reactivated' by the author. This is done periodically in order to maintain it as the backdrop for several different textual units, some of which may not be contiguous. It is obvious that this sort of thing is very likely to occur in long and complex books like Revelation.

Much has already been written about the parallelism between the bodies of these cycles, especially between the Trumpets and the Bowls and so the detail which is available elsewhere will not be presented here. The important point which needs to be made clear, is that there is so much lexical and conceptual repetition, that parallel connections of all kinds can be found between all of the five central cycles.

As Bauckham 1993,22 says: 'these repetitions create a complex network of cross-reference, which helps to create and expand the meaning of any one passage...'. In the context of the present study, it is not so much the expansion of meaning which is of interest. In this case, these repetitions are of interest for confirming the reality of the structural organization which is being proposed. These serial repetitions demonstrate that the central cycles are not only tightly bound together by reason of their overlap links, but that they also function together because of the complex interweaving of lexical parallelism which occurs.

For example, the word 'sign', is clearly important for the central Cycle 4, being the dominant motif of this cycle, but in addition to this, it occurs exactly seven times in the whole book, with those occurrences being in Cycles 4, 5 and 6. Consequently, these three cycles are linked together by this important lexical parallelism. Similarly the word 'earthquake', also occurs seven times in the book and occurs in Cycles 2, 3 and 5, while the word 'woe', occurs fourteen times in Cycles 3,4 and 6.

By contrast, the name 'Babylon', occurs six times and, like 'sign', links Cycles 4, 5 and 6 together. The word 'war', occurs nine times in Cycles 3, 4, 5 and 6 and a synonymous concept (take peace from...) occurs in Cycle 2. The verb 'slay', occurs eight times in Cycles 2, 4 and 6, and the two nouns (and the cognate verb) translated by 'anger' and 'wrath' occur a total of eighteen times in Cycles 2, 3, 4, 5 and 6. In addition, 'torment' (noun and verb), occurs eight times in Cycles 3, 4 and 6, plus one occurrence in the setting of Cycle 7. 'Plague', occurs thirteen times in Cycles 3-6 plus two in the setting of Cycle 7, and 'beast', occurs 36 times in Cycles 2-6 inclusive, plus two in the setting to Cycle 7, while 'throne(s)', clearly a dominant preoccupation in the book, occurs 46 times.

The evidence of the overlap links suggests that Cycles 2-6 belong together; and should be interpreted as all contributing to a single larger whole. As a complement to this, the evidence reviewed in this section suggests that each cycle should be viewed as being in parallel to all the others. For each of them is connected by way of their individual settings to the larger original setting of the Throne Room in Heaven portrayed in Chapters 4 and 5. This is not to deny that there is also linear progression in these cycles, but this issue will be discussed in Chapter 5, section 7.

3.6.3 The Relationship Between Cycles 1 and 2

There is agreement that there is a major division between Cycles 1 and 2 (between 3:22 and 4:1), and the primary linguistic data which supports this observation has already been presented in section 3.2 above. The objective here is to make some remarks concerning the connections, and therefore the relationship, which exist between these two cycles. The aim will be to make the point that there is both a division between two cycles at this juncture and also a linear flow of thought across the unit boundary. This implies in turn, that the ordering of the two cycles is intentional, and that their respective messages should not be interpreted as if they are two separate, and unconnected, blocks of information.

Firstly then, let's consider the notion that there is a clear distinction between Cycles 1 and 2, because there is objective linguistic evidence available to support this hypothesis. Longenecker 2001, as mentioned above, has discovered that, for ancient writers, making connections clear, was at least as important as making divisions clear. Furthermore, his application of the intermingling connection principle, in the form of the Ab/aB formula, to this junction between 3:22 and 4:1, is enlightening. He understands that Chapters 2-3 (the body of Cycle 1) form a unit (A), while Chapters 4-5 (the beginning of Cycle 2) form another major unit (B). Then he makes the insightful remark that 3:21, being the promise to the overcomer, instead of drawing from its preceding context as the previous such promises do, talks about sitting on thrones and, in so doing, previews material (b) which is central to the following unit (B).

However, Longenecker's contention that the material which is 'a' in his formula is 3:21 (ibid.,114) indicates a misunderstanding of the system. According to the formula which he uses, the 'a' part must come after the division between the units thus: Ab/aB, and this is not the case for 3:21. His contention that there is an overlapping link here is correct but the correct formula for his data is Ab/B as per Parunak 1983a,532.

In reality, the connection is more complex, and the 'craftsmanship' more 'studied' (ibid.,113) than Longenecker realized. In 3:20 there is reference to the **opening of a door**, which concept is taken up in 4:1. This concept is not central and, therefore, is not repeated more than once in Cycle 1 (A) and Cycle 2 (B), and so the notation for this kind of transitional repetition is 'c'.

Next, in 3:21, as Longenecker correctly remarked, is the reference to God's **throne** which occurs once in Cycle 1 (A), but is a central, repeated concept in Cycle 2 (B). This, therefore, is a candidate for being the ‘b’ part of the formula. Next, in 4:1 there is a reference to **the voice** which John heard at first, which is a central concept in Cycle 1 but only occurs in this place in Cycle 2, and so would be represented by ‘a’ in the formula. These features indicate that the transitional connection between the two cycles is a complex, balanced one, of the type Acb/caB, as visually laid out in the following chart, which is Chart 19.

Chart 19.
The Connection Between Cycle 1 and Cycle 2

The Connection is of the Type Acb/caB

A. = **Cycle 1** when Jesus is **speaking** to John, and to the churches 1:9-3:22

c = the reference to an opening **door** in 3.20

b = the reference to sitting on God’s **throne** in 3:21

Division Between Two Major Units

c = the reference to an opening **door** in 4:1

a = **a heavenly voice** speaking to John, being **the same voice** as in Cycle 1 4:1

B. = **Cycle 2** when all that occurs emanates from **the heavenly throne room** 4:1-8:6

This insight into the art of connecting together different units of a discourse in subtle but evocative ways, enables the modern analyst to make two firm deductions. The first is that there is indeed a transition between two distinct units after 3:22. It could be objected that since the junction is so obvious, such complex extra details are redundant. However, in response to the objection, it needs to be reiterated that this was apparently good style at the time of writing.

In addition to that, it may be, that at this point early on in the book where the division is obvious, the author is setting up a pattern to guide the listeners in other places where the signposts may be less obvious. This possibility is confirmed when it is realized that this kind of tail-head link which has been observed between Cycles 1 and 2, also occurs between Cycles 6 and 7.

As a consequence, this feature sets Cycles 1 and 7 apart, as distinct from Cycles 2 to 6 which are all tightly joined together by overlap links. To make this point easier to grasp, let's lay it out in visual form, as in Chart 20. In this chart you will see each of the seven cycles laid out in order, with indicators in the surrounding text which describe the exact kind of connection which links them to their neighbors.

Chart 20.

The Differences in the Connections Between the 7 Cycles

Cycle 1 – 1:9-3:22

A Tail-Head Link which marks the connection between 3:22 and 4:1

All of	**(Cycle 2 – 4:1-8:6)**	these Cycles
are	**(Cycle 3 – 8:1-11:19)**	tightly
joined	**(Cycle 4 – 11:15-16:1)**	together
by the means	**(Cycle 5 – 15:1-16:21)**	of
Overlap	**(Cycle 6 – 16:17-19:21)**	Links

A Tail-Head Link which marks the connection between 19:21 and 20:1

Cycle 7 – 20:1-22:7

The point which this chart makes clear, is that Cycles 2-6 are tightly bound together in a group, such that they cannot be reasonably be split apart into separate units. This is because the overlap links overlap, as their name indicates. As such, the extremities of each cycle are so tightly interwoven together that they cannot be separated without doing an injustice to the text as the author set it out. By contrast, the links at the end of Cycle 1 and at the beginning of Cycle 7 are only simple tail-head links. These features are also links, or connections, as their name indicates. Nonetheless, they have the advantage that the exact point of the division between the units so linked, can be located with precision. In these cases, the extremities of the units intermingle to some extent, but not to the degree that it is no longer possible to discern the boundary between them. The details of the link between Cycles 6 and 7 will be explained in Chapter 5.4.

The second deduction concerning the significance of the Tail-Head link between Cycles 1 and 2 is as follows. It is that there is an intentional flow of thought, linearly, across the unit boundary, and that this thought includes the concept of sitting on thrones and thence reigning.

Study of the book as a whole indicates that this is a major, book-level theme which begins, therefore, in Cycle 1, flows through all the other cycles, and terminates at 22:5 with the last words of the body of Cycle 7, where it says that God's people will reign with Him for ever. Since this refers to the saints, or the overcomers, it is in direct parallel with 3:21. This latter verse tells us that the overcomers (who are members of God's people in Asia Minor at that time) will be granted the privilege of sitting on thrones with Jesus, just as He Himself, was granted to sit with the Father on His throne. Sitting on thrones clearly implies reigning.

The transition between Cycle 1 and 2 is dependent on the specific words 'to sit', and 'throne', and is therefore a bona fide tail-head link in its own right. However, at the thematic level, the concept of overcoming also participates in the development of the theme of reigning, and this concept is to be found throughout Cycle 1, overcoming being the first phase of becoming rulers. In addition, the first reference to Christ as ruler is in the Prologue at 1:5, which verse is paralleled in the Epilogue (22:16 and 20), by the re-occurrence of Christ in his function of the faithful witness. The first reference to God's throne also occurs in the Prologue at 1:4, in tandem with the verse just cited.

These observations indicate that Cycle 1 is in direct relationship with Cycle 2 and, as such, is an integral part of the book and should in no way be detached from it, and treated as a quite separate unit. On the contrary, being the first Cycle it serves as an introduction and, as such, initiates the themes and issues which are important in the book as a whole. Even though more research is needed, it seems likely that, at the higher levels of discourse, overlapping connections of this sort regularly introduce important themes.

INFORMATION

Very little research has been done into these kinds of connections between units at the upper level of the discourse hierarchy. Two hypotheses arising out of this study can be formulated for further investigation. The first is that the more complex a transitional link is, the larger the units which it is connecting. The second is that the transitional links of large units will usually contain material which is important for the organization of the book as a whole. In the above case, it will be seen in Chapter 5 that the apparently innocuous 'door' has a high level function. This hypothesis is complementary to the widely-held opinion (see Parunak 1983a,531-32), that lower-level tail-head links are created by using features which have little or no other importance, an example of which is the repetition of 'sea', in Revelation 12:18 and 13:1.

3.7 The Seventh Cycle: The Seven Characteristics of the New Creation 20:1-22:7

The seventh cycle is also a seventh unit in a series and, like the seventh units of Cycles 2-6, it is different from its predecessors. The purpose of this section is to make some general statements about it which are easily supported by the data, and then to propose a hypothesis for the things which remain. A complete understanding of this cycle will not be possible until after other important issues have been discussed and clarified, and this will be accomplished in the course of the following chapters.

As a starting point for this preliminary discussion, the limits of the seventh cycle can be established by default. Thus far the process of analysis has proceeded by establishing the internal coherence of each cycle. The result is that six cycles have been found, each with a setting, and a body with a seven-fold motif. The last unit of the sixth cycle is embedded in a linguistic unit which terminates at 19:21. Inspection of this section of text confirms that, according to all the usual linguistic criteria, a new linguistic unit does indeed begin at 20:1.

This new beginning is signaled by a change in location, primary participant(s), and topic. There are no compensatory words, such as 'another', which link backwards to a previous section of text, which could, therefore, be evidence for some kind of continuity between 20:1 and what immediately precedes. The continuity of theme and of lexical chains between the passage beginning at 20:1 and what immediately precedes is very weak. More detailed discussion of the division between 19:21 and 20:1 will be found in Chapter 5.4.

The thematic similarities which are clearly present are between 19:20-21 and 20:10 and 20:14-15, which all contain references to the lake of fire. This suggests that the passages which terminate with these references, are in parallel to each other, as illustrated by Chart 21. The repetition of the theme of the Lake of Fire is objectively present in the text, that is for sure, but that alone does not prove any linear movement which flows inexorably from Chapter 19 through to Chapter 20, as some have tried to argue. All it proves is that there are four sub-sections which are in parallel with each other, as a result of this repetition of lexical items and of the underlying theme concerning the final judgment. The other thing which it proves is that some sub-topics and themes do flow over from Cycle 6 to Cycle 7, but this is a totally normal phenomenon. Some topics and themes flow from near the beginning of the book only to be completed in the final cycle, which is a totally normal function of a conclusion for a whole book. But it does not prove that there is a direct grammatical or semantic connection between Cycle 6 and Cycle 7 which establishes a linear relationship.

This observation that these sub-sections are in parallel with each other also serves to confirm that 20:1 must be the beginning of a new unit. However, it is clear that not all the units in Chart 21 can be major units like a cycle. This is not possible given the brevity of the sections in question, and given the fact that the concept of the lake of fire is not more pervasive than it is. So this evidence only confirms that there is a new beginning at 20:1, and not automatically that it is the beginning of a new cycle. The fact that it is the beginning of a new cycle can only be demonstrated when all the available evidence is taken into consideration, at a later stage in the process.

Chart 21.
The Parallelism of the Lake of Fire Motif

New Topics Introduce New Sections	**Closures End a Topic and Make Way for New Sections**
19:11 A New Topic: One Sitting on a White Horse	**19:20-21 Closure 1:** Lake of Fire Motif: The Beasts are Judged
20:1 A New Topic: The Imprisoned Dragon	**20:10 Closure 2:** Lake of Fire Motif The Dragon is Judged
20:11 A New Topic: One Sitting on a Throne	**20:14-15 Closure 3:** Lake of Fire Motif Death, Hades, the Dead are Judged
21:1 A NewTopic: A New Heaven & Earth	**21:8 Closure 4:** Lake of Fire Motif A Specific List of the Dead

In Chapter 2 it was proposed that the closing section of the Narrative Framework (i.e. the Epilogue) begins at 22:6. This means that a section of text beginning at 20:1 running through to at least 22:5, remains to be analyzed. From a linguistic point of view, it is clear that, regardless of whatever specialized function it may have, this passage must certainly function, in whole or in part, as a conclusion to the book.

This implies firstly, that any problems or conflicts which have been initiated and not previously terminated, are likely to be resolved in this section. Then secondly, any book-level themes which have been introduced and not fully developed, will be brought to closure in this passage as well. In addition, if there are any hidden ironies or special twists in the plot, they will also be brought to light before the book closes.

To summarize this preview of Cycle 7 then, it can be said that like its predecessors, this cycle has a setting and a body. It also has a brief conclusion (22:6-7) which stands outside the organization of the body, but this feature is consonant with its role as the concluding cycle. By nature of its position at the end of the book, it is in parallel with Cycle 1 at the beginning. Not surprisingly, therefore, these two cycles are similar in structural organization and have no interlude encased within the body of the cycle.

3.7.1 The Setting of Cycle 7 20:1-15

The setting of the cycle can be distinguished from the body for two complementary reasons. Firstly, its own internal integrity can be established on the basis of a parallel ABA'B' pattern, as displayed in Chart 22.

Chart 22.
The Setting of Cycle 7 20:1-15

A. Satan's Imprisonment and Temporary Demise 20:1-3
(An angel *comes down* from Heaven: Satan is bound, and thrown into the pit so that he may not deceive the nations for 1000 years; afterwards he will be released for a short time.)

B. The Martyred Witnesses Sit to Judge 20:4-6
(I saw thrones: the martyred witnesses have the right to judge; they live and reign with Christ; this is the first resurrection and the second death has no power over them; the remainder of the dead do not live again until after the 1000 years.)

A' Satan's Release and Final Destiny 20:7-10
(Satan is released after the 1000 years and once more deceives the nations who *go up* against the saints, but fire *comes down* out of Heaven, and the devil who deceived them is thrown into the lake of fire.)

B' The (Other) Dead Stand to be Judged 20:11-15
(I saw... a throne and one sitting on it; the dead (now restored to life) stand before Him and are judged by the books and their works. Those not found in the book of life are thrown into the lake of fire. This is the second death.)

This pattern interweaves references to:

- Satan's demise
- the thousand year period,
- the first resurrection and the second death,
- thrones and those seated on them exercising judgment and ruling power,
- the judgment of the dead on the basis of books and their works, and
- the final destiny for some in the lake of fire.

Secondly, this topical and thematic coherence, which deals primarily with judgment issues and the final solution for evil in the context of the lake of fire, sets it apart from the following text (21:1-22:7). By contrast, the following text deals primarily with salvation issues and the eternal destiny of the people of God in the context of a new creation and a new Jerusalem.

The second sub-title concerning the martyred witnesses assumes a particular interpretation of the identity of those sitting on the thrones. However, this interpretation is one of those widely held by others, according to Beale's (1999,995-1001) discussion of this issue. The position proposed above was chosen on linguistic grounds, namely that 20:4 is a chiasm featuring the same generic-specific linear development which is typical of Cycle 7, and linked by a complex repetition of 'and', 'and not' and 'nor'. This chiasm of 20:4 can be seen graphically presented in Chart 23.

Chart 23.
The Chiastic Structure of Revelation 20:4

A. And I saw thrones, And they (people-generic) sat on them
And (authority to pronounce) judgment was given to them 20:4a-c

> **B.** And the souls (specific 1) of those killed because of their testimony about Jesus, And because of the Word of God 20:4d-e
>
> > **C.** And who did **not** worship the beast, **nor** its image,
> > And did **not** receive its mark on their forehead, and **(nor)** on their hand 20:4f-i (specific 2)
>
> **B'** And they lived (again or still) 20:4j

A' And they reigned (= pronounced judgment) with Christ (on thrones) for 1000 years 20:4k

The parallelism inherent in this chiasm suggests that the concepts of sitting on thrones and being given authority to enact judgment (Part A. of the chiasm 20:4a-c), describe the same situation as living and reigning with Christ (Part A' 20:4j-k). Part B. (20:4d-e) is logically the detailed definition of the specific identity of those introduced generically by 'they' (pronominal suffix) and 'to them', in 20:4b-c. The linear development between A. and A' is generic-specific, that is to say that, those who were seen seated, in general terms, on the thrones to act as judges, were the same people who had specifically come back to life and reigned with Christ for a 1000 years.

It can be observed that the word 'thrones' is fronted, which means that it is designated as the topic of the whole unit. This tells us that the whole concept of ruling and reigning, which in turn, implies sitting in judgment, is what this section is all about. Yet, the center of the chiasm, and, therefore, the most important piece of information about the topic, is that these people did not worship the beast, nor did they obey it in any respect.

In other words, they overcame the dreaded beast, which is all part of their ruling and reigning. This picks up, and repeats in other words, the theme of overcoming which is dominant in Cycle 1.

It repeats the message of the double interlude in Chapters 10 and 11, which informed us that reigning with Christ can have its bitter moments, and may even involve suffering to the point of losing one's life, physically speaking. It also repeats the triumphant message sounded out in 12:11, that these same people overcame their accuser by their testimony, and by being willing to resist even if it cost them their lives. So there is great deal of thematic richness in this verse, and it is not pedantic to insist that the martyrs who were made alive to reign with Christ, are the same as the people who were seen seated on thrones in the heavenly places.

3.7.2 The Body of Cycle 7 21:1-22:5

The limits of the body of Cycle 7 can be defined by default, since it is the only text which remains between the setting of the cycle and the Epilogue.

Nonetheless, detailed analysis confirms that it is a coherent unit with a basic, parallel framework and a complex, parallel internal structure. This structure is based on the interplay between generic and specific statements concerning a series of related sub-topics. This basic framework is displayed in Chart 24, and the details contained within it will be filled out in Chapter 5.

The development of these sub-topics proceeds according to a symmetric organization (abb'a'), with the new creation (a) and the new Jerusalem (b) being introduced in this order and then developed in the specific sections in the opposite order (b' a').

Nonetheless, the internal structure of the body is not as immediately obvious as it is in other cycles. The text material is mainly descriptive in nature, and some of it is also detailed and repetitive. As a consequence, it creates an impression of what the author wants to communicate, rather than setting out an orderly, logical argument. It is not a criticism to say that only an impression is created. This may be entirely intentional on the author's part, and so the hearer and/or analyst may be reacting appropriately to the text by making this observation.

Chart 24.
The Body of Cycle 7

A. Generic Introduction to the Characteristics of the New Creation and the New Jerusalem 21:1-8

B. Specific Development 1: Detailed Description of the Characteristics of the New Jerusalem 21:9-21

C. Specific Development 2: Detailed Description of the Characteristics of the New Creation as Associated with the New Jerusalem 21:22-22:5

Given the other-worldly nature of the vision, it is possible that an impression is all that the narrator was able to create, in describing what he experienced. The point here is to be realistic about the nature of the text, and to accept what it communicates on its own terms, and not to try and make it accomplish more than it really does.

However, the principal impression created is clear. There is little dispute among commentators that this passage gives an insight into the nature of the New Creation in general, and the New Jerusalem in particular.

QUOTE
The theme of the New Creation dominates chapter 21, though the preceding idea of judgment is not altogether forgotten.
Beale 1999,1039

The ethos of the whole cycle is aptly summed up in the text itself, when God Himself speaks in no uncertain terms and declares in 21:5, **'Behold, I am making all things new'**. However, this English translation does not do justice to what was actually said. In literal terms the Creator actually said: **'Behold, NEW, I am making all things'.**

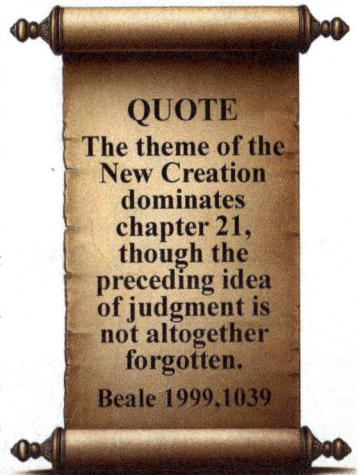

As this version indicates more clearly, the word 'new', is made specially prominent by being fronted and by being marked by 'behold'. This occurrence of 'new' is also the last, and probably the most important occurrence, of a lexical chain containing nine appearances of the word. The nine references are 2:17; 3:12 (x 2); 5:9; 14:3; 21:1 (x 2); 21:2 and 5. In total, seven different referents are qualified by the adjective 'new'; these are a name, my name, Jerusalem, a song, heaven, earth, and all things. The last one, being a generic summary, would seem to be the most important.

Overall then, it can be stated with some confidence that at least one part of the message of Cycle is 7 is clear: the chief characteristic of the world which is being described, is that everything in it is **'new'**.

Even if the general theme is clear, can it be said that a seven-fold motif dominates this cycle as in the others? It is obvious that there are not seven discrete units as in Cycle 1, neither is there a clear numbering system as in the Seals, Trumpets and Bowls Cycles. Even though the word 'new', is obviously a key word, the author gives no clear path to follow as he does in the Signs Cycle, and there does not appear to be seven occurrences of any other word or grammatical form, which could be a guide as in the Proclamations Cycle. Nonetheless, the constant repetition of the word 'seven' and the seven-fold organization throughout the book create a considerable amount of expectation.

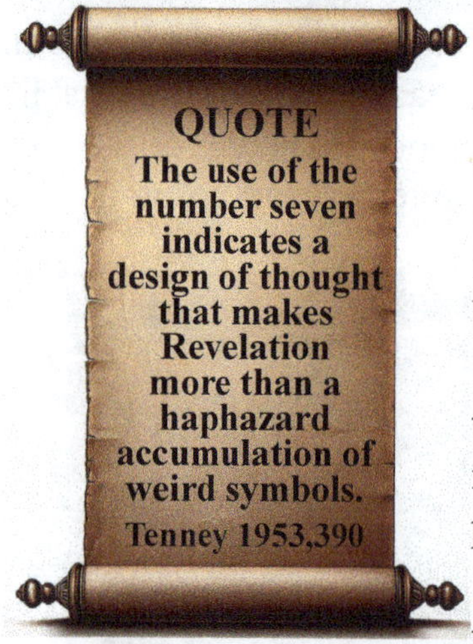
QUOTE
The use of the number seven indicates a design of thought that makes Revelation more than a haphazard accumulation of weird symbols.
Tenney 1953,390

The word 'seventh', occurs five times and the word 'seven', occurs 54 times in the whole book. Fourteen of these (over 25%) occur in the first 21 verses of the book and so it is hard to avoid the impression that an intentional pattern is being established as has been recognized by many.

So it may be that it is entirely intentional that the seven-fold motif of the seventh cycle is a final mystery, which is left for those who persevere to the end to discover.

In any case, this omission of an expected feature, is a regularly occurring characteristic of discourses, which should not cause any surprise. But, nonetheless, it needs to be understood that such surprising mysteries, especially at the end of a discourse, are intended to provoke appropriate reflection. The purpose at this stage, is to ensure that the reader stays engaged right to the end, and does not miss the final thrust which the author will leave with him.

From a discourse analysis perspective the Callows 1992,15, put it very comprehensively like this:

> Language is flexible, and mismatch is possible. Whenever mismatch occurs it has significance, and this must be assessed. The fact that there are several ways of saying the same thing means that the communicator is always choosing between options to best express his meaning. The analyst most clearly discerns the communicator's purpose when he compares what the communicator did say with what he might have said.

The working hypothesis then, with which this discussion will be temporarily terminated, is that, by one means or another, the author intended for the hearers to expect and look for a seven-fold motif in this cycle. Some hearers may just be left with this impression, in line with the superficially at least, impressionistic nature of the text as whole, while others may actually find enough evidence in the text to bolster this impression to certainty. The evidence which is available will be presented in Chapter 5.

3.7.3 The Parallelism Between Cycles 1 and 7

Just as Cycles 2-6 are markedly in parallel with one another and form a group, so also Cycles 1 and 7 have particular affinities with each other and speak to some of the same issues, either directly, or antithetically. Briefly, it can be noted that the settings of the two cycles are antithetically in parallel. The setting of Cycle 1 presents Jesus Christ in all his glory, who is the undisputed hero of the book, while the setting of Cycle 7 presents Satan, the principal villain, in all the ignominy of his failure to achieve his goals and his final defeat. This failure is highlighted even more by the contrastive vignette at 20:4 where the very people whom he sought to destroy (cf. 12:17), rise up to final glory and victory.

In the body of the two cycles, it is the word 'new', which establishes the most striking parallel. Of the nine occurrences in the book, three are in the body of Cycle 1 and four in the body of Cycle 7. All the references concern the privileges of the people of God in their glorified state and, as such, represent the conceptual parallel between the main themes of the two cycles.

It is the imperfect state of the earthly church which is under the microscope in Cycle 1, yet they can, nonetheless, aspire to greater things. These new things are promised in advance in Cycle 1, but the full and final acquisition of that new state is only fully laid out in Cycle 7. Once the overcomer reaches that ultimate glory, he will have finally left behind all the imperfections of life on the first earth.

In reality, Cycle 7 is full of parallel references which relate to all the cycles in the book. This is not surprising since it functions as the conclusion to the seven cycles. As such, it not only brings to closure the major themes, but many of the sub-themes as well. Nonetheless, the most striking correspondences are with Cycle 1, and these will be discussed in more detail in Chapter 4.4.

3.8 A Summary of the Issues which Have Been Resolved

A guiding principle in seeking out the major units of the book has been the principle of comparison, as features which are the same are grouped together, and features which are different are noted and their significance assessed. In this chapter it is the similarities which have been the primary focus. As a result of the work accomplished so far, the analysis which seems to best account for the data discovered in the text, is that the body of Revelation is composed of seven major units, which have been labeled Cycles.

These cycles are almost identical in basic structure, being composed of a setting, a body dominated by a seven-fold motif, and in the case of most of the five central cycles, the body also includes a contrastive interlude. A corollary of this similarity of structure is that the cycles may also have similar functions in the overall organization of the book. The evidence for this so far, is that each has its own setting and each contributes something distinctive to the overall topic of the book. This implies that each one is, in some ways, an autonomous unit, and is not directly dependent for its internal coherence and its informational contribution to the book as a whole, on any other cycle.

Even though the questions of topic and themes have not yet been addressed, it has been noted that there are considerable lexical links between the cycles, along with its concomitant parallelism. This combination of structural similarity and lexical similarity is pointing towards the conclusion that the cycles relate to each other as a series of parallel units. This parallel organization is visually represented in Chart 25

The chart also indicates that Cycles 1 and 7, being the first and last units, function as the introduction and the conclusion of the visionary content which is contained in the body of the book, while Cycles 2-6 are set apart as particularly belonging together as a group. The primary evidence so far noted for this latter organizational feature, is the fact that they are bound together by overlap links as indicated by the asterisks.

In addition to the above remarks, the analysis of the book which is emerging from the study so far, has contributed a number of other improvements to the consensus which had emerged previously.

Firstly, the divisions between the major units have been clarified in two ways. It has been confirmed that the boundaries between Cycles 2-5 are not clearly delineated as has been intuited by many commentators. However, with the definition and systematization of the overlap links it is possible to go beyond the previous intuitions on this matter.

Chart 25.
The Parallel Organization of the Body of Revelation

Cycle 1 1:9-3:22	**The Seven Letters**
The CONTEXT of the Book:	The Church on Earth Caught Up in Time
Cycle 2 4:1-8:6**	**The Seven Seals**
Cycle 3 8:1-11:19**	**The Seven Trumpets**
Cycle 4 11:15-16:1**	**The Seven Signs**
Cycle 5 15:1-16:21**	**The Seven Bowls**
Cycle 6 16:17-19:21	**The Seven Proclamations**
Cycle 7 20:1-22:7**	**The Seven Characteristics of the New Creation**
The CONCLUSION of the Book:	The Church in Heaven Released into Timeless Eternity

(** A double asterisk indicates that an overlap link connects these units with the unit which follows.)

With insights derived from the concept of an overlap link, it is possible to define with precision the boundaries of the transitional link unit, even if it is still impossible to state that one particular point in the text is the definitive boundary point between the individual cycles. At the same time, it is also now possible to state with certainty, that a link which may incorporate a certain amount of intermingling of the unit extremities, is not an overlap link, but is something different.

This contributes to a growing awareness of what modern theories of discourse analysis permit, or even predict, when assessing texts which defy more straightforward analysis based primarily on division into discrete units alone. This kind of analysis supports the notion that 'there is, of course, no theoretical objection to saying that the boundary (between units of text) is indeterminate', but it also avoids the 'real danger ... of brushing under the carpet of indeterminacy valuable evidence as to the progression of the writer's thought...' (K and J Callow 1992,26).

By contrast to the particularities of the overlap links, the other kind of connections can now also be discerned with more clarity and precision.

The most obvious (once they are seen) and contrastive of these, are the simpler tail-head links which connect Cycles 1 and 2, and Cycles 6 and 7. The other types of connectives, which occur in Revelation, are asyndeton (absence of any overt marker), and *kai* 'and', and both these connectives were briefly discussed in Appendix A2.2.4.

Secondly, it has been proposed that settings are a significant feature of this book. In many other discourses just one initial setting may be all that is provided and required. However, in this case, there are very many settings, and some of them are quite lengthy and complex in nature, and have a very significant function in the development of the message of the book.

Perhaps the most significant proposal is that each cycle has its own setting, in addition to the one which serves the whole book. This insight helps to describe and explain the fact that similar elements (e.g. references back to the heavenly throne room) reoccur periodically throughout the text.

Previously, the anomaly was that such references were apparently not connected to one another, and did not contribute any significant narrative or thematic development to the whole. However, it can now be perceived more clearly that these settings have an influence beyond their strict linguistic boundaries; and pervade whole stretches of text, which may not be directly contiguous.

As this phenomenon is considered, it can be observed that with a cyclic, non-linear, text such as this, settings of this nature are much more necessary than in linear type texts. This is because the author takes more time to say what he wants to say, because he is intentionally repeating himself, and, because, therefore, he is presenting his discourse in the form of a series of cycles. As a consequence of this choice, he needs to constantly remind the reader of the setting, so that it is obvious against which background context the information being received should be interpreted and understood.

Thirdly, there is recognition that there is indeed a sequence of interludes. These have now been clearly defined, so that they can be identified where they exist. They all have similar positive content and the same function, which is to contribute to the Salvation Theme. All of them also abruptly interrupt the flow of the main body of the cycles where they occur, which body material is focused on the Judgment Theme. This clear definition has made it possible to weed out the impostors, and to start making more sense of those other texts, which also seem to break up an otherwise homogenous pattern, and yet are not interludes.

Fourthly, the unnumbered series of visions have been more clearly defined. The Signs Cycle has been more clearly defined by recognizing that the signs are personages, each with their own story. Then, for the Proclamations Cycle, this one has been defined with reference to recurring grammatical features. These are, specifically, the present participle of the verb 'to say', forceful doublets, and reason clauses. In both cases, by using these more objectively obvious characteristics, it has become possible to avoid the problem of appealing to a phrase like 'and I saw' for discovering the cycle boundaries, and their internal sub-units.

This latter practice, in the past, has never been a satisfactory solution for dividing the discourse into units. This is because, really and truly, This phrase 'and I saw' is part of the Narrative Framework, as was explained in Chapter 2, and it is in this context that its true function is best understood. In this context then, it can be seen that it is a cohesion marker, like a thread in a tapestry, and is not a division marker at all. All these insights help to explain why it does not consistently mark the beginning of cycle-level sub-units, and why this proposal in the past has never been satisfactory, and has never generated a consistent consensus.

Fifthly, the final cycle, Cycle 7, has now been defined with much more precision and much less ambiguity. The first key has been the more precise delineation of the six previous cycles, and the analogous example of their structure. These insights have contributed to a better understanding of the outer limits, and the internal structure, of the last major part of the book, which had previously been the subject of much debate. It is possible now to identify its boundaries and to propose that it has a setting and a body the same as all the other cycles. In addition, this combination of a setting and a body is in direct contrastive parallel with the setting and the body of Cycle 1, which is most appropriate for the conclusion of a discourse.

3.9 Where Do We Go from Here ?

Although these improvements are considerable, there are still unresolved difficulties and textual features, which have not yet been fully accounted for, or described.

The issues concerning topics, themes and interludes, which have been alluded to in passing in the previous discussion, will be taken up in Chapter 4. The matter of the sub-topics of the book is another complex matter needing attention, for there are nine of them, and each of them have numerous references scattered throughout the book.

This means that the topic and the sub-topics may have to be dealt with separately to make the discussion manageable. So this will be attempted in Chapter 7. In any case, once the main topic and the themes have received a preliminary treatment and have received a certain amount of clarification, it will be possible to return to the remaining structural issues concerning the seven cycles in Chapter 5.

In that context then, it will be seen that the grouping of Cycles 2-6 also have their own setting and conclusion. The organization of Cycle 7 will be developed in much more detail, the motifs of the seven cycles will be established and explained, and the chiastic arrangement of the whole book will be demonstrated.

When all that ground-work (so to speak) has been accomplished, then it will be necessary to address the topic of prominence, which will show us which are the most important parts of the author's message. So, in Chapter 6, this topic will be discussed in detail, because, it is obvious, that in dealing with any discourse, when all is said and done, it is essential not to miss the point!

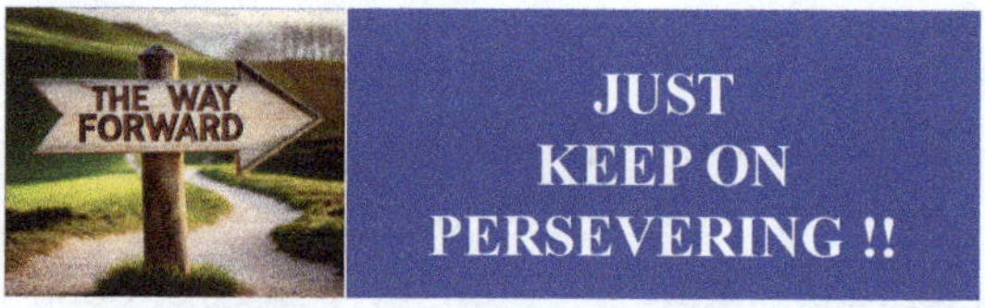
THE WAY
FORWARD
JUST
KEEP ON
PERSEVERING !!

APPENDIX 3

PREFACE

This Appendix has been placed here to provide extra technical information relating to the analysis of the Seven Cycles for those who wish to explore these matters further. There is no need to read this Appendix if this extra information is not required, for the technical information already given in the main text is sufficient for the general purpose of understanding the structural organization of the book.

The Appendix just broadens out what has already been explained and makes more specific connections with the methodology used, and the commentators who have gone before.

The extra contents are as follows :

1) Precise information to explain and support the division into units of the Seals Cycle, since it is the most difficult of Cycles 1-6 to analyze

2) A review of remarks by previous commentators concerning the overall organization of the book, with special reference to the presence of the seven cycles.

All other readers are invited to move on straight away to Chapter 4, where we will start explaining and exploring the Main Topic of the book. With the topic established, we will investigate the Themes which color in the details of the topic. This will include, in particular, a study of the Interludes, which carry the Salvation Theme through the choppy waters of the bodies of the Seven Cycles.

APPENDIX 3
Ancillary Information Pertaining to the Analysis of the Seven Cycles

A3.1 Evidence for the Division into Units

A3.1.1 A General Explanation

In this appendix evidence will be provided in summary form, to indicate on what basis the text of the Seven Cycles was divided into units for this study. In order to keep the material manageable, the information will be provided in abbreviated form, and not all the cycles will be presented. The most well delineated Cycles, namely, the Letters, Seals, Trumpets and Bowls will not be show-cased here. However, a sample analysis of the Signs Cycle, which is the most difficult case (apart from Cycle 7) will be provided, in order to show what is possible. Cycle 7 will be explained in more detail in Chapter 5, and the interludes will be presented in more detail in Chapter 4.

The main aim at this stage is to demonstrate that text can be divided into units on the basis of linguistic evidence, and that this evidence can be made available for perusal by other analysts. For more detailed explanation of this nature please refer back to Appendix A2.1.1.

The abbreviations used in the presentation of the data are as follows:

D = Differences permitting a division into distinct units. Normally reference is made to the division at the beginning of the unit and also to that at the end of the unit.

IC = Internal Coherence requiring that similar units be grouped together.

F = Function of the unit.

A3.1.2 The Signs Cycle 11:15-16:1

D: A new major unit linked to what precedes and what follows by overlap links.

IC: An autonomous major unit with the same structure as preceding ones of similar size and function, namely a setting, and a body which presents a seven-fold motif and an interlude.

F: Functions together in a coordinated relationship with the other cycles to create the body of the book which presents the content of the visions received by the narrator. This cycle also contributes special prominence to the body of the book.

The detailed analyses of the sub-units of the Signs Cycle may be found in Chapter 7.

A3.1.2.1 The Setting 11:15-19

D: Beginning of a new numbered sub-unit (7th Trumpet). Change of topic, principal participant and situation.
IC: Embedded narrative with chiastic structure.
F: Overlap link: Conclusion to the Trumpets Cycle and the Setting for the Signs Cycle.

A3.1.2.2 The Body 12:1-16:1

D: Beginning of a series of seven signs.
IC: Composed of a series of sub-units containing seven signs and a contrasting interlude.
F: Head of the Signs Cycle contributing special prominence to the book as a whole.

Sub-Unit 1: Signs 1 and 2 12:1-17

D: Marked introduction of a new topic ('a great sign was seen'). New participants.
IC: Embedded narrative with symmetric structure.

Sub-Unit 2: Sign 3 13:1-10

D: Change of topic, primary participant and situation. Introduction of new personage.
IC: Embedded narrative with symmetric structure.

Sub-Unit 3: Sign 4 13:11-18

D: Change of topic, primary participant and situation. Introduction of new personage.
IC: Embedded narrative with symmetric structure.

Sub-Unit 4: Interlude 14:1-5

D: Change of topic, primary participant and situation. Introduction of different personage.
IC: Embedded narrative with symmetric structure.

Sub-Unit 5: Sign 5 14:6-13

D: Change of topic, primary participant and situation. Introduction of new personage(s).
IC: Embedded narrative with chiastic structure.

Sub-Unit 6: Sign 6 14:14-20

D: Change of topic, primary participant and situation. Introduction of new personage(s).

IC: Embedded narrative with a double chiastic structure but with the same topic.

Sub-Unit 7: Sign 7 15:1-16:1.

This is also the Setting of the Bowls Cycle

D: Change of topic ('another sign'), and situation. Introduction of new personage(s).

IC: Embedded narrative with chiastic structure.

A3.2 A Review of Existing Structural Insights

A3.2.1 The Seven Cycles, The Overlap Links and the Interludes

It is undeniable that at least some of John's material is organized on the basis of the number seven, and a number of commentators have proposed that the book may be coherently divided into seven major parts. Others have agreed with Spinks 1978,220 who said that 'it is possible that after having given us three obvious sets of seven in a row, John expected us to be able to see for ourselves the other sets of seven', and have presented outlines composed of seven major visions divided into seven sub-units. With the passage of time a consensus has built up concerning the boundaries between the first five major units, which corresponds to a large degree with the outline developed in this book, but from Revelation 17 onwards the consensus is far from complete.

Many writers, with Lohmeyer 1926 being perhaps the first, have observed that the latter part of Revelation 1 serves as an introduction to the following seven letters. However, Loenertz 1947 went further and perceived an introduction to each of the seven visions and Bowman 1962,64-5, possibly in parallel to Loenertz, formalized this insight even more by specifically describing these introductions as 'Settings'. This innovation contributed greatly to the impression that the first three-quarters of the book at least, were more highly organized than previously supposed, but it still left additional text (e.g.7:1-17) summarily included in the macro organization of the book which was not appropriately accounted for.

Spinks 1978 saw potential in Bowman's work and tried to improve its short-comings in a number of ways. His most useful improvement was to include interludes in his revised outline at 7:1-17 and 10:1-11:14 (ibid.,216-17), and yet this is ironic because it is not one of the improvements which he discusses. In fact, many decades previously Moffat (n.d.,289) had suggested that these passages should be treated as 'intermezzos' and since the 1970s a growing number of commentators have followed the same line of reasoning, although they have not always used the same terminology.

Tenney 1953,392 included 'parentheses' in his analysis, while commentator Ladd 1972,14-16 and 110-11 and Ryken 1974,336, in the domain of literary criticism, had already begun to use the term 'interlude'. Fiorenza 1976,744 and 1977,360-61 was also using the term 'interlude' at about the same time as Spinks, while Collins 1976,19 dealt with material which did not fit into her outline by assigning them to 'appendices'.

Spinks 1978,215, once again building on Loenertz 1947, made a further contribution by shedding more light on the phenomenon of 'dove-tailing', by which means the author uses a single stretch of text to link together major components of the book. Collins 1976,49 at the same period as Spinks, was using the term 'interlocking' to describe the same phenomenon. According to McLean 1991,143, this term was borrowed from Allo 1933. Fiorenza 1977,360-61 also following Loenertz 1947 used the term 'intercalation'. However, it was Moffat n.d.,288 and 297 once again who had foreseen this issue with his references to units being 'closely welded together' and to 'dove-tailing'.

A consensus is now also developing on this issue, with more scholars taking account of this literary phenomenon. Some, nonetheless, subsequently reject its more obvious interpretive implications, as, for example, Thomas 1995,525-43.

Among those scholars who tried to combine the notion of a seven-fold structure with that of a concentric organization, Welch 1981,242-48 produced a seven part chiasm, while Strand 1987 concentrated on incorporating the settings and the interludes and produced an eight part symmetric analysis. Kline however, succeeded in doing both and produced a seven part chiasm which takes account of the settings and interludes as well. Kline is quoted in Beale 1999,130-31. Welch and Kline's seven part analyses and Strand's eight part analysis, do not include the Prologue and the Epilogue. See also Beale 1999,141-44 for a review of Snyder 1991.

A3.2.2 Unresolved Issues Still Remaining for the Seven Cycles as a Whole

The history of research summarized above is doubtless typical of many such processes, as the boundaries of knowledge slowly expand and the new insights are gradually accepted by the majority. However, the disadvantages of such early stages of research are twofold, firstly, that only some of the issues are somewhat dimly discerned, and secondly, in concentrating on the smaller elements of information, researchers tend to overlook the larger picture. In the case of Revelation, the discoveries noted above are helpful and have contributed to a growing consensus on several important issues, and yet other issues still remain unresolved.

Firstly, the exact position of the boundaries of the textual units at various levels is still a moot point, especially in the latter part of the book. Moffat n.d.,292 stated the issue in this way: 'where the problems of structure arise... (it) is in the juxtaposition of disparate materials'. Many decades later these 'disparate materials' still appear side by side and no theory has yet been applied to the book, which both accounts for the difficulties and also gets close to convincing the majority of analysts. Some commentators have commendably tried to find objective markers in the text to alleviate this problem, but for the moment the attempts are still not rigorous enough to withstand close scrutiny.

For example, Bowman 1962,62 followed by Spinks 1978, and also Wendland 1990, have tried to use 'and I saw', and similar phrases to help define major divisions for the latter part of the book. However, even using these objective markers they do not find the same major divisions but only a series of lower level ones. Wendland's use of 'and I saw' is less clearly articulated than Spinks'. He seems to use it as a division marker when it suits him (e.g. 1990,381,384-5 and 386) and to ignore it when it does not. The fact that this system is unreliable is demonstrated by the fact that for the section from 17:1 onwards his analysis is quite different from Spinks' even though in theory they both use this phrase to guide their analytical decisions.

Spinks 1978,218 freely admits that his hypothesis is not water-tight for as he says, 'and I saw' is not used with regularity and precision' and that in 9:17, 'I saw is used 'inconsistently'. Consequently, he can only claim that 'and I saw' (and 'after these things I saw') assumes an *almost* technical character' (emphasis added). The hypothesis is 'almost' viable but not quite, because as well as 9:17, the occurrences in 6:2, and 6:8 do not 'introduce' (ibid.) a scene, as he claims, but fall in the middle of a sub-unit, while the occurrence in 6:5 is ignored entirely. Likewise at 1:12 and 17, 'I saw' does not 'introduce the setting to Act 1' (Spinks 1978,218) because according to his analysis (ibid.,216) this setting is 1:9-20. Consequently, neither verse is near the beginning of the section. These exceptions indicate that this is not yet a consistent analysis which accounts for all the uses of this phrase.

Another difficulty with his analysis is that he makes a major division between Acts in the middle of 17:3 (ibid.,217) and so divides a section of text which otherwise would appear to belong together more closely than his analysis implies. Elsewhere (e.g.18:1-19:10), he unites texts which are clearly different (cf. the clear change of topic and theme at 19:1). In this latter case, he also ignores 'after these things I heard', even though he uses 'after these things I saw' elsewhere (e.g. 18:1) as a division marker and 'I heard' is identical to 'I saw' in function and parallel in meaning. Where not otherwise indicated, the data for these remarks are all drawn from the outline presented in Spinks 1978,217.

A second related point is that more balance is needed in applying a range of complementary principles to the task of text analysis. In the past, commentators seem to have concentrated almost exclusively on trying to divide the text into units, and once this has been accomplished they move on to the tasks of interpretation and exposition. However, there is a lot more to text analysis than just dividing into units. Even this latter task is best accomplished by both looking for evidence for divisions between textual units while at the same time looking for indicators of cohesion which bind parts of the text together.

It is in maintaining a balance between these two complementary phenomena that the ultimate goal of a systematic outline of the book is best achieved. This specific issue is particularly relevant to Revelation since it is a book which seems to have an above average number of markers of cohesion relative to the number of unambiguous division markers.

Consequently, ignoring issues of cohesion can be a considerable impediment to the task of producing a viable analysis of this book. A notable cohesion feature which inextricably links the whole of the middle of the book together (Chapters 4-19) is the phenomenon of dove-tailing or interlocking mentioned above. In contrast to the argument cited in the text above, if the phrase 'and I saw', and similar phrases are interpreted as markers of cohesion rather than markers of division, as is preferred in the present analysis, then the result is much more systematic. See also the note on connectives in Appendix 2.

As Fiorenza 1977,362 insightfully remarks:

> The author of Revelation does not divide the text into separate sections or parts, but *joins* units together by interweaving them with each other... It is therefore more crucial to find out the *joints* of the structure which interlace the different parts than to discover 'dividing marks'.

Thirdly, when special features like interludes are posited, there is a lack of rigor in defining them and ensuring that all units bearing the same label really do resemble each other and function in a similar way. The consequence of this oversight is that textual units which do not neatly fit into the overall plan can too easily be camouflaged by a convenient label, when in fact their actual role in the overall scheme of things remains unknown. In other cases, the result is that the text is unjustifiably truncated or dislocated in order to fit a preconceived idea. So for example, Strand 1987,115 makes

16:15 an interlude on a par with the whole of Chapter 7, but the differences in size, position in the Cycle, text-type and content are considerable. It is, therefore, difficult to justify the implication that these two texts belong to the same category of unit.

Wendland 1990,384 does the same by suggesting that 20:7-10 is an interlude. Another case is Spinks, who, having noticed the feature of 'dove-tailing' in the middle of the book (1987,217, following Loenertz 1947), tries to apply it also to his sixth and seventh Acts where it is not justified. The result is that the end of Act 6 is 20:1-10, but then 20:4-6 is truncated and re-used as the setting to Act 7. Both these examples overlook the fact that 20:1-15 is a complete unit and so there is no serious attempt to support the unjustified division into smaller units.

Fourthly, there is often a failure to distinguish primary structural features which contribute to an understanding of the book at the macro level and secondary features which elucidate the structure at subordinate levels. In such cases, the structural insights may well be valid but confusion arises from a failure to correctly discern their role relative to other features in the overall plan. Care always needs be taken to let the data speak for itself, and this includes allowing the primary structural features, which form the main skeleton of the book, to come to the fore naturally, and not to force secondary data into a mold where it does not fit.

For example, Strand 1979,43-52 and 1987,107-9 perceives a linear movement throughout the book from a predominantly historical perspective to a predominantly eschatological perspective, and he also perceives a matching series of references to an 'Exodus from Egypt/Fall of Babylon' motif in 8:2-14:20 and 15:1-18:24. These observations are probably correct, but they do not warrant making an important book level division between 14:20 and 15:1, which is essential for his analysis.

This does an injustice to the text which refers to 'another great sign', in 15:1, which must, in some way, be related to the preceding references which are very similar in 12:1 and in 12:3. It seems doubtful whether such a major division can be justified in this position. This is precisely because the features which he has observed, are not contributing to the macro structure of the book but are merely secondary features.

The same conclusion is also valid for Bauckham 1993,4-5 and Smith 1994 who, having correctly observed the similarities between the Babylon vision (17:1-19:10) and the Jerusalem vision (21:9-22:9), then inappropriately proceed to try and make these two passages key components in their overall plan. Aune 1997,xciii-xcvii makes similar remarks although his final outline of these passages (ciii-civ) is much more complex. Hall's proposals (2002) concerning Chapters 10-11 are also addressing secondary features of the book as a whole.

Fifthly, one of the indicators that an analysis is reaching maturity is that there are no significant units which are left unaccounted for. For example, Tenney 1953 presents a neat outline with six main parts which each have seven main sub-units. But then the last section 21:9-22:5 has to be left outside of this orderly plan almost as if it was an afterthought.

On a smaller scale texts like 16:15 and 18:20, and even 8:13 and 9:12, do not obviously fit in their contexts and cause explanatory problems for commentators. Usually, authors say what they mean to say and so each part of the text has a contribution to make to the overall effect. As Smith 1994,389 correctly says 'we should not blame a careless redactor, as some commentators do', and, to attribute data which does not fit our thesis to 'an excusable blunder' (Bowman 1962,63), is a way of placing responsibility onto the author, which really belongs to the analyst.

Pauses, or even incoherence, can have their planned place in a text, but their intended role should be discernible within the overall context, and it is the task of the analyst to understand how all the pieces fit together.

Finally, any valid structural hypothesis ought to support and contribute to the stated aims of the book, and should certainly not be running counter to those aims. Since the Prologue, Epilogue and other texts within the body indicate that the overall aim was to influence the behavior of the hearers, initially Christians of the first century, outlines which emphasize other issues to the detriment of this central purpose will always tend to be found wanting, and will not attract the support which they may otherwise deserve.

For example, Bowman's ground-breaking analysis (1962) is cast as a drama, even though he himself fully admitted that the book could never have been originally conceived, nor enacted as a proper play (ibid.,59). Although his thesis is courageous and certainly dramatic, it is, nonetheless, not very credible, and this may be why it has not drawn wider support, even though the analysis itself is basically sound.

Snyder 1991 sees the structure of Revelation as producing a special kind of liturgy for an 'end-time Feast of Tabernacles' (quoted in Beale 1999,142). This also is a bold idea which is not very credible in its context, and likewise will probably not gain many supporters.

The results of the linguistic analysis which is presented in the main text of this book, will serve to confirm the most useful insights of earlier scholarship. However, it also aims to be more rigorous in its use of definitions and other analytical tools. As a consequence of this extra rigor, the present study aims to clarify many of the unresolved issues and thereby to produce a more complete and a more elegant end result. This end result needs to be attained without fudging, without fuzziness around the edges, and without fiddling the books, as it were.

A3.2.3 The Signs Cycle 11:15-16:1

A number of commentators, apparently independently, have recognized that the author of Revelation introduced the motif of 'a sign' at 12:1 and have sought therefore to discover a series of seven signs to match the other septenaries. These are Loenertz 1947 (cited in Ford 1975), Tenney 1953, Morris 1969, Johnson 1981, Ryken 1974, Wendland 1990, Morey 1991, Hayford 1995, and Kuen 1997. Bowman 1962 followed by Spinks 1978 also divided this passage into seven parts but each part was called 'a pageant', with no particular reference to the signs motif.

There is general agreement on the division into units, and the discrepancies which occur are regularly the same, and can be explained and thence improved by reference to other linguistic features in the text, which the writers did not discern, as will be indicated below. Tenney went further and also recognized that the signs are actually represented by personages.

However, he then went too far by making the child in 12:5, and Michael in 12:7, two of the signs without justifying why this should be so. These personages, are only minor participants in their immediate context, and no reason is provided as to why they should be elevated to the same level as the other sign personages. In addition, this proposal means that there are four signs in the passage 12:1-7 and only three in the whole of 12:9-14:6, which creates an unbalanced analysis.

Bowman, Wendland, Hayford and Kuen propose that the body of the unit is preceded by a one verse setting (11:19). The difficulty with this is that most other commentators recognize 11:15-19 as a complete unit, and so to divide it at verse 19, would seem to be rather arbitrary. This is ultimately unnecessary when the concept of overlap links is understood. This was foreseen by Loenertz, who was beginning to perceive the overlap links and who apparently made the whole of 11:15-19 the setting to the Sign's Cycle.

The other major difficulty is that none of these commentators take account of the system of interludes, even though some of them recognize the earlier interludes (ch.7 and 10:1-11:14). Since there is no recognition of a system and no definition of an interlude, the passage which fits into this system (14:1-5) is not recognized as such, and is included as one of the seven signs. This creates a discrepancy in the numbering of the signs and also a mixing together of the major judgment and salvation themes under the rubric of the sign's motif.

There is nothing to prevent an author mixing his themes together if he wishes, but it would appear that in the body of the central cycles (2-6) the author does not actually do this. So, this is an example of where the author is made to bow to the constraints of the analysis, instead of the analysis being adapted to what the author actually put in the text. See the chapter on themes for more discussion of this issue.

As a consequence of the above, some juggling is necessary to obtain seven signs which is the cause of the other discrepancies. Some commentators ignore Sign 2 which is actually indicated by the author (12:3) and which would, therefore, seem to be a rather major error, but such is the case for Wendland, Ryken, and Hayford. Bowman also puts the Woman and the Dragon together under one sub-title, although he does not call them signs, as indicated above. Morris (1969, 44) accepts that the Dragon is the basis of the second sign, but rather arbitrarily interprets the sign as being 'Satan Cast Out' and assigns it to 12:7-12. Others ignore the last sign which is also indicated by the author at 15:1, and such is the case for Tenney, Johnson, Ryken and Morris.

Johnson 1981,414 and 510, is a special case because he has two systems which do not harmonize. In his outline he presents a system of seven signs, which is very similar to that of the other commentators cited. However, in his commentary he takes no account of the outline for the development of the sign motif, but presents another system based on the seven occurrences of the word 'sign' in the book. This latter insight is a valid one, but it is not directly relevant to the structure of the Sign's Cycle as such. See the chapter on prominence for discussion of this issue.

Another result of juggling the text in order to obtain seven signs is that Loenertz, Morris, and Johnson, combine the whole of 14:6-20 into a single unit, when the linguistic evidence and the consensus of opinion solidly support the view that 14:6-12/13 and 14:14-20 are two discrete units. Conversely, Ryken divides 14:14-20 into two separate units, when the evidence suggests that it is a single complex unit.

Wendland 1990,381 proposes that 14:12-13 is an 'insertion', but he does not explain why this should be so. Neither does he explain why he does not treat 13:18 in the same way, even though it is a similar kind of verse also beginning with 'here...'.

In summary then, these writers have discerned the importance of the seven units of seven for the structure of the book as a whole, and have tried to take account of it in their analysis. The discrepancies noted above can be eliminated and a coherent analysis of this cycle can be obtained by taking account of the insights obtained from linguistic features like the interludes, the overlap links, and the codas. The resulting analysis is also enhanced by better definitions of all the various features involved, and by a more systematic application of those definitions, as is explained in the main text.

A3.2.4 The Seventh Cycle

Discussion of the last part of Revelation is a complex matter since there is less consensus of opinion concerning the issues involved than for other parts of the book. Consequently, it is not possible to undertake a full survey, and so attention will be directed mainly to those commentators who have either tried to divide the book consistently into seven main sections, or have proposed main sections composed of seven sub-units. The main issues arising are firstly, where the main division should fall which indicates the beginning of the last main section of text prior to the Epilogue. Secondly, on what grounds to divide the text into sub-units, and thirdly, whether there is a seven-fold motif in the last part of the book.

The Initial Boundary of the Last Main Section

Some have proposed 17:1 as the initial boundary of the last main section of Revelation, since this is the place where the seven bowls come to an end. This is the case for Lund 1942/1970, Ryken 1974 and Kuen 1997, and for them the last section is 17:1-22:5. However in order to illustrate the uncertainty and the variety that there is even for the major divisions, it can be noted that Morris 1969 proposed 17:1-20:15 as the last major section, while Tenney 1953, Ladd 1972 and Beale 1999 proposed 17:1-21:8. What is left over is tacked on the end as a much smaller unit.

Others propose that the final boundary falls at 19:11, but here again there is no significant consensus. Loenertz 1947, Fiorenza 1977, and Johnson 1981 propose that the last section is 19:11-22:5, but Loenertz also includes 19:6-10 as a setting. Meanwhile, their colleagues Lohmeyer 1926, Wilcock 1975, Collins 1976, Bauckham 1977, Giblin 1991 and Aune 1998b propose that the section runs from 19:11 to 21:8, while minority viewpoints are held by Wendland (19:11-20:15) and Mounce (19:6-20:15). These latter have a further 'last' unit (usually 21:9-22:5), which in some cases may be divided into seven sub-units to make it stand on a par with previous larger sections. This is the case for Wendland and Wilcock, yet in order to accomplish this the latter makes his last section run on until 22:19. Collins, on the other hand, frankly calls this last section an appendix.

Moving on further, Hendriksen 1940 and Metzger 1993 analyze the last section as being 20:1- 22:5, while Bowman1962, Spinks 1978 and Hayford 1995, all of whom produce creditable seven-fold structures, work with 20:4-22:5.

The remarks which can be made concerning these different analyses are as follows. Firstly, the lack of consensus speaks for itself, especially as the above summary is only partial in scope and by no means presents all the options. Whereas everyone is agreed about where the first letter begins and the seventh ends, in this case there is no consensus about where the last main section of Revelation begins, nor even where it ends. This implies that there is still considerable uncertainty concerning the structure of this part of the book and commentators still seem to be at the stage of groping for solutions.

Secondly, more clarity could be obtained if the seven-fold structure of the Babylon section (16:17-19:21) were to be accepted. This involves understanding the system of settings and the discernment of the seven proclamations. Quite a number of commentators observe the parallel between Babylon and the new Jerusalem, but in reality this is only one of a large number of parallels which exist in the book. The parallelism is certainly there, but it is not one which contributes directly to the macro structure of the book. The point then, is that the seven bowls section is not the penultimate seven-fold unit and does not, therefore, usher in the last section of the book.

A third key issue is the linguistic function of 19:11-21. One point of consensus is that 19:11 is perceived to be a new beginning. However, the reality is more complex than that. It is indeed a new beginning but according to the argument presented in the main text it is only the beginning of a conclusion, which is a special kind of beginning under any circumstance. It is to be granted that it is the beginning of a unit which is operating at a high level in the linguistic hierarchy. Therefore, the impression expressed that it initiates a 'major' section of some kind, and the confusion which this impression has engendered, are understandable.

The problem in the past is that the full range of linguistic evidence present in the text has not been fully explored and understood. Once this has been done, a coherent analysis of the role of 19:11-21 can be obtained, whose insights are validated by the fact that it explains why many have felt intuitively that 19:11 begins an important segment of text, even though it is, in fact, a conclusion and not the beginning of a new major section.

A fourth issue is the role of 20:1. In amongst all the debate it is interesting to note that there is no disagreement that 20:1 is also a new beginning. The point of disagreement is whether it is the beginning of a new major section, or just the beginning of a sub-unit. This is closely linked to the theological debate over whether 20:1 is sequential to what immediately precedes, or is recapitulative.

This debate is too vast and complex to even resume here, but in any case it has been well documented elsewhere (see for example Clouse 1977, Lewis 1980, Grenz 1992, White 1994 and Beale 1999,972-83). Nonetheless, it is probably reasonable to conclude that, over the centuries, biblical scholars have been fairly evenly divided over whether 20:1 is attached sequentially to 19:21 as a narrative continuation of what is described in the preceding passage, or whether there is a distinct break at this point. In this latter case, this verse begins a separate entity, which in the view of most proponents of such a division, is recapitulative in nature.

The main remarks which can be made of a general nature, which can perhaps guide the debate through to greater agreement is the insistence that firstly, the full range of linguistic evidence available should be taken into account. Then secondly, that the linguistic evidence should be allowed to constrain the theological conclusions rather than vice versa.

It is not sufficient to merely debate in a vacuum whether 20:1 is sequential or recapitulative as do the documents cited above. In such a situation, it is hardly surprising that an approximately equal amount of data can be adduced to support each of the positions. The contribution of such verses at the micro level can only be fully appreciated if they are assessed within the context of an adequate analysis of the macro structure.

This latter implies the prior existence of a complete and internally harmonious analysis of the whole book, which is linguistically viable, and which takes account of all the significant data (cf. the remarks in Callow 1999,406). To the extent that the work is not done to accomplish this goal, the debate runs the risk of going on ad infinitum.

The Division into Sub-Units

A general problem with all the analyses mentioned above, whether the authors are specifically seeking to divide their major units into seven sub-units or not, is that the division into sub-units tends to be arbitrary and artificial. There are many examples, but for the sake of illustration the two principal texts 19:11-21 and 20:1-15 will be taken as representative of the general problem.

Both these texts have a complex, but coherent, parallel internal structure. The former is an ABCB'A' chiasm and the latter is an ABA'B' parallel structure (see Chapter 5 and its Appendices for the details). This means that even though each passage can be divided into its constituent parts (sub-units), they cannot be divided into separate autonomous units which function together as constituents of another higher level unit. Similarly, even if such sub-units can be perceived, it is nonetheless, not appropriate to suggest that they function on the same level with much larger units which are not divided in such a way (e.g. 21:1-22:5).

So, for example, in all the outlines surveyed, all the commentators divided both the passages cited into at least three or four smaller parts. Having said that, not all the outlines provide that amount of detail so these remarks are not directly relevant to such analyses. Giblin is also an exception in that he did not divide 19:11-21, but he did make a major division at 20:11. In the main, the divisions proposed are 19:11-16, 17-18, 19-21 and 20:1-3, 4-10, 11-15.

So, for those who did make these divisions, many of them made these small units function at the same level of their analysis as a long passage like 21:1-22:5. Yet this passage itself, is composed of three major units and a total of fifteen sub-units which are on a par with the sub-units of the passages under discussion.

One problem underlying these observations is that the divisions proposed are not supported by linguistic evidence and so it is not being unreasonable to label such analyses 'arbitrary' and 'subjective'. As such, they do not take account of the complex interweaving of parallels which creates remarkably balanced and complete structures as will be demonstrated in Chapter 5. In the case of 19:11-21, careful observation of these parallels leads to an analysis with five sub-units, whereas the commentaries only present three (19:11-16, 17-18 and 19-21).

A second problem is that such analyses do not take account of the notion of a linguistic hierarchy (see Chapter 1.3 of this book), or, in more graphic terms, the analysts do not appear able to distinguish the wood for the trees. The impression given is that almost the entire effort of analysis is devoted to dividing the text into units (i.e. it is as if 'individual trees' are isolated and studied), without taking into account the notion of coherence within a hierarchy.

This coherence addresses how the various units fit together to create larger units, which are themselves coherent within themselves. These units, in turn, fit together to create yet more coherent units, so that the final, largest possible combination of units (the book in the linguistic sense, or the 'wood' in terms of the metaphor), is also a large unit which can be apprehended and appreciated as an entity, with its own beauty, balance and unity.

The consequences of such inadequate analyses are particularly unfortunate, especially when it is realized that the structural organization of the text is based primarily on an interplay of parallelism and symmetry of various kinds, as is the case for biblical literature in general, and Revelation in particular.

For example, Aune 1998b, 1114 suggests that 21:1-5a can be analyzed as a symmetric structure ABCDD'C'B'A'. This is almost certainly correct and confirms the analysis in the text in Chapter 5, that the concepts of 'a new creation' (21:1a) and 'all things being made new' (21:5a) are prominent. This is contra Aune himself, since he himself claims that 21:3a-4 are the most important verses. However, this overlooks that fact that with symmetric structures of this balanced kind, the outer wings are usually considered to be thematically the most important parts. The center is only the most important part when it is a true chiasm with an unequal number of sub-units (e.g. ABCB'A'). See Breck 1987 and Wendland 1998,119-20.

Such an analysis, therefore, is useful as a secondary, confirmatory piece of evidence, which can help to isolate prominent points in the text. However, it is not useful for the primary analysis, because it destroys the coherence of the overall passage which, for Aune, is 21:1-8 (ibid.,1113). His symmetric structure straddles the three sub-units of his principal analysis and leaves a final part unaccounted for. The parallel structure proposed in this study, is based on generic/specific semantic relationships and takes account of all the data in this passage in a single coherent system. Symmetric and other kinds of parallel structures are indeed helpful for confirming the validity of an analysis, but this is only true when they all fit together neatly, leaving no 'bits left over'; in other words, when the total 'wood' is as tidy and symmetric as the constituent 'trees'.

As Wendland 1998,110 puts it (with italics added):

> The well-formed literary discourse is built up into a hierarchy of larger and smaller units from a diverse assortment of components and interrelationships on a number of different levels of textual organization. The analyst must look to see how they *all* operate *in concert* to communicate the original author's message.

Returning then, to the two illustrative passages cited above, it has to be concluded that the division into sub-units proposed in the works listed, at best, rides roughshod over the symmetry and parallelism which can be observed in the text, and at worst, demonstrates a basic ignorance of some of the essentials of the linguistic architecture of a text.

Cotterell and Turner 1989,244, having struggled with the same kind of issues, made the following remark and proposed their own solution:

> The ... pericope has its own structure, its own transitions, its own peak, all within the larger structure of the (total) narrative. To deal with these complex structures a new kind of commentary is needed which can place lexical studies in their appropriate place but can give to the larger structures more careful consideration.

The Seven-Fold Motif

The notion of not seeing the wood for the trees also applies to how the possibility of there being a seven-fold motif in the last part of Revelation has been handled. For example, Johnson 1981,411 and 573, like many others, seems to be totally absorbed by the need to divide into units. Each of his seven 'Last Things' (19:11-22:5) is therefore restricted to a separate unit of text. This overlooks the fact that an author is able to communicate his motifs and themes in many different ways, not just by a one-to-one relationship between referents and text units. It also overlooks the fact that already in Revelation 12 the author himself placed two signs together in a single textual unit. The consequence of this preoccupation with division into units is that the text is forced into a preconceived system, rather than the system being adapted to take account of the text.

On the one hand, Johnson allots a great deal of space and importance to the events of judgment including separate slots for both the binding and the final defeat of Satan, (20:1-3 and 7-10). Yet, at the same time, he only assigns one slot to all the detailed description of the new creation in 21:1-22:5.

The question remains as to why he divided one section of text into as many small units as possible and not also all the rest. On the other hand, Ryken1974,337 proposes a very similar organization and yet he includes the judgment of Babylon (Ch.17-18) which is logical, since in this way all the final judgment events are included in the schema and not just some of them. However, neither of them include the judgment event in 21:8 as a separate part of their seven-fold plan.

Hayford, and Bowman and Spinks propose better overall titles for their final section ('The Church in the Millenium', and 'The Church Triumphant') which is, moreover, limited to 20:4-22:5, a passage which is rather more homogenous. But even so, it is hard to avoid the impression of arbitrariness. This is because Bowman and Spinks' preceding major section has judgment as its main theme and included various judgment events, and yet, judgment events continue on into their last section before giving way to more positive, re-creative events. See Spinks 1978 for a comparison of the analyses of both Hayford and Bowman.

Hayford 1995,475-6 does something similar but gets around the problem by calling the preceding section 'The Seven Spectacles' and the last section 'The Seven Sights...', and yet, superficial analysis of these titles suggests that they are synonymous. In both cases, the question still remains as to why all the judgment events should not be grouped together, and all the events of 'The Consummation' (their term) be grouped together separately.

Wilcock 1975,17 and Wendland 1990 384-5 limit their scope even more to 21:9-22:19 and 21:1-22:5 respectively, but still cannot avoid this same basic problem even though the details are different. Both entitle their last section 'Seven Revelations' and the preceding one 'Seven Visions' or 'Sights', which sub-titles also seem to be synonymous. The double problem is that the whole of the book is a revelation (1:1) so why assign this title to just the last part and not all the other parts, especially as they do not even agree as to which sub-unit corresponds to a particular revelation?

This issue is further complicated by the fact that some of their revelations are also sights or visions (for example 21:1 and 2), so why call some things which are seen 'sights' and some of them 'revelations'? Tenney 1957,38 does better by trying less hard in that he proposes a list of 'Seven New Things' which at least form a homogenous group which is consonant with its proposed title. Nonetheless, arbitrariness still lingers since there are other 'new things' in the text which he did not include in his list.

Clearly, the last section of the book will not give up its treasures easily, since despite all these attempts, there is no consensus to speak of, and considerable arbitrariness still to eliminate. These superficial issues are probably due to a failure to come to terms with a number of underlying issues.

The first one, as mentioned at the outset, is the concentration on the small units (the trees) to the detriment of being aware of, and even being guided by the overall thrust of the author's purpose (the wood). When the larger picture is considered, (Longacre's 'top-down' approach), there are certain important issues in the book which come to an end. In particular, it is the judgment issues which come to an end, and this observation goes together with the contention that 19:11-21 is a closure and not a new beginning, as will be explained in Chapter 5.

Overall then, the book provides a revelation that God's plan for judgment and for eliminating evil has an end in view and, therefore, there are some things which will be literally 'last things'. To this extent the commentators who use this phrase are correct. However, the particular role of the last part of the book in this context is to demonstrate that just as (and this may be simultaneous as well as complementary) some things come to an end, so, by the same token, some new things will be created which will then exist for all eternity. These latter 'new' things can hardly be called 'last things'.

At the macro level of the book these two issues represent the two major themes of the book, and, therefore, for obvious reasons, should be considered as two distinct features of the book. This means then, that it is not appropriate to mix them together on the micro level, and treat them as if they belonged to the same logical strand of development. That is, they should not be mixed unless the author himself does so, for, in fact, one of the complications is that these two strands are intertwined in the last part of the book by the author himself.

However, if he does so, then what he actually does should be analyzed and described, rather than imposing an organization on the text which neither recognizes, nor reveals, what the author was doing. The solution is firstly, to keep the ending of the 'last things' distinct, as something which is primarily communicated by the ending of Cycles 2-6. Then secondly, to recognize that Cycle 7's main purpose is to inform the reader about a new beginning following on from, and complementary to, what has gone before.

Having kept those larger issues distinct, it is then necessary to recognize that within the scope of Cycle 7, the author uses a system of antitheses to make his point. This is a complex method of communicating to be sure, but that is what he did. Not only that, but the antitheses are also double negatives, that is to say, that the negative elements are negated or removed, which results in a positive end result. So it is then, that as a consequence of this rather convoluted procedure, his overall point is entirely positive and has the 'new things' in focus.

Nonetheless, when we finally get to this point of understanding, the genius of the author's craftsmanship becomes discernible. This is because the antitheses can be seen to be a clever piece of sleight of hand, whose purpose is to highlight even more, the magnificence of the new world to come.

The second underlying issue is the failure to carefully define how divisions are made in the text and then remain consistent to the definition. Closely linked with this is **a third issue** which is the similar failure to define a seven-fold motif, if such is proposed, and likewise to remain consistent to the definition in elucidating it.

What needs to be done in order to forge a greater consensus concerning the structure and, thence, the intended communicative purpose of the final part of Revelation, is to pay greater attention to these foundational issues of definition and consistency. These, in turn, ought to be rooted in objective linguistic data (whether lexical, grammatical, or semantic) which can be found in the text. It is only by justifying a structural proposal with data which can be reviewed by others, that arbitrariness can eventually be eliminated, and a growing consensus can be created.

There are some other views of seven-fold structures which are not dependent on dividing the text scrupulously into units and which, by the same token, have a measure of textual objectivity. It can also be said that their proponents do not force the rest of the text to fit into the seven-fold structure and therefore resist the temptation to use them as a template for the organization of the whole of the larger unit when this is not warranted by the data.

The first of these is presented by Aune 1998b,1113-5 who points out that the speech by God in 21:5-8 can be divided into seven parts. This is an interesting observation, because it is one of only two speeches by God the Father in the book, and because (as was previously demonstrated in Chapter 5) this passage is in large part generic, and therefore includes most of the essential material of the body of Cycle 7. As Aune himself says, 'the number is probably intentional' (ibid.1114) confirming once more, that the whole of the structure of the book is permeated with seven-fold structures of different kinds. Yet, at the same time, it is not possible to say that this structure is like the other seven-fold, cycle-level, motifs, since it does not dominate and constrain the structure of the whole of the body of the cycle.

Ironically on the following page (1115), Aune observes that 'the term "Lamb" occurs no less than *seven* times (his italics) in 21:1-22:5', and yet he concludes that 'the phrase was added to the text... since (it) always appears to be tangential and secondary'. As a result of this subjective impression he uses this seven-fold repetition as evidence to support his ad hoc source-critical approach, which is another example of an arbitrary and unverifiable approach to text analysis.

Another example is that proposed by Welch 1981,245, and this one is noteworthy because it takes into account the broad sweep of the book, and is not blinded by the details. He correctly observes that 'the rewards for faithfulness and endurance' given to the overcomers in Cycle 1 (his section B in a chiastic structure) are specifically fulfilled in Cycle 7 (his section B'). These similarities provide clear evidence for parallelism between the beginning and the end of the book. Welch actually lists seven promises but he does not go so far as to make this an essential component of his structure.

The parallelism is undoubtedly an objective feature of the text. As Welch points out, at least some of the promises given in Cycle 1 are specifically fulfilled in Cycle 7. Furthermore, 21:7 states that 'the overcomer will inherit these things', the antecedent of which is the 'all things' of 21:4, and in the specific development of this generic statement in the following text, will be found some of the promises which Welch enumerates.

So there is plenty of data to support his view that 'the evidence continues that this (parallel) relationship is in no way coincidental' (ibid.,245). Intriguing as this may be, it is still not possible to use this data as support for a seven-fold motif in Cycle 7 as well. In reality, Cycle 1 lists more than seven distinct promises to the overcomers, and Cycle 7, in turn, does not clearly reproduce just seven of them, nor even one drawn from each of the seven letters. Convenient as this would have been if the data had supported the idea, it has to be concluded that this parallelism was not intentionally placed in that position to serve as a seven-fold motif for the whole cycle as well.

In summary then, it can be seen that no consensus at all has been built up concerning the last part of the book. It is not at all clear that there is a seven-fold motif at all, and for those who believe that this is so, there is no meaningful consensus as to what it is exactly. To clarify these questions, it will be necessary to take account of the obvious linguistic features which are present in the text, as will be described in Chapter 5 of the main text.

It's All About

The One Who

Holds the Seven Stars

In His Right Hand

CHAPTER 4
Topics, Themes and Interludes
4.1 Introduction
In Chapter 3 it was observed that some of the cycles contain long sections of text, which interrupt the orderly progression of the seven-fold motif of the cycle. Consequently, because they occur between sub-units which otherwise belong together, they have been called interludes. In this chapter the reasons why John may have included such apparent interruptions in the organization of his discourse, will be explored. In the process, the function of these interludes will be elucidated. However, in order to accomplish this task, it will first be necessary to make some observations concerning the topic and the major themes of the book.

In the preceding chapters, the focus was on the more formal aspect of analysis, which concentrates on defining the constituent parts of the text. This includes defining their structure, and how they function in relation to one another, as they combine together to form the book, as a complete textual unit. By contrast, a discussion of the topic and themes has the more conceptual aspect of analysis in focus, which concentrates on elucidating the meaning of the text. These two aspects are complementary, and both are needed for an analysis to be complete. So then, the following discussion of the interludes will provide a concrete example, which can serve as an illustration as to how these two aspects of text analysis come together and inform each other.

4.2 Topics and Themes
The topic of a text is what it is primarily 'about'. As Callow 1998,218 explains more specifically:

> By 'topic' we mean conceptual material which is of central importance throughout a unit - what a unitary stretch of text is primarily about. This important material is quite complex, but in all its varied manifestations it will be found to be always referential (about some unitary thing or situation), always important (by comparison with the rest of the unit), and always extensive (occurring several times through a stretch of text).

In the following discussion, the topic which is of primary interest, is the topic of the book as a whole. This should be kept distinct from the topics which occur on the lower levels of the hierarchy, namely at the cycle, paragraph or sentence level. Confusion can arise when the use of the term at the macro level and the micro level are not kept distinct. This is because on the macro level there is usually only one topic, while on the micro level there will be many different ones. Furthermore, what is thematic material (i.e. is non-topical) in one lower-level unit of text, may become the topic in subsequent units.

DEFINITION
A Topic
is the subject of a discourse : what the author wishes to talk about and is trying to describe, explain, or otherwise elucidate.

Another important point to be retained is that a topic, especially at the macro level, is a concept held, firstly in the mind of the author, and thereafter, in the mind of the hearer, and not a particular lexical item in the surface structure. This means that the topic must, necessarily, be indicated near the beginning of the discourse, and the concept so invoked must remain implicit right to the end. However, at the same time, it does not mean that it will be specifically referred to more often than any other referential item in the discourse. On the contrary, it may be explicitly referred to only rarely, or even not at all. As Callow 1998,219-20 explains:

> The topic of a configuration (unit of text) is a concept which, whether it is signaled overtly or indirectly, or even by zero, is conceptually present throughout the whole unit. Those who like language to be very tidy may at this point be more than a little uneasy. Without one-to-one correspondence with surface structure signals, how are we to identify a topic at all? But... surface-structure signals abound... A message sender signals his topic overtly just as often as he needs to in order to get his message across. Normally, clear initial signals are given, and then the topic is frequently referred to using surface-structure forms appropriate in the particular language.

This is why a discourse topic can be overlooked, or even be incorrectly identified. Therefore, this is why, in a thorough analysis, any topic which operates for the most part as an implicit assumption at the conceptual level, with only indirect signals in the surface structure, needs to be explicitly identified.

If the topic of a discourse is whatever is being talked about, then the theme (or themes, since there may be more than one), is whatever provides pertinent information concerning the topic. The notion of a theme is better known than the notion of a topic and is more widely used. Nonetheless, identification of themes can also be a subjective process unless clear definitions and appropriate criteria are used. In the context of discourse analysis, the definition of themes, which was an intuitive process in the field of literary criticism, has become a more refined and objective process.

DEFINITION

A Theme

is a central, unifying idea in a discourse :

It is the bigger issue, which the author is trying to transmit to the reader, as he talks about the topic of his discourse.

This is important because the thematic material is what embodies the main content of a message. It is, therefore, what carries the weight of accomplishing the author's communicative purpose. Callow 1998,230-1, for example, takes a considerable amount of space to define what themes are and what they accomplish in a discourse. This is so important to understand, that it is worth the effort to take the time to digest her explanation in detail. She says, for example:

> The prominent core of the developing message is its theme. ... The theme is prominent material which moves the message towards the communicator's goal.... The communicator plans beforehand what he will say, not in detail, but in broad outline It is on this planned line of development that he constructs his message as he presents it.
>
> This line of development is what we are calling the theme. The unfolding thematic content is a cognitive reality to the addressee also, who needs it in order to locate incoming parts of the message correctly within the whole. ...
>
> But theme is not simply a set of relationships. It has content. The theme of a configuration consists of that prominent referential material in the unit which carries its purposive thrust. Since, in any configuration, the referential material is organized as relating directly or indirectly to the topic, it is obvious that the theme of a configuration will include the topic as its referential base.

Just as topics occur at all levels of the discourse hierarchy, themes do also, and so it is important to distinguish thematic material which is relevant to the author's purpose for a discourse as a total unit, from that which is only relevant at a much lower level. The lower level themes have their contribution to make to the whole, but it would be a mistake to treat them as if they carried the dominant message of the book. Callow 1998,231 explains this as well, in the following way:

> It is not only the total message which has a theme. Configurations within it can each have their own theme; the message exhibits a layering of themes within themes, the lower-level themes contributing to the prominence and purposive development of the main one(s).

4.2.1 The Topic of Revelation

Authors can never succeed in communicating something worthwhile unless their addressees know what it is they are talking about. Logically, as indicated by Callow above, this has to be established near the beginning of the discourse. So, what then, for Revelation, is the 'cognitive material available as a matrix into which to plug the new message elements (the recipient) receives' (Callow 1998,219)?

It is not necessary to search far, for the first word of Chapter 1, 'a revelation', establishes the topic of the book as a whole. The context provides a considerable amount of information in order to help both the reader and the listener establish the appropriate grid, or 'matrix' in Callow's terms, which is going to enable them to make sense of the thematic information, which is to follow. They need to be able to make sense of this information, because it will embody the crucial components of the communication process.

This information was previewed very briefly in Chapter 3.1.2, but will be developed here in a bit more detail. The first part indicates that the revelation is a message whose originator is God Himself (1:1) and whose original recipients were Christians in general, 'his slaves/servants' (1:1) and, more specifically, those located in seven churches of Asia Minor (1:4). The message involves Jesus Christ in some way (1:1-2) and was transmitted by intermediaries who included at least one angel and the narrator John (1:1). This is a message which contains a plan with a goal in view, as is revealed little by little in verses such as 15:1 and 8, 16:7 and 17, 17:17 and 21:6, and it is a message which should be listened to carefully and is intended to elicit an appropriate positive response (1:3).

Although the word, 'revelation', is never used again in the book, the concept remains present. The whole concept of communicating a message to others dominates Cycle 1, and reoccurs in the central interlude (10:8-11). Most of the topic-related issues initiated in the Prologue are also reviewed in the Epilogue, as a final reminder before the book ends. In addition to these surface structure features, which continue to maintain the concept of a message in general, other details of the content indicate that it was a message communicated by unusual visionary means (4:1). These included sights (1:12), sounds (1:10), and even smells (8:1-4).

This means that one of the functions of the phrase 'and I saw' (and other similar phrases), which occur repeatedly throughout the book is that of a topic marker. Although the word 'revelation', is not used again after the first verse, the phrase 'and I saw', is a surface-structure reminder of the underlying concept that a message from God is in the process of being revealed and transmitted. This is an example of 'surface-structure forms appropriate in the particular language' which Callow referred to in the second quotation in section 4.2 above, concerning topics. It may be added that it is also a form which is appropriate to the literary context.

Having said all that, it has to be admitted that the word 'revelation' is quite a vague word with very little specific information contained within it in isolation. A revelation could be about anything. Consequently, for a word such as this to be useful to the listener, especially, as in this case, it represents the topic of a whole book, it needs to be qualified in some way. As we look again at Revelation 1:1, we find that this is exactly what happens. The word for 'a revelation' does not appear in isolation but we are immediately told that it is about Jesus, the Christ. In the Greek the grammatical connection between Jesus and the word for 'a revelation' is the genitive case. The genitive has many possible meanings in Greek, as in most languages, but meanings of possession (i.e. 'belonging to'), relative to people, or 'concerning', in the case of messages as we have here, are among the most obvious meanings and the most common. Nonetheless, it can always be argued, as some do, that there is ambiguity inherent in this phrase, but the appropriate response to this ambiguity is not to be dogmatic and to insist against all the evidence, that it can only mean one particular thing.

The beauty of language is that it is very fluid and can quite readily carry several meanings at once with no difficulty. In this case, as mentioned elsewhere as well, the ambiguity needs to be embraced and allowed to do its full work of giving us a variety of insights into the author's intended message.

It is simplistic and unnecessary to insist that it is only permissible for him to say one thing at a time. If we embrace the ambiguity, then it serves to put Jesus fully into the picture right from the first sentence of the book, which only serves to enhance our understanding and appreciation of the revelation.

So, whichever way you look at the genitive relationship here, it serves to show us that Jesus is fully wrapped up in, and involved in, this process of communicating this revelation from God. In short, He is both the Messenger and the Message. The fact that Jesus is central to the message of the book is confirmed by the fact that He is actively present throughout the book, and that He overtly appears as a participant at regular intervals.

This then, is the topic of the book: from His heavenly vantage point, God is in the process of revealing some things, which only He sees and knows, and which have been largely hidden from humanity up to this point. This revelation is primarily about Jesus, and, in addition, He actively participates in transmitting and explaining this message to its intended recipients.

This revelation about Jesus is what John is talking about from the beginning of the book to the end. After that, the rest of the informational content which follows, is the theme, namely the particular content of the message which John was entrusted to communicate. More details about the topic of the book will be developed later on in Chapter 7.3.

4.2.2 The Principal Themes of Revelation

The message, which is the topic of Revelation is long and clearly complex, and so it is to be expected that the thematic material of the book will be composed of a compilation of sub-themes, each of which contributes something to the whole. To do full justice to an analysis of the themes of the book it would be necessary to take all of this into account. However, it is not possible to accomplish this within the confines of this chapter. So the aim here is to define the principal themes from which all the sub-themes can be derived.

According to Callow 1998,232 the themes of a discourse can be ascertained in the following way:

> To establish the theme of a text we need clear criteria. We here suggest a practical approach that has proved useful in the analysis of widely varying languages; it is a two-pronged approach, consisting of excluding certain material from thematic status for specific reasons, while at the same time including other material as thematic, again for specific reasons.

On the basis of the criteria proposed by Callow 1998,230-40, the material which can be excluded from consideration for thematic purposes is all the support material which provides orientation, a setting, or amplification.

This means that the Narrative Framework, which in large part at least, is support material will be excluded, and its relationship to the principal themes will be taken up later. In addition, the settings to each of the cycles will be excluded for the same reason, that they are support material and therefore non-thematic.

This leaves, in general terms then, the body of each of the seven cycles, which is where we may expect to find the thematic material. Having said that, the body material needs to be perused in order to find any relatively short texts which do not contribute to the themes, because they have a different discourse function.

In Revelation, there are some such texts which are functioning, for example, as 'authorial signposts' (Callow 1998,235), as in the case of 'the woes' in 8:13, 9:12 and 11:14. Other elements, which are not contributing directly to the cognitive development of the message, are the codas of Cycle 4 (e.g. 13:9-10), and the motivational elements such as the blessings or exhortations (e.g.16:15 and 18:20, see Callow 1998,247).

The body of each cycle then, is included in the discussion of thematic material, because it contains referential material which contributes to the cognitive development of the message as a whole, and, as such, contributes the primary information concerning the discourse topic. Since the seven cycles are in a coordinate relationship to one another, they are presumed, for the moment, to contribute information of approximately equal importance concerning the topic.

In reality, it is unlikely that all the major units in a discourse would have the same degree of importance, but any nuances which may exist can only be defined in the context of a detailed discussion of prominence, which will be presented in Chapter 6. For the moment, the aim is to simply delimit the places in the text where the primary thematic material is located, in order to define the principal themes of the book.

The texts concerned are: 2:1-3:22, 6:1-7:17, 8:7-9:21, 11:1-13, 12:1-14:20, 16:2-16, 18:1-19:21 and 21:1-22:7, excluding the short texts indicated in the preceding paragraph. Perusal of these parts of the books indicates that there are two contrastive types of referential information which are presented.

Firstly, there are a series of negative events, which emanate from God's heavenly throne-room and manifest themselves, for the most part, as catastrophes in the context of the human referential world. Consequently, those catastrophic events are experienced by those living on the earth (3:10).

These catastrophic events are described in the main body of the book, that is, in Cycles 2 to 6. These catastrophic events are orchestrated and overseen under the leadership and all-seeing eyes of Jesus, in His persona of the Lamb.

Secondly, there are positive events which are also linked with God's throne-room and, for the most part, are limited to this same referential world. These events are experienced by certain people who are followers of the Lamb (14:4). For the most part, these positive events are described in the Interludes and Cycle 7. Cycle 1, being an introduction to the book as a whole, provides previews of both the positive and the negative events.

For the sake of simplicity and ease of reference, the theme concerning the negative events will be called **the Judgment Theme** and the theme concerning the positive events will be called **the Salvation Theme**. Between them, these two themes provide the basic referential information which describes God's plan. This plan is revealed in the message, centered around Jesus, which is the topic of the book, and which is transmitted by John. The two principal themes by definition include all the possible sub-themes.

The Salvation Theme

Whenever the Salvation Theme is referred to, it should be understood to include any, or all, of the features included in the following definition:

> The Salvation Theme is represented by any event which is designed to promote the well-being (i.e. the salvation) of any part of God's creation (but particularly God's people), or any positive response to such events.

The general context for this theme is the heavenly referential world (or the new creation), and the primary situation is God's heavenly throne room.

The Judgment Theme

Whenever the judgment theme is referred to it should be understood to include any, or all, of the features included in the following definition:

> The Judgment Theme is represented by any event which is designed to cause harm to any part of God's creation (but particularly to God's enemies), or any negative reaction to such events.

The general context for this theme is the earthly referential world (or the old creation), and the principal situation of the activity is also usually on, or in close proximity to, the physical earth.

As mentioned at the outset, the terms used to denote the themes are chosen as much for convenience as anything. The term 'judgment' was therefore chosen in order that it may specifically contrast with the term 'salvation'. However, in some cases the detrimental activity affects the people of God and appears to be initiated by Satan (see for example 2:10 or 12:17), in which case it may be considered that the label 'judgment' is inappropriate.

In response it can be noted firstly, that book-level themes of the type under consideration here are, by definition, very broad and will encompass many sub-themes. Secondly, the more specific rationale is that in the immediate context of the second letter, and also in the broader context of all the letters, Satan's attacks on God's people actually serve the purpose of God's plan, which is his benevolent chastisement of his people.

This kind of event is, by definition, God's provisional, short-term judgment on his people, which is necessary for their correction, strengthening and purification. In the specific context of 2:10, the phrases concerning testing and being faithful, even if death threatens, indicate that there is a plan hidden behind the external suffering. The wider context, as, for example, in 2:16 or 2:20-23, indicates clearly the implicit element of judgment per se.

4.3 Literary Architecture and the Organization of Themes

Text material as it was created and presented in biblical times was unidimensional. This means that it was a challenging task for a writer to recreate in his readers' imagination the multiple dimensions of external reality, or of a complex communication.

If he wished to develop, for example, two major themes, he only had two basic patterns available to him. These patterns are a simple alternating pattern, AB,AB,AB, etc., where A represents one theme and B the second, or an inverted pattern, ABA, or ABBA.

As Parunak 1983b,8 says: 'mathematically these are the only ways to duplicate a pattern in one dimension'. Nonetheless, variations on a theme are possible, and so these two basic patterns can be adapted and combined to create a number of other possibilities. The basic combinatory techniques are embedding, where one pattern is placed within another, or concurrence, where a given unit of text is simultaneously organized according to two or more different patterns. In addition, these various patterns can, and do, occur simultaneously at the different levels of the discourse hierarchy. By means of this repertoire of devices, limited though it may be to a unidimensional format, an author was able to go some way towards re-creating a multi-dimensional world in the hearers' imagination.

Needless to say, as Parunak (op.cit.11-12) himself points out, a reader would not be consciously aware of the literary devices being used, but only of the net result as presented by the textual unit as a whole. However, as in the case of all artistry, it is possible for an analyst to go much further than the average reader, and both discover, and reconstruct, the devices used by the author to communicate his overall message.

INFORMATION

Parunak's argument is that the biblical text is unidimensional because it was the vehicle for a primarily aural communication. However, written text as it was presented at that time, was unidimensional in any case, even though text may not be unidimensional in our day and age. This observation is already implicit in Parunak's article of 1981. The term 'unidimensional' describes the fact that the only communication tool available to ancient authors was the process of inscribing letters and words one after the other in a single string on an appropriate support. Only one element of communication was available for use at any one time, which makes it unidimensional. This is in contrast with modern technology where, in addition to the lexical dimension of writing, an author can provide other simultaneous means of contributing nuances of meaning to his message by the use, for example, of bolding, underlining, italics, capitals, numbers, headings, white spaces and paragraphs, and even colors and pictures.

Furthermore, John's experience, in line with most real-life experiences, was a multi-media event, during which the original message was transmitted to him using a variety of methods including sight, sound, taste (10:9), question and answer (7:13-17) and other forms of active participation (21:9-10). The challenge for John then, was to reduce this multi-dimensional message, which would require modern interactive computer or TV techniques to adequately reproduce, to a single dimension, that of words written one letter at a time arranged in one line at a time on a page. This insight is derived from Parunak (1981 and 1983b).

So, for example, in the domains of music and visual art, the products of such artistry can be both appreciated, and analyzed into its component parts, just as literature can be. Likewise, it is possible to drive a car, or ride in an airplane, without understanding how they work. Nonetheless, an engineer can also take these vehicles apart and show in a comprehensive way how, and why, they work as they were designed to do.

As far as Revelation is concerned, two major themes are in view, the Salvation and the Judgment Themes, and the aim of the following discussion is to demonstrate how the author organized these two themes in the discourse as a whole. Is the book as it stands truly 'an unintelligible mystery', as some would have us believe, because it is no longer in its 'legitimate order', (this is the viewpoint of Charles 1920,xxii-iii.)? In today's world we now have the linguistic tools which enable us to elucidate the structure of the book as it stands, and thereby perceive that there is, in fact, an inherent organization, which is both legitimate and coherent.

As indicated above, on the basis of mathematics alone, John's organizational choices were limited from the start. He either had to deal with the whole of one theme first and in isolation, before expanding on the second theme in a second block of text. Or, he had to deal with them one at a time in alternating segments of text. If he chose the latter system, then the organization has to be a parallel pattern (AB,AB), an inverted pattern (ABA or ABBA), or some combination of the two. In addition, these different possibilities of textual architecture can be operative at any level of the discourse hierarchy, whether, for example, at the cycle level, the cycle sub-unit level, or the paragraph level.

It is to be expected that, in some places in the book, each theme in turn will be clearly presented, but in addition, there will be places where the two themes are present concurrently and will give the impression of merging or overlapping. It is inevitable that they should meet at certain points and, that this point of juncture, should create some linguistic turbulence, which may even throw up new ideas, sub-topics and sub-themes.

If there were no points of convergence like this, then there would be no obvious reason why an author would place them together in the same work. In reality, however, the primary interest of a discourse is created when two such, seemingly opposing, themes, come together. Far from being an unfortunate anomaly, creating these points of convergence is usually one of the author's main objectives. This convergence between the Judgment and Salvation Themes happens to a limited extent in Cycle 1, as a kind of preview. However, the primary point of convergence is in Cycle 7. Since this is the conclusion of the book as a whole, this is not surprising, and this observation lends credence to the notion that this convergence was the goal of the author as he reached the climax of his book.

4.3.1 The Thematic Organization of Revelation

The Thematic Organization of Cycles 1 and 7

The referential material which is thematic in the body of Cycle 1 (2:1-3:22) concerns the church, as its members live out their lives on earth, and is of three kinds. For the sake of completeness and clarity it needs to be said that there is another element of the letters, which is not included in this discussion here. There are also clearly instructions concerning what the Christians should do in order to avoid the acts of judgment and to benefit from the acts of salvation. However, this is volitional import material and is not part of the referential thematic information under discussion. See the section at the end of this chapter for a brief discussion of the function of the volitional material.

So, in terms of the thematic material then, there is information concerning what Christ knows about each church (cf. 'I know', at 2:2,9,13,19; 3:1,8 and 15). This information serves as a basis for presenting the two principal things which are part of his plan, which are either acts of salvation or acts of judgment.

So, for example, in 2:18-29 he says to the church at Thyatira that he knows their works, love, faith etc. But then, he warns the person called Jezebel and those associated with her, that he will throw her into a bed... into great affliction, which is an act of judgment. After that, he indicates to the other Christians what future acts of salvation are prepared for them.

In terms of order, as a general rule, the words concerning judgment come first and are followed by the words of salvation. Having said that, however, the two themes are closely associated and sometimes completely intertwined in the same textual unit. So, in 2:10 he warns the Christians of Smyrna that the devil will throw some of them into prison, and that they will have affliction. This is a negative event and fits the definition of a judgment type event. However, salvation is also implicit in the same event, for they are promised that it will be of short duration with the expectation of release (salvation) after ten days. Even the phrase 'that you may be tried/tested', implies salvation for those who pass the test.

Overall then, this Cycle contributes material relevant to both the major themes in an alternating (AB,AB etc.) pattern which is repeated seven times (one major pattern per letter) with just some slight variations.

Traditionally, it is considered that the letter to the Christians at Philadelphia (3:7-13) contains no word of reproach or warning of judgment. Nonetheless, this letter still contributes information to the judgment theme: the fact that they kept Christ's word and did not deny his name (3:8) implies that they had previously known their own testing judgment events. The fact that their enemies would submit to them implies the same (3:9), and the fact that the whole earth is due to go through a time of trial is specifically indicated (3:10), and this would include them. But, there is also evidence that the same referential event can be both a salvation event and a judgment event, at the same time.

The detail of the way in which Jesus addresses the seven churches in the seven letters of Cycle 1, will be developed further in Chapter 7.5.

Cycle 7, despite its different structural organization, displays a thematic organization which is similar to Cycle 1. In the first instance, it contains information which is about the church and is of direct interest to the church. Referentially, it indicates how some parts of God's plan, which were still future in Cycle 1, actually work out in practice, when the time is right.

In addition, it contributes to the development of both the themes, for, throughout the body of the cycle (21:1-22:7), there is a series of contrastive statements concerning the positive things which John saw in the new Heaven and earth, followed by complementary negative statements. So, for example, the first statement at 21:1 concerning his vision of the new creation, is followed by the statement that the former heaven and earth had passed away, and that there was no more sea.

Where the thematic material comes to an end at 22:5, there is a final negative statement indicating that there will be no more night and no more (created) light sources, followed by a complementary positive statement indicating that God Himself will be the source of light. In terms of the general discussion of themes which is in view here, the positive statements contribute to the Salvation Theme, because they concern things which God plans to accomplish for the benefit of his people. The negative statements contribute to the Judgment Theme, because they concern the plan to remove things belonging to the first creation which are either inadequate (e.g. 22:5) or are clearly tainted by sin (21:8). In effect then, there is, once again, an alternating (AB) pattern, which is repeated seven times in the course of the series of antitheses which are presented in this passage. The issues surrounding this series of antitheses will be taken up in more detail in Chapter 5.

The general principles which can be deduced from the organization of Cycle 7 are as follows. There is alternation and intermingling of the two main themes as there is in Cycle 1. Nonetheless, it begins (21:1) and ends (22:5c) with the Salvation Theme, which is also the theme of the single largest central unit (21:9-21). It can be observed also that, just as in Cycle 1 so here, a single event can be construed as both a salvation event and as a judgment event, depending on the point of view. Thus, for example, in 21:4 and 8, two lists are given of negative aspects of the old creation which will be removed as part of God's plan of judgment. Yet, at the same time, it is clear that this removal of negative things also contributes positively to God's plan of salvation for his people.

The Thematic Organization of Cycles 2 to 6

The organization of Cycles 2 to 6 is similar in each case, but at the same time it is different to that of Cycles 1 and 7. In the latter, there is continual alternation and even intermingling of the two themes, while in the former, they are kept quite distinct.

It was proposed in Chapter 3 above, that the body of each of the central cycles is organized around a seven-fold motif, namely the seals, the trumpets, the signs, the bowls and the proclamations. Perusal of the texts concerned indicate that, with only one or two apparent exceptions, they all contribute exclusively to the Judgment Theme. The exceptions are firstly, that the fifth seal (6:9-11) is thematically ambiguous. This is because it points towards an event which will be another example of a single event being both a judgment event (for those who killed the martyrs), and a salvation event (vindication for the martyrs). Then, in addition to that example, Signs 1 and 2 (12:1-18) and Bowl 3 (16:4-7) also contain similar elements of ambiguity.

In terms of quantity, the Judgment Theme dominates the development of the thematic information communicated in these central cycles.

However, that is not all that can be said, for in four of the five cycles the repetitive insistence on judgment is broken up by distinct blocks of text, which present dramatically contrastive material. This contrastive material contributes to the development of the Salvation Theme. These are the blocks of text which have been previously referred to as the Interludes. Their contribution to the development of the themes will be discussed next.

4.3.2 The Organization and the Function of the Interludes

The observations which were made in the course of the analysis of the seven cycles in Chapter 3, were that an interlude is a unit of text which is clearly different from its immediate context. As such, it breaks up, and creates a pause, in a series of units which otherwise belong together. Further observations were that the interludes are usually located in the heavenly realm and project a sense of certain hope for God's people.

In summary, it can now be said that there are four clear interludes which occur in Cycles 2,3,4 and 6. Cycle 5 (the Bowls Cycle) does not have an interlude like the others even though it has one verse, 16:15, which is quite different from its immediate context. In Chapter 3.4 some reasons, based on the immediate context, were proposed why this verse was not intended to be an interlude. Now two more can be adduced from the broader context.

The first is that a similar verse occurs in Cycle 6 (18:20) and this cannot be an interlude, since an interlude already clearly occurs at 19:1-8. Both these verses (16:15 and 18:20) are clearly exhortations which are aimed primarily at the hearer These verses, therefore, are volitional import texts, designed to motivate a positive response to the information being presented. As such, these texts are not contributing to the thematic development (see the definition of thematic material above) as the other interludes do, and this provides another reason why these texts are not interludes. The function of 16:15, 18:20, and other such verses, will be discussed in section 4.6 below and again in Chapter 6 below.

In contrast to this viewpoint, Wendland 1990,382 considers that the interlude for the Bowls Cycle is located at 16:5-7. However, this ignores the internal cohesion which binds together the whole of the third bowl (16:4-7).

The judgment event described is the pouring of the bowl onto the rivers and fountains of (drinking) water thereby turning them into blood (16:4). The following verses are a descriptive commentary which explain the reasons for, and the implications of, this event. The commentary picks up the concepts of drinking water, and blood, and explains that it is appropriate that those who spilled the blood of the martyrs should be made to drink blood in return.

It is not appropriate, therefore, to divide this unit into two parts. On the contrary, there is probably a good reason why this commentary is placed here as will be proposed in Chapter 6. In addition, Wendland fails to propose a reason why his interlude occurs between the third and fourth sub-units of the cycle instead of in its usual position between the sixth and seventh sub-units.

In the earlier discussion of the Narrative Framework, in Chapter 2.3, it was proposed that 10:1-11:2 be analyzed as a book level interlude. In the light of the more detailed information which has been subsequently presented, it can now be observed that it does, in fact, match the definition of an interlude. This is because it interrupts the trumpets motif and contributes positive information concerning God's plan, namely that it will soon be brought to completion (10:7). Furthermore, it is contiguous with the interlude of the Trumpets Cycle (11:1-13) and functions in tandem with this unit of text to provide a unique, double interlude near the middle of the book.

If this passage is also included in the list, then there are five interludes in the central part of the book, each of which contributes to the development of the Salvation Theme, in contrast to the Judgment Theme. Since the number five is symbolic of the concept of grace, this is a very appropriate numerical organization for a theme which is all about salvation.

4.3.3 The Structure of the Interludes

Some aspects of the structure of the interludes were presented in the general discussion of the overall organization of each cycle in Chapter 3. In the following sections a more complete discussion of their internal organization will be presented.

The Seals Cycle Interlude 7:1-17

This interlude can be divided into two main parts (7:1-8 and 9-17), on the basis of a different location, different participants and different topics. In addition, even though the function of 'after these things', is ambiguous in the book as a whole, in this instance its presence at the beginning of 7:9 seems to establish a clear parallelism with 'after this', in 7:1. Furthermore, the passage beginning at 7:9 is also set off as markedly different by the presence of 'and behold'. The structure of the two parts is as presented in Chart 26.

There are some clear similarities between each part, in that each has a combination of description and direct speech, and both have a coda, which completes the basic parallel structure. The unity of the two parts is established by the fact that, neither of them contributes to the sequence of the seven seals, and both of them contribute to the Salvation Theme.

Chart 26.
The Structure of the Seals Interlude 7:1-17

Part 1. 7:1-8

A. Description: John sees four angels holding the four winds back from harming the earth, the sea and trees 7:1

B. Description: Another angel with a seal of the living God, who cries out with a loud voice to the four angels who have power to harm the earth and the sea 7:2

C. Direct Speech: The angel says: 'Do not harm the earth, the sea or the trees until we have sealed God's people on their forehead.' 7:3

Coda: John is made aware of the result of this sealing activity. 7:4-8

Part 2. 7:9-17

A. Description: John sees a great crowd standing before the throne in Heaven with palms in their hands 7:9

B. Direct Speech: They cry out with a loud voice: 'Salvation to our God, sitting on the throne and to the Lamb'. 7:10

A' Description: The angels standing round the throne, the elders and the four creatures fall before the throne and worship 7:11

B' Direct Speech: Blessing, glory, wisdom, thanks, honor, power and strength (7 items) to God for ever and ever. 7:12

Coda: John is made aware of the identity of the principal participants in this worship activity. 7:13-17

Once this is noticed, further coherence between the two parts can be adduced from the fact that Part 1 is a description of activities designed to promote the well-being of God's people (and temporarily other parts of creation as well 7:3), and that Part 2 is a positive response to God's salvific activity. There is nothing in the text which clearly indicates that the worship in 7:9-12 is directly stimulated by the activity of 7:3-8, although 7:15

('therefore') indicates that the service of those in white robes is a response to some aspects of God's plan of salvation. However, the above insights into the structural coherence of the whole passage, taken in the context of the Salvation Theme, tend towards an understanding that a direct linkage between the two parts was intended.

There are three prominent points, which all combine together to create one harmonious thought. The prominent points are the three direct speeches. This is because they are the last in a linear series, because direct speeches are always more important than any surrounding background or introductory material, and because the speeches contain commands, or forceful declarations.

These three prominent direct speeches are supported by the two codas. These are also prominent because they come last in a linear structure, and they are unusually long for a coda. In addition, in the first one John hears the numbers of those who were sealed, which means that he was listening to another direct speech. Then, in the second one, it is composed almost entirely of another direct speech, which makes five direct speeches in all.

The combined message is that the people represented by the 144,000 people seen in the vision, are protected in some way from the judgment which is due to come on the earth. Secondly, that salvation in general, and this would include the preceding component of salvation in particular which has just been described, comes from God and the Lamb as part of their plan for their people.

It is to be noticed that the verb 'to seal', which is the key action in this part of the vision, is exactly the same word as the noun 'a seal', which is the key component of the surrounding narrative concerning the opening of the seven seals. This is the only cycle where this direct lexical relationship is made between the two parts of the cycle. However, this is the first cycle with an interlude, so it seems as if the author is purposely indicating that there is an intentional connection between the interlude and the rest of the cycle, even though the two parts give us information on two quite different themes.

This insight and understanding results in the tumultuous praise and worship which goes up to God and to the Lamb, from these people who are the beneficiaries of their plan of salvation for them.

Finally, at a secondary level, it should be noted that, on account of the sheer number of repetitions in such a short space, the number 12 is also being highlighted as important. The number 12 is representative of the concept of government. In addition, in this case it includes the multiplication operation of 12 times 12, and also the magnification produced by the application of the largest number available at the time, which is 1000. So, we are talking here then, of government at the highest level imaginable. This is not surprising since this is all taking place in the throne room of Heaven, which is the highest source of authority which has ever existed.

In this case then, the sub-theme of government is not evoked explicitly in this interlude, but it is hard to deny, that in a Hebrew worldview context, it is certainly being evoked implicitly. This insight is supported by the fact that the great multitude are portrayed as serving God before His throne (the word 'throne' being used three times in the speech of 7:14-17), which is a governmental situation. Then, a few lines later, it says that the Lamb leads them, and this idea is taken up again in the central, Signs Cycle interlude, also with governmental implications.

Anyone reading this text today would automatically understand that these people whom John saw, were, or represented in some way, the Church. However, in English this word has taken on a very specific meaning, and so we understand it to refer to an assembly of people grouped together for religious, or spiritual purposes.

But, the point is, that, in John's day, that would not necessarily have been the case. In the New Testament the first time that the word translated 'church' is used, is when Jesus lays out the blue-print for the organization of the group of people, which He was assembling for His Kingdom purposes, as described in Matthew 6:18. The Greek word used there for 'church' is the word *ekklésia,* the primary meaning of which, at the time, was a governmental assembly. So it appears that He was organizing a shadow, or alternative government, as much as He was organizing a band of followers.

Noticing these implicit references is useful, even necessary, for discerning book level threads, and the one in question here is the whole thread of ruling and reigning. This thread is actually very important for the book as a whole, even though it is somewhat hidden, as it is here in this interlude. But this is precisely why it needs to be noticed, and taken account of in an appropriate way. Since it is so important, will be developed with a little more detail in Chapter 7.4.

Meanwhile, we could sum up the message of this interlude in this way:

The Redeemed from all the nations are Sealed and Singing, Protected and Praising.

Having persevered through their time of tribulation, and having washed their robes in the blood of the Lamb, they now joyfully serve in the government of Heaven and faithfully focus on allowing the Lamb to lead them.

The Narrative Framework Interlude 10:1-11:2

This unit of text is both an interlude and a part of the Narrative Framework, at the same time. It is part of the Narrative Framework because it recounts John's participation in his own vision, and not just what he actually saw in his vision. It is an interlude, because it breaks up the sequence of the seven trumpets and contributes to the Salvation Theme. It is a coherent unit because of the presence of the phrase, 'a little scroll', which first occurs in v.2 and is last referred to in v.10, and because of John's active involvement in 10:4 and 10:8-11:1. See Chapter 2.5.2 for a display of its internal organization.

As with other narrative passages in Revelation, there is a linear chronological format, but this is also overlaid by a coherent concentric pattern. This parallel structure is a simple A.B.A' chiasm, with A. being 10:1-4, B. is 10:5-11, and A' is 11:1-2. This interlude has already been described in some detail in Chapter 2.5.2. Within this framework two prominent points can be located. The first (10:6-7) is what may be called the referential prominence of the unit, because it is concerned with communicating important new information concerning God's plan, that it will definitely be accomplished, and soon!

The second prominent point (10:11) is a place where the volitional import of the text is made explicit, and John is told that he must prophesy again. It is prominent because it is at the end of, and so, is the culmination of, the narrative unit. It is treated as the end of the unit, because the following verses (11:1-2) are not considered to be part of this narrative thread. This is because it provides no significant new information, for we have already been informed in 10:11, that John should continue his prophetic work, and the extra instructions in 11:1-2 are never referred to again. Therefore, since these verses contribute nothing to the thematic development, they appear primarily to have the function of providing a bridge between Chapters 10 and 11. For discussion of this overlap link see Chapter 2 sections 5.2 and 5.3.

Chapter 10:11 is also prominent because it is in direct speech. It is clearly a commentary on the preceding symbolic action and, as such, it is reasonable to suppose that it was intended to be the interpretation of this act. The interpretative function of this verse, therefore, also makes it prominent.

Symbolic material (the taking of the scroll and eating it) is not treated directly in semantic analysis, but only an interpretation which is expressible in referential terms, which is what is given in verse 11. This means that, within the context of this view of discourse analysis, the referential explanation is automatically more prominent than the symbolic vehicle. See Callow 1998,331-2, for more explanation of this issue.

So it is then, that this is a section of text which conveys a volitional import, because it is hortatory in nature, and is concerned with what John was supposed to do. What is of interest is not that he should prophesy, since this is not new information. Rather it is the 'again', which is of interest, because this is the new information and, therefore, the focus of the exhortation. Since 'again' is the important word, John is clearly presented with an exhortation to *persevere* in what he is already doing, namely doing the work of a prophet and witness. Perseverance, even under pressure of suffering, is a major sub-theme of the book (see for example 2:10 and 21:7). So, once again, John's personal experience serves to illustrate and reinforce this thematic strand.

It could also be deduced that he was to persevere in what he was doing, even though it may cause him to suffer. This can be deduced from the referential context because he is already suffering in exile for his previous work as a prophet (see 1:9), and also from the symbolic context, namely the suffering that eating the little scroll would engender 10:9-10.

This interlude is attached by an overlap link to the following interlude of the Trumpets Cycle, as mentioned above. For this reason, and since they also communicate the same basic message, they create a doublet of constituents at the book level, which mutually reinforces the significance of the message of each of them. A summary of the message of the interlude of the Trumpets Cycle will be given below. Meanwhile, the message of this Narrative Framework interlude can be summarized in this way:

Perseverance is the Priority for a Prophetic Witness

INFORMATION

It is reasonable to suppose that the first readers would have easily made this deduction about John's example, without the author having to specifically spell it out to them. This is because they should have had such a template in their worldview, derived from their knowledge of the Old Testament. So, for example, the book of Isaiah can be divided at the macro level into three concentric parts: A. *The Book of Condemnation* (ch.1-35), B. *The Book of Confirmation* (ch.36-39), and, A' *The Book of Consolation* (ch.40-66). The center of the chiasm (B) is the historical section of the book. These personal experiences serve to illustrate and confirm the reality and reliability of the prophecies given in the other parts of the book. (Schooling, personal research based on the outline in Motyer 1993 cf. pp. 276 and 286). Dorsey 1992,319 makes a similar observation concerning Amos 7:10-17. He also actually calls this passage 'a narrative interlude' and he suggests, in addition, that it serves to illustrate the message contained in the prophecy. In this case, it is 'a revealing sample of Israel's response to (God's) warnings'.

The Trumpets Cycle Interlude 11:1-13

This section has been defined as an interlude because it is not part of the sequence of the seven trumpets, and because it contributes to the Salvation Theme. It is preceded by a section of the Narrative Framework to which it is attached by an overlap link (11:1-2). The three woes are not included in this discussion for the reasons given in the preceding sections.

The overall structure, as presented in Chart 27, is that of a chiasm which is in the form of an embedded narrative. In keeping with its narrative text type, the center sections (11:3-12) are ordered according to a chronological format. Even so, there are enough parallels to support the overlaid chiastic structure, including the word ‘enemies’, in B and B', which are the only two occurrences of the word in the book.

Chart 27.

The Structure of the Trumpets Interlude 11:1-13

A. Setting 11:1-2
  B. The miraculous ministry of the two witnesses 11:3-6
    C. The earthly destiny of the two witnesses 11:7-10
  B' The miraculous confirmation of their ministry 11:11-12
A' Conclusion 11:13

Other evidence for the internal parallelism is as follows:

- the contrastive repetition of, ‘the holy city’, referring to Jerusalem in 11:2 (A), and ‘the city’, which is either referring again to Jerusalem or to its antithesis Babylon in 11:13 (A'), and a third reference to ‘the great city’, referring to physical Jerusalem in its unholy state in 11:8 (C).
- There is the reference to 1260 days (which is 3.5 years) in 11:3 (B.), which is matched by the reference to 3.5 days in 11:9 (C) and 11:11 (B').
- There is the reference to ‘standing’, in 11:4 (B.) which is paralleled by ‘stood’, in 11:11 (B').
- Each of the sub-units have a time reference (11:2,3,9,11,13).
- Each of the sub-units have a reference to ‘God’, or ‘the Lord’, (11:1,4,8,11,13).

This interlude would also seem to have two prominent points, one drawn from the linear chronological structure, and one from the parallel structure. It is usually the conclusion of a linear structure which is the most naturally prominent, which in this case, would be the end of the narrative per se (11:11-12), supported by the conclusion (11:13). This indicates that the two witnesses will be vindicated and saved, in spite of their apparent defeat, and that their enemies will in turn be punished.

The center of a chiasm is its most important sub-unit and in this case (11:7-10), it describes the death of the two witnesses. Superficially, these two prominent points would seem to be in conflict, but this is an example of where two contrasting themes come together and create some unexpected turbulence, but which, in turn, leads to a deeper understanding of the author's overall purpose.

In this case, the point being highlighted is that the two witnesses really do suffer a major defeat in this world's terms, and even lose their lives as a result of their ministry. However, in the context of the following sub-units, which have their own prominence as indicated above, it can be seen that this defeat is, in fact, only a gateway to a greater and more dramatic salvation, which overcomes suffering in this world, and even physical death.

Even though there are references to suffering and judgment in this passage, the interlude as a whole is, nonetheless, contributing to the Salvation Theme. This is because, in this passage, it is demonstrated that God's plan of salvation is more powerful than suffering, and can overcome even real, human defeats. Then, secondly, we are beginning to observe here, that part of that salvation, is the ultimate judgment of those who inflicted, or rejoiced over, the defeat in the first place. It is an example of a double negative creating a positive.

Finally, it should be noticed that the governmental thread is implicit in this interlude, as well as in the previous one. Even though the work of the two witnesses is portrayed as being an example of prophesy (11:6), and of speaking out words of testimony (11:7), in actual fact they are deciding what will happen and what will not. This is, in reality a governmental function, just as Jesus ruled over the natural elements, as well as over human circumstances during His earthly ministry. Just as Jesus was King while on earth, and, as such, was totally in charge of what happened to Him, and what happened around Him, He trained His disciples to do the same.

These two witnesses are only prophetic representatives of those same 12 disciples (note the number 12), and, as such, represent all disciples of Jesus, of all times, as illustrated by the innumerable cloud of witnesses described in 7:9. They are so trained and skilled in this ability to decide and govern, that they even have power over death. Death no longer has absolute power over them, but they continue to be overcomers in, through, and after, the process of physical death, just as Jesus demonstrated as the First-Born from the dead.

So then, we could sum up the message of this interlude in this way:

Perseverance is the Price to Pay for Prophetic Witnesses

The Signs Cycle Interlude 14:1-5

The structure of this interlude, as presented in Chart 28 below, is in the form of a simple ABA' chiasm with a coda, which is organized according to a similar, inverted (ABB'A') pattern.

Constituents A and A' of the interlude are in parallel because of the specific repetition of the 144,000 each time qualified by a passive perfect participle. Constituents a and a' of the coda are in parallel because of the similarity of the central concept (undefiled/unblemished), and also because of the similarity of their grammatical construction (negative statement + plural adjective + 'they are').

Constituents b and b' are in parallel because they amplify information previously given in constituents A and A' of the body of the unit. As mentioned in Chapter 3.5.2, the presence of the coda means that the interlude participates in the internal structural coherence within the Signs Cycle as a whole. This is because all the principal sign units, which incorporate Signs 1-6, are also characterized by this structural feature.

Chart 28.
The Structure of the Signs Interlude 14:1-5

A. The Lamb Standing on Mt Sion with the 144,000 14:1
  B. The Sound in Heaven of a New Song 14:2-3a
A' No one could Learn the Song except the 144,000 who are Purchased from the Earth 14:3b

Coda: John is made aware of the identity of the principal participants in this activity 14:4-5

a. They are not defiled, for celibates they are 14:4a
  b. They are the ones who follow the Lamb wherever He goes 14:4b
  b' They are the ones who were purchased as first-fruits 14:4c
a' No lie was found in them, unblemished they are 14:5

The new song of the 144,000 (14:2-3), which is, once again, a positive response to God's acts of salvation, is the most prominent feature of the unit, being the theme of the central unit of the chiasm. The coda also plays a part in the prominence matrix, since it is the last unit and brings closure to the narrative aspects of this interlude. It is noticeable that it has the same type of content as the codas in the interlude of the Seals Cycle, since, once again, John is made aware of additional aspects of the identity of the main participants in the preceding body of the interlude.

It is interesting to note that all the Signs sub-units, which immediately precede the interlude, have an A.B.B'A' structure, plus a coda, as their internal organization. See Appendix 3 for the details. Both these structures are unusual in Revelation, and so this kind of organization marks the Signs Cycle as being different from the others.

Yet, as can be seen above, the interlude also contains both of these unusual structures. It is possible, therefore, that the detailed similarity between the Signs sub-units and the Signs Cycle interlude, is an extra structural clue, which John provided to compensate for the absence of an overt numbering system. It is certainly a variation on a theme which is remarkable.

As before, the governmental thread is present implicitly in this interlude. This is because the main piece of new information contained in this text is that the Lamb is seen standing on Mount Sion along with His followers. Mount Sion symbolically represents the highest possible position of authority in the universe. This is the heavenly throne room, the location of the government of God's Kingdom. The 144,000 redeemed singers are specifically present, since they follow the Lamb wherever He leads them, and they are all in a standing position in this vision. In this governmental context, the position of standing is that of a king who has made his decision, and now is ready to act.

So then, we could sum up the message of this interlude in this way:

The Saved Singers Now Stand With the Lamb and Share His Authority

The Proclamations Cycle Interlude 19:1-8

The structure of this interlude is somewhat complex, and yet it mimics in great detail the structure of the proclamations which precede it. It is possible, once again, just as was noted for the Signs Cycle above, that the detailed similarity between the proclamations and the interlude, is an extra structural clue which John provided to compensate for the absence of an overt numbering system.

As with the proclamations themselves, the structure of the interlude is organized around a series of direct speeches, which are introduced by the present participle of the verb 'to say'. The main difference is that it is followed by a coda, which is a minor component of the Narrative Framework, as indicated in Chart 29 below.

The concentric structure confirms the internal integrity of the interlude, and the fact that it terminates at verse 8. With an ABB'A' structure of this sort, the most prominent part is considered to be the A and A' sections combined, but with significant support provided by the B and B' sections combined. In other words, there is not the same peak of prominence as in chiastic structures. In this particular case, the distinction between the two sets of parallels is not great, since the primary sub-theme of worship addressed to God is carried by each of the constituents.

Chart 29.
The Structure of the Proclamations Interlude 19:1-8

A. 19:1-3 **Personage:** 'a great crowd'. Present participle: 'saying'
Direct speech 1: 'Hallelujah'
followed by TWO reason clauses introduced by 'because'
Direct speech 2: 'Hallelujah...'

B. 19:4 **Personages:** The 24 elders and the 4 living creatures (before) the throne. Present participle: 'saying'
Direct speech: 'Amen, Hallelujah'

B' 19:5 **Personage:** 'a voice from the throne.'
Present participle: 'saying'
Direct speech: 'Praise God...'

A' 19:6-8 **Personages:** 'a great crowd.' Present participle: 'saying'
Direct speech 1: 'Hallelujah'
followed by TWO reason clauses introduced by 'because'

Coda: 19:9-10 Being part of the Narrative Framework.
Personage: The Bowl Angel of 17:1
Direct speech 1: indicative verb: 'he says to me'
'Write: Blessed...' 19:9a
Direct speech 2: indicative verb: 'he says to me'
'These words of God are true' 19:9b

(Transitional element of the Narrative Framework 19:10a)

Direct speech 3: indicative verb: 'he says to me'
'Don't (worship me)...Worship God' 19:10b
followed by a commentary/explanation introduced by 'for'

A and A' are in parallel because of the repetition of 'a great crowd'. They also have a similar structure, particularly remarkable being the repetition of 'hallelujah', with its concomitant reason clauses. It is noteworthy that this is specifically stated to be a second speech (19:3).

Although the conjunction 'because' is not repeated, the clause which follows the second hallelujah, is implicitly another reason clause, with *kai* 'and', indicating a parallelism with the last preceding reason clause at the end of 19:2. B and B' are in parallel because the personages are directly related to the throne, because of their similar structure, and because the speeches do not provide more reason clauses but, rather, support for the reason clauses.

The prominence is, therefore, flatter in profile but it is also more forceful, because there is a four-fold repetition of the same theme which makes the whole unit prominent. This prominence is further reinforced by the validating nature of the coda.

The coda is clearly distinct from what precedes because it does not fit into the concentric structure and, even though it contains direct speech, the introductory speech form is different, with the indicative present form of the verb 'to say', being used, instead of the present participle. The coda is an embedded narrative unit and is, in fact, part of the Narrative Framework. As such, it is organized according to a chronological format, rather than a concentric format. Consequently, its most prominent point is the final main event, which is the third direct speech in 19:10b. This is confirmed by the fact that this speech contains two complementary imperatives, which carry the same message, that only God is worthy of worship.

Despite the coda's differences, including the fact that it is operating at the level of the Narrative Framework, the unit, nonetheless, is tightly integrated into its context and is intentionally attached to the interlude unit which precedes. This is firstly, because there is a clear tail-head link attaching the two units. This is indicated by the repetition of 'the marriage of the Lamb', in verses 7 and 9.

In addition to this clear cohesive feature, both the main body of the interlude and its coda have similar structures, organized around a series of direct speeches. Then, to top it all off, all the sub-units of the interlude, including the coda, contribute to the sub-theme of worship as previously mentioned in the preceding paragraphs.

The fact that this unit is part of the Narrative Framework provides two further insights. In 19:9 the speaker is not specifically identified, although the following context indicates that it must be an angel. The fact that this unit is part of the Narrative Framework indicates that it relates in the first instance to other units of this framework, and only secondarily to its immediate context. This means that the speaker at 19:9 must be the currently active speaker within the context of the Narrative Framework.

This proposal is confirmed by the fact that this thread is continued, in subsequent sections. So it is then, that in the next unit of the Narrative Framework (21:5-10), one of the seven Bowl Angels is once again identified as an active speaker (v.9). He is specifically identified again, because, in the meantime, there has been another speaker active in the Narrative Framework. This was the one sitting on the throne at 21:5. This is why it can be stated with some confidence that the speaker is one of the seven bowl angels, who was the active speaker in the previous Narrative Framework unit at 17:1.

Secondly, this unit provides another example of how John's personal experience, as recounted in the Narrative Framework, illustrates the message of the book. The whole thrust of the proclamations interlude is that a whole range of beings should, and do, worship God. As if to reinforce the point, John himself is also specifically told that he should do the same in 19:10. So we can see quite clearly here that John's personal experience is indeed intended to contribute to the message of the book. This is in parallel to his personal experience in the interlude unit of the Narrative Framework, which was described above, where he was shown that he needed to persevere in his service as a prophet.

The governmental thread does not appear in this interlude as it does in some of the preceding ones. However, this time there is another surprise, and another piece of new information concerning God's plan for the role and destiny of the Church. This time a wedding is in view, and the marriage of the Lamb is mentioned for the first time in 19:7 in a doublet.

In terms of quantity, this thread is very briefly stated and could almost pass unnoticed. In total, there are only five propositional references to either the wedding itself, or to the bride in 19:7 (x2), 19:9, and 21:2 and 9, although this number is, of course symbolic of grace and very suitable for evoking the Salvation Theme.

This paucity of references would seem surprising since we are given enough information to know that this wedding is the summum bonum, the high point, where everything is going to end up. The wedding is the end of the narrative thread which tells the story of the Lamb and His relationship with His followers. Since this is the conclusion to this most important story, it is very prominent, and extremely important, for an understanding of the whole book.

So, it may seem surprising to us that such an important topic receives such little attention. However, it is not so surprising considered from a Hebrew world-view perspective. In their system the most important items of information were often couched in brief, and even mysterious forms, in order to oblige the student to do the work to perceive and understand what was being communicated, for what you learn for yourself you remember the best. This topic will be discussed again in Chapter 8.

This passage where the wedding thread is first referred to, is also the only passage where the comparison between the bride of the Lamb, and 'that other woman', known as Babylon, is implicitly put in place. This is because a final derogatory reference to Babylon occurs in 19:2, which prepares the way for the introduction of the glorious bride of Christ in the following verses. This is the same literary device as is used in Chapter 20, which follows, when the demise of the dragon is briefly described, in order to prepare the way for the more detailed description of the new era under the leadership of the Lamb in Chapter 21.

So then, in the light of these two prominent points which are presented by this interlude, we could sum up its message with this sub-title:

The Wedding and the Worship.

4.3.4 The Function of the Interludes

The one thing which the above units of text have in common, is that they all interrupt the development of the Judgment Theme. Furthermore, the interruption is rather abrupt, and begins and ends without any kind of transition, introduction, or closure. Historically, this feature of the interludes has been one of the main reasons for the difficulty in developing a consensus of opinion concerning the structure of the book.

This is because when the development of a linear analysis is in view, anything which interrupts an obvious logical flow, also automatically disrupts any attempt to produce a neat, linear analysis, with clear relationships between each succeeding segment of text. When it is not possible to draw the lines of demarcation clearly, it is inevitable that consensus on where to draw them will be more difficult to attain.

This problem, nonetheless, is not as difficult to overcome as may at first appear. This is because the same kind of alternation between contrasting segments of text is a literary phenomenon which still occurs. For example, this feature is particularly common in novels or similar works, which have a distinct conflict in the plot, or contrast in the themes. An author may present the hero and his associated circumstances and themes in one chapter, and then, without explanation, present the villain and his associated material in the next. This alternation could continue for several chapters until the dénouement approaches, when the two are bound to come together in some way or another.

The only difference is that in our modern era, specific conventions have developed which indicate to the reader the author's purpose. In this case, an author would usually put contrastive material in a new chapter, for example. By means of this convention the reader knows that a completely new set of information may be presented in a new chapter, even though nothing is specifically said in the text to this effect.

Once it is recognized that different conventions are operating, it is not so difficult to discern that the pattern of alternating material is not so unusual after all. This process of moving from the familiar to the unfamiliar helps, in turn, to discern the function of these interludes.

In the first instance, the most obvious point which can be stated is that, if an author wishes to present two contrasting themes in the same work, it is necessary to choose to place information relative to these two themes at some point in the text. When and how this is done is a choice, but once the choice has been made, it is to be expected that the reader will be able to discern the difference between the two sets of topics and themes, otherwise clear communication would not be possible.

It is clear that, regardless of what other conventions are used to signal the switch between the two themes, the net result will be blocks of text which alternate, according to the main theme which they are developing.

So, in Revelation, after presenting aspects of the Judgment Theme in the body of the Seals Cycle, for example, John then chose to present material relative to the Salvation Theme. This new block of text is what is being called the interlude for that cycle, and so on, for the other cycles where an interlude occurs.

Secondly, it can be stated that the interlude texts interrupt and create a pause in the organization of the body of the seven-fold cycles within which they occur. So, for example, in 6:1-17 the first six seals are opened, and the accompanying text presents a series of events which concern deprivation, destruction and death. On the basis of the precedent set by the first cycle, a hearer would expect a seventh seal, but before that is presented, the interlude inserts material which is hopeful, salutary and glorious (7:1-17).

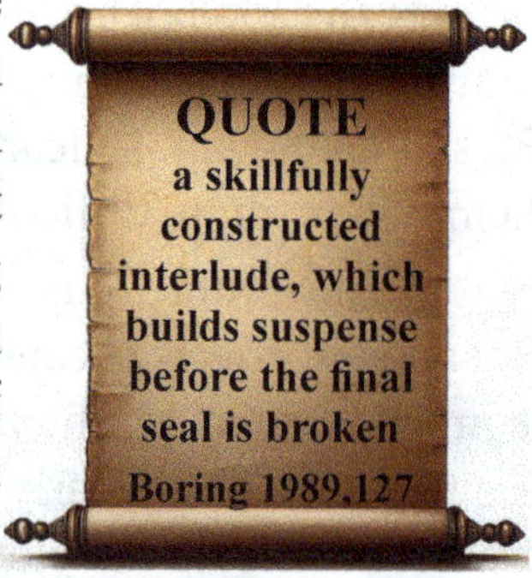
QUOTE
a skillfully constructed interlude, which builds suspense before the final seal is broken
Boring 1989,127

As if this literary pause was not enough to signal the author's intention, the notion of a pause in the series of negative events is specifically stated in the text as well, for the opening of the interlude revolves around the temporary halt of the judgment events (7:1-3). There is also a pause in the Narrative Interlude where John temporarily halts his prophetic work in order to receive personal instruction and exhortation (10:1-11:2). This is of interest, because it is only in the context of passages designated as interludes, that this kind of hiatus in the flow of the action happens.

With regard to the interlude in Chapter 7, it can also be observed that the first main event is left incomplete. That is to say that the narrator does not explicitly recount what happened after the process of sealing the 144,000 people, nor whether the four angels were released to continue their work or not. This means that the event which caused the pause, is as much in focus as the sealing event itself. Consequently, this must, therefore, have some significance within the context of the narrator's overall purpose.

The objective data which is available here is that right at the beginning of the first interlude, which is already remarkable for its size and complexity, the narrator specifically sows the notion of a pause into his hearers' minds. It is certainly possible to conclude that this was not just a coincidence, but was an intentional signpost. This is especially so, considering that John did not have available modern conventions like paragraph spacing, or a new chapter, which would create pauses for those listening; and he certainly did not have the ability to create any sub-headings to help him guide his hearers into the right path of understanding.

Thirdly, it can be stated that breaks in the normal flow of text are usually inserted to create tension, which is a classic method for getting the reader emotionally involved with the text, and, thereby, to maintain motivation to keep reading to the end. In this case, three tension creating factors are discernible, namely conflict, suspense, and unfinished business.

The conflict is set up and maintained by the fact that a contrastive theme is presented and developed by the five interlude units. For each theme, there is a set of protagonists, and these two groups of personages are clearly in opposition and incompatible with each other.

In the first interlude (7:1-17), two groups of people are described who are clearly different from, and in contrast to, the people alluded to in Seals 1-6. Furthermore, the underlying conflict has already been hinted at in Seal 5 (6:9-11). The other major protagonists who are in conflict are the dragon and the Lamb, the former being present in the body of the Signs Cycle 12:3-18, and the latter being present in the Signs Cycle interlude 14:1.

Boring 1989,127 understood the function of 7:1-17 in a similar way, although he made no distinction between the concept of 'suspense', and that of 'unfinished business', observing that :

> Instead of seeing the expected End, what we see is the church.
> This is literary craftsmanship, ...what seems at first to be a

> postponement...turns out to be a skillfully constructed interlude, which...builds suspense before the final seal is broken'.

Suspense is created by the fact that situations described in the interludes are quite different from those described in the surrounding text. The result is that an element of uncertainty is injected into the discourse. This is because no explanation is given at first, as to what the relationship is between these two sets of circumstances, and only hints are given as to how it will all work out in the end. The element of suspense is essential to any well-organized plot, and it is usually maintained right until the end, when everything is fully resolved.

The element of unfinished business is a more short-term feature. In this case it is created by the fact that an expectation is aroused that there will be seven seals, seven trumpets and so on. But, in actual fact, this sequence is interrupted by the interludes, leaving the reader waiting for the completion of the series.

4.4 The Salvation Theme Seen as a Whole

4.4.1 The Interludes Contribute the Most Information to the Salvation Theme

In the discussion of the interludes above, it has been seen that each of them is composed of a large body of material which contributes significantly to the development of the Salvation Theme. The primary function of these units of text then, is to be the vehicle throughout the middle part of the book whereby the author communicates this positive aspect of the message. The fact that they are interspersed in the bodies of the cycles which develop the judgment theme, merely indicates that John chose an alternating ABA'B' system of ordering his material.

In fact, a great deal of orderliness can be observed in all the details which have been discussed so far. This suggests that this is an intentional arrangement rather than a haphazard one. So, in summary then, all of them as a group, contribute to the development of the Salvation Theme. In addition, the four cycle interludes normally occur in the same position relative to the other parts of the body but the exceptions are explicable. The normal position is between the sixth and seventh parts of the seven-fold motif of the body, and the issues concerning the different position for the interlude in Cycle 4, and its absence in Cycle 5, will be explained in Chapter 6.

4.4.2 The Arrangement of the Interludes

The arrangement of the interludes is not linear and, as a consequence, a coherent linear analysis, where the primary relationship of every unit of text is with its immediate neighbors, is not possible to obtain. However, as has been indicated above, strict linearity is not the only textual architecture which is possible, and evidence is accumulating that this was generally not the preferred textual architecture for biblical writers. So, for example, Bailey 1983,50, in discussing New Testament literature says: ‘the use of the inversion (i.e. non-linear) principle is relatively universal and often subconscious’, and Baldwin 1972,9 and 74-5 in the context of the Old Testament sums up her conclusions as follows:

> It is my hope that others will be helped to understand Zechariah as I myself have been by discerning its symmetry of structure... one of the important contributions of modern scholarship to our understanding of the Bible is the realization that its truth is expressed in literary forms and structures as well as in words...an explanation of the apparently chaotic order of events, and the abrupt changes of subject-matter...(is) found... in a literary unity built on a chiastic pattern.

In the case of the interludes of Revelation, the relationships between them are neither linear nor symmetrical, but instead there is a network of relationships comprised of numerous cross-references and parallels of all kinds. The result is like a patch-work, which can, indeed, seem chaotic and relationally abrupt when considered one part at a time, with linearity as a grid. But even so, such an artistic product is, nonetheless, complete, and visually pleasing when considered as a whole, and with principles such as are used in flower-arrangements, as a grid.

Using more technical terms drawn from the field of sociolinguistics, the semantic and structural relationships between the interludes can be characterized as being relatively dense and multiplex. This is in contrast to their relationships with the body of cycles other than their own, which are sparse and uniplex. See Schooling 1990 for a discussion of sociolinguistic issues relative to social network theory.

The relationships are dense because all the interludes as individual units are related in some way to every other interlude, and they are multiplex because, in all cases, there is more than one relationship between each interlude. By contrast, apart from the fact that they arise out of the same setting in Chapters 4 and 5, the interludes have no clear relationships with the bodies of the central cycles other than their own. Those semantic relationships which do exist, do not express exact correspondences. For example, several interludes have references to God’s servants e.g. 7:3 and 19:2. By contrast, the body of some central cycles also use the word for ‘slave/servant’, but with reference to servants of human masters e.g. 6:15.

4.4.3 The Hubs and Spokes of the Network Arrangement

This network organization has two main hubs, the seals interlude (7:1-17) and the proclamations interlude (19:1-8), being the first and last of the series. Despite the distance separating them, these two units of texts are connected by three elements of structural similarity, and over ten clear lexical or conceptual parallels. These two units also have multiple relationships with all the other interludes, including the Narrative Framework interlude (10:1-11:2). See the Appendix following this chapter for more details on these issues.

The Narrative Framework interlude and the trumpets interlude (11:1-13), are quite different in basic content from the other interludes. Nonetheless, together they form a third hub of relationships since they are bound together structurally by an overlap link and are connected by four semantic parallels. Despite their differences, they both have multiple links to the seals and proclamations interludes, as mentioned above, and the trumpets interlude has a more distant link with the signs interlude.

In addition to these relationships among themselves, the interludes are also connected by being mutually connected to other passages in the book. The most important of these is the general setting of Chapters 4 and 5, to which all the interludes are connected, most of them by multiplex relationships. This is followed in importance by connections to the Prologue and the Epilogue.

In this latter case, the Narrative Interlude has the most connections because it is also part of the Narrative Framework, along with the Prologue and Epilogue, as has been previously discussed in Chapter 2 above. Nonetheless, most of the other interludes have direct connections with the beginning and the end of the book as well.

The seals, proclamations and narrative interludes also have connections with the body of Cycle 7. However, this is not altogether surprising since, in its function as a conclusion, the body of Cycle 7 has connections with most other major parts of the book. What is more surprising, however, is that the interludes have dense, multiplex relationships with 12:10-12, which is a small part of the body of the Signs Cycle. Furthermore, this sub-unit also has relationships with the Prologue, the Epilogue and the general setting of Chapters 4 and 5. Phenomena which are surprising, and which seem to intrude into an otherwise homogenous pattern, are often indicators of special prominence as will be discussed in Chapter 6 below.

It is true that Revelation, as an entire book, is characterized by a large number of parallel references which create a network of cross-references. But, even in this context, the interludes, being relatively short passages compared to the rest of the body of each cycle, have a noticeably large number of connections between themselves and other important parts of the book. The network is so dense and complex that it cannot even be conveniently displayed in a diagram.

This density of organization is highlighted by the following facts. Each interlude has many connections between itself and the body of its own cycle, and, therefore, clearly belongs in its own cycle, as was indicated in Chapter 3. However, apart from that, the overt connections between the interludes and the bodies of the other cycles are almost negligible.

4.4.4 The Main Points Arising

The main points arising from this discussion are three-fold. Firstly, the interludes are neither in a linear relationship like links in a single chain, nor even in a clear set of parallel or symmetric relations, as is typical of other parts of Revelation. However, they are, nonetheless, arranged in a systematic pattern, this pattern being characterized as a network. Complex as this pattern may be, it is possible to distinguish it from other patterns in the book.

This objective reality, along with the fact previously mentioned, that the interludes harmonize with the context of their particular cycle and clearly 'belong' in that place, constitute more evidence that this is not a haphazard arrangement. So, therefore, we can conclude that this arrangement is intentional, and, as such, contributes appropriately to the overall communicative purpose of the book.

Secondly, study of the detail of the interludes indicates that they are not independent texts, floating in an unattached way relative to what surrounds them. Even though they are not attached linearly, they nonetheless arise directly out of the general setting established in Chapters 4 and 5. This is made clear by considerable explicit repetition, and so the seals, signs and proclamations interludes all make reference to the heavenly throne room of Chapter 4. The Narrative Interlude, in turn, makes reference to the one living for ever who created the heaven and the earth (10:6//4:9 and 11), and the voice out of Heaven (10:8//4:1). Meanwhile, the Trumpets Interlude refers to the witnesses who are standing before the Lord of the earth, who also hear a loud voice out of Heaven saying, 'Come up here' (11:4 and 12//4:8,11 and 4:1), just as happened to John in Chapter 4.

This means that they are all anchored to the same starting point. Not only that, this anchor point is the same one to which the seals, the trumpets the signs, the bowls and the proclamations cycles as a whole are all also attached. See Chapter 5 for more discussion of these points.

This means, in turn, that the series of interludes are, in fact, in a parallel arrangement with the totality of the parts of the central cycles taken as a set, which are organized around the seven-fold motifs. In some ways, the interludes are more closely associated with the basic setting than the content of the seven-fold motifs, since, in most cases, what is described in the interludes actually takes place in the throne-room itself. In contrast to this, the events described in the rest of the bodies of the central cycles unfold, for the most part, on the earth.

Thirdly, as indicated at the outset, the interludes contribute to the Salvation Theme and move the communication flow of the book forward in a positive direction towards its ultimate goal. As Callow 1998,231 admits, 'it is not always easy in practice to decide what is thematic and what is not'. This is because it tends to be a process of gradual elimination as more and more aspects of the content, which contribute to the theme, are analyzed in detail, and are compared with the developing matrix of 'the prominent core' (ibid.,230) of material which comprises the theme of the book.

4.4.5 A Summary of the Content of the Salvation Theme

It is not possible to analyze all the sub-topics, and their concomitant sub-themes here, and thereby, create a complete picture of the book's theme. However, it is possible to draw out essential material from the interludes in order to create a basic overview of the Salvation Theme.

Being in a network arrangement then, each interlude contributes some information to the Salvation Theme, which confirms what is already known, or which will be confirmed by subsequent interludes. In addition, each one also contributes some unique information. It is interesting to note that in line with its function as part of the book's highest level of structure, the Narrative Interlude provides the most generic aspects of the thematic material.

In 10:7 reference is made to 'the mystery of God'. According to the context, this mystery was proclaimed by God himself to his servants the prophets. This is another way of referring to the topic of the book which was called a 'revelation' in 1:1. This is because the 'revelation' referred to in 1:1 is something which God also gave to his servants (cf. 'prophecy', in 1:3), in order to inform them about something which was previously hidden and, therefore, an unknown mystery to them . See also Paul's testimony in Rom. 16:25-6.

If this is the case, then the thematic information given concerning the topic is that it is certain to be accomplished and that the end, or the accomplishment, of this plan, is associated with the seventh trumpet. Within the literary context, this implies an element of rapidity since the seventh trumpet is sounded immediately after the double interlude, of which 10:7 is a part. The rest of the interlude, although couched in symbolic terms, suggests that, either the content of this mystery/prophecy, or the process of bearing witness to it (10:10-11 cf. 1:2,9 and 11:3-11), will be comprised of both pleasant (sweet) and unpleasant (bitter) aspects. This is confirmed by the following interlude (11:1-13), which takes up the sub-theme of the work of the prophetic witness and indicates that it is composed of both bitter apparent defeat (11:7-10), and sweet victory (11:5-6 and 11-13).

As is often the case with ambiguity, it may not be necessary to limit the referential meaning of the metaphor to one or the other of these alternatives. If the content of the message is being referred to, then the two apparently conflicting, but, nonetheless complementary, aspects of the theme are those being labeled 'judgment' and 'salvation'. As Beale 1999,546 has correctly pointed out 'The "gospel" of Christ, including both salvation and judgment, was prophetically "announced" by God...to his prophets in the Old Testament, and its inaugurated fulfillment ...to the prophets of the new age.'

> **QUOTE**
> **The 'mystery of God' has been called 'God's plan of redemption'... (which) we... do not know except by a revelation which God has supplied.**
> **Lenski 1943,319**

The extra information provided by this interlude is that the war waged by the beast against God's people, and even physical death, cannot be avoided. However, in spite of all that, God's plan of salvation will not be hindered. It will still be accomplished in and through, and over and above, those negative experiences, and that those responsible for the bitter experiences will suffer the consequences of His judgment.

The first part of the Seals Interlude (7:1-8) reveals that God's people will be protected from some or all of the judgments visited on the earth by direct decree emanating directly from God's throne-room (cf. 7:1,3,5 etc.). Even so, suffering due to other causes is still possible as 6:9 and 7:14 indicate.

The rest of the Seals Interlude (7:9-17), along with the Signs Interlude (14:1-5), and the Proclamations Interlude (19:1-8), indicate that God's people have a place in His throne room, which is the location of His government. In this haven of rest, they are beneficiaries of His presence and all His promises (7:9,14-17). From this vantage point, they recognize that their salvation comes from God alone (7:10; 19:2), they discover that the crimes committed against them have been avenged (19:2), and they rejoice in the accomplishment of all these blessings (14:2-3; 19:6). Two significant aspects of those blessings are that they are mandated to rule and reign with the Lamb, as they follow Him wherever He goes, and that they will end up being the bride at the wedding, with which the story ends.

Here in the interludes then, the majority of the thematic material concerning the Salvation Theme is presented. The same material is previewed in the Letters Cycle but is presented in terms of promises, which are motivational in nature rather than informational. As a consequence of this viewpoint, therefore, their accomplishment is seen as still future. Once again, with just a few extra details, the thematic material is reviewed in Cycle 7, being presented at this concluding point as if the accomplishment is already past and certain.

This then, is an outline of the referential information, which Revelation provides concerning the salvific aspects of God's plan. One thing is left ambiguous and that is whether the blessings can be enjoyed by the people of God in the immediate present, or whether they are reserved only for the future. This is where the objectivity of what the text actually says shades over into the interpretation of what the text means. However, Wilcock 1975,82-3 (quoting Maycock nd,89) is one interpreter who does not hesitate to claim a beginning for these blessings in the present:

For the vision of verses 13 to 17 of Chapter 7, 'refers, not only to the glory of the blessed ones in heaven, but to the life of the Christian soul in the world here and now. And who that, in this present pilgrimage, has been granted some glimpses of the "unsearchable riches of Christ" will affirm that the language of the seer is extravagant?'

Perhaps this is what the ambiguity is intended to imply.

Whether or not one agrees with this interpretation, what has been established with some degree of objectivity, is that the interludes are not unwanted intrusions which destroy the harmony of the text. On the contrary, they belong together as a series, are anchored in the same setting, and, between them, contribute a considerable part of the thematic information concerning God's plan of salvation. This is a plan, which not only enables God's people to survive, but also to rejoice even though surrounded by catastrophic judgment events and pursued by a deadly enemy.

4.5 The Relationship Between the Salvation Theme and the Judgment Theme

4.5.1 Some General Issues

The Salvation Theme has been explored in some detail because, historically, the interludes form part of the structure of the text which has not been well understood or explained.

By contrast, even if the seven-fold structure of each cycle has not been fully appreciated, the basic organization (seven seals followed by seven trumpets and so on) of the rest of the text in Chapters 4 to 19 has, nonetheless, already been elaborated many times over. There would be no debate either that, with the interludes removed from consideration, with only minor exceptions, what remains of the body of each of the five central cycles clearly talks about judgment.

Consequently, a brief statement of the prominent core of the Judgment Theme will be presented, without going into any more detail than is necessary for that, to serve as a prelude to the following discussion.

The passages under consideration are the body of each of the five central cycles after the interludes have been removed, because they were discussed above, and after the seventh sub-unit of each of Cycles 2-5 have been removed, because they form the setting to the following cycle. These texts are:

- the first six seals (6:1-17),
- the first six trumpets (8:7-9:21),
- the first six signs (12:1-13:18 and 14:6-20),
- the first six bowls (16:2-15), and then,
- the seven proclamations including their conclusion (18:1-24 and 19:11-21).

The significant referential information which is provided by these passages concerning the judgment aspect of God's revelation (the topic of the book 1:1) is set out in the following list. Because these passages are cyclic in nature, some of the information is presented more than once, even if embodied in different surface structure forms. Consequently, only representative references are given.

1) The judgments occur on the earth as a direct result of events happening in heaven (e.g. 6:1,3 etc.).
2) The judgments are catastrophic events which affect all domains of the physical creation including human beings (e.g. 6:2,4 etc., 16:2-15).
3) Some judgments only affect parts of creation or humanity (6:8; 8:12), while ultimately others affect the whole of the domain concerned (16:3), and will constitute a final judgment (6:12-17; 16:12-14; 19:11-21).
4) Spiritual beings who, either directly or indirectly, have caused some of the suffering on the earth, will be included in God's plan of judgment (12:5-10; 18:2; 19:19-20).
5) Judgment will also be a vindication and a victory for the people of God (16:4-6, 19:14).

4.5.2 Some Complications

It has been said before, and so it bears saying again, that Revelation, whichever way you look at it, is a complex book. Consequently, even though we have provided a simple and straight-forward summary of the Judgment Theme above, nonetheless, it has to be admitted that there are some complications. With regard to establishing the theme of a text Callow 1998,232 says that:

> 'in practice we will probably find a residue, the status of which seems initially uncertain. Indeed our final decision may depend on just how detailed we want our theme to be, depending on the purpose of our analysis'.

Difficulties often arise in the case of reason-result and generic-specific semantic relationships, because it is not always immediately obvious which side of the relationship is the most prominent. Generally speaking, the result part of the relationship is more prominent, and is what is included in the theme. However, if the reason part is accorded special prominence in some way, then it too may be a candidate for inclusion in the theme. Likewise, the generic part or the specific part of the relationship may be more prominent, depending on which other indicators the author has placed in the context.

In Revelation 12, the dragon is formally introduced into the narrative and reappears again in 20:2. Referentially at least, he would appear to be an important personage, and so the question arises as to whether he, and the events he is involved in, should not be included in the theme.

In Chapter 12 his appearance is necessary as a reason to explain other events. The conclusion of his story in 12:17, which is the most naturally prominent part of a sequential embedded narrative like this, but in the context of the whole book, it is actually an explanation. This explanation provides the *reason* why the people of God suffer unjustly. Furthermore, within the immediate context of the chapter, the presence of the word 'because', in verses 10 and 12 also indicate that what happens to the dragon is a *reason* for other events which are more important.

Since the activities of the dragon provide reasons for other events, his role is consequently downgraded in importance and is not a candidate for thematic status. In 12:12, however, this lack of importance is balanced by the fact that the reason clause provides support for a volitional text. It is the motivation for the direct command ('be glad') and the warning ('woe to,' or, 'lament') which precede it. In such a case, it shares in the prominence of the volitional text and, therefore, could be a candidate for thematic status.

In Chapter 20 certain aspects of the dragon's career are again described, and this includes his final end (vv.7-10), which would seem to be naturally prominent. Once again, however, in the context of the whole book, this is only a reason which explains why the people of God can hope for an eternity unmarred by the presence of evil and persecution, as the following body of Cycle 7 makes clear.

In the context of the overall ABA'B' structure of Chapter 20 itself, the presence of volitional import material in verse 6 accords special prominence to verses 4-6. This, in turn, puts the victory of the people of God in section B in focus. This is in opposition to the defeat of the devil in section B' .

Finally, for other reasons, Chapter 20 has been analyzed as a setting, which means that it is not a candidate for thematic status at all. The conclusion then, is that, from a literary point of view, the author has organized the structure of the text in such a way so as to downgrade the importance of this personage. This, in turn, communicates the message that he is relatively unimportant in the overall scheme of things.

This is the case from a linguistic point of view, even though from a theological point of view, the identity, career and final end of the dragon would seem to be important. This apparent clash of viewpoints gives pause for thought, and is one of the reasons why this book has been written, as will be developed further in Chapter 8.

It is for the above reasons then, that the dragon is not included specifically in the thematic material contributing to the Judgment Theme.

In the light of these considerations, the generic information which is included in the body of Cycle 7 is deemed to be more prominent than the specific information included in the setting, and this is reflected in items 4 and 5 in the listing in the previous section. The dragon is, therefore, included in the theme (in item 4 above), but only as an implicit member of a generic grouping. This is a balanced solution which takes account of the fact that there are reasons for according this personage thematic status, but at the same time it takes account of the fact that the author seems to have intentionally down-graded his status, within the context of the book as a piece of literary architecture.

Heimerdinger 1999 provides a wide-ranging discussion of the notion of foregrounding in the Old Testament. The corollary of his discussion, is relevant here. What he says is this: by an 'array of pragmatic, semantic and grammatical criteria' (op.cit.263) an author can intentionally bring a particular personage or element of the discourse into the foreground in the hearer's mind. If that is the case then, by the same token, he can also do the opposite and cause a personage or event, to be relegated firmly into the background in the readers' appreciation of the total discourse.

4.5.3 Some Conclusions

The aim of the present study is to elucidate the structure of Revelation rather than explain all the aspects of its message. Nonetheless, the structure of a book cannot be reasonably discussed in a vacuum without some reference to the message it carries, since a linguistic structure has no reason to exist if it is completely divorced from its message.

Consequently, in the present chapter the main themes of the book have been evoked, in an attempt to clarify some of the structural issues, especially those concerning the interludes. At the same time however, a great deal more could be said about the detail of those themes which must be left unsaid at this point.

What needs to be said, even so, is that some conclusions concerning the major themes can be derived from an understanding of the structure. What has been observed is that the two themes are presented alternately throughout the book. In Cycle 1 and Cycle 7 they alternate many times at the sub-unit level throughout the cycle. In Cycles 2-4 and 6 (Cycle 5 having no interlude) they alternate just once in the cycle with the seven-fold motif part carrying the Judgment Theme, and the interlude carrying the Salvation Theme.

In this way, the two themes, to a large extent, are developed separately, and if each of the different parts is taken in isolation, then each theme could be studied and described separately. However, this is not the whole story. As mentioned above, there would be no great interest in developing the two themes in total isolation, and little point in putting them in the same book, if they never related to each other in some way.

The themes come together closely in Cycle 1, which foresees the possibility that the judgment of one group of people implies salvation for another. This concept is taken up in the conclusion of the book (Cycle 7). Here it is made clear that the banishment of evil, as a result of God's plan of judgment, is the direct corollary of, and the necessary condition for, the full enjoyment of His plan of salvation.

The themes also come together in the middle of the book in Chapter 12. Here, the first two Signs are entwined together in the same narrative, and it is the only place in the first six cycles where more than one element of the seven-fold motifs co-occur in the same sub-unit. The woman and child clearly benefit from God's gracious plans for good, since they are protected and provided for (12:5,6,14-6), while the dragon justly suffers the opposite. In the middle of the story, and the center of an ABA' structure, a clear statement is made that one event, the throwing down of the dragon from heaven to earth, is, at the same time, a salvation event for some, and a woeful catastrophe for others (12:10-12).

This insight leads to a reevaluation of the two themes as it becomes clear that, in reality, there are not two distinct themes, but two strands contributing to a single, more complex theme. In other words, there is only one plan, not two separate ones, and there is only one series of events not two.

This view of judgment as an integral part of God's plan of salvation for his people is not a new insight, but has its roots in the Old Testament. Nahum is just one example of this, as explained in Schooling 2024b.

However, the plan is a double-edged sword which cuts in two directions and each individual event can be viewed from different points of view, depending on the standing of the witness. So, for example, the judgment and eventual banishment of evil from the world is a liberation and a victory for the followers of the Lamb (e.g.16:4-7, 19:11-21). Yet, at the same time, the salvation of the people of God is a defeat, and a source of chagrin, for those left behind, or outside this plan (e.g.11:11-13, 21:7-8).

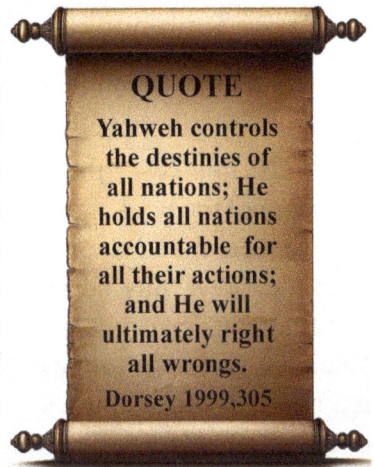

> **QUOTE**
>
> **Yahweh controls the destinies of all nations; He holds all nations accountable for all their actions; and He will ultimately right all wrongs.**
>
> **Dorsey 1999,305**

When this is understood, it can be seen that, things are not exactly as they may seem to be at first glance. The salvation aspect of the message is in second place, in terms of the quantity of text devoted to this issue, but in terms of overall importance it ranks in first place. This is because the judgment aspect contributes to the completeness of God's plan of salvation. Thus, salvation, and not judgment per se, is the final goal of the plan, and an appreciation of God's plan of salvation is the main aim of the referential part of the message of the book. This is confirmed by the way the book ends in Cycle 7, where the grandeur and the splendor of the ultimate phase of God's plan of salvation is clearly in focus.

4.6 The Function of the Volitional Import Material

The thematic material which has been discussed above, has been limited to those parts of the texts which are referential in nature and contribute to the informational development of the text. However, there are also portions of text which do not contribute directly to the informational flow of the message, but rather to the volitional nature of the message. That is, the part of the text whose function is to influence the behavior of its readers/hearers.

For the most part, it is the Narrative Framework which carries the volitional import material but, this is a distinct part of the structural organization of the book as has been previously discussed in Chapter 2.

Since this is so, the volitional material could possibly be described as another theme which overlaps with the salvation/judgment theme. Having said that, however, it must not be overlooked that the volitional material is also presented in other parts of the book. For example, a large proportion of the body of Cycle 1, the seven letters, is composed of exhortations, promises and warnings.

In addition, volitional text re-appears in 12:12 in a strategic place in the middle of the book, where the judgment and salvation strands come together as mentioned above. Then there are also other texts like 16:15, 18:4, 18:20 and 19:5 which contain volitional import material, and all contribute to a build up of momentum towards the end of the book.

In this case, the volitional material is not following the general structure of the book, nor even one part of it, like the Narrative Framework, but weaves in and out and appears in different places in the structure. In such a case, it may be preferable to analyze this aspect of the book as a simultaneous prosodic theme. It would be a good candidate for a prosody since the volitional import is signaled at the beginning of the book and is maintained throughout as an important aspect of the text, without being overtly indicated very often. As such, it runs like a prosody in parallel to all aspects of the text including the structural organization and the thematic development.

An alternative solution would be, therefore, to not treat the volitional import material as a theme at all. Since it is a different kind of material, it is best to keep it separate, and to not treat it as part of the structural, nor even the thematic development. Instead, it can be characterized as the body of data which indicates the author's *purpose* in writing the book in the first place. As Callow 1998,132-33 explains:

> Human beings are purposive. Speech and all other human activity have some purpose behind it. Usually we know the purpose or can make a good guess. ... the mental transition towards purposes is an underlying and permanent trend in human thinking.

Any of the above proposals could be used to relate the volitional material to the rest of the book, depending on the exact purpose of the analysis. However, it is the latter solution which is the preferred one here. This is because, in this way, it is easier to maintain an element of hierarchy and to emphasize the point that the volitional material is more important than the thematic material. This is true precisely for the reason that it embodies the author's ultimate purpose and goal.

The reason why Revelation exists is not merely to provide information, even though knowledge of God's plan for the universe is a fascinating and amazing possibility. This information is only present to act as a vehicle for the author's more far-reaching purpose, which is to radically influence his hearers' behavior on issues that are literally issues of eternal life and death.

His desire is that his hearers should benefit positively from the salvation aspects of God's plan, and avoid the negative aspects of judgment. But, in order to do so, they have to react appropriately to his message. Thus, it can be seen, that the salvation and judgment thematic strands are only planks in a larger structure. That structure is a message which is almost exclusively intended to bring about change (or to confirm an already existing appropriate life-style) in the people who receive it. It is only secondarily intended to provide them with interesting information.

Heimerdinger 1999,221-2 referring to Labov's insights (1967 and 1972), has this to say about narratives:

> Labov explains that a narrative which contains only informative material is not a complete narrative. It may perform a referential function, but it lacks significance. Evaluation is the means by which the significance of the story...is indicated. In other words, the narrative has a point, a raison d'être, and the speaker (or author) uses certain evaluative devices to establish and sustain the point of the story. Evaluation involves the interference of the speaker in the factual report and as such it belongs to the expressive import of a narrative.

Revelation is not a true narrative and does not contain much expressive (i.e. expression of emotion) import material. Its informative material may be characterized rather, as a dramatic exposition, which has a volitional import, but, nonetheless, Heimerdinger's remarks apply equally well. This is because an exposition without a point does not have a 'raison d'être'. Revelation is not simply a theological treatise, which expounds the content of God's plan for the world, with its judgment aspects and its salvation aspects. In reality, it is an *exhortation* designed to touch the heart of God's people and to influence them to seek after his salvation.

Exhortation, like evaluation, involves the 'interference' of the author in the narrative which is exactly what happens in the Narrative Framework, and the other places where hortatory material intrudes into the overall, informational development. This interference, and involvement, by John in his message, is the signal that there is more than one thing going on at once. This, in turn, reminds the reader that the primary purpose of the book is not to convey content, but to convince the consciences of those who will hear the message.

Kathleen Callow, in personal communication, has suggested that grammatical imperatives like 'Rejoice' (12:12, 18:20) or 'Praise God' (19:5) may also be interpreted as expressive import material since they address attitudes and value systems. This is no doubt true, as it would be true of imperatives like 'Repent' in Cycle 1. However, this does not rule out the possibility of treating this material as volitional, since in the context of the book itself (see, for example, some of the interludes like 14:1-3 and 19:1-8), the attitudes, which are underlying the above words, are clearly lived out by means of specific actions.

However, this suggestion does raise an important point that Revelation, as a whole, is not devoid of expressive material, even if it is mainly implicit. Consequently, it can be deduced that John believes that his hearers should take note of what he is saying, and do as is as being suggested in the book. This issue of the expressive strand which pervades the whole book deserves further elucidation.

This then, is the role of the volitional import material. Because this function has such an over-riding importance, it is helpful to keep it separate in the analysis, rather than treating it as another aspect of the thematic material. For this reason it will be discussed further in Chapter 6.

4.7 Conclusion

The aim in this chapter has been to explore certain aspects of the thematic content and development of the book, in order to arrive at a more complete understanding of certain aspects of the structural organization of the book. The primary concern was to confirm the existence of the interludes and to clarify their function.

It was observed, firstly, that most of them fit into a regular structural pattern in a predictable place, in the seven-fold organization. The exceptions of Cycles 4 and 5 have been noticed in passing, and will be discussed further in Chapter 6 below.

But then, secondly, there is also a regularity about their function, in that they all contribute primarily to the Salvation Theme. Not only that, but they are the only parts of Cycles 2-6 which exclusively contribute to the thematic development of the salvation aspect of God's plan.

There is a network of semantic relationships between them all. This indicates that, in addition to the structural pattern, there is also a thematic or conceptual pattern, which all serves as evidence to support the view that the presence of the interludes is not haphazard but is intentional.

Even though their relationship is not linear, the point has been made that alternating thematic emphases in separate blocks of text, which are in an ABA'B' pattern, is a form of literary architecture which is just as valid as the form, which relates and advances the thematic material like the links of a chain. For the sake of completeness, it should also be noted that networks of relationships, which are even more difficult to discern and describe, are equally valid types of relationships. This is so, because, in fact, they represent more accurately the real nature of human relationships and experience, than do the more simplistic, linear or alternating patterns.

In this discussion of the interludes, it was not possible to take account of the more formal structure of the cycles without also taking some account of the primary themes and their inter-relationship. This is appropriate since a linguistic structure, even if it can be easily observed and described, cannot exist and has no meaningful function, apart from the content of the message which it is serving to communicate.

Similarly, the study of a structure can be an interesting challenge, but it has no real usefulness, unless it serves as a vehicle to a better understanding of the content of the text which it embodies. This also needs to be stated and borne in mind as the discussion advances, that the real purpose underlying a study of the structure of a book is ultimately to better understand and appropriate its message.

In the case of Revelation, progress is being made on this score, because the study of the thematic material gave rise to the observation that there were elements of the text, which did not contribute to the information flow of the book. These parts of the text were analyzed as contributing explicitly to the volitional import of the book as a whole.

It was proposed that the most helpful way of understanding the function of these texts was not to treat them as another aspect of the thematic development, but rather to see them as an embodiment of the author's overriding purpose. They do not contribute so much to the *how* of the author's work of construction, but instead they reveal *why* he wrote his book in the first place.

Discussion of the thematic development and the volitional import necessarily involved making distinctions between some things, which are more important for the author's purpose, than others. This has, therefore, provided a brief preview of, and an insight into, the importance of the notion of prominence, which will be developed in more detail in Chapter 6.

Thus far then, a general overview of the book has been completed at the structural level and also in terms of content and purpose. However, as has often been repeated, this book is fascinatingly complex, and so, even though a general overview serves to clarify some issues in order to understand the book in terms of general principles, by the same token it has not taken care of all the details by explaining the exceptions.

Neither has it fully accounted for parts of the text which do not fit neatly into the broad outline so far described. This exploration of the finer detail, and a clarification of the different levels of emphasis and prominence, will be the subject of the following chapters.

THE WAY
FORWARD
EXPLORE MORE
CAREFULLY SOME OF
THE FINER DETAIL...

APPENDIX 4

PREFACE

This Appendix has been placed here to provide extra technical information relating to the analysis of the Interludes for those who wish to explore these matters further. There is no need to read this Appendix if this extra information is not required, for the technical information already given in the main text is sufficient for the general purpose of understanding the structural organization of the book. The Appendix just broadens out what has already been explained.

In particular, it contains more precise information to explain and support the division into units which was described in Chapter 4.

All other readers are invited to move on straight away to Chapter 5, where we will be reviewing, and exploring some of the finer details of the seven cycles.

APPENDIX 4

Ancillary Information Pertaining to the Analysis of the Interludes

A4.1 Evidence for the Division into Units

A4.1.1 A General Explanation

In this appendix evidence will be provided in summary form, to indicate on what basis the text of the Interludes was divided into units for this study. In order to keep the material manageable, the information will be provided in abbreviated form.

The main aim at this stage is to demonstrate that text can be divided into units on the basis of linguistic evidence, and that this evidence can be made available for perusal by other analysts. For more detailed explanation of this nature please refer back to Appendix A2.1.1.

The abbreviations used in the presentation of the data are as follows:

D = Differences permitting a division into distinct units. Normally reference is made to the division at the beginning of the unit and also to that at the end of the unit.

IC = Internal Coherence requiring that similar units be grouped together

F = Function of the unit.

A4.1.2 The Interlude of the Seals Cycle 7:1-17

D: Change of topic, participants and situation. A break in the sequence of seven seals.

IC: Parallelism between 'after this' and 'after these things' (7:1,9),

The whole interlude is composed of salvation theme material as opposed to judgment theme material in the preceding and following passages. Although it is not obvious in the surface structure the consensus of opinion is that the topic of both parts of the interlude are the same, namely, the people of God seen as a complete group. The structure of both parts is a combination of a parallel structure composed of description and direct speech followed by a coda. Even though description and direct speech occur in the preceding seals, these constituent parts are not in a parallel relationship. The fifth seal possibly has a parallel structure but the evidence is weak.

Part 1. 7:1-8

D: Change of topic, participants and situation.

IC: Same participants and same basic event (sealing) throughout. The parallelism is established by the repetition of the reference to harming (synonyms) the earth, the sea and the trees (7:1,2 and 3). There is no good reason for this extensive repetition in such a short span except for the intention to create a parallel structure.

> **A. Description**: John sees four angels holding the four winds back from harming the earth, sea and trees v.1
>
> > **B. Description**: Another angel with a seal of the living God who cries out with a loud voice to the four angels who have power to harm the earth and the sea v.2
> >
> > > **C. Direct Speech:** The Angel says: 'Do not harm the earth, the sea or the trees until we have sealed God's people on their forehead.' v.3

Coda: John is made aware of the result of this sealing activity. Namely, 144,000 people are sealed v.4-8. The Coda is composed of a generic resume (v.4) and a specific list (vv.5-8).

Part 2. 7:9-17

D: Change of grammatical subject (even though the underlying topic of the whole section remains the same), participants and location.

IC: Same situation and same basic event (worship) throughout.

> **A. Description**: John sees a great crowd standing before the throne in Heaven with palms in their hands v.9
>
> > **B. Direct Speech**: They cry out with a loud voice: 'Salvation to our God, sitting on the throne and to the Lamb'. v.10
>
> **A' Description:** The angels standing around the throne, the Elders and the four creatures fall before the throne and worship v.11
>
> > **B'** Direct Speech: Blessing, glory, wisdom, thanks, honor, power and strength (7 items) to God. v.12

Coda: John is made aware of the identity of the principal participants in this worship activity, namely the people dressed in white robes v.13-17. This Coda forms part of the Narrative Framework (see Chapter 2).

A4.1.3 The Interlude of the Trumpets Cycle 11:1-13

D: 11:1-2 is interpreted as an overlap link. In this passage John's involvement fades out, apparently uncompleted. The same passage sets the stage for the following description of the two witnesses which introduces a new topic, participants and situation.

IC: The narrative concerning the two witnesses along with parallel references to 'the city' at 11:2,8 and 13.

A. Setting 11:1-2
B. The miraculous ministry of the two witnesses 11:3-6
C. The earthly destiny of the two witnesses 11:7-10
B' The miraculous confirmation of their ministry 11:11-12
A' Conclusion 11:13

Notes: Being an overlap link, 11:1-2 can be viewed in different ways. The imperatives (rise, measure, leave out, do not measure) would seem to be dominant, but they only concern John's story and, as such, are only relevant to the conclusion of the passage 10:1-11:2. As far as the interlude as a whole (11:1-13) is concerned, the dominant concepts in vv.1-2 would seem to be God (in Heaven), those worshiping Him, the city, the nations and the time period.

The parallels between A and A' are God (in Heaven), the response to Him of worshiping or giving glory, the city. The parallels between B and B' are the concept of miraculous activity, standing//stood, enemies, a time frame stated in days. Each of the sub-units have a time reference which is unusual since time references are rare in the book. 'The Lord' or 'God' occur in each of the sub-units.

A4.1.4 The Interlude of the Signs Cycle 14:1-5

D: Change of topic, participants and location. A change from the judgment theme to the salvation theme.
IC: A single embedded narrative with a single set of participants. A coherent parallel structure with significant cross-references throughout.

A. The Lamb standing on Mt. Sion with the 144,000 14:1
B. The sound in Heaven of harps playing 14:2
B' The sound in Heaven of a new song 14:3a
A' No one could learn the song except the 144,000 who are purchased from the earth 14:3b

Coda: John is made aware of the identity of the principal participants in this activity 14:4-5

a. They are not defiled, celibates they are 14:4a
b. They are the ones who follow the Lamb wherever he goes 14:4b
b' They are the ones who were purchased as first-fruits 14:4c
a' No lie was found in them, unblemished they are 14:5

Notes: Constituents A and A' of the interlude are in parallel because of the specific repetition of the 144,000 each time qualified by a passive perfect participle. 'The Lamb' also occurs in A and also in the coda as does 'his Father' and 'God'.

Constituents a and a' of the coda are in parallel because of the similarity of the central concept (undefiled/unblemished) and also because of the similarity of their grammatical construction.

Constituents b and b' are in parallel because they amplify information previously given in constituents A and A' of the body of the unit. Constituent b. of the coda says that the 144,000 follow the Lamb wherever he goes, while in Body A. they are with him on Mt. Sion. The reference to the Lamb's name being marked on their foreheads (v.1) could well be interpreted as signifying ownership in the case of slaves/servants, or as a commitment to follow in the case of soldiers who would wear their master's colors.

Coda b' says that they are the first fruits of those purchased from humanity, whereas in Body A' they were previously described as those purchased from the earth.

A4.1.5 The Interlude of the Proclamations Cycle 19:1-8

D: Change of topic, participants and location. Change from Judgment Theme to Salvation Theme. It is followed by a coda which is a section of Narrative Framework, which also contains direct speeches, but these are preceded by full forms of the verb 'to say' rather than participles.

IC: A series of direct speeches each with a similar internal structure. The structure of the whole is a concentric structure followed by a coda. The coda, nonetheless, is tightly integrated into its context and is intentionally attached to the interlude unit which precedes. This is because there is a clear tail-head link attaching the two units (the repetition of 'the marriage of the Lamb' in verses 7 and 9), because they both have similar structures organized around a series of direct speeches, and because they both contribute to the sub-theme of worship.

A. 19:1-3 Personage: 'a great crowd'.

Present participle: 'saying':
direct speech 1: 'Hallelujah',
followed by TWO reason clauses, introduced by 'because',
direct speech 2: 'Hallelujah'.

(Note: this is NOT introduced by a participle and is specifically stated to be a 'second' speech by the same participants)

B. 19:4 Personages: The 24 elders and the 4 living creatures (before) the throne.

Present participle: 'saying':
direct speech: 'Amen, Hallelujah'.

B' 19:5 Personage: 'a voice from the throne'.
Present participle: 'saying':
direct speech: 'Praise God...'.

A' 19:6-8 Personages: 'a great (synonym) crowd', present participle: 'saying'
direct speech 1: 'Hallelujah' followed by a reason clause, introduced by 'because'
direct speech 2: 'Let us Rejoice' followed by TWO reason clauses, introduced by 'because'.

Coda: Being a Minor Component of the Narrative Framework 19:9-10
Personage: The Bowl Angel of 17:1 (implicit)
direct speech 1: indicative verb: 'he says to me' 'Write: Blessed' v.9a
direct speech 2: indicative verb: 'he says to me' 'These words are true' v.9b, followed by John's response as an element of the Narrative Framework v.10a
direct speech 3: indicative verb: 'he says to me', 'Don't worship me, Worship God' v.10b, followed by a commentary/explanation introduced by 'for'.

F: Its primary function is that of the interlude of Cycle 6

The Narrative Framework unit contributes to the overall thrust of the cycle and the interlude, in that it continues the motif of the proclamation, being a series of direct speeches. It is, at the same time, a book-level prominence feature contributing to the hortatory objective of the book. The interlude is the last and, therefore, the concluding interlude, and the entire unit (19:1-10) contributes to the complex preliminary conclusion at the end of Cycles 2-6 (19:1-21).

A4.2 The Relationships Between the Interludes

A4.2.1 The Seals Interlude 7:1-17 & the Proclamations Interlude 19:1-8

There are 3 structural similarities between these two interludes. These are: direct speech as a major component, the presence of an element of the Narrative Framework, and codas. In addition, there are more than 10 semantic relationships including references to the general setting of Chapters 4 and 5, and references to God's servants, glory and power, salvation, Amen.

A4.2.2 The Narrative Framework Interlude 10:1-11:2 and the Trumpets Interlude 11:1-13

There is 1 structural relationship (overlap link), and 4 semantic relationships: prophesy, nations and tongues and peoples, finish (referring to an aspect of God's work/plan), and the concepts of bitter/unpleasant experience and sweet/pleasant experience. The concept of witness is central in 11:1-13 and also implicit in 10:1-11:2 since John is designated as a witness elsewhere in other parts of the Narrative Framework (1:2).

A4.2.3 The Seals Interlude

The Seals Interlude has 3 relationships with the Trumpets Interlude, 4 with the Narrative Interlude including 1 structural, and 5 with the Signs Interlude including 1 structural.

A4.2.4 The Proclamations Interlude

The Proclamations Interlude has 2 relationships with the Trumpets Interlude, 3 with the Narrative Interlude including 1 structural, and 7 with the Signs Interlude including 1 structural.

A4.2.5 The sub-unit 12:10-11

The sub-unit 12:10-11 is connected to the interludes and the Prologue, the Epilogue and the cycle settings, by the presence of a loud voice from Heaven, the Lamb, salvation, power, be glad, witness and tabernacle.

LIFE IS NOT LINEAR

My two daughters are adamant. Adamant and in agreement about one thing in particular : the straight-line theories of ivory-tower academia do not match well with the intricacies of real life.

They both decided individually to train to become teachers, and so they both quickly learned that lesson plans are an essential part of the teacher's equipment. What they were taught was 1,2,3 ducks in a row, like all good well-formed discourses, of course. An Introduction, the Body of information to be transmitted, and a Conclusion. Then once you have done one, you do another one and so on until the whole unit is taken care of – all lined up neatly like beads on a string, straight lines in a series, one after the other.

Sounds really good, it's all neat and tidy. You know exactly what you are doing and where you are going. The theory was that a straight line gets you the fastest from the beginning to the end, as economy of effort was in view. The purpose, in theory at least, was that this method would require less work and effort for the teacher, and also for the students.

So, as long as they themselves were confined inside the walled enclosure of the ivory tower, carefully shielded from the vicissitudes of the real life beyond, they believed all this nonsense. This innocence continued for quite some time until the fateful day arrived when they had to sally forth and, courage in both hands (or lost somewhere in the depths of their bulging brief-case), to face the… yes, what was it you said ?

Yes, a real live classroom. A classroom full of chaos, uncertainties and a cacophony of noise. Oh the noise! Impossible to even think in a straight line, let alone talk in a straight line, can't even walk in a straight line! Why? Because a normal classroom is full of bodies. Little bodies, which writhe and move in all directions with most unexpected noises of all kinds emanating from those little mouths, with such a high pitched squeaking velocity: it was enough to drive you mad !! (For myself, I still remember the antics which we used to purposely get up to in order to make the student teachers' life a misery !!)

In no time at all, they found that the linear plan idea did not work. Barely had the first few words of the introduction trickled from their mouth when that grinning little toothless monkey over there (there must be one permanently in residence in every classroom) put their hand up and interrupted you in the middle of a sentence (would you believe it, in the middle of a sentence no less) and declared in a loud screeching voice for all to hear that they needed to make an emergency visit to the bathroom – right now!

You have barely got over the embarrassment of the long litany of titters, and barely muffled comments on the matter, and barely managed to get the monkey ushered back into his seat, when you try to start again. But horrors, you have forgotten where you were in this beautiful linear plan, and have to go back to the beginning and start again !!

Enough said. The most important skill, they discovered very quickly, was not so much creating a lesson plan, but learning how to repeat yourself creatively, in such a way that no one ever really notices !!

It was the same in John's day. He was a teacher too, confronted with the same task of transmitting important information to real life people. It is not surprising then, that he repeated himself, and made progress by talking in cycles.

Yes, life is like that – it is full of curve balls, variables of all kinds and repetitions. We cannot live without repeating ourselves many times over. So it is not at all surprising either, that we cannot talk to each other, in real life that is, without repeating ourselves in many and various ways.

That is one thing which we can be adamant about : life is not linear.

It is ridiculous to try and insist that it is.

CHAPTER 5
The Seven Cycles Revisited
5.1 Introduction

In Chapter 3 the more obvious issues concerning the body of Revelation were discussed and it was proposed that it is composed of seven cycles, each of which is organized around a seven-fold motif. Then, in Chapter 4, the organization and the function of the interludes was discussed. With these principal features of the structure in place, it is now possible in this chapter to review the seven cycles in more detail. This will be in order to present the more complex features which contribute to a full understanding of the organization of the book. This will include clarification concerning the settings, the setting and closure of Cycles 2-6, the organization of Cycle 7, and the contribution of the seven-fold motifs.

5.2 The Settings

It was proposed in Chapter 3 that each cycle is introduced by a setting. Having said this, it is important not to succumb to the temptation to use this label as a convenience. That is, to use it to categorize parts of the text whose function may be unclear, but which, in fact, are not settings at all. Although this term is well-known, within the context of discourse analysis it has become something of a technical term with its own particular definition.

No message can be communicated in a vacuum, for of necessity it has to come out of somewhere, and that 'somewhere' is called a setting. As Callow 1998,175 puts it, 'the milieu of a communication is its locational or notional setting...(it) pervades the whole and sets its distinctive mark on each message'. Callow goes on to say (ibid.) that 'each writer selects a sub-world as the milieu of his communication'. The reason for this is because there are many possible settings. Therefore, it is clear that the setting for a particular message is not arbitrary, but it is the one which best suits the message which is to follow, and the one which best suits the author's purpose.

Callow refers here to a 'sub-world' which is the same as the different referential worlds which were previously described. In the case of Revelation, the book makes reference to two different referential worlds (or sub-worlds). The book, as a whole, is set in the human, physical universe, more specifically on the island of Patmos. This basic fact is established by the setting for the book as a whole which is called the Prologue (1:1-11) as was described in Chapter 2.

The content of the visions which comprise the body of the book, however, refer to, and therefore, need to be understood, in the context of another referential world, namely a heavenly, spiritual world. This is also already indicated in the Prologue (1:1-2), although few details are given at this point, of the nature of this other world. This particular referential world is then described in more detail in the settings which prepare the way for each cycle of visions. Thus, it is by keeping track of the settings, that it is possible to keep track of the framework of interpretation, which should be used to understand any particular part of the text.

Going on further, it should be borne in mind that most of the research accomplished so far in the domain of discourse analysis, has been based on narrative texts. Consequently, it is usually assumed that settings are components of the narrative-type text. As Callow 1998,291 explains:

> In general, the term 'setting' has been used for the introductory configuration in a narrative unit, usually identifying the main participants in the major configuration which follows, and frequently giving locational and temporal information also... The setting configuration foregrounds a total scenario in the light of which the message that follows is to be understood.

Even though Revelation as a whole is not a true narrative, it, nonetheless, has close affinities with narrative because of the all-pervasive influence of the Narrative Framework described in Chapter 2. This impression is further reinforced because many of the visions, which John sees, are presented in the form of embedded narratives. Even if this were not the case, all texts have to be located in the context of some sub-world or another, and this would have to be indicated by the author at the outset.

As Callow 1998,292 summarizes this area of on-going investigation: 'It is assumed that setting and circumstance relations will be found to have a counterpart in theme-based texts, (for example, hortatory and expository texts) but more research will be needed before this can be adequately demonstrated'.

In resume then, a setting has two primary functions. Firstly, that of identifying an appropriate frame of reference, or referential world, within the context of which, the following message should be understood. Then, secondly, that of introducing the most significant personages who either participate in (if it is a true narrative), or, influence in some way, the content of the text which follows.

Looking back then at the setting of Cycle 1 (1:9-20) in the light of the above comments, it can be seen that it does provide an appropriate context for the body of the cycle. In the first instance, there is the situation of John on Patmos (1:9), which identifies the person who received the vision, and the physical place where it all unfolded.

> **QUOTE**
>
> **Timelessly, for the Christians of all the ages, it is true that: '*En Patmo* we suffer; but *en Pneumati*, we reign'.**
>
> **Wilcock 1975,42**

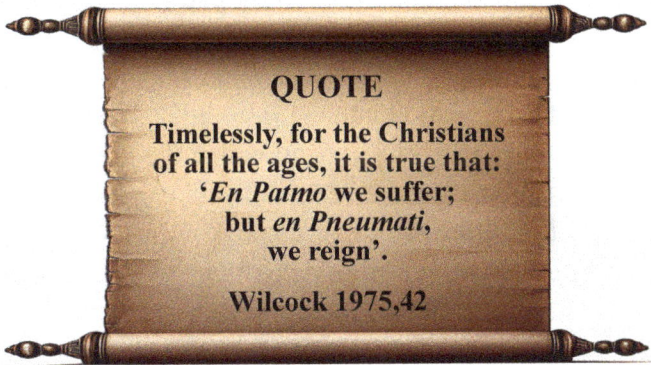

This situation is the context for the whole book, and not just the first cycle. This is why, as previously noted in Chapter 2 section 5.3, the best way to account for all that the data implies, is to interpret 1:9-11 as an overlap link. This link unit then functions both as part of the Prologue and also as part of the setting to Cycle 1, at the same time.

It is into this situation which the glorified Christ then comes (1:10-13), bringing something of the heavenly realm down into John's physical world. This personage in this particular form (for the Risen Christ pervades the whole book, but in different forms in different places) then dominates the rest of the cycle, being the participant who dictates the messages. Then, as indicated in Chapter 3, he has aspects of his being, as described in the setting (1:13-16), reiterated in each of the seven parts. The same is true for the settings of the other cycles, since each one provides an appropriate frame of reference for what follows.

Within the constraints of this study, it is only possible to establish the main points of each issue. In this case, as in many others, a lot more could be said. For example, the fact that Christ was dead but is now living (1:18) is a significant motivation for the exhortations which follow. The Christians who are imperfect and struggling against persecution, can be encouraged to go on to glory by this example of one who passed through death, and then went on to live for ever.

5.3 The Setting of Cycles 2-6

Chapters 4-5 is one of those passages in Revelation, which are quite literally awesome. Firstly, it is because their content is awe-inspiring. Then, secondly, because there is a sense of mystery and uncertainty about the author's method of presenting his material and, therefore, about how the hearer is intended to understand his message. As usual, it is helpful to begin by taking account of those things which are obvious, and then building by increments towards an understanding of those things which are less obvious.

It is not difficult to discern that 4:1 is a new beginning in that the seven messages, which the hearer was told to expect in 1:11, have been completed and something else begins. Nonetheless, a sense of connection and transition with what precedes is provided by the phrase 'after these things'. This sense of connection is confirmed by the indication that the voice which John hears in the context of 4:1, is the same voice that had spoken to him previously. In technical terms, it is still the same voice speaking, which was introduced in the setting of the previous cycle at 1:10. So then, it can be stated that the first two participants remain the same, and this sameness establishes a connection with what precedes, but for the rest, everything else changes.

The most important change is the change of situation or 'milieu' in Callow's terms (1998,175), which, in this case, also involves a change of referential world. In the first cycle, John was on Patmos and, although he had a heavenly vision, it was because the heavenly personage invaded his world and spoke to him in that context.

Now, in 4:1 it is John who leaves Patmos behind and is invited to visit the heavenly realm. It is in this new context that the next series of visions unfold, and, as far as can be deduced, so do all the other visions in the book. After this initial transition, the first two participants fade into the background, and a completely new set of participants are introduced (4:2, 4 and v.6, and again at 5:6). Even though one of these participants is, in fact, the Christ, He is revealed in a different form in 5:5-6. John is told that it is the Lion of Judah who is being presented to him, but when he turns to look, he discovers that this very mysterious Lion looks exactly like a Lamb. From an analytical point of view, he is clearly presented as if he is a new participant, namely in the indefinite form (***a*** Lamb 5:6) on the first occurrence, and, thereafter, in the definite form (***the*** Lamb 5:8).

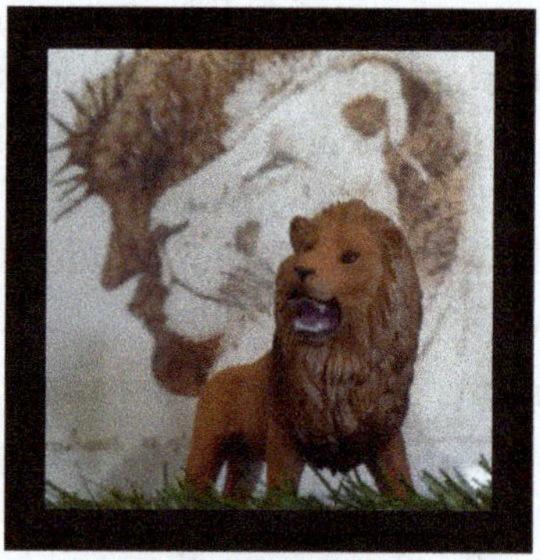

Therefore, since Chapter 4 presents the hearer with a new milieu, a new referential world, and new participants, it is clearly a setting. But the question which remains unclear, and which will be developed below, is whether it is just the setting for what immediately follows (i.e. the Seals Cycle) or for a longer passage than that.

5.3.1 The Structure of Chapters 4 and 5

It is also not difficult to establish that Revelation 4 and 5 belong together and form a single unit. This is because the setting established in general terms at 4:1, and then developed in more specific terms at 4:2, remains the same throughout. The participants introduced in Chapter 4, namely, the one sitting on the throne, the 24 elders and the four living creatures, also continue through to the end of Chapter 5. In addition to that, the content is organized according to a parallel, chiastic pattern which interweaves recurring motifs and participants as illustrated in Chart 30.

Chart 30.
The Structure of Revelation 4 and 5

Introduction: Transition from Cycle 1 and General Setting 4:1

A. The One Sitting on the Throne is Introduced and Described 4:2-3

B. The Next Participants, the 24 Elders and the 4 Living Creatures are Introduced and Described 4:4-7

A' The Worship Ascribed to The One Sitting on the Throne is Introduced and Described 4:8-11

A'' The Issue of the Scroll held by the One Sitting on the Throne is Introduced and Described 5:1-3

B' The Next Participant, the Lamb, is Introduced and Described, and the Elders and Living Creatures Respond 5:4-7

A''' The Worship of the Lamb is Introduced and Continues as does that of the One Sitting on the Throne 5:8-13

Conclusion: The Closure of the 24 Elders and the 4 Living Creatures 5:14

In this Chart all the four A sub-units are in parallel with each other. This is because of the specific reference to the one sitting on the throne. This is the reason for the unusual notation: A, A', A"and A'". The two B sub-units are also parallel with each other, which repetition is marked by the usual notation: B. and B'. This is because both sections introduce the next new participants, and also because of the specific references to the elders and living creatures.

There is adequate evidence for arguing for the internal cohesion of the whole of Chapters 4 and 5, at the same time. However, it is not difficult to perceive that this passage can be divided into two distinct sub-units, each with its own internal cohesion and distinctive message. In support of this, it can be noted that the larger passage divides structurally into two major parts, as displayed in Chart 30. Then, after that, each of these parts has their own indicators of internal cohesion and each contains different, even if complementary, content.

That is, Chapter 4 serves as a generic setting for all that is to follow, and this setting is the Throne Room in Heaven. Then Chapter 5 contributes a specific event arising out of the general setting, which serves as the specific setting for the Seals Cycle which is to follow.

This specific setting presents the Lamb to us, as the one who is worthy to open the seven seals. As mentioned above, the Lamb is introduced as if he was a brand new participant in the unfolding drama. This means that he is specifically being introduced as a new participant, or even, we could say, as a new topic, even though the same person was introduced previously under his name 'Jesus'. This is important because it raises the level of prominence of this description of the Lamb.

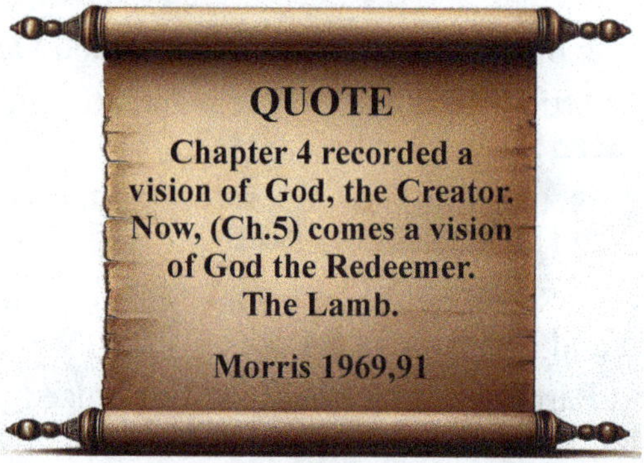
QUOTE
Chapter 4 recorded a vision of God, the Creator. Now, (Ch.5) comes a vision of God the Redeemer. The Lamb.
Morris 1969,91

The internal structure of each chapter confirms this observation. This is because Chapter 4, when viewed in terms of its detail, has a modified chiastic structure, which is not unusual for texts which are primarily organized according to thematic criteria. Such texts are, by nature, descriptive and more general in nature.

On the other hand, however, Chapter 5, is quite different, being an embedded narrative with a clear problem/resolution plot, and having a linear structure, which is typical of true narratives. Narratives, by nature, are dramatic and full of action. When occurring at the beginning of a lengthy section of text as in this case, they serve to prepare the way for some important activity. In this case, a new participant is introduced for the first time, and so, in the context of a narrative, this participant is likely to be a main participant, or even, *the* main participant, in the action which is to follow. As it turns out, this is exactly the case, because the Lamb reappears regularly as the most important, active participant right through to the end of the book.

So then, Chapters 4 and 5 can be viewed in two different, but complementary ways, either as one whole unit or as two closely related units. Chart 30 above, shows what it looks like when considered as one complete unit. In the following charts it will be seen what the two parts of it look like, when considered as two distinct units. This is an example of complementary analyses, which look at the same texts from slightly different points of view, and, thereby, bring to our attention different aspects, or emphases, of the same material. Supplementary notes on these issues are provided in the Appendix following this chapter.

Chart 31.

Part 1: The Generic Constituent of the General Setting of Cycles 2-6 4:2-11

A. Introduction/Description of the One Sitting on the Throne and the 24 Elders. 4:2-4

B. Special description of the Throne 4:5-6a

C. Introduction/Description of the 4 Living Creatures and their Activity. 4:6b-8

B' # (missing)

A' Description of Activity of the Elders in Worship of the One Sitting on the Throne 4:9-11

Firstly, it can be noted that sub-unit B' is missing. The implications of this will be discussed below.

Secondly, this structural organization suggests that, even though the whole unit is generic in nature, the introduction of the four living creatures is, nonetheless, the most prominent part of this section. This is confirmed when it is noted that they play an important secondary role in the development of the body of the following cycle. See 6:1,2,5 and 7.

Having said that, however, the prominence of the four living creatures is a low level prominence and not a book level prominence. When all is said and done, the book is about the Lion who looks like a Lamb.

In summary then, Chapters 4 and 5 serve as a complex setting with several functions at once. Firstly Chapter 4 is a setting for what happens in Chapter 5, and for this reason the four living creatures are introduced as a localized sub-topic, within the wider context of the Throne Room. This is why they are made to be prominent within that context. Then secondly, all that serves to prepare the way for reintroducing Jesus in His persona of the Lamb, which happens in Chapter 5. Then the two chapters together serve as a setting for all that follows right up to the end of Chapter 19.

Chart 32.
Part 2: The Specific Constituent of the General Setting of Cycles 2-6 5:1-13

Narrative Structure with Plot

1. **Setting** for what is to follow. Specific development of one aspect of the description of the One Sitting on the Throne, namely the introduction of the scroll with seven seals. 5:1
2. **Inciting Moment.** The problem is identified: A qualified person is needed to open the scroll 5:2
3. **Developing Conflict.** There is no one available who is worthy to open the scroll. 5:3
4. **Climax.** A climax of tension is reached: John is so disappointed that he weeps. 5:4
5. **Dénouement.** A solution is identified: The Lion of Judah can open the scroll. 5:5
6. **Final Suspense.** The execution of the solution is delayed and an element of uncertainty introduced. When John looks, he does not see a Lion, but a Lamb, who looks as if he is mortally wounded. 5:6
7. **Conclusion.** The immediate problem is resolved and the immediate effect of that resolution is described, namely the Lamb steps forward, takes the scroll and worship ensues. 5:7-13.

5.3.2 The Function of Chapters 4 and 5

It has been seen then, that Chapters 4 and 5 both contain setting material, with the first part being more generic in nature, and the second part being more specifically related to what follows in Chapter 6. There is further evidence in the details which supports this observation. Perusal of the internal organization of Chapter 4, reveals that it has an incomplete chiastic structure, ABC-A'.

Unfortunately, it may never be possible to discover if such broken patterns were systematically used to intentionally create particular expectations in the mind of the hearers. Nonetheless, in support of this idea, Dorsey 1988 and 1999,246-52 proposes that a particularity of the structure of Lamentations is that expected parts of the patterns previously established by the author, are missing. This gives a sense of incompleteness or loss which correlates with the content of a lament. This pattern with a missing part occurs at the book level and also at lower levels in Lamentations, much as the seven-fold pattern in Revelation occurs both at the book level and also at lower levels of the structure. In this case, the number seven correlates with the concepts of completeness and perfection. See also Parunak 1981,166-68 on these issues.

Nonetheless, it can be deduced that in a system of parallel, matched pairs such as is created in a chiasm, similar expectations are created. The simple fact of a first occurrence of a particular element, automatically creates the expectation of the occurrence, sooner or later, of a matching occurrence to complete the pair. In this case it is a reference (4:5) to the throne in Heaven which generates awe-inspiring lightnings, voices and thunders. Whether the second matching pair is provided by synonymous repetition or by complementarity, is of no consequence, the main thing is that an opening bracket should always, normally, be completed by a closing bracket. So when this does not happen, turbulence, and unfulfilled expectations are created in the mind of the reader, and this may be fully intentional on the part of the author.

Similarly, the fact that a problem is introduced into the plot of a linearly organized narrative, creates the expectation of a resolution. A narrative which ends without resolving any, or all, of its problems, would be considered to be incomplete by most readers, or listeners, familiar with this system of text organization.

In this case, the One Sitting on the Throne and the 24 Elders are introduced in 4:2-4, and then, after the occurrence of other elements, these two personages reoccur together at 4:9-11, thereby completing the system with a matching pair. However, this is not the case for 4:5-6a which is a specific description of the throne itself, and not merely a reference to the throne in preparation for the introduction of a personage, as is the case elsewhere in this passage (4:2, 4, and 6b).

The only way to circumvent this issue would be to make 4:5-6a belong with one of its neighboring sub-units. This is difficult because, as a description of the throne, it is autonomous in its own right. Furthermore, it has no clear connections with the primary content of the other two sub-units, both of which have the introduction of personages as their primary function. It is also difficult to interpret these verses as a setting to the presentation of the four living creatures, since they have their own introductory reference to the throne in verse 6b in a manner analogous with verses 2 and 4.

So, in the first instance, it can be concluded that no matching pair for the sub-unit 4:5-6a occurs within the immediate context of Chapter 4, nor even within the larger context of Chapter 5. The reference to the seven spirits of God in 5:6 (cf. 4:5b) is not considered to be sufficient reason to posit a full matching pair, since it is an explanation and, therefore, peripheral to the description which is the primary content of this sub-unit. In addition, it is appended to a different referent (the eyes of the Lamb) in 5:6, which further attenuates its impact.

A reference to the seven spirits of God (4:5b) occurs three times in the book as a whole (cf. 1:4 and 5:6). In terms of the major content of the book, this is only a detail even if it is rich in implied theological significance. It would seem to confirm that Chapters 4 and 5 are connected as has been stated above. In addition, it implies that there is also a connection with the Prologue, which is, of course, the setting for the book as a whole. If this detail is added to the discussion previously presented, it can be concluded that the Prologue, the setting for the book, is connected to Chapter 4, the setting for Cycles 2-6 (cf. also the connection between 1:10 and 4:1). This latter then, in turn, is specifically connected to each of the individual settings of Cycles 2-6. In addition, the setting of Cycle 7 contains a reference to thrones, with only a very slight difference in meaning, and then the throne of God is again centrally in view in the body of Cycle 7.

If these observations are accepted as valid, then the result is that this book has an unusually large mass of related setting material. This starts in the Prologue, is significantly enhanced by the material in Chapters 4 and 5, and then is systematically re-activated all the way through Cycles 2-7. This fact then raises the level of prominence of this setting material above its normally rather low level of importance. This, in turn, makes it a candidate for being included in the thematic material of the book and for being included in a summary of the book's overall message.

However, just to finish off the thread of the missing B' sub-unit, it can also be noted that the central content of 4:5-6a (thunder, lightning etc., and the sea) is explicitly repeated elsewhere in the book, and it is of more than passing interest that these places are the settings of Cycles 3-6. Thus it is, that the reference to these audio-visual events reoccur at 8:5, 11:15 and 19, and 16:18 which are part of the settings of Cycles 3, 4 and 6. In addition, there is also the antithetical, or complementary, silence, which occurs in the setting of Cycle 3 at 8:1. Then, finally, to complete the list, the reference to the sea around the throne reoccurs in 15:2, which is in the setting of Cycle 5.

Two conclusions can be drawn from these observations. Firstly, the settings of Cycles 3 to 6 are not just settings by convenience, or by coincidence, but they are, in fact, reactivated settings. This reactivation specifically situates their following content in the context of the heavenly throne room originally described in Chapter 4. This concretizes in observable practice what Callow 1998,291 described theoretically in the following way:

> A setting is held constant throughout the unit which follows... If the same setting is operative for a long time, or if it is reverted to after another has intervened, it becomes necessary to reactivate it: usually a few words are sufficient. Sometimes we assert explicitly that the setting has not changed... Such reaffirmed settings contain little or no new information. **Many languages use complete or partial repetition** with the same context-providing function. (Emphasis added.)

Secondly, this reaffirmation of the setting material of Chapter 4 in the following settings provides the closure, which the presence of 4:5-6a without a matching pair immediately following, seemed to require. The conclusion is that Chapter 4 as a single unit is, in fact, incomplete, as was originally hypothesized. Its incompleteness thus gives rise to an expectation that something more should be provided to meet this need.

This kind of signal is typical of a textual unit which is introductory, since, by definition, an introduction gives rise to an expectation that more is to follow, just as a conclusion indicates that the intended message has been completed. So, Chapter 4 communicates that it is the beginning of a larger unit, which will be completed in due course, not only by its content, as explained above, but also by its structure. Furthermore, the references provided above indicate that what is missing in Chapter 4, is completed by what is provided in the following series of settings, and the last of those is the setting to Cycle 6. So, it is here then, in 16:17-18, in particular, that there is another reference to lightnings, voices and thunders, which, in the context, are clearly coming out from the throne.

Once again, it can be observed that within Revelation there is a remarkable weaving together of details, which creates a complex, but consistent pattern, and, at the same time, communicates a coherent message. In this particular case, the settings, beginning with the Prologue and continuing through Chapters 4 and 5 and then on through, at least as far as the setting of Cycle 6, create a consistent, coherent pattern.

As would be expected, the first settings in a series (i.e. the Prologue and Chapter 4) are more general in nature, and those which follow are more precise. Chapter 4 provides a general description of the heavenly throne room, and this general context carries over naturally into Chapter 5 by virtue of its contiguity, and is reactivated by virtue of a brief repetition in the settings of Cycles 3-6. In addition, the setting of each of these later cycles also provides material which is relevant as a setting for the specific content which is to follow.

On the basis of the above discussion then, it would seem natural to treat Chapter 4 as a separate unit which acts as a general setting to the whole of Cycles 2-6, and Chapter 5 as a specific setting for Cycle 2. The problem however, with this neat solution is that there is still some data which remains unaccounted for. An important component of the setting to Cycle 3 (8:1-6) is the phrase 'the prayers of the saints'. If this were just part of the specificity of Cycle 3, there would be no particular problem. Yet perusal of the following body of the cycle (8:7-11:19) reveals no overt connection between the prayers of the saints in the setting, and the outworking of the trumpet judgments in the body.

There is a reference to the prayers of certain of the saints (11:5-7) in the trumpets interlude, but this reference is not clear. What is clear, is that this reference does not permeate the content of the seven-fold judgments. The reference which does, is the reference to the seven angels with their seven trumpets.

The connection which does exist is with 5:8, which makes reference to the prayers of the saints, and this is the only overt connection with the setting material of Chapters 4 and 5. This is because the fact that the altar in 8:3 is part of the throne room furniture has to be deduced, and is not a specific back-reference. Since all the settings under discussion have some overt reference back to the generic setting, it would seem as if this reference to the prayers of the saints in the setting of the Trumpets Cycle is following the same pattern. Therefore, its intended function is to create a direct link with this generic setting as well. Since this would seem to be the case, then Chapter 5, as well as Chapter 4, contains material which is part of the generic setting for the following cycles.

Once again the interweaving of motifs is present and in this case it is more complex than one would have wished. In this case, where the data is complex, the concomitant analysis also has to be more complex, in order to take account of all the data observed. This is because an analysis which does not account for all the data is 'inadequate'.

As a consequence, the analysis which would seem to best account for all the data is that Chapters 4 and 5 should be viewed as a single bipartite unit with a double function. This is not very surprising, and serves as a confirmation for the proposed analysis, because this also occurs elsewhere.

Similar complex interweaving of different kinds of text resulted in a similar interpretation for the setting of Cycle 1, as discussed in Chapter 3. Another example, occurs in Chapters 10-11 where the Narrative Framework Interlude is connected to the Trumpets Interlude by an overlap link.

In summary then, the total unit of Chapters 4 and 5 together, functions as a generic setting for Cycles 2-6. Each of these cycles, in turn, reactivates this generic setting in its individual setting, as well as adding new setting material, which is relevant to the following cycle. At the same time, it also functions as a specific setting for Cycle 2 and prepares the way for the events which occur as a result of the opening of each of the seven seals. An alternative solution would be to view Chapter 5 as another overlap link, being part of the generic setting and the specific setting for Cycle 2 at the same time.

5.4 The Closure to Cycles 2-6

5.4.1 Unfinished Business

It was noted in the above discussion that Revelation 4:1 is a sub-unit which serves as an introduction to what follows, being both a transition from the previous cycle and also a general setting of all that follows.

It can now be noticed more specifically that the general setting is provided by the phrase 'and behold, a door was/stood open in Heaven'. This new setting information is clearly marked and, along with its parallel phrase 'and behold, a throne was set/stood in Heaven', it creates a memorable doublet. The evidence for being a marked constituent is as follows: after the introductory phrase, the word, 'a door', is the first item presented, being fronted. It is also marked by *idou*, 'behold', and there is repetition of a similar form thereby creating a doublet: 'and behold a door', which is paralleled by, 'and behold a throne' in 4:2.

What is of interest is that this new beginning is well developed and memorable, and yet is not of crucial importance for the rest of the long setting unit (Chapters 4-5) to which it belongs. The throne is important, but the door being open in Heaven is not, since it could be left out and not change the communicative value of Chapters 4-5 in any way.

Two questions arise from this observation: Firstly, is there any particular reason why this extra information should be supplied at this point in the text? Secondly, the whole unit to which 4:1-2 belongs is a long, and presumably important, new beginning, yet without being placed at the beginning of the book. So the question arises then, as to whether the following material will continue through to the end of the book, or will it be brought to closure before the end ?

5.4.2 The Particular Role of 19:11-21

In Chapter 3 it was noted that 19:11-21 was a separate unit, whose relationship with its context was not clear. With this context, and the above discussion, in mind, it can now be noticed that there are similarities between 19:11 and 4:1. In both cases, John sees Heaven opened. In 4:1 his attention is particularly drawn to a door which reveals a scene behind it. Whereas in 19:11, his attention is drawn to what is to be seen through the opening in the heavens.

Smith 1994 claims that the feature of doors opening in Heaven was common in apocalyptic literature. If so, the original recipients of Revelation may have already been aware of this device. In addition, Smith notes that it was not a fixed convention in that the word for a door did not have to be used on every occasion, but rather it was another example of 'structural conventions (being) established only to be varied' (ibid.,382).

The object which John sees in 4:2 is a throne, and in 19:11, it is a horse, both referents being marked by the phrase 'and behold'. In each case, there is someone, who is not immediately identified, sitting on the item in view. These features are all in parallel with each other and were probably clear enough, at least at the period when the text was first written, to indicate to the reader/hearer that they should be associated in some way.

Discussing the features of oral literature, Harvey 1998,58 makes a very interesting comment about literary 'echoes' which are separated by long expanses of intervening material. This is what he has to say about this phenomenon:

> It seems...that the aural audience was capable of recognizing such echoes over a considerable expanse. Whitman (a modern editor of Homer) cites Odysseus's recognition by Eurycleia as an example: 'Between the discovery of the scar and the old woman's instantaneous gesture of surprise, Homer inserts a seventy-five-line episode about the origin of the scar, returning with perfect ease to the moment in hand by the mere repetition of the single verb *to recognize*'.

So, in the light of this external confirmation, it is not surprising to observe a similar feature in Revelation. However, 4:1 is not a text in isolation, but serves to introduce a complete unit which runs through to 5:14. It is, therefore, the beginning of a generic-specific development, the culmination of which, is that John eventually comes to recognize the Risen Christ in his newly revealed form, which is that of a lamb (5:6).

Likewise, 19:11 is part of a complete unit, one of the main purposes of which, is to provide another description of the Risen Christ, this time in the form of a victorious warrior (19:11-21).

Identification with the Risen Christ is made clear by the reference to His eyes as a flame of fire (19:12) and the sharp sword which proceeds from his mouth (19:15, cf. 1:14,16). The description in 5:6 of the Lamb who looks as if he has been killed identifies Him as the Christ described in 1:5, 7 and 18. The reference to faithful and true (19:11) is evocative of the faithful witness in 1:5, and the reference to shepherding the nations with a rod of iron (19:15) is evocative of 1:5 and a direct parallel with 12:5. The name King of kings and Lord of lords (19:16) is the same as that ascribed to the Lamb in 17:14. These descriptions along with other evidence for parallelism are laid out in Chart 33.

Chart 33.
The Conclusion to Cycles 2-6 19:11-21

A. A Description of the Risen Christ Seen as a Victorious Warrior 19:11-13
parallels: 'one sitting on a white horse', 'having a name written... his name was the Word of God', 'garment dipped in blood', 'he makes war'.

B. A Description of the Armies of Heaven and their Leader 19:14-16
parallels: '(those) followed (sitting) on white horses', 'out of His mouth proceeds a sharp sword', 'He treads the winepress...,' 'He has on His garment...a name written: King of kings and Lord of lords'.

C. Proclamation 7: The Summons to the Final Conflict 19:17-1
parallels: 'assemble', 'the flesh of horses and those sitting on them', 'kings and those (following) sitting on horses', 'all the birds...', 'Come... eat'.

B' A Description of the Armies of the Earth and their Leader 19:19-20
parallels: 'the kings of the earth and their armies assembled to make war with the one sitting on the horse and his army'.

A' A Description of the Warfare and the Victory of the Risen Christ 19:21
parallels: 'the rest (the kings of the earth and their armies) were killed (war made and accomplished)', the one sitting on the horse', 'the sword...proceeding from his mouth', 'all the birds were filled by their flesh'

Since the parallelism between Chapters 4-5 and 19:11-21 has already been noticed, it can now be remarked that there is also a probable parallel between the reference to the Lion of Judah in 5:5, and the description of the victorious warrior. Similar to the missing B' sub-unit mentioned above, in the same way, in 5:5 the lion is presented but is then left in abeyance. This is because it is a lamb which is described in 5:6, when John was expecting to see a lion. When a personage is introduced it leads to an expectation that he will participate in the discourse at some point. It would seem then, that the Lion of Judah and his function is, in effect, described in 19:11-21, thereby fulfilling the expectation created in 5:5, and completing the sub-topic thereby initiated.

The conclusion being drawn from this discussion, therefore, is that the data described above is evidence for an ***inclusio*** structure. This means that the whole of Chapters 4 and 5 provide an opening bracket, or a setting, for the whole of Cycles 2-6 as was proposed in section 3.2 above. Then, in line with the expectation created by the opening of this bracket, the whole of 19:11-21 functions as the corresponding closing bracket. This closing bracket, therefore, forms a conclusion for this same central part of the book, Cycles 2-6, just as Chapters 4 and 5 formed an introduction and setting for these cycles.

DEFINITION

An Inclusio

is a parallel structure with two constituents. The two constituents are placed near the beginning, and near the end of a particular section of text. By this means the author indicates, that everything in between these two opening and closing brackets, are included in the bigger unit thus bracketed. This is why it is called an inclusio. Even though this feature is a marker of cohesion first and foremost, it can also be used, secondarily, as a confirmation for establishing the unit boundaries.

Consequently, the preferred solution being proposed here, is that 19:11 is the beginning of a sub-unit which is functioning as a conclusion to a major segment of the book. The evidence that it is a conclusion is considerable, as will be seen in the course of the ongoing discussion below, but the evidence supporting the contention that it is the beginning of a major unit is weak and unconvincing. Further brief discussion of this difference of opinion is provided in the Appendix at the end of this chapter.

The contention that 19:11-21 is a conclusion rather than a new beginning, can be supported by the following points. Firstly, the dragon, the two beasts and Babylon, being the primary opponents of God's people on earth, are introduced in the above order, and then their demise is described in the reverse order. Lenski 1943,547-8 appears to be the first to have noticed this phenomenon and so, as he himself says:

> All of these three go down together even as they appeared together. The circumstance that each of the three is revealed in a separate vision should not lead us to think that there is an interval... between their appearance... The same method is followed in showing the end of the three. In reality all perish together... Yet each ends in a distinct way... Differentiated and shown as three, their end, as was their appearance, is represented separately... But in reality they end at the same time by the same hand and power, by the Parousia of the Lamb.

Chart 34.

The Rise and Fall of the Dragon, the Two Beasts and Babylon

A. The dragon is previewed in Cycle 1 & formally introduced in 12:3-4

B. The two beasts are formally introduced 13:1-18

C. Babylon is previewed in 14:8 and mentioned in 16:17-20, but not formally introduced

C' Babylon is described in 17:1-18 and her judgment is proclaimed in 18:1-24

B' The two beasts and their followers are judged 19:11-21

A' The dragon's failures are reviewed and his judgment described 20:1-10

In other words, even though the appearance and the end of these three personages (the two beasts being treated as a single personage), are probably simultaneous, the fact that they are described separately is a textual phenomenon, and contributes to the structure of the book as a text.

So then, according to Lenski (ibid.), the dragon (A) and the beasts (B) are introduced in Chapters 12 and 13 and their demise in the lake of fire is described at the end of the book. It is described in 19:20-21 for the beasts, and in 20:7-10 for the dragon. Babylon (C) is described and destroyed 'in an unbroken line' in 16:17-18:24, thereby creating an ABCC'B'A' pattern, as demonstrated in Chart 34.

QUOTE

No reader could expect the conclusion to the vision of the fall of Babylon to be the end of the whole prophecy.

Bauckham 1993,5

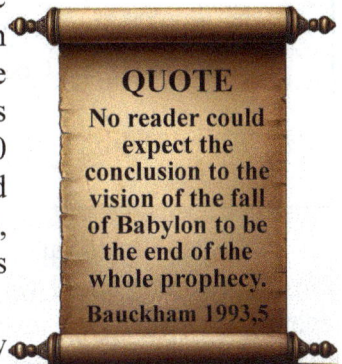

The B' part of the pattern is clearly a closure, being the second of a matched pair and

corresponds to 19:11-21. This closure is the conclusion of the story of the beasts, which unambiguously began within the context of Cycles 2-6, and now ends at the end of Cycle 6. But at the same time, it is not the end of the total story.

According to the above schema, the end of this story of judgment would be with the demise of the dragon in 20:10. So the question arises as to whether this should belong with Cycles 2-6 or not. This is because, according to Lenski, he is introduced in Chapter 12, which is Cycle 4. In terms of a formal introduction, this is correct, but, in fact, Satan and his goals are previewed extensively in Cycle 1.

There are six references to 'Satan', or 'the devil', at 2:9,10,13 (x2), 24, and 3:9 in Cycle 1. These are the only such references in the whole book, and it can be noted in passing that there are only six references in this lexical chain (six being the number of incompleteness, or failure to reach the perfect standard), and not seven. Elsewhere he is referred to as the dragon – thirteen times in all, thirteen being the number for depravity and rebellion.

This is in contrastive parallel to the references to Christ, who is referred to as Jesus Christ seven times in the whole book, at 1:1,2,5,9 (x 2), 12:17 and 22:21, and also as Jesus seven times at 14:12, 17:6, 19:10 (x2), 20:4, 22:16 and 20, which makes for fourteen times in all, with fourteen being the number for deliverance and salvation. The references to Jesus Christ are mainly in the Prologue, and then, for most of the rest of the book, He is referred to as the Lamb.

From these references it can be seen that Jesus dominates the Prologue and, as such, is clearly established as the topic of the book and the most important participant in the drama which follows.

Chart 35.
The Thread Containing Satan's Story

A. Satan's Goals Summarily Previewed (Cycle 1)

B. Satan, his Goals and Failure Formally Introduced and Described (Cycle 4, 12:1-17)

A' Satan's Ultimate Failure Summarily Reviewed (Setting of Cycle 7, 20:1-10)

By contrast, Satan does not appear here at all. He is only belatedly introduced in a formal way in Chapter 12, halfway through the book. But even then Jesus pops up again in a very isolated reference at 12:17. By literary sleight of hand the author seems to make him taunt the dingy dragon, who cannot do anything right.

If all these references are taken into account, an example of taking account of all the data and not just part of it, Satan's story is organized as an ABA' chiasm, as displayed in Chart 35. Since this is the case, then it is logical that Satan's story, begun in the first cycle, then figuring with a little detail, in the central cycle, should eventually be concluded in the last cycle. Appropriately enough then, his story begins near the beginning and ends near the end. However, the chart shows that his story is very threadbare.

Chart 36.

The Rise and Fall of Satan and his Cohorts

a. Death and Hades, and Jesus' conquest of them, previewed 1:18

b. Satan previewed and denounced by Jesus in Cycle 1,

A. Death and Hades formally introduced 6:8,

c. One beast previewed 11:7

B. Satan formally introduced, his defeat by Jesus and His followers announced Ch.12

C. The 2 beasts formally introduced Ch.13

D. Babylon previewed at 14:8 and 16:19, described in Ch.17 and Judged in Ch.18

C' The 2 beasts seized and judged 19:11-21

b' Satan's failure reviewed 20:1-3

c' The beasts' failure reviewed 20:4

B' Satan's final failure and his judgment 20:7-10a,

a' Death and Hades' final failure reviewed 20:13a and

A' Death and Hades are judged and destroyed 20:13b-14.

Coda: All evil doers (i.e. all those who did not learn to overcome Satan and his cohorts) will be consigned to the Lake of Fire, which is the Second Death 21:7-8

What has been described above is, nonetheless, only part of the story. Revelation truly is a complex book, as many commentators have noticed. So, to do it justice, our analysis also needs to be well developed and somewhat complicated as well.

So it is, that the Judgment Theme parallelism is even more complex than just the elements described above. But, in order to make it as clear and as simple as possible, all the elements were laid out together in Chart 36.

In this chart, lower case letters (a,b,c) are used as well as capitals (A,B,C). The small letters denote minor semantic components, which are either brief, or have been downgraded in importance because they are only previews, reviews, or are consigned to a setting. The capital letters denote the more important semantic units, where, for example, a protagonist is formally introduced, or is described at length.

As can be seen in the chart, the organization of these particular, and related, elements is certainly complex. Yet, at the same time, it is clearly not random either, but is contained within a clear system, which is based on the usual conventions of repetition and parallelism.

QUOTE

Since we are finding a lot of repetitions as we go, This quote is worth repeating:
'The book of Revelation is a remarkably well-constructed literary piece, containing a multiplicity of neatly intertwining patterns.'
Strand 1987,107

The main body of each of Cycles 2-6, as depicted by the sevenfold motifs, is devoted to developing the Judgment Theme, as previously explained in Chapter 4. Furthermore, most commentators are agreed that the sixth sub-unit of each of these cycles depicts the final judgment, and some also think that the seventh unit continues and completes this same sub-theme.

If this is the case, then the sixth Proclamation (18:21-24) is the last of these references and, in effect, it completes the references to the destruction of Babylon as a type of 'the fall of the final world kingdom' (Beale 1999,918). It is only followed by an Interlude (19:1-8), which develops the contrasting Salvation Theme, even as it makes a final reference to Babylon in 19:2. Then, after that, a section of Narrative Framework (19:9-10) reappears, and the completion of the battle which was announced in Bowl 6 (16:12-16), is described in 19:11-21.

With this in mind, three details need to be made clear. Firstly, the sixth sub-units actually refer to the final judgment as it affects people still living on the earth and, as Beale 1999,512 indicates, refers to 'torment preceding death'. Secondly, the seventh units of Cycles 2-5 are transitions over to the next cycle, so their contribution to the description of the process of judgment is not entirely clear. With complex linguistic units of this nature it is important to avoid being prematurely dogmatic, but to be open first of all to the nuances of meaning which the author has placed in his discourse.

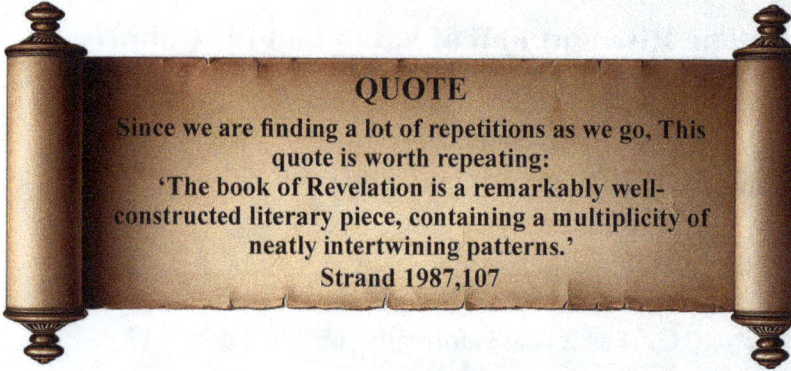

The clearest of the seventh units, in terms of content, is the seventh Proclamation and its context (19:17-21), which is the only seventh unit of Cycles 2-6 not to be a transition to another cycle. Here there is a mixing of the eternal judgment of spiritual beings, the beasts, and the death in battle of human agencies, the kings of the earth. However, even this is ambiguous since they are killed by the sword proceeding from the mouth of the rider on the white horse, so it may possibly be referring to a post-death, spiritual experience similar to the one in 20:11-13.

Thirdly, it should be remembered that the text under discussion is only a preliminary conclusion of part of the book, and is not the final conclusion.

Having established these issues, it can be concluded that the issue of the final judgment on earth, which is the topic of the sixth sub-units, is concluded, appropriately, in Cycle 6. More specifically, the issue of the final battle raised in Bowl 6 (16:12-16) is completed in 19:11-21, which is the passage under discussion. So then, this brings to closure issues of earthly judgment which have been an important theme in Cycles 2-6. The only issues of judgment which remain, concern the judgment of a spiritual being, Satan, in 20:10, judgment occurring after physical death as a preliminary to the eternal state (20:11-15), or reviews of previously described events.

For example, 20:7-9 refers to the destruction of the armies of the nations. Since these same armies have already been destroyed in 19:21, it seems clear that 20:7-9 is a review. Note also that Satan is active in assembling the armies in the preceding narrative in 16:13 which also supports the view that 20:7-9 is a parallel review. This event provides a context for the following point which is Satan's eternal judgment in 20:10. For, although his judgment is described separately from that of the beasts, as mentioned previously, it is reasonable to suppose that, in reality, their judgment will occur at the same time, according to earthly time that is.

Since these verses recapitulate the same events as those described in 19:17-21 they serve analytically, as a tail-head link with that passage. Other reviews are at to be found at 21:8 and 21:27a. This system of picking up once more topics, which have been previously dealt with, in order to provide a clear context for the following main point is appropriate for a conclusion. So, in this case, the author is picking up a number of sub-themes already initiated earlier in the book, and bringing them to an appropriate conclusion. Everything that is, except for the final main point. This system of review prior to completion, which occurs throughout Cycle 7, lends credence to the proposal that 20:1-5 is also a backward-looking review of previous events.

In summary then, these reviews provide a necessary context for the issues which will come into focus in Cycle 7, which, of course follows, and completes Cycles 2-6. It is logical that such final, eternal, issues should be left for the final conclusion of the visionary material in this last cycle.

More evidence will be presented below to support the division between Cycles 6 and 7, but the conclusion which has been reached in this section concerns the role of 19:11-21. It is being proposed that, just as Chapters 4 and 5 provided an opening setting for the whole of Cycles 2-6, so also, 19:11-21 acts as a matching closing bracket or *inclusio*, and thereby provides a conclusion for these central cycles.

Once again, in summary, these central cycles had as their dominant theme, in terms of quantity at least, judgment events as they pertain to life on earth. Consequently, it can be seen that 19:11-21 has a double function: it contains the seventh proclamation (19:17-18) and thereby brings to an end the Proclamations Cycle, and, as a total unit, it also serves as a closing bracket for the whole of Cycles 2-6. It is, in effect, a kind of overlap link, but this time the overlap shows that the seventh proclamation is tightly integrated into the organization of Cycles 2-6 as a whole, and does not overlap with the following cycle.

5.4.3 Evidence for the Division Between Cycles 6 and 7

There has been considerable debate in the past, as to whether 19:21 is the end of a major unit and that, therefore, 20:1 is the beginning of another major unit at the book level of the hierarchy. The alternative viewpoint is that 19:21 just marks the end of a lengthy paragraph, and 20:1 continues on the flow of thought where the preceding verse ended.

This is a very important issue, because the viewpoint which you take on this issue, will very much influence your interpretation of the message of the whole book. If this debate is ever to progress towards a consensus, then it seems clear that the full range of linguistic evidence which is available, needs to be considered. This is so that the author himself can guide us to the correct interpretation, rather than it being left to an ad hoc personal opinion. Please feel free to consult the Appendix at the end of this chapter for more information on this debate.

The aim here is to review some of the wide variety of evidence which is available in the text. As has been noticed elsewhere, it is not the evidence which is lacking, since Revelation is composed of many linguistic strands which are intertwined with each other with considerable intricacy, and yet, with remarkable consistency.

Firstly then, the evidence reviewed above, suggests that at this point in the book a complex conclusion has been reached. But yet, at the same time, it is not the conclusion of the whole book. The conclusion is complex because it is both the conclusion of the sixth cycle, and also the conclusion of Cycles 2-6 as a total unit. At the highest possible level then, 19:21 is the end of a cycle, which is the largest possible unit in the book. Any proposal which situates a break of this magnitude at another point, would also have to propose a more convincing analysis of the macro structure on either side of the break.

At the next level of clear thematic flow, there is no question that 19:21 brings to an end the story of the two beasts, which were introduced in Cycle 4. The subsequent reference to them in 20:10, looks back on their demise, and is a clear example of a review of previously completed events. The function of this final reference will be discussed in the next main section below.

What happens next in 20:1, is a switch back to the story of the dragon, and the parallelism of the evidence suggests that the hearer is intentionally invited to mentally pick up this story from where it was left unfinished in Chapter 12. The repetition of the verb 'to throw', in 20:3 (// 12:9 twice and 12:10), and more particularly the lengthy repetition of the definition of who Satan is in 20:2, which is clearly in parallel to his formal introduction in 12:3-10, provide the surface structure markers which invite this mental reconnection. This must be the purpose of this detailed repetition, because, from a literary point of view, it is completely unnecessary for a participant who has already been introduced.

This repetition reactivates this known information as the setting within which the hearer should receive and interpret the new information provided in 20:1-3. Therefore, the setting and the connection for 20:1 is Chapter 12, rather than Chapter 19. This evidence of parallelism is clear and needs to be accounted for in some appropriate way, and not just cursorily swept aside, as if of no consequence. Meanwhile, there is an interim reference to Satan at 16:13, but this reference also arises out of the setting in Chapter 12.

In terms of the description of Christ in 19:11-16, which is a significant part of this unit, it can be seen as the last in a series of five passages where Christ is described in some detail. The previous passages were:

- 1:9-20 in Cycle 1
- 5:5-7 which is part of the setting to Cycles 2-6
- 7:17, which is the conclusion to the first interlude, and
- 12:4-5, which is in Cycle 4 in the immediate context of the descriptions of the dragon and the two beasts.

In 5:5 reference is made to 'the Lion of the tribe of Judah', but when John looked, what he saw (5:6) was a Lamb, and no other reference is made to the Lion. As mentioned above, one possible way of viewing 19:11-21 is that it is a synonymous description of Christ as the Lion of Judah. This then resolves the problem for the hearer, as to why this participant was introduced, and then left hanging with no further explanation.

In support of this contention, Beale 1999,951 proposes that the 'judicial action' carried out by Christ in 19:11, is an allusion to the Hebrew Scriptures. That is to say that 'Psalm 72 applies it to the "king's son" and Isa.11:4 applies it to the messianic "shoot...from the stem of Jesse"' (cf. 'the root of David', in 5:5). Furthermore, in both 19:15, and also in the parallel in 12:5, it says that Christ will *shepherd* the nations with a rod of iron, whereas in the Hebrew source (Ps.2:8-9) the equivalent verb is 'to break'. This double change in Revelation is clearly intended to create another allusion to King David.

With this final description of Christ, and the concomitant event of the battle completed (19:21), it is not unreasonable to switch attention back to Christ's antagonist in the following segment of text.

However, this is a switch and not a continuation, because none of the participants of 19:11-21 are maintained as active participants in Chapter 20. This is because their story has already come to an end. Once again, the point is, that this part of the previous story, Christ's in this case, has ended. This is an accurate statement because even if Christ is implicitly present in Cycle 7 (e.g. 20:11, 21:2 and 21:22) he is not an active participant, as He was previously. So then, with His part of the story completed, it turns out that in 20:1, the hearer is invited to pick up the threads of the dragon's story again, so that it too can be brought to a conclusion, which is what happens in 20:10.

At another level down in the thematic development, the parallel and contrastive presentation of the stories of the city/woman Babylon, and the city/woman Jerusalem is to be found. It is clear that, 17:1-3, which contains the phrase 'Come, I will show you...', referring to Babylon, is in direct parallel with 21:9-10, which introduces the description of Jerusalem, with exactly the same phrase. Then, in turn, 19:9b-10 is in parallel with elements of 22:6-9, since there is the repetition of a blessing, and references to the truthfulness of God's word, and to angels coming to show God's servants what they need to see.

These two sets of parallels create, therefore, two sets of brackets which, according to some writers, mark the beginning and the end of significant parts of the text. This observation is partially correct but needs to be modified to fully account for the data, as is explained in more detail in the following Appendix. The main point of interest here, is that the closing brackets are not at the end of a major section of text, but rather that they are *near* the end of a major section, and contribute to a complex, multi-stranded conclusion.

In the case of 22:6-9, it is an overlap link which contributes to both the conclusion of Cycle 7, and also to the conclusion of the book as a whole, as was explained previously in Chapter 2. In the case of 19:9b-10, it contributes to a complex series of conclusions which runs from 19:1 to19:21 and which, taken all together, provide the conclusions for several thematic strands. So included in this multi-stranded part of the discourse, are a preliminary conclusion for the major Salvation Theme, the conclusion of Cycle 6, and also the conclusion of Cycles 2-6 as a larger unit.

In support of this counter-proposal that 19:9b-10 contributes to a complex conclusion rather than being itself a conclusion, it can be noted that it is not an autonomous unit but belongs with verse 9a and thus, creates a minor part of the Narrative Framework. So, for example, it is the same speaker in 19:9a and 9b, but introduced twice with two identical, parallel introductions 'and he says to me'. Therefore, the following phrase 'these words' (19:9b), must, in the first instance, refer to the words in 19:9a, even though, by extension, they may also refer to the preceding words in the larger context.

Furthermore, this section of Narrative Framework cannot reasonably be detached from its context because of the double reference to 'the marriage of the Lamb', in 19:7 and 9. This double reference to 'the marriage', could be interpreted as a tail-head link, in which case a division between units would fall at the end of 19:8.

However, 19:9 is clearly not introducing another new section which is on a par with 19:1-8 or 19:11-21, since it is short, and its whole tenor is commentary and conclusion. What the tail-head link indicates, therefore, is that there is another new sub-unit coming up, which, in this case, is a Narrative Framework sub-unit. Nonetheless, even though it is a new sub-unit, it is attached to, and belongs with, the preceding interlude.

This is because it provides a pause and a commentary at the end of the interlude (19:1-8), and, as such, an element of closure. In addition, it picks up from the previous section of Narrative Framework at 17:1-18, and can reasonably be construed to be a continuing and, for the moment, closing speech, of the same bowl angel, who was active back in Chapter 17. Since this is the same bowl angel who initiated the dialogue with John at this latter point in the framework, then this passage, in itself, is also a conclusion.

The final observation which can be made concerning these intermediate size units of text, is that the interlude in 19:1-8, is the last in the series of interludes, which carries the Salvation Theme forward in the central part of the book. This means then, that this unit is also a conclusion.

As well as the above thematic indicators there are also indicators in 19:1-21 that certain lexical strands are brought to closure here, in addition to the larger units mentioned above. The most striking of these are:

- the references to 'a great crowd', 'the four creatures', and 'the elders', which all occur for the last time in 19:1-6.
- the important seven-fold sequence of the word 'sign', which ends at 19:20,
- the final five of fifteen references to 'a horse', which occur in 19:11,14,18,19 and 21.
- the strands containing: 'clothed', and 'dressed' (19:13-14), 'garment' (19:13 and 16), 'supper', 'winepress' (19:15), 'blood' (19:2 and 13), and 'birds' (19:21).

Earthly kings are referred to many times, mainly in Cycles 2-6 in a context of judgment. The last of these, which brings closure to this sub-theme, is in 19:19. However, the final reference of all, is at 21:24 but is in a positive context. This reference is parallel to another one in a positive context at 1:5 and brings the kings theme to an end, on a positive note, for the book as a whole. Thus, the beginning and the end of the book provide brackets of positive references, whereas the references in a context of judgment occur in Cycles 2-6 and come to an end at 19:19.

It can be seen then, that there is **concurrence,** and complexity, in the passage 19:1-21, and all these features lead the hearer to understand that certain elements of the message are being brought to a conclusion.

DEFINITION

Concurrence

is the co-occurrence of several different linguistic features in the same section of text.

When there is a particular concentration of evidence occurring in the same stretch of text like this, then this is a place where the author is at pains to make an important point. In this case, it is to communicate that an ending of some significant proportion has been reached. This is even more striking when it is noticed that the following passage (20:1-3) has none of these concluding features. On the contrary, this next section contains several features which mark a new beginning, or provide new information, or reactivate information which appeared in parts of the text which are prior to 19:1-21.

This new information, or reactivation of known information, is as shown in the list which follows:

- There is a reference to an angel descending from Heaven (20:1), which is in parallel to 18:1 (inter alia), which was at the very beginning of the seven proclamations.
- The word 'a chain', made prominent by the adjective 'great', is used in 20:1 for the first and only time.
- The concept of one thousand years occurs for the first time.
- The main event of putting Satan in the pit is new information, while
- The word 'a key', is cognate in Greek with 'shut', and this latter reoccurs in 21:25, while a synonym for 'a pit', (i.e. 'a prison') reoccurs in 20:7, so these two words are not final elements in a lexical chain.

It is noticeable that there are very many different features co-occurring here, plus the fact that the stretch of text concerned is relatively long (21 verses). These two facts strongly support the proposal that 19:21/20:1 is a high level division between large units of text.

So then, 19:1-21 is a complex conclusion containing at the same time a whole list of conclusions as follows. It contains:

- the conclusion to the series of interludes (19:1-8), and at the same time
- a final bracket for the Babylon story (19:2)
- a conclusion to an intermediate part of the Narrative Framework (19:9-10)
- the conclusion to the story of the beast and the false prophet (19:17-21)
- the conclusion of the Proclamations Cycle (19:17-18)
- the conclusion to Cycles 2-6 (19:11-21), and last, but not least,
- the final description of Christ in the last of his clearly described roles

It is a quite remarkable, once again, that there happen to be seven of these conclusions, all wrapped up, as it were, in the same package.

As regards the last item in the above list, the descriptions of Christ, here is a brief reminder of what those descriptions are about and where they are to be found:

- His incarnation and faithful witness to God (12:1-5, 1:5, 3:14, 19:11, 13b)
- His eternal divinity evoked (1:8, 1:12-20, 2:8, 2:18, 21:6, 22:13)

- His ruling over the nations is evoked (1:5, 2:12, 3:7, 12:5,10, 19:11-12,15-16)
- His sacrificial death to redeem mankind (1:5, 5:6, 12:11, 14:4, 19:13a)
- His resurrection and headship of the Church (1:5, 1:12-20, 2:1, 2:8, 3:1, 7:16-17, 14:1-5)
- His second coming (1:7, 22:12,20)
- His final triumph over evil in righteous judgment (19:11-21)
- His role as bridegroom, and eternal sustainer of the saints in glory, is implicit in 19:7, 21:2,23 and 22:3 but is not described in any detail.

If all these allusions are included in the count, then there are eight of them, which, at the symbolic level, is the number 7 + 1, with the role of bridegroom being the eighth. In this role He ushers in the new beginning, as explained in section 5.5.5 below.

Being a complex conclusion of this nature, it clearly has an important function in the book. It cannot, therefore, be signaling a low level junction between paragraphs, or even paragraph clusters, but must indicate a higher level division than that.

In terms of the nomenclature used in this study then, one cycle, or even a set of cycles, concludes at this point, and the new beginning which clearly exists at 20:1 must, in turn, be the beginning of another cycle.

5.4.4 Evidence for a Tail-Head Link Between Cycles 6 and 7

In previous discussion it was noted that ancient writers apparently took pains to connect different parts of their discourse together by various kinds of overlapping links, and a connection of the type Acb/caB was previously posited for the transition between Cycles 1 and 2, as explained in Chapter 3 section 6.3. A similar kind of transition can also be posited for the connection between Cycles 6 and 7, as is being discussed in these sections.

It is of considerable interest, and probably no coincidence, that the same features which were used to form the connection between Cycles 1 and 2, also occur in the transition between Cycles 6 and 7. See Chapter 3, sections 6.1 and 6.3 for an introduction to the general issue of ancient transition techniques, as well as a full discussion of the transition between Cycles 1 and 2.

Two of the key words which contributed to the tail-head connection between Cycles 1 and 2 were ‘a throne’, in the context of reigning, and ‘a door’, in the context of Heaven being opened. John sees Heaven opened again at 19:11 and this provides a link back to 4:1. However, this same concept also provides a link forward because in 20:1-3 the word 'a key', is used in the context of its cognate in Greek 'to shut', and 'to seal' - no doubt the equivalent of 'to lock', in relation to 'the pit'. This is a contrastive concept, or even the direct opposite, of the concept of unlocking and opening a door in Heaven.

Christ is dominant in the context of Cycle 1 and the beginning of Cycle 2, and even participates in the section of text where the intermingling link (3:20-21) is operative. By contrast, Satan is the principal participant in 20:1-3 and 7-10, so it is appropriate, therefore, that the transition feature should also be an example of a similar contrast, and include the latter participant. The clear contrast between opening and shutting was previously set up in the hearer's mind by the repetition of these words in 3:7-8, in a context which also uses the word 'a key'.

Since the word 'key' is only of secondary importance in each of the Cycles being connected (19:11 and 20:1-3), and is not typical of either, its notation is the letter 'c'.

The concept of reigning and judging is central to the final interlude (19:1-2 and 6) and the Cycles 2-6 conclusion (19:11-21). This is actually a key concept for the whole book and, as such, occurs in all the cycles including both 6 and 7. However, it is not evenly spread and occurs in clusters, the major ones being Chapters 4-5, 19:1-21, and 20:4-6 and 20:11-15.

So it is due to the fact that it occurs in concentrated form at the end of Cycle 6, and also near the beginning of Cycle 7, that it becomes a candidate for use as a transitional link. In addition, the specific word 'throne' also reoccurs in 19:1-6 (twice) and again in 20:4 and 11 (twice) which reinforces the overlapping connection.

The word 'a throne', in various forms, also occurs throughout the book, but again in clusters. Prior to the double use in 19:1-6, its previous usage was a single occurrence at 16:17. The previous reference to God sitting on his throne was right back at 7:15. As regards the concept of reigning prior to 19:1-21, the previous brief allusions to the concept, not the use of the word, were at 17:14 and 15:3. The word was previously used at 11:15 and 17.

This connection, based on the important concept cluster of reigning/judging/thrones, will be represented by (bolded with an apostrophe) '**c'**'.

In addition to the above words and concepts there are a number of other, less important words, which occur near the end of Cycle 6 and near the beginning of Cycle 7, and which, therefore, contribute to this overlapping link. These other words are as shown in this list:

- 'the witness of Jesus' (19:10 - reinforced by a previous plural occurrence at 17:6, and 20:4);
- 'the word of God' (19:13 and 20:4);
- 'bride' (18:23 at the end of the body of Cycle 6), 'wife' (19:7), and then 'bride' again (21:2 at the beginning of the body of Cycle 7), with 'bride' and 'wife' co-occurring in 21:9;
- 'assemble' (19:17,19 and 20:8);
- 'the rest' (19:21 and 20:5), and
- the combined concepts of a marriage and close communion in the same context at 19:7-9 and 21:2-4.

These will all be globally represented by 'xyz' in the formula.

Another concept cluster which is important for this linkage is the combination of the beast, the false prophet, the mark of the beast and the worship of its image. As mentioned above, the story of the beast and the false prophet is brought to a conclusion in 19:20, but there is a further reference back to this same detailed concept cluster in 20:4 and 10 together. From the point of view of telling the story, there is no need to repeat this information, but it is repeated, and in doing so it creates a link between the two cycles.

Since this information is dominant in Cycle 6 and only repeated once in Cycle 7, the notation is 'a'.

Another link word is 'white'. It is not a dominant concept but it occurs three times in 19:11 and 14, and is repeated just once in 20:11, meaning that it could also be included in the material represented by 'a', for, after all, it is really all about the Rider on the *White* Horse

Conversely, 'the lake of fire', and the concept of clothes or adornment which is bright, light and clean, occur briefly in Cycle 6 and extensively in Cycle 7. The concept of the lake of fire occurs once at 19:20 and then at 20:10,14,15 and 21:8. Clean, fine linen occurs in the description of the wife of the Lamb at 19:8 and of the followers of the one on the white horse at 19:14, then the bride's adornment reoccurs at 21:2 and the lengthy description of the adornment of the new Jerusalem continues in 21:9-22:1 with the concepts of brightness, lightness and cleanness being particularly noticeable. Consequently, these concepts which are dominant in the second of the two cycles are represented by 'b' in the formula.

What all this data indicates then, is that the author has constructed a remarkably balanced, complex link between Cycle 6 (**A**) and Cycle 7 (**B**), which can be represented by the formula **Ac**'bc,xyz/**c**'ac,xyz**B**. This formula is similar in type to the connection which was previously noticed between Cycles 1 and 2 (Acb/caB), and includes the same major concept clusters (thrones/reigning and door/key/open/shut).

This strongly suggests that the author created a pattern, a lower level template, you could say, at the beginning of the book, which was repeated later on. However, the connection between Cycles 6 and 7 uses many more features than the connection between Cycles 1 and 2. This suggests that this complex arrangement of features was intended to be prominent and, therefore, was intended to indicate that a significant transition was taking place.

Once this system is understood, it indicates clearly that an important division between two major units occurs between 19:21 and 20:1. So, it bears repeating, that the linguistic data which is available needs to be accounted for in an appropriate way. Consequently, any analysis which places the last major division of the book in another place, must also account for this detailed repetition in this part of the book in some other more convincing manner.

5.5 The Structure of Cycle 7 in Detail 20:1-22:7

The previous sections above sought to demonstrate that Cycles 2-6 are a complete unit, bounded by a general setting (Chapters 4-5), and a conclusion which is 19:11-21. This analysis is, in turn, confirmed by the fact that, what follows, namely 20:1-22:7, is also a coherent unit with its own setting, body and conclusion as illustrated in Chart 37.

Chart 37.

Overview of the Structure of Cycle 7

1. Setting: A Description of how the Ultimate Problem of Evil is Resolved 20:1-15

2. Body: A Preview of the New Creation 21:1-22:5

A. Generic Introduction to the Characteristics of the New Creation and the New Jerusalem 21:1-8

B. Specific Development 1. Detailed Description of the Characteristics of the New Jerusalem 21:9-21

C. Specific Development 2. Detailed Description of the Characteristics of the New Creation Associated with the New Jerusalem 21:22-22:5b

Coda: A Summary of the Eternal Destiny of the People of God 22:5c

3. Conclusion: The Veracity and Reliability of the Vision 22:6-7

A brief overview of this Cycle was presented in Chapter 3. The charts displayed there are reproduced in the Appendix at the end of this chapter for your convenience. Following on from that, and to complete the picture, the more complex issues concerning this cycle will be elucidated in the rest of this chapter.

5.5.1 General Principles Constraining the Structure of Cycle 7

There are four general principles which appear to have a major influence on the organization of this cycle.

Firstly, it is self-evidently the last cycle and therefore has to function as a conclusion to the series of cycles. More than that, it is the last in a series of seven, in a book, in which the number seven is clearly important. Not only that, but the seventh sub-unit of four of the five preceding cycles has been a unit, which is clearly, at the same time, both a conclusion to what precedes, and a new beginning for what is to follow.

Even Cycle 1 has a less obvious overlap connection with Cycle 2, as was previously explained in Chapter 3.6.3, being of the type which is called a Tail-Head Link. As a consequence, even the seventh letter can be interpreted as, at least presaging a new beginning, even though the structural organization is not the same as for the other seventh units in the following cycles.

By virtue of its position, Cycle 7 provides a conclusion for the visionary content of the seven cycles, and this is confirmed by some of its content, yet at the same time the main component of its content (21:1-22:5) describes a radical new beginning. It has not escaped the notice of the commentators that this is hardly a coincidence, but is directly linked with the symbolic message which has been drummed out, throughout the book, by means of the repeated seven-fold structures.

Even though his concept of the book, as a whole, and his division into major units are different to what is presented in this analysis, Wilcock 1975,197-8, nonetheless, very aptly explains this insight as follows:

> As most of the sixth sections seem to deal with some sort of finality, so most of the seventh sections seem to look past the 'end' to what lies beyond... Scene 7 [19:11-21:8] follows suit. It has described the whole drama of sin and redemption in the most basic terms, and now in its seventh section [21:1-8] looks forward into the distances of eternity. Here is the new world... It is as if we have passed through a series of seven-sided rooms, in each of which one window has looked onto eternity; and in a moment we shall step out of the seventh room and find ourselves in the open air.

If the occurrence of the number seven has any symbolic significance at all, and this is hard to deny, then the seventh in the series ought to be important. In this case, which is a series of *seven* sevens, the seventh of the series, far from being outside the system, ought to contribute something very significant to this symbolic aspect of the book.

A second related point is that conclusions, in and of themselves, are specialized features of a text. All texts must have 'purposiveness' (Callow 1998,149-50), and if authors are going to succeed in communicating their message then they must reveal their purpose by the conclusion, at the latest. Having said that, they, by no means, have to reveal their purpose in the most direct way possible. Callow (ibid.,160) goes on to say that purists like to have everything neat and tidy, but that 'speakers of languages are not purists'.

On the contrary, conscious ambiguity plays an important role in language. This is particularly true with conclusions, when an author may hold something back, in order that the readers be obliged to contribute something themselves, to the process of comprehension. What the author does is to set up a pattern, which creates the possibility of predicting how it will end. Thus, alert listeners are capable of deducing for themselves what may happen, from the information given. For there to be a pattern, there needs to be some repetition, and for the listener to be able to correctly provide the missing piece to complete the picture, the ending, even if it has a twist in the tail, must be a continuation or a completion of the pattern previously used.

Callow 1998,216 illustrates this at some length with an example of English humor. She says firstly, that 'the repetitive nature of the story has built up an expectancy that the culmination will fit into the pattern established'. But then she concludes: 'An important aspect of this kind of humor is that the readers must be left to make the final humorous connection themselves. A final explanation... would have drained all the humor away'. Some more detailed examples of this principle are provided in the Appendix at the end of this chapter.

It is not so much humor which is in view in Revelation, although irony is definitely present. So, for example, there is a case in point which actually provides yet another connection between Cycles 1 and 7. In Cycle 1 the Christians at Smyrna are warned that the devil will try to put some of them in prison, but that this will only last for a period of 10 days (2:10). By contrast, when it comes to his turn, the devil will be held in prison for 1000 years (20:2 and 7), which is, 10 multiplied by 100, and years, in his case, instead of days. Meanwhile, the Christians who have suffered, will be seated in positions of supreme authority, on heavenly thrones, during this same very long period of time (20:4). It is to be noted that the word 'prison' is only used with its primary meaning in 2:10 in Cycle 1 and 20:7 in Cycle 7.

So the issue here is not humor per se, but rather, the principle which is at stake. This is the fact that conclusions will often both play on the patterns already established in the book, and yet also be thought-provokingly different.

Thirdly, one way in which Cycle 7 is different is its structural organization. The previous cycles all had a systematic seven-fold structure, even if the superficial manifestation was more obvious in some cases and less obvious in others. This is not the case for Cycle 7. The body of Cycle 7 particularly, is primarily composed of description, and, as such, is less systematic, and more impressionistic than the other cycles. See Chapter 3.7.2 for previous discussion of this issue.

Fourthly, the primary semantic relationship which links together the various parts of the body of the cycle is the generic-specific relationship (see Chart 37). In conjunction with this, there is a pattern of thesis-antithesis which also runs through the whole cycle - but this basic pattern also has a twist to it, as will be seen.

5.5.2 The Setting of Cycle 7 Revisited 20:1-15

In previous discussion in Chapter 3.7.3, it was observed that the setting of Cycle 7 is the antithesis of the setting of Cycle 1. This is because the former is a summary of Satan's failure and final defeat, which is in direct contrast to the latter which portrays the Risen Christ in all his glory of victory.

Following on from this, it can now be observed that the setting of Cycle 7 is also in an antithetical relationship with the body which follows. As mentioned, it provides a review of Satan's downfall but the culminating point is that he ends up in the lake of fire (20:10). This preview of his ultimate fate, provides helpful long-term hope, but it is not much help in the short-term. However, if it is accepted that 20:1-3 is recapitulative, and, therefore, covers the same time period as the life of the Church on earth, then this same section also provides an interim, limiting solution to the problem of evil. This information is of immediate short-term benefit to the people of God on earth, because they learn in this way, that the dragon can no longer deceive them, which is surely better than nothing (20:3).

Thus it is, that the originator of evil, the one who stood behind the perpetrators of evil on the earth, whose ultimate goal was the persecution and the destruction of the people of God (12:17), is finally both definitely, and definitively dealt with. This not only brings to a conclusion an important theme in Revelation, it also brings to a conclusion a basic issue which has perplexed humanity since the beginning of time.

In parallel with the general problem of evil, the more specific, and final, problem of death is also resolved in 20:14. Even though death as a personified entity is not a major theme in Revelation itself, it is, nonetheless, a major, on-going ontological issue. Since it is stated that death is 'the last enemy' to be destroyed in 1 Corinthians 15:26, it is reasonable to assume that this awareness of death as a personified enemy, may have been present in the reservoir of general knowledge for the first readers of the book, as well as for its modern readers. Consequently, the announcement of the resolution of this problem is of considerable significance.

The two related issues which are addressed are what happens to human beings who have been responsible for evil acts, and what happens to those who have been the victims of evil. The vindication of the people of God who have suffered persecution is established in 20:4-6, which provides a final response to the cry which went up in 6:10, and the final end of all evil-doers is described in 20:12-15. In this way, the setting of the cycle provides a brief, but comprehensive statement concerning the resolution of the problem of evil, which indicates that it will be, once and for all, put to rest. Considering that the following body presents, for the most part, a positive picture of future bliss, this is an appropriate setting, for it is clear that paradise could never be fully paradise unless it was apparent that the problem of evil had been previously resolved.

The setting with its removal of evil then, is the antithesis of what follows, but, as such, provides the context within which the quintessence of the New Creation and the New Jerusalem can be fully appreciated. At the same time it also sets a pattern, for the interplay of thesis and antithesis continues in the body which follows.

5.5.3 The Body of Cycle 7 and its Seven-fold Motif 21:1-22:5

An overview of this unit was previously presented in Chapter 3, section 7.2. The primary issue which was raised and left unanswered was whether it can be truly said that Cycle 7 continues, completes, or contributes in some way, to the series of seven-fold motifs, which have been evoked in the previous cycles. It was remarked that the seven-fold motif is manifested in different ways in the earlier cycles, so it can be deduced that there is no unwritten law stating that it must be manifest in a particular way. It was also observed that the methods previously used are not obviously reproduced in Cycle 7, which leads to the deduction that, if it is present at all, it must be in some different form.

Before proceeding to answer this question some aspects of the structural organization need to be clarified. The primary semantic relationship which links together the various parts of the body of Cycle 7 is the generic-specific relationship, which creates a three part parallel structure with a coda as demonstrated in Chart 37 above.

In addition, the first unit (**A.**) has an almost identical internal organization which is a double **A.** (Generic) **B.** (Generic) **C.** (Specific) parallel structure, plus a coda for each part. This organization is displayed in simplified form in Chart 38.

Chart 38.
The Structure of the Body of Cycle 7 as a Complete Unit

A. Generic Introduction 21:1-8
B. Specific Development 1. 21:9-21
C. Specific Development 2. 21:22-22:5b
Coda. Summary 22:5c

In actual practice, the internal organization of all the units A. B. and C., as displayed in Chart 37 above, is very complex. But it is amazing to find that, even though there is an enormous amount of detail provided, the internal organization of each unit is remarkably coherent and consistent. The details are not randomly heaped up like a pile of dead leaves, but display rather, the dynamic artistry of a carefully woven pattern. For those interested in such details, the full displays of these units are provided in the following Appendix.

Generic-specific relationships, since they cover the same ground, can be ambiguous when it comes to deciding which part is the most important, but as a general rule, the generic part is more naturally prominent than the specific. This means that section **A.** (21:1-8) is more important than sections **B.** and **C.**, and this is confirmed, because it is also the section which contains the most indicators of marked prominence.

The concept of prominence was explained briefly in Chapter 1 and it will be taken up in more detail in Chapter 6. However, since the organization of Cycle 7 is unique in the book, and since the generic-specific relationships are somewhat complex, with regard to prominence, we will take a moment here to explain the issues involved.

The first sketches of the theory of semantic relationships underlying this study (Beekman et al. 1981,112) indicated that the generic was naturally more prominent. See also Cotterell and Turner 1989,224 where each 'HEAD' which is paired with a 'specific', is in fact the generic partner. More recently, Callow 1998,285 has mitigated this position by saying that the context is the deciding factor especially 'in cases where the generic precedes a single specific'. However, where several specifics amplify the generic as in Cycle 7, it seems clear that the generic would be more prominent being, in effect, a more memorable summary of the concept(s) concerned.

The first two generic statements in Chart 39, present the new Heaven and the new Earth, and the new Jerusalem as being the topics of the following section (21:1-2). This is followed by a specific description of aspects of the new creation (21:3-4), which is marked for prominence by being a direct speech and by the presence of 'behold'.

Chart 39.
The Internal Structure of Unit A. of the Body of Cycle 7
21:1-8

A. Generic Vision of the New Creation 21:1
  B. Generic Vision of the New Jerusalem 21:2
    C. Specific Descriptions of the New Creation 21:3-4b
Coda. Repetition of Summary Explanation 21:4c

A. Generic Statement Referring to Renewal 21:5
  B. Generic Statement Referring to Completion 21:6a
    C. Specific Descriptions of the New Creation 21:6b-8a
Coda. Repetition of Summary Explanation 21:8b

This is the beginning of a build up of prominence markers which culminates in 21:5-6b, where there is a repetition of 'behold', and three direct speeches in a row.

Two of these are generic summaries, and one of them is a part of the Narrative Framework which contains volitional import material plus the imperative 'Write!'.

All three are followed by the book level prominence marker 'I am the Alpha and Omega'. After this, the text flattens out again into specific description 21:6c-8, which runs to the end of the section, although there is a further reference back to the 'all things' of 21:5 in the repetition of 'these things', in 21:7.

This evidence indicates that it is the first and last direct speeches of this group of three, which are the most important part of the section, and thence, of the whole body of Cycle 7. These are: **'Behold, I (am) make(ing) all things new'** (21:5a), and, **'It has been done/finished'** (21:6a).

The first of these is prominent because it is marked by 'behold'. Then secondly, it is because it is God Himself speaking directly from His position of authority on His throne. This is only the second time in the book where

He unambiguously speaks directly like this, the previous occurrence being at 1:8, right at the beginning of everything. If the less specifically identified voice in 16:17 is also considered to be the voice of God Himself, then this declaration would be the last of three.

The verb of the second direct speech is in the perfect form, and, therefore, it has a definite sense of finality and completion. Since the use of the perfect indicative is very rare in the book, this contributes to the prominence of this statement.

The direct speech (21:5b) is support material, since it is acting as a signpost, pointing away from itself, in order to enhance the prominence of the other two speeches.

The first of these declarations, being in the present tense unambiguously refers to the immediate situation of the New Creation and the New Jerusalem. The second is ambiguous, and perhaps intentionally so. It could be referring back antithetically to the completion of the work of judgment previously summarized in the setting of the cycle. This is possible, because it is in parallel with the same verb at 16:17, where the completion of judgment is in view.

On the other hand, it could refer to the completion of all the events recorded in the book. This is possible because it is in parallel with similar usages of the same verb at 1:1,19 and 4:1, where all the action described in the book is in view. Or, it could just refer back to the previous verb, such that God says ‘I am making all things new’, and then barely an instant later he declares that this work of new creation is already completed. In this case, the parallelism would go all the way back to Genesis 1 where God spoke the word and, with the same, each part of the original creation immediately came into being.

This grand ambiguity makes the statement timeless, and all-encompassing in its sweep, which is fitting for a statement of such finality in such a grand finale.

Here then, in this doublet, is expressed the underlying meaning of the seven-fold symbolism. To put it in terms of the logical progression of the book, the repetition of the seven-fold motifs and structures has prepared the hearer for this final revelation. This final revelation is a revelation of the ultimate, perfect (cf. the number 7) reality. This reality, which everyone needs to be aware of, is that God not only has a plan, but that it is also perfectly certain that He will actually execute this plan, and finish everything which He has started, in order to turn everything into ultimate perfection.

There is little disagreement that in Scripture the number seven, symbolically understood, represents 'fullness' or 'completeness'. The whole book has been permeated with this symbolic message. But now, right at the end, God Himself speaks, albeit briefly, but in unmistakable terms, as if to say: 'Everything has been completed, finalized, finished; now everything has been newly re-created, everything is perfect and complete. Everything is ready for occupation and eternal enjoyment'.

This then, is the 'seven' of the seventh cycle: it is different, it is striking and, appropriately for the seventh in a series, it completes the pattern with a final conclusion. The connection between this double statement and the previous symbolic message is not explicit: it is there to be perceived by those who will perceive it. It is like the archetypical joke cited above. To try and fully explain this connection, even in the context of a text analysis, would be to destroy its effectiveness. Explaining it would destroy the power and persuasiveness of a communication, which derives its dynamism from a complex play on words, concepts and symbols.

5.5.4 Detailed Development of the Seven-fold Motif

As was observed above, the whole of the body of Cycle 7 is organized around the generic-specific semantic relationship. The main generic part has been dealt with first, because it is considered to be the most important part of the whole. As such, it provides a cogent summary of the primary point of the whole passage. However, the specific part also has its place and, by definition, it contributes finer detail to the generic summary already provided.

Any text is composed of old, or known information, plus new information. For obvious reasons, the ratio of old to new information increases as the text develops, until by the time the conclusion is reached, the author has said all that needs to be said. Consequently, there is usually very little new information in a conclusion. Cycle 7 is no exception.

The body alone contains between forty and fifty propositions. The word 'proposition' here is being used in a technical sense to represent a complex grouping of concepts, which is functioning as a unit in its context. For example, the proposition, 'I saw the holy city, the new Jerusalem', is composed of at least six concepts but is functioning as a single unit in 21:2. See Callow 1998,60-2 on concepts as units, and pages 154-55 on propositions.

Most of these propositions are repetitions of previously introduced information. This repetition creates a series of parallels with all the previous cycles. There are approximately 120 parallels in all. The fact that a conclusion should make a final reference to a number of concepts previously discussed in the book should come as no surprise. But the fact that there are direct connections with all the cycles, underscores the parallel nature of the structural organization of the book.

If, in addition to being a conclusion, Cycle 7 contributes some final new information to the overall message, this information can be derived with reference to the propositions which are unique to the cycle. Otherwise, it may be that some propositions were introduced in a preliminary way elsewhere, but only developed in detail in this cycle. As Alter 1981,97 explains: 'what you have to look for... is the small but revealing differences in the seeming similarities, the nodes of emergent new meanings in the pattern of regular expectations created by explicit repetition'. This process reveals that the proposition, the new creation (i.e. the new heaven and earth 21:1), with its synonymous proposition, I make all things new (21:5), are unique to Cycle 7.

The new Jerusalem was summarily introduced in Cycle 1 (3:12) but is described in detail in Cycle 7. This confirms the two major generic topics which were previously proposed. If the same process is applied to the detail, then the propositions which contain significant new information are,

- God living/being very close to people (21:3,22, 22:3-4),
- the nations are present in God's presence in the new Jerusalem (21:24-6, 22:2),
- God is the source of light for his people (21:24, 22:5),
- fountains and/or a river of living water will be present (21:6, 22:2), and
- a life-giving tree will be present (22:2).

The reference to 'fountain', at 21:6 is the last of five references, the first (7:17) and the last referring to living water, and the others being references to earthly fountains. Similarly, 'river', at 22:1-2 are the last two of eight references. The last two are the only ones to refer to living waters, the others referring to earthly rivers.

This process of distinguishing the new information from the old can be quite productive and, in this case, this process has already provided confirmation for the main topics of the cycle, which were previously deduced according to different criteria. However, for the detail, it runs the risk of being too subjective, since, at times, it is a matter of opinion exactly what constitutes 'significant new information'.

This may not be a problem if the text is intentionally impressionistic as was suggested previously. But since more evidence is available, then a more objective viewpoint can be constructed, for complementary analyses contribute their particular insight to the total picture, as Longacre 1999a,144 has previously explained in detail.

One of the general principles mentioned above, was that the whole cycle is marked by a series of antitheses. These antitheses throw into perspective at least six, and possibly seven, positive characteristics of eternity as illustrated in Chart 40.

Chart 40.
The Antitheses of the Body of Cycle 7

Antitheses	Thesis Being Highlighted
The first/former things passed away, no more sea 21:1 and 4	There is a new heaven and earth, including a new city 21:1-2
No more death, sorrow...or pain 21:4	God is present (dwelling with) His people 21:3; 22:3-4:
No more people destined for the second death, none of those not in the book of life 21:8, 27	Life is present and abundantly available 21:6c; 22:1-2
No (physical) sanctuary, so the shutting of the gates is no longer operative 21:22 and 25a	God and the Lamb are sanctuary, the nations have access to God and to healing 21:23-6; 22:2
No more curse 22:3	All good things will be there, including healing 21:5,7; 22:2
No more night 21:25b	God and the Lamb are the light and glory of the city 21:23; 22:

In the first instance, the body and its setting are in an antithetical relationship, and this linguistic feature is continued in the detail of the body. In effect, there are seven passages which provide contrast within the body by means of antitheses. So, just as shadow helps to highlight any object of interest, in 21:1-22:5 the antitheses throw into sharp relief the glories of the New Creation and the New Jerusalem, which are the main topics of interest.

As the chart indicates, six positive characteristics explicitly occur in semantic relationship with, or, in the immediate context of, the antitheses. The disappearance of Babylon is a seventh antithesis which is not explicitly stated, but which would highlight the appearance of the New Jerusalem.

Nonetheless, this antithesis is clearly implicit in the author's choice of words throughout this cycle.

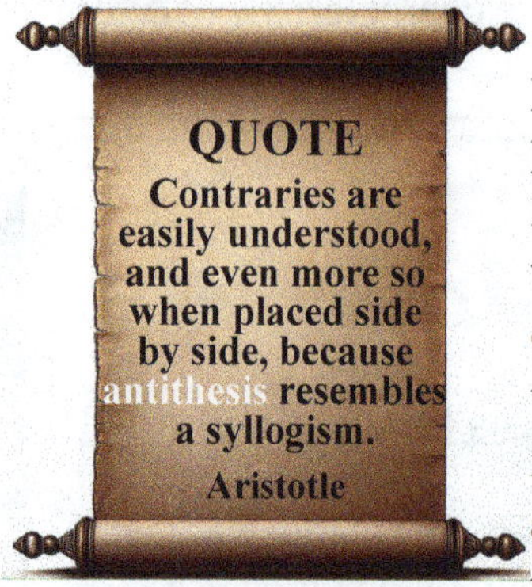
QUOTE
Contraries are easily understood, and even more so when placed side by side, because antithesis resembles a syllogism.
Aristotle

Spread through the seven antithetical passages there is a seven-fold repetition of the phrases 'no longer', or 'not at all' (21:1,4 x2, 25,27; 22:3 and 5), which is clearly reminiscent of the striking six-fold use of the same phraseology concerning Babylon in 18:21-3. In 21:8 and 27 the Greek root for 'abomination', is used which is in parallel to the references to Babylon in 17:4 and 5. These are the only occurrences of this root. In addition, in 21:8 there are references to fornication, murder and sorcery as in 17:4,6, and 18:3,9,23,24, and in 21:19-21 there are references to the precious stones which Babylon once had and lost, as per 17:4 and 18:16-17.

Before moving on, it can be observed that what have been called antitheses are, in reality, double negatives. That is, they describe the removal or disappearance of something negative. The only possible exception is the reference to the sanctuary in 21:22. However, within the broader biblical context, it could be understood that this reference was intended to evoke the earthly Temple, which had been defiled by sinful people, and the destruction of which, having been predicted by Jesus, had possibly been accomplished by the time Revelation was written. The physical building was, in any case, an imperfect and inadequate representation of God's true dwelling place, cf. Acts 7:48-50.

Since a double negative makes a positive, these references actually contribute to the overall positive tenor of the seventh cycle. This is the twist in the antithetical tail.

The above study of the antitheses is already leading in a certain direction, but it is the structural organization of the body which makes it possible to assert, with some conviction, that there is a seven-fold pattern woven into this cycle, as in the others. As noted above, the body of the cycle (21:1-22:5) is organized on the basis of generics and specifics. The two generic topics, the New Creation and the New Jerusalem, are in focus at the beginning of the body, while the specific details are described in the rest of the sub-units of the body as indicated in Chart 41.

The New Jerusalem is also the topic of 21:11b-21. Internally this unit has a mixture of generic and specific information. Overall, it contributes to the notion of the New Jerusalem as 'a city' and, as such, is considered to contribute generic information. At the specific level, it contributes to the proposition that the city is characterized by light, airiness, brightness and glory (21:11,18-21), which contributes to Item 7 in the chart.

Chart 41.
The Seven Characteristics of Eternity as Portrayed in Cycle 7

The Characteristics	The Textual Units
1. A New Creation	21:1 and 21:5
2. A New City, the New Jerusalem	21:2 and 21:9-11a
3. God is Personally Present with His People	21:3-4b,21:6b-7, 22:3b-5b
4. Water of Life is Abundantly Available	21:6b, and 22:1-3a
5. Healing is Abundantly Available	22:1-3a
6. The Nations are Present	21:24-27 and 22:1-3a
7. God and the Lamb are the Light and the Glory of the City	21:22-3 and 22:3b-5b

Since there are some concentric structures embedded within the larger passages, there is inevitably some informational repetition. But the result is that, when this repetition is taken into account, reference is made to five significant characteristics of the generic topics. When these are taken together with the two generic topics, it makes a total of seven pieces of information (or propositions) which, together, provide a picture of eternity as John glimpsed it from his visionary vantage point.

Since the whole body of the cycle is constructed around the generic-specific relationship, it is totally appropriate that the seven-fold motif should also be constructed around the same semantic relationship.

Comparison of these proposals with Chart 40, and its accompanying discussion, demonstrate that the seven characteristics are to be found in both charts. Thus it is, that two complementary methods of analysis have led in the same direction and, taken together, they provide solid evidence that the proposed organizational motif is objectively present in the text. In this final cycle John presents a seven-fold view of eternity, and since this other world is characterized by its newness, the seven-fold motif may be summarized more memorably as the motif of **the Seven New Things**.

The final conclusion is two-fold. Firstly, the symbolic import of the seven-fold motifs used throughout the book is completed, and as it were, interpreted by the double statement in 21:5-6, *'I am making all things new'* and *'(These things) have been done or completed'*. In addition to this play on symbols (as opposed to a play on words), it has also been demonstrated that the cycle contains descriptions of seven new things (two generic and five specific) which will characterize the eternal world, which will replace the actual imperfect world.

It can be freely admitted that a casual reader or listener may well not have been immediately aware that John described exactly seven new things, since this motif is not as clearly delineated as in previous cycles. However, if John's objective was primarily to create an impression of this new world, then the absence of an obvious, numbered organization may have been part of his intention. Be that as it may, the impressionistic nature of the surface structure does not invalidate the fact that careful analysis can uncover this pattern of seven new things, which is woven into the warp and woof of the text. The discovery that there are seven of them, just serves to confirm the dominant concept of completion and perfection.

5.5.5 The Coda and the Conclusion of Cycle 7

The analysis of the body of Cycle 7 has been completed, but there is still one phrase, *'and they will reign for ever and ever'* (22:5c), which remains unaccounted for. This has been analyzed as a coda to the body, as was previously presented in Chart 37 above, for the following reasons.

It is a clause with informational import and so it belongs with 22:5 rather than with 22:6. Nonetheless, it does not fit into the parallel structure of 21:22-22:5b. The coda cannot be construed as being semantically parallel to the reference to God's slaves in 22:3, even though this noun is the immediately preceding grammatical antecedent of the pronominal suffix 'they'. These slaves have the privilege of standing upright in the presence of their Master and being beneficiaries of his largesse (v.4), but, under no condition, could slaves be normally considered to have the right to reign together with their Master. The concept of reigning, by definition, implies a different sort of relationship.

So, even though the coda contributes new information, the seven-fold motif previously described is complete without it. Consequently, it appears to fall outside of both these organizational systems.

Grammatically, the antecedent of the pronominal subject 'they', which is included in with the verb 'to reign' in 22:5c, would seem to be the direct object pronoun 'them' at the end of the previous verse. This, in turn refers back to God's 'slaves', in 22:3b, but, semantically speaking, the content of the coda bears no direct relationship with this sentence.

The semantic relationship between the coda and what precedes, would seem to be that of a comment, and, in effect, the comment refers just as naturally to the whole of the body as it does to the preceding unit of text. Consequently, the pronominal subject 'they', in its ambiguity, may refer quite naturally to the people of God in general, as they are referred to throughout the body of the cycle. Furthermore, it can be observed that this system of providing a concluding comment in a coda is not unique, but is a system which was previously used throughout Cycle 4, and also occurs within the sub-units of Cycle 7 itself.

Functionally, the coda contributes to the whole of the body and, in fact, to the whole of the seven cycles, much as the well known coda, 'And they all lived happily ever after', does in English literature. It is the final piece of information which the author leaves with the addressees at the end of the 'story' before the concluding part (22:6-21), which contributes nothing more to the 'story' as such.

This coda is short, it is cogent, and it is entirely memorable; to such an extent that it will remain ringing in the ears of the listeners long after the discourse has been terminated. Implicitly, it suggests that there has been a past, but one which is now finished and soon to be forgotten. More explicitly, it is totally positive in its forward-looking perspective on out into eternity. This is a direct, and cogent, reminder that this whole book is not an end in itself, but that its informational purpose is to bring its hearers to an end, which turns out to be a new beginning.

In a much briefer manner, this coda is communicating the same message as the overlap links of Cycles 2-6. In those previous cases the reader was informed by the structural organization, that they had reached the end of a stage, but they also discovered, at the same time, that, that end point was also ushering them into a the beginning of another new stage in their journey.

In this case, the coda is in parallel to those previous end units, because it has the same function, but this time, the message is slightly different. It is still indicating that an end has been reached. This time it is the end of the whole book, but, even so, it is not the end, but just the point of departure for a new beginning. However, this time, it is the beginning of timeless eternity, and so it will never have an end. It is not so much that they will live happily ever after, but, in this case, they are destined to happily rule and reign over everything, with their Master, for ever and ever, in a world that has no end. All this is entirely appropriate for a coda and for a book of this kind.

The coda does not contribute to the whole by its content alone but also by virtue of its place in the overall structure. The sevenfold motif of the seventh cycle was described above and it was remarked that it is complete without the coda. Yet, in this case, the coda contributes to the seven-fold motif, in that it also contributes some new information concerning the characteristics of the new creation.

This new information is that the people referred to in the body of the cycle, will reign for ever and ever. In this case, then, it is an eighth element which also contributes to the seven-fold motif. Since this is the first time that this has occurred in the book and, since there are seven, seven-fold motifs (which produces a total of forty-nine occurrences of such a feature in the book), then this coda is also a fiftieth element with regards to the book as a whole.

It was Wilcock 1975 who made a particular contribution with regards to this insight. According to his analysis the whole book is divided into eight scenes with a total of fifty visions, and so he explains the phenomenon of an eighth and of a fiftieth in this way.

> Why is there an eighth scene?... there is an outstanding 'eighth' in Scripture... it is ... to be found at the centre of biblical revelation, for he has ratified it in his work of redemption. It is on Good Friday, the sixth day of the week, that the redeeming work of Christ reaches its climax: "It is finished" (Jn.19:30)... and the Saturday is the day of rest... But of course there was something else to follow. The seventh day proclaimed the end of the law ... and the reign of sin... But Sunday the *eighth* day did more. It proclaimed Christ to be "Son of God in power... by his resurrection from the dead" (Rom.1:4). ... Scripture goes even further... no Jew could doubt the significance of 'forty-nine', and what should follow it... "You shall count seven weeks of years, seven times seven years, so that the time of the seven weeks of years shall be to you forty-nine years. Then you shall send abroad the loud trumpet...And you shall hallow the fiftieth year...a jubilee..." (Lev.25:8-10). With the year of jubilee comes the release of every slave, ... the restitution of all wrongs. The eighth which follows the seven, and the fiftieth which follows the seven times seven, are alike symbolic of a glorious new beginning. (Wilcock ibid.202-3).

Wilcock ibid.,203 then goes on to quote a passage from C.S.Lewis 1956 (1980),171-2 in which Lewis says: 'The things which began to happen after that were so great and beautiful *that I cannot write them...* and we can most truly say *that they all lived happily ever after'*.

The words which have been italicized, independently support insights expressed in the text above, namely that John was unable to clearly describe what he saw of the New Creation. The result, which we have observed, is that this last set of sevens is rather impressionistic in nature. Then, after that, he appends a coda, which is indeed appropriate, and even better, than the one which Lewis also refers to.

In the case of the present analysis, it has been proposed that the macro structure of the book is composed of a series of seven sevens. In the light of the above quotation from the Pentateuch (Lev.25:8-10 cited by Wilcock above), an organization of seven times seven for Revelation would seem to be symbolically the most appropriate of all the possible systems.

In support of this, the reference to a loud trumpet, can be cited. In the context of the Jubilee celebrations of the Old Testament, the blowing of the trumpet was an essential and a crucial feature of this, once in fifty years, event. But, remarkably it is also a crucial feature of Revelation, for it rings out as a semantic prosody, right from the Prologue (1:10) on through, in effect, to the end of the book.

So it is at the end then, the Jubilee concept is reactivated once again, for the series of seven sevens is completed by an eighth, and a fiftieth feature, just as in the Jubilee. Then, as if that was not enough, 22:14-15 in the Epilogue also makes allusive reference to the Pentateuch, namely Deuteronomy chapters 27, 28 and 30.

So then, the present analysis, being more systematically in line with the data, does not confirm Wilcock's overall analysis. But, at the same time, it does confirms that all that he says about this particular feature, is entirely appropriate, and in line with the overall tenor of the book.

In this present case, in the form of this coda to the seventh set of sevens, there is also an 'eighth' and a 'fiftieth'. In the seven sevens, all of God's work to deal with the issues of the first creation with regards to the problem of evil is finished (cf. 'It is finished' in Wilcock's quotation and at 21:6). It is reasonable to assume that all His work to fashion and prepare the New Creation, is also finished.

All that remains is for the liberated slaves to leave Babylon and Egypt behind, and to enter fully into the great privilege of reigning with Christ for ever and ever.

It is remarkable that in his commentary Wilcock makes specific reference to the release of the slaves, which was indeed a prominent feature of the year of Jubilee. This is remarkable, since it is precisely the word 'slave', which appears in 22:3 in the immediate context of, and almost in parallel to 'they will reign', in the coda.

The juxtaposition of these two seemingly contradictory concepts now becomes clear, since in this final and ultimate Jubilee, it is true that the slaves of God are now those who become the rulers of the new universe. So, the work of dealing with the past is done, but, in addition, all the work of preparing the new creation is also finished, so all that needs to be done in the context of the eighth and the fiftieth, is to enter in and enjoy this new beginning, in a way never previously imagined before the revelation of this final mystery.

The whole book is about Jesus and the revelation of the mysteries concerning Him, but for most of the book He is presented as the Lamb, who had been sacrificially killed. Now, in this last part of the book Jesus, raised from the dead and vibrantly alive once more, is revealed as the Lamb for an eighth time. His appearances in different personas are as follows:

- The Lamb who had been Sacrificed, Chapter 5
- The Lamb who Stewards God's Plan of Judgment, Chapter 6
- The Lamb, the Savior of His people, Chapter 7
- The Lamb, the Symbol of their Success, 12:11
- The Lamb, the Source of Life, 13:8, 21:17
- The Lamb, the Supreme Authority on God's Mountain, 14:1-15:4
- The Lamb, the Suzerain Warrior King, 17:14-19:21
- The Lamb, the Shepherd Bridegroom of the Bride 19:7,9, 21:9

On this occasion He is revealed only very subtly, but, nonetheless, in an implication which cannot be denied. In 21:2 reference is made to the Bride, who has prepared herself to meet her Husband. Even if the husband is not explicitly named here, it is obvious that it is none other than the Lamb, who has now taken on the role of the Husband of the Bride, who in her turn, represents the people of God.

So with this extra insight included, the story is now complete: the former slaves have been liberated to reign with their former Master, but that is not all. The Jubilee trumpet has sounded and this is also to herald the fact that the newly freed slaves are destined to marry their Master, and so to co-reign with Him as His wife.

Jesus, in His role as the Bridegroom, is there to usher them into this new beginning which surpasses all previous beginnings, for it is the beginning of an eternity of happiness, for now and ever after. To use Lewis' words once more, all that needs to be done is to go 'further up and further in' (C.S.Lewis 1956 (1980),165).

After the coda, all that remains is the conclusion of Cycle 7, which is to be found in 22:6-7. This passage stands apart from what precedes, in that it no longer continues the communication of referential information, as is the case for the setting and body of each cycle of visions. At this point, the author returns to volitional import text which is designed to encourage the hearer to take the message seriously and to act accordingly, and this continues through the Epilogue to the end of the book.

Nonetheless, 22:6-7 is clearly connected to the body and the coda by the phrase 'These words', which must, in the first instance, refer to what immediately precedes. Consequently, 22:6-7 is analyzed as being one of the many overlap links in the book, being both a conclusion to Cycle 7, and also the beginning of the Epilogue, as was explained in Chapter 2.5.3.

5.6 The Function of the Motifs of the Seven Cycles

The word 'motif' which has been used to describe the repetition found in the body of the cycles has been chosen with care. It is a word which implies repetition but which otherwise adapts to its circumstances. A motif may be concrete and definite, and, in linguistic terms, such a motif would be represented by a specific lexical unit, or word. Otherwise a motif may be evocative and elusive, in which case it is more likely that an author will be making allusion to a concept, which may be represented in the surface structure in a variety of ways. In Revelation both types of motif occur as the dominant characteristic of each cycle.

It is of note that the motif of the first Cycle is a conceptual motif. The word 'letter' is never used by John. Nonetheless, by using the verb 'to write', and by evoking the presence of a writer and of recipients of a message, he had no difficulty in evoking the concept of a letter, and of repeating the concept seven times. Since this understanding of the letter concept is well established, it is not difficult to go a step further and establish a similar understanding for the sixth and seventh cycles.

> **QUOTE**
> **Metaphors and symbols are a deliberate transgression of a word's boundaries of meaning.**
> **Beale 1999,55**

In the case of the sixth cycle, the word 'proclamation' is never used either. However, as with the first cycle, the lexical terms used (i.e. many different verbs of vocal expression, and various participial forms of the verb 'to say') set the tone. In addition, the context of speakers and addressees, and a common preoccupation which provokes comment, make it obvious that the concept of a proclamation is underlying this grouping of speeches.

Similarly, in the seventh cycle, the word 'new', is used and it is also used in connection with the word for 'all things' (21:5). This surface structure usage specifically orientates the hearer towards the underlying motif, even though not all the seven things presented in the cycle are individually qualified by a word indicating newness.

The other motifs used, those of the seals, the trumpets and the bowls are concrete and definite and, consequently, they have long since been recognized by generations of Bible students. The motif of the sign is more ambiguous. The word 'sign', is present and is clearly applied to a certain number of personages, but nonetheless, the concept of a sign is rather more amorphous and difficult to concretely imagine, than a seal, a trumpet or a bowl. This may explain why its presence has generally been overlooked.

A motif is like a sauce poured as a topping on a meal. It is not an obligatory ingredient, but it definitely adds noticeable spice and zest to the main content. In linguistic terms, motifs almost always have a metaphorical function, regardless of whether they are concrete or conceptual in form. However, unlike regular metaphors, they do not operate as lexical items at the sentence level but more as a thematic component at a higher level of the discourse.

In the case of Revelation, the seven-fold motifs under consideration are clearly limited to the confines of one particular cycle. They are not obligatory components, in and of, themselves, in that they contribute nothing significant to the cognitive content of the cycles. However, they clearly have a function of bringing together in conceptual unity, the various components of the body of the cycles which, otherwise, do not have clear logical or semantic connections.

In addition, it can now be noted that they add a metaphorical flavor which contributes to the thematic significance of each cycle. In talking of metaphors, it is not intended to imply that the letters John wrote were not truly real letters.

It is obvious that he wrote and sent real letters to the churches in Asia Minor. Then, for the trumpets which he heard, and the bowls which he saw, they were not just metaphorical, nor imaginary either. They were almost certainly not physical objects, but they were, nonetheless, 'real' objects, in the context of the heavenly world in which his visions unfolded.

What is being said, is that, in the context of the analysis of a text, any element in the text, whether it be real physically, or real spiritually, has the potential for communicating a message by metaphorical means. This continues to be true, even if the feature being used as the basis for the metaphor is entirely imaginary, in purely referential terms.

Revelation is well-known for being a book full of symbols. Symbolism is a universal feature of language, which provides life and color to material which would otherwise be prosaic and even pedantic. Since it is so universal, symbolism must be an effective form of communication, otherwise it would not be used so widely. This means that it must be comprehensible, at least by those people who were the original, intended recipients of the communication. Over time, the consensus which has developed among linguists, is that a meaningful metaphor consists of three basic ingredients, the topic, the image, and a significant point of similarity between the two. This insight into the nature of language is also recognized and accepted by many biblical scholars,

John was not obliged to organize his material around this particular set of motifs, nor around any motifs at all. The fact that he did, nonetheless, use the motifs of letters, seals, trumpets, and bowls is incontrovertible, and the evidence for the other three motifs is substantial as well.

This leads to the question of intentionality once more, for if an element clearly appears in a text, it is reasonable to ask what the author intended to accomplish, and how precisely that element was intended to guide the understanding of the message.

The way forward, in the case of motifs, is to seek out the point of similarity which is the basis of the metaphorical function, and which is intended to illuminate the intended topic. Obviously it is not permissible to select points of similarity arbitrarily. They must have clear relevance to the underlying image, and must be guided and constrained by the content of the text and any other clues which the author has provided.

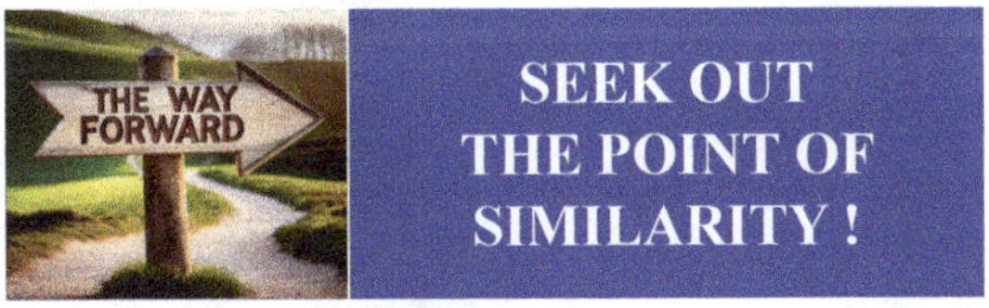
THE WAY FORWARD
SEEK OUT THE POINT OF SIMILARITY !

5.6.1 The Motifs of Cycles 1 and 7

The key characteristic of a letter is that it is a personal, even informal, means of communication. The problem is that the general concept of a letter implies nothing about its content, since a letter, by its very nature can contain any kind of content. The more specific concept of a letter written to first century churches implies that it is likely to contain both teaching and exhortation, whose combined purpose is to motivate a certain kind of behavior. The content of the seven letters confirms this general orientation since the central message of the whole series is a call to repent, and to persevere. In addition, they all contain warnings and promises, which urge the hearers to seek after the promised salvation, and to do the necessary to avoid impending judgment.

The first cycle provides an introductory context to the visionary content of the whole book by virtue of its position at the beginning. In a very real sense, the messages of the first cycle prepare the way for all that is to follow. The letter motif contributes a context of personal communication to a group of people, which has the intent of motivating them to a positive response to the author's desires for them. The group of recipients are a group of churches on earth and, as many commentators concur, it is not unreasonable to assume that the numerical aspect of the motif may be intended to imply that they are representative of the Church as a whole, as it is on earth.

As has been noted above, the body of the seventh cycle is almost entirely descriptive, but the dominating motif, that of newness, has, as its point of similarity, the concept of change - that things will be different from what they have been previously. In the context of the whole book in general, but of Cycle 1 in particular, the new things are the realization of the promises made to the churches in the first cycle. So, for example, in each letter the overcomer is promised that he will inherit certain things, and all these things, are fulfilled either generically, or specifically, in Cycle 7.

Promises are motivational types of communication and, once again, in the context established by Cycle 1, these particular promises are designed to urge the hearers to enter into the fullness of the salvation, which God has prepared for his people. However, a further element in the point of similarity, which is more than implicit (see 21:1,4,27; 22:3 and 5), is that the old, or former, things must pass away to make room for the new. The most important of these former things, which will not continue into the new era, are the problems of pain, persecution, judgment and death.

In addition to the backward-looking references cited above, the relevance of the setting to Cycle 7 can once again be highlighted. This is because it is in this particular part of the whole discourse, that the hearers are specifically told that the final phase of judgment has taken place, firstly on an interim basis, and then definitively. So it is that we are specifically told in Chapter 20, that the devil has been defeated, and has had his power seriously reduced for a temporal period, and then after that he is consigned permanently to the lake of fire. As a result, both the original, and the final, sources of all pain and persecution, namely, the devil and death itself, have been taken care of (20:10 and 14).

So then, Cycle 7 by virtue of its position, is the conclusion to the book. Once again it concerns the Church. It aims to motivate the Church as it is, by describing the Church as it will be, or, as God sees it from His heavenly viewpoint. The motif provides a means of looking back, to old things which are no more, and forward to a new era, all at the same time.

5.6.2 The Seals Motif of Cycle 2

The point of similarity for the seals motif of Cycle 2 which is highlighted in the text, is the fact that they are broken (see 6:1,3 etc.). A seal when it is intact contains, and keeps hidden, whatever message is inside. Once the seal is broken however, the message is revealed.

It would seem clear, in this case, that the message of the motif is intended from the outset to be metaphorical. This is because the document to which the seals are attached is never in view, once the process of opening the seals begins. Consequently, whatever written message it contains is never divulged. It is obvious that that part of the scenario is not important - it is simply part of the setting to prepare the way for what is important, namely the fact that the seals are broken one by one.

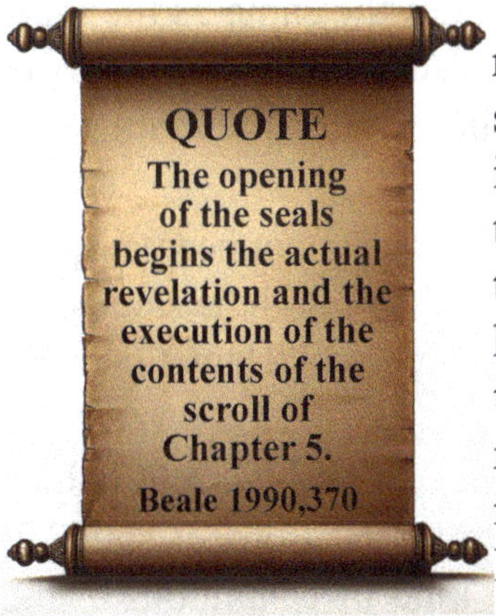
QUOTE
The opening of the seals begins the actual revelation and the execution of the contents of the scroll of Chapter 5.
Beale 1990,370

The message which is revealed as a direct result, even though it is presented in the form of a series of events, rather than in purely verbal form, is a message of judgment. The overall effect of the seal motif then, is to indicate to the hearer that God's plan of judgment which, presumably, had been prepared beforehand, is now about to be initiated. This is because, implicitly and metaphorically at least, it is being opened and revealed by the process of breaking the seals. In His mercy then, God reveals this plan in advance, so that everyone may know about it ahead of time

5.6.3 The Trumpet Motif of Cycle 3

The trumpets of the third cycle were objects in common use which had a variety of uses and, therefore, a variety of possible points of similarity. The context of judgment suggests that the point of similarity is that of a warning of danger. This hypothesis is supported by the fact that the judgments in this cycle are partial (see 8:9,10,12 etc.). A major purpose of a calamity, which affects only a minority of the people concerned, is presumably to warn those who remain that worse is to come.

This concept is taken up in the three Woes (8:13, 9:12, 11:14) which are clearly a warning that worse is indeed to come. Discussion of the three Woes will be taken up in more detail in Chapter 6, where it will be proposed that the whole of the Trumpets Cycle is designed to prepare the way for, and hence warn about, what is to be revealed in the following cycles.

Finally, it can be noticed that within the Trumpets Cycle, two different reactions to the events described are recorded. At the end of the sixth trumpet (9:20-21), within the more pessimistic ethos of the Judgment Theme, it is recorded that people took no notice of the calamities around them, and did not repent. The implication is that they heard the warning but they decided to ignore it. By contrast, within the more positive ethos of the cycle interlude (11:13), it is recorded that some people took notice of the warning implicit in the events, which were occurring around them. As a consequence, they made a more conciliatory response.

There is once again, an accumulation of evidence which guides the reader's reaction to the metaphorical aspect of the trumpet motif. This leads him to understand that, as a group, the trumpets are intended to warn about the judgments which are yet to come.

Just as the breaking of a seal is not the same as reading the whole document, since it is only a preliminary part of the process, so the blowing of the trumpet (in a biblical context at least), is not the same as the main event which is to follow. The trumpet blast is also a preliminary part of a longer process whose purpose is to prepare the way for the main event by announcing it.

If the main event is viewed as negative, then the announcement may be called a warning. However, if the main event (even if it is the same one) is viewed as positive, the announcement may be called an acclamation or an invitation to rejoice.

In Revelation the trumpet blasts take place in Heaven and belong to that referential world, whereas, in earthly terms, the trumpet sound is manifested, or perceived by witnesses, as some kind of calamitous event. However, the point is, that the trumpet blast is not the main event. Even if it is worked out in human terms as a partial judgment event, its primary purpose as a metaphorical means of communication, is to point to the main event which is yet to come.

The main event is the final, definitive, judgment, which is portrayed by the pouring out of the seven bowls. These events are representative of the final judgment, from which there is no escape, and no possible return. The trumpets give due warning, to those who will listen to them, that this final judgment is on its way.

The only part of the process which remains to be completed, in between the warning of the trumpets and the completion of the bowls, is the need to elucidate the underlying reasons for the necessity of this process. This part of the process is accomplished by the Signs Cycle.

5.6.4 The Bowls Motif of Cycle 5

Bowls are an even more common object of everyday life, whose use and purpose are rather limited, but in this case the point of similarity is made clear by the extra information provided by the author. The use of bowls revolves around three features, namely that they can be filled, can contain something for a time, and then are emptied.

The setting of the Bowls Cycle explicitly indicates that these bowls are filled with God's anger (15:7), but the primary feature of the metaphor is the fact that their contents are poured out, as is repeated several times (e.g. 16:1,2). This is the last phase of the process and, with that completed, there is nothing more to be said, for the use of the bowl is finished.

It is possible, if not probable, that the concept of pouring out the contents of the bowls was intended to be evocative of drink offerings, which were poured out to the gods in that era. If this hypothesis is accepted, the same underlying concept is implied, since the pouring out would have been the last act which completed this particular ritual.

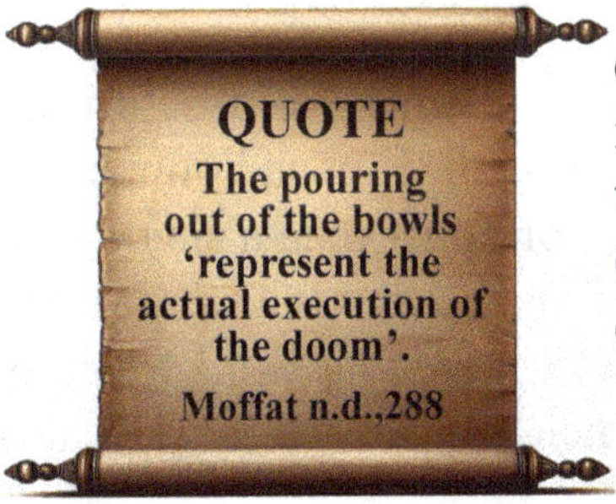
QUOTE
The pouring out of the bowls 'represent the actual execution of the doom'.
Moffat n.d.,288

This concept of something being executed and thereby finished, is also explicit in the setting where it is stated that with/in them the anger of God is completed or ended (15:1), and this is then confirmed by the loud declaration at the moment of the seventh bowl: 'It has occurred/has been finished' (16:17).

The first verb in the Greek (15:1) is actually in the aorist and the second (16:17) is in the perfect form. These two verbal forms contribute directly to the sense of finality and certainty implicit in the whole cycle. The use of the perfect is of particular interest, since perfect indicative verbs are rare in Revelation. This concept of God's plan being finished or completed is taken up again, and repeated at the end of the book, in a parallel reference to this one in 21:6.

Consequently, the metaphorical importance of the bowls would seem to revolve around the concept of completion, or consummation of judgment. There will come a time when what has been revealed, and warned about, and explained, will take place and be completed.

5.6.5 The Proclamation Motif of Cycle 6

The metaphorical aspect of the speeches in the sixth cycle can be interpreted in two similar ways. They could be understood as the proclamations of a herald, or, given the nature of some of the speakers, they could be understood as the testimony of witnesses. In either case, the common factor is that most of the speeches are presented as if they are commenting, after the fact, on an event already completed.

The exceptions are the third and sixth proclamations where a future tense is used in the main speech. However, the third Proclamation has a forceful reason clause whose first cause is the strength of the Lord God (18:8), and the sixth Proclamation (18:21-24) is also a strong statement because of the repetition of the words 'by no means...any longer'. The seventh Proclamation (19:17-18) is also slightly different, for it is an invitation, yet the intended action is definitely completed in 19:21. Consequently, even though the connotations of an invitation are slightly different from those of the previous proclamations, the overall thrust, that the action in view will certainly be completed, is the same.

The overall contribution of the proclamation motif to this cycle then, is that the judgments described are so certain to take place that they are described, and reacted to, as if they had already been accomplished. The Proclamations indicate that the judgments described are certain to take place.

5.6.6 The Signs Motif of Cycle 4

The Signs Cycle motif is harder to analyze than the others because it is an abstract concept and therefore more difficult to visualize. In addition, by its very nature, it presents a double layer of metaphor rather than a single one. This is because the word 'sign', is itself a metaphor in that it is a word which represents something else. So, here in this cycle, there is a word which is already a metaphor being used as a motif, which at a second level is also being used to illustrate a deeper reality.

Since the whole issue of Cycle 4 will be a major topic of discussion in Chapter 6, further analysis will be left in abeyance for the moment. In the meantime, it can be simply stated that Cycle 4, even though it is unified by a seven-fold motif, is, nonetheless, different from the other cycles. This difference is based on the type of motif which is being used, and also by its complexity. However, the main point is that, like a seal and a trumpet sound, a sign is not, in and of itself, the most important thing. By definition, it is a linguistic signpost pointing towards something else more important than itself, which something needs to be discerned and understood.

So then, in Cycle 4 the signs are personages. However, the concept of a sign as a motif indicates that it is not the personages which John actually saw (or the form in which he saw them), which are the most important part of the message. Apparently, these personages are illustrations, like well-developed painted sign-boards, which point to, and perhaps help, the hearer better understand, deeper and more complex truths.

The bottom line is that judgment has been prepared and is on its way. If anyone is curious enough to think about these things, then these signs will point them in the right direction. By this means of obtaining a heavenly perspective (or worldview) on the events happening in the earth realm, they will get some insight into exactly why this plan of judgment must, and will, be accomplished.

5.6.7 The Function and the Message of the Motifs taken as a Group

It is self-evident that the analysis of motifs is more subjective than other kinds of linguistic analysis. It is on the border of where more objective analysis shades over into the domain of interpretation. Even though this study is not intending to provide a full interpretation of Revelation, it does intend to bring the analysis right to this border point, from which interpreters of the text can carry on their work, on the basis of a systematic analysis of the text.

The main points which can be stated in summary is that, in the first instance, the existence of a seven-fold motif in each of the seven cycles can be supported by objective evidence drawn directly from the text, as has been discussed throughout this chapter. The second point is that, if John took pains to create this rather complex structure, it must have been to contribute something to the overall effect of his organization and message. The deduction which has been drawn from these observations is that the motifs contribute a metaphorical layer to each cycle, which provides an orientation for the hearer, which is intended, in turn, to influence his understanding of the content.

Not only that, there is not just one motif, but a complete series with seven large parts, and forty-nine smaller parts. So then, the final question which needs to be addressed: What is the purpose in the author's mind, of having a large series of seven times seven like this.? Clearly his purpose is to communicate a message; this is the obvious function of these motifs. So what then, is the aggregated message of the complete group of seven?

The Combined Effect of the Motifs of Cycles 1 and 7

As has been repeated several times already, these two cycles create an opening bracket and a matching closing bracket for the whole book. As such, they provide us with the introduction for the whole book, as well as its matching conclusion. The importance here of using the metaphor of a pair of brackets, is that it reminds us of the function of an introduction and of a conclusion for any discourse. It reminds us that everything which falls between the two brackets is encompassed by, and contained within them. This means, practically speaking, that anything which the two brackets contribute to the message of the whole discourse, is automatically true of what is contained within the external packaging.

In the case of these two cycles, they contain two, very broad, all encompassing messages which are relevant to the whole of the book. The first is that the book, in its entirety, is a personal message to the Christians on earth from the Risen Christ, who is now ruling and reigning over the affairs of the earth, as the Alpha and the Omega, and as the King of kings and Lord of lords. His goal is to comfort and console them. By the same token, He also wishes to encourage them to carry on following Him, so that they will fully succeed in their mission, and fully live out their God-ordained destiny. We know all this because of the motif of a letter.

Secondly, He gives them a clear picture in Cycle 7 of what that destiny is supposed to be, according to the plan and purposes of God. In summary, it is that, through all the trials and tribulations of life on earth, they should be trained and prepared to rule and reign with Him for all eternity.

The way that many people have written about Revelation in the past, has left us with an enduring impression that the book is all about judgment. But this is not the case. Cycles 1 and 7 show us that it was written for the Church: for her benefit and consolation. It was written for her so that she could know for sure that our Heavenly Father had endowed us with a future and a hope. We know all this because of the motif of everything being made new, combined with the final coda.

The Combined Effect of the Motifs of Cycles 2 to 6

So then, how do the motifs of Cycles 2-6 fit in with what has just been stated in the previous paragraphs?

Starting with the seals, there is little difficulty in discerning that the opening of a seal implies that the contents of a previously written document are now being revealed. This is only repeating what was stated by the very first word of the book, right at the beginning. Likewise, with the trumpets, the sound of them is clearly heard, and can serve as a warning to those who will take note of their message.

Let's not forget, even if it is in passing, that these motifs also communicate something about God's grace and mercy. Whenever a severe penalty is legitimately due to catch up with somebody, it is an act of mercy to tell them about what will happen, *before* it happens. If, in addition to that, the guilty party receives a clear warning of what is awaiting him, then that is also an act of mercy and grace.

So it can be seen then, that, even though Cycles 2-6 are ostensibly all about judgment, the motifs used reveal to us God's heart of love, and His compassion for all humankind. This is because by this revelation of

His viewpoint on the matter, He has told us ahead of time, and with many warnings, about what His plan of judgment looks like. But also, extremely important, He has also shown us how to avoid that final judgment entirely, having paid the total price for that forgiveness and pardon Himself.

Similar remarks can be made about the other motifs, as each of them reveals something significant about the total process of judgment. Each of them also contain a hidden echo of God's kindness. Consequently, each have a part to play in communicating the entire message about judgment, on the one hand, and also about God's kindness revealed in the total process, which includes revelation and warning, among other things.

As explained previously, all of these motifs are similar in that, whenever any of them are activated, or referred to, people on earth witnessed a calamity. But John is saying that in Heaven, that same event was caused by, or simply was, the opening of a seal, a trumpet blast, or a bowl being poured out, and so on. So, there are two levels here which need to be kept distinct. In general terms we have a single 'event' which is equally real for all concerned, but just seen from two different viewpoints, namely the heavenly and the earthly.

But then there is a third level, in that when John reports in his visionary narrative what he saw, heard and understood, he also makes a connection between a trumpet (or a seal etc.), and a calamity. This is the level which is of concern to those who wish to understand the text as text. So what then does this mean? What did John intend to communicate in bringing these different concepts together into one whole series of metaphors?

It is clear that the overarching message is one concerning God bringing about His judgments on the earth, in response to human failure to live according to His intended standards. This, of course, has been understood by all succeeding generations of Christians. This is true whether it is the initiation of the event, as evoked by the seals and trumpets, or whether it is the explanation of those events by the signs, or the completion of those events as evoked by the bowls, or the certainty of those events as evoked by the proclamations.

However, having read or heard John's text, a human witness of such an event, can now interpret it on the basis of information received from Heaven. If it is the first time the witness had ever thought about such things and reached more than just a superficial conclusion, what may happen as a result, is that suddenly he gets a flash of insight into what is really going on. For the first time, he gets a revelation, that God has a plan to judge evil and that includes human beings.

At a deeper level, as the witness contemplates the fact that certain people have come to the end of their life in the judgment event, and have been suddenly projected unprepared into eternity, more may happen. He might take it as a *warning* and start thinking about avoiding such a fate himself.

If he was a follower of the Lamb, however, and knew his Bible well enough, he might interpret the event as a sign. In other words, he might now begin to put the pieces together and come to *understand* what is really happening. Namely, that there is a cosmic war going on and that he is caught up in it, whether he likes it or not.

If he is a bit further along the road of life, he might even take a measure of comfort from the judgment events which he has observed. He might hear the proclamations ringing out across spiritual space, and be comforted to think that his final vindication was both getting closer (cf. Luke 21:28 in context), and was *certain* to be accomplished. It would encourage him to see that God was on the move and that He was actually carrying out what He said that He would do.

If, on the other hand, he was a direct victim of the judgment event and lost his life, then, in his case, he would have gone through his own particular final judgment here on earth. For him it would be the *consummation* of judgment, after which the only thing which would follow, would be the judgment of the 'dead' in Heaven.

So it is then, that each and every one of these calamitous, judgment events, whenever they happened in history, could be understood from different points of view. It would be the same event, but the point of view would depend on the experience and the stand-point of the person concerned.

Whichever way Revelation is interpreted, the judgments described in Cycles 2-6 are clearly cyclic (i.e. similar judgments occur more than once) even as there is a sense of progression towards a final end. That means, they will eventually come to an end - there will be a 'last' one - for everyone and for all time. If this is the case, then perhaps this is what John intended to communicate through the various motifs.

A judgment event as seen from an earthly stand-point is very similar every time it happens: it is calamitous and brings earthly life to an end for some. But each such event, with heavenly insight, can communicate a slightly different message to different people. Some may interpret it from the standpoint of an opened seal, others may perceive it as a sounding trumpet, while for others, it is too late, for the bowl has already been emptied.

Because these earthly events originate in Heaven and can be viewed from outside time, and from the heavenly viewpoint of eternity, it is reasonable to deduce that they are, therefore, timeless. What this means in practice, is that the overall message of the writers of this book, is to show to us that, all that is contained in this book is intended to be helpful and relevant to anyone who reads it. These messages are rooted in eternity, and flow out from the eternal heavenly realm. As a consequence they are eternally relevant.

These calamitous, judgment events then, have taken place all through history, and we have all been witnesses of at least some of them. This means that anyone, at any point in history, can read this book and benefit from its message. This message is, therefore, timeless, in the sense of being always true and always relevant throughout the entire time frame of life on earth.

5.7 The Chiastic Organization and the Linear Development of the 7 Cycles

In the process of discussion so far, it has been continually observed that the seven cycles which have been delineated, appear to be functioning in parallel to each other. This is further confirmed by the presence of the motifs. The motifs, as a set, do not logically belong together. For example, reference to a seal does not automatically lead one to think about trumpets, and talk of bowls does not engender reflections about proclamations.

On the contrary, each cycle, being unified around a distinct motif, stands apart from its neighbors, and could even stand alone as an autonomous unit. Grammatically, the cycles are in a coordinate relationship and contribute to the content of the book much as the sections in a pie-chart contribute to an understanding of the total message of the chart.

Cycles 2-7 are linked by *kai* 'and' (8:1-6;11:15-19; 15:1-16:1; 16:17-21; and 20:1), with Cycles 2-6 also being joined by an overlap link. Cycles 1 and 2 are connected in the surface structure by 'after these things' (4:1), and in the deeper structure by a tail-head link. The function of this phrase 'after these things', in the discourse as a whole remains unclear, but at the lower level it is clear that it also contributes a coordinating connection (cf 20:3 and also 7:9 where 'after these things' is functioning in tandem with 'after this' (7:1)). See the note on connectives in Appendix 2 for more detail. The semantic relation is an additive one. See Callow 1998,282-83, and Dooley and Levinsohn 2001,92-93 on this topic.

The outer reaches of the first and seventh cycles have their special focus on the career of the Church, which contributes primarily to the Salvation Theme. In contrast to that, the most immediately obvious contribution of the inner grouping (Cycles 2-6), influenced as they are by their seven-fold motifs, is to the Judgment Theme. This observation leads to the possibility that the cycles are organized in a concentric manner as will be developed below. At the same time, it will be observed that a linear development is also discernible which is complementary to the concentric structure, and which provides an additional insight into the message of the whole book.

To posit concentricity and linearity at the same time is not contradictory. This has been observed elsewhere (see Bailey 1983,50, Wendland 1985 and 1999, Longacre 1999a,144 and Schooling 1998) and is an example of the complex, multi-layered nature of language. The two complementary strands (or overlays) illuminate the central message together, much as two headlamps contribute complementary physical illumination.

5.7.1 The Chiastic Organization

Whenever a text is composed of an uneven number of parallel units, as is the case for Revelation, it is reasonable to wonder whether it is not, in fact, a chiasm. Other commentators have pursued this possibility but their attempts have failed so far to reach a convincing conclusion, and to promote consistent consensus. This is because, to the extent that a chiasm becomes complicated, or its creator resorts to dislocating the text in order to make it fit the analysis, it loses credibility.

The consensus among commentators is that Cycles 1 and 7 are clearly parallel to one another and that Cycles 3 (the Trumpets) and 5 (the Bowls) are more obviously parallel to each other than the other members of the central series. The problem remaining is that there is a multiplicity of lexical and thematic features which links all the cycles into a complex matrix of relationships.

This gives the impression that there ought to be a series of clearly matching pairs, but at the lexical level, the evidence for linking Cycle 2 and Cycle 6 together as a matching pair remains elusive. At the high level of analysis which is in view here, parallels between matching units ought to be clear, and close to being unique to the units concerned. The parallelism ought also to permeate the whole of the unit concerned, and not just be an incidental detail. The conclusion is that, although low-level lexical links can be established between Cycles 2 and 6, this only establishes their general parallel relationship with the other cycles. However, there is not sufficient evidence of this type to establish a clear matching-pair relationship between the two individual cycles.

This is where awareness of the motifs becomes important since they dominate the whole of the body of each cycle, but at the same time are unique to the cycle concerned. Viewed from the broader, metaphorical perspective of a motif, Cycles 2 and 6 can be considered to be in a unique parallel relationship. Cycle 2 is the beginning of a series of cycles in which the judgment theme is quantitatively dominant. The motif of opening a seal promotes the idea of revelation: it is a preliminary act which gives a first glimpse of a plan of judgment, which has just begun or is about to begin.

Chart 42.
The Chiastic Structure of Revelation

The Prologue 1:1-11*

A. Cycle 1 1:9-3:22	**The Seven Letters**
The CONTEXT of the Book: The Church Living in Earth-Bound Time	
B. Cycle 2 4:1-8:6*	**The Seven Seals** Revelation of Judgment
C. Cycle 3 8:1-11:19*	**The Seven Trumpets** Warning of Judgment
D. Cycle 4 11:15-16:1* The CLIMAX of the Book:	**The Seven Signs** Explanation of Judgment
C' Cycle 5 15:1-16:21*	**The Seven Bowls** Consummation of Judgment
B' Cycle 6 16:17-19:21	**The Seven Proclamations** Certainty of Judgment
A' Cycle 7 20:1-22:7*	**The Seven New Things**
The CONCLUSION of the Book: The Church Living in Timeless Eternity	

The Epilogue 22:6-21

(* an asterisk indicates that an overlap link connects the units so marked with the unit which follows)

By contrast, Cycle 6 is the conclusion to this series and the motif of a proclamation, taken in context as being the declarations of witnesses to an event, promotes the idea that the judgment events are now past and have been completed. Similarly, the motif of the trumpet (Cycle 3) and its inherent warning, promotes the idea of imminence with the totality of the judgment events still future, although on the verge of being completed. In parallel to this, the bowls motif (Cycle 5) and its concept of consummation, promotes the idea of imminence in the immediate past, namely that at that point, the judgments have just been completed. It could have been at the very instant even that the event is being described. This reinforces the lexical parallelism which has already been noticed about these two cycles.

The discussion above is intentionally broad in its view of the motifs, since the aim is to establish the inherent parallelism which exists between certain pairs. At the same time, it should not be forgotten that these motifs are communicating quite complex messages at the semantic level. In particular, they are a hinge between Heaven and earth and are interpreting events which take place in Heaven (e.g. a trumpet blast) as events which are actually perceived and experienced on earth as some kind of calamitous event.

Finally, it can be remarked that these two pairings leave the Signs Cycle standing alone in the middle of the structure. In effect, this cycle has no clear parallel links with any other cycle of the judgment series and is different in a number of ways from its neighbors in the central grouping. By contrast, the clearest parallels (based on references to Satan, (2:13 (inter alia)//12:9//20:2) and the Christ who rules (1:13-18//12:5, 14:14//22:3)) link it with Cycles 1 and 7, thereby creating a stepping-stone type connection with these two outer cycles.

The motif of the sign itself is ambiguous in terms of what it communicates. What it primarily suggests is that it is a signpost pointing towards realities other than itself. Inspection of the content of the cycle indicates that the signs provide explanations concerning various aspects of God's plan of judgment. The fact that this cycle occurs as the centerpiece of a chiasm suggests that it is the climax, or peak, of the book.

As a consequence of these insights derived from this review of the motifs, the whole book can be analyzed as a chiasm as presented in Chart 42. The sub-headings for Cycles 1 and 7 have been intentionally updated in this chart, relative to what they were in Chart 1 in Chapter 1. This is to reflect the progression of thought which has developed in the course of the discussion in the intervening chapters. This, in turn, is intended to reflect the likely interpretation that this book is intended to be viewed as timeless, and, therefore, as relevant to every generation of Christians, from John's time until the present.

Cycle 1, therefore, is not just about the Church as it lives out its life on earth from an earthly viewpoint, but it also describes it as God sees it from His heavenly viewpoint, even though the people concerned are still living in earth-bound time. Similarly, Cycle 7 does not just describe the state and the status of the Church as it will be in the future, although it does that; but more importantly, it describes it again as God sees it, and how He always, timelessly, sees it. But this time He is seeing it from the perspective of the people who have learned to be overcomers.

This status of being overcomers is the result of them having learned to operate in the realm of the heavenly throne room, as they have dared, like John, to go up higher 'in the spirit', and to be followers of the Lamb in all situations. Those situations could be totally earth-bound situations, as largely described in Cycle 1, or they could be more other-worldly, like the situations described concerning the two witnesses in Chapter 11.

These latter overcomers produced miraculous signs, and served the Lamb, even while on earth, and then continued to operate from the heavenly realm, even after they had passed through physical death. They were overcomers in both life and death, in the time-bound earth realm, and also in the timeless, eternal, heavenly realm.

5.7.2 The Linear Development and the Progression of the Plots

Repetition in any text is never entirely exact. Consequently, therefore, even when there are multiple repetitions, there will always be some new elements added and a consequent linear development.

Speaking of poetry, Alter 1981,97 explained this linguistic phenomenon in this way:

> The parallelism of biblical verse constituted a structure in which, through the approximately synonymous hemistichs, there was constant repetition that was never really repetition. This is true not just inadvertently because there are no true synonyms, so that every restatement is a new statement, but because the conscious or intuitive art of poetic parallelism was to advance the poetic argument in seeming to repeat it - intensifying, specifying, complementing, qualifying, contrasting, expanding the semantic material of each initial hemistich in its apparent repetition. Biblical prose...operates stylistically in the opposite way, word-for-word restatement rather than inventive synonymity being the norm for repetition; but in both cases...the ideal reader...is expected to attend closely to the constantly emerging differences.

Even though his position on repetition in prose is rather over-stated, the basic principles are correct. That is to say that, in repeating material, an author is, nonetheless, advancing the linear logic of his discourse, at the same time.

So then, it has long since been recognized that there is linear movement within the repeated judgment cycles from partial, preliminary judgments, to complete, and final, judgment in the sixth sub-units. In the same way, there is also linear movement through the seven, cyclic, major units of the book.

At the outset, the Church is in its earthly context, with its imperfections and with plenty of work to do in order to conform to the wishes of her Master. The Church at this stage is depicted as it is in the here and now of this current age. Sin has invaded God's Garden, and the dragon-shaped serpent is still able to beguile and deceive by various secondary means. Consequently, they are bound into this earthly system by what we call time. What this means is that they can only ever fully escape from this prison, by coming to the end of time. This could be the end of their time on this first earth, as they pass through the door called death. Otherwise, it could be at the end of the present age as a whole, when Jesus comes back again to usher in the eternal, timeless age of the new Heavens and the new Earth. Or it could be, as indicated in the preceding paragraphs, that they learned to go up higher in the spirit, and to operate in the heavenly realm, even while they are still living in their physical earth-suits.

As a result of this earth-bound situation, the followers of the Lamb still have many trials and tribulations to contend with, and many obstacles to surmount. Their task then, is to learn to be overcomers by putting into practice the twin principles of repentance and perseverance.

At the end of the book, the Church is seen from a different, heavenly perspective. From this viewpoint, the followers of the Lamb have reached the end of their earthly journey. The problems of the past are put behind them, and nothing but future perfection and the fulfillment of all the promises are in view, as they enter into the coming age, when time will be no more.

Meanwhile, although it is not explicit in the outline presented above, the Church continues to be a secondary participant in the central cycles. This is usually in her position of bearing the brunt of the backlash of the judgment going on around her, as, for example, in 12:17. This is part of her preparation for glory, as evoked in the first cycle, and as indicated, for example, in 2:10.

With this information in view then, it can be seen that the Church also, in a sense, passes through the Judgment Cycles. There is no direct leap from Cycle 1 to Cycle 7. On the contrary, the Judgment Cycles describe the path which each member of the Church must take in their progression towards perfection, all through the period governed by time.

Total perfection is only acquired when they reach the end of their earthly career, as is described at the end of the book. But in the meantime, everyone is obviously expected to grow in grace and maturity. The Lord of the Church clearly encourages them all to show more and more signs of perfection, as they progress step by step towards the end of time, and towards the end of their life here on this earth.

In addition to all that linear progression through time, the Church also appears periodically in the interludes, but in this case she is seen from the heavenly point of view. From this point of view, we can observe another feature which is true of the Church, namely, that, from this point of view, she is already sealed, protected, praising God and following the Lamb wherever He goes (7:1-3, 11:3-6 and 14:1-5).

Within the confines of the central Judgment Cycles the same combination of features can be observed. The metaphorical coloration provided by the motifs helps to confirm, first of all, the internal parallel arrangement, but it also contributes to the linear movement.

The Revelation of Judgment Cycle (Cycle 2) is an initial insight into the fact that God has a plan prepared and that this plan involves judgment. This revelation can be viewed in two different ways. It can be seen as something to be feared by those who will suffer the consequences, or it can be seen as a consolation and encouragement for the people of God, since the judgment of their persecutors heralds their own salvation. There are two different reactions, but the unifying concept of revelation which is inherent in the motif of the seal remains the same.

This insight helps to understand the fifth seal (6:9-11) which is superficially different from the others, in that it does not describe the actual outworking of a judgment. In the fifth seal, judgment is still central in the direct speech of 6:10, but otherwise the main event is the comforting of the martyrs as they continue to wait patiently for justice to be done. However, the thread which unifies all the seals is the concept of revelation, for in this segment the main message is that it is revealed to the martyrs that God has a plan of judgment, which will satisfy them when the time is right.

This promise is specifically consummated in the outworking of the third Bowl (16:4-7), where it is declared that the blood of the saints and prophets will be avenged in a symbolically appropriate manner. This reference, in turn, establishes another parallel internal to this set of cycles. Other references to, and parallels established by this sub-theme of the avenging of the death of the martyrs, are to be found in 17:6, 18:24,19:2 and 20:4.

The Seals Cycle then, views judgment from the point of view of the beginning of the process. Even though it is implicit that the process of judgment begins already with the opening of the seals, it is also clear that a great deal of it is still potential rather than actual. In addition, at this stage it is partial and not complete.

As well as the fifth seal, already discussed, where the judgment is clearly potential and future, the first and second seals are characterized by a purpose clause which maintains the same concept. The fourth seal has an implicit purpose contained in the words, 'given... authority'.

The judgments of the third and fourth seal are clearly partial. The only exception is the sixth seal but, since this is prominent and evokes the final judgment, the difference is explicable.

The same pattern of partial judgments is continued in the Warning of Judgment Cycle (Cycle 3) but this time there is a greater sense of urgency. This is because, even though the final judgment is still future, time is now getting short (8:13; 9:12; 10:6-7 and 11:14).

By contrast, the sixth cycle, which by virtue of its position as the last of the judgment cycles, looks at judgment from the opposite point of view, namely from after the fact. Final judgment at this point is now past history, having been unleashed in the Bowls Cycle. Now from this perspective, what was once potential and had to be taken by faith, has now been realized, and the awesome truth has the certainty of an accomplished mission.

Thematically then, the linear movement of the five central cycles as a whole, repeats the same internal linear movement of each of the individual judgment cycles.

This linear movement corresponds with the concept of a plot in a story. In the field of discourse analysis Longacre 1983,22 has developed a template with seven components to aid in charting the flow of a narrative. Even though Revelation is not a true narrative, it does have many elements which are similar to narrative, and this is particularly true of the linear movement under discussion, which creates a thread in the book which can be usefully understood as a plot.

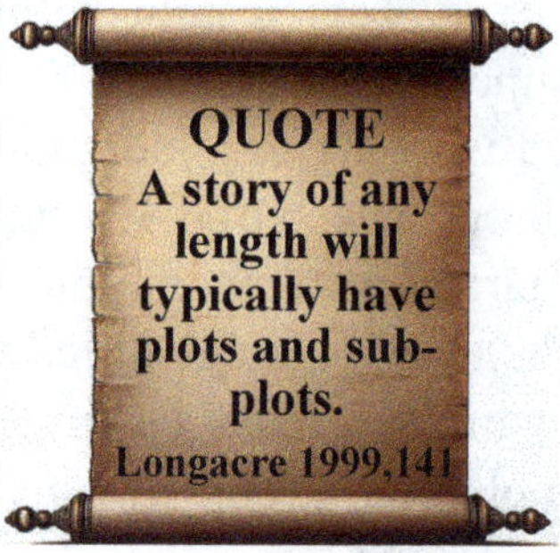
QUOTE
A story of any length will typically have plots and sub-plots.
Longacre 1999,141

In reality, it is rare to find a single plot in a complex discourse. In Revelation, there are two main plots. The first concerns the interaction between Jesus, the Commander in Chief, and the members of His Church who are to obey Him and follow Him wherever He goes. The second one concerns the interaction between Jesus, the Victorious Conqueror, and the arch-villain, the dragon. In addition, on the sub-plot level, John's own story has a minimal plot, as developed in the Narrative Framework, and a plot of some sort could be discerned for each of the other characters who appear in the book, if this amount of detail was ever needed.

The two main plots which concern the Church, on the one hand, and the dragon, on the other, are presented in Chart 43 below, with the components of Longacre's plot template laid out in the middle. See also Longacre 1999 for additional discussion of his plot template.

Since God's plan, through Christ, is to bring about salvation for the Church, it is not surprising that the Church's story is very much tied up with the Salvation Theme. Naturally enough then, the plot which concerns the dragon, is intertwined with the Judgment Theme. This latter story describes, in effect, the problem of evil as it is seen with the dragon at its center, and how God's plan will be worked out so that this problem will be resolved.

It can be noticed in the chart that the Christ features as a participant in both of the plots illustrated. This demonstrates in an objective way how it is that He is the dominant character in the whole of the book. Yet, at the same time, the book is not a story about Him in particular as, for example, the Gospels are, nor is He the main character in either of the major plots.

Longacre also includes in his template the possibility of a plot structure being preceded by an Aperture and terminated by a Closure. In Revelation these two elements also occur in the form of the Prologue at the beginning and the Epilogue at the end, as was previously illustrated in Chart 42 above.

It is not possible to develop all the implications of asserting that Revelation has one or more plots, which progress linearly through the book. The main purpose here is to demonstrate that structurally, this can be observed and that, in particular, the seven cycles coincide with, and embody, all the components of the seven elements of Longacre's plot template. This would seem to be no coincidence, but, on the contrary, serves as confirmatory evidence that Revelation is indeed composed of these seven major parts. These seven cycles are clearly distinct, in terms of their internal organization and content. Yet, at the same time, nonetheless, they also clearly contain linear threads which connect all of them together.

In the previous two sub-sections then, it has been seen that Revelation is, primarily, cyclic in nature, being composed of a series of autonomous units arranged in a parallel, chiastic pattern. Yet, at the same time, the series of seven cycles project a definite sense of linear development towards a final conclusion. This conclusion however, is not a catastrophic annihilation of our world, nor does it even have judgment primarily in focus. The end goal is complete victory for Christ and His Kingdom, and for all those who choose to follow Him wherever He goes. At the same time, this complete victory includes the complete defeat of the enemy of all humankind and the destroyer of the earth. So it is all good news for those who are on the winning side.

A cyclic motion which also makes linear progress is, in effect, a spiral. So, in this case, the analysis which is being proposed, confirms the intuitions of earlier generations of scholars. This is because some of them had previously proposed the spiral imagery to describe the way the message of the book is progressively revealed.

Please see the Appendix at the end of this chapter for more detail concerning these important details.

Chart 43a.
The Two Major Plots of Revelation
The Church's Story

Cycle	The Church's Story	Longacre's Plot Template
1.	The Church on earth is presented. She is imperfect and persecuted, but is encouraged by warnings and promises given by the Risen Christ.	**1. Setting the Stage**
2.	Some have died as martyrs and await their vindication. In this context the Church is both sealed and already praising.	**2. The Inciting Moment**
3.	The Church (incl.John) is seen as in danger, yet praying and protected; persecuted yet vindicated.	**3. Developing Conflict**
4.	The dragon makes war on them and overcomes them, and yet they sing, follow the Lamb, and persevere.	**4. The Climax**
5.	The martyrs are vindicated; otherwise the Church is absent and unaffected by these judgments.	**5. The Dénouement**
6.	The Church again seen as persecuted by Babylon, but they are still praising, and their Savior, the Victorious Christ, is revealed.	**6. The Final Suspense**
7.	All her enemies are dealt with and, as overcomers, the Church inherits all the promises, is married to the Lamb, and lives happily ever after.	**7. The Conclusion**

Chart 43b.
The Two Major Plots of Revelation
The Dragon's Story

Longacre's Plot Template	The Dragon's Story	Cycle
1. Setting the Stage	The Risen Christ is the master. The dragon is not formally introduced, but his presence is assumed and he is the persecutor of the Church.	1.
2. The Inciting Moment	The Lamb opens the seals and reveals and inaugurates a plan of judgment.	2.
3. Developing Conflict	The tempo and imminence of judgment increases, and the warnings get clearer.	3.
4. The Climax	The true nature of the dragon is revealed. He provokes cosmic war and the Church is the main target.	4.
5. The Dénouement	God's plan of judgment is accomplished, and the problem of evil on the earth is resolved.	5.
6. The Final Suspense	Babylon is introduced as another source of evil but is rapidly dealt with.	6.
7. The Conclusion	The dragon is finally dealt with and all evil is banished for ever.	7.

5.8 Conclusion

There is an accumulation of evidence then, which demonstrates that the body of Revelation is composed of seven major parts. These seven parts function in parallel to each other, elaborating the same themes from different points of view.

The first and last cycles are particularly in parallel to each other and refer primarily to the Church and its salvation, although references to judgment and persecution are not absent. The central group of five cycles also belong together, being set apart by their own opening and closure, and being joined together by overlap links. The most space is devoted to issues of judgment, but the Church is not totally absent in that it reappears in interludes in four of the five cycles.

The motifs which give each cycle its own specificity, make it possible to discern a chiastic arrangement, which further enhances the parallel organization of the total structure. Looked at in terms of parallelism, the fact that the cycles are, in effect, autonomous textual units standing in a simple coordinate (or additive) relationship to each other is what is the most striking feature. However, in reality, they are subtly joined together by the plots which are developed throughout the book and which create connecting threads. This objective observation demonstrates that the arrangement is not haphazard, but that there is a linear logic which also pervades the whole, and maintains its unity from the beginning to the end.

What is of particular interest in all this from an analytical point of view, is that the structure of the text mirrors and communicates the same message as the content of the text. As Breck 1987,70 puts it:

> Form expresses content, therefore content determines form. The author of a literary work, whether it be an epigram or an epic novel, chooses the particular structure that best expresses the meaning he or she wants to communicate.

The author of Revelation seems to have taken this principle and applied it with a great deal of specificity to his particular communication. Structurally, the book proceeds cyclically, by means of seven parallel units, and yet at the same time there is a linear movement not unlike the development of a plot in a narrative.

Semantically, the same phenomenon is woven into the fabric of the message being communicated: in God's plan the judgments are cyclic, in that there always have been judgment events which affect some people on the earth, and there always will be. Yet, at the same time, events are moving towards a culmination and, eventually, there will be a final judgment and an end to the whole process.

In parallel to all this, the Church is moving on a linear path from imperfection to perfection. Even as the judgments cyclically repeat themselves, the Church on the earthly level passes, as it were, through them and is partially affected by them. But, at the same time, on the heavenly level it passes, as it were, above them, and is unaffected by them.

This story of the Church is carried by the interludes through the middle of the book. These are a structural feature which punctuates five of the central cycles. They appear and disappear again in such an unannounced manner, and so unadorned by any special features, that they could almost pass the reader by unnoticed. In fact, they have indeed gone unnoticed by many commentators in history. But, if this is true from a structural point of view, then semantically, the same phenomenon is at work.

The deep message concerning the Church in Revelation, is buried virtually unnoticed in the bowels of the book. This message would seem to be that the Church exists and lives in two dimensions at once. On the earthly level it is imperfect, in process, and constantly surrounded by the dangerous fall-out of God's plan of judgment.

Yet, at the same time, that dark reality is punctuated by the illumination that there is also a heavenly dimension within which all is perfection and glory. The presence of the interludes in the text, appearing unannounced and disappearing again almost immediately, is a graphic illustration. It is an illustration crafted into the form of the text, which contributes to the communication of the overall meaning.

That is, for the followers of the Lamb, even though life on earth may seem to be dominated by doom and gloom, yet, at the same time, there is another glorious, heavenly reality. This heavenly reality awaits them at the end of their journey, that is for sure, but that is not all. From time to time it is possible to glimpse at a distance, as it were, down the passage-ways which connect the two worlds, this heavenly reality, even from here on the earth. In order to confirm this world-view shattering idea, we only have to consider the example of John, which is also recorded in this book. For he, himself, visited the heavenly realm and learned to see things from that point of view.

The overlap links are yet another example of how the structure contributes to the communication of the overall message. Five times in a row (Cycles 2-6) the major units of the book are connected by overlap links. These links are, at the same time, both an ending to what preceded, and also an introduction to what is to follow. It is as if the hearer is consciously being prepared for what is to follow, because the main point about the grand finale of Cycle 7 is to communicate the message that there will come a point in human experience, which will be unique.

The cyclic progression will finally come to an end. At that point, all at the same time, 'in the twinkling of an eye' according to Paul in 1 Corinthians 15:52 , all that has been previously known in the old heavens and earth will come to an end. Yet, that will not be the end, because all that is yet to be discovered in the new heavens and earth will be inaugurated. This will be the end to end all ends, and the beginning which will surpass all previously known beginnings.

This understanding of how the form of the discourse contributes directly to an appreciation of the content illustrates what Alter 1981,112 previously declared:

> Language in the biblical stories is never conceived as a transparent envelope of the narrated events or an aesthetic embellishment of them, but as an integral and dynamic component - an insistent dimension - of what is being narrated.

Indeed, we have said it before, and it bears repeating again: 'the book of Revelation is a remarkably well-constructed literary piece' (Strand 1987,107).

LOOK FOR THE BITS WHICH STICK OUT ABOVE THE REST !

APPENDIX 5

PREFACE

This Appendix has been placed here to provide extra technical information relating to the analysis of the Seven Cycles for those who wish to explore these matters further. There is no need to read this Appendix if this extra information is not required, for the technical information already given in the main text is sufficient for the general purpose of understanding the structural organization of the book. The Appendix just broadens out what has already been explained and makes more specific connections with the methodology used, and the commentators who have gone before.

The extra contents are as follows :

1) Precise information to explain and support the division into units which was described in Chapter 5.

2) A review of remarks by previous commentators concerning various aspects of the structural issues underlying an analysis of the Seven Cycles.

All other readers are invited to move on straight away to Chapter 6, where we will continue explaining and describing the issues concerning the semantic notion of prominence – the mountains and valleys woven into the texture of the text.

APPENDIX 5

Ancillary Information Pertaining to the Analysis of the Seven Cycles

A5.1 Evidence for the Division into Units

A5.1.1 A General Explanation

In this appendix evidence will be provided in summary form, to indicate on what basis the text of the Seven Cycles was divided into units for this study. In order to keep the material manageable, the information will be provided in abbreviated form, and not all the cycles will be presented.

The information provided here will not be the same as that provided in Chapter 3 and its Appendix, but will be complementary to it. The purpose is to provide extra information concerning the units of text specifically discussed in Chapter 5 above.

The aim is to demonstrate that text can be divided into units on the basis of linguistic evidence, and that this evidence can be made available for perusal by other analysts. For more detailed explanation of this nature please refer back to Appendix A2.1.1.

The abbreviations used in the presentation of the data are as follows:

D = Differences permitting a division into distinct units.

Normally reference is made to the division at the beginning of the unit and also to that at the end of the unit.

IC = Internal Coherence requiring that similar units be grouped together

F = Function of the unit.

A5.1.2 The General Setting of Cycles 2-6 4:1-5:14

D: Change of topic and situation. Introduction of new participants. Ends when setting material ends and the main topic introduced (the opening of the seven seals) is taken up in detail.

IC: Parallel chiastic structure. Coherence of general situation (throne-room), purpose (setting material including introduction of new participants) and content (continuation of references to the one sitting on the throne, and to the 24 elders and 4 living creatures). The relationship between the two major parts is that of generic-specific.

Introduction: Transition from Cycle 1 and General Introduction 4:1

A. The One Sitting on the Throne is Introduced and Described 4:2-3

B. The Next Participants, the 24 Elders and the 4 Living Creatures are Introduced and Described 4:4-7

A' Worship Ascribed to The One Sitting on the Throne is Introduced and Described 4:8-11

A'' Issue of the Scroll held by the One Sitting on the Throne is Introduced and Described 5:1-3

B' The Next Participant, the Lamb is Introduced and Described, and the Elders and Living Creatures Respond 5:4-7

A''' The Worship of the Lamb is Introduced and Continues as does that of the One Sitting on the Throne 5:8-13

Conclusion: The closure of the 24 Elders and the 4 Living Creatures 5:14

F: It functions as both the general setting to Cycles 2-6 and the specific setting of the Seals Cycle. Alternatively, 5:1-14 can be viewed as an overlap link being both part of the general setting and also the specific setting of Cycle 2.

Part 1 (Generic) of the General Setting of Cycles 2-6 4:2-11

Structure: thematic with chiastic arrangement

A. Introduction/Description of the One Sitting on the Throne and the 24 Elders 4:2-4

B. Special description of the Throne 4:5-6a

C. Introduction/Description of the 4 Living Creatures and their Activity 4:6b-8

B' # (missing)

A' Description of the Activity of the Elders in Worship of the One Sitting on the Throne 4:9-11

Note: Leaving aside the issue of B' which is missing and which is discussed in Chapter 5.3.2 above, the structural organization suggests that the introduction of the four living creatures is the most prominent part of this section. This is confirmed when it is noted that they play an important role in the development of the body of this cycle. See 6:1,2,5 and 7.

Part 2 (Specific) of the General Setting of Cycles 2-6 5:1-13

Structure: narrative structure with plot

1. Setting: for what is to follow. Specific development of one aspect of the description of the One Sitting on the Throne, namely the introduction of the scroll with 7 seals. 5:1

2. Inciting Moment: The problem is identified, namely that there needs to be someone who who will step forward who is qualified to open the seals of the scroll. 5:2

3. Developing Conflict: No one is worthy to open the scroll. 5:3

4. Climax: A climax of tension is reached, namely John is so disappointed that he weeps. 5:4

5. Denouement: A solution is identified, namely the Lion of Judah can open the scroll. 5:5

6. Final Suspense. The execution of the solution is delayed and an element of uncertainty introduced, namely when John looks he does not see a Lion but a Lamb who looks as if he is mortally wounded. 5:6

7. Conclusion. The immediate problem is resolved and the immediate effect of that resolution is described, namely the Lamb steps forward, takes the scroll and worship ensues. 5:7-13.

Notes: 1. Following the usual logic of problem/resolution type narratives, and because of its extra length, the conclusion would be considered to be the most prominent sub-unit.

2. Since the above text is only a setting, the actual working out of the problem of the opening of the seals is contained in the body which follows. The above text is an embedded narrative, that is, it is a complete narrative in its own right but it is functioning as part of a larger unit (Cycle 2) which in this case is also in narrative form.

3. The analyses presented in Parts 1 and 2 above are different from the analysis of the same texts presented in the preceding paragraph. These are examples of complementary analyses which look at the text from slightly different points of view and bring to the fore different aspects or emphases of the same material. The first analysis looks at Chapters 4 and 5 as a total unit and proceeds from that point of view. As such, it presents the broad outlines of the structure and does not take account of all the detail. By contrast, the following two analyses look at the individual parts of the larger text and treat them in turn as individual units, rather than as a parts of a larger whole. By the same token it also enters into finer detail and takes account of smaller sub-units (e.g. 4:5-6a) which are beyond the scope of the higher level analysis. See Longacre 1999a,144 for more comment on complementary analyses.

A5.1.3 The Conclusion to Cycles 2-6 19:11-21

D: Change of situation, topic and participants. No continuation of any significant theme or sub-theme from the preceding passage.

IC: Interweaving of several sub-themes and lexical chains which complete sub-themes or motifs initiated in sub-units prior to the immediately preceding context. The interweaving begins in verse 11 and continues through to verse 21.

F: Closure to the sixth cycle, since it contains the seventh Proclamation (vv.17-21), but at the same time it is also a conclusion to the whole Cycles 2-6, being in parallel with and forming an *inclusio* with Chapters 4 and 5. Structure :

A. A Description of the Risen Christ Seen as a Victorious Warrior 19:11-13
parallels: 'one sitting on a white horse', 'having a name written... his name was the Word of God', 'garment dipped in blood', 'he makes war'.

B. A Description of the Armies of Heaven & their Leader 19:14-16
parallels: '(those) followed (sitting) on white horses', 'out of His mouth proceeds a sharp sword' 'He treads the winepress...,' 'He has on His garment...a name written: King of kings and Lord of lords'.

C. Proclamation 7: The Summons to the Final Conflict 19:17-18
parallels: 'assemble', 'the flesh of horses and those sitting on them', 'kings and those (following) sitting on horses', 'all the birds...', 'Come... eat'.

B' A Description of the Armies of the Earth & their Leader 19:19-20
parallels: 'the kings of the earth and their armies assembled to make war with the one sitting on the horse and his army'.

A' A Description of the Warfare & the Victory of the Risen Christ 19:21
parallels: 'the rest (the kings of the earth and their armies) were killed (war made and accomplished)', the one sitting on the horse', 'the sword...proceeding from his mouth', 'all the birds were filled by their flesh'.

Notes: The system of parallels is complex and complete: A. is in parallel with all other sub-units ('one/those sitting/ following on (white) horse(s)'); A//B: 'name.. written..., garment...blood/winepress...garment'; A//B'//A': 'make war/killed'; B//C//B': 'armies'(stated or described); B//A': '(sharp) sword...out of his mouth'; C//B': armies of 'the kings' of the earth, (specific/generic); C//A': 'all the birds', 'the fleshes of the rest/armies of the earth'. This means that even though sub-units can be recognized according to the changes in topic, as per the schema above, at the same time 19:11-21 is a complete unit and cannot be sub-divided into several units of the same semantic weight functioning at the same level of the discourse hierarchy.

Proclamation 7 (19:17-18) is at the middle of a chiasm and is therefore the most important sub-unit.

A5.1.4 The Seventh Cycle 20:1-22:7
The Seven Characteristics of the New Creation or The Seven New Things

D: Change of topic, participants and situation. It follows the end of a set of seven which is marked by special features (e.g. *inclusio* 19:11) which confirms that it is the end of a major section. It is followed by the Epilogue which is the concluding unit of the book composed of Narrative Framework material, to which it is attached by an overlap-link.

IC: Composed of two major units with contrastive primary topics which function together as setting and body with a seven-fold motif, followed by a conclusion which overlaps with the Epilogue. The organization of the whole cycle is based on generic/specific relationships and antithetical contrasts.

F: Conclusion of the body of the book composed of seven major cycles which contains the visionary content of the book.

Structure:
1. Setting 20:1-15
2. Body 21:1-22:5
3. Conclusion 22:6-7

Note: This linear structure throws the natural prominence onto the conclusion which emphasizes the veracity and the reliability of the preceding vision. This kind of material is volitional import material which is, in any case, always more prominent than informational import material.

The detailed structural analyses of all the components of Cycle 7 are to be found in Chapter 7.9.

A5.1.5 The Setting of Cycle 7 20:1-15

D: Change of topic, participants and situation.

IC: Parallel structure interweaving references to the demise of Satan, 1000 years, first resurrection/second death, the lake of fire, and thrones and judgment/reigning.

A5.1.6 The Body of Cycle 7 21:1-22:5

D: Change of topic and situation. Continues until the end of the visionary content when the final section of Narrative Framework begins (overlap link).

IC: Parallel Structure. Coherence of general topic and theme, the new creation. The structure is as follows:

A. Generic Description. 21:1-8
B. Specific Description 1. 21:9-21
C. Specific Description 2. 21:22-22:5

A5.1.7 The Conclusion of Cycle 7 22:6-7

D: Change of topic and import. Beginning of a new direct speech by the angel of 21:9.

Followed by a new section where John is explicitly named and is the speaker.

IC: Complete unit of direct speech which is all volitional import material.

F: Conclusion of Cycle 7 and also first part of the Epilogue at the same time. (Overlap).

Note: the antecedent for 'these words' v.6 grammatically has to be the preceding words in the first instance, which is why v.6 is logically attached to 22:1-5. However the words are ambiguous and can also be interpreted by extension to refer to all the words in the whole book. In support it can be noted that the verse as a whole is in parallel to similar verses spanning the whole book (cf. 1:1,5, 3:14, 19:11 and 15:3,16:7, 19:2,9). Therefore, it is only possible to adequately take account of all these features of the text by interpreting 22:6-7 as a transitional unit with a double function (i.e. an overlap link), a conclusion to Cycle 7 and also the beginning of the Epilogue which is attached by this means.

A5.2 A Review of Other Opinions Concerning Topics Discussed in Chapter 5

Some topics concerning the seven cycles were previously discussed in the Appendix following Chapter 3. In this present Appendix the items discussed will be those referred to in this chapter.

A5.2.1 The Significance of the Trumpets Motif

A brief review of the literature suggests that most commentators interpret the trumpets in Revelation 8-11 as having primarily a warning function.

Beale 1999,468 rightly suggests that the Old Testament is the appropriate context within which to search for the point of significance for this metaphor. He goes on to say that 'the OT trumpets predominantly indicate: a warning to repent, judgment, victory or salvation, enthronement of Israel's king, eschatological judgment or salvation, or the gathering of God's people'. On the surface then, there appear to be a number of options to choose from when seeking to ascertain the point of similarity for the trumpets as a motif in Revelation.

Beale 1999,468-72 provides a long and complex discussion of the use of trumpets and in this section argues against the majority viewpoint (ibid.,469 note 9) and states: 'we have concluded above that the trumpets represent punitive judgments against hardened unbelievers instead of mere warnings to induce repentance' (ibid.,471). However, detailed perusal of his argument would suggest that in some places it is based on non-sequiturs and, overall, it seems to be unnecessarily fastidious. So it is that, elsewhere (ibid.,787), he says that 'the trumpets primarily warn unbelievers'.

For example, he cites the example of the fall of Jericho in Joshua (ibid.468-9) and agrees that 'the first six trumpets in Joshua 6 announce the judgment to come on the seventh day' but tries to argue from this absence of judgment events during the first six days to support the claim that in Revelation 6-8 'the first six trumpets...are punishments preliminary to a climactic judgment' with the emphasis on 'punishment' rather than on 'preliminary'. Within the context of Joshua itself this argument overlooks two important facts.

Firstly, the first six trumpets did not actually provoke any punitive act against the people of Jericho. Then, secondly, Rahab and her family understood the message of her visitors and of the subsequent trumpets, reacted positively, stayed obedient to God's word to her right to the end, and so were saved in the midst of judgment all around them. The fact that the majority did not heed the warning did not make the trumpets any less a warning. The point about a warning is that it says something about the graciousness of the person giving it in good time. It does not, in and of itself, imply anything about the eventual reactions of those who hear it. Furthermore, a warning is of no value if there is no execution of the announced calamity. A warning implies that real danger will be encountered in due course, and so the accomplishment of this negative event, far from contradicting the basic intent of the warning, is what actually validates it.

Wilcock 1971 takes a more open-handed approach to symbolism in Revelation and suggests that, far from being forced to take one rather limited point of view with regards to symbolism and metaphor, John is saying that 'here are two things which correspond to each other, being *equally real from different points of view* ' (ibid.,154 his italics). Further on he concludes that many of the symbols used in the book are 'different descriptions of the same thing' (ibid.,156). Symbols and metaphors are by nature very fluid uses of language which, in Beale's own terms, are 'a deliberate transgression of a word's boundaries of meaning' (1999,55). Therefore, it would seem more appropriate, with Wilcock, to be open to all the possible nuances which may be inherent in the comparison, rather than somewhat pedantically arguing that its message should be limited to a narrow semantic field.

More practically speaking, it has been observed both in the structure, and also in the content of Revelation that a single feature can be accomplishing more than one thing at a time (e.g. the overlap links), and this may be the case with the cycle motifs. In the case of the trumpets, it may well be that they should be understood as both punishments and warnings at the same time, and to exclude one part of the meaning would be to diminish the richness and communicative impact of the metaphor.

Pursuing this line of thought, one may also ask what there is to prevent the trumpet from being a warning of judgment, and an acclamation of victory at the same time, since this possibility can be found equally well in the Old Testament context. In support of this idea we can even cite Beale 1999,469. This is because, even in spite of his desire to remove the element of warning from the trumpet metaphor, he does actually allow that the trumpet can indicate both judgment and victory at the same time.

Giblin 1991,158 in fact takes this position and suggests that the trumpets 'herald deliverance'. In one event, Christ's death on the cross was at the same time a defeat for some, and a victory for others, just as it is in any battle or modern day sports event. In the same way, the events presaged by the trumpets are both a judgment event for some, but at the same time a deliverance event for others. This is because the judgment of God's enemies is, at the same time, a victory for God's people. There is nothing from a linguistic point of view to prevent an interpreter from suggesting more than one interpretation for a particular linguistic feature. This means in this case that, on one level, the seven trumpets are warnings of judgment with the negative connotations which that implies, and, at the same time, it is also an evocation of the trumpet of the Jubilee, with all its positive connotations. All that can justifiably be discerned in the same motif.

It would seem, however, that there is a deeper reason yet why Beale's argumentation is short-sighted. This is because there is a confusion of referential levels which leads to an incorrect matching of the metaphorical aspect of the motif with its meaning in its relevant referential world.

The first point of information (topic) is that John saw trumpet-wielding angels, and heard the trumpets sound. All these things, however, took place in the referential world which is called 'Heaven' and were 'real' in the context of that world. However, the result of the trumpet blasts, or their manifestation as it was felt and experienced in the referential world known as the 'earth', was perceived as a series of calamities, which we are calling judgment events.

People on earth witnessed a calamity, but John is saying that in Heaven, that same event was caused by, or simply was, a trumpet blast. So there are two levels here which need to be kept distinct. In Wilcock's terms we have a single 'event' which is equally real for all concerned but just seen from different viewpoints, namely the heavenly and the earthly.

But then there is a third level, in that John reports in his visionary narrative what he saw, heard and understood, and makes a connection between a trumpet and a calamity. This is the level which is of concern to those who wish to understand the text as text. So what then does this mean? What did John intend to communicate in bringing these different concepts together into one metaphor?

The answer to this question can be best understood by bringing into the discussion the concepts of the seals and the bowls, since, in effect, the same principles are operative in each case. Whenever a seal was opened, or trumpet sounded, or a bowl emptied in Heaven, the result on earth was much the same. It was a catastrophic judgment event - and this is what was perceived by the human witnesses.

A5.2.2 The Issue of Motifs, Symbolism and Imagery in General

Metaphors occur in all languages, without exception, because this is the way human beings are wired. As a consequence, there will always be some form or other of imagery and symbolism, including what we have called and described as motifs in the preceding pages. Anyone who tries, in any shape or form, to argue otherwise, is going to have an uphill battle against history and against the basic shape of the human psyche itself. There are countless authors who have expounded on this phenomenon of the human condition, of whom we give just a few examples here.

Alter 1981,95-6 and Callow 1998,177 make specific comments on motifs. For more general discussions on metaphors and imagery in general, see, for example, Beekman and Callow 1974, 124-50 and Larson 1984, 246-55, for a linguistic viewpoint. Then, Beale 1999,50-64 and Wilcock 1975,151-7 for discussion from the biblical studies viewpoint.

See Lenski 1943,61 for reference to the symbolism of the seven letters and Wilcock 1975,59-64 for a discussion of the issue of number symbolism in general in Revelation .

As regards the symbolism of the seals, see Morris 1969,92 and Beale 1998,264. Strand 1979,48 using a will as his referential starting point suggests that 'the breaking of the seals was preliminary to the opening of the will and disclosing who would inherit and who would not'. See Daniel 10:21 for a reference to a similar document or scroll which is either a metaphor or a reference to a spiritual reality. Beale 1999,370 comments concerning the seals: 'the opening of the seals begins the actual revelation and execution of the contents of the "scroll" of ch. 5'.

As regards the bowls, Ryken 1974,354 and Beale 1999,788 also agree that the point of similarity is that of completion or consummation. Moffat n.d.,288 suggests that the bowls represent 'the actual execution of the doom'.

A5.2.3 The Issue of the Last Major Division in the Book

Wilcock 1975,17 and 175 and Aune 1997/1998,civ and 1040-46 are two, among many, who propose that the last major division in the book is at 19:11. However, little evidence is provided to support this view. The best evidence is reviewed by Aune who argues (ibid.,xcv-xcvii) that since 17:1-19:10 and 21:9-22:9 are in parallel, therefore 19:10 must be an ending and thence 19:11 must be a new beginning.

However, this evidence only seems to suggest that there is a major beginning at 21:9, but not necessarily straight after 19:11. In addition, as has been proposed elsewhere (Appendix A3.2.2), this parallelism is a secondary feature of the text and therefore permits the establishment of secondary boundaries, but it does not contribute usefully to the construction of an outline of the macro-structure.

Beale 1999 is rather contradictory for he claims that 19:11 is 'the beginning of another major literary segment' (ibid.,949) but it is not the beginning of a major segment in his overall outline (ibid.,136). However, he does provide more evidence for a major division, even though it is weak and does not bear close scrutiny (ibid.,949). Firstly, he says that the presence of 'and behold', 'indicates the beginning of another vision'. However, this is not consistently true throughout the book (cf. the occurrences at 6:2,5 and 8) and even if it were true, the data does not support the idea that this phrase, in and of itself, introduces a major part of the book.

Secondly, he says that the concept of 'the opened heaven' (19:11) introduces a 'major' unit of the book, citing three other occurrences of the concept (4:1; 11:19 and 15:5) in support. However, inspection of these references reveal that they are not all the same. In the first and last the verb is a perfect, passive participle, whereas the middle two are identical indicative aorists. In addition, in the first and last it is a door to, or heaven itself, which is opened, and in the middle two it is 'the sanctuary...' in heaven which is opened. This creates an ABB'A' pattern, so that even if these phrases occur near the beginning of a segment and create a series of parallels, the segment A' (which is in 19:11) is at the end of the lexical chain and therefore, logically, is likely to be part of a conclusion, rather than part of a new, major beginning.

The basic problem with these analyses, along with many others like them, is that they assume that these features are operating at the macro level and treat them as such, but they are really functioning at a lower level of the hierarchy. These differences can only be discerned and accounted for, by doing a full discourse analysis of the text ,which takes account of each of the levels of the discourse hierarchy which are in operation.

Here is another example. Ladd and others of his school of thought hold the view that 'chapters 18-20 appear to present a connected series of visions' (1972,261). In other words, he is saying that there is no major, book level division within this sequence of chapters.

However, the connection only 'appears' to be present, and that appearance is due to the literary structure. The sequence of the judgment of Babylon, the two Beasts and finally Satan is objectively present in the text, but that, by no means implies that 20:1 follows 19:21 in direct sequence in some kind of chronological plan. In any case, as has been explained in the main text, there is no way of proving that events which take place partially, or in whole, in the heavenly referential world have an earthly chronology at all.

The underlying problem, once again, is that Ladd does not assess the full gamut of linguistic evidence which the author provides, but bases his arguments almost entirely on theological presuppositions. See, for example, the arguments presented in Clouse 1977. By contrast, Lewis 1980, also approaching the subject from a theological point of view, provides detailed arguments as to why 20:1 cannot be interpreted as following 19:21 sequentially, but argues that 'there is good reason to conclude that at this point John broke the sequence to reiterate the great themes of victory...' (ibid.,49). See also Erickson 1977, White 1994 and Beale 1999,974-76 on these issues. This issue was also presented, with other examples, in Appendix A3.2.4 which follows Chapter 3.

A5.2.4 The Issue of Missing Components in a Discourse

As mentioned in the main text, Dorsey 1988 and 1999, explains how one of the key features of the book of Lamentations is that a number of different components, which one would expect to be there, are missing. In fact, he says that this system of missing pieces, or incomplete patterns, are typical of eulogies, or laments, in that era.

From my own personal research on Lamentations, I found an example of a missing component which he does not mention. It is to be found in Chapter 2, which is also poem 2 of the series of five. The poem should be a seven part chiasm (A.B.C.D.C'B'A') but the C' unit is missing. The missing component reduces the poem from being made up of seven parts, as the previous one is, down to six parts.

So there are two signals here operating together. The first signal is that the poem is incomplete, compared to the template in the first poem, then secondly, it is composed of six parts instead of seven. In both these cases, it indicates incompleteness and imperfection, a missing of the mark, which is strongly supportive of the content which is about judgment and loss, with no spark of hope. As it happens, this is the most negative of all the poems, and the most lacking in any element of hope, so these structural features are entirely appropriate.

In the case of Lamentations, the missing component is compensated for in the next poem (Chapter 3) which is the most hopeful one of them all. In the case of the missing component in Revelation 4, it is a reference to God's throne and its associated thunder and lightning which is missing, and this lack is also compensated for later in the book.

A5.2.5 The Issue of Number Symbolism in Revelation

In general, there is little disagreement that numbers in Scripture are used symbolically and that the number seven, symbolically understood, represents 'fullness' or 'completeness'. So, Davis 1968,154, Beale 1998,203, Giblin 1991,165 quoting Beasley-Murray 1974,256-7, Bauckham 1993,30 and Aune 1997,xciii inter alia.

Davis 1968 actually wrote an entire book on numerology only to conclude that the Bible does not use numbers symbolically. But even he was forced to admit that an exception to this rule was the number seven (op.cit.,154).

For completeness we can also remind ourselves here that, in contrast to the number seven, the number six symbolically represents incompleteness and imperfection, and that the number five represents grace. However, there is less consensus on these latter numbers.

There is a reference to the number six with regard to Lamentations in the section above. In addition to that example, it can be added that there is another number six in the same chapter as the one mentioned above, i.e. Chapter 2. In this chapter, God addresses the nation of Israel by the term 'daughter of Sion', which is a rather affectionate and even intimate appellation. However, the term is (only) used six times – six times all together in the space of one chapter. By contrast, it only occurs once more in all the rest of the book. So, in the book as a whole, God uses this affectionate term seven times, which is what one would expect. However, in this single chapter which presents everything negative which you can imagine about Israel, it is used six times. This also is appropriate symbolism at work.

Further comments regarding the use of the number six in Revelation can be found in the section below. A more extended discussion of the use of numbers may also be found in Chapter 7.8.

A5.2.6 The Issue of the Spiral Development of the Book.

One of the key features discussed and proposed in the main text is that the book of Revelation progresses as a whole, in a spiral fashion. That is, that the book as a whole is composed of seven cycles, which go over the same ground from different points of view and are, as such, in parallel to one another. Yet, at the same time, without creating any impediment or contradiction, the book, as a whole, also progresses by means of a linear development from the beginning to the end.

This spiral development can be discerned the most easily in those cycles where the seven-fold motif is delineated the most clearly, that is to say, in the Seals, Trumpets and Bowls Cycles. The main body of each of Cycles 2-6 as depicted by the seven-fold motif is devoted to developing the Judgment Theme, as previously explained in Chapter 4. Furthermore, most commentators are agreed that the sixth sub-unit of each of these cycles depicts the final judgment, and some also think that the seventh unit continues and completes this same sub-theme. See, for example, Beale 1999, 129,400-1,505-15,770,827,918-24.

In terms of number symbolism, as mentioned above, it is entirely appropriate that the final judgment, from which there is no hope of escape, should be depicted by the sixth sub-unit of the cycles. Likewise, it is symbolically appropriate that the seventh sub-unit should complete the cycle and usher in a new beginning.

For the same reason, it is very logical and reasonable, to suppose that the entire organization for Revelation, based on a structural system of seven times seven, is entirely intentional. Considering the content of the book, it would seem to be much more satisfying, and much more symbolically appropriate, than any other system. Other analyses, based on other numbers, are always going to be inherently lacking this crucial ingredient.

Others who were aware of the parallel or cyclic nature of the book and even discerned its spiral progression are Collins 1976,111-6, Fiorenza 1977,360, Morris 1987,41, Boring 1989,32, Ryken 1993,466, Metzger 1993 and Strand 1979,49-50.

A5.2.7 The Issue of the Comparison between Babylon and Jerusalem

A number of commentators discern that there is a similarity between the way Babylon on the one hand, and Jerusalem on the other, are presented. As a consequence of this observation most such commentators continue that line of thought by accepting that they are implicitly being compared to each other. Some of these, for example, are Bauckham 1993,4, Smith 1994, Aune 1997,xcv-xcvii and Longenecker 2001,106.

What they notice, in particular, is the parallelism between the phrase 'Come, I will show you' in 17:1-3, and the similar phrase in 21:9-10. Then, in the same general context there are the two references to John falling down to worship an angel in 19:9b-10, and 22:6-9. In their case, they think that this repetition indicates book level divisions in the text.

However, the writers cited above, overlook a number of points. Firstly, the passages in question are all part of the Narrative Framework and need to be understood in this wider context as discussed in Chapter 2.

Secondly, the parallels 'Come, I will show you...' (17:1, and 21:9), and 'I fell at his feet...(to worship)' (19:9-10 and 22:8), are not unique. The former also occurs at 4:1 and the latter at 1:17. These six references undoubtedly are in parallel to one another, and form a pattern at the book level. However, this series of parallels does not appear to provide a key to the analysis of the book at the macro level. On the contrary, it is more likely that their function is to provide cohesion rather than to mark divisions, as is the case for many features of the book.

Thirdly, the opening brackets are not at the beginning of the relevant sections, but rather they are *near* the beginning. Thus, 17:1-3 is preceded by 16:17:21 which is the true beginning of the Babylon story, and 21:9 is preceded by 21:1-8.

Fourthly, the closing brackets also include a blessing (cf.19:9a and 22:7) and are in the immediate context of the concept of the witness of Jesus (19:10 and 22:16,18,20). This observation strengthens the case for parallelism but also underlines the fact that these texts are not isolated, but are attached to a context and have, therefore, a more complex function than would first appear. This leads into the last point, that the authors cited separate these texts from their context instead of interpreting them as parts of the larger units of text around them, to which they belong.

A5.2.8 The Issue of Ambiguity

On a number of occasions reference has been made to ambiguity, because, like it or not, ambiguity seems to be a common characteristic of human communication, across the board. The problem for the analyst who comes along behind is to decide firstly, whether the ambiguity was intentional on the part of the author, then secondly, to decide which aspect of the ambiguity should be given the most weight in the analysis. As a rule of thumb, in this analysis it has been proposed that all the aspects of the ambiguity should be included in the analysis, to the extent that that solution is possible.

Other researchers have investigated this issue and have come to the conclusion that ambiguity is often intentional, and, in some cases, is even considered to be good style. So, for example, the phenomenon of leaving a conclusion unstated or ambiguous is widespread. Ford 182,75 notes it with regard to English folk-tales, Callow 1998,172 with regard to Kazakh folk-tales and it is true of New Caledonia folk-tales (Schooling personal research).

In a biblical context it may have been an important, if not obligatory, feature of parables to leave their conclusions unstated or ambiguous, (see, for example, Frankovic 1995 including notes 22 and 26). Schooling 1998,31 proposes that the book of Micah ends with a pun based on Micah's name. Alter 1981,96 writing about literary conventions says: 'repetition tends to be at least partly camouflaged, and we are expected to *detect* it, to pick it out as a subtle thread of recurrence in a variegated pattern, a flash of suggestive likeness in seeming differences'.

Sandford 1977,74 writing as a pastoral counselor comments more generally on the human condition in the following way: 'We generally delight to tell others things directly because it is self-exalting. And the learner has not been invited into the process of discovery. However, a man dead to self teaches whenever possible by parable and analogy, that others may learn by discovery. Though Jesus could have announced "I am the Son of God", He did not take such a short cut. Men must go through inner stages of learning, voluntarily, on their own'.

See Ceresko 1976,309-11 for some other examples of word-play parallels in the Old Testament. Parunak 1981,166-68 also provides considerable discussion of how the subtle changing of a pre-established pattern contributes special emphasis.

Harvey 1998 has done us a great service in investigating literary styles and conventions which were regularly used before, and during, the period when Revelation was written. So, one of his observations is that the placing of antitheses next to each other without any other explanation is a linguistic feature which was not uncommon in ancient literature. The point about this practice is that it creates ambiguity and forces the reader to do some work to understand what is being communicated. The quotation from Aristotle which appeared in the main text above, was taken from his book (ibid.74). Bailey 1983 has also made a useful contribution to this issue.

A5.2.9 The Issue of the Function of Chapter 20

One of the key points about the analysis of Cycle 7 presented in the main text above, is that the setting of Cycle 7 (ch.20) is in a contrastive, or antithetical, relationship with the body of the cycle.

Wilcock 1975,198 has the same understanding of the role of this text, except that for him the passage begins at 19:11 and ends at 21:8. It is true that 19:11-21 also deals with the theme of the end of evil, but it has been argued in the main text above, that it is an interim conclusion which is in parallel to and prepares the way for 20:1-15, rather than being an integral part of the same textual unit. Giblin1991,158-9 also perceives the importance of describing the defeat of God's enemies as a preliminary to describing the 'necessary corollary', which is the New Creation and the New Jerusalem.

Otherwise, commentators seem to have overlooked the subtle ambiguities of the antitheses which are present in the last part of the book.

A5.2.10 The Issue of When God Speaks from His Throne

In the analysis of Chapter 21 presented in the main text, the moment when God speaks from His throne is a key moment, both in Cycle 7 and in the whole book. It can be noted here that this insight was independently contributed by Metzger 1993,99, where he says that 21:5 is only the second place in the whole book where God Himself, sitting on his throne, unambiguously speaks. Moffat n.d.,480, also made this remark and noted that the first instance was at 1:8, thereby providing another parallel between the beginning and the end of the book.

However, they both overlook the voice from the throne, which is referred to at 16:17. It is true that this is not an explicitly, exact repetition. Nonetheless, it is a clear, synonymous repetition, which is perfectly acceptable, and normal, for Hebraic type texts like this one. The fact that the result is a threefold repetition creates a more elegant and satisfactory overall result, with one reference being near the beginning, one reference being near the end, and one near the middle.

Broadly speaking, doublets are rare at the book level in Hebraic discourses in general, and in Revelation in particular. The only exceptions, generally speaking, are when the doublet is clearly functioning as an *inclusio*, which this one is not. To have a threefold repetition when referring to God in such an important way as this, is much more symbolically appropriate.

A5.2.11 The Issue of Whether the Book is a Chiasm or Not

The consensus among commentators is that Cycles 1 and 7 are clearly parallel to one another and that Cycles 3 (the Trumpets) and 5 (the Bowls) are more obviously parallel to each other than the other members of the central series. See for example, Beale 1999,132-35. However, even in recognizing this amount of parallelism, most stop short of positing a chiastic structure for the whole book.

Nonetheless, some do claim to discern a chiastic structure. Unfortunately, Lund 1970 and Fiorenza 1977 resort to emending the text. Others tend to be rather complex, relying on relatively minor details as evidence for the parallelism involved. However, most do point to the Signs Cycle as being the central part of the structure.

Kline (in Beale 1999,131) has the most credible proposal for a chiasm, which I have managed to find so far, yet his evidence for this pairing is still flimsy. It is dependent on a parallel vision of the Risen Christ (5:5-6//19:11), but this fails to account for the role of 19:11-21 and is not clearly a unique parallel since there are other visions of Christ in the book. It is also dependent on the parallel of horsemen (6:1-8//19:11-21) which is also not self-evident. In 19:14 the horsemen are clearly the saints and are in parallel to other references to the saints. In 19:18 the horsemen are obviously in parallel with passages like 16:14 but it is not clear that a parallel can also be established with Chapter 6. The fact that the word 'horse', is repeated does not, in and of itself, establish a semantic parallel relationship especially at this important, book level of analysis.

See Man 1984 for discussion of the importance of chiastic structures for exegesis and interpretation. This issue will be taken up again in the following chapter. Bailey 1983 claims that 'inversion as an overall outline' is the most common form of concentric type structures, and provides evidence that it was widely used in ancient literature. See ibid.,49-52 and notes in loc.

CHAPTER 6

Prominence

The Mountains and Valleys of Text

CHAPTER 6
Prominence: the Mountains and Valleys of Text

6.1 Introduction

A well-formed text is a work of art. Consequently, there are discernible contrasts, similar to topographical mountains and valleys in any such carefully textured work of art. This is essential, because an author of necessity must organize his discourse in such a way that some parts of the text strike the reader, or hearer as the case may be, as being relatively more important for the communication of the inherent message than others. This feature of the organization of a text is called prominence and as Longacre 1985,83 aptly describes the issue:

> Discourse without prominence would be like pointing to a piece of black cardboard and insisting that it was a picture of black camels crossing black sands at midnight.

Even though, with the advantage of hindsight, this characteristic of a discourse would seem to be self-evident, nonetheless, in the past it has been overlooked. Thus, for example, an early text book on discourse analysis (Brown and Yule 1983) passes over the subject in silence. Biblical commentators are usually interested in elucidating the detail of a text and only rarely lead the reader to perceive the high points or peaks in the text, which embody the most important part of the writer's overall message. When some reference is made to this issue, it is usually in the context of discussion of lower levels of the analysis, and is not supported by appropriate argumentation.

The most developed theory of semantic prominence has been made available in Callow 1974 and 1998. The notion of prominence affects a discourse in many different ways, but the two principal categories are those of natural prominence and special prominence. Natural prominence refers to the difference in importance that arises naturally out of the relationships, which exist between various units of text. As Callow 1998,156 puts it herself:

> When two units are related to each other, one of the two is normally relationally dominant, that is, it is more prominent than the other because of the relationship between them. Thus an effect is normally more prominent than its cause, an appeal than the grounds on which it is made.

Special prominence is attributed to certain parts of the text whenever the author decides to draw special attention to them. Sometimes these special features enhance the existing natural prominence, and so cause those units of text to be even more noticeable than usual. In other cases, it may draw special attention to parts of the text which would not otherwise be considered prominent.

Authors have at their disposal a wide range of features with which they can attract attention to units of text, which they wish to be recognized as prominent. In effect, anything which creates a contrast with the mass of material which surrounds it, is potentially an indicator of prominence.

> Anything unanticipated always carries with it a degree of prominence, hence special prominence is often conveyed by unexpected lexical and grammatical choices. Writers frequently build in the recipients a certain expectation, only to conclude with a totally unexpected outcome... Surface structure devices for signaling special prominence fall into three main categories: **lexical devices**, **rhetorical devices** and **departure from norms.** Callow 1998,164 and 182.

Longacre talks about 'the peak' of a discourse which is where it builds up 'to some kind of climax' (1985,84), and, in general terms, this often corresponds with an area of special prominence in the text. He has observed that there will be clues, even many clues, to indicate where the author is marking his text for prominence. In the course of this study of Revelation, this observation has been confirmed, for the author is indeed,

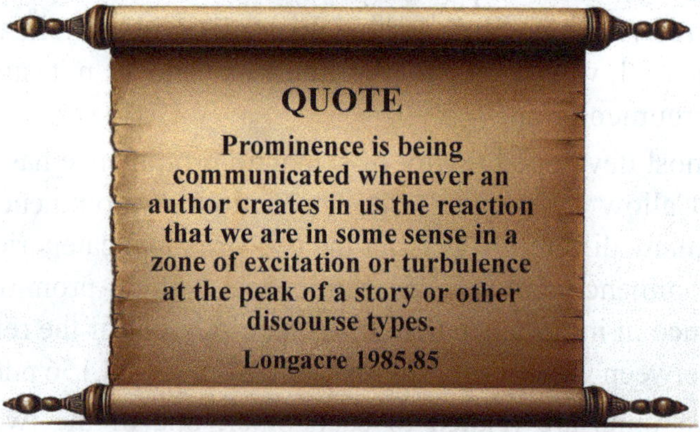
QUOTE
Prominence is being communicated whenever an author creates in us the reaction that we are in some sense in a zone of excitation or turbulence at the peak of a story or other discourse types.
Longacre 1985,85

both liberal and lavish, in his use of prominence markers. The only caveat is that an analyst who approaches the book with a different worldview in tow, and with different reading habits, needs to learn to read these prominence markers for what they are. Then, having done that, he needs to endeavor to not force them to accomplish something which they were not designed to communicate.

Even though the indicators which an author can use in any given language to mark special prominence are 'legion' (Callow 1974,51), they are nonetheless recognizable. This is primarily because they are unexpected, as Callow indicates, and their unexpectedness tends to create some disturbance or 'turbulence' in the normal flow of the text, as Longacre has explained.

Prominent parts of the text, however, do not exist for their own sake, but together they create a network of important points, by which means the author makes his overall purpose clear. As Callow 1998,187-8 explains:

> A well-structured message does not present an overall uniformity; rather, it has development and thrust. The sender communicates the message as a directional entity, developing towards a communicative goal, and the addressee is drawn along this purposive pathway as he receives the message... (the) elements that carry the purposive flow of the message and combine to form *the significant patterning of the message...* (are) its **schema.**

DEFINITION

A Schema

embodies the purpose of the author in presenting a particular discourse. It is the combination of structural components used to communicate the main point of the discourse.

In simplified terms, the schema of a text corresponds with the author's main point. Clearly, writers fail in their task if their readers miss the main point. However, getting the point does not depend on the reader's opinion, or subjective intuitions, but rather on correctly assessing the prominence indicators which the writers have placed in their text. As Callow 1998,152 sums it up:

> A pure hierarchy, without prominence, might suffice for the analysis of a railway timetable or the multiplication table; but for the analysis of communications steeped in the purposes and personalities of the communicators, we must allow for the constant and generous use of prominence devices.

The purpose of this chapter is to describe the principal areas of natural and special prominence in Revelation. Once these areas of prominence have been identified then, in the context of the relevant schemas, it becomes possible to propose an objective appraisal of the main points of the message of the book. As a result of this process, this appraisal is based on data from within the text, and is no longer subject to the whims and fancies of personal opinion, or theological persuasion, as it was in the past.

6.2 Natural Prominence in Revelation

Every semantic unit from the shortest proposition upwards, has a pattern of natural prominence, but in this study only two main patterns will be discussed. These are the patterns of natural prominence to be found within the book viewed as a total unit, and within the grouping of Cycles 2-6, which is the largest individual component of the book.

6.2.1 The Pattern of Natural Prominence for the Book as a Whole

As indicated previously, the body of Revelation is composed of seven cycles of approximately equal size. Each of these cycles, being complete in itself, could theoretically stand alone as a complete discourse. It has also been noticed that, in terms of grammatical connections at least, the seven cycles are in a coordinate relationship to each other.

More specifically, the grammatical connections are:

- the phrase 'after these things' at 4:1, linking Cycles 1 and 2,
- 'and I saw' at 15:1 and 20:1, linking Cycles 4 and 5, and 6 and 7, and…
- *kai* 'and' plus another verb at 8:1, 11:15 and 16:17, linking Cycles 2 & 3, 3 & 4, and 5 & 6.

These coordinate relations imply also a sequential relationship, but, as indicated in Chapter 2, this sequencing is part of the Narrative Framework. Thus, it can only be interpreted unambiguously as indicating the order in which John received, and recounted, the series of visions. The sequencing does not unambiguously imply any other kind of temporal relationship between the referential content of the cycles. Other data must be adduced in order to support any analysis which is dependent on a particular temporal view of the organization of the book. For Cycles 2-6 the issue is complicated by the overlap links. However, the cycles are still connected by *kai* 'and', regardless of whether the grammatical link between the cycles is considered to be at the beginning or the end of the overlaps.

By definition, a coordinate relationship implies a relationship between units of equal weight and importance operating at the same level of the linguistic hierarchy. The terms used to designate this relationship at the semantic level (in order to distinguish this level from the surface structure grammatical level), are those of an addition or additive relationship. More information on this particular point is provided in the Appendix following this chapter. Units in such a relationship are normally considered to have equal natural prominence. However, in a case like Revelation where the whole discourse is linked together by such a relationship, it is not sufficient to stop the analysis at that point. This is because to do so would suggest that the book was simply a listing of items of equal importance, which is clearly not the case. Such an analysis would be akin to painting a picture of black camels on black sand, as mentioned above.

In the case of an additive semantic relationship like this, the conclusion of the discourse is considered to be the most naturally prominent part of the whole. This is because it is in the conclusion that the author's communicative purpose is the most fully developed and, by this time, the most complete amount of information concerning the topic has been presented.

In the case of Revelation, therefore, it is Cycle 7 which fulfills this role. This is because at this point, the most complete amount of information concerning the revelation, which John received, has been presented. By the end of Cycle 7 the hearer knows that God has fully dealt with the problem of evil, and that He has established a completely new creation.

Since the communication of information is in view here, the schema which the author is using to accomplish this purpose, is called an informational schema. As a general rule, informational schemas will be linear in nature, and the end point of that schema, corresponding with the conclusion of that linear structure, will be the most naturally prominent part of the discourse.

It should be noted, however, that the conclusion of a text is not necessarily the last unit to be presented, even if this is often the case. In the example which Callow 1998 discusses on pages 191-3 and 297-300, the semantic conclusion which fulfills the conditions of completeness and purposiveness, is presented near the beginning of the text. In this case the conclusion is presented immediately after the presentation of the topic, and the material which follows is supportive, explanatory detail.

Callow 1998,198 also indicates that the true conclusion may also be followed by additional text which stands 'a little apart from the main schematic structure'. This is the case in Revelation, where the Epilogue follows the main informational conclusion contained in the body of Cycle 7, along with its coda.

In the discussion in previous chapters it has been noted that Cycle 1 and Cycle 7 are in a direct relationship with one another. On a structural level it is because they function as the introduction and the conclusion to the body of the book, and on an informational level it is because they both address issues concerning the people of God.

As the detail of Cycle 1 is considered, it can be noted that it does not just contain information but it is also volitional in nature. Each of the seven letters are similar in structure and intent, and each of them addresses the will of the recipients and urges them to a particular set of related actions. As Callow 1998,190 says, ‘the only essential element in a volitional message is the proposed action’, as a consequence it is the commands which are the most naturally prominent part of each letter. The introductory part (beginning ‘I know’), therefore, provides the grounds for the following exhortation, along with the motivational promises and warnings. Consequently, these are all classified as being, less prominent, support material.

So, for example, the verb ‘to repent’ occurs eight times in total, four times as a command:

- twice in Letter 1,
- once in Letter 3,
- three times in Letter 4, and
- once each in Letters 5 and 7.

There are sixteen references to endure or remaining faithful in different forms, all of which occur in a context of exhortation or instruction:

- four times in Letter 1,
- once in Letter 2,
- twice in Letter 3, and
- three times in Letters 4, 5 and 6

In addition, the concept of endurance is also implicit in all the letters in the promise to the overcomers near the end of each letter.

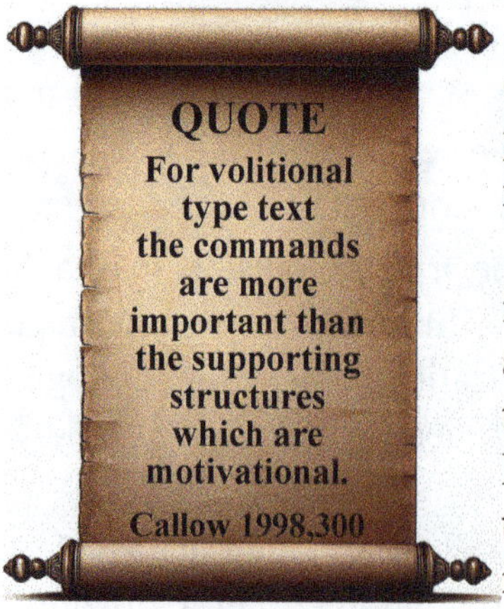
QUOTE
For volitional type text the commands are more important than the supporting structures which are motivational.
Callow 1998,300

Even though other exhortations also occur, the ones concerning repentance and perseverance are considered to be the two most prominent aspects of Cycle 1.

Even though they are less prominent in the context of the first cycle, the warnings and promises are, nonetheless, important in that they provide the primary link with Cycle 7. In Cycle 1 these motivational messages point towards the future and are not yet fulfilled, but in Cycle 7 they are described as having been fulfilled.

Thus, for example, in Letter 6 (3:12) the overcomer is promised that God’s name will be written on him and this is fulfilled in 22:4. In 2:11

the overcomer is promised that he will avoid the second death, and this is confirmed in 20:14-15, with extra support in 21:27.

When taken together as a pair then, the semantic relationship between Cycle 1 and Cycle 7 is that of condition-consequence. In other words, the primary message of Cycle 1 in the context of its relationship with Cycle 7 could be restated as a condition as follows: 'If you do the following things then ...'. The consequences which will be enjoyed as a result of fulfilling the previous conditions are then described in full in Cycle 7. Here, the consequences are no longer simply motivational - promises with merely the potential for realization - but they are described, from the viewpoint of the narrator at least, as events which have already been accomplished.

Once again, Cycle 7 is the more naturally prominent of the two since it is the more prominent consequence aspect of a condition-consequence relationship. See Callow 1998,261 and 357 for discussion and examples of the condition-consequence relationship.

So it is then, that each of the issues which have been discussed above, point in the same direction. They indicate that it is Cycle 7, in its position as the conclusion to the whole of the body of the book, which is the most naturally prominent of all of the seven cycles.

6.2.2 The Pattern of Natural Prominence for Cycles 2-6

As mentioned above, at the grammatical level Cycles 2-6 also stand in a coordinate relationship with one another, but with the added complication that they are also connected by overlap links. Internally, the structure of each cycle is similar, in that each of the seven sub-units and their respective interlude also stand in a coordinate relationship to each other.

The semantic relationship, once again, is additive, being a sequence as considered from John's viewpoint of observer and narrator, as he witnesses the parade of each segment of each vision. However, 'simple succession does not make either (or any) element relationally subordinate' (Callow 1998,299). So, even at this lower level in the hierarchy, there are no individual units which can be interpreted from a relational point of view, as being naturally more prominent than any other. This is true for the sub-units of each of these cycles, and also for the relationship between the cycles themselves.

Using the same argumentation as above then, it can be proposed that when a series of units appear to have the same natural prominence, then it is usually the conclusion which is the most naturally prominent. This is because that is where the author's purpose reaches its fullest development. In the case of these cycles, this would naturally be the seventh unit where the author reaches the end of what, in the majority of cases at least (i.e. the seven seals, trumpets and bowls), is clearly intended to be a consecutive series of seven.

However, as discussed in Chapter 3 above, these cycles are connected by an overlap link in that the conclusion (the seventh sub-unit) of Cycles 2-5 is, at the same time, the setting for the following cycle. This linguistic phenomenon has two consequences for the issue of prominence. Firstly, the natural prominence of cycles 2-5 is pushed towards the end, so that in effect, the whole of the following cycle is acting as a literary conclusion to what precedes, and not just the seventh sub-unit. But this happens repeatedly, so it is as if one never quite gets to the conclusion, but the semantic development continues until the final conclusion of the whole series is reached.

However, at this point another surprise is encountered. This is because Proclamation 7, which is the conclusion to the last of this series of cycles, is embedded in another linguistic unit. This unit is 19:11-21, which is the conclusion to the whole of Cycles 2-6, as discussed in Chapter 5 section 4. This previous discussion revealed that the unit in question is actually part of a complex set of seven interim conclusions. This would be appropriate, seeing that it is actually serving as the final conclusion to each of the cycles from Cycle 2 through to Cycle 6. So then, we can see that not only has the natural prominence of this whole section of the book been pushed towards the end, but that its natural prominence has, at the same time, been considerably expanded.

The second consequence is that a setting is less naturally prominent than the body which follows. This means that the natural prominence which may otherwise have been attributed to the seventh sub-units of Cycles 2-5, is down-played by John who, by his structural organization, makes it function as a setting. This downgrading of the prominence of each of the seventh sub-units serves as well, to further enhance the prominence of the final conclusion, when it eventually arrives.

Once the combination of these phenomena is discerned, it is possible to start putting into words a subtle message, which John is communicating by means of his discourse structure. It is as if he saying something like this to the hearer: 'You thought that you were coming to the end of the series of seven, and that here you would find the conclusion and the answer to all your outstanding questions. But you are mistaken. I have postponed the ending and we have started again without fully finishing what went before. This is because I want you to keep on reading a bit longer until you reach the final end, the conclusion of the whole series, which will be the most important part of all'.

Callow 1998,185 indicates that there can be varying degrees of prominence. She says that 'milder forms of prominence are used, not to arrest attention, but to convey a certain atmosphere, to elicit a certain kind of response, without the reader's awareness'. See also Bergen 1987,328-29 on the subliminal aspects of communication.

This implicit transmission of an author's intentions and how this should be incorporated in some way into a complete analysis has been crystallized in this way:

> A discourse is not simply an organized collection of words, it is the distillation in verbal form of the thoughts and outlook of the communicator... It is the intended meaning of the speaker which controls the selection of specific verbal forms, and any analysis of the resultant discourse which does not give due weight to that intended meaning will be inherently incomplete and defective. K. and J. Callow 1992,5.

In the light of this quotation it can be seen that it is one thing to observe 'verbal forms' as they occur in the surface structure of the text. However, it is another more important process, to come to terms with the intention of the author when he chose to express himself in that particular way. The point that is being made here, then, is that if the author went to considerable trouble to link Cycles 2-6 together in the way which has been previously described, then it must have been with some discourse related purpose in mind.

The proposal being presented then, is that the writer has intentionally canceled out the natural prominence of Cycles 2-5, or, at the very least, has significantly down-graded it. By this means, he has also attributed this prominence to the conclusion for the whole series, which is 19:11-21.

It may be objected that, since there is such an accumulation of special effects, this phenomenon is really an example of special prominence. However, there are many other examples of special prominence in Cycles 2-6, as will be discussed below. In addition, it would be very unusual for there to be no locus of natural prominence at all, in a section of text this long. For these reasons, therefore, it is being proposed that this phenomenon is, in fact, an example of natural prominence, even if it is an unusual one.

This complex conclusion at the end of Cycles 2-6 (19:11-21), reintroduces the risen Christ in his role of conquering hero, as an echo of both the initial vision in 1:9-20, and the throne-room scene of Chapters 4-5. Having re-activated that background setting, against which this part of the discourse should be understood, it then proceeds to bring to closure both that vision of the victorious Christ, but also some subsidiary but, nonetheless, important thematic strands.

If the above argumentation is valid, then it also serves as secondary confirmation for the remarks made previously in Chapter 4 above, concerning the setting of Cycle 7 (20:1-15). Firstly, since John appears to have downgraded the importance of some material (namely, the conclusions of Cycles 2-5) by making them settings, this lends credence to the idea that he has done the same thing to the dragon by assigning the description of his final doom to setting material.

Secondly, if it is accepted that 19:11-21 is marked by an accumulation of natural prominence, then this, in turn, overshadows the following setting section composed of 20:1-15, just as a higher mountain peak throws shadow on the neighboring valley. This then constitutes extra evidence that, in the writer's view, Chapter 20 is less important than the nature of its content might superficially imply.

As mentioned in Chapter 4 section 6, Revelation does not contain any overt expressive import material. However, as Manabe 1984,4 points out, in reality 'every text, in some way, manifests the belief or value system of its writer'. This is because it is hard to imagine that any serious person who took the time to put together a well organized discourse, did not do so without some conscious, or unconscious, intention of communicating to others what he felt about the subject matter.

Manabe goes on to argue that this is particularly true of third-person narratives (such as are found in the section under discussion in Revelation 19:11-20:15). This is precisely because the surface structure of the genre makes it appear that the author is distant and disinterested, when, on the contrary, the author's primary intention is to communicate his world-view without overtly showing his hand. No serious novels would exist if this were not the case.

The discussion in the text above provides some insight as to how the author of Revelation has subtly communicated his opinions concerning his subject matter, by the way in which he has arranged his material. That is to say that he has caused some parts, concerning Christ, to be upgraded in prominence, and others, concerning the dragon, to be downgraded in prominence status. Cf. Dooley et al. 2001,105.

Finally, before terminating this discussion, there is one more thing to be said which goes along the same lines as what has been explained above. In Chapter 4 the interludes contained within Cycles 2-6 were discussed.

At that time, it was pointed out that, for various reasons, the interludes, and the Salvation Theme which they carry, were more important than the constituents carrying the Judgment Theme.

In addition, it was also pointed out that any volitional import material, which is, for the most part, carried by the Narrative Framework, is more important than any of the thematic material.

Now, in the context of the present discussion, it can be noted that the last interlude, that is to say, the conclusion to the whole series of five interludes, occurs at 19:1-8. This is immediately followed by a portion of volitional import material in 19:9-10. This is also an intermediate conclusion and, both together, these two units immediately precede the section we are currently discussing which is 19:11-21. As such, they belong to the set of seven intermediate conclusions mentioned in Chapter 5.

As we have said before, conclusions in a linear system are the most prominent units in the series. This means that the last interlude at 19:1-8, is the most naturally prominent of them all, and that the volitional import material in 19:9-10 should also be the most naturally prominent of all the volitional import material, up to that point, at least.

6.2.3 A Summary of the Points of Natural Prominence

Since we will need to refer to this information again later on, we will list here all the points of natural prominence which we have found so far.

Bearing in mind that we have been dealing with the linear structures which are present in Revelation, the main point is that conclusions are the most naturally prominent constituents of a discourse of that nature. In the case of this book then, for the book as a whole, Cycle 7, being the conclusion to the whole book, is the most naturally prominent unit.

Secondarily, the complex set of conclusions at 19:1-21 is the next most naturally prominent constituent. This implicitly includes the insight that the last interlude has natural prominence, as does a portion of the Narrative Framework.

To complete this summary, we will add here the point that introductions can also have a second lower level of natural prominence. This is particularly true in the case where the introduction makes a connected, complementary, contribution to the overall import of the conclusion. This is usually the case, because it is extremely rare that an introduction would have no connection, or correlation, with its matching conclusion at all.

These then, are the main points of natural prominence in order of importance:

- Cycle 7 (this may include the Epilogue as per 6.4.2)
- The complex set of conclusions at 19:1-21
- Cycle 1, being the matching introduction for Cycle 7
- Chapters 4 and 5, being the matching introduction for the conclusion to Cycles 2-6 at 19:1-21
- The Prologue, being the introduction for the whole book, and the matching, introductory bracket for the book's ending

6.3 Special Prominence in Revelation

As explained at the outset, the passages in a discourse which are specially prominent are in 'zones of turbulence' created by the author. He accomplishes this effect by inserting into his text one, or more, unexpected, or unusual, linguistic features whose purpose is to stick out above the rest of the discourse.

This literary ploy is designed to attract the readers' attention, either consciously or unconsciously. This is done in order to make them realize that something special is happening and that, therefore, they should pay special attention to what is being said, at this point in the discourse.

A Prominence Feature

These special prominence features may occur in a portion of text which is already naturally prominent, for the reasons discussed above. In such a case, the level of prominence will be raised even higher.

Obviously, prominence features can also occur elsewhere in the text, thereby raising that unit's level of importance relative to its normal level of importance. In addition, its importance will also be raised relative to surrounding parts of the text which are not so marked. The different kinds of special prominence features, which regularly occur, will be described below.

6.3.1 External Special Prominence Features

Authors have two possibilities for indicating that a particular text is intended to be prominent. They may provide indicators directly at the point of prominence or they may provide markers prior to the point of prominence. These latter markers act as signposts alerting the hearer in advance that something important is going to be communicated in a forthcoming section of text. They are being called external prominence features here, because they occur prior to, and outside of, the section of text which is being made prominent. Such signposts occur in Revelation and they indicate that the Signs Cycle is particularly prominent and is, therefore, the peak of the book.

The most striking set of signposts which John provides are the passages collectively known as The Three Woes (8:13, 9:12 and 11:14). These passages have been notoriously difficult to interpret and to relate adequately to their context. This difficulty of analysis is already advance warning that prominence markers may be influencing the flow and form of the text, and is already a clue to the analyst that something of this nature may be taking place.

The three woe passages are all prominent in their context. These passages are prominent by virtue of being different, in the following ways, as compared to their immediate context.

- The first two woes occur in the middle of an otherwise unbroken sequence of 6 trumpet units.
- They make an unexpected appearance, with no introduction, explanation, or other obvious attachment to their preceding context.
- They are all in the form of direct speech, introduced by asyndeton, even though the speaker is not specified in the last two occurrences.
- The first occurrence is marked by the double introductory formula, 'and I saw and I heard...' (8:13), which only occurs twice in the whole book (cf. 5:11).
- This is also marked by the triple repetition of the word 'Woe', while the second two are marked by 'behold', which is a prominence marker in its own right.

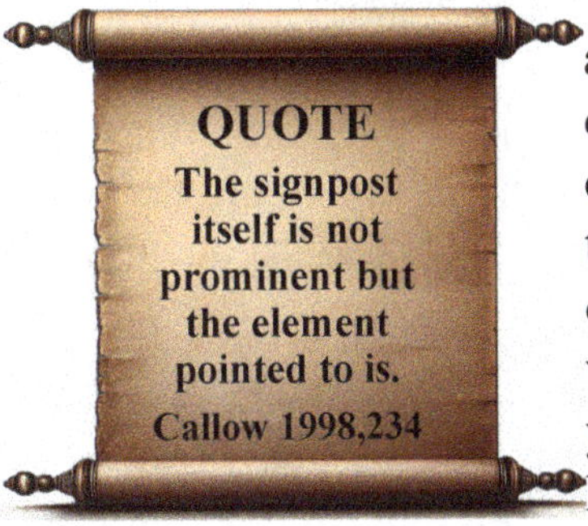
QUOTE
The signpost itself is not prominent but the element pointed to is.
Callow 1998,234

Yet it is clear that, in and of themselves, they are not important, because they are only commentaries and do not make any significant contribution to the referential content, or the thematic development, of the book. A piece of text which is not naturally prominent by virtue of its basic content and function, and yet is marked for special prominence, must have a special function. In this case the function is that of the signpost.

A signpost or, in more technical terms, an orienter, must be prominent in order to be noticed, but it is not otherwise important. The fact that there are three similar signposts functioning together indicate that the eventual communication, which is being drawn to the reader's attention, must be particularly important. The fact that they obviously belong together, even though separated by intervening text, indicates that they are operating at a higher level of the hierarchy than the surrounding text. As Callow 1998,292 says, 'This material is prosodic: it stands outside the hierarchical structure of the message proper'. This suggests that their function is not to point towards a prominent point within the Trumpets Cycle alone, but to draw attention to something which is prominent in a broader context, which, in this case, is at the level of the book as a whole.

Further evidence to support this proposal is that there is another text, which also indicates that something special is going to happen at the time when the seventh trumpet is blown. This feature occurs in the same context, but is also not part of the Trumpets Cycle, since it is part of the Narrative Framework. It occurs at 10:7 and will be discussed in detail later on. Meanwhile, it can be noted that this feature and the three woes are functioning together, but not as part of the Trumpets Cycle, but at a different level, in order to draw attention to its ending.

Analysis of the content of the woes also indicates that, even though they are superficially commentaries on the last three trumpets, at a deeper semantic level they are actually pointing beyond these last three trumpets. The first of the woe signposts (8:13) is the longest and contains the most information. The four concepts which are contained in the direct speech are:

- the woe concept,
- the addressees, who are the inhabitants of the earth,
- the concept of what yet remains to be accomplished, namely the sounding of the last three trumpets, and
- the concept of sounding the trumpets itself.

The last two of these signposts (9:12 and 11:14) continue the woe concept. Otherwise, their main thrust, as marked by the presence of 'behold', is to build anticipation as regards the things which are to happen soon. These events, as previously established in 8:13, are the sounding of the final trumpets.

However, the trumpets themselves are not inherently important, since they are also signposts pointing to something else. What is important in the whole context of the Trumpets Cycle, is not the actual sounding of the trumpets, but what happens afterwards, as an immediate consequence of each trumpet blast. Furthermore, the consequence of the seventh trumpet is particularly complex. This is because the seventh trumpet is the setting for the following cycle, as has been explained above, and before that, in Chapter 3.

As a result of this merging of the seventh sub-unit into the setting of the following cycle, the whole of the Signs Cycle is, in effect, the outworking of the seventh trumpet. This is why it can be said that the woes are not just pointing towards the trumpets, as their superficial content suggests, but are actually pointing beyond them, to the Signs Cycle.

It is of interest, therefore, to note that, within the context of the early part of the Signs Cycle, the word 'woe', reoccurs at 12:12. In actual fact, the word 'woe', occurs fourteen times in the book, which is 2 x 7. The first seven occurrences are in the three woe signposts previously discussed. The last six all concern Babylon and are closely grouped at 18:10-19 in Cycle 6. This leaves 12:12 as a single isolated occurrence in the center of this lexical chain thereby creating an ABA' chiasm. This suggests that the occurrence at 12:12 is the most important of all the occurrences.

These occurrences of 'woe', are in direct contrast, semantically, to the seven blessings, which also create a similar thread spread throughout the book. This contrastive set of key words gives this particular lexical thread, consisting of the seven woes, an antithetical impact which is greater than might have been otherwise the case.

The reference in 12:12 is specifically directed towards the earth and the sea, however the following context indicates that it is people, to whom the woe is directed. The reference is therefore either a metonymy (the earth representing all of the earth including its inhabitants), or it is an example of ellipsis. This is because the sentence forms part of a parallel doublet. The first part is 'Be glad, heavens and those who live there', while the second part is 'Woe, earth and sea', and by completion of the ellipsis, we could add 'and those who live there'. These same people, from land and sea, eventually express their woe in 18:10-19.

Upon investigation then, it can be seen that this woe of 12:12, is actually directed at the inhabitants of the earth. This insight totally coincides with the expectation created by the first woe in 8:13, which was explicitly directed towards the inhabitants of the earth. So, the expectation is created in 8:13, compounded by the two following woes, and then in 12:12, the cause of the anticipated lamentation is explained.

The reason why the inhabitants of the earth are going to want to lament and bemoan their lot, is because the devil has been thrown down to the earth. Not only that, but he is in great anger and is going to vent his anger upon them.

So then, by following the directions contained in the signposts, the hearer is led to look for a culmination of something which is a cause of woe, in the context immediately following the seventh trumpet. That is exactly what is to be found in 12:12.

In passing it can also be noted that the preceding context in 12:1-10, explains subsidiary reasons for the cause of the woe. These concern the birth of the male child, who was destined to shepherd the nations with a rod of iron, and the subsequent war in Heaven. Then, in the following context in 12:13-13:18, the implications of this event for the inhabitants of the earth are explained. These are, that the dragon will vent his anger on them, and particularly on the followers of Jesus.

However, in addition to the concept of woe, these signposts also point to the importance of the notion of a trumpet, which is the motif of the cycle which forms the immediate context. As mentioned above, a trumpet is not used to draw attention to itself since its primary function is that of an audible signpost. Its main purpose is to alert its hearers to prepare themselves for what will happen immediately afterwards, whether it is a particular action which is required, or whether it is to pay attention to some more important communication which is to follow.

INFORMATION

Here are another couple of details, which reveal how remarkably well this book is crafted. The word 'a trumpet', and the verb 'to trumpet', occur sixteen times in the whole book and yet all the occurrences are situated before the opening of the Signs Cycle. The last occurrence is at 11:15, which is the transition verse between the end of the Trumpets Cycle and the setting of the Signs Cycle. This is textual evidence that the arrangement of the trumpet motif at the book level, is intended to bring the reader's attention to bear on the information revealed in the immediately following Signs Cycle. The word 'trumpeters', also occurs once at 18:22, but it is used in quite a different context, and may be intended to be seen as a specific contrast to the previous use of the trumpet motif, in the earlier part of the book.

Within the context of the Trumpets Cycle alone, each trumpet blast does indeed prepare the way for at least one event which follows. However, in addition to the warning function of each individual trumpet, within the context of the cycle alone, it is also possible now to perceive that the cycle, as a whole, has the same function at the book level. This means that the series of seven trumpets as a complete cycle, can be understood as a major signpost preparing the hearer to pay special attention to the next unit to occur, which is functioning at the same level in the book, and this is the Signs Cycle.

Within the Trumpets Cycle itself, it is noteworthy that the first four trumpets are briefly described, and follow each other without any extra material between. However, the fifth and sixth trumpet passages are longer and more detailed than their predecessors. This phenomenon of a longer fifth and sixth unit also occurs in the Seals Cycle, even if not to the same degree. This demonstrates that there is a pattern in the author's organization, and it can be inferred that already in the Seals Cycle, the author is setting up a pattern to prepare the hearer for what is to follow, just as he set up more basic patterns in the Letters Cycle.

So it is then, that as the reader advances through the Trumpets Cycle, his rate of progress slows down. This is because these latter judgments are described in such graphic detail, that it takes longer to recount, which slows everything down. The net effect of this literary device is to raise the tension in the emotions of the hearer. At the same time, the greater length of the passages postpones the arrival at the end of the cycle where a dénouement, or a release of tension, may be expected.

The first two woe passages (8:13 and 9:12) which occur just before and after the fifth trumpet, as discussed above, also contribute to this slowing down process. So it can be seen that all these devices are working together with the same purpose in mind.

In addition, the process of slowing down progress, and the consequent postponement of a possible resolution, is made more dramatic by the fact that the Signs Cycle is immediately preceded by not just one, but two contiguous, and overlapping, interludes (10:1-11:2 and 11:1-13). Pauses in the communication flow are often intended to be signposts pointing towards a prominent part in the text. Pauses of this length and complexity then, must be pointing towards a major point of prominence.

The content of the interludes also confirms this point of view. Taking the second interlude first, briefly to say that it will not be discussed in detail here, because it contains no book level prominence markers. There is a flash forward reference to the beast in 11:7, but it is not sufficiently clear to say that it is a signpost directing the reader's attention towards the Sign Cycle. The function of this interlude at the book level is that it contributes to the slowing down of the pace of mainline information flow prior to the peak. Other than this, its function is limited to its role as the interlude of the Trumpets Cycle.

The first one of the pair, on the other hand, has been previously analyzed in Chapter 2, as part of the Narrative Framework. In it John is encouraged to continue on in his prophetic task (10:11). Perhaps now it can be deduced that this was necessary because the most important part was yet to come. However, prior to that, John was told to seal up, and not write down something which he had heard (10:4). This is unusual in this book of visions wherein, on several occasions, John was instructed to carefully record everything which he saw and heard.

Anything unusual is already an indicator of prominence and, in this case, the actual event (not recording a dramatic utterance) is also designed to provoke curiosity and tension in the hearer. In this particular case, the tension is not resolved, since it is not indicated that John ever revealed what the thunders said. However, this does not nullify the fact that, in the meantime, tension has been created.

The prominent part of this first interlude of the pair, is the direct speech at 10:7. Here the hearer is informed at what point he may expect to find out what he wishes to know. In any dramatic literature, where there is a build up of tension and uncertainty, what motivates the reader is finding out how it all works out in the end. In the case of this particular book, the topic of which is the revelation of visions from God, the goal of discovering how God's mysteries will work out, is a compelling motivation.

The information given here then, is that the reader will have his curiosity satisfied, and his emotional tension released, at about the time when the seventh angel blows his trumpet. As previously noted, the last trumpet blast ushers in the Signs Cycle and so the reader does not, in fact, get to the end of the story on arriving at the end of the Trumpets Cycle.

It is true that a great deal of the mystery of what is going on behind the scenes in the spiritual world is explained in the Signs Cycle. However, the specific development of the ending of God's plan (of judgment in this case) only occurs with the seventh sign (15:1), and it is only finally completed with the seventh bowl.

Further reference to the completion of God's words occurs in 17:17, and the final 'It is done' in 21:6, is reserved for the conclusion of the book in the last cycle. All this demonstrates that the beginning of the Signs Cycle is the point of highest tension in the book. This is because the reader has been led to believe that all will be revealed at the time of the seventh trumpet, but this is only partially true, since it is only the beginning of the end, and not the end in itself. Anticipation has been built up to such a point that the reader will be at the peak of his emotions upon discovering that he is not going to be satisfied immediately. However, at the same time, he will be relieved to know that he is now on the downward slope towards the conclusion.

For those interested, a detailed analysis of 10:1-11:2 is provided in the following Appendix.

6.3.2 A Summary of the Special Prominence Features

It can be seen then, that in the first part of the book the author provides a number of special prominence markers, in order to guide the hearer's attention towards the content of the Signs Cycle. The combined effect of these prominence features clearly indicate that the Signs Cycle is intended to be interpreted as a specially prominent part in the book. There are other book level prominence markers which occur after the main peak, at 16:15, 18:20 and 19:9, but these will be discussed later after the role of the Signs Cycle has been more fully described.

Meanwhile, as a reference point, we can bring these external, special prominence features together in a list, as follows :

- the three woes, complemented by their fulfillment in 12:12, inside the Signs Cycle
- the seventh trumpet'
- the whole of the Trumpets Cycle as a complete unit
- the extra length of the fifth and sixth trumpets
- the complex combination of the two interludes contained within the Trumpets Cycle
- the direct speech in 10:7, being also the center of a chiasm
- the fact that John was told to stop writing his visions in 10:4

It is once again remarkable, without intention aforethought, or any manipulating of the evidence, that there appear to be precisely seven such prominence features. Barring any human error, that is !

6.3.3 Internal Evidence for the Prominence of the Signs Cycle

There is also a considerable corpus of data to be found within the Signs Cycle itself, which confirms that the author intended for this part of the book to be recognized as being particularly important.

For ease of reference this will be divided into the three categories of special prominence devices proposed by Callow 1998,181-5, namely lexical devices, rhetorical devices and deviation from norms.

Lexical Devices

This category concerns words which, by virtue of their meaning, are more prominent than other words in the context, because they express a superlative, a strong emotion, or a particular forcefulness of some kind.

This kind of prominence occurs at the end of the setting of the Signs Cycle at 11:19 with a dramatic listing of five forceful words, the last of which is also qualified by the adjective for 'great'.

These words are

- 'flashes of lightning',
- 'voices' (or 'noises'),
- 'peals of thunder',
- 'an earthquake', and
- 'a great hail storm'.

This list is also a rhetorical device in its own right, at the same time as the prominence of its content, because it is a repetition of a similar listing, which occurs in the setting of the Trumpets Cycle at 8:5. The fact that there is repetition of such striking words makes it even more prominent, and the fact that the list at 11:19 has an extra item, 'and a great hail storm', makes it more prominent still. Like the trumpet blasts referred to earlier, these dramatic audio-visual effects, nonetheless, contain no important referential information, but are acting as tangible signposts to prepare the hearer for what is to immediately follow.

What follows is the lexical item 'a sign', in 12:1. This word is prominent because it has an air of mystery about it, which arouses the curiosity of the hearer. In effect, it is also a lexical signpost because it does not reveal directly what the author is talking about. By its very nature the word 'sign' indicates that there is yet more of importance to come. That is, what the sign actually is, and also whatever it is that the sign represents.

This is significant in the context of the book, since the word belongs to the same lexical field as the main topic stated at the beginning of the book. This topic, of course, is 'a revelation from God', which occurs right at the beginning of the book in 1:1, and which has been restated in the immediately preceding context, as the mystery of God (10:7). The word 'sign', is also fronted and qualified by the word for 'great' which provide two more indicators of prominence.

Chart 44.
The Organization of the Seven Occurrences of the Word 'Sign'

A. A GREAT SIGN IN HEAVEN... 12:1

B. Another **Sign** in Heaven... 12:3

C. It (the second beast - i.e. the false prophet) does **Great Signs** to impress people 13:13

D. The **Signs** which it (the false prophet) had power to do 13:14 (in context of the deception of those who make/worship the image of the beast)

B' Another **Sign** in Heaven… 15:1

C' Spirits of devils working **Signs** come out of the mouth of the dragon, the beast and the false prophet to assemble people 16:14

D' The false prophet who did the **Signs** 19:20. (in context of the deception of those who make/worship the image of the beast)

In addition to its semantic importance, the occurrence of the word 'sign', at 12:1 is significant because it is the first of a series of seven occurrences of the word in the book. Not only is it the first occurrence, but it is also the most prominent of all the occurrences, when seen in the context of the total pattern of the seven occurrences which create a parallel pattern, as summarized in Chart 44.

After the first occurrence in 12:1, the word is repeated again immediately afterwards in 12:3. In this case, it is not fronted but is qualified by the contrastive word 'another', which raises its prominence by specifically linking it back in a pattern to the previous prominent occurrence. In addition, the definition of the sign, which is 'a dragon' in this case, is marked for prominence by the word 'behold', which is the only occurrence of this word in the body of this cycle before it reoccurs at the beginning of the interlude at 14:1.

Rhetorical Devices

This category concerns special patterning which can be limited to lexical items, as in the case of figures of speech, or can extend to the organization of long stretches of text. In Chapter 5 section 7.1 it was proposed that the whole book is organized according to a chiastic structure. Since the Signs Cycle is at the center of this chiasm, this special arrangement makes the whole of the Signs Cycle specially prominent relative to the rest of the book.

Within the context of the cycle itself, the first three units of the body of the cycle are embedded narratives (12:1-18, 13:1-10 and 13:11-18). Although they have been analyzed as separate units, they are nonetheless logically and semantically connected and form, as it were, a mini-novel with three chapters. Since narrative is the most vivid of all the text-types it naturally contributes to the prominence of the text, and is one of the many devices for marking the peak of a text which is not otherwise a true narrative.

Longacre (1983a,11) comments at length on the reasons why a narrative is noted for its vividness. The most vivid form of all narratives is drama. Revelation is, in many places, very vivid and dramatic, so much so that some commentators such as Bowman (1962 and 1968), and Wilcock (1975) suggest that the book should be read and interpreted as a drama in order to be properly understood. Such a proposal is not necessary since it is sufficient to make a claim which is more easily supported, namely that in writing his letter, John uses narrative text-types which are dramatic. Neeley (1987,56) observes that the 'quasi-narrative' text of chapter 11 of Hebrews forms the peak of that book as well, which serves as an additional illustration that narrative style texts can, and do, occur at peak points in non-narrative style literary works.

Revelation has a number of embedded narratives, or texts which simulate the form of narrative (see for example, 14:1-5 and 14:14-20), but this text (12:1-13:18), is the longest and most highly developed of them all. This embedding of one text type within another creates what is called 'skewing'. This inevitably happens when the surface form is representative of one text-type (narrative in this case), and the underlying objectives of the author in the book as a whole (hortatory and expository), are different. It is as if the content does not fit properly inside the larger packaging of the book as a whole; as if, for example, you are trying to put your hand in a glove which is not the correct size.

This kind of stretching and skewing also creates linguistic turbulence and, therefore, often occurs at peak points in the text.

It can also be noted that an important element of suspense is created by the fact that the storyline of each of the three units is broken off, and not completed until later in the book. In 12:17, after telling us that the dragon was 'enraged' and was going off 'to make war' the author quite literally leaves him standing on the beach, at the end of 12:18. In 13:7 the saints are told that the first beast is also going to make war on them, but those who are reading/listening and most concerned about this plan, are left in suspense, not knowing what happens next. Likewise, in 13:16-17 they are told that there will be dramatic economic restrictions, without being told how it will work out.

Creation of tension is exactly what occurs at the peak of a text.

Within this narrative context there is also an unusually great concentration of personages who are directly involved in the events described. The principal personages are the woman clothed in the sun and her child, the dragon and the two beasts. If the child is taken as a representation of Christ, then the Lamb, in another form, is also present. If so, then this is the only place in the whole book where he is 'on stage' with the dragon. In any case, he is not far distant for two reasons.

Firstly, in the explanation of why the dragon lost the cosmic war (12:10-12), both the Christ, and the Lamb, are referred to within the space of about 25 words. Although they are not directly 'on-stage' in the narrative, so to speak, it is clear that the victory over the dragon is directly due to what Jesus, as the Christ (or the Messiah), and as the Lamb, accomplished.

Secondly, the Lamb is the first personage to be reintroduced at 14:1 at the end of the first three units, which contain the sorry story of the dragon and his two proxies. In this instance the Lamb is marked for prominence by 'behold', as was the dragon previously at 12:3.

God is also a participant (12:6) although he is not directly 'on stage'. Other participants are the people of God and the nations under different descriptions (12:10,11,17 and 13:7; 12:5,13:3,7-8,11,16), the inhabitants of Heaven (13:6), the dragon's angels, and Michael and his angels (12:7-9).

The plot organization is also very compact, particularly for the first unit (12:1-18). A large number of events are rapidly described, with little extraneous detail, within a relatively short span of text. So, it can be seen then, that there are many evidences of turbulence and tension in the text at this point, and so all of these features confirm that this is a major peak of prominence in the book.

Further investigation will show that there is actually nothing else quite like this in the whole book. Consequently, we can safely propose that the Signs Cycle is *the* main point of special prominence in the whole book.

Deviation from Norms

To help the audience figure out which portions he considers to be more significant, the author drops certain hints in the text. These hints are often based on what may be called the 'norm-deviation principle'. This is a term coined by Bergen 1987,331 who develops this idea in some detail.

For her part, Kathleen Callow 1998,184 explains this concept of deviation from norms as follows:

> Any deviation from an unexpected norm exploits the element of surprise. It catches the attention, and is thereby prominent. The unexpectedness may be syntactic or lexical...but it also occurs whenever any element stands out as different from its surroundings, even though there is nothing inherently surprising about it otherwise.

The following examples of features which deviate from norms previously established can be observed in the Signs Cycle. Firstly, the pattern of the repetition of the phrase, 'and I saw...', is broken, with the pattern ending at 10:1 and recommencing at 13:1. The last occurrence of the dominant 'and I saw...' pattern is at 10:1, but the narrator actually fades gradually from the scene throughout the narrative interlude with the phrase 'and I heard', at 10:4 and the phrase 'and the angel whom I saw', at 10:5. Other first person singular phrases also occur throughout this interlude which ends at 11:2.

The occurrence of a long break in such a pattern, which otherwise occurs throughout Cycles 2 and 3 and continues to the end of the book, is, in itself, an indicator of prominence. Secondly though, this normal active phrase is replaced on three occasions within a short space, by the passive form of the phrase, 'and ... was seen...' (11:19, 12:1 and 12:3). By this means, the author provides a more precise indicator of prominence at the end of the setting and at the beginning of the body of the Signs Cycle.

This is accomplished in a number of complementary ways. One way is that the passive form causes the narrator to be eclipsed, thereby provoking a change of viewpoint, which is another prominence indicator. In the case of the central reference (12:1), the grammatical subject slot is filled by the phrase, 'a great sign'. This change brings the word 'sign', into focus thereby enhancing its preexisting lexical prominence.

As Callow1998,225 points out, the passive form 'topicalises' the grammatical subject, that is, it clearly marks it as the topic of the section (a narrative in this case) in question, thereby 'giving it greater initial prominence'. This effect, in turn, is completed by the fact that the verb is moved down from second place to fourth place in the sentence, thereby downgrading its level of prominence in a complementary relationship to the fronted and upgraded subject.

Secondly, this is the first series of visions whose constituents are not clearly demarcated by identical introductions or numbering. A number of earlier commentators have made reference to this fact without understanding its linguistic significance. So, it was, for example, that Collins 1984,111 included two series of 'unnumbered' visions in her outline.

Apart from the issue of prominence, another linguistic reason why John could not specifically enumerate the seven signs is because the word, 'sign', is a key word, and is used in a lexical chain with exactly seven occurrences in the book as a whole, as was indicated in Chart 44 above. Since this is the case, and since it would seem to be a part of the intentional structure of the book, it was not possible for John to use the word to introduce each of the seven signs. He chose, therefore, to introduce just the first, second and last sign. In this way he made his plan obvious to those who were used to, and able to discern, this kind of lexical organization.

In addition, the organization of the body of this cycle is different. Instead of being in the form of a series of compact, discrete units which follow each other in an orderly fashion, the organization is based on a series of personages. These personages do not follow each other neatly, but are introduced in different ways, and then sometimes reappear in different places in the cycle, and interact with each other.

In linguistic terms it could be said that the Cycles 1-3 and 5-6 are organized according to the concept of 'particles' and thereby appear in a neat, linear order like beads on a string. In contrast to that, Cycle 4 (and also Cycle 7) is organized according to the concept of a 'field'. This form of arrangement creates the possibility of the personages being in multiplex and multidimensional relationships, as if they were units all situated on the same plane, or pieces on a chess-board.

Thirdly, it should not be overlooked that the interlude (14:1-5) is fronted and so, instead of appearing between the sixth and seventh occurrences of the motif, it is placed between the fourth and fifth occurrences. This makes the interlude particularly prominent within the context of the cycle alone, by bringing it to the hearer's attention sooner than would have been expected. However, it also makes the whole cycle prominent since it is the only one which deviates from the usual pattern for the placement of the interlude.

Finally, it is the only cycle to have a series of three specific exhortations directed to the hearer beginning with the word 'here' (13:10,18 and 14:12). The word 'here', occurs a total of seven times in the book. In its first occurrence in a hortatory phrase at 13:10, it is preceded by another hortatory phrase 'if anyone has an ear let him hear'. This is a variation of the similar phrase which occurs in all the seven letters but, otherwise, nowhere else in the book. At the same time it is reminiscent of what Jesus is reported as saying in the Gospels

A key word in both the first and third occurrences is 'endurance', which word also occurs seven times in the whole book, but only in these two places and in the Letters Cycle. The third occurrence (14:12) also contains a reference to those who hold fast to God's commands. The underlying verb 'to keep', occurs many times in the book, but only in the seven letters, and in other hortatory units like the Prologue, the Epilogue, and 16:15. This establishes a clear link between the Signs Cycle and the other hortatory units in general, and the Letters Cycle in particular.

The Signs Cycle is the first of the central cycles to contain exhortations and the only one to have such a sustained series. The only other occurrence of this kind of exhortation is at 17:9, which is in the long Narrative Framework passage, in which John is receiving special instruction concerning Babylon. In this context, the exhortation is directed at him and is fully integrated into its context. This makes its function different from that of the three exhortations in the Signs Cycle. However, there is a similarity in content, which suggests a parallelism between 17:9 and the second occurrence of the series of three at 13:18. The latter invites reflection on a riddle based on the number six, and the former invites reflection on a riddle based on the number seven.

It is also the first cycle to have one of the seven blessings embedded in it at 14:13. This blessing, although embedded in a minor piece of the Narrative Framework, is directly attached to the third 'here' exhortation and so reinforces it. The previous blessing was back at the beginning in the Prologue (1:3).

The internal evidence listed above strongly supports the contention that the Signs Cycle is a zone of turbulence. A large number of linguistic features co-occur, particularly near the beginning of this cycle, which disrupt the patterns which had been previously established for the book. This kind of departure from norm, and the kinds of features themselves, regularly mark prominence wherever they may be found. When they co-occur in this way it is an indicator of a significant point of special prominence in the text.

Cotterell and Turner 1989,312, using linguistic analysis as their starting point, perceive the importance of the Signs Cycle and remark that 'in studying the allegory (12:1-14:2 sic) we are at the same time studying the central theme of the book, which is *not* "the end of the world" but something like "an explanation of the cosmic battle in which the church is necessarily engaged".'

Using insights drawn from a chiastic arrangement of the book Welch 1981,246-7 calls Chapter 12 'the crux' and 'the substantive centerpiece of the entire book'. He also remarks that Chapter 12 is the physical center of the book with 194 verses preceding it and 193 verses following it.

It was observed previously that the dragon, especially in his appearance in Chapter 20, seems to be intentionally downgraded in importance by the author. However, in this case it is now being proposed that the Signs Cycle, and especially Chapter 12 which primarily describes events concerning the dragon, is marked for special prominence. There is, nonetheless, no contradiction between these two conclusions, because what is being marked as specially prominent in Chapter 12, is the story of the dragon's failure and defeat.

This is another example of the author's calculated use of language, for to herald with trumpets, as is literally the case here, the defeat of one protagonist, is another subtle way of proclaiming and emphasizing the victory of his opponent. The victorious opponents are both the Lamb and His followers, who are crucially central to the all-important explanation in 12:9-12. Having directly participated in the dragon's defeat, they triumphantly reappear in the interlude at 14:1. These are the very ones who were previously represented as the primary targets of the dragon's spite, in the form of the newborn child in 12:4-5, and the rest of the children of the woman in 12:17.

The irony is huge, and the impact of this part of the message can hardly be missed. You just have to have eyes to see, as well as ears to hear.

6.3.4 Other Points of Special Prominence in Cycles 2-6.

The discussion above presented evidence for the contention that the Signs Cycle (which is the central, fourth cycle in the series of seven), contains the main peak of special prominence in the book as a whole. However, there are other points of special prominence which occur in Cycles 2-6, and these will be discussed below.

Each of these central cycles is composed of a series of sub-units in an additive relationship, which creates a text which is little more complex than a list (seven seals, seven trumpets etc.) in its overall arrangement. Mention was made previously, of the fact that the natural prominence of the final sub-unit of each list, is reduced by the fact that it is also the setting of the following list. The consequence of this feature is that the whole of the section from 4:1 through to 19:10 has no naturally prominent part, until this function is filled by the final conclusion at 19:11-21.

This lack of natural prominence is, nonetheless, compensated for by the presence of a number of specially prominent points. The primary manifestation of special prominence, which is of particular interest for an appraisal of the book as a whole, is the occurrence of the interludes.

The pattern of seven similar sub-units is established in Cycle 1 and is repeated at the beginning of Cycle 2, but then it is interrupted at 7:1. Not only does the interruption break the series of seven similar sub-units, but it also brings to the fore a different theme, which is in direct contrast to the theme developed by the seven sub-units.

As Heimerdinger 1999,239 remarks, using the slightly different terminology of salience, rather than prominence:

> The foregrounding of informative material occurs principally through the inherently unexpected or disruptive nature of an event recorded. An event which is unexpected is salient [i.e. prominent] against the background of more predictable happenings.

In addition to that, the first interlude at 7:1-17, which establishes this new system of a break in the repetitive pattern, is particularly long. It is also composed of two complementary parts, is marked by 'behold' at 7:9, and is concluded by a part of the Narrative Framework (7:13-17). Please see the following Appendix for more details on the complex use of 'behold' in Cycles 2-6.

The second cycle interlude, which is the interlude of the Trumpets Cycle (11:1-13), is also marked for special prominence by virtue of the fact that it is attached to the Narrative Framework interlude (10:1-11:2) by an overlap link, thereby creating another long, double interlude.

The next interlude, which is in the Signs Cycle (14:1-5), is much shorter and simpler in its internal organization. However, it is fronted and is also marked by 'behold', this being the next occurrence of this marker after the occurrence at 12:3.

The final interlude at 19:1-8 does not have any noticeable internal markers of special prominence. But, by this time, the system of interruptions in the general flow of thought has been well established, and so special marking does not need to be repeated. However, this interlude is introduced by the phrase 'after these things', which may be an intentional indicator of a link with the first interlude (7:1). It is also concluded by a part of the Narrative Framework (19:9-10), which is also the same as the first interlude.

The main point then, is that, within the general flow of Cycles 2-6, the interludes are points of special prominence. This observable fact confirms the proposition made in Chapter 4 above, that the Salvation Theme, which is developed by this series of interludes, is the most prominent of the two contrastive themes developed throughout these cycles. The other theme concerning God's plan of judgment, which is developed throughout the rest of the bodies of these cycles is, therefore, of lesser importance, despite the greater amount of text assigned to its development.

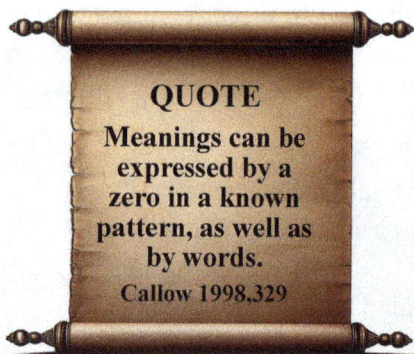

> **QUOTE**
> **Meanings can be expressed by a zero in a known pattern, as well as by words.**
> **Callow 1998,329**

This observation is further confirmed by the data available in Cycle 5, the Bowls Cycle, which is the one cycle of the central group which does not have an interlude at all. This then, is an example of a situation where the absence of a feature which otherwise may have been expected, contributes to the organization of the whole, 'for the omissions of biblical narrative are as cunning as its repetitions', as Alter 1981,98 insightfully remarked.

Perusal of the content of Cycle 5 indicates that it is the culmination of the events of judgment and, as the bowl motif indicates, it represents the consummation of God's plan of judgment. The setting at 15:1 indicates that with the completion of the bowl judgments, God's anger is finished. The following cycle does not describe further outpouring of judgments as such, but for the most part, presents the testimonies of witnesses of this final judgment. Clearly then, the Bowls Cycle is the darkest and most terrible part, where final judgment falls and there is no more hope of escape for those upon whom it falls.

This message of unavoidable doom is made even more weighty by the fact that there is no compensatory message of hope in this cycle, because there is no interlude. In Cycles 2-4 the messages of judgment and salvation counterbalance each other to some extent, with the Judgment Theme having a greater quantity of text assigned to it, and the Salvation Theme a greater degree of prominence. In these cycles the advance warning of God's plan of judgment is clearly given, and the judgments are limited in scope. At the same time, the presence of the interludes provide evidence that an alternative, positive destiny is possible, for those who take notice of the warnings and react accordingly.

In Cycle 5 the message moves on to a further stage: the ultimate judgment falls and there is no longer any hope of salvation to mitigate the solemnity of the message. Using once more the metaphor of mountains and valleys, it is as if the Bowls Cycle is the deepest and darkest of all the valleys, with no nearby peak (interlude) to reflect light into it. However, if the shadow is darkest here, it is not to draw attention to the shadow itself. Rather, the function of the shadow is to throw into relief the nearest and biggest peak. In this case, that peak is the preceding Signs Cycle with its particularly prominent interlude.

In summary then, the interludes of Cycles 2-4 make a positive contribution to the message of these cycles. This is reinforced by the contrastive negative implications contributed by the absence of an interlude in Cycle 5. These two contrastive and complementary contributions both point towards the plan of salvation as being the part of the informational schema which is of greatest interest and value for the hearer.

6.4 The Importance of Schemas

An analysis of prominence in a discourse and an understanding of its schema work together in two complementary ways. Firstly, an appraisal of the prominent elements of a text is the basis for formulating a first hypothesis concerning the schema. Then secondly, consideration of the purpose of the text as formulated in the schema, permits a more reliable interpretation of those passages which are marked for prominence. Exploring each in turn, until all the data has been accounted for, is a means of reaching the most complete analysis possible.

The previous discussion proposed that Cycle 7 is the most naturally prominent part of the book, while Cycle 4 is marked with the greatest special prominence. In the previous stage of analysis it was necessary to make appeal to the author's purpose in order to identify the natural prominence of Cycle 7 in the first instance. In the same way, it is also necessary to continue to develop an awareness of the schema, in order to more fully understand why these two parts of the book are prominent, and what message they are intended to communicate.

Perusal of the content of these two cycles indicates that they are primarily composed of informational import material, which describes various aspects of God's plan of judgment and of salvation. Since there is so much information contained in these cycles, and in the book as a whole, it is clear that the book must contain at least one informational schema. So this will be explored first.

6.4.1 The Informational Schema of Revelation

The informational schema of a text is the pattern of organization which an author uses in order to communicate new information to the addressees. The schema which best fits the informational purpose of Revelation is the Mystery-Explanation schema.

Discourses may have more than one informational schema, as explained in Callow 1998,197-200 and the most common of these are those which create, and resolve, some kind of problem and tension (ibid.,190). Revelation also has elements of problem and tension, notably the introduction of the dragon in 12:3, whose goal is to destroy God's people (12:17). In addition, there is the belated description of Babylon in Chapter 17, who is also portrayed as an enemy of the people of God (17:6). These subsidiary schemas can also be fruitfully analyzed in their own right but, for the sake of simplicity, they are included under the broader mystery-explanation schema being discussed.

This particular schema is being proposed because the topic of the book, as indicated by the word 'revelation' at 1:1, implies that something which is currently mysterious and unknown, is about to be revealed. This sense of anticipation is confirmed by the use of the word 'mystery', itself, with reference to what God is doing at 10:7.

The rest of the book is taken up with the gradual unveiling of this mystery, which is brought to completion in Cycle 7. This is where the author describes the final removal of all evil, and the eternal salvation of God's people. This then, is where his message, at the informational level, comes to its culmination and is, therefore, the furthest point along the purposive chain which the book as a whole brings the hearer.

The mystery aspect of the book will be developed and explained in more detail in Chapter 8.

However, in addition to this point of natural prominence, there is also the point of special prominence which occurs at the beginning of Cycle 4 in Chapter 12. This is the point where the most tension is created by the author. By this point the underlying problem which is crucial to most informational schemas, has been sufficiently well developed for the hearer to have a good idea of the issues at stake. It is also a time of suspense, for it is a time of maximum complication, when the hearer is left wondering how things may turn out, with only a few clues, for the moment, as to what the dénouement may be. Please look back at Chart 43 in Chapter 5 to see exactly where the points of suspense are in the two main plots.

The principal complication which is introduced at the beginning of the Signs Cycle, is the revelation that there is a cosmic battle going on behind the scenes, which contributes to the uncertainties of life on earth. These were previously alluded to in the Letters Cycle, so the reader has been prepared to some extent by this preview glimpse of the behind-the-scenes conflicts. These back-room battles also explain to a large extent the chastisements raining down from Heaven, as are described in the Seals and Trumpets Cycles.

At the center of this battle is humanity's arch-enemy, the devil himself, who, the hearer is now told, has been thrown down to earth, apparently free to vent his fury on whoever comes across his path (12:9, 12-17). The only things which are worse, are to know that he has two powerful colleagues as revealed and described in Signs 3 and 4 in 13:1-17. Having said that, however, things get worse again. This is because we discover that God will punish those who decide to follow Satan and his colleagues, as indicated in Sign 5 14:9-11. Then, as if that was not enough, the final straw is that God has a plan to reap the whole of the earth in final judgment, as described in Sign 6 14:14-20, and this will include everyone, with no exemptions and no exceptions.

As well as introducing complications, the author is also explaining, in effect, why there is so much evil in the world, why judgment is necessary, and why God's people are persecuted. The fact that the dragon is thrown down to the earth is a direct cause of why God's people are persecuted, and otherwise suffer unjustly. It is also a direct cause of why people rebel against God and so invite his judgment upon themselves, as indicated in passages like 13:3-4,8,14,16; and 14:9-11.

This means that Cycle 4 provides some reasons for the things which are revealed concerning God's plan, and Cycle 7 describes the end result. Normally in a reason-result relationship, if the primary aim is simply to provide information, the result part of the relationship is the most prominent, as explained by Beekman et al.1981,112 and Callow 1998,257-8.

This is borne out by the fact that the conclusion of the book is the most naturally prominent part, as has been previously observed. However, the author also chose to mark the Signs Cycle for special prominence, which both raises its level of importance and also raises the question as to why this was done. The answer to this question is connected to the next subject of discussion which is the volitional schema of the book.

6.4.2 The Volitional Schema of Revelation

Cycles 4 and 7 certainly contain a lot of information, but they also contain some volitional import material, as is exemplified by the conclusion of Cycle 7 (22:6-7), and as complemented by the Epilogue. Further study reveals that, although less in quantity, volitional import text, nonetheless, can be found throughout the book.

This means that in addition to the informational schema, the book must also have a volitional schema which will be composed of one or more elements as Callow 1998,190-1 explains:

> The only essential element in a volitional message is the proposed action... Supporting elements, however, are frequently found.

The principal element in such a schema then, is the exhortation which directs the hearer towards the desired course of action. The supporting elements may include validation of the message sender, extra information to explain the reasons for the commands given, advice as to how to put into practice the instructions, promises, which are positive motivators, and warnings which serve as negative motivators.

Chart 45.
The Imperative Doublets in Revelation

Direct Imperative Doublets	Echoes Elsewhere
Repent and Persevere – Cycle 1	They did **not** repent : 2 doublets 9:20 & 21 and 16:9 & 11
Rejoice and Lament, 12:12	A Reverse Echo: Lament & Rejoice 18:19 & 20
Fear God and Worship Him 14:7	Two Echoes as Examples 19:10, 22:9 John is Instructed not to worship the angel but to worship God alone.
Come Out of Her, My People and Give Back to Her... 18:4-7	The Echoes are in the same context

The Same Passage Includes Four Double Echoes
- Give back to her as she gave to you
- Double to her the double of what she has done
- Mix in her cup the double of what she mixed for you
- Give her torment and sorrow for the things she gloried in and luxuriated in

In the body of Revelation, the most dense cluster of exhortations is to be found in Cycle 1 and this is completed by a number of other exhortations in the central Signs Cycle. The setting of Cycle 1 (and the Prologue to which it is attached by an overlap link) provides validation concerning the identity and authority of the divine author of this revelation, the Risen Christ himself. The passages which develop the Judgment Theme provide negative motivation by indicating what will happen to those who do not heed the exhortations. Then to complement that, the passages which develop the Salvation Theme, provide positive motivation by indicating what will happen to those who do take notice of the exhortations.

The principal elements of this volitional schema are the passages which contain the exhortations. These exhortations are laid out in visual form in Chart 45. Consideration of these imperatives, which are the means of communicating the exhortations, will prepare the way for the ongoing discussion, which will be developed in the following paragraphs.

It is interesting to note that they are all doublets, which add to their natural prominence. Most of them also have echoes in other parts of the book, which expand their influence beyond their immediate context. These basic ingredients of the volitional schema will be referred to and developed in more detail in the following sections.

6.4.3 The Exhortations to Repent and to Persevere

In the body of the book, it is in Cycle 1 that John the most comprehensively transmits the volitional purpose of the divine author in the series of seven letters, which are seven exhortations all pointing in the same direction. Each letter has a similar volitional schema, even though there is some variation in the placement of each of the elements. These details will be expounded in more detail in Chapter 7.

Each letter begins with a formal introduction and a description of the sender, who is the risen Christ in each case. This serves to authenticate each letter, validating its source and the right of the sender to address himself in this direct way to the addressees. This is followed by a statement concerning the current situation, which is accompanied at some point in the letter by either a commendation, a reproach or both. These elements serve as both a grounds for the following exhortation but also as a motivator. On the basis of their current situation, the addressees can either feel encouraged that they are already doing well, or they can sense the implicit warning that they need to change. The primary exhortation occurs in the middle of each letter and is in the form of one or more direct imperatives.

Further motivating elements occur in the latter half of the letters. These are condition-consequence sentences which are either warnings or invitations, depending on whether they are couched in negative or positive terms. There is also at least one promise to those who overcome the obstacles before them, which is a motivating element. Then finally, there is another more general level of exhortation, which urges the hearers to take seriously the primary exhortation, which has already been communicated. This element has been called a hortatory orienter in this analysis, and is composed of the stylized phrase 'he who has an ear, let him hear what the Spirit is saying to the churches'.

The most important part of the schema, as indicated in the quotation above, is the primary exhortation. Throughout the seven letters there is considerable repetition and several different verbs are used, but they can all be reduced to two principal concepts, which are the concept of repentance, and the concept of perseverance. The verb 'to repent', used as a direct command and a positive exhortation only occurs in Cycle 1, which indicates that it is a dominant theme for this cycle, and one of the unique elements which it contributes to the book as a whole. For the rest, the word is only used negatively, 'they did not repent', four times in the rest of the book. A doublet at 9:20-21, and another doublet at 16:9 and 11. These negative uses act as a kind of contrasting echo and counterpoint to the uses in Cycle 1.

On the other hand, the concepts of endurance and holding fast, as well as occurring many times in Cycle 1, also reoccur at strategic points in other parts of the book. The concept of patient endurance occurs at 13:10 and 14:12, which are the codas to Signs 3 and 5. This new information validates the analysis of these codas, made previously on other grounds. Now it can be seen that these are volitional import texts, which are contributing, primarily, to the development of the volitional schema of the book as a whole. As such, they stand outside the referential development of their immediate context, and so, the function and relationship of a coda is appropriate.

The coda at 13:9-10 includes a repetition of the hortatory orienter 'he who has an ear...' which occurs in all the seven letters. This is the only other place in the book where this phrase re-occurs, thereby creating a clear link with the volitional import texts of Cycle 1.

The sentences concerned are those which begin with the phrase 'here is the endurance... of the saints', and, as such, they are not direct commands but mitigated exhortations. This means that they do not contain any grammatical imperatives. Nonetheless, the intended meaning in their context, is that the saints *should* persevere and remain faithful (13:10), if they wish to benefit from the promises which God has offered to them.

6.4.4 Other Components of the Volitional Schema Occurring in the Body of the Book

In addition to the principal exhortations mentioned above, which are directly addressed to the Christians who were the intended recipients of this book, there are other elements situated elsewhere in the body of the book. These additional elements also contribute more to the volitional schema than they do to the informational schema.

Firstly, there are three texts 16:15, 18:20 and 20:6 which are difficult to analyze because they do not fit neatly into their immediate context. These may be compared to the three woes which occurred in the first part of the book. The latter are also texts which only fit loosely into their context, and they were interpreted as being prominence markers preparing the way for what was to happen when the seventh trumpet sounded. The three texts under discussion are like a matching set, which occurs in the second half of the book. They are also prominent, being part of the volitional schema.

The first and last of these, are two of the seven blessings, concerning the need to keep one's garments pure (16:15) and concerning the importance of participating in the first resurrection (20:6). On the other hand, 18:20, the middle one, is an exhortation to rejoice directed to the people of God, who are not participants in the activities described in the immediate context. It is actually functioning in tandem with, and as a contrast to, a previous exhortation, which is directed in general to whoever will listen. This is an exhortation to be woeful or to lament in 18:19. This is a reverse echo of an otherwise identical doublet in 12:12. See Chart 45 above.

There is another, somewhat similar, pair of exhortations in 18:4-6, but this is addressed to people who, implicitly, are inside Babylon. They are, therefore, direct participants in what is happening in the immediate context. In their case, they are exhorted to 'Come out' of Babylon, and then to participate in her retribution, by giving her back the double of what she had done to them.

There is another blessing at 19:9 but this is a part of the Narrative Framework and will be discussed below.

It has been said before, but it is an important point which bears repeating: the practical fact of the matter is, that analytical difficulties are often indicators of points of prominence. So it was with the three woes, and it is the same here, with this matching set of three more prominence features.

As indicated then, the best analysis which handles the data in the most reasonable and coherent way possible, is that these three texts are also book-level prominence markers. Whereas the three woes were preparing the way for what was to happen in the middle of the book, these latter three are preparing the way for important issues, which will come to completion at the end of the book.

As is the case for all prominence features, they are, in and of themselves, prominent by virtue of being different relative to their immediate context. This prominence is heightened because they contain direct, or mitigated, commands. Yet, at the same time, as has been explained before, they are signposts or markers of prominence. As such, they point beyond themselves to events which are yet to be fully realized. In this case, the events in view, which concern the completion of the joint plans of judgment and of salvation, will only reach their culmination at the end of the book. The culmination of the volitional schema, to which these texts contribute, also occurs at the end of the book, in the conclusion to Cycle 7 (22:6-7) and in the Epilogue (22:6-21).

So then, the important issues, which these prominence features are bringing to the readers' attention, are specifically volitional in nature. The function of these texts, embedded as they are in the middle of other material, which is primarily informational in nature, is to periodically bring back to the hearer's attention the overall purpose of the book. This purpose is volitional. By that we mean that, the author's goal is to persuade his readers to make certain decisions, and to take a certain direction along life's path. In more modern terms, we could say that he is urging them to review their world-view and, if necessary, to re-work it.

So with this purpose in view then, these short, but punchy, texts are placed strategically in exactly the right places for this one purpose. That purpose is to gradually build up an expectation that the full force of the volitional impact of the book will become clear, as the book draws to a close.

So it is then, that the two texts, 16:15 and 20:6, are blessings. The significant thrust of the blessings in Revelation is that they point towards the future. They can be interpreted as invitations or as mitigated exhortations. The implication is that, if the hearers accomplish what is described in the immediate context, then they will obtain good things, or blessings, in return.

The blessing of 16:15 continues the concept of perseverance previously mentioned. This is because the verb 'to watch', previously occurred in the fifth letter (3:2), and the verb 'to keep', occurs many times in the book, but including Letter 4 at 2:26, and Letter 5 at 3:3. So, by the means of these parallel links, a direct connection is made with the exhortations contained in Cycle 1.

So, in this one in particular, the overcomers are invited to watch out, in order to avoid being caught in an embarrassing state of undress. They can accomplish this by persevering in what they have previously been taught, but especially with regard to what (spiritual) clothes they are wearing. The positive complement of this concept is brought to completion in the seventh cycle, where one of the main features of the New Jerusalem is that she is beautifully and appropriately clothed (21:2 and 9-11).

The blessing of 20:6 is specifically directed towards those who persevere in their attachment to Christ and who remain obedient to the word, or commands, of God and do not worship the beast (20:4, cf. 2:10-11 and 26). The commensurate promises of serving in God's presence, and reigning with Him, come to full completion in 22:4-5. This time around, they will not just reign with Him for 1000 years, but for ever.

There are many more things which could be said, because there are many parallels and links between strategic texts like these, and other parts of the book. Suffice it just to note that one of the exhortations to persevere at 14:12, which was discussed previously (see sections 6.3.3 and 6.4.3 above), is placed in the form of a coda to a passage which provides considerable information concerning the worship of the beast, and what will happen to those who fall into this trap (14:9-11). This exhortation also makes specific reference to remaining faithful to Jesus and keeping God's commands, which are the same concepts as those expressed in 20:4.

The volitional nature of 18:20 is fully apparent since its main component is an exhortation to rejoice. The exhortation 'Rejoice!', can also be translated as 'be glad'. As mentioned elsewhere, this is not interpreted as an expressive import text because in the context of the book, the concept of being glad implies definite actions, like singing and bowing down cf. 4:9-11; 15:3 and 19:1-8.

The supporting reason, that full judgment will be meted out in due course, is also brought to its full end in Cycle 7. This exhortation is the same as the one in 12:12 and thereby provides a link with this central part of the book, which also has a significant amount of volitional import material. At the same time, there are links with the end of the book, where the final purposes of the God's plan are brought to completion.

Secondly, there is another set of exhortations at 14:6-7, and it is to be noted that this also contributes more volitional material to the central Signs Cycle. These exhortations are different to those discussed previously, since they are not directed towards the Christians who are the intended recipients of the book, as in the Letters Cycle for example. Neither are they even addressed to the Christians who are already in Heaven as in 12:12 and 18:20.

These exhortations are much broader in scope and are addressed to all the inhabitants of the earth (14:6). Even though different words 'an eternal gospel' are used, it is clear, by the nature of the exhortations, namely 'Fear God... and worship (Him)' 14:7, that these are, in effect, all the commands of God summed up in a brief resume. Nonetheless, they are connected to the other exhortations, because within the scope of the concept of perseverance, there are several references to the concept of persevering by fearing God and always keeping His commands.

These references are as follows:

- The references to God's commands are in 12:17 and 14:12. (In passing it is interesting to note that this phrase also occurs at 22:14 in the Textus Receptus. Since this creates a series of three, this would be a reason for considering its inclusion in the text, contra its omission in the Nestlé-Aland 27 version.)
- There is also a reference to the words of the prophecy at 1:3 and 22:7,10,18 and 19, which make five references in all.
- There is the example of John in the Narrative Framework, when he is told twice to continue worshiping God alone, and never another being, not even an angel. 19:10 and 22:9
- There are references to the words of Christ at 3:8 and 3:10
- There are references to 'the word(s) of God' at 6:9, 19:9 and 20:4
- To conclude, there are seven references to the words in the book, which are also God's words, at 21:5 and 22:6,7,9,10,18 and 19.

It is notable that the two best attested references to keeping God's commands occur in the Signs Cycle at 12:17, and at 14:12. The first is in the context of the exhortations at 12:12, which is one of the volitional import codas mentioned previously. The other one is in the context of 14:6-7. This is where the eternal gospel is proclaimed so that, if anyone reading this book feels convicted in any way, about the need to keep God's commands, this angelic announcement provides a clear statement of how to do that. It thereby provides support, by amplification, for the exhortations which are more central to the author's volitional purpose.

In the body of the book then, the volitional purpose of the author is clearly established in the seven letters which, in form and function, are like smaller versions of the entire book. This volitional purpose is taken up again in the Signs Cycle by means of the exhortations which occur at 12:12, and in two of the codas, and supported by a more general exhortation in 14:6-7. This purpose is then brought back to the hearer's attention three times, by small units of volitional text before the expectations aroused by this schema, are brought to closure in the course of the final cycle.

6.4.5 The Place of the Signs Cycle in the Volitional Schema

Evidence was presented in section 6.3.3 above, that the Signs Cycle is marked for special prominence. In the subsequent sections on the volitional schema it was observed that the Signs Cycle is the only one of the five central cycles to have a significant body of material, which contributes directly to the hortatory aspects of the volitional schema. The material which contributes information concerning the judgment and salvation themes does also provide motivational support for the volitional schema, but, otherwise, its primary purpose is to contribute to the development of the informational schema.

It was observed in the context of the informational schema that the Signs Cycle provides reasons why certain other events described in the book, and which come to completion at the end of the book, form part of God's mysterious plan. In the context of the discussion of natural prominence it was proposed that the end result (i.e. Cycle 7), should be more prominent than the reasons in Cycle 4. But this left unanswered the reasons why Cycle 4 is marked for special prominence.

The first thing to be clarified is that 'schematic prominence outranks other kinds of prominence' (Callow 1998,360). In a complex text such as Revelation there are many different things going on at the same time at different levels, in order to create a complete communication package.

In principle, all these things can be studied and appreciated, but, nonetheless, 'the major elements in the writer's developing purpose' (ibid.) will always be more important than the elements which are only secondary to his main purpose. This means, that the parts of the text which contain major elements of the schema of the text, are more important than other parts, regardless of their content.

A second thing to be clarified is that the kind of schema being developed may well influence the decisions as to which information is deemed more important. Callow 1998,300 remarks in particular, that in volitional texts, reasons become more important than results.

This is because the writer's purpose is to influence his hearers' behavior and to get them to do something. The problem in such situations is that people do not see the need, or, do not want, to change. A great part of the writer's task in such a case then, is to provide adequate motivation in order to persuade the reader to choose to do what is appropriate.

In the case of Revelation, the indicators in the text which have been discussed above, show that Cycle 4 is particularly important in the author's purpose. This is due to the presence of the special prominence markers which bring it to attention, but also by the presence of several hortatory features. It can now be appreciated that the reasons which John lays out in this central cycle, are intended to be important motivational factors in his overall communicative purpose.

In other words, it needs to be understood that there are supernatural reasons why certain things happen on the earth. As a consequence, humanity's destiny is not entirely in their own hands, since there are powerful spiritual forces at work, which directly influence people's decisions but, over which, they have no direct control. It can also be said that, most people are blissfully unaware of these cosmic events, which have such a major influence on world affairs.

Once it is understood that nobody can change the course of these events and, by their own action, avoid the negative consequences of these events, it is clear that this information becomes a motivating tool. The only way of escape is to listen to the seer, act upon the instructions given, and thereby benefit from the plan of salvation, which God has prepared for those who fear Him and keep His commandments. Thus it can be seen that, even if knowing how everything will work out in the end is useful and interesting information, what is more important is to be motivated to listen and obey now, before it is too late to benefit from God's plan of salvation.

Being aware then, that Revelation is primarily a volitional import text, and as a corollary of that, being able to perceive the volitional schema which reveals the author's overriding purpose, is essential for gaining an accurate understanding of the book's ultimate message. As Callow 1998,147 explains in some detail:

> The import of a message is determined by the speaker's intention... It is important, then, to bear in mind that the weaving together of certain conceptual threads does not in itself carry import: the same concepts can be woven together in a variety of ways. It is the speaker's **purpose**... that determines the pattern of the weave, and hence its interpretation and analysis. (Emphasis added)

This is why everything in Revelation must be interpreted in the light of the understanding that the writer's overriding purpose is firstly, to persuade his hearers to think about making decisions that are literally of life and death importance. Having accomplished that part of the task, he then wants them to *do* what is necessary, in order to ensure that they obtain an eternal destiny which is full of light and glory, rather than one which is full of flames and fury.

This is also why it will be necessary to return to the subject of the Narrative Framework and reassess its role within the context of the volitional schema in section 6.5 below.

6.4.6 The Place of the Letters Cycle in the Volitional Schema

The head of a volitional schema is that part of the text which contains the primary exhortations, since this is the only obligatory part of such a schema. In Revelation this role is filled by the Letters Cycle, since its main purpose is to communicate the double exhortations of repent and persevere. In this case then, the volitional head occurs at the beginning of the book and the following material provides support for these principal exhortations.

This means that overall, the first and last cycles have approximately equal natural prominence. This is because the conclusion is the most naturally prominent part of the informational schema, while the introductory cycle is the most naturally prominent part of the volitional schema. The Signs Cycle still retains its function as the most specially prominent part of the book as discussed above, since it is specially prominent at the informational level and also at the volitional level.

6.5 The Role of the Narrative Framework in the Volitional Schema

The Narrative Framework of the book was previously described in Chapter 2. As the label implies, these texts are grouped together on the grounds that they are the places in the book where the narrator, John, actively appears and participates in his own vision. As such, it provides a framework for the book as a whole, which provides support for the informational content of the rest of the book.

Within this context it was observed that, in its role as support for other parts of the book, the Narrative Framework is backgrounded. Consequently, it would normally be viewed as less prominent and less important than the material which it supports.

However, this is just a general overview which is useful as a starting point, for the reality is, in fact, more complex than that. As was also observed in Chapter 2, the Narrative Framework does not only provide information, but it also contains a great deal of hortatory material. As we have been explaining all through this chapter, this hortatory material is intended to influence the hearers' behavior and so, therefore, contributes to the volitional schema of the book.

6.5.1 A Summary of the Volitional Aspects of the Prologue and Epilogue

Chart 3 in Chapter 2 provides a listing of the constituent units of the Prologue and the Epilogue which can be referred to for convenience. This list indicates that each sub-unit has a volitional function. By means of these passages, John does several things which contribute directly to the volitional schema.

- He provides validation of the message senders.
- He appeals to the highest possible authority and indicates that the revelation contained in the book comes from the almighty and eternal God (1:1,8; 22:6) and from Jesus Christ (1:1,5,10-11; 22:16).
- He also validates himself as a reliable narrator by identifying himself as one who is known by, and in a relationship with, the addressees (1:1,4,9).

- He is one who understands and shares their suffering (1:9).
- He is one whose testimony is reliable (1:2; 22:8).
- He validates the message by reporting an angelic declaration that his message is reliable and true (22:6).
- He also validates it by making reference to the Old Testament (e.g. 1:7; 22:14-15,16) which would have been accepted as an authoritative source by the addressees.

As if that were not enough, his interaction with the angels in the vision also gives him an opportunity to repeat a double foundational instruction, which occurs in the body of the book. This is, that he and, implicitly his hearers also, should worship God, and not worship any other being, 22:9 repeating 14:7-10 and 19:9-10.

Instructions are also implicit in the blessings (1:3; 22:7,14) for the thrust of their message may be paraphrased in the following way: 'If you wish to be blessed then you *should do* what is stated in the immediate context'. At the same time, the blessings contain promises, and either implicit or explicit warnings, for they indicate that *if* the hearers do certain things then they will receive the promised benefits (e.g. 22:14). Conversely, if they do not, then they will receive the opposite (e.g. 22:15 cf. 22:18-19). These promises and warnings are motivational in nature, as are the reminders that there is not much time left and, therefore, those who wish to respond positively should do so quickly (1:3,7; 22:6,7,12,20).

Other invitations to respond positively are provided at 22:17b and c, and verbatim positive responses, which presumably, the hearers are expected to echo, occur at 22:17a and 20b.

6.5.2 A Summary of the Volitional Aspects of Other Parts of the Narrative Framework

As a reminder, the various components of the Narrative Framework can be found in one place in Chart 2, which is in Chapter 2.

The central interlude of the Narrative Framework (10:1-11:2) provides two more supportive elements which contribute to the volitional schema. The direct instructions given in this passage are to John in his function as the narrator. However, the second series of instructions (10:8-11) can be interpreted as being an enacted parable, which is intended to serve as an example to the hearers. By this indirect means, they are exhorted to persevere and to continue their work for God, even though it may not always be palatable.

In addition, the primary informational content (10:5-7) indicates that the accomplishment of God's plan is certain and that time is running out. This information is not simply interesting, it is arresting, and for those who have ears to hear, it indicates that it is important to take notice of this message and to act quickly.

This constituent of the Narrative Framework interlude is considered to be primary because it is the middle part of an ABA' chiasm. Then, in addition, its level of importance is raised because of the special prominence contributed by words like, 'he swore' (10:6), and by phrases like, 'the mystery of God is finished' (10:7).

Blessings also occur in smaller parts of the Narrative Framework (14:13 and 19:9-10) and, as mentioned above, these provide both implicit instruction as well as motivational promises and warnings. The first of these is in the direct context of other volitional material (14:12) which was discussed previously, and is also a recasting of volitional material previously encountered in Cycle 1 (2:10,13,26). Within this immediate, and wider, context it clearly contributes to the same hortatory thread that the Christians should persevere and remain faithful to Christ right until their death.

The second of these blessings occurs in the immediate context of an interlude and develops the positive motivational material contained in the interlude. In this case, the Narrative Framework material continues with further validation of the veracity of the message, and exhortations concerning whom one should, and should not, worship.

The overall impression provided by the element at 1:17-20 is that of reassurance in an overwhelming situation. This is accomplished by the exhortation 'Do not be afraid!', which, although it is expressive in import rather than volitional, it is reminiscent of how Jesus greeted his disciples when he was on earth (e.g. Mt:14:27; 28:10). In addition, the presence of 'behold' (v.18), underlines the fact that Jesus is no longer dead, but is truly risen and personally present. The final reference to the keys of death and hades is a reminder of his supreme authority. This not only serves to reassure John, but as others read about his experience, they are also reassured and, therefore, better prepared to receive the exhortations which are to follow in the seven letters.

The element at 5:4-5 contains an exhortation to John 'Do not weep!', which is similar in tone to the one cited above, and is likely to have the same reassuring effect, since most people relive vicariously the personal experiences which they hear about. Like the above example, it also contains positive information about Jesus, which indicates that he is strong, reliable and competent. This implies, in turn, that it is well worthwhile for those who receive these exhortations to put their confidence in Him.

The element at 7:13-17 is expository in nature, containing explanatory information concerning the people who John saw around the throne. It contains information which contributes to the positive motivational component of the volitional schema, since it describes what the addressees can aspire to, if they take notice of the exhortations.

By contrast, the element of the framework at 17:1-18 provides information which contributes to the negative motivational component of the schema, thereby making clear certain dangers concerning involvement with Babylon, which the addressees would logically want to avoid.

Finally, the element at 21:5-10 contributes a repetition of volitional import texts which have been previously surveyed. There is a message validator, 'these words are reliable and true' (21:5b), and a negative reminder of what will happen to those who do not heed the warnings (21:8), both of which are repeated in the Epilogue. There is validation of one of the message senders 'I am the Alpha and Omega' (21:6b), the same as in the Prologue and Epilogue, and a confirmation of the promises offered to the overcomers (21:7) which is the fulfillment of the promises in Cycle 1.

This survey demonstrates then, that all of the eleven components of the Narrative Framework, except one (4:1), contribute something to the volitional schema of the book.

6.5.3 The Particular Contribution of the Narrative Framework to the Volitional Schema

For the most part, the Narrative Framework repeats and confirms elements of the volitional schema which occur elsewhere in the book.

The primary exhortations in the book are the doublet, Repent! and Persevere! which are addressed to Christians. These were, at the time, those living in Asia Minor, but by widely accepted interpretive extension, it may also apply to all Christians living on the earth at any time in its history. Then, in addition, there is the doublet, Fear God! and Worship Him alone! which is addressed to everybody on the earth, with the non-Christians probably being particularly in view (14:7).

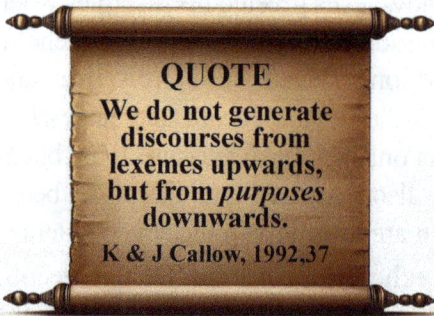

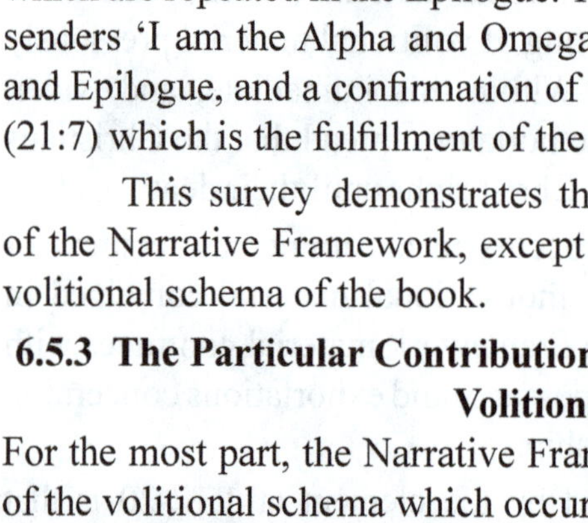
QUOTE
We do not generate discourses from lexemes upwards, but from *purposes* downwards.
K & J Callow, 1992,37

If the exclamation, Woe! is interpreted as an exhortation meaning 'Lament!' in contrast to 'Rejoice!', then this produces a contrastive doublet at 12:12 . This doublet is addressed to the inhabitants of Heaven in terms of a reason to rejoice, and to the inhabitants of the earth in terms of a reason to lament. It is then repeated in reverse order in 18:19-20.

Finally, there is the doublet of 'Come out of her', and 'Give back to her...', referring to Babylon in 18:4 7. This double exhortation is addressed, presumably, to God's people, and other interested parties, who have not yet made the crucial decision to part company with Babylon, and to be fully committed to following Jesus, the Lamb of God.

Two of these exhortations, namely Persevere! and Worship God!, also occur in the Narrative Framework. Cycle 1 provides validation of Christ as a message sender, promises and warnings, and various parts of the body of the book indicate what will happen to those who obey the above instructions as well as what will happen to those who do not.

This leaves four elements of the volitional schema which are unique to the Narrative Framework.

- Firstly, there is the validation of John himself as a reliable witness. This is not surprising since the Narrative Framework, by definition, is that part of the book where John personally appears.
- Secondly, however, what is more striking, is that the validation of Jesus in his all-encompassing sovereignty expressed by the phrase 'I am the Alpha and Omega', also occurs in this context. It has been previously proposed in Chapter 2, that this is a book-level prosody. However, it now can be noted more specifically, that it is a prosody which contributes to the volitional schema of the book, and not just the referential schema. This is because its purpose is the validation of one of the message senders.
- Thirdly, it is to be noted that the validation of the message, namely, the affirmation that it is reliable and true, is also limited to the Narrative Framework with references to this issue occurring at 19:9, 21:5 and 22:6. This illustrates how it is that the Narrative Framework is a message within a message. It is as if at these points in the discourse, the narrator stands to one side and provides comments on the message of the book as a whole, rather than continuing with the main thrust of his narration. So then, it is not just the words in the immediate context, which are in view when these comments are made, but the message of the book as a whole.
- Finally, the Narrative Framework provides a unique exhortation which occurs in two particular blessings, which invoke special blessings on those who read this book and keep, or take to heart, its words. One of these occurs in the Prologue at 1:3 and one in the Epilogue at 22:7. These two

blessings also form part of the message within a message, which contributes a commentary on the principal message of the book.

As indicated above, the blessings are, in effect, mitigated exhortations. This is because the message, which is clearly implicit in them, is that one should do what is proposed in order to be blessed.

In the case of the body of the book, a number of specific exhortations are addressed to the hearer as indicated above, but in the case of the two blessings just listed, the hearer is exhorted to keep the words of the whole book. In other words, in hierarchical terms, this is another, higher level of exhortation, namely an exhortation to obey exhortations given elsewhere. This is so important, that some of the warnings and promises contained in the Epilogue (22:18-19) are actually specific support for this higher level of exhortation, whose purpose is to promote respect for another exhortation..

So then, overall, the Narrative Framework has a double function like some other parts of the book. Firstly, at the level of the informational content of the book, it provides support for the principal content of the body of the book as explained in Chapter 2 above. Secondly, it contributes to the volitional schema of the book, because most of its constituent parts are volitional import texts, and, as such, they contribute to the volitional purpose of the book as a whole. In addition, it provides its own unique volitional contribution, since it contains a higher level exhortation to heed the other exhortations contained in the book.

6.5.4 Volitional Thrust and Special Prominence Relative to the Narrative Framework

One of the major principles which has been developed in this chapter is that a well organized discourse has many peaks and valleys. In other words, there are many points, at all the levels in the discourse hierarchy, which are signaled by the author as being more important than the rest of the text which surrounds it. However, the principle of prominence also applies to the discussion of prominence itself. In other words, among all the elements of a book which are prominent, some will be more important than others, and possibly, one of them will be the most important of all.

If arbitrariness is to be avoided, there must be some underlying theory, which provides principles to guide the decision as to what is more prominent than the rest. All through this book it has been argued and explained, that discourses start out as concepts in a person's mind. These concepts are then transferred by the author into words, which are either spoken, or written on a page. Then, when this process is complete, another person can read the words on the page and, if the communication process is successful, the words will generate similar, or even identical, concepts in the mind of the reader.

At this point, the cycle is complete, and the discourse has accomplished its purpose.

Having said that, let's not pass over this word too quickly, but let's take some time to digest the concept which lies behind this word 'purpose', for nothing can be successfully accomplished without a purpose. A purpose is an intentional goal which is formulated in the creative recesses of the human soul. This may be quite formless and undefined to begin with, but as the mind cogitates and the spirit processes, this purposeful goal is gradually put into words and can be expressed to others. As any writer knows, these words may then be worked, and re-worked, until the end result is to the author's satisfaction.

This is the way the human psyche works, as anyone who has practically tried to communicate any kind of message, knows full well. Books do not miraculously appear out of thin air, and words do not magically materialize onto a page out of nowhere. All messages, however short or long they may be, start in the mind of a person with a purpose, a person who wants that purpose to be known by others.

This means, for our purposes here, that anything which contributes directly to the author's purpose must be more important than ancillary, support material. This is why exploring and discerning the schemas in a discourse is important. It is because they chart what the author is doing, where he is going, and they may even explain why he expressed himself in the way in which he did.

This is also why Callow 1998,360 states that 'schematic prominence outranks other kinds of prominence'. In her discussion of a text with a volitional schema she goes on to say (ibid.), that 'the writer's main purpose is not to send out information... but to receive donations. The real purpose of the message is to issue an appeal, not to make promises'.

If these principles are applied to Revelation the following deductions can be made. The main purpose of the book is not to provide information about the future, nor even about God's plan for the world. If this had been the case then John would have limited himself to providing the necessary information, as would be found in an encyclopedia, or a text book.

He did not do this however, but he also provided extensive hortatory material which has a volitional intent, in that it is designed to persuade the hearers to undertake, or maintain, a certain course of action.

Within this hortatory material there are a large number of promises, but promises which are unattached to the real experience of the people concerned, have little value.

Discourses which are like this often occur in modern political contexts and could be classified as propaganda. Revelation is not like that: its aim is not to get the hearers excited about what may happen, and then to leave them without any control over the fulfillment of those promises.

On the contrary, the author provides considerable instruction as to what the hearer can, or must, do, in order to benefit from the promises. This instruction is summarized in the concept of overcoming the various difficulties and suffering, which the addressees have encountered and will continue to encounter. So then, as a consequence of all this explanation, it can be stated with conviction that the promises are not the most important parts of the letters, as some have suggested, nor of the whole book. By the same reasoning, it can be deduced that the warnings of judgment are not the most important part of the book either, even though many commentaries certainly seem to imply that.

The information provided about God's plan, along with the promises and warnings, are not present simply for their own sake, but to provide motivational support for the primary goal which is to influence the addressees' behavior. Part of the information helps to validate the overall message, and part of the information addresses the recipients' intelligence, so that by better understanding the issues at stake, they can be helped to make a better decision. The promises and warnings, even though they contain information, by their very nature, are intended to appeal primarily to the addressees' emotions. In this way, the writer has used several communication tools and has addressed both parts of the addressee, intelligence and emotions, which are capable of receiving and processing a message.

All that is left after this process of elimination, are the elements of text containing the commands or exhortations, whether in direct imperative form or in mitigated form. These then, are the most important parts of the book wherever they may be found.

This is because the commands are the furthest point along the author's purposive chain, which it is possible to reach using the material provided in the book. As mentioned above, the promises are not the end of the chain, because they point towards something beyond themselves, namely what the hearer must do to obtain them. In contrast to this, the actions recommended do not point to anything else beyond them to results or events which also occur in the book. John himself cannot decide and act in place of the addressees, only they can do that for themselves. This can only happen after they have finished reading what he had to say.

So he goes as far as he can, which is to recommend, or even command, what should be done. Then, in order to cement in place what he has accomplished so far, he adds a second level of exhortation, which is to strongly encourage his hearers to keep the other commandments expressed elsewhere, and that is where he stops. As far as the book, as a discourse, is concerned, the furthest point in the process which it is possible to reach is the expression of those exhortations. This is still true, even if, having heard this book read, the hearer may well continue the process by deciding for himself, and by acting out the exhortations.

These then, are the most important parts of the book, followed in order of importance by the other elements which contribute directly to this volitional purpose.

As noted above, the Narrative Framework is the principal element in the structure of the book which is devoted almost exclusively to providing material which is volitional in nature. As a result, it contributes proportionally more material of this kind to the book than any other part of the structure.

It can be seen then, that the Narrative Framework does indeed have a double function. On the one hand it provides pertinent information which contributes an appropriate context for the book. This includes information concerning its narrator, its ultimate source, its addressees and its general geographical and social context. This information provides the support at an informational, and referential, level, which all discourses need and usually provide.

However, the point now being emphasized is that it also has a second function, which is to be the primary conduit for the channeling of the volitional purpose of the message from the author to the hearers. In particular, it contains the higher level, generic exhortations, namely the command to keep the commands contained in the book as expressed by 1:3 and 22:7b. It is true that these are mitigated exhortations, which perhaps reflect the respect and the brotherly relationship which existed between the narrator and his addressees, but, nonetheless, their purposive thrust is not difficult to discern.

The narrator was not obliged to express his volitional purposes in this particular place in the book, for he could have done this at any point using some other structural form. In fact, he did place some volitional material in other places, for example in Cycle 1, in Cycle 4 (12:12), and by means of signpost-type texts like 16:15. However, what can be observed from the data, is that he did, in fact, choose to put most of this kind of material in the

Narrative Framework. By this means, he not only endowed the Narrative Framework with another function, but also upgraded its importance from being mere support material to being, in effect, one of the most important parts of the book. In addition, within the Narrative Framework, he set the example as a model to follow, for he also gave personal examples of how he himself received instructions and put them into practice.

So it is then, that within the context of the Narrative Framework, John expresses the most clearly, his ultimate communicative purpose, which is to influence the decisions and behavior of his listeners.

6.6 Some Final Comments on Prominence in General

We have endeavored in this chapter to cover the issues of prominence in Revelation as thoroughly as possible. Nonetheless, in order to be complete the picture, there are a number of points which still need to be included in the discussion.

The first point in general to be made here then, is that anything and everything in a discourse has an automatic degree of prominence. From that starting point, anything can be made more, or less, prominent, if the author so chooses. This is why it is very helpful to distinguish between natural prominence and special prominence, as we have already done in the preceding discussion.

The second point is that, in our analogy of the mountains and valleys, not all the mountains are the same height. Obviously, they are not all the same. This means that throughout the book, there are all sorts of gradations of prominence, from very prominent to not at all prominent, possibly even down to a negative prominence, down in the depths of a valley.

It is part of the artistic skill of a writer to provide all these different nuances. With words and meanings he accomplishes what a painter does with paint. A painter does not necessarily paint with stark colors and obvious contours between them, but shades the parts together in unobtrusively blended patterns. A skilled writer does the same. Then, by the same token, it is the artistic appreciation of the readers which is brought into play to correctly recognize and interpret what the artist has presented to them. This is one of primary the goals of this book, and of all the discussion which it contains. That goal is to try and recognize and appreciate what the co-authors of Revelation have accomplished, and from there to try and encourage other readers, in their turn, to correctly appreciate and understand the message of this mysterious, yet, magisterial book.

6.6.1 The Participants

All narratives, in particular, have participants who are active in the story, or maybe, in some cases relatively inactive. Since Revelation has a

Narrative Framework, and many embedded narratives, there are a number of participants, who appear for longer or shorter periods of time, in the various stories. It is also obvious, once the obvious is stated, that not all these participants have the same level of importance, or prominence, in the book as a whole. Nonetheless, this obvious point is basically never referred to in the traditional commentaries on the book.

There is a very good reason why all this is important. It is because it is very easy to attribute to a particular participant, like the dragon, for example, an unduly high level of importance. Intuitively, this often happens because we are easily impressed by brawn and braggarts. However, we have found that, linguistically speaking, the dragon is specifically downgraded in importance by the author.

In the same way, there may be a participant who has a very high level of importance, like God the Father, for example, who is, nonetheless, often overlooked. God the Father only participates in the action, by clearly speaking, twice at 1:8 and 21:5-6. Since He does not take up much space, but remains, for the most part, in the background, in most writings by far which exist about this book, He hardly gets any mention at all.

However, such a state of affairs can hardly be reasonably justified. Just because of who He is, He ought to get the most attention of all, and be raised up to the highest level of prominence in the book. This level of prominence is raised even higher by the author, because he is at pains to inform us, right at the beginning at 1:1, that this eternal, Creator God, is the sole source of all the mysteries revealed in this book .

For this reason, therefore, because of the over-riding natural prominence of this participant, enhanced further by the special prominence attributed to Him in 1:1, what He says in Chapter 21 is probably the most prominent part of the book, at least at the informational level. This is so important to understand, that we will come back to it again, and spend more time on this topic before we get to the end.

Here then, is a list of all the individual, active participants in order of importance:

- God the Father
- Jesus, the Messiah, who is also the Lion who is a Lamb
- John, the narrator
- Satan, or the dragon
- The beast from the sea
- The beast from the land
- Babylon

It is interesting to note that there are, once again, seven of them.

In addition to these specific, individual participants, there are also some groups of participants who are present in the book, without being very overtly active in the purposive thrust of the book. These include the people of God, the 24 elders, and the angels to name but a few. The angels may seem to be an exception to this general statement, since they are very numerous, and very active, in the book. But, in this case, they are being analyzed as a group, as opposed to one of the individual participants listed above. For those readers interested in these details, the different groups of participants and, especially the angels, will be discussed in more detail in the following Appendix.

6.6.2 The Topics

The notion of the topic of the book was introduced and reviewed in some detail in Chapter 4 above. However, in addition to the broad topic of the book as a whole, there are also some more detailed sub-topics, and these also can be arranged in an order of importance, according to their level of natural and/or special prominence. For those interested in this question, the most important sub-topics will be presented and discussed in more detail in Chapter 7 which follows.

But the point which we are making here, is about prominence. Since the topic of a book is the main thing which the book is all about, and since it must, by definition, pervade the whole discourse, then quite naturally it is important. If it were not important, then the book would not exist, and the discourse would disappear into oblivion.

A consequence of this observation is that any part of a discourse which introduces, and/or significantly develops, the main topic of a whole discourse, will naturally be more prominent than other texts around it, which do not do this. So, in the case of Revelation, this happens in the Prologue, and also in Chapters 4 and 5, which is the introduction to, and the setting for, the whole of Cycles 2-6.

This is one important reason why introductions are also considered to be prominent. They have a prominence which is in second place to their matching conclusion, even though setting material is not normally considered to be thematic, as previously discussed. They can be prominent because of their relationship to the topic, even while not being thematic. That is to say, that they may introduce the topic, and therefore be prominent, without contributing any new, or significant thematic information about the topic.

The Prologue then, is to be considered to be among the more prominent parts of the book, even though it is an introduction and a setting. This is for the following reasons:

- It introduces the main topic of the book, which is a revelation about Jesus, the Messiah

- God Himself is part of that topic, being the source of the revelation
- God Himself participates and is recorded as speaking – one of two times in the book
- It contains a significant amount of thematic material about Jesus, the topic of the book.
- The Prologue is connected to Cycle 1 by an overlap link and so shares some of the prominence of that cycle
- It is part of the Narrative Framework, which contains the volitional import thread

Chapters 4 and 5, being the setting for Cycles 2-6, can be considered also to be among the prominent parts of the book, for these reasons:

- The settings from the Prologue onwards are well developed, with many repetitions and re-activations and are, therefore, all-pervasive. This is unusual and raises their level of prominence.
- This setting is based in the Throne Room of Heaven. This is arguably the most important, and therefore, the most prominent location in the universe.
- This setting re-introduces the main participant and main topic for a second time. This is unusual, and normally unnecessary, and so it is prominent.
- He is introduced as a completely different person, ostensibly another participant, but it is still the same Jesus who is in view. Once again, very unusual, and prominent.
- This introduction is very developed with a lot of significant thematic material.
- This introduction is composed of a very unusual mystery which is revealed. Namely a lion is introduced, but John sees a Lamb. This Lamb looks as if it should be dead, but it is, nonetheless, very much alive, and receives enormous acclaim.
- The lion is introduced but then, no more is said about it. This is tension building, and therefore, prominent.

The purpose of the discussion in the preceding paragraphs then, has been to point out that there are a few extra areas of prominence in a book like Revelation. These are, in particular, areas of text overtly dealing with the main topic of the book, and those participants in the storyline who are particularly prominent for various reasons. These should all be included in their appropriate place when evaluating a discourse's prominence, and before moving on to matters of interpretation.

6.7 A Summary of Prominence Issues in Revelation

This investigation of prominence has revealed that Revelation has four major loci of prominence at the macro level, plus a prominent strand which pervades the whole book. These points of importance have been located by three complementary methods as follows:

- A study of the Natural Prominence of the book
- A study of the Special Prominence of the book
- A study of the Volitional Import Schema of the book

In Chart 46 these various prominent parts of the book, are laid out for ease of reference, in approximate order of importance. The chart is set out under two headings, which separate the major prominent parts from the minor prominent parts. The division into these two sections may appear, at this stage, to be rather arbitrary. This is because, as far as I know, nobody has yet pursued this topic sufficiently far, to be able to establish such parameters as these, by means of clear data and examples.

Chart 46.

The Most Prominent Parts of the Macro-Structure of Revelation

The Major Prominent Parts

Cycle 1, being the main component of the Volitional Schema, and also being the matching introduction for the main conclusion, Cycle 7

Cycle 7, being the naturally prominent conclusion to the Informational Schema

Cycle 4, being the most specially prominent cycle, and center of the main chiasm

Complex Conclusion 19:1-21, being naturally prominent as a conclusion, with additional special prominence features

The Minor Prominent Parts

Chapters 4 and 5, being the matching introduction for the conclusion of Cycles 2-6, and being specially prominent in relation to the topic of the book

The Prologue, being naturally prominent as the introduction for the whole book, and the beginning of the the Narrative Framework and of the Volitional Schema; supported and confirmed by **the Epilogue**.

The Interludes, being the most prominent thematic strand, with the last interlude in the series being particularly prominent, being part of the complex conclusion of 19:1-21

My thoughts on the matter are that Natural Prominence should be given slightly more weight than Special Prominence. This is because Natural Prominence will always occur in a discourse, but Special Prominence may not. In addition, it seems likely, for the reason just given, that the author's purposive thrust is most likely to be accomplished in a zone of Natural Prominence. This is certainly the case in Revelation, and, I suspect that further investigation will demonstrate that this is a general rule.

Special Prominence, of course, can always increase the Natural Prominence, to a level higher than it would be normally. In addition, it can even trump it, and, by this means, a zone of text which is not naturally prominent, could still become the most important part of a discourse. Special Prominence can upset the normal order of things, and turn frogs into fairies, or lions into lambs, because that is what it exists for. However, I deduce that this will only happen, at the highest levels, on an exceptional basis, so it will never be the general rule.

The second criterion is that larger constituents should be given greater weight than smaller constituents, which have the same level of prominence attributed to them. This is because larger size is naturally, in itself, a prominence feature, in most cases. So that is certainly one way of distinguishing between constituents which have the same level of prominence per se.

Thirdly, however, when all is said and done, any constituent, however large or small, will have its level of prominence raised, if it is a component of a volitional import schema. As indicated above, a larger constituent with this characteristic, should be given more weight than a smaller one.

All this may seem like very unimportant, arcane details, but such details are more important than might first appear. This is because this discussion of prominence brings us right to the border of the task of interpretation, and explanation, for a modern day audience. When a Bible teacher teaches, or a Bible commentator comments on a biblical text, he or she, is taking on the very big responsibility of telling people what they think God is saying through His Word. To do this they must decide which is the most important part of the message. From there, they will expand on this insight or intuition, whatever it may be, and build the main thrust of their teaching on this understanding.

But what if they have got it wrong ? What if some kind of personal or theological bias causes them to give more weight, or, the most weight of importance, to parts of the text, which are not actually important, from the author's point of view? Whose opinion, and whose perspective are they actually transmitting? Enough said. I will leave it to you to answer those important questions.

It can be seen in Chart 46, that the four main points of prominence are Cycle 1, Cycle 7, Cycle 4, and the complex conclusion at 19:1-21.

6.7.1 Cycle 1, Cycle 7 and 19:1-21

Two texts provide complementary elements of natural prominence at the informational level. These are firstly, the conclusion to Cycles 2-6 (19:1-21), which brings to closure important aspects of the Judgment Theme. Secondly, in order of placement in the book, but more important in terms of prominence, is the body of Cycle 7 (21:1-22:7), which confirms the closure of the Judgment Theme, and also brings to closure the Salvation Theme. These passages are prominent because they bring to closure the informational development and, consequently, they jointly provide a complete conclusion for the book.

By contrast, Cycle 1 has been elevated to a higher rank of importance than its natural prominence would normally permit. It does have some natural prominence because it is the introduction for the whole book at the thematic level. However, normally speaking, it would only rank in second place to its matching conclusion. In spite of all that, it has been placed in pole position, because it is the most naturally prominent part of the volitional schema. This is because it provides the most information, and the most specific instructions, as to how the addressees should respond to the total message.

6.7.2 A Review of the Special Prominence of Cycle 4

Cycle 4 is the cycle which is marked for special prominence and, therefore, can be considered to be the peak of the whole book. Since it contains both information and instructions, it contributes prominence to both the informational and the volitional schemas. Since it is in the middle of a chiasm, it is automatically more prominent compared to the other cycles. Since this is normal for such a cycle-based discourse structure, this could be considered to be an example of natural prominence. However, since it is a cyclic structure embedded in an overall linear information schema, it could be considered to be an example of special prominence. Whichever viewpoint one prefers on this detail, it does not make much difference, since the cycle is clearly marked for prominence in a number of ways, as has already been explained in the preceding sections.

Since it is marked for prominence in the context of an informational schema, then it can be assumed that it contributes very important information. It can be deduced, therefore, that this information concerning the cosmic war which is going on behind the scenes, as it were, is crucial for a correct and complete understanding of the total message.

6.7.3 The Role of the Interludes

The interludes are also specially prominent within the context of each cycle, which means that for Cycle 4, the interlude of this cycle is the prominent part of the most specially prominent cycle. The conclusive evidence for this, is the fact that the interlude of Cycle 4 bears the highest possible level of marking for prominence, since it is an example of deviation from previously established norms.

The previously established norm was that the first two interludes occurred between the sixth and seventh sub-units of their cycle, whereas this one is fronted (a mark of prominence in itself), so that it occurs between Signs 4 and 5. It is also marked for prominence by 'and behold', which occurs in second position in the first sentence.

The prominence of the interludes signals that the Salvation Theme which they carry, is to be viewed as more prominent than the Judgment Theme material. This supports the observation above, that the conclusion of the Salvation Theme is not contained in an interim conclusion, but in the conclusion of the book as a whole, in the most naturally prominent position.

6.7.4 The Importance of Understanding the Relationship Between Cycle 4 and Cycle 7

Important as it may seem to be, the closure of the Judgment Theme as it is presented in the setting for Cycle 7, is less prominent than the closure of the Salvation Theme, which comes to completion in the body of Cycle 7. In summary, the point which is being made here is that, throughout the book the Salvation Theme is always more prominent than the Judgment Theme. This is in spite of the fact that the Judgment Theme clearly seems to get more air time.

In Cycle 7 the Judgment Theme is once again downgraded in importance, and is clearly made structurally subordinate to the Salvation Theme. This subordination is evidenced in a number of ways.

Firstly, the Judgment Theme is brought to closure first and this information is consigned to the setting of the cycle. A setting, as we have seen before in Chapter 5, usually has a much lower level of prominence than the body which follows it. By contrast, the Salvation Theme is developed in great detail and brought to closure in the body of the cycle, and, as a consequence, is brought to closure last, in the position of highest prominence.

Secondly, by means of this literary organization, the story of the temporary and eternal fate of the dragon is presented in Chapter 20, as a necessary context for the full maturity of God's plan of salvation. In other words, the plan of judgment has to be completed first, in order for the plan of salvation to blossom in all its fullness. This is because the plan of salvation will only be complete, and resplendent in all its glory, when evil has been fully eliminated and completely eradicated.

This means that the plan of judgment never had an end in itself, and by no means was ever considered to have an eternal aspect about it. On the contrary, evil, and its collateral judgment, must end and not continue to exist. So the purpose of the plan of judgment was always subservient to the plan of salvation, and it only existed to serve as a plank upon which the plan of salvation would be built and come to eternal fullness.

Thirdly, the part of the dragon's story which is presented in 20:1-3 is presented as a review, and not as a primary component in his story. There are a series of reviews towards the end of the book as was previously explained, so this is just one in a series of them. The point about a review is that it is an optional item in a narrative sequence. It is, therefore, automatically less prominent than the obligatory, primary components. In this case, the obligatory part of the dragon's story is described in Cycle 4, and this is in a context marked for prominence.

In a cyclic, repetition-based discourse, the logical understanding of the extra piece of information given in Chapter 20, is that it is a repeat of what has gone before and is, therefore, a review. The story in Cycle 4 is that the dragon is defeated and falls from grace, literally downwards in direction. The review in Chapter 20 recounts the same story of downward defeat and disgrace, but just in a shorter form and with a slightly different point of view.

It is true that many people have had, and may continue to have, difficulty in adjusting their world view in order to perceive that 20:1-3 is a review. However, in this context of explaining the details of the prominence of Cycle 4, it is possible to contribute some more evidence to support this viewpoint. So, let's not forget that the whole of Cycle 4 is marked for prominence, and so this means that everything which happens within it, is prominent to some degree or another.

The linguistic fact of the matter is that the turning point, or, the peak, of the dragon's story in Chapter 12 is in to be found in verses 7-9. To use modern non-technical terms, this description is the crux of the matter. This whole passage is oozing with prominence markers as follows:

- It is very dramatic, even for a narrative, describing a war, a cosmic war at that.
- The main participant, Michael, just unexpectedly invades the situation, unannounced.
- His identity is not explained; the readers are left to use their own general knowledge (which they would have had in that era) and to make the connections for themselves.
- The good guys win, and the bad guys lose, but, above all else…

- This dramatic part of the story *is left unfinished*, thereby creating suspense and readership angst. This feature is always a marker of prominence in a narrative.

But, why would we say that it is unfinished, since, superficially at least, 'the end' of the story is described in verses 10-17. But is it ? Remember, that a component of dramatic suspense is created when the author does not say everything which could be said, but leaves some things to the readers' imagination, as mentioned in the list above.

It says in Chapter 12 that the dragon was thrown down to the earth, and went about enraged, trying to make war on the people of God. But in the meantime, having explained what happened in 12:7-9, the reason why it happened is given in 12:10-11. Please see Appendix 3 for the division of the sub-units as needed.

The reason why it happened is because the power and the authority over the earth had been given over to Christ, the Lamb. As a consequence of this, the dragon no longer had the same power and authority as before (12:10). The direct practical result of this switch over in the earthly power structure, was that the people of God would now be able to defeat the dragon and overcome him, whenever they came into conflict, as described in 12:11. This dramatic, revolutionary, change was to result in great joy for those whose home base was the heavenly Kingdom of God (12:12).

So the end then, of the dragon's story was that he was left standing, rather sheepishly (please excuse the pun!), on the beach. By any dramatic or literary standard, this is a way of saying that his story was left unfinished. Consequently, the reader is left in suspense: the terrible, arch-villain, the dragon, was roaming around on the earth somewhere in a great anger, but nobody quite knows what he is doing exactly, nor where he is. What we do know is that his time was limited and short (12:12b), so this was not a definitive, eternal solution that is being described. We also know that he whistled up three stooges, the two beasts and Babylon, and it is clear that they are the ones who, in actual practice, persecute God's people. So what is happening here ?

In 12:12b-17 we are told that the dragon was enraged and wanted to exact vengeance on God's people, but we are not actually told that he did so. In fact, we are told that what he attempted to do failed, and this seems to imply that he was not actually able to do any harm at all. This would explain why he empowered his two principal proxies to do his dirty work for him. Why would any-one with any sense give their authority over to somebody else? One answer is because the dragon had lost his power to do serious harm himself. So, consequently, he was obliged to give over whatever authority he had left to these other beings, to actually cause harm on the earth in his place. This is the kind of thing which you have to do if you end up in some kind of prison, and this is the process of what happened next, which is described in Chapter 13.

So then, even if it has taken a few lines to explain the details, the sum of it is that, the dragon's story is left unfinished, and we do not know exactly what became of him in the end. So it is then, that when his story is specifically picked up again in Chapter 20, obviously, this is of great interest, because now, that suspended need-to-know, will be satisfied. In brief then, the dragon's story is reviewed, as we have said before. That is, we are told, in summary form, that there has been a conflict (implied) and, as a result, the dragon has been dis-empowered and defeated.

Let's take note that we are told some specific things. This loss of authority is for a short time and is not an eternal solution. The dragon's imprisonment is for only 1000 years, which is totally in line with what was said at 12:12b. During this time he has lost the power to deceive the nations as indicated in 20:2-3. But this neither says, nor implies, anything about whatever other damage he could still do by using the two beasts in his place.

So then, this review of what happened to the dragon is fully consonant with what was recounted in the fuller story. The only new information which is added, comes right at the end at 20:10, where the final solution for the dragon is described. At this point the reader is, at last, informed of the dragon's demise, and relieved to finally find out what will happen to him in the end.

In summary then, in case it is not clear: the dragon was defeated and thrown out of the heavenly places by Michael and his angels. This is an event which apparently was closely linked to the birth of a boy, who was protected from the dragon's attack and was taken back up to Heaven. It is also coincidental with a time when Christ's power to reign in the Kingdom of God began, and when the people of God could defeat the dragon by using the power of the blood of the Lamb.

These elements are all described in Chapter 12. The events described in 20:1-3 are a review of those previous events, and there is no textual support for the idea that they are a new set of events due to happen thousands of years later than the previous events of Chapter 12.

6.7.5 The Connection Between Cycle 4 and the Volitional Schema

Cycle 4 is also specially prominent because it contributes more directly to the volitional thrust of the book than the other central cycles, having, as it does, a double exhortation at 12:12. The combination of all the prominence features suggest that the author is bringing special attention to the dragon's expulsion from Heaven as a reason why many of the other things described in the book happen. In the context of the volitional schema, this reason was seen to be an important motivator and more important than the consequent results.

6.7.6 The Role of the Narrative Framework in Creating Prominence

Finally, the prominent strand is created by the Narrative Framework. This part of the text causes the volitional schema prominence, which outranks all other types of prominence, to come to the fore at the beginning and end of the book, and also at regular intervals throughout.

In it, John provides an extra level of exhortation by which means he insists that the hearers should respond actively to the other, more specific exhortations. As a consequence of this, all parts of the Narrative Framework are interpreted as being prominent themselves, and also as being markers of prominence.

They are prominent, in and of themselves, because they constantly remind the hearer of the volitional purpose of the author. By virtue of their prominence they also tend to make whatever they are linked to (usually their immediate context) more prominent also. In effect, they are acting as signposts. Signposts are prominent so that they are noticed, but their primary function is to point at something else thereby making it prominent also. Thus, for example, the narrative interlude (10:1-11:2) contributes to the prominence of the following Signs Cycle, while the minor element at 19:9-10 prepares the way for, and points towards, the following prominent text in 19:11-21.

It is for this reason that the Prologue is included in the list of prominent parts of the book, as listed in Chart 46 above. This is because it introduces and launches the Narrative Framework and so, as such, is a prominent part of this supporting, structural skin of the discourse. It is also where the topic of the book is first introduced.

Continuing on in a similar vein, Chapters 4 and 5 are also included in the list of prominent parts for similar reasons. Firstly, it is because they incorporate an unusual, and therefore prominent, re-introduction of the main participant, Jesus, who is also, actually, the most important aspect of the topic. Secondly, apart from linking back to the Prologue, since it develops the topic in more detail, Chapter 5 is also, technically, a part of the Narrative Framework, since in this passage John participates in his own narrative. Notably, in this part of the chapter (5:4-5) he receives an instruction in the form of an imperative, and is told to stop weeping. This is a contrastive echo of the later imperative doublet, Rejoice/Lament which occurs at 12:12 in the specially prominent Cycle 4.

So for all these reasons, it is clear that these two chapters are specifically marked for prominence. They are, therefore, moved up the prominence ladder to a higher position of importance compared to their more normal, lowly position as a setting.

6.7.7 Conclusion

Thus it can be seen, that deciding what the main point of a discourse is, does not have to be left to intuition or to the discretion of the hearer. There are indicators of various kinds which the author considered appropriate to place in the discourse. These guide a careful listener to an appropriate understanding of his message.

It is true that these indicators still have to be interpreted, and there may be differences of opinion in this realm, but undoubtedly, it is an important step forward to discern and classify these indicators. This is because, from that starting point, a consensus can truly develop, based on data drawn from the text, rather than on supposition and personal opinion. In any eventuality, the debate will be best served by interpretations and supporting theoretical justifications which provide 'superior explanatory power for particular features of the Biblical text', as recommended by Bergen 1987,336.

6.8 Revisiting the Notion of the Topic of the Book

Since the book of Revelation is most definitely a complex discourse, the approach taken in this study has been to decorticate it, and then to study its various levels, from the outer structural skin, on down to the more hidden levels. Every attempt has been made to start with what are the most obvious elements which can be more easily understood, before passing on to the more subtle, and less well-known elements.

So it is then, that back in Chapter 4 we started out by introducing the notion of the topic of the book. Because of our desire to keep things simple and to progress step by step, we limited our definition of the topic of Revelation to the most obvious, and the most general version of it. So, we proposed back then that this general definition revolved around the key word, which introduces the whole discourse at 1:1, which is the word 'a revelation'.

In this current chapter we have been exploring the notion of prominence. However, no discussion of prominence is complete without making reference to the notion of the topic, for without the topic, any discussion of prominence makes no sense and has no meaning. This is because a book, or discourse, is *about* something, or someone. That is the topic of the book. The purpose of prominence is to be able to locate the places in the discourse where the author is indicating to us that these passages are where he is telling us some particularly important things *about the topic*. That is the basic definition of prominence: it shows us what the author considers to be important *about the topic*.

So then, there are two particular things which can now be elucidated about the topic of the book. The first thing is that it is God Himself who is the source of the revelation which is the topic of the book. Now, as it happens this is a very unusual feature, because normally, in most books, the author gives no direct indication of where his idea for the topic came from. It is usually just because he wanted to write about this idea or that person, and that is all there is to it.

But in this case we are specifically told that the idea for this book came from God Himself. What we have reminded ourselves in the discussion of the preceding paragraphs above, is that, God by the very nature of who He is, is automatically prominent in any discourse where He appears. The fact that He appears very few times in this book is of no relevance. On the contrary, this means that when He does intervene, then it is even more important than ever, to take note of what He said or what He did. In this case, this understanding reminds us that His brief double intervention in the middle of Cycle 7, is supremely important for an understanding of this book. Therefore, it should not be passed over lightly and quickly, as it usually is.

The second issue to clarify is what the specific topic of the book really is. All we proposed earlier was a very general topic, namely that it was a revelation and that is all. But obviously, we can go further than that, and ask, 'Well, what is the revelation *about* ?'

When we ask this question, the answer becomes immediately clear, because we are not left to guess as best we can, because we are told right at the beginning at 1:1, that it is about Jesus the Christ, or Jesus the Messiah. Even though the genitive in 1:1 is technically ambiguous, in the context, it is obvious that the primary meaning is that the revelation is about Jesus. This is confirmed in no uncertain terms soon after in Chapters 4 and 5, where, as explained previously, this primary participant, who is the topic, is introduced again with much fanfare and many details. This also is unusual, so it is clear that we are not supposed to miss this point. Then after that, perusal of the rest of the book shows that Jesus is always present, overtly or covertly, in one form or another, and that is exactly what you would expect for the topic.

So then, in case we had not fully grasped this point before, Jesus is the topic of the book. Since He is the topic of the book, then it is self evident that the author is going to be constantly talking about Him, in one way or another. As he talks about Him then, at certain points, the author is bound to indicate that some parts of this revelation about Jesus which he is presenting, are more important than others. He does this by inserting elements of prominence into his discourse, by all the different means which have been discussed throughout this chapter.

So then we can now ask the crucial question : 'What then, is this book really all about ?'. Because, of all the work which we have done to bring us to this point in our understanding of what the topic of the book really is, and which parts of it the author considers to be the most important, we can now answer this question with some confidence and clarity.

This book then is all about Jesus. Jesus, plus a combination of all the important things about Him. These are the things which God has shown the author, and which he has shown to us, by indicating that they are more important than all the other things which he has said.

When I first got to this stage of the process myself, I followed it up by doing an experiment. I forewarn you that, although it was very enlightening, the result surprised me quite a bit. So what we are going to do now is repeat the experiment and you can follow along.

The experiment is this. We are going to take the topic of the book, which is Jesus, as has just been explained, and then we are going to summarize what the author said about Him. To be more precise, we are going to see exactly what God the Father sought fit to reveal about Him, so that John could pass this revelation on to us.

As was explained in Chapter 4, the basis of our summary is the thematic material which was discussed in that chapter, because the thematic material is what the author says about the topic. But within that thematic material, we are going to focus on the prominent parts of it. This is because, as we have been explaining all through this current chapter, the prominent material reveals to us the most important parts of what the author has to say about the topic.

So we will start with the topic, and work our way through all the prominent parts listed above, linking it all together with the non-prominent thematic material, which has been placed in between the prominent parts.

6.8.1 The Prologue : Jesus is King

The Prologue provides the topic of the book, which is to be found in the opening paragraphs, as is the case with most discourses. In this case the author tells us that he is transmitting a revelation concerning Jesus (1:1). In the immediately following paragraphs (1:4-20) it becomes clear that the revelation is specifically a revelation of Jesus as King. We are specifically told that He has passed through death and is alive again, and that He is the ruler of the kings of the earth.

Secondarily, it also becomes clear in these same verses that the recipients of the letter are the seven churches. These are the people who, having been liberated from their sins by the King's blood (1:5), are now supposed to read the letter and to take note of its contents (1:3). The specific application of this topic for them, is discovering that their role is to be kings and priests together with Christ (1:6).

6.8.2 Cycle 1 : The King is the Commander In Chief

Jesus is King over the Church, and each of the seven letters reveals a facet of His kingship, and of His undisputed right to rule over their affairs.

In these seven letters Jesus, as King and, therefore, as Commander in Chief of the Church, brings correction and encouragement to the individual churches and gives them instruction as to what they should be doing. In particular, they should be continuing in a spirit of repentance, and they should also continue to persevere in obeying Him, and in following Him wherever He goes.

The Church is supposed to rule and reign with the King. As such, its members are supposed to learn to be overcomers by becoming victorious over their enemies, in and through all the difficulties of life. They should do this, even if they are faced with the prospect of physical death.

6.8.3 The Setting to Cycles 2-6 : The King's Credentials

The Kingdom's HQ is in Heaven. The King is therefore a heavenly being who is perfectly at home in the glorious, spiritual world surrounding the throne of God. There is no other higher or greater place of authority than this, as indicated in Chapter 4. He rules from there.

The King is declared worthy to rule over the whole universe. He is worthy because He willingly chose to give Himself as the sacrificial lamb, in order to redeem all men for God by shedding His own blood, as revealed in Chapter 5. The purpose of this was so that they, in turn, could become kings and priests in the service of their God (5:9-10). As Jesus is to rule over the affairs of Earth, so His followers also are to reign on the earth.

6.8.4 Cycles 2-4 : The King's Compassion

The King's function is to govern or reign. There are two principal aspects of this reigning task which are developed in Cycles 2-6. One of these is the judicial task. It is the King's task to uphold and implement the law of the Kingdom, which is, in this case, the Law of God. This involves bringing to account and dealing with those who have broken God's law, and so have been in rebellion against Him. This is what is meant by the phrase "the time has come for judgment…". See for example 11:15-19.

However, it is very noteworthy that He goes about this task with great compassion. He does not just arbitrarily impose His judgments as He would normally have the right to do. But instead, He first **reveals** what is going to happen (Cycle 2). Then He **warns** about what He is going to do (Cycle 3). Finally, and most importantly, He then **explains** how the most basic level of this judgment has already been accomplished, and how the ongoing aftermath of this cosmic war will play out from then onwards (Cycle 4).

These are all indicators of His compassion for, by these means, He gives the inhabitants of the earth the opportunity to understand what is happening to them. From the basis of that revealed understanding, they can then, if they so choose, repent and avoid His final, irrevocable judgments which are still to come.

6.8.5 The Interludes of Cycles 2-6 : The King's Companions

The second aspect of a monarch's function is the executive task. This means that He is the leader of the Kingdom and so He needs to organize the life of the Kingdom for the protection, the benefit and for the inclusion of His loyal subjects.

So it can be seen then, that the King does not rule alone, but that He has companions who He leads and takes care of. These are the people who have been redeemed from the earth, who are faithful to Him, who share in His sufferings and who follow Him wherever He goes. These companions are described in the Interludes.

6.8.6 Cycles 4-6 : The King's Combat

Since Cycle 4 is particularly prominent it is included here as well as in the section above. Warfare is an integral part of any king's responsibility for He has to protect His people from harm and to defend His Kingdom from attack. King Jesus' combat is against evil in all its forms. The war takes place in the heavenly realm but the principal enemy and his minions have already been defeated. They have been (and are continuously) defeated by the authority and the blood of the King, and by the cooperation of His companions (ch.12-13). This is all explained in Cycle 4.

Another realm of combat is the demonic infrastructure, known as Babylon, which the devil has constructed on the earth in order to rule over it. Babylon has also been defeated and will be completely destroyed (ch.14 & 17).

The Church's task is to learn how to defeat these same enemies for themselves and thus they govern with the King, even though they may go through tribulations themselves, at the same time. Ultimately, all evil will be punished and eradicated for ever (Cycles 5 & 6).

6.8.7 Closure for Cycles 2-6 : The King's Conquest

The King has totally conquered all His adversaries. There is no escape and no second chance. The King is accompanied in this conquest by His companions. In the prominent Narrative Framework component in 19:10, John is specifically told that the essential part of his work as a prophet is to testify, that is, to declare truth, about Jesus. This is one way in which the companions overcome their enemies, as was previously stated at 12:11b.

6.8.8 Cycle 7 : The King's Crowning Glory

The primary enemy is defeated for time and eternity (ch.20). The redeemed share His eternal glory in the New Jerusalem on the new earth (ch.21). They will reign there in peace as the bride of the King (22:3-5).

6.8.9 The Epilogue : They All Lived Happily Ever After

The 'book' of Revelation is primarily a letter, which was written to Christians in Asia Minor during the first century AD. As is true with all biblical letters, the purpose is a combination of teaching and exhortation. The purpose of this letter is to teach about Jesus in His role as the King, and to encourage and exhort the Christians to align themselves with this teaching and thus, to learn to reign with Him on the earth. Having done that, they will be ushered into a new world and a new era in which they will live happily ever after.

6.8.10 The Coda : The King is Coming Soon

The King is coming soon, as we are reminded by the very last piece of information provided in the book at 22:20. When He comes, He is coming to bring rewards both for His companions (22:12), and disciplinary action for those who chose not to follow Him (19:11-16 and 20:11-15).

All that is taught here is timeless. This is because it is all true in every generation. The practical outworking of it may be slightly different at different generations, but the basic principles revealed in this book are always true. Jesus is the King. He has already conquered His enemies, and is in charge of everything else which will happen until the end of time. He is coming soon, and He will bring His rewards with Him: Final, and eternal, judgment for those who deserve it, and vindication and great blessing, for those who have followed Him down the narrow path to safety.

The Church, in fact anyone who has an ear to hear, should take seriously what is taught in this book and put it into practice.

6.9 A Final Word

We have now completed our discussion of the notion of prominence in a discourse, and the explanation of how semantic prominence is actually manifested in the book of Revelation.

To conclude this explanation we reviewed the results of an experiment. The experiment was to follow the logic of an analysis such as this, to whatever conclusion it would lead us. The results which the experiment produced were laid out in the preceding paragraphs, and as such, they can be reviewed and evaluated by any one who cares to make the effort. As I said myself at the outset, I found the results to be surprising. Revealing, in line with the book being a revelation, but not at all confirmatory of the theology and the understanding of the book, which I had inherited from my forebears.

What about yourself, how does it sit with you ?

So, please permit me to have the last word on the matter with a few more concluding remarks before we put the final full stop to this chapter.

One of my first surprises was to notice that this summary, based around the topic of the book, has nine components. The tenth item above is a coda, so is not included in this review. This happened quite naturally, just by trying to include all the prominent points, and it happened without any preconceived forcing, or after-the-fact re-arranging, on my part. Yet, it is remarkable to consider that the whole book is also composed of nine parts, namely the seven cycles, plus the Prologue and the Epilogue. But that is not all. This story about the King provides for us eight (symbolic of new beginnings) notable characteristics of this King, composed of one generic statement at the beginning, and seven specific statements.

This list is then followed by a coda. This feature in turn, synchronizes totally with the body of the book, where codas can be found in several strategic places including at the very end of the body of the book at 22:5c.

Many people, maybe most, would just dismiss this as an unremarkable coincidence, I am sure. But for myself, having spent many years being constantly surprised by the amazing intricacy of this book, with all sorts of coincidental numbers, and quite remarkable repetitions and parallels turning up everywhere, I am not so sure. But anyway, this is not something which can be objectively proven, so I will just make my point and leave you to make your final decision.

My final point is much more objective and rooted in the data. The whole purpose of the analysis described so far in this book, has been to examine the data, and let the data speak for itself without any intrusions from the outside. As a result, based on good evidence, it was found that the book is composed of nine major parts, as already mentioned. Then from there, following a linguistically viable trail, the various parts of those nine components, which are the most prominent, were laid out for all to see and to consider.

Then, finally, just by using the topic stated in the book and the prominent points, and nothing else, a summary of the message contained in that raw data, was drawn up. There may well be differing opinions about the result, and I am fairly confident about that. But the point which I want to make in conclusion, is that that summary was totally based on the data and nothing else, and it will be hard to disprove that statement.

As a consequence, that summary needs to be taken seriously and not dismissed too quickly and too thoughtlessly. This is because the best way to construct a meaningful consensus about what this book is really all about, is by going over the data again and again, and letting the information provided by the author guide us to our conclusions.

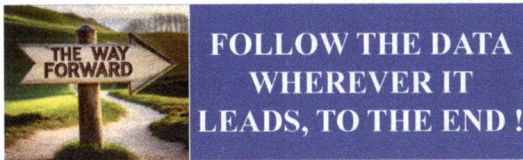

FOLLOW THE DATA WHEREVER IT LEADS, TO THE END !

PREFACE FOR APPENDIX 6

The extra contents for this Appendix are as follows :

1) The notion of prominence as referred to by the biblical commentators.
2) The notion of prominence as referred to by other linguists and translators.
3) Some technical discussions concerning the surface structure causes of semantic turbulence, which occurs at points of prominence in a discourse like Revelation.
4) A detailed review of the groups of participants to be found in Revelation, with special reference to all the angels.

If these topics are of no particular interest to you, please feel free to move on straight away to Chapter 7. In that Chapter we will endeavor to demonstrate how the various parts which we have studied so far, all fit together into a coherent and harmonious whole.

APPENDIX 6
Ancillary Information Pertaining to the Discussion of the Notion of Prominence

A6.1 The Notion of Prominence in the Biblical Commentaries

It would be an impossible task to consult in detail all the works which have ever been written on the book of Revelation. The full list of the ones which I was able to consult can be found in the bibliographies of Schooling 2004.

However, there were very, very few references to climaxes, peaks, or even important points, in these discussions presented by previous generations of scholars. Such an idea was passed over in silence, as if to locate the important parts of a text, was just not a relevant task for them.

An exception to this general state of affairs is Dorsey 1999, whose work is grounded in modern linguistic theory, and who, therefore, tries to take account of a number of issues dealt with in this book. Among earlier commentators Baldwin 1972,80 is one, for example, who discerned a 'theological climax' in a major part of Zechariah, but this is not developed or explained in any detail.

On the other hand, Aune 1997 and 1988, produced over 1000 pages of commentary on Revelation but, according to his eight page index of principal topics, he makes no reference to the notion of climax or anything similar. Citing Aune again, we find that in his volume 1998b,1022, he does make reference to 19:7-8 as being 'the main part of the hymn' in 19:5-8. But this is at a very low level of the discourse and not at all important for the book as a whole, and, once again, there is no argumentation to support why it should be considered the main part.

Then, another example is Beale 1999,226, who makes reference to 'the main point' of each of the seven letters. He claims that the promises are the 'main point' of the letters, but his viewpoint is not buttressed with data either. This means that a reader has no idea why exactly this particular part should be considered to be important, because the analysis is based on intuition and personal opinion, rather than on data to be found in the text, or on credible linguistic theory.

As regards the pause created by the two middle interludes in Chapters 10 and 11, Strand 1987,111 claims that the interludes 'enhance or intensify the thrust of the immediately preceding material'. This is a muted kind of reference to the notion of prominence. If, however, it is clear that a pause in the flow of a text builds anticipation and even a sense of impatience in a reader, it is not at all clear how a switch to a different topic intensifies the impact of the *preceding* topic. In such a case, a contrast is created, but not an intensification.

As regards the fact that the signs are explanations and are, therefore, important. Beasley-Murray 1974,191 could see that 12:1-14:2 (sic) 'provide an explanation of the nature of the conflict in which the church is engaged' but he was not able to fathom its full importance, because his analysis constrained him, nonetheless, to view this part of the book as 'a parenthesis' (ibid.).

A6.2 The Notion of Prominence Among Linguists and Translators

Linguistics in general is a very recent discipline, and the analysis of whole discourses, as in this book, is even more recent. As a consequence, as the pioneers have broken into new territory, they have needed to invent new technical terms in order to describe what they were finding.

As a result, different technical terms have been used to describe similar linguistic features. In terms of semantics, the term 'prominence' to describe a place in the discourse where the meaning of the text was more important than in other parts, was already being used by Kathleen Callow in 1974. She has since then developed these thoughts in more detail in her later books and articles.

Levinsohn 1992 also began using the same term, although in his case, he was only working on narrative at the sentence level. As a consequence, his reference to the term is very limited and does not apply, to any great extent, at the higher levels.

For a general overview of the notion of prominence see Callow 1974,49-68 and 1998,151-52. For more detail, see Callow 1998,155-56 for an introduction to natural prominence, 164 for comparison with special prominence, 181-85 for a description of special prominence, 218-19 for topical prominence and 230-31 for thematic prominence. See also Bergen 1987,331-34.

See Callow 1974,50-51, Longacre 1983a,25-38 and 1985 in toto, Bergen 1987,331-34, Cotterell and Turner 1989,246-47, and Dorsey 1999,39-41 for some inventories of surface structure features which have been found to mark prominence. Levinsohn 1992,168-70 provides a few examples of such devices in NT Greek. More recently, Levinsohn 2020, has provided considerable insight into the various prominent parts of the Epistle to the Galatians.

Longacre, on the other hand, concentrated more on producing 'a surface grammar of discourse' (1985,97), rather than on identifying the underlying semantic relationships. Consequently, this is the main difference between his approach and Callow's. In addition, being an early pioneer in this field, he concentrated mainly on narrative texts. As a result, he came up with the word 'peak', as referred to in parts of Chapter 6 above, which is the term which he used the most consistently. The review of 'peak' and 'peaking' by Cotterell and Turner (1989,244-8) reflects Longacre's viewpoint.

However, in the domain of special prominence, his viewpoint coincides with Callow's to a large extent, since they are both seeking to take account of the same linguistic surface structure phenomena. One of the reasons for the coinciding of the two viewpoints, is because some features of narrative can reoccur in other kinds of discourses, which are not strictly narratives per se, as we have already noticed in previous discussion of Revelation.

This is because, as Longacre, from the outset of research into this subject, has recognized (1976,212), when it comes to discussion of the peak, other kinds of texts may have characteristics which resemble those of plot in narrative. Since Revelation is a complex text containing elements of narrative, it also has some plot-like elements. As a consequence, even if the term 'plot' is usually considered to be a characteristic of narrative, it can also occur in a text like Revelation. This feature was previously discussed in Chapter 5 and is illustrated by Chart 43. See Callow 1998,198. and Longacre 1983,20-38 and 1985 for more discussion of this point.

Surprisingly, little progress seems to have been made on these matters in the last fifteen to twenty years. There appears to be very little which is strikingly new, which has been produced on this subject, since the early 2000's. One of the most recent handbooks on Hebrew discourse, Patton and Putnam 2019, barely gives the notion of prominence a mention, and that is only prominence at the sentence level. Scacewater's collection (2020) does somewhat better, but the results are patchy because there are many different contributors and different methodologies used. But, nonetheless, the references which are to be found in this volume are very cursory in nature, and are only less informative reviews of what had already been set out in the older works mentioned above.

A6.3 The Notion of Prominence and Turbulence

In our previous discussion, we have already pointed out that any unexpected turbulence in a discourse could already be advance warning that prominence markers may be influencing the flow and form of the text. Longacre (1983a,25-6 and 1985) makes reference to this in his discussion of 'peak' and it was also a helpful clue in the analysis of Micah (Schooling 2024b).

A surefire way of locating turbulence in a biblical book is to take note of where there is consistent disagreement amongst commentators. By this I mean disagreement which has lasted for many decades, if not centuries, with no clear consensus in view. The turbulence which provokes disagreement can be of many different kinds. I will comment on a few of them below, because they are all topics which could be researched and clarified further.

A6.3.1 The Prominence Implications of Additive Relationships

See Beekman et al.1981,79, Callow 1998,282-3 and 297-300, and Dooley and Levinsohn 2001,92-93 for definition and explanation of additive relationships. Additive semantic relationships are marked in the surface structure by coordinate grammatical relationships. These relationships would normally be considered to create no great difficulties, as they imply relationships between units of equal weight and importance. Consequently, they would have equal natural prominence.

This is straightforward when dealing with narrative type texts, which are usually linear in organization, and chronological in sequence. However, in non-linear texts like Revelation it is a different matter. Even though almost everything in this book is linked by the conjunction *kai* 'and', it is not at all reasonable to assume that everything therefore, is of equal weight and value, as in a list. In addition, one of the major points of disagreement about this book, is whether it is organized linearly, sequentially and chronologically, or whether it is organized on the basis of repetition, recapitulation and reiteration.

When a discourse is laid out in a series of parallel cycles, it is a moot point as to what is being joined to what, exactly, by the conjunction which has been placed between them. So this question remains to be elucidated further: What exactly is the function of *kai* 'and', in a book like Revelation? I have briefly made some remarks on this issue in Appendix 2, and I plan to produce a longer article on the subject of connectives in NT Greek which will be forthcoming shortly.

A6.3.2 The Prominence Implications of Features Such As 'Signposts'

In this present analysis of Revelation, it was most helpful to have in mind, the notion of prominence features like 'signposts'. See Callow 1998,180-1 and 292-3 for discussion of this issue of prominence marking signposts.

Another major source of disagreement among commentators in the past, has been how to explain the textual items, like the Three Woes, and other such textual anomalies, which are to be found in this book. The problem is caused by the fact that such texts stand outside, as it were, the general flow of the rest of the discourse. As a consequence, they do not fit neatly into a linear structure, if that is what you are looking for, but they disrupt it, thereby causing turbulence.

This issue was dealt with in some detail in the main text of this chapter, so we will not go over all that again here. The main point to be made is that, when the notion of prominence was introduced into the discussion, then a huge amount of light was beamed on these difficult to analyze texts. As a result, when all these extraneous pieces of text were considered to be prominence features, then all the outstanding difficulties and disagreements were resolved.

The term 'signpost' in and of itself is very graphically helpful, because everybody knows that a signpost is intentionally made to be different, and to stand out from its surrounding context. This is because it is pointing at something else, and that something else is usually something important that the passerby, or the reader in this case, may want to look at carefully.

A6.3.3 The Prominence Implications of Alternative Analyses

The Narrative Framework Interlude was discussed in Chapter 2, and, in Appendix 2, two alternative analyses were presented, to help demonstrate the reality of the overlap link between Chapter 10 and Chapter 11.

As a brief reminder those two analyses were as follows:

1) The passage can be analyzed as a chiasm based on the speeches of the angel with the little scroll thus:

A. 10:1-4 The angel is introduced

B. 10:5-7 The angel speaks very strongly (he swears): There will be no more delay, but at the time when the seventh trumpet is sounded, at that time the mystery which God proclaimed to His servants the prophets, will be accomplished.

A' 10:8-11 The angel concludes his intervention

2) The passage can be analyzed as a chiasm based on the actions of John:

A. 10:1-4 John stops his prophetic activity

B. 10:5-11 John takes and eats the scroll and is re-commissioned in his prophetic activity

A' 11:1-2 John re-commences his prophetic activity

At the time when we first discussed this issue, the approach was to say that there were two possible analyses for the same section of text, but that there was no real difference between them. Consequently, we just picked the one which suited us best, depending on which details we were focusing on at that time.

However, now that we are looking at everything in the light of the notion of prominence, we can see that they are not identical in terms of overall importance and semantic weight. The first one is clearly more prominent than the second one and, therefore, should be attributed more weight and importance in any subsequent analysis or commentary.

The prominence markers for vv.5-7 (section **B.** in the first analysis) are as follows:

- the fact that it is the center unit of a chiasm,
- it is in direct speech,

- there is a strong speech verb, 'he swore',
- it has an accompanying dramatic gesture - i.e. lifting his right hand,
- he swears by God Himself,
- the presence of the key phrases 'it is finished', and, 'the mystery of God'.

So by concentrating on these aspects of the text it brings God Himself, into focus. As we saw in the previous discussion of the relative prominence of different participants, when God is involved, everything becomes more prominent than anything else where He is not directly involved. By contrast, John and his participation are in focus in the second analysis. But compared to God Himself, John is clearly not as important as all that. As a consequence, the first viewpoint is more prominent than the second one.

This is an example of how it is possible to discern different levels of prominence in a text by taking account of the relative prominence of the different aspects of the text. It also demonstrates how a shift in the reader's point of focus and can also change what comes out at the other end, as the most important part of the text in question. However, when these more subtle issues are understood, our viewpoints and interpretations are no longer dependent on unsubstantiated intuition. In place of that, our arguments and explanations can be reasoned out, based on objective data, and can be demonstrated with care, depending on which precise point one wishes to make, and how convincing one wants to be.

This example also illustrates the value of alternative analyses. Once you have established that different, legitimate analyses are possible, it is then possible to compare them and discern their different points of focus. From there it becomes possible to make more refined decisions regarding which parts of the text, or, which insights derived from the same text, are more important than the others.

A6.3.4 The Prominence Implications of 'Fronting'

In some cases, a word, usually a key word in its context, is moved nearer to the front of a sentence than would usually be the case, for a given language. This is called 'fronting' and has long since been recognized by linguists as a means by which, extra attention is brought to bear on this word. See, for example, Levinsohn 1992,83 on fronting in NT Greek, and Dooley and Levinsohn 2001,66 for general comments.

Fronting creates prominence, because, by definition, it is unusual and runs counter to the norms of the language. This in turn creates literary and linguistic turbulence, which are the classic signs that a prominence feature has been placed in the text.

In the earlier references given above, the examples given are usually only at the sentence level, and only concern slight differences in emphasis at that lower level. However, when analyzing whole discourses, as in the case of this study, it is possible to find examples of fronting which clearly are intended to influence the prominence flow of the whole discourse. There are at least two such examples in this book.

The first is right at the beginning at 1:1, where the whole general topic of the book is established by the very first, 'fronted', word which is 'a revelation'. The second one is at 12:1 where the word 'a sign' is moved up to second position, after the conjunction 'and'. At the same time it is made the grammatical subject of the following passive verb, thereby buttressing its position at the beginning of the new paragraph. As has already been discussed, Cycle 4, which starts at 12:1, is very particularly marked for special prominence, and this is another example of that phenomenon. In this case, the concept of 'a sign', which is the topic of the whole cycle, is brought immediately to the reader's attention by this prominence feature.

More recently, Levinsohn 2020,299, mentions how fronting can draw attention to the start of a whole new theme, which implies that it is the beginning of whole new major constituent of a discourse. However, at this point in his discussion he is more interested in establishing constituent boundaries, rather than in prominence per se.

A6.3.5 The Prominence Implications of Embedding

Embedding is the technical term used to describe a situation where an author embeds a particular text type into a discourse which is, for the most part, made up of a different text type. In many cases it is narrative which is embedded in another text type, because it is generally accepted that stories are more vivid and more memorable than other text types.

Heimerdinger 1999,247 cites an example from the OT of a story embedded in the middle of a chiasm which contributes a particular highlighting force to the message of the total textual unit to which it belongs. Once again, this kind of unusual disturbance in the normal flow of a discourse, and in the normal patterning of a linguistic structure, creates turbulence and, therefore, often occurs at peak points in the text. See Longacre 1983a,10-12.

This supports the contention set out in section 6.3.3 above, that the embedded narratives of Chapters 12-13 are a particularly important component of the overall message. These narratives not only disrupt the basic hortatory nature of the book, as established in the Prologue and in Cycle 1, but they also disrupt the flow of the Lamb's story, which had started in Chapter 4 and was continued right through to the end of the preceding Trumpets Cycle, which is Cycle 3.

A6.3.6 The Prominence Implications of the Use of *idou* 'behold' in Cycles 2-6
Another manifestation of special prominence in Cycles 2-6 is as follows: Cycle 2 has a series of three occurrences of *idou*, 'behold', at 6:2,5 and 8, which mark the first, third and fourth seal respectively.

The horse in the second seal is separately marked by the word 'another'. There would seem to be two possible explanations for this grouping of prominence markers. It could be drawing attention to the repetitive, numbered, list-like internal organization of the cycle. This, in turn, would confirm the norm established in Cycle 1, and prime the hearer's expectation regarding the intended organization of the cycles. Otherwise, it could be bringing attention to the repetition of the word 'horse', in readiness for its climactic reappearance at 19:11 where it is also marked by 'behold'.

The Textus Receptus has an extra 'behold' at 6:12, which suggests that at least one copyist had noticed the series earlier in the chapter and thought that it should be continued. More recent versions do not retain this occurrence of 'behold'. If this TR view of the text is correct it suggests that this marker in Chapter 6 is drawing attention to the series of horses rather than to the series of seals.

The use of 'behold' at 7:9 is the only occurrence in Chapters 6-12, apart from those in Chapter 6 discussed above, and those which contribute to the prominence of the woe passages (9:12 and 11:14) and the beginning of Chapter 12. In this isolated position and in its context, its function is not clear.

The most obvious hypothesis is that it is marking the great crowd for special attention. One could object that this is a bit unnecessary since the concept of a great crowd had already been evoked in 7:4-8, which just precedes it. In reply it could be countered that it must, therefore, be drawing attention to the fact that this great crowd was composed of all the nations, and not just the tribes of Israel. To put prominence on the crowd, which, in other terms, is the massed multitude of the redeemed saints, puts it in line with previous key words which were marked by 'behold'. These were, a door in Heaven (4:1), a throne in Heaven (4:2), and the Lion of the tribe of Judah in 5:5.

Apart from that hypothesis, it can only be that the presence of 'behold' here, suggests that the author was intentionally drawing attention to the double interlude by this means.

The two occurrences of 'behold' at 12:3 and 14:1 are almost certainly drawing attention to the two contrastive sets of protagonists of the first part of this cycle, the dragon and his followers, and the Lamb and His followers.

If this is so, then it strengthens the case for the fact that the followers of the Lamb needed to brought to our attention in 7:9, as discussed above. This is because both the Lamb, and also His followers, are the ones who overcome the dragon.

A6.3.7 The Prominence Implications of Evaluation

For the reasons explained above, that semantics is a new discipline, with a number of different pioneers, prominence has also sometimes been called 'salience'. So, for example, Heimerdinger was using already this term in his 1999 book.

An interesting point is when he argues at length 1999,240-59, that evaluation is an indicator of foregrounding which is a form of 'special salience' (p.240) or prominence. The key indicator of evaluation is that 'evaluation marks the interference of the speaker in the factual report' (p.241). This is exactly the same criterion (intrusion of the narrator into the text) as the one which has been used in this study to define the Narrative Framework.

Even though it has not been observed that the Narrative Framework is consistently used as a means of evaluating what has been recounted in the body of the text, nonetheless, it does happen. At 19:9-10 the fact that those who are called to the marriage supper previously referred to at 19:7, are blessed, clearly implies a positive evaluation of this event. In addition, the fact that John is specifically told again to write down this particular statement also has an evaluative implication that it is particularly important. There is further evaluation implicit in the expressive import command to not be afraid at 1:17, and in the warnings at 22:18-9.

If this line of reasoning were developed further, it could be argued that the Narrative Framework, in and of itself, is prominent even without the presence of the volitional import material.

A6.3.9 The Prominence Implications of the Volitional Schema

The introduction of the notion of the volitional schema and how that influences our views of prominence is a new, and quite revolutionary, step forward in our understanding of semantics.

The interested reader, therefore, is invited to pursue this topic further by consulting Longacre 1992,110, for his hortatory schema, Sherman and Tuggy 1994,7 for a resume of common volitional schemas and Callow 1998,191-2, for more detailed descriptions of different schemas.

The fact that volitional import text, or exhortations, can be communicated using different surface structure forms is explained in Callow 1998,191, where she refers to 'muted or subliminal' appeals. Sherman and Tuggy 1994,6-7 and Longacre 1983b also refer to mitigated exhortations when what is intended in the purpose of the author to be understood as a command, is not grammatically expressed by an imperative.

A6.3.10 The Prominence Implications of Numbers

Throughout this book many references have been made to numbers. Not just to the use of actual numbers in the text, but also to the number of times a particular feature is used, either in the book as a whole, or in a particular context. What has been called lexical chains, that is the repetition of a particular word or phrase, is one of the most obvious examples of this phenomenon. This is because key words are usually repeated a significant number of times as, for example, 3 times, 5 times or 7 times.

These references have been necessary just because there are such a large number of clearly observable occurrences, and other occurrences, which some may call ‘coincidences’. Therefore, in order to be consistent in talking about Revelation, some mention must be made of this phenomenon to be accurate, honest and complete.

So it is then, that most of these references to the numbering systems which are present in Revelation have only been made in passing, and have not been fully defended with detailed argumentation. This is because it is just not possible in the space which we have available, to explain and defend the importance of lexical chains in general, and the occurrence a certain number of times of an individual item, in particular.

However, in line with others who have observed this feature in biblical texts, it is assumed that this linguistic feature is significant for a full understanding of texts such as Revelation. It is assumed that the presence of a lexical chain with a significant number of components, must be adding prominence and semantic weight to the words and phrases concerned, or to the contexts in which they occur.

The interested reader is referred for more information on this topic to authors such as these. Please see, for example, Bauckham1993,29-37, Bliese 1993,210-26, Davis 1968, Hamilton 2023 and 2024, Terry 1992, Parunak 1983a,529-40 and Vallowe 1984.

An interesting example of this phenomenon is discussed in the following section.

A6.4 The Groups of Participants in Revelation

In the course of the discussion in the main text of Chapter 6, an explanation was given about the relative prominence of the different participants in the discourse. At that time only the seven principal, individual personages were discussed. So now, for the sake of completeness we will make mention of the groups of participants. At the same time, we will also make some interesting observations on the subject of numbers.

A6.4.1 A General Listing of the Groups of Participants

Here is a list of the groups of participants as they appear in order in the book.

- The people of God as they are referred to as the members of the seven churches 1:4-3:22. It is assumed for the sake of this study that this group is representative of the universal church at large. Consequently, the people referred to at 5:9, 7:3-17, 8:3, 12:11,17, 13:7, 14:1-5,12, 15:2, 17:14, 18:4, 19:1-8,14, 20:4-6, 21:1-7, 22:3-5,9,14,17 are considered to be the same group of people. In any case, there seems to be little additional value to be obtained by differentiating them further.
- The 24 Elders 5:6 et al., 19:4, who perhaps represent a larger heavenly parliament.
- The 4 Living Creatures 5:6 et al., 19:4, who perhaps represent all the creatures in heaven and earth as in 5:13.
- The dragon and the two beasts, and Babylon, Chapters 12,13 and 17.
- Many angels 5:11. See below for all the details on the angels.
- The horses and horsemen in Chapter 6.
- Death and Hades 6:8, 20:13.
- The kings, princes… every man of the earth 6:15, 9:4, 11:9-10,18, 13:7-8,16, 14:6, 15:4, 16:16, 17:2,8, 18:3,9-21, 19:17-21, 20:12-15, 21:8,24, 22:2.
- Locusts like scorpions 9:3.
- The 2 witnesses 11:3.
- The woman with child 12:1-6.

If this count is correct then there are eleven different groups of beings, human or otherwise, who participate in the various plots and sub-plots in Revelation. Regardless of your views on the symbolism of numbers in the Bible, it can hardly be overlooked that the numbers 24 (as for the 24 Elders), 4 (as for the 4 Living Creatures), and 2 (as for the 2 witnesses) are highly symbolic and significant in Scripture as a whole.

A6.4.2 Individual Angels and Groups of Angels as Participants in Revelation

Summary

Amazingly the word 'angel(s)' occurs **70 times** in Revelation, referring to good or bad angels. This includes 4 occurrences only occurring in the Textus Receptus. In terms of any specific, individual angel, who participates in the action of the book, **there are 50 of them,** as detailed below.

Detailed Count of the Individual Good Angels Only

Prologue

1 the one angel who brings the message to John

Cycle 1

7 The 7 angels of the 7 churches. Total 7. Plus the one from the Prologue, makes 8.

Cycle 2

1 A strong one who starts things off 5:2 (+ many in Heaven)
4 The 4 holding back the 4 winds 7:1 A Total of 5 different angels.

Cycle 3

7 The 7 Trumpet Angels 8:1
1 Another angel 8:3 A Total of 8 different angels.

Narrative Interlude

1 Another one, who held the little scroll in Chapter 10

Cycle 4

(Michael and his angels and the devil and his angels 12:7)
1 The one who proclaimed the eternal gospel 14:6
1 + a second one 14:8
1 + a third one 14:9
3 + 'another' one, three times 14:15,17, & 18. All of these in Signs 5 & 6
This makes a total of 6 different individual angels in this cycle, not counting Michael and his Cohort.

Cycle 5

7 The 7 Bowl Angels 15:1

Cycle 6

1 another one, 18:1. Otherwise, the other ones are counted as one of the Bowl angels, as at 16:5.

> Then specifically at 17:1 it is one of the Bowl angels, followed at 18:21 and 19:17 where they are said to be 'one' angel. This is taken to be a deliberate repetition of 'one' in 17:1, and so, therefore, refers to another 'one' of the bowl angels. In Greek, the first occurrence of 'one' is *heis,* which is the normal word for 'one', then the second time it is *hena.* In context, this means: 'one'..., and another 'one', with the noun being elided. These are the only places in the book, where it says 'one angel'.

Cycle 7

1 The angel who came to put the dragon in the pit 20:1
12 The 12 angels, one at each gate of the New Jerusalem 21:12

Epilogue

The very first angel from the Prologue reappears at 21:15, and 22:1,6,8 & 16 = 5 occurrences. This makes a total of 14 different angel occurrences in Cycle 7 plus the Epilogue together, but only 13 new ones.

TOTAL of all these definite positive occurrences = 49 = 7 x 7 !! So far, that is.

In addition: at 8:13 the Nestlé text has an eagle flying in heaven but in the TR it is another angel !!

So this would make 50 positive occurrences, if all are counted.

Then at 9:11, there is a bad'n mentioned (Abaddon), but he is only mentioned in passing and is not a direct participant in the book. However, if he were included that would be another way to make 50 !!

You are free to make of these numbers what you wish, but all I can say is that, over the many years during which I have studied this book, I have been constantly amazed. Constantly amazed at how even the smallest details fit together in a harmonious and coherent whole. It seems as if everything has a place and everything is in its place !

HIDDEN TREASURES

I was pushing a trolley with a few other people. It was some kind of dream or half-asleep, early morning impression. It was a flat-bed type trolley, an old fashioned kind, made of wood and solidly built, not like you would see today. There was something important on it, and we were clearly on a mission to take it somewhere. The object was medium sized but it was 'weighty' so that the trolley was quite heavy. Not so heavy that it was impossible to push, but it took a good effort, nonetheless.

The object was nondescript from the outside, like an old wooden box; yet it had some kind of shape to it that made you think that it was casket, but not ornamented or very pretty in any sense of the word. Just ordinary. But, nonetheless, I knew that there was a valuable treasure inside it. In addition, there were four Bibles placed on the four corners of the bed of the trolley, around the casket. They were big, old fashioned, leather bound family Bibles.

So we were on a mission, and were pushing the trolley at quite a rapid, determined pace down a fairly smooth but ordinary pathway. When suddenly we looked up and saw that there was, what appeared to be a big stone wall built right across the pathway from one side to the other, completely blocking it. Obviously, one's natural reaction would be to slow down a bit. But immediately, the Lord spoke very clearly. He said; 'No, don't stop; keep on going, and push on through. That is not a real wall, it is a fake wall, so keep going and push on through.'

So we kept on going and soon we were right up against the wall and about to crash into it. Then the Lord spoke again, 'Don't stop now, but push on through. Don't be afraid but trust me. I will take care of it.'

At that point, the trolley hit the wall and we immediately realized that it was a big sheet of glass, painted to look like a wall. Because the trolley was so heavy and solid it just smashed the glass to smithereens and we just went straight on through without any loss of momentum.

I share this story because it illustrates in graphic form what I experienced in writing this book, and what you, the reader, may be vicariously experiencing as you read it.

For me the casket on the trolley was clearly the book of Revelation. Rather nondescript on the outside, but clearly containing some hidden treasures on the inside. Our mission was to take these treasures where they needed to go. It was not an impossible task, but there were obstacles along the way, and perseverance and determination were required to complete the journey.

But the story is always the same. We have pushed on through. With the Master's help, the obstacles have always disappeared, and He has always pulled us through and given us success.

Life is like that and that is a timeless fact. Two thousand years ago, John received a similar message for the people of God: follow the Lamb wherever He goes, do what He says, and, above all else, keep on persevering. Press on through, regardless of the obstacles, whether real or imagined, and He will give you success.

It is a responsibility, but it is also a great honor and privilege to work together with the King, learning to rule and reign over all the obstacles that life throws at you. But I have found this process to be well worth all the time and all the effort invested.

I trust that you will find that to be true for yourself as well.

CHAPTER 7

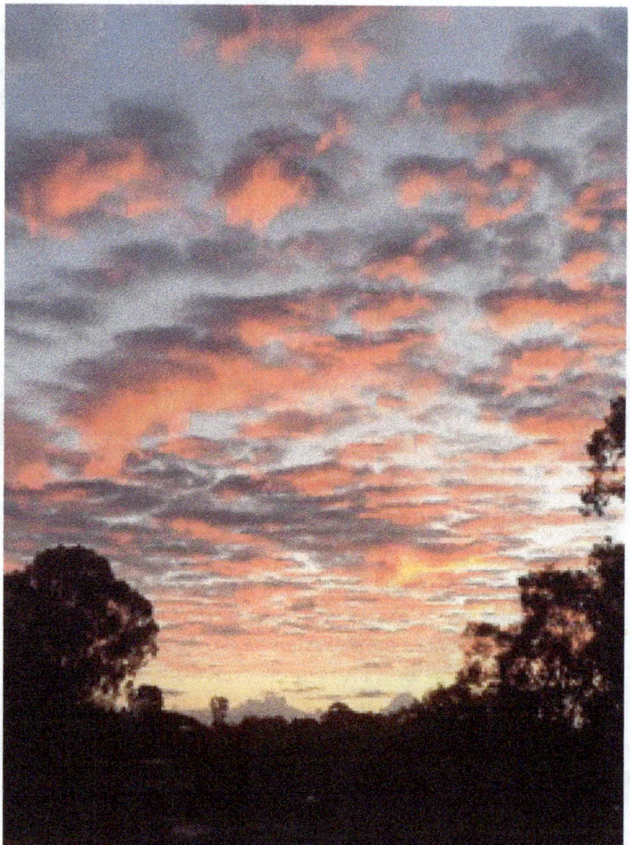

CHAPTER 7a

The Proof of the Analysis: The Harmony of the Macro Structure, the Topic and the Sub-Topics

7.1 The Story So Far and Where We Go From Here

The process of dismantling the text in order to define and investigate each of its parts has come to completion. This process has made it possible to go beyond the outward form of the surface structure, and to get a glimpse of the inner workings of the semantic structure.

In such a case as this, the proof of the analysis resides in the real life test as to whether it can all be successfully put back together again, such that it all still 'works' properly, with no inexplicable gaps, and no parts left unaccounted for. So, it is now time to put the pieces back together in order to obtain an overview of the behind the scenes workings of the text, and with the same, to gain a better understanding of how the various parts fit together to form a single, coherent whole. This understanding of the 'how' also leads, to some extent, to an understanding of *why* the text is presented in this form. However, a more detailed development of the implications of the structure for the overall message of the book, will only be presented in Chapter 8.

Firstly, the various components of the macro structure which have been discussed and explained in the previous chapters, will be brought back together in one place. This is in order to show how they all fit together, and relate to each other.

Secondly, we will revisit once more the notion of the topic of the book. This is because the topic is the most important part of the book, for, without it the book could never exist. Consequently, it is of considerable importance to state clearly what the topic is, to say everything which needs to be said about it, and to examine all its different facets.

Thirdly, some of the lower level detail of Cycle 1, Cycle 4 and Cycle 7 will be examined, in order to demonstrate that the macro structure does, in fact, harmonize with the micro structure. For the overall analysis of the book to be proved accurate, it needs to be demonstrated that there is no conflict or contradiction between it, and the lower level organization of the sentences and paragraphs, with which it is constructed.

Then finally, with the same goal in view, a few interesting, smaller details will also be presented, in order to make everything as complete as possible. Along with the data drawn from Cycles 1, 4 and 7, these smaller details will also be drawn from other parts of the book which are among the most prominent.

By consulting the following charts, the reader will now be able to look for any particular verse, which may be of interest to them, in the left hand column. Then by reading across to the central columns, you will be able to locate exactly where it fits in the macro structure of the book. Then, by consulting the right hand column, you will also be able to see what its precise function is, in the overall scheme of things.

7.2 An Overview of the Macro Structure

For ease of reference an overview of the organization of the whole book is laid out graphically on the following pages, in Charts 47a and 47b.

The main observation is that the macro structure of the book is organized according to three principal, hierarchical levels. The highest level is that of the book as a whole. The primary constituents of the book are the Prologue, the Epilogue, and the Seven Cycles. The next level down after the book level, is the level of the cycles, and these are composed of smaller constituents, which are generically called sub-units. The sub-units, in turn, are composed in semantic terms, of clusters, or groups, of propositions. In traditional grammatical terms these propositions are communicated by means of words, sentences and paragraphs.

Chart 47a provides, within the scope of one page, a summary of the entire infrastructure, so that it can be taken in without the distraction of all the finer details. At this highest, birds-eye-view, level of the book as a whole, it can be seen that the discourse is composed of a three-part ABA' structure. This is composed of the seven-part central body of the book (B.) bracketed by the Prologue (A.) and the Epilogue (A'). This creates nine major constituents in the book as a whole, with the introductory Prologue and the concluding Epilogue being obviously in parallel to each other.

This chart also displays the setting and closure of Cycles 2-6, as well as the chiastic structure of the Seven Cycles, which are the constituents of the body of the book (B.). In addition, the placement of the overlap links, and the complex Tail-Head links, is the most clearly laid out. These are the connections which glue together all the main nine constituents of the book. As a reminder, the detailed explanation of the Tail-Head links can be found in Chapters 3.6.3 and 5.4.4.

Chart 47b contains all the detail concerning the book down to the sub-unit level, and including the prominence features. The purpose of this chart is to display all the components of the book in one place, so that it is possible to locate and see any part of the book in its context. From there it can be discerned what its function is, and what part of the overall message which it carries. More information concerning the lay-out of the charts will be found in the text which follows them.

Chart 47a.
A Simplified Outline for the Whole Book of Revelation

Ref.	PROLOGUE	Function and/or Thematic Résumé
1:1-11		**Setting for the Whole Book** Initiates Narrative Framework & Volitional Import.

Ref.	BODY OF BOOK	Function and/or Thematic Resume
1:9-11	Over-lap Link Between the Prologue and Cycle 1	
1:9-3:22	**A. CYCLE 1**	**The Church Living in Earth-Bound Time**
	A Complex Tail-Head Link Connects Cycle 1 to Cycle 2	
4:1-5:14	**SETTING TO CYCLES 2-6** **Heaven is Opened to Reveal a Person Sitting on a Throne**	**Introduction to Cycles 2-6**
5:1-14	Over-lap Link Between the Setting of Cycles 2-6 and Cycle 2	
5:1-8:6	**B. CYCLE 2**	**The 7 Seals: Revelation of Judgment**
8:1-6	Over-lap Link Between Cycle 2 and Cycle 3	
8:1-11:19	**C. CYCLE 3**	**The 7 Trumpets: Warning of Judgment**
11:15-19	Over-lap Link Between Cycle 3 and Cycle 4	
11:15-16:1	**D. CYCLE 4**	**The 7 Signs: Explanation of Judgment**
15:1-16:1	Over-lap Link Between Cycle 4 and Cycle 5	
15:1-16:21	**C' CYCLE 5**	**The 7 Bowls: Consummation of Judgment**
16:17-21	Over-lap Link Between Cycle 5 and Cycle 6	
16:17-19:21	**B' CYCLE 6**	**The 7 Proclamations: Certainty of Judgment**
19:17-18	Overlap with the Closure of Cycles 2-6 by embedding Proclamation 7 within it	
19:11-21	**CLOSURE FOR CYCLES 2-6** **Heaven is Opened to Reveal a Person Sitting on a White Horse**	**Conclusion for Cycles 2-6**
	A Complex Tail-Head Link Connects Cycle 6 to Cycle 7	
20:1-22:7	**A' CYCLE 7**	**The Church Living in Timeless Eternity**
22:6-7	Over-lap Link Between Cycle 7 and the Epilogue	

Ref.	EPILOGUE	Function and/or Thematic Résumé
22:6-21		**Conclusion for the Whole Book** Concludes Narrative Framework & Volitional Import.

Chart 47b
A Complete Outline of the Whole Book of Revelation

Ref.	PROLOGUE	Function and/or Thematic Résumé
1:1-11**		**Setting for the Whole Book** Initiates Narrative Framework & Volitional Import.

1:9:22-7	BODY OF BOOK		
Reference	**Book Level**	**Sub-Units**	**Function and/or Thematic Résumé**
1:9-3:22**	**A. CYCLE 1** **The 7 Letters to the 7 Churches**		**The CONTEXT of the Book:** **The Church Living in Earth-Bound Time**
1:9-20		Setting	The Risen Christ Appears in Glory
2:1-7		Letter 1	a. The Letter to Ephesus
2:8-11		Letter 2	b. The Letter to Smyrna
2:12-17		Letter 3	c. The Letter to Pergamum
2:18-29		Letter 4	**d. The Letter to Thyatira**
3:1-6		Letter 5	c' The Letter to Sardis
3:7-13		Letter 6	b' The Letter to Philadelphia
3:14-22		Letter 7	a' The Letter to Laodicea
4:1-5:14**	**SETTING TO CYCLES 2-6** **Heaven is Opened to Reveal a Person Sitting on a Throne**		**Introduction to Cycles 2-6**
5:1-8:6**	**B. CYCLE 2**		**The 7 Seals: Revelation of Judgment**
5:1-14		Setting	Drama in the Heavenly Throne Room
6:1-2		Seal 1	The White Horse: Conquest
6:3-4		Seal 2	The Red Horse: Power to Remove Peace
6:5-6		Seal 3	The Black Horse: Partial Famine
6:7-8		Seal 4	The Dappled Gray Horse: Death and Hades
6:9-11		Seal 5	The Martyrs Appeal for Justice
6:12-17		Seal 6	Cosmic Catastrophes
7:1-17	**INTERLUDE**		**The Redeemed from all Nations** **are Sealed and Singing**
8:1-6		Seal 7	Overlap Link with the following cycle

BODY OF BOOK (cont.)

Reference	Book Level	Sub-Units	Function and/or Thematic Resume
8:1-11:19**	**C. CYCLE 3**		**The 7 Trumpets: Warning of Judgment**
8:1-6		Setting	Silence in the Heavenly Throne Room
8:7		Trumpet 1	A Third of the Earth was Burned Up
8:8-9		Trumpet 2	A Third of the Sea was Turned to Blood
8:10-11		Trumpet 3	A Third of the Rivers were Made Bitter
8:12		Trumpet 4	A Third of the Light Sources Darkened
8:13	Prominence Feature		1st Woe (A Warning)
9:1-11		Trumpet 5	Torment Released on the **UnSealed** People
9:12	Prominence Feature		2nd Woe (A Warning)
9:13-21		Trumpet 6	A Third of Humanity was Killed
10:1-11:2**	**Interlude of Narrative Framework**		**Perseverance is the Priority**
11:1-13	**INTERLUDE**		**Perseverance is the Price**
11:14	Prominence Feature		3rd Woe (A Warning)
11:15-19		Trumpet 7	Overlap Link with the following cycle
11:15-16:1**	**D. CYCLE 4**		**The 7 Signs: Explanation of Judgment**
11:15-19		Setting	Hubbub in the Heavenly Throne Room
12:1-18		Sign 1	The Woman with the Child
12:12	Prominence Feature (Embedded)		Exhortation & Warning 'Be Glad... Woe...'
12:1-18		Sign 2	The Great Red Dragon
13:1-10		Sign 3	The Beast Out of the Sea
13:11-18		Sign 4	The Beast Out of the Earth
14:1-5	**INTERLUDE**		**The Saved Singers Stand With the Lamb**
14:6-12		Sign 5	A Group of 3 Angels with Messages
14:13	Prominence Feature		Blessing in Narrative Framework
14:14-20		Sign 6	The Glorious Reaper with Angel Helpers
15:1-16:1		Sign 7	Overlap Link with the following cycle
15:1-16:21**	**C' CYCLE 5**		**The 7 Bowls: Consummation of Judgment**
15:1-16:1		Setting	Victory Songs in the Heavenly Throne Room
16:2		Bowl 1	Judgment Falls on the Beast Worshipers
16:3		Bowl 2	Judgment Falls on the Seas
16:4-7		Bowl 3	Judgment Falls on the Rivers
16:8-9		Bowl 4	Judgment Falls on the Sun
16:10-11		Bowl 5	Judgment Falls on the Beast & his People
16:12-16		Bowl 6	Judgment Falls on the Kings of the Earth
16:15	Prominence Feature (embedded)		Blessing with Warning implicit
16:17-21		Bowl 7	Overlap Link with the following cycle

BODY OF BOOK (cont.)

Reference	Book Level	Sub-Units	Function and/or Thematic Resume
16:17-19:21	**B' CYCLE 6**		**The 7 Proclamations: Certainty of Judgment**
16:17-21		Setting	Loud Voice & Noises from the Heavenly Throne Room, then Cosmic Catastrophes
17:1-18	Prominence: marks final suspense		Narrative Framework: Extra explanation re Babylon; Serves to slow down forward movement of Judgment Theme
18:1-3		Proclamation 1	a. An Angel: Babylon is Fallen !
18:4-8		Proclamation 2	b. A Voice from Heaven: Come Out...
18:9-10		Proclamation 3	c. The Kings of the Earth Weep...
18:11-17a		Proclamation 4	**d. The Merchants Weep Over Her**
18:17b-19		Proclamation 5	c' All the Sailors Weep Over Her
18:20	Prominence Feature		Command to 'Be Glad..'
18:21-24		Proclamation 6	b' A Mighty Angel: Never Again...
19:1-8	**INTERLUDE**		**The Wedding and the Worship**
19:9-10	Prominence Feature in Narrative Framework		Blessing with more exposition and exhortation
19:11-21	**CLOSURE FOR CYCLES 2-6**		**Conclusion for Cycles 2-6**
19:17-18		Proclamation 7 (embedded) a'	**Heaven is Opened to Reveal A Person Sitting on a White Horse**
20:1-22:7**	**A' CYCLE 7 The 7 New Things:**		**The CONCLUSION of the Book: The Church Living in Timeless Eternity**
20:1-15		Setting	The Defeated Devil Disappears in Disgrace
20:6	Prominence Feature		Blessing with Warning Implicit
21:1-22:7		Body	The 7 New Things
21:5b	Prominence Feature in Narrative Framework		Command to 'Write'
22:6-7**		Conclusion	These Words Are True: Keep Them

Ref.	EPILOGUE	Function and/or Thematic Resume
22:6-21		**Conclusion for the Whole Book** Concludes Narrative Framework & Volitional Import.

** The texts marked by ** are connected to the following unit by an overlap link.

NOTE: The reference 12:1-18 is correct following certain versions, and primarily because, from a linguistic point of view, 12:18 is the end of a semantic unit. Many translations incorrectly label it 13:1. Please bear this in mind when comparing the charts to source texts or translations in any other languages.

AN EXPLANATION CONCERNING THE ORGANIZATION OF CHARTS 47a AND 47b

Since the organization is rather complicated, a color coding system has been provided to clarify matters as much as possible. Each major constituent, therefore, has its own color. This means that, at a glance, you can see where it starts and where it ends, and where it is interrupted by other constituents. In this way, each cycle has its own color, and, where two cycles are in parallel with each other, for example Cycle 1 and Cycle 7, then they have been assigned the same color to demonstrate this parallelism.

Where an interlude, or a prominence feature, interrupts the linear flow, then this can be seen immediately, by means of the different colors which are used, being green for the interludes and yellow for the prominence features. The colors which go right across the page, from the reference column on the left to the far right, indicate that the units concerned are book level features.

The positioning of the references has the same purpose. Those which are positioned to the left of the reference column, indicate a text which is operating at the book level. Those which are positioned to the right of the reference column, indicate a text which is operating at the cycle level.

It is in the context of a chart like this, that a number of smaller parts of the text which do not fit neatly into their immediate context (e.g. 8:13; 9:12; 11:14; 14:13; 16:15 and 18:20), find their raison d'être. These small parts have been analyzed as prominence features operating at the book level. When these parts are studied in isolation it is difficult to discern why they should have been placed in the context where they are found. It is not self-evident why they should have been included in the book at all, since they contribute little to the informational import of their immediate context.

However, when they are seen as contributing to the impact of the message of the book as a whole, then it is much easier to understand how they fit into the whole, and also why they occur in that particular place in the text. Those occurring in the first half of the book bring to attention the peak of the book, which is Cycle 4. Those occurring in the latter half, highlight the volitional nature of the book and prepare the way for the conclusion.

The larger constituent parts of the structure of the book will be reviewed in the following sections.

7.2.1 The Narrative Framework

The book gives the impression of being a narrative, yet closer inspection reveals that it is not a true narrative, but an exhortation with many expository components. Consequently, it is not structured according to events on a time-line, but rather according to topics on a theme-line as the charts, which are laid out above, illustrate.

The reason why the book appears to be in narrative form is because the volitional and informational content is linked together by a Narrative Framework which begins with the Prologue, ends with the Epilogue, and reoccurs periodically throughout the book. This framework provides a general context for the narrator's prophetic experience, and also provides a sequential progression, within which his visions are recounted.

7.2.2 The Seven Cycles of Seven

The body of the book is composed of seven cycles which relate to each other in a parallel, chiastic arrangement. Each of the cycles is dominated by a different seven-fold motif, most of which are developed in linear form. However, this is not an obligatory condition, and so there is slight variation in Cycle 4, and quite a different organization of the motif in Cycle 7.

The motifs, which are self-evidently the primary unique characteristic of each cycle, form the basis upon which a chiastic structure can be discerned. Each cycle is introduced by a setting and the last one is completed by a conclusion. In complement to that basic structure, four of the central cycles contain an interlude which develops the Salvation Theme, which is in direct contrast to the Judgment Theme of the co-occurring seven-fold motifs.

7.2.3 The Interludes and Themes

The two primary themes of the book have been labeled the Judgment and Salvation Themes. As would be expected, both are introduced in the first cycle and brought to a final conclusion in the last cycle. In between, in Cycles 2-6, the Judgment Theme is dominant in terms of quantity, being brought to the hearers' attention by the seven-fold motifs. However, this is counterbalanced by the Salvation Theme which occurs in the more prominent interludes.

7.2.4 The Structural Complexities

It is not surprising that in a discourse of this length there are some complexities. However, these complexities are not just redundant features. In actual fact they reinforce the message in subtle ways, as well as contributing to the structural patterns of the book.

The Overlap Links

The most pervasive complexity is the phenomenon of overlap links. This term describes the situation where a single unit of text serves, at the same time, as both the conclusion of one unit and also the setting or the introduction to the following unit. The Prologue is attached to what follows, and the Epilogue to what precedes by this means, and the whole group of Cycles 2-6 are joined together in this way.

This feature supports the contention that the book is not just a collection of discrete visions but is an organic whole. It was clearly intended from the outset to be read and understood as a complete unit.

The overlap links can be easily located in Chart 47a above, and in Chart 47b they can be located by means of the double asterisks.

The Unity of Cycles 2-6

The chiastic nature of the macro structure leads to the expectation that the first and last cycles should be in parallel, and inspection of the content confirms that this is the case. This is because they both concern the Church in its complementary situations of physical life on earth, and spiritual, new-birth life, as seen from the heavenly point of view.

By contrast, Cycles 2-6 present various aspects of God's plan of judgment, with the Church and the Salvation Theme being developed in some detail in the interludes. This proposition that Cycles 2-6 be viewed as a separate unit, is further confirmed by the fact that they have their own setting and conclusion. It is of note that the structure of the highest levels of the discourse creates similar patterns.

So, the book has a setting, body and conclusion in an ABA' format, while the body (B), of the book also has this same structure. Thus, Cycle 1 is the introduction, or setting for the body, while Cycle 7 is its conclusion. Similarly, Cycles 2-6, which is the center part (B) of the body of the book, also has the same ABA' (setting-body-conclusion) structure.

The structure of the individual cycles is a variation on the same theme. The first cycle being the introduction to the body has no conclusion, whereas Cycle 7 being the conclusion to the body also has its own conclusion. Cycles 2-5 have a conclusion which is at the same time a setting for the following cycle, while Cycle 6's conclusion is embedded in the conclusion for Cycles 2-6 as a complete unit.

The Chiastic Structure

The chiastic structure overlays the whole of the rest of the structural features and, consequently, influences the interpretation of different parts of the whole in different ways, as has already been illustrated in the preceding summaries. However, the most important contribution which it makes is in the domain of prominence, since its presence makes it clear that the central, fourth cycle must be specially prominent relative to the other cycles.

Patterns of Prominence

In a way that is consonant with its structural complexities, the book also has a complex pattern of prominence. Cycle 7, being the conclusion of the body, is the point of greatest natural prominence at the informational level. This is because, it is at this point where the principal themes are brought to conclusion, and the hearers' curiosity the most fully satisfied.

At the same time, numerous special features indicate that Cycle 4, the Signs Cycle, is the most specially prominent, thereby drawing special attention to the explanations which are presented in that cycle. However, there is also a volitional schema, which is more important than the informational schema. This creates another strand of prominence which links the Prologue, Cycle 1, Cycle 4 and the Epilogue, as well as smaller parts in between. This point will be reviewed further in the next section.

The Hortatory Intent

The ultimate importance of a discourse is directly related to its primary purpose. In the case of Revelation it is clear that the author's main purpose is to exhort the hearers, in order to influence their decisions and their way of life. This intention is made clear in the Prologue and the Epilogue in particular, although most of the elements of the Narrative Framework contribute in some way, to the volitional schema and the hortatory intent of the author.

This means that the Narrative Framework is not just a convenient structural convention, but is also an essential component in communicating the main point of the author's message. This is also why Cycle 1 has a particularly important place in the book as a whole. Introductions can be important in their own right, although they are not usually more important than their matching conclusion. However, in this case, the cycle of the Seven Letters contains the primary exhortations to repent and persevere, to which the divine author wants his hearers to respond positively.

For this reason, it is the head of the volitional schema, while all the rest of the book is support for these principal exhortations. This hortatory intent then, is the most important aspect of all the different aspects of the book, and the most complete expression of why the author undertook this communication enterprise.

7.2.5 The Final Word on the Analysis

As far as the story of this present stage of study is concerned, the process of analysis is complete. It is not complete in an absolute sense, since more could be done to explore additional aspects of the structure, especially at the micro level. This part of the task will be taken up in the following sections of this chapter. However, exploration of the macro level in terms of taking the text apart (dividing it into units) and putting it back together again (proposing how the parts relate to each other and to the whole), has been taken as far as is possible, for the moment.

The features in favor of the resultant description are that all the units of text which are candidates for analysis at the macro level have been accounted for – none have had to be displaced, ignored, or otherwise explained away, in order to accommodate the analysis. On the contrary, the analysis has demonstrated that, far from being incoherent, Revelation has a very coherent and reasonable structure. It may not appear very coherent to anyone reading it solely from the point of view of modern, western traditions, but, as we have been trying to make clear throughout this study, the book was written a long time ago in the context of ancient middle-eastern traditions. Viewed from that perspective, it is very coherent and very skillfully constructed.

Within the context of this structure, each part has its place, and its contribution to make to the overall message. Furthermore, as questions of the function of some of the key parts of the structure have been explored, it has been possible to at least propose why the author placed those particular constituents, in that particular place in the discourse. This, in turn, provides insight into the whole question of intentionality – what the author intended to communicate, and to accomplish, by means of this particular discourse in this particular form.

Following Callow's expressed hope (1999,406) 'that discussion of differing structures will be solidly based on the linguistic data, and accepted, rejected or modified on that basis', an attempt has been made to do that as fully as possible. Therefore, every effort has been made to ensure that the interpretations are subordinate to the data, which can be observed in the text itself, rather than to subjective impressions, personal opinions, or pre-existing theological commitments.

This is because, as Callow 1999,ibid., goes on to explain:

> If the analysis contradicts the data, it is wrong; if it does not account for all the data, it is still inadequate; if it goes beyond the data, that is, it is not supported by the data, it is speculative.

Despite all the precautions which may be observed, any of the above inadequate scenarios are possible, and so it would be helpful for the analysis presented in the previous chapters to be reviewed by others. This is so that those parts, which have stood the test of independent scrutiny, may be used with confidence to influence future exegesis of this important book. Then, in the case of those parts which do not pass the test, those aspects of the analysis may be modified in appropriate ways, so that they, in due time, may also be helpfully influential.

Significant parts of the above analysis are new in that the process has asked different questions and, consequently, has produced results which differ in a number of ways from the traditional way of viewing this book. As such, it is to be expected that it may produce as many negative reactions as positive ones, and for the same reason it may take time for the results to be assimilated and eventually to be accepted.

This is viewed as a positive and necessary process as long as it is pursued in good faith. As Reed 1999,62 puts it:

> The results of such New Testament linguistic research, of course, will not go without challenge. When linguistic analysis supports common belief, many reply that 'everyone knows that'. When it provides an unexpected finding, the response is that 'you can prove anything with linguistics'. Rather than respond in isolationism, those who are convinced that New Testament interpretation necessitates an analysis of a text's lexico-grammar must be explicit about their linguistic method and apply it to actual texts (preferably whole texts...) so that it may be critiqued and improved upon or discarded.

This study has sought to respect the conditions which Reed has proposed as an appropriate way forward, and it is to be hoped that those who may study it, and even critique it, will do so in the same spirit.

However, even when this has been accomplished, it will still not be the end of the journey, for a study of the structure of a book can never truly be an end in itself, but simply a means to an end, and this end is to influence and constrain any subsequent interpretation. Axiomatic to this study is the truism that people do not make the effort to create a complex discourse like Revelation for no reason at all, but on the contrary, they do so with a clear purpose in mind. The purpose of the writer of this book at the outset then was to influence the original recipients of his work. These were the people who would read it, and also those who would hear it read. The author's aim was to encourage them to make every effort to live according to God's eternal purpose for them, and, from there, to fully benefit from the blessings, which He had prepared for them to enjoy, both in the here and now and also for all eternity.

Continuing in this same train of thought then, the purpose of the present study of discourse structure is that modern-day readers may better understand the message of Revelation. The goal is to permit the original author's intended purpose to be optimally accomplished even in this day and age. It is to be hoped then, that the linguistic features of this book which have been presented, will serve to facilitate the understanding, and enhance the appreciation, which future hearers and readers of the message of Revelation may have. May it be that this, in turn, will fulfill a practical purpose for all those who have ears to hear, for

> Whoever reads the word of this prophecy will be blessed, and those who not only pay attention to what is written in it, but also take it to heart, will be blessed even more, because the time available to respond is now very short. Rev.1:3.

7.3 A Review of the Topic of the Book

In Chapter 4.2.1 the issue of the topic of the book was previewed. At that point, it was proposed that the topic of the book is the 'revelation' given by God to John, which showed him what God's plans are for this world and for the world to come.

Then, in Chapter 6.8, we took another step along this path of exploring the various facets of the topic, by looking at it again in the context of the most prominent parts of the discourse. On this occasion, it was pointed out that Jesus is really and truly the topic of the book, because He is the focus of the revelations given by God. In addition to Him being the subject of the revelations, Jesus is a participant who is prominent just because of who He is, and this important detail should not be overlooked.

For these reasons then, the topic, Jesus, in this case, was explored through the lens of everything else which is prominent in the book. This produced a surprising, but very enlightening, ten part description of the person, and of the accomplishments, of Jesus the Messiah. Since the number 10 is symbolic of a testimony, we could also say that this is a testimony abut Jesus .

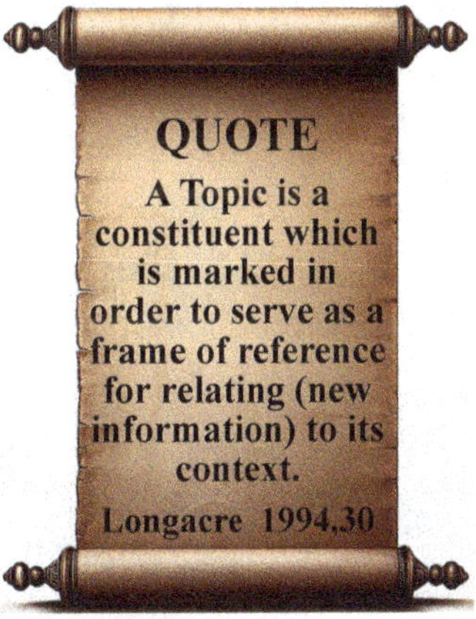
QUOTE
A Topic is a constituent which is marked in order to serve as a frame of reference for relating (new information) to its context.
Longacre 1994,30

So now, in this following discussion, we are going to review the topic for a third time. The goal this time is to pick up on the broad notion of a revelation, and explore how its roots go down into the deeper parts of the book. In short, it will be found that the broad, upper-level, notion of the topic, connects very harmoniously and specifically, with the detailed outworking of the topic at the sentence and paragraph levels.

7.3.1 The Detailed Development of the Topic of 'a Revelation'

As indicated in the discussions cited above, the topic of a text does not need to reoccur overtly on many occasions. Nonetheless, evidence that the topic is maintained and carried through to the end of the discourse ought to be discernible. The principal features on the micro level which demonstrate that the topic of a 'Revelation of God's Plan for the World' is maintained throughout the book will be presented in this section.

The principal lexical items which allude to the topic of the book are 'a revelation... (of God)' in 1:1, 'the mystery of God' in 10:7, and 'the words of God' in 17:17. Verbs which co-occur with the above lexical items are the verbs 'to happen' and 'to finish'. Both these verbs have a meaning which is relevant to the concept of a plan.

The texts where the verb 'to happen' co-occurs with references to what God is doing, or saying, are as follows:

- 1:1 A Revelation of/about Jesus the Messiah, which God gave to him to show to His servants, (namely) the things which *are due to happen soon.* John was witness to (this) word of God sent by His angel.
- 1:19 The things which *are about to happen*, after this
- 4:1 The things which *are due to happen* after this
- 11:15 The world's kingdoms *have become* God's and Christ's kingdoms, and He will reign for ever (i.e. timelessly: for all time and for eternity)
- 12:10 Now, the salvation, the power, the Kingdom of God, and the authority of His Christ *has happened* (or *become*)
- 21:6 God said: '*It has happened*'

  (Note: literally the Greek is: 'These things (implied) have happened', i.e. a finished, completed work of things, plural)
- 22:6 These words are reliable and true, which the Lord God sent His angel to show to His servants, (namely) the things which *are due to happen soon*
- 1:18 I (Jesus) am the first and the last, the alive one; I *was* (same verb: 'to happen') dead, and *have now become* (same verb: 'to happen' implied but elided and replaced by a synonym) alive for ever (i.e. timelessly: for all time and for eternity)

  (Note: the occurrence of this same verb in 16:17 is interpreted as only referring to the pouring out of the bowls, and not to the totality of God's plan. Consequently, this reference is not included in the above list.)

7.3.2 The Detailed Development of the Topic of a Revelation Based on the Verb 'To Happen'

The verb listed above is *ginomai* in Greek, which can have various meanings in English like 'to become', 'to happen', or even simply, 'to be'. It is used many times in Revelation but these are the occurrences which are relevant to our discussion about the topic.

As you can see in the above list, there are seven very similar references, which have to do with the things which God revealed to John. If we look closely, we can see that the parallels are such that they create a chiasm, as displayed in Chart 48.

Sub-units **A.** and **A'** are clearly parallel to each other, based on multiple similarities, and the verb phrases, in particular, are identical. In sub-unit **B.** it is a generic statement (the things), and the happening is still future. In **B'** the happening has emphatically happened, for the verb is in the perfect past tense. In the context of Cycle 7, where it occurs, we know specifically what it is that has happened. This movement from generic to specific is something which occurs elsewhere in the book, notably in Cycle 7.

In sub-unit **C.** the happening is still future, as are all the sub-units in the first half of the complete structure, and it is also generic in nature. In sub-unit **C'** the happening has happened, just like in sub-unit **B',** the only difference being that the past tense is communicated by a slightly less emphatic aorist verbal form in the Greek. It also specifically tells us exactly what the things are which were due to happen.

Chart 48.

Chiasm of the Topic Based on the Verb *ginomai* 'to Happen'

A. 1:1 A Revelation of/about Jesus the Messiah, which God gave to him to show to His servants, (namely) the things which ***are due to happen*** soon. John was witness to (this) word of God sent by His angel.

> **B.** 1:19 The things which ***are about to happen,*** after this
>
> > **C.** 4:1 The things which ***are due to happen*** after this
> >
> > > **D. 11:15 The world's kingdoms have become God's and Christ's;**
> > > **He will reign for ever (i.e. timelessly)**
> >
> > **C'** 12:10 Now, the salvation, power, the Kingdom of God, the authority of Christ ***has happened (or become)***
>
> **B'** 21:6 God said: ***'It has happened'*** (a finished, completed work)

A' 22:6 These words are reliable and true, which the Lord God sent His angel to show to His servants, (namely) the things which ***are due to happen soon.***

But then we come to sub-unit **D.** (11:15), which is, of course, the center of the chiasm and the most prominent part of the complete set. There are several things which this sub-unit tells us, as follows:

- It specifically links everything back to Jesus, who was set out as the topic of the book, and of this topical thread in **A.** (1:1).

- It provides the specific elements of God's plan, which had only been presented in general terms up until then. Those specific elements are that God's plan is for Jesus to take over all the world's kingdoms, and that He will reign as supreme authority, from then on, and for ever.
- Yet, at the same time, this is only a generic statement, because the four specific facets of this rule over the earth, are laid out in the following sub-unit, **C'** (12:10).
- In these two sub-units (**D.** and **C'**), the aorist verbal form is used. By convention this is interpreted as implying a past tense, so this means that, whereas everything was previously still in the future, from constituent **D.** onward, God's plan is now viewed as having already been accomplished. In more general terms, the aorist form focuses on the actual events described rather than the timing of the event. This is very appropriate considering the specific information which is communicated in these units. By contrast, the verb in **B'** (21:6) is in the perfect aspect which brings more into focus the actual past timing of the events in view.
- The above statement in **D.** is at the very beginning of the setting to the Signs Cycle. This is another example of the settings in the book being given unusual extra prominence. In this case, it also increases the prominence of the whole cycle. Then, in addition, the whole of the rest of the setting continues to confirm and add extra details concerning Christ's eternal reign.
- This setting brings together the two themes, entwined in one statement (11:17-18): references to both the judgment foreseen on the rebellious nations, and the salvation or reward, promised for God's people. The connection between them is the fact that God, through Jesus, has taken up His right to reign over the earth.

However, there is an eighth occurrence of the same verb at 1:18, but the reference is slightly different. This should not surprise us as it is an example of the 7+1 principle (which creates an eighth), as we have already seen in previous discussions.

This reference is included in this list for several reasons. Firstly, it is because it is about Jesus and He is always going to be prominent, being the topic of the book. It is the first use of the verb in reference to Him after His introduction in 1:1. It is the first, of only a very few occurrences in the book, when He speaks directly for Himself, and about Himself. By the repetition of this verb, He makes an indirect, but, nonetheless, a very clear, connection between the 'happening' of God's plan, and the fact that He 'happened' to have died, but was now alive again. It is for the same reason that I have 'happened' to use various forms of the word 'happen' throughout this discussion, in order to make the repetition of this thread obvious in English, just as much as it is in the Greek.

So it is that, the specific context of the use of this verb is different in this case, compared to the previous seven. Yet, at the same time, it is clearly referring to the topic of the book and so belongs in this topical thread. It belongs with the seven, and yet it is different, which makes it a good candidate to be an 'eighth'. Furthermore, this example of an 'eighth' is all about a new beginning, after a significant ending.

7.3.3 The Detailed Development of the Topic of a Revelation Based on the Verb 'To Finish'

In addition, to the previous seven references based on the verb 'to happen', there are two more references to God's plan based on the verb 'to finish'. These are:

- 10:7 The Mystery of God is/was *finished* (aorist verb: tense is therefore ambiguous)
- 17:17 The Words of God will be *finished* (future tense)

All together then, these references to the topic of the book occur at the very beginning of the book, and close to the very end, and there are nine of them. This detail is consonant with other book level features previously encountered.

In between these two extremities, the thread reappears regularly throughout the book, and always in contexts which are already prominent for other reasons. This is exactly what you would expect in a case like this, where the topic is regularly being re-activated and having significant thematic material attributed to it.

In the case of the occurrence in 10:7, we are told that this mystery revealed by God to his servants, the prophets, will be accomplished at the time when the seventh trumpet is blown. In Chapter 6 it was explained how various prominence features alert the reader to this fact, that something important will happen at the time of the seventh trumpet.

In this verse we are told generically what that something important is: it is that God's plan will be accomplished and finished. When this generic 'something' is put in the context of the other topical threads, we can state without any shadow of doubt, that, in specific terms, the accomplishment of God's plan is completely integrated with the fact of Jesus taking His authority to reign on the earth, as per 11:15 and 12:10.

In 17:17 we are given an extra piece of information about this accomplishment of God's plan. We are told that when this plan is accomplished, that is to say, when Jesus is authorized to take over the power of the world's kingdoms, another important event will take place. The beast, who as the dragon's proxy had been able to rule the earth up until then, will be defeated and dethroned *at the same time*. So it is then, that by the same event (the fact that He was dead, and is now alive again), and at the same time, Jesus will start to reign, and the beast's reign will also be brought to an end.

Further examination reveals that the verb 'to finish' also occurs in 15:1 and 15:7-8 with reference to the anger/plagues of God. In the context of this verb it is clear that the plagues expressing God's anger are part of His plan, and so these texts also make reference to the main topic of the book. These texts can be treated as two separate occurrences of the same collocations, but since they form an *inclusio* around a complete unit of text (15:1-8), it is probably more revealing to treat this reference as a complete complex unit, with two parallel references to the same concept cluster, framing the complete sub-unit.

Chart 49.
A Chiasm of the Topic Based on the Verb 'to Finish'

A. A Revelation about Jesus the Messiah, which God gave to… to show to His servants, (namely) the things which ***are due to happen soon*** 1:1

B. The Mystery of God ***is/was finished*** 10:7

C. The Plagues/Anger of God ***are finished*** (two occurrences) 15:1-8

B' The Words of God ***will be finished*** 17:17

A' These words, (which) God sent… to show to His servants, (namely) the things which ***are due to happen soon*** 22:6

If these four occurrences of 'to finish' are integrated into a simplified form of the topical thread previously described, another chiastic arrangement can be perceived, as portrayed in Chart 49. This is another example of a complementary analysis of the same basic data.

A and A' are in parallel because of the verb 'to happen'. These two infinitives are in the aorist aspect, with a future sense implied by the context, i.e. the events are not yet accomplished.

B and B' are in parallel because of the presence of the verb 'to finish'. The first occurrence is in the aorist with a future, imperfect sense implied by the context, (i.e. the events are not yet accomplished), while the second occurrence is in the future form, which projects forward to a time when the events will have been accomplished. In addition, the lexical items 'the mystery of God' and 'the words of God' are in parallel since they both refer to the underlying concept of God's plan.

The central unit (C) also has 'to finish' in the aorist on both occasions (15:1 and 15:8). On the first occasion the completion of God's anger is potential, but is not yet actualized, since the plagues are being prepared and have not yet been poured out. On the second occasion, although the plagues have still not been poured out, the verb in its context projects forward again to a time when they will have been completed. Since it is larger, and more complex, than the other units, C is a natural candidate for being the central, and therefore, the most important part of a chiasm.

It can be seen then, that even though there are only five references in this particular display, there are a total of nine overt references to the topic of the book, when all the references are counted. As mentioned previously, these references create a remarkably systematic thread which maintains the presence of the topic of the book (a revelation or mystery) in an overt way.

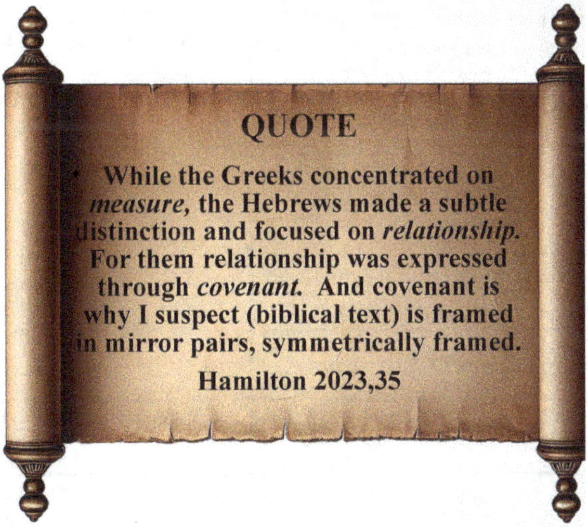
QUOTE
While the Greeks concentrated on *measure,* the Hebrews made a subtle distinction and focused on *relationship.* For them relationship was expressed through *covenant.* And covenant is why I suspect (biblical text) is framed in mirror pairs, symmetrically framed.
Hamilton 2023,35

The most notable feature is the fact that these references are not only in parallel to one another, which is not totally surprising seeing that they refer of necessity to the same underlying concept, but that they also create a clear chiasm as demonstrated above. Actually it is not just one chiasm, but there are, in fact, two complementary ones, as illustrated by Charts 48 and 49 above. This is intriguing, and further analysis and interpretation of these chiasms, could lead to some pertinent theological insights. We will explore these possibilities a little more at the end of this section. But, before we do that, let's just note, in more detail, how this topical thread intertwines with most, if not all, of the prominent parts of the book.

As mentioned above, the most obvious references to the topic occur right at the beginning of the book, in the Prologue (1:1), and at the beginning of the Epilogue (22:6) which is the conclusion for the whole book. It is notable that these two passages along with the Central Interlude (10:7) are all major components of the Narrative Framework, while 17:17 is the last, and the largest, of the minor components of the framework. This phenomenon supports the view presented in Chapters 2 and 6 above, that the Narrative Framework has an important supportive role for the book as a whole.

Chart 50.
References to the Topic of the Book

1:1	A Revelation of/about Jesus the Messiah which God gave	**THE PROLOGUE**
1:18	I (Jesus) *was* dead and *have now become* alive for ever	**THE PROLOGUE**
1:19	The things which *are about to happen* after this	**THE SETTING TO CYCLE 1**
4:1	The things which *are due to happen after this*	**THE SETTING TO CYCLES 2-6**
10:7	The Mystery of God is/was *finished*	**NARRATIVE FRAMEWORK INTERLUDE**
11:15	The world's kingdoms *have become God's and Christ's kingdom and He will reign for ever and ever*	**TRUMPET 7** which is **THE SETTING TO CYCLE 4 – The Signs Cycle**
12:10	The salvation, power, Kingdom... and authority of Christ *has happened*	**SIGN 2**
15:1-8	The Plagues/Anger of God are *finished*	**SIGN 7**
17:17	The Words of God will be *finished:*	**NARRATIVE FRAMEWORK COMPONENT**
21:6	God said: '*It has happened*'	**THE MOST PROMINENT PART OF CYCLE 7**
22:6	These words are reliable and true which the Lord God sent His angel to show to His servants (namely) the things which *are due to happen soon*	**THE EPILOGUE**

In addition to the beginning, the middle and the end of the Narrative Framework, the other places where the topic is, either overtly or covertly, referred to, are in the Signs Cycle and in Cycle 7. These cycles, of course, are the most naturally and the most specially prominent of all the cycles. All that leaves are the settings of Cycle 1 and Cycles 2-6, which are part of the series of specially prominent settings, which introduce the topic, as explained in Chapter 6. Apart from that, 11:15 is immediately preceded in 11:14 by a prominence feature which points forwards, and 12:10 is followed in 12:12, by a prominence feature which points backwards. See Chart 50 for the references and a summary of the content.

These observations lead to the conclusion that the linguistic organization of this feature of the book is systematic. There is a clear sense that, whether it was accomplished consciously or unconsciously, the author leads the reader along a clear path towards his final destination. In this case, references to the main topic of the book are placed in a systematic way, in strategic places, so that at each significant moment; the reader knows what the author is talking about.

The result is a textual thread which weaves its way through the whole discourse, thereby knitting everything together into a coherent and harmonious whole. Exactly where this thread appears, in observable form, in the surface structure is indicated in the list which is laid out above.

This study of these micro issues confirm two of the major assumptions underlying this study, that discourses in general, and Revelation in particular, are organized in a systematic way. The result is that this organization can be analyzed and described, by means of appropriate linguistic tools. This means, that even though the analysis of a complex discourse such as this is a challenge, it is by no means impossible. Consequently, careful study of each, and any, of the components of the discourse, whether large or small, will reveal their own treasures of truth and insight.

7.3.4 The Theological Implications of this Discussion of the Topic

In the previous parts of this discussion of the topic of the book we have identified all the smaller items in the surface structure where the reader is reminded of, and instructed about, what the author has in mind as he is writing. So this, in turn, leads to the all important semantic question. How does this organization influence the meaning of the message, and constrain our understanding of what it is all about?

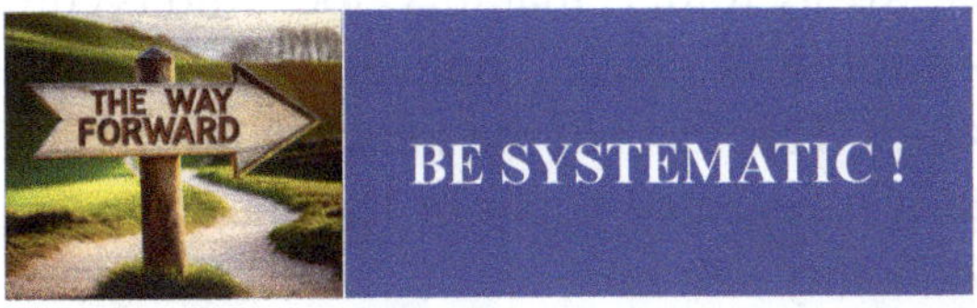
THE WAY
FORWARD
BE SYSTEMATIC !

The way forward is to copy the author's example and to be systematic, without rushing, and without hastily skipping over important parts of the puzzle.

A couple of principles drawn from general knowledge of how discourses work, and also from particular examples of what we have found in Revelation so far, can guide us in this task. They are as follows:

- The most important facets of the topic will be established at the beginning.
- These are likely to be repeated, in order to make the point clear.
- Less important facets of the overall message are not likely to appear at the beginning
- These will be included much later than the important facets.
- The basic topic will be consolidated with an accumulation of details as the discourse progresses
- In the case of Revelation, we have noticed that there is often movement from generic statements about the topic, or sub-topic, to subsequent revelation of the specific facets of the topic.
- There is likely to be some linear development as the discourse progresses.

So let's systematically work through the list of eleven surface structure appearances of this topical thread, as laid out in the previous section.

The Introduction of the Topic 1:1-4

We can see that, naturally enough, the topic is first set out in the Prologue. It is stated in generic terms in the very first line in 1:1. Here we are told that this book is all about a revelation of information which God gave to His people, via his servant John, about Jesus the Messiah, or the Christ. This information was communicated in words, which were then to be written down by John, as indicated in verses 2-3. Once this, and other, generic statements have been communicated in 1:1-4a, then the author moves on immediately to start providing some specific details about the main topic.

The Primary Position of God the Father 1:1 and 1:4

The first details are actually about God the Father, in the first instance, and this fact should not be overlooked. Ultimately, it is God Himself who is the most important part of the topic, and the most important participant in the whole book, for He is the supreme authority over all things, and He is the source of everything else which we are told. So it is then, that the very first specific thing which we are told, is that this God, who is communicating His revelation to us, is a spiritual, eternal, timeless being, who always was, and always will be (1:4b-c). This facet of the treasures which are being revealed, is so important that it is repeated again in 1:8, thereby creating an *inclusio* for this whole introductory sub-unit.

The Centrality of Jesus, the Messiah 1:1 and 1:5-6

But in the next breath Father starts talking, through John, about Jesus. This is totally in line with what we would expect from the rest of the Bible. Our Heavenly Father does not take up much time and space to talk about Himself, but instead, we can see that He wants to get on and talk about His favorite subject, which is His Son, Jesus.

In verses 5-6 these are the things which are revealed about Jesus:

- He is The Faithful Witness
- He is The First-Born from the dead
- He is The Ruler of the kings of the earth
- He is The One who loves us
- He is The One who set us free from the bondage of our sins by His blood (death)
- It is He who made us to be kings and priests for the Father
- It is He who is worthy of glory and praise

By a remarkable coincidence, we were told basically three things (or perhaps five things) about the Father in verse 4, but then we are told seven things about Jesus in verses 5-6, plus an eighth. This eighth item is that He is coming again, and it is added on the end like a coda in verse 7. Of course, His second coming will usher in a whole new beginning after the closure of this current age, which we now live in.

The seven attributes listed above do, of course, contribute new information about the main topic of the revelation, which is Jesus, but these are still very generic in nature. They are only brief allusions to seven facets of who He is. Consequently, we have to add the specifics on the basis of the Gospels, which are also about Him, and on the basis of the specifics which are supplied later on in Revelation itself.

So then, the fact that He is *The* Faithful Witness, must refer to His time on earth when He faithfully revealed, and bore witness to, the Father and His Kingdom. The fact that He is The First-Born from the dead obviously must refer to His death and resurrection. As a consequence of that, He has become The Ruler of the kings of the earth, as will become clear in Revelation. Obviously again, He did all that because He loves us, which is a well-known fact, but not one to be skipped over lightly, especially as it happens to be in the middle of the set of seven, and not at the beginning as our logic might have suggested.

Then, as a result of all those steps, we humans can be set free. The text says generically that we are set free from our sins. However, the more detailed explanation given later, is that the dragon has been defeated, and so we are actually set free from all the bondage resulting from his dominion over us. This includes our sins, but everything else as well.

At the sixth point, which is the number for us humans, the crowning glory for us is that He has arranged it for us to become kings and priests. Not just any old kings and priests, but ones who are authorized to minister to, and to serve, the Living God, the Eternal One, who created and rules over everything. Amazing !!

The seventh point brings us full circle and returns us, appropriately enough, to the God-head. I have interpreted this to refer to Jesus as well, since He is the topic of this whole section, but in its ambiguity, it can obviously refer to God the Father as well, which is not a problem at all.

This whole section which is an accolade to Jesus, is brought firmly to an end with an 'Amen!' after the final full stop. This is one good reason why verse 7 has to be interpreted as a coda, that is as an eighth, which does not belong directly with the seven, but, nonetheless, is still telling us something about Jesus.

In conclusion, it can be noted that there is a telling absence in all this introduction of the topic of the book. This too should be included in our review of what we are being told, because, as we have seen previously, something which is *not* said, can be just as revealing as those things which *are* said. So, there is no direct reference to the dragon at all. The best mention which he gets, is in the fifth item, where implicitly, and only implicitly, we are told that he is a loser. The dragon is not a part of the topic of the book, and the only relevance he has, is that we need to know that he has been dispatched and dealt with. He is the forever loser who never gets anything right. No, it is clear that Jesus is the topic. He is the one who is given maximum air time. So, after a brief introduction of John, in last position, in verses 9-10, attention is once again focused on Him.

Previously, there was a list of seven of His attributes (plus an eighth), this time there is a list of nine attributes in verses 13-16. Then after a break with a reference to John, there is still an extra reference added on about Jesus, just as there was for the list of seven attributes.

This extra reference is in 1:18 and, as we have seen before, this is the second item in the list of eleven above, which we are systematically working through. It is also the extra eighth element added to the series of seven references, which we found right at the beginning, as explained in section 7.3.2 above.

This reference is also a repetition (repetitions are always worthy of note) for it refers to the fact that Jesus had died and was now alive again. This is a more detailed, synonymous repetition of the statement that He is the First-Born from the dead, as given in 1:5. So, in this repetition, which fixes our attention on the primordial nature of His death and resurrection, God reveals to us an extra detail of information. He tells us that Jesus has won such a victory, that He now owns the keys to both death and Hades.

In other words, with the Cross as His weapon, He has not only dispatched the dragon – who is not even worthy of a direct mention, but He has also bludgeoned into submission, humanity's ultimate and greatest enemies, death and hades together.

The Things Which Are Due to Happen Next 1:19 and 4:1

So now, let's take the next two references, 1:19 and 4:1 together since they are the same, and their purpose is not to provide new information, but to guide us to where we will find the next new information. After 1:19, the things which happen next are in Cycle 1. This is so important that we will devote considerable space to this in the next main section.

As regards 4:1, this is introducing both Chapter 4 and Chapter 5. So the next new information is that Jesus is re-introduced, but this time as the Lamb, who had died and yet was alive again. Immediately, we can see that this is a repetition of the most important facets of Jesus' life and ministry, as already described in the Prologue. So the things which happen next, that is, the new information which is revealed to John, are that the Lamb is the only being, in the whole of the universe, who is deemed worthy to take the scroll from God's hand, to open it, and reveal its contents. Although it is not explicitly stated, it is a reasonable deduction from all that follows after, that this scroll contains God's plan of judgment, at the very least. It is possible that it also contains the details of His plan of salvation as well, since the two are intimately entwined with one another.

However, the point in all this, and the connection with what has gone before, is that there is only one single, and sole reason, why Jesus, as the

Lamb, had acquired sufficient authority to do this. It is because He willingly and sacrificially gave His life on the cross to buy the human tribe back for God. In doing so, because it was a redemption procedure, it automatically meant that Jesus had, in one event, canceled out and replaced, the previous authority which existed over the inhabitants of the earth. This authority, of course, had been previously held by Satan, the serpentine dragon, and by death and Hades, and all their cohorts, since the beginning of time, and since the beginning of all sins.

Once again, neither the One dictating, nor the one writing, deign to spell all that out, as if it is beneath them, but, nonetheless, it is obviously true within the full context of the whole of Scripture. This is because nothing can be done without the appropriate authority to do it. If you do not have that authority, then it is necessary to acquire it by legal means. Then it is possible to remove the previous authority from office, so that they can no longer operate as they used to.

When Will God's Mystery Come to Completion? 10:7

As so often happens in any discourse of any complexity, an element of uncertainty and suspense is injected into the 'story'. In 10:1 this segment of text begins with a very dramatic description of a very radiantly coiffured angel, who then, in due course, raises his voice to make an earth-shattering announcement. He is clearly speaking on behalf of the Timeless Creator God (10:6), and he is referring to the very same words, which have been entrusted, as we were informed previously, to His servants, the prophets (10:7b). So we know that this is all about the topic of the book.

Then he makes his announcement that the mystery of God which is contained in this revelation, composed of words; that this mystery of God, will be brought to completion. However, he does not say exactly when this will happen. All he says is that it will come to completion when the seventh trumpet is sounded. So suspense is established, and consequently, we have to persevere, in order to uncover the rest of the hidden gems. What on earth is the seventh trumpet all about?

The Seventh Trumpet 11:15

Fortunately, we do not have to wait too long to find out about the seventh trumpet because we are informed about this event in 11:15-19. The sounding of this trumpet is another very dramatic event, and, fortunately for us, it does tell us some very important things about God's mystery. So this is the information which the seventh trumpet brings to our attention, as follows:

- It stirs up a great commotion in Heaven 11:15a and 11:19.
- The voices talk about the kingdoms of the earth. This refers to the government of the earth, and to who is in charge 11:15b.

- Although not mentioned by name, the earth, had, presumably, been previously governed by somebody or other.
- But the main point is that this government has now been transferred (has become) to God and His Christ 11:15b.
- From this point on Jesus, the Christ, will govern the earth for all time and for ever 11:15c.
- The people already in Heaven think that this is a great idea, and confirm the basic fact that this transfer of power has already taken place 11:16-17.
- The new information is that this new government will bring judgment on all those associated with the old regime, and who did not willingly accept the authority of Jesus. He will destroy those who destroyed the earth 11:18a and c.
- We are also told that Jesus will give rewards to those who had been his servants, and who had feared, or honored, Him 11:18b.
- Chart 48 indicates that 11:15 is at the center of a chiasm as regards the thread of the topic. This implies that, whichever way we look at it, this text is important for the development of the topic.

In spite of all this information, this passage gives us no definite chronology and does not spell out exactly when all this would take place. In both 10:7 and 11:15 it is the aorist verb form which is used. As mentioned previously, the actual tense is somewhat indefinite, and is dependent on the context. So it would seem that the event of the transfer of power is what is in focus, and not the actual timing of the event.

However, in the context of all that has gone before, it would seem apparent that the transfer of power took place at the time of the death and resurrection of the sacrificial Lamb, who paid the price for this transfer. But what about the judgment of the dead and the distributing rewards to those who had been faithful?

If we are fully honest with the data, it has to be said that there is no clear indicator of time in the text. The interpretation is dependent on the analyst's viewpoint. Traditionally, it has always been assumed that this refers to future events, because from our viewpoint, some of us are not dead yet, and so have not yet faced our final judgment, or received our final rewards. However, the viewpoint of the text is presented as the viewpoint of those who are in Heaven already.

From their point of view it may be that those already dead, and who were involved in destroying the earth, have now been summoned to their final judgment by the new King. After all, new kings, when they take office, normally have to clean house quite a bit, and resolve the problems left by the previous regime. Then, as a complement to that, those who had always been faithful to the new king, and were also dead, would have now also received their rewards. This would explain all the rejoicing and praising going on in Heaven, because prior to that, they had been treated like dirt by the previous tyrant.

The practical implications of this viewpoint would be that those who died from this point onwards (i.e. from John's time onwards), would receive their judgment or reward, upon passing through death to the heavenly realm, where they would meet the King who now governs the earth from Heaven. Let's keep an open mind on this point, and be willing to modify our worldview, if needs be, on the basis of what else we learn as we pursue our quest for hidden gems.

We also need to bear in mind that 10:7 told us that, at the time of the seventh trumpet, God's mysterious plan would be finished or complete. However, having said that, we know from our discussions in previous chapters, that the seventh trumpet's main function is to usher us into the Signs Cycle!! So, in other words, we cannot know exactly what all this means and implies, until we have explored the Signs Cycle at least. So, let's do that now.

The Signs Cycle 12:10 and 15:1-8

As we have seen previously in Chapter 6, the Signs Cycle is very important, so it is to be expected that we will find important information tucked away here somewhere. As is often the case, some of that important information can be found right at the beginning, and, in this case, this is immediately after the end of the seventh trumpet. Hidden in plain sight, as it were. These are things which are more hidden from us in our day and age, but were undoubtedly more obvious to those living in John's culture 2000 years ago.

The first sign which John saw was a woman who was about to give birth to a male child. Obviously, by its very nature, a sign needs to be interpreted. So, who, or what, does this sign represent, and what does this mean in the context of this revelation? Undoubtedly there are different opinions with regard to the answer to this question, and it is possible that more than one of them can make a legitimate contribution to our understanding.

However, in favor of the interpretation which I am going to propose, I would like to appeal to the principle of the law of the first mention, and invite you to come with me back to the very beginning. If we go back to the beginning, we will find certain things which were present on the earth back then, but interestingly, they are repeated by direct references or by allusive echoes in the book of Revelation. Not only that, but those references in Revelation are very closely connected with this topical thread, which we are in the process of studying. Here are the allusions which I have found, along with their references.

- The Eternal Creator God 4:11 and 10:6.
- He made the earth, notably the heavens, the land and the sea. There are three references together to the land and the sea, at 10:2,5 and 6, plus two references to the heaven (sic) in 10:1 and 10:6.
- He placed the sun, the moon and the stars in heaven in order to govern, or rule over, the operation of the earth. In other words, they were the very first earthly authorities, three of them, to be put in place by the Creator.
- He placed a man and a woman on the earth to govern it as well. In due course the woman produced a son, and the three of them were the first human authorities to be put in place. The first sign in 12:1 & 2 is a woman who brings to birth a son. In this case, she has no husband present, and so her child is miraculously produced from a seed whose source is unknown, humanly speaking. She was clothed with the sun, had the moon under her feet, and had 12 stars in her crown. Since time immemorial the zodiac has been composed of 12 heavenly bodies, or stars.
- There was also a snake (12:9), or a dragon, present, the very same one who reappears in 12:3-9, as the second sign out of the seven.
- God spoke to those first servants of His, just as He is doing again in Revelation, and, in particular He spoke prophetic words to them in order to tell them what He planned to do. He said that there would be constant trouble between the serpent and the offspring of the woman, but that ultimately her seed (fathering source unknown) would destroy that troublesome dragon. The exact outworking of this prophetic picture is described in Revelation 12.
- Revelation is full of prophetic words entrusted to God's servants and are directly referred to, for example in 1:1-3 and 22:6. These prophetic words explain what God is in the process of accomplishing. In particular, He is accomplishing and bringing to completion, the prophetic words given about the woman's Seed and the dragon-snake, to the first humans, right at the time of Creation.

What has been described here in this list is exactly the scenario which is described in the first two signs which are presented in Chapter 12, at the beginning of the body of Cycle 4, the Signs Cycle. In other words, for those who have ears to hear, we are being told through this prophetic revelation, that Father God is in the process of accomplishing the very first prophetic words which were given at the beginning of time, for the benefit of the whole of humanity. For the benefit of all, without exception, the Lion of Judah, who is the Seed of the woman, has crushed the head of the serpent, and completely defeated him.

So all this review of the first two signs, brings us to the next part of our topical thread which is 12:10. This occurs right at the moment when the dragon's defeat is being announced with great drama, and great detail, in 12:7-9. At that moment, following on from the end of the seventh trumpet, the most specifically detailed announcement concerning the transfer of power is sent out, for all who will listen to it. We are given several pieces of crucial information in this announcement, as follows:

- Now is the time. No more waiting 12:10.
- It has happened. In this context of the dragon's defeat, what everyone has been waiting for, has happened.
- Salvation has come, and all that that rich word implies.
- The promised power of God has been seen.
- The Kingdom of God has been established.
- Authority (for the earth presumably) has been transferred to God's Messiah, or Christ.
- This has all happened specifically because the accuser has been defeated and dethroned.
- From now on, the followers of the Lamb can overcome the dragon 12:11.
- They can do this by means of the blood of the Lamb, which means that He has already given His life for them, to buy their salvation, and to give them overcoming authority as well.
- This is a cause for great rejoicing, especially for those already in Heaven 12:12. But also, presumably, for those who are overcomers and are aligned with Heaven's worldview while still on the earth.

So then, when did this defeat of the dragon take place? In the light of this crucial component concerning the main topic, the defeat of the dragon has obviously already taken place as John is writing. Then secondly, it is obvious that this defeat took place at the time when the blood of the Lamb was shed for all humanity, as previewed already in the Prologue and Chapters 4 and 5.

Then, following on from that, this passage also tells us that the followers of the Lamb can now also overcome the dragon, whenever he shows up. Consequently, they no longer have to be victimized by his accusations, lies and tricks, in any shape or form, nor do they need to fear death any more. This is because, even if they sacrificially give their lives in service of the Lamb, as He did for them, then they will be raised to life again as overcomers, just as He was.

However, we now come to 15:1-8, which is the seventh sign, but also, at the same time, the beginning of the Bowls Cycle. This passage tells us by repeating the message twice, that in the course of the seventh sign, and the seven bowls together, God's anger as a result of evil, will be finished, accomplished, terminated. This includes the avenging of the unjust deaths of His people 16:6, as well as bringing joy to the overcomers in Heaven 15:2-4.

So, if we previously answered the question of when exactly the dragon was defeated, now we have another question to answer. In the light of the whole of the Bowls Cycle, when exactly will the pouring out of the bowls be finished, thereby completing the execution of God's anger and judgment against evil? In Chart 49 this passage was at the center of a chiasm, so we should not pass over it too quickly and too lightly, but we owe it to ourselves to give it, and its implications, appropriate consideration.

Traditionally, it has always been considered that this particular ending must still be future. This is because, from our point of view once more, these judgment events still seem to be taking place right up until the present time. So, therefore, according to our logic at least, this is a series of events which will only be completed at some time in the future.

Another way of looking at it, from Heaven's point of view this time, is that the full weight and extent of God's anger against evil in general, and humanity in particular (as represented by 'the earth' in 16:1), was poured out on Jesus on the cross. He took the punishment and paid the price for all the offenses which had been committed against God, in the past, certainly. But He also took care of the future, and paid for all the ones which would still be committed after the moment of the crucifixion, from our point of view.

Since God is timeless, He sees the past and the future from His point of view, and not from ours. Jesus, in His humanity, was the representative of all human beings who have ever existed, from the time of Adam, Eve and Cain and Seth, right through until the end of time as we know it. Most would agree, that from God's point of view, the price was paid once, but it covered all the eventualities for the whole of earthly time. This is why we can still hope to be forgiven and saved, even though we live 2000 years later, and why also we can hope to avoid the final judgment altogether. Jesus has paid the price for all that, so it does not have to be paid again. No double jeopardy here.

There is definitely an element of mystery here, for, after all, the book tells us directly, that these revelations are also mysteries, as indicated in 1:20 and 10:7 for example, so if we have a job to figure it all out, then that is understandable. In a sense, it would be to profane it, to try and explain it, just as explaining a joke drains all the humor away. Food for thought.

It Has Happened : Cycle 7 21:6

At this point, in order to keep things as simple as possible we will move on to consider 21:6, which is not the next one on our list. This is in order to keep going down this particular track, and to finish this train of thought. Up until now we have been making an effort to see things from God's point of of view, since He is the most important participant in the events and declarations, which we are considering. Consequently, we have been pursuing the line of thought that the revelation of this book, is in the process of informing us that the mystery of God's plan concerning Jesus has been completed at the time of writing.

This point of view then, seems to be clearly confirmed in this current passage when God declares quite emphatically, using the perfect aspect of the verb, which implies a past tense, that 'It has happened', or by implication, and in line with its parallel verb, 'It is finished'. This is the most prominent point in the whole of Cycle 7 and, arguably, it is also the most prominent point in the whole book.

All this was fully discussed in Chapter 5 already, and it was noted back there, that the difficulty with understanding this statement, lies in the difficulty of knowing what the 'it' refers to. So in summary here then, our suggestion is that we should choose the generic option. This is because the generic-specific semantic relationship predominates in Cycle 7, and because the generic expression of a matter naturally takes priority over anything which is more specific. The additional advantage is that the generic option contains within it, all the more specific options, and so nothing is therefore excluded from this interpretation, but all the possibilities are given their chance to have their say.

The difference here is that we are now reviewing Cycle 7 in the light of this discussion of the topic of the book, and this has included a look at the antecedents of the revelatory explanations contained in Cycle 4. We have observed therefore, that the defeat and dethroning of the dragon described in Cycle 4, are best understood in the light of the first prophecy entrusted to the human race, by God Himself once again, concerning the woman's Seed.

We can observe now with more clarity that the first few chapters of Genesis are really all about who has authority over the earth realm, and who, therefore, would be responsible for its government. The answers to these questions are that God Himself is the ultimate authority over the earth, because He created it, and is therefore, by divine right, its owner. But then, secondly, He decided to delegate its actual government to humans. However, as we know according to the story, all did not go smoothly, and the government of the earth actually ended up for a time in the hands of the serpent, otherwise known as the dragon.

But that is not the end of the story, because the Seed of the woman would deal with the problem and put things to rights. So we can pursue this further by now considering that Jesus was born, not by human effort, but by supernatural supply of the Seed to a woman.

Then, as we observe Jesus' ministry on the earth, we notice that He apparently only ever talked about the Kingdom of God. Now, why would He do that? What was that all about? Well, a kingdom is a system of government, so the Kingdom of God is a system of government, which is under God, and accomplishes the purposes and decrees of God.

As we pursue all this further in the light of the information given in Revelation, we find that Jesus, who is the Lamb of God, but who is also the Lion of Judah, has succeeded in wresting this governmental power and authority from the grasp of the dragon. As the representative of the whole of humanity, He has won the victory, bringing salvation and restoration to all of mankind.

As a consequence, He now rightfully and legally rules over the earth and will do so for ever. This is possible because He Himself, in His own body, suffered the consequences of humanity's sin, and had all the bowls of God's anger poured out on Him, instead of on them.

But He is not alone, for He has companions with Him. As a consequence, God's original plan for the earth has been re-established. The earth will indeed be governed by human beings, but they are the ones who willingly and freely choose to follow the Lamb wherever He goes, and who, therefore, operate under and by His authority. With this authority, represented by His blood, they can now successfully and systematically resist, and overcome, the dragon and all his minions.

So, from God's point of view then, He can rightfully and triumphally proclaim, 'It has been accomplished'. This is because the problems of the past, the problems of sin and evil, have been dealt with, and the new system, the new Kingdom, has been prepared and inaugurated. The bride-price has been paid and there is nothing left now to do, but to enjoy the party.

Some Loose Ends to Tidy Up 17:17 and 22:6

All of the above sounds really good, and even quite convincing. However, we have to be true to the data and, unfortunately for us, the data is not as tidy as we might have hoped. One of the loose ends is literally right at the end in 22:6, where we are reminded again, for this is also a repetition and not an isolated statement, that Jesus is coming again, and in that context, there are some things which are yet to happen. The verb 'to happen' is not in a direct future tense, but the contextual implications are still clearly future in nature – and this is right at the end of the book.

So then, Jesus has been to earth once and, at that time, He accomplished a huge amount, such that nothing will be the same again, for ever. However, He is also coming again, and this promise is alluded to several times. This certainly implies that there will be some things happening at that time as well, which implies in turn, that there is some unfinished business which can only be taken care of at that future date.

Cycle 7 actually tells us what some of that unfinished business is. Once again, it is the dragon who is causing us these extra difficulties and headaches. This is because Cycle 7 tells us quite clearly that the dragon has only been taken care of temporarily, and that he is limited in authority at this time, but not totally eliminated. His final and definitive fate is obviously still future (20:10), and, by the same token, he can still apparently operate on the earth through his proxies at least, such that he can even persecute and cause the death of God's people, as per 11:7, for example.

This then brings us back to the reference in 17:17 which we have not previously dealt with. Admittedly, this whole passage is not easy to understand and to explain, but let's have a look at it and see what we can discover, and better comprehend.

In a very broad, generic sense, first of all, we can discern that, from God's point of view, there are basically only two kinds of people living on the earth, at any one time. Firstly, there are His people. These are the ones who have freely chosen to follow the Lamb, as we have established previously. As a consequence, they benefit totally from God's plan of salvation which has been accomplished by Jesus. As part of that, they avoid large parts of His plan of judgment, and in particular they will avoid totally the final judgment, and the second death, even though they may have to persevere through persecution, and its concomitant suffering on the earth, as mentioned above.

Then, secondly, there is the other group of people, and they are specifically defined and described in Chapter 17. Remember that all human beings were designed to govern the earth, and, as a result, they have free-will, and the ability to decide how they are going to organize their life, and their circumstances. So it is then, that in 17:17 (and also in 17:13), we read that these people decide to give their authority (it is literally 'their kingdom') over to the beast, who is the dragon's proxy.

Human beings decide. This is what governing is all about. So we can either decide to align ourselves with Jesus' authority and do things His way, and for Him; or we can vote/decide to give our authority to those who represent the dragon, and do things his way, and for him. It seems fairly obvious, therefore, that this state of affairs will continue, and has to continue, for as long as humans roam the earth, and still have the freedom to know about, and to choose between, good and evil. The verse in question, 17:17, specifically tells us that this state of affairs, of choosing whom we will serve, will continue *until* the words of God's plan *will be finished*, with this verb being in the definite future tense. This must mean, therefore, that there is still a sense in which God's plan is not yet fully accomplished, and will only be fully accomplished, presumably, when Jesus comes back again.

This insight helps us to now resolve more fully, the enigma which was left in abeyance, when we previously discussed the bowls of God's anger in 15:1-8. When we discussed this passage previously, we suggested that from Heaven's point of view, the bowls of God's anger were fully poured out upon, and borne by, Jesus on the cross. If this were not the case, then there is no guarantee that everyone who wants to, can be saved, and so avoid that fate for themselves. From a theological point of view, there is really no problem with this understanding of the bowls.

However, the problem arises when we continue on past the setting of the Bowls Cycle, as laid out in 15:1-8, and press on into Chapter 16 where the body of this cycle is presented. In this chapter it is clear that some people, while still living on the earth, do suffer the consequences of God's anger being poured out. However, it is also clear who these people are. They are specifically the ones who chose to worship, and to serve, the devil's proxy, the beast, as in 16:2 and elsewhere.

Meanwhile, God's people are nowhere to be found in this chapter, because they do not belong in this category. The main theological point is this. Jesus died on the cross and took the full punishment so that anyone, and everyone, can benefit from His representative death if they so wish. But, because God, in His love, respects the free-will which He has given us, we have to choose to receive and benefit from this great blessing, for ourselves.

REMINDER

Whoever you choose to follow and obey, you end up at the same destination as them, whether it be good or bad.

Rev 3:21 & 20:10-15

This means equally, that if anyone does not decide for the Lamb, but by design or by default, chooses to go with the beast, then the opposite is true.

The Lamb offers a free pass, but if you do not take it, then you do not get a free pass. Unfortunately, there will still be some in that category. For them there is no free pass, so they do not avoid the results of God's anger being poured out. Since Jesus is not there to take the hit for them, they have to take the hit themselves. As a result, they have to bear the full consequences, and to bear the full punishment intended originally for the dragon and his minions, along with them. This is because they chose to follow them and throw their lot in with them. It is simple. Whoever you choose to follow and obey, you end up at the same destination as them, whether it be good or bad.

The Kingdom Now and the Kingdom Future

So then, in summary, we have ended up by saying that everything about God's plan is finished and complete, and yet, at the same time, we have also said that there is some unfinished business, which will only be completed in the future. So have we created an insurmountable dilemma here? Not really. It is only a dilemma if we are incapable of getting outside of ourselves, in order to assess and appreciate a worldview which is different from our in-built worldview.

The solution to this apparent dilemma is contained already within the book of Revelation itself, and something which we have been explaining from the beginning. One of the unique features of this book is that it is firmly based in two referential worlds at once. The first of these is the heavenly world, where God Himself has His throne, and where Jesus is currently situated, along with those of His followers, who have already passed through the gates of death and successfully survived them.

The other one is our well-known earthly one, where John was situated at the beginning of the book, and where the still-living earthlings have their abode. Both of these referential worlds, of necessity, have their own, almost completely opposite view of the world. This latter one is dominated by time, with a tangible past and present, and a more subtly anticipated future, but the heavenly one is different, and, admittedly it does take some effort and imagination, to align oneself with its viewpoint.

Traditionally, it has always been said that God is eternal and that the world in which He lives is, likewise, eternal. In this book we have been developing the habit of saying rather, that God and His world are timeless, in the hopes that this terminology might break through the worldview barrier more readily. As a consequence, from Heaven's timeless viewpoint, God's plan as worked out by Jesus, is indeed complete, for nothing else needs to be added to it, to bring it to perfection.

But from a human, earthly, time-dominated viewpoint, it is not the same perspective, for there are still countless millions of people who are alive or yet to be born, who have not had their chance to make their decision. Since God respects our free-will choices, and that is all part of His plan, then He still makes it possible for us to work out our own salvation in earthly terms, even though the gift of salvation is already paid for, and available to be received in its totality, in heavenly terms.

Likewise God's judgments have already fallen upon Jesus in their entirety. Yet there are still people, both now and in the future, who will decide to go it alone. Consequently, therefore, they will have to tough it out in the face of God's judgments without any help from anyone.

In confirmation of this understanding of the teaching of the Scriptures, Jesus, when He was here on earth before, said some very similar things. When talking about God's Kingdom, or the Kingdom of Heaven, He made it clear that it had been inaugurated and was already operating, right at the time when He was teaching about it.

Yet, included in those same teachings, was the notion that some aspects of this heavenly kingdom would only be completed in the future. This also has created a dilemma for many, and yet most people nowadays accept that both those perspectives are true, even if it is hard for us to understand, and to explain all the details.

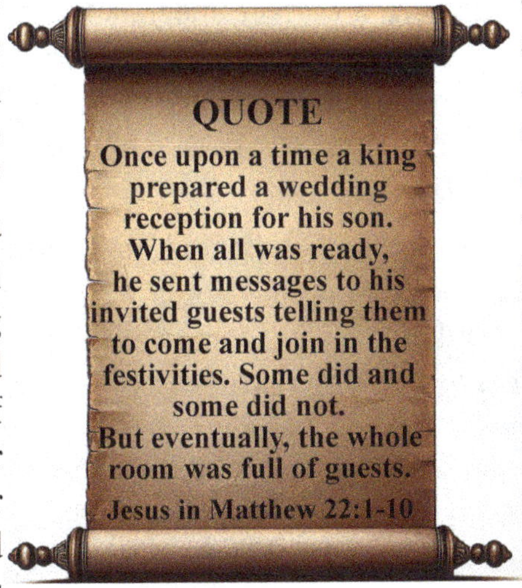
QUOTE
Once upon a time a king prepared a wedding reception for his son. When all was ready, he sent messages to his invited guests telling them to come and join in the festivities. Some did and some did not.
But eventually, the whole room was full of guests.
Jesus in Matthew 22:1-10

So, as we draw a conclusion then, let's take a very human situation as an example, which Jesus used in the Gospels and which reoccurs in Cycle 7 of Revelation – the illustration of a wedding.

We all know that arranging a wedding is a big deal, and costs a lot of money and effort. Someone has to do that work of preparation and it is usually either the father of the bride, or the father of the groom. So, over a long period of time the person responsible does all the work, and pays out all the money, until finally everything is taken care of. The room is ready and decorated. The cake is there, along with the champagne and the glasses. The tables are laid out and carefully set, with a place for each guest. Finally, the father can shout out with great delight: 'It's done, I have made everything perfectly ready, just as I planned!'

All this may be totally true, and yet the room may well stay empty and unoccupied for another twelve, or even twenty-four, hours. This is because the work of preparation is indeed finished, but the guests… nothing can happen without the guests. Naturally, the guests have to make their own individual decisions, whether they are going to turn up or not, and even if they turn up, they have to make their journey and get there. In some cultures, the festivities will not start until everyone has safely arrived.

So it is with our Heavenly Father. It is true that everything has been thought of, and everything is ready. There is not a single detail which needs to be added to make the plan complete. Yet, in His great long-suffering, grace and mercy, He patiently waits for each invited guest to make his or her choice. He waits, not only for them to decide, but also while they get themselves ready, and make their journey to their heavenly destination.

7.3.5 Lessons to be Learned from this Review of the Topic

There are a number of important lessons to be learned from this review of the topic of the book. Firstly, it demonstrates quite clearly the theoretical principle that the topic will, most definitely, be traceable, in some way, right through the book. This is important because if there is any doubt or debate about what the topic actually is, then it can be demonstrated by undertaking an exercise, such as we have done in the preceding paragraphs.

Linked to this, is the reminder that the topic, and knowing exactly what it is, is fundamental for a correct understanding of any discourse. In times past, the topic of Revelation has never been a serious subject of either definition, or of discussion. It was always just assumed that a brief statement about it was enough, if anything was said at all, and that everybody, just intuitively, would understand the rest.

However, this study has indicated that assumptions of such a nature, are really not good enough. This is because in a complex book like this, a topic is also likely to have some complexities attached to it. As the study in Chapter 6 has shown, as well as the one in this chapter, the deeper details of a topic can contain some hidden gems, as well as some worldview bending surprises. Nothing can really be taken for granted about a book level topic, until you have done the work to demonstrate exactly what it is, as we have done here.

The next item of note is that the study of the details of a topic thread, as we have seen in this discussion, reveals new, extra, details about the topic, as you work along the thread. In this case, it is stated quite clearly that Jesus, has taken up His right to reign over the earth and, as such, this gives Him the right to execute both God's plan of judgment, and also His plan of salvation.

This information totally confirms what we learned about the themes of the book, as explained in Chapter 4, which is what would be expected.

However, at the same time, it brings to our attention specific information, which was not totally clear in just studying the two themes separately. This is because this study of the topical thread shows exactly where the two themes come together, entwined in one statement. This happens at 11:17-18, and so, thematically speaking (and themes are the information provided about the topic), this is probably one of the most important parts of the book, because when an author brings two contrastive themes together in one place, that is always significant.

In this case then, in the context of the whole unit, which is 11:15-16:1, we are told that the Lord God has taken control of the whole earth, and it has become His Kingdom. All this has been, and is being, accomplished through Jesus, His Christ, as per 11:15. The result is that the rebellious nations and all their dead denizens can be legitimately judged, and by the same token, His faithful people can be rewarded.

This observation therefore, brings us to another point which is worthy of note. This passage, 11:15-16:1, is a setting. Normally, settings are not considered to be thematic, and would technically be excluded from such consideration. As a consequence, this information which has just been elucidated, would not be included in the thematic statements at all. Yet, this complementary study of the topic thread, brings this important information to our attention, by another means. Consequently, the prominence of this setting is raised considerably, and so it can be fully taken into account, as it deserves.

Next, this study of the topical thread confirms that there is linear movement in the course of the progression of the discourse. The first kind of progression is from generic to specific, for the topic is introduced generically, and then more specific information is added to it as it progresses, culminating with the most amount of information becoming available in Cycle 4, which is the peak of the book.

In addition to that, there is a kind of chronological progression as well, if one can call it that. This study of the topic has forced us to confront the reality that the book has a foot in two different referential worlds at the same time, and these have different viewpoints as regards time. From the heavenly, timeless, point of view, everything has already been accomplished, and the end point of the whole process is already in view. Yet, at the same time, it still leaves room for the earthly, time-based viewpoint, which observes that some things are still in the process of being worked out to completion, in earthly and human terms.

To use a different metaphor, there is also a movement from dark to light, from despair to liberation. At the beginning, Christ's first coming is in focus, and, as we all well know, this ended in the greatest crisis of all of human history. As Chapter 12 explains, there was a huge, cosmic conflict being choreographed, and consummated. This is because the dragon had been in charge of things on the earth for as long as anyone could remember, and he could only be dislodged if an innocent victim willingly confronted, and endured, unimaginable torture, and the most agonizingly drawn out, painful death that humans had ever managed to invent.

Fortunately, this was accomplished, and the victory of light over darkness was secured. As a consequence, as the book progress, this passage from dark to light becomes more and more obvious. This continues until, at the end, it is Christ's second coming which is in focus, and all becomes light and glory.

Finally, last but not least, this kind of detailed study of the topic not only confirms what the true topic is, but it also makes it clear what the topic is not. The topic of the book is Jesus, and the most important information about Him is that He won the victory over sin and evil, and so lives to reign for ever. His reign will be marked by the removal of evil and the establishment of all that is right and good. Under Him, things do not get worse and worse so that humanity needs to be rescued in extremis from the ravages of the devil. This has been accomplished already, and the purpose now of His reign is to bring all the positive promises of God to fruition.

It is all about the one who holds the seven stars in His right hand. As such, He rules with benevolence over the Church, first and foremost, but also with them and through them, He reigns in like manner over the whole world.

So this means that this book is not about the devil, and what he does or does not accomplish. On the contrary, he only barely gets a mention, and that is out of necessity in order to describe his defeat, rather than for any positive reason. Likewise the book is not all about judgment either. This subject too, is an unfortunate necessity, because the removal of evil is a necessary precursor to the full flowering of God's Kingdom of grace and glory. It cannot, and does not, and should not, ever take precedence over the fact that it is God's plan of salvation, accomplished by and through Jesus, which is paramount, and which is the goal of the whole of history, from the Garden of Eden, right through to the Garden of the Heavenly City.

For the same reason the book is not about the end times either. To focus on the end times of this current era is to focus on the negative, and on the outworking of the plan of judgment. It gives more credit to the devil's successes in his attempts to destroy the earth, along with its inhabitants. Instead the goal of the book is to give credit to God that He always had a plan to turn things around for good. Then also to give full credit to Jesus, who paid the price and did the work, to make the salvation and grace of God the pinnacle of history. When He did this, He also opened the door, for anyone who may desire it, to aspire to, and to enjoy to the full, the greatest, and longest, wedding party which the world has ever known.

So then, to sum it all up, this process of testing out the out-workings of the topic has been a success. The more that we have delved into the bowels of the book, the more we have discovered the beauties of God's timeless word, and not the opposite. There have been some difficulties and dilemmas to consider and to corroborate, but the end result has always been a harmonious and consistent confirmation of the insights which had previously been uncovered, and predicted, by the top-down overview of the macro structure.

Yes, there are definitely some complexities which stretch our analytical capacities, and even our worldview. But, nonetheless, this process has only served to refine and to enhance our ability to appreciate the scope and the splendor of the message of this amazing book. This is hardly surprising because it reveals to us eternal mysteries, hidden from view since the dawn of time. But now that that mysterious plan is all complete, there is no need to keep it a secret any more, and so Father God has revealed it to us, through His servant, the prophet, John. As a result, we have the privilege of being party to those mysteries about Jesus, those very glorious gemstones of truth that the prophets of old, and even the angels, longed to see and understand, but could not (1 Peter 1:10-12). Thanks be to God for His grace and kindness to us all.

7.4 A Review of the Sub-Topics of the Book

In the above section we took another look at the topic of the book. However, that is not all that can be said, because the main over-riding topic can often be broken down into complementary sub-topics, and Revelation is no exception to that general rule.

In Chart 51 then, the Prologue is reproduced once again, but this time the purpose is to show where the sub-topics are located, and what they are. In addition, in the right hand column the references are given to show where they also come to a conclusion. It can be seen that they all come to a conclusion in the Epilogue, right at the end of the book.

This means that the sub-topics are book level sub-topics, which run right through the book.

Chart 51.

The Seven Sub-Topics of Revelation

Unit	Sub-Topic Start	Sub-Topic Description	Sub-Topic Conclusion
1.	1:1-2 The Topic is introduced. Plus the first reference to John. He is the witness to God's Word and to what he saw concerning Jesus Christ	1. **John's Personal Example**	22:8 This is the last specific reference to John but he probably also pronounces the final doxology blessing in 22:21.
2.	1:3 Blessed are those who read, hear, and keep the words written in this prophecy.	2. **The Blessings**	22:14 is the final specific blessing but this is preceded by another blessing for those who keep the words of the prophecy in 22:7. It is complemented by the final solemn warnings to everyone who hears the words of this prophecy in 22:18-19.
3.	1:4-5a The Church as represented by the seven churches of Asia Minor is introduced.	3. **The Church's Career**	22:16-17 contain the last specific references to the Church as represented by the (7) churches. It is also referred to as the bride, and as those who hear these words. They are also implicitly present right to the end.
4.	1:5b-6 The first example of worship and praise ascribed to Jesus by John on behalf of himself, and the churches	4. **Worship of Jesus**	22:8-9 is the last specific reference to worship when the angel corrects John again, and tells him to worship God alone
5.	1:7 Behold Jesus is coming again. This declaration contains the first allusions to the Old Testament.	5. **Jesus is Coming Again**	22:12-20 contain the last references to Christ's second coming and the last allusions to the Old Testament.
6.	1:8 I am the Alpha and Omega, the One who is, was, and is to come.	6. **Jesus is Timeless**	22:13 is the last reference to the Alpha and Omega, the first and the last, and completed by extra allusions to His eternal being in 22:16.
7.	1:9-11 Write down what you see and send it to the churches.	7. **The Written Word**	22:10 Do not seal what you have written but reveal it.

This means in turn, that they are not just communicating minor details which could easily have been left out all together. It means that these sub-topics contribute something important, in their own right, to the total message of the book. As such then, they should not be passed over with no comment at all.

The Prologue of the book has already been described in detail in Chapter 2, and several charts of its organization can be found there. The main thing to be said here in review, is that, as soon as the main topic, Jesus, has been introduced at 1:1, the rest of the Prologue through to verse 11, is presented like a list. This is because the series of items which are presented subsequently, have no surface structure, grammatical connections between. The use of *kai* 'and', as a conjunction to connect sentences and paragraphs then starts at the beginning of verse 12, once this list has been completed.

What we can now posit with some confidence, is that this particular grammatical organization shows us where the sub-topics are introduced. It so happens, and this should not surprise us any more, that there are seven of them, and they also happen to correspond with the seven sub-units with which the Prologue is constituted.

It will not be possible here to give a full exposition, and draw out all of the implications, of these seven sub-topics, but, nonetheless, here are a few fun facts about each of them. This will serve to demonstrate that the topic and the sub-topics are all also intricately woven together, such that they inform and support each other, and create a consistent, harmonious whole

7.4.1 John's Personal Example

As has been previously explained, John, being the narrator, is intimately connected with the Narrative Framework, and all this has been explained in detail already in Chapter 2. As such, he is implicitly present in the text every time the verbs to write, to see, and to hear are used, with reference to the development of the narrative. However, it can now be noted that his name is specifically mentioned five times at 1:1,4,9, 21:2 and 22:8. Five, of course is the symbol for grace and John's name also means 'God is grace'. For the Hebrews the meaning of names was very important.

Furthermore, he specifically intrudes into the narrative sequence, and participates actively in what is happening around him, seven times. No more, no less. This is remarkable, but here are the occurrences if you wish to check it out:

- In the Prologue and the setting to Cycle 1, when everyone important is introduced 1:1,4,9,17.
- In the introduction to Cycles 2-6 in Chapters 4 and 5.

- In the Narrative Framework Interlude in Chapter 10.
- In Chapter 17 when he was taken to see the woman known as Babylon
- In 19:11 when he saw Heaven opened for a second time.
- In 21:10 when he was taken to see the heavenly woman, the New Jerusalem.
- In the Epilogue when all the sub-topics are brought to a conclusion.

In the Prologue, we see that John has a personal relationship with Jesus, and is able to interact with Him and receive instruction from Him directly. When John first sees Him directly he falls prostrate in worship. It will be seen that John's experience is intimately bound up with the sub-topic of worship in other places too.

In Chapters 4, 5, 17, 19 and 21, we observe that John is enabled to travel to the heavenly realm, and also to see into it, either directly from inside it, or from outside it. This demonstrates that, even though he was human and, normally speaking, was rooted in the human, physical referential world, he was not limited to that world. In spite of his humanness and his intimate connection with the physical word, he was also capable of experiencing the heavenly realm, and of understanding his visions in the light of the heavenly worldview. This is what enabled him to be a prophet, and so to receive communications of various kinds from Heaven, and then to transmit them to the rest of us.

Then, perhaps the most poignant of all his experiences, which speaks deeply to those of us following the same trail, is in Chapter 10. In this chapter John recounts two complementary, bitter-sweet experiences which summarize his experience as a servant of God and as a prophet. His task from the beginning had been to take careful note of everything, and then to write it all down. But, in Chapter 10, he experiences an apparent contradiction, when he is told not to write down, and record, something which was obviously important.

Then, in the second of his experiences, when he eats the scroll, he finds that his obedience to his calling results in some things which are sweet, but also some things which are bitter in nature.

This is of interest and an encouragement to those following on behind, who get caught up in important service for God. This is because it is, by definition a challenge to follow after God and serve Him. The living God lives in another world and has His own way of doing things, according to His own logic. For us humans, we often do not understand what is going on, and often find ourselves confronted with apparent contradictions like this one. Some things are sweet and thoroughly enjoyable, while other things are bitter and barely palatable.

John's example and advice helps us to know what to do. We are to persevere come what may, putting our trust in the One who loves us and gave His life for us, and staking our lives on the spoken and written promises of God. This is mirrored by the example of the two witnesses in the matching interlude, which follows in Chapter 11. They too have seemingly contradictory, bitter-sweet experiences, but they also come through them victorious, as John did, and as Jesus did before that.

John's example is an example for all of us who come after, and are willing to learn from him. Whatever may happen to us in this earthly referential world, the heavenly referential world lies open before us and is accessible to us. From there we can be resourced and motivated to keep on going, and as we do so, we learn to become overcomers and, in the end, we actually will be overcomers. Having pressed on and made our way to that point, we will be qualified to receive the reward prepared for such faithful witnesses, who testify on behalf of the word of God and of Jesus as he did (1:2).

7.4.2 The Blessings

There are seven specific blessings spread throughout the book from the beginning to the end as follows:

- A blessing comes to those who read, hear (this implies understanding) and keep the words of this book 1:3.
- A blessing comes to those who die "in" the Lord.
  They will receive rest and reward 14:13.
- A blessing comes to those who remain vigilant and who take care to keep themselves properly covered 16:15.
- A blessing comes to those who are invited to the Lamb's wedding party 19:9.
- A blessing comes to those who benefit from the first resurrection. The second death has no authority over them, and they will reign with Christ 20:6.
- A blessing comes to those who keep the words written in this prophecy 22:7.
- A blessing comes to those who have learned how to do their laundry, because they are the ones who will have access to the heavenly city and to the tree of life 22:14.

One particular blessing is repeated almost verbatim. That is the blessing which comes to those who read, make an effort to understand, and respond positively to the words in this book. This speaks directly to all of us, who have come this far in our pursuit of understanding the mysteries being revealed in it. This is both a challenge, and also an incredibly motivating encouragement, for that is the purpose of these promises of blessing.

There are another two which are very similar. These are the ones which encourage us to pay attention to our clothing. This would seem to be another of those mysteries with which this book is replete, so I won't try and explain it, but leave it to you to delve into it further.

The second blessing about those who die in the Lord, confirms and supports part of the wisdom to be learned from John, as we saw in the previous section. So the encouragement is that, even though a life of following Christ may have its bitter, sorrowful times, even ending perhaps in a premature death, it will be worth it all in the end.

So these then, are the seven specific blessings, but there are many more in the book, tucked away in various places. This is because the whole purpose of carefully writing these things down, as we have been discovering together, is to reveal to us all the blessings which God has prepared for us in Christ Jesus. Most of the words in this book, by far, point us in the direction of some blessing or another. So it is not surprising that we are constantly encouraged to discern those blessings, and to do all that is necessary, with great determination, to benefit from them.

7.4.3 The Church's Career

The first things to note as we consider this sub-topic, is that the word 'church' occurs seventeen times in Revelation. Sixteen of those occurrences are in Cycle 1, which is all about the Church, of course, and then once more, to conclude, at 22:16. I don't know about you, but in the course of this study I have gradually come to see that numbers were very important for the authors of this book. This is true to such an extent, that one begins to expect that anything important in the book will be connected, in some way, with a significant number.

QUOTE

Numerical literary style **is a term used... to describe the way scenes in the (Scriptures) are structured according to clearly defined arithmetic patterns.**

Hamilton 2023,27

As I was doing this research, I had been doing a lot of counting. I had found sevens – lots of them everywhere – a 24 and some 12s, not to mention 3 and 5. But seventeen ! Even in the work I had done on the Old Testament, I had never come across a seventeen! So it would have been easy to shrug and just say it was an anomaly, and not worry about it any further. But the thing is with research, if you are truly seeking after truth, then there is a curiosity which drives you on.

So I made the effort to get down my book on numbers in the Bible, and, to my amazement, I saw that ten whole pages had been devoted to this unlikely number, instead of the more usual three or four. So I discovered that one reason why this number is important, is because it is the *seventh* prime number. This symbolically, must mean that if seven represents perfection, then the seventh prime must represent the quintessence of perfection. In addition, seventeen is created by the addition of 7 and 10. Seven, of course means perfection or completeness, and ten represents a testimony, usually a human or earthly testimony. Seventeen, therefore, is a totally complete testimony to something or someone, which implies a complete story, and if it is a good story, then it also implies a complete victory.

A testimony then, is a story, and seven plus ten means a complete story, which is finished and nothing else needs to be added to it. This is a word which occurs in different forms in Revelation. With all examples taken together of the verb *martureo* in Greek, and its related noun *marturia*, when a testimony about Jesus, is clearly and particularly, in focus, it occurs twelve times. This symbolizes governmental perfection, or a complete, reliable authority. So this testimony which we are talking about here, is a story of a complete victory which is coming from the most reliable possible governmental authority.

INFORMATION

If all the occurrences of the root ***martur-*** are counted, then there are a total of 19 occurrences in the whole book. The number 19 symbolizes faith. For the testimony about Jesus to be effective in a person's life, in order for their name to be written in His Book of Life, and in order to become an overcomer, then this testimony needs to be received by faith.

The governmental authority is God Himself, and the testimony is about Jesus who won the most complete of all possible victories. In the Old Testament, the number seventeen is associated with the perfect testimony of the likes of Enoch, Noah and Joseph. It is associated with the crossing of the Red Sea which happened on the seventeenth day of the month, which in turn prefigures the resurrection of Jesus, which also happened on the seventeenth day of the month.

So then we might ask, why is this significant number assigned to the Church? The answer probably has two aspects to it. Firstly, the Church is a testimony to what Jesus has accomplished. They/we are the fruit of His labors, and stand as a living testimony to His complete victory over the dragon, sin and evil of all kinds. In addition, part of their task, as John himself exemplified, is to continually, all through the ages, speak out words of testimony about Jesus.

Secondly, the Church has its own testimony, and this is worked out particularly in Cycle 1, where the word is grouped together in a cluster of sixteen occurrences. Sixteen is the number of love and, in particular, of mutual love, where we love one another. The total story, or testimony, of Cycle 1 is that imperfect people who become followers of Jesus, the Lamb, and who listen to what He says and do it, become like Him. In other words, they can aspire to become overcomers like Him, which concept is clearly repeated in each letter. The word 'to overcome' occurs 12 times in the book. As noted previously, this symbolizes governmental perfection, and it occurs 10 times with reference to the Church overcoming, which brings us back again to the number for a human testimony.

So it is then that by the blood of the Lamb, by the word of their testimony, and by loving the Lord so much that they are willing give their lives for Him (12:11), they become overcomers. They learn to overcome all opposition and achieve complete victory over all their enemies. Hence, seventeen is their number.

QUOTE
(In John's Gospel) there are 7 different summations of 17 words, either uttered by Jesus or in the combined dialogue between the Baptiser and his disciples.
Hamilton 2024,30

However, the Church is not just present in Cycle 1. It is implicitly present throughout the book, because they are the people to whom all the words of testimony are addressed. They are therefore present, and quietly listening, from when the very first word is uttered, until the last one has gone out into the atmosphere. But, in addition to that, they are also specifically present in all the interludes. There are five interludes in all, which is the number for grace.

Interlude 1.

The Redeemed from all Nations are Sealed and Singing 7:1-17

The people of God are known and numbered by God, sealed and set apart for God, and ultimately protected from all harm. They include both those who trusted in God for their salvation in the Old Testament, as well as those who have joined their ranks since then. They are a crowd so huge that they cannot be counted from a human point of view, from every tribe and nation. They may have suffered temporarily, but they have understood about being dressed in the right clothes.

So they shout out their words of testimony about God, and the Lamb, and, as overcomers themselves, join with the government of Heaven (the 24 – 2 x 12 – elders) and the angels in worship. The number 144 is 12 x 12, which is the ultimate in governmental perfection. The number 1000 can symbolize the ultimate in divine perfection, or it can represent a number which is so big that it cannot be counted, humanly speaking.

Interlude 2.

The Narrative Framework Interlude: Perseverance is the Priority 10:1-11:2

John, as one member of the wider church, gives us an example of what it means to be a servant of God, and a follower of the Lamb. Nobody said that it would be easy, just that it is worth the cost. So he faced apparent contradictions and delays, in his work as a prophetic mouthpiece for his Master. He also found that it was a bitter-sweet experience at times, but he persevered, and was given words of encouragement saying that he would yet prophesy before nations, speaking different languages, and before many kings. It is our turn now to testify, and to declare that this word has become totally true, and that John's words have been read and heard all through the world, in all the nations, and before countless kings over a period of 2000 years !! Is God faithful to His promises or what?

Interlude 3.

The 2 Witnesses: Perseverance is the Price to Pay 11:1-13

The number 2 represents the basic human team working in unity, and this is particularly true of the followers, or disciples, of Jesus. Their task is to prophesy and to testify for Jesus. They are overcomers in life and in death, because even though the beast overcomes them physically, they overcome it spiritually and eternally, and have the last word. He who laughs last, laughs longest!

Interlude 4.

The Saved Singers Stand with the Lamb on Mount Sion 14:1-5

This interlude confirms that the 144,000 are those who have God's and Jesus' name marked (sealed cf. 7:3) on their foreheads, because they are the ones purchased from the earth. They sing a song which only they have the right to sing. They follow the Lamb wherever He goes, and share in His authority, since they stand with Him, and rule, from Mount Sion, the place of highest governmental authority in the universe.

It needs to be said, so that there is no misunderstanding, that the ruling and reigning which we are talking about here, is that which takes place within the Kingdom of God, which is ruled over by the Lamb. As Jesus, the Lamb, said Himself in Matthew 20:25-27, neither He, nor His followers, were to use the methods of the nations, which degrade and denigrate people. They were to use the methods of government which He Himself had used while on earth.

As far as Revelation itself goes, Jesus gives detailed instructions to His followers as to how they were to conduct themselves in Cycle 1. Then in the preceding interludes, summarized above, the examples of John himself, and the two witnesses, were given as models to follow. These examples are followed closely in 12:11 by the clear, outright instructions as to how the overcomers were to win their victories and use their authority. Confidence in the blood of the Lamb, authority in the word of their testimony, and power in their perseverance in the face of death, are their methods. These are not the violent and domineering methods of the world, but are clearly a world apart from that, being the methods of God's Kingdom.

Interlude 5.

The Wedding and the Worship 19:1-8

Along with the 24 Elders and the 4 Living Creatures, this huge crowd constantly worships God and praise Him, for the things which He has done for their benefit. There are five of them as follows:

- He is righteous and true in His judgments and He has judged all who defiled the earth
- He has avenged the blood of His people
- He, the Lord God Almighty, reigns and this is a cause for celebration
- He has prepared the wedding party for the Lamb and His bride, which is anticipated with joy
- He has clothed the bride, the Church, in beautiful clothes, prepared in readiness

As we read through these summaries, it can be seen that the interludes are not hermetically sealed units, which function in autonomous isolation. Like so many elements of this book, they are like threads which weave in and out, and which make connections with other units. So it is that, any given interlude may make reference to other interludes, thereby reinforcing the message of that interlude. Then, by the same token, they also contribute support to some of the book level themes.

Here are seven of these strands which can be found in different places:

- The authority, rule, and reign of God and of His people
- God's determination to judge all evil, but also to protect His people from that judgment
- Worship of God and of the Lamb
- Rejoicing over the blessings which God has provided
- Overcoming the difficulties and obstacles
- The Church's need to be redeemed, cleansed, correctly clothed, and sealed
- Shouting, singing and writing words of testimony

Once again, a more detailed study of the sub-topic of the Church's Career, reveals a harmonious, consistent, and coherent message, full of encouragement and promises of blessing.

7.4.4 Worship of God and Jesus

Once again this sub-topic pervades the whole book. The first reference to worship in 1:5-6 is an actual demonstration of worship in practice, and not just some theoretical reference to it. As such, the concept is unmistakably present, and the sub-topic is thereby introduced. However, in addition to that first occurrence, the word 'worship' then occurs 23 times in the book, which makes a total of 24 references.

This corresponds well with the 24 Elders. Even though they are the highest human governmental authority (12 x 2), they spend most of their time in worship of God and the Lamb.

INFORMATION

The number 23 represents death. What we can deduce from this interesting anomaly, is that a theoretical knowledge about worship, or just the word 'worship' on our lips, does not constitute true worship. This is just a dead work. True worship is only that which is produced in practice from the heart as John demonstrated for us in 1:5-6.

Within that total there are 9 (10 including 1:5-6) references to worship of God and/or the Lamb, and including also an unusual example in 3:9, which is, nonetheless, an example which is considered to be an acceptable kind of worship. In addition, there are 10 references to the wrong kind of worship, which demonstrates that it is possible to worship the wrong person or thing, and in context, this is obviously not acceptable. Finally, there are 4 references to the word 'worship', where John is personally involved in worship. These references are two double references in 19:10 and in 22:7-8.

The 4 references to John's worship experience correspond well with the 4 living creatures, who represent the earth realm, and who also spend their time in worship. Then, if 1:5-6, which we have already noted, is also included, then that makes 5 references in total, which brings us back to the symbol of grace once more. In the total inventory of John's experience, we find that in his humanity, he does not always get it quite right. He is so overwhelmed by his heavenly experiences at times, that he is sorely tempted, on more than one occasion, to worship the angel sent to serve him. But he is immediately corrected, and told to only worship God. So, once more, he is an example to all of us, who are listening in to his testimony.

Biblical worship, as exemplified in the 10 positive examples, is a very complete activity, involving the whole of the person, body, soul and spirit, we could say. On a physical level it includes shouting, singing, declaring, as well as falling down, or bowing down, and other prophetic actions. Chapters 4 and 5 give a particularly complete overview of what worship is all about in practice.

7.4.5 Jesus is Coming Again

There are many references in the book to 'coming' in various contexts, so for simplicity's sake I have not counted the ones referring to Jesus coming to the churches in Cycle 1 to bring specific correction to them, nor the reference to Him coming as a thief in 16:15. So just counting the references which specifically say that he is coming on the clouds, or that He is coming quickly or soon, in a general, indefinite sense, then there are 5 of them, and they occur at 1:7, which initiates this sub-topic, 3:11, 22:7,12 and 20.

So this sub-topic does not occur all through the book, as most of the others do, but the references certainly create a clear set of brackets, or an *inclusio*, at the book level. The information which is provided about this second coming is as follows:

- He is coming on the clouds, as the disciples were told at His ascension 1:7
- Everybody will see Him come, and it will not be a joyful time for everybody 1:7
- Since He is coming soon, the Christians should persevere and particularly they should keep hold of their crown, which is the symbol of their right to rule and reign on the earth 3:11
- Since He is coming soon, everyone who reads this book would do well to put into practice what is revealed in it 22:7
- When He comes back, He will bring a reward for everyone, according to what he has done in his life. The context of the whole book suggests that this 'reward' could be negative or positive 22:12

So there are five items here, which are, once more, the symbol of grace. But there is also a sixth in 22:20, because the grace of God invites a response from those of us in the '6' category, namely, us humans. How do we respond to the declaration that Jesus is coming back again and will be bringing rewards with Him for everyone? The response which is suggested by this book of testimony, is that we should say 'Amen!', which means 'I agree! Let it be so!'

7.4.6 Jesus Is Timeless

There are three phrases used in the book which are used to describe or evoke, the difficult to conceptualize notion, that Jesus lives in another world and is therefore, outside of time. As mentioned previously, this characteristic of the Godhead has traditionally been described by the word 'eternal' and its derivatives. However, in this study I have used the word 'timeless' in an effort to break through the semantic fog which generally cloaks this concept, and to bring more clarity into the thinking of a twenty-first century readership.

Before getting fully into this discussion, we need to clarify a complicated detail. In Chapter 5 we pointed out that God the Father, the Almighty, is an important participant in this discourse, even though He does not appear very often, and is not the topic of the book. As a consequence, He is present in the text in some strategic places, including within the domain of this current sub-topic, which concerns eternal timelessness.

So it is then, that in 1:4, where we have the introductory greetings typical of a letter, but which, in this case, introduce the whole book, John firstly brings greetings from God the Father, designated by His title the *One who Is, who Was and who Is to Come.* We know that this is referring to the Father because, His greetings are then followed by greetings from Jesus. On three occasions, here in 1:4, then in 1:8 and 4:8, God the Father is referred to by this title which obviously refers to His timelessness. Since this phrase is only used with regard to Him, it is not otherwise included in this review of Jesus' timelessness, apart from noting that this mention of His eternal nature does occur and actually occurs three times in the book.

The surface structure components which we are going to consider in more detail are the following three phrases: *I am the Alpha and the Omega,* which occurs in 1:8, 1:11 (TR only), 21:6 and 22:13, *I am the Beginning and the End,* which can be found in 1:8, but only in the Textus Receptus, 21:6 and 22:13, and *I am the First and the Last,* which occurs in 1:11 (TR only), 1:17, 2:8 and 22:13. Conceptually they are all synonymous, since they all indicate, in different ways, that the person concerned has always been there.

This is because He was there at the beginning of time and of Creation, will still be there at the end of time and, in the meantime, is always present with us, wherever we may be, and whether we are thinking about it or not.

The complexity which we need to elucidate arises from the fact that the first reference to the Alpha and Omega, in 1:8 also clearly refers to God the Father. However, Jesus is also referred to by these three titles. In 22:13 they all occur together in the same verse as a synonymous triplet, where they clearly refer to Him. However, this is not always the case, because in four cases, these titles are applied to God the Father as well.

Now Revelation is not a handbook on theology and should not be treated as such. It does not explain why Jesus and the Father are given the same attributes, it just puts them both together in the same basket and leaves the reader to figure it out. Clearly then, this unexplained juxtaposition implies that Jesus and the Father, are on the same footing with regard to the eternal being, or the timelessness, of their nature.

The reason which would best explain this phenomenon is that, this is the expression of a worldview, which is showing through the texture of the surface structure. In other words, on the basis of Heaven's worldview, from which vantage point this book is being written, both God the Father, and Jesus, are considered to be timeless. Consequently, this fact is assumed, and, therefore, does not need to be explained. As a result, these titles can be ascribed to either one of them, as needs be, with no difficulty.

On the basis of this understanding of what is being communicated then, we are going to look at all the occurrences of these titles which are attributed to Jesus, regardless of whether they are attributed to the Father as well, or not. Jesus is clearly considered to be timeless by the authors, and that is what we are interested in exploring.

The Alpha and the Omega

This title refers to the first and last letters of the Greek alphabet, just as we might say, 'the A and the Z'. There are apparently 4 uses of this title, in the Greek version of the text as we have it today. This is a problem from a numerical point of view since the number 4 is considered to represent Creation, which is clearly finite, and not timeless. This is obviously not appropriate when talking about timelessness, which is an attribute which can only be applied to the Creator, and not to the Creation itself. So, for the moment, suffice it to say that all references to the number 4 in this section are anomalies. The reason why they are anomalies will be elucidated further in the final chapter.

The Beginning and the End

This title is in plain English, as is the next one, and so neither of them require any further explanation as regards their meaning. This title is used 3 times in the Greek versions of the text, but the occurrence in 1:8 is only to be found in the Textus Receptus.

The First and the Last

This title refers to Jesus on all occasions and occurs 4 times. As mentioned above, this is considered to be an anomaly. However, in this case the anomaly can be smoothed out in two ways. Firstly, if all the references of these last two titles are taken together, then there are 7 of them. The second possibility is, that if all the cases where these last two titles are applied to Jesus, are counted, then there are 5 of them.

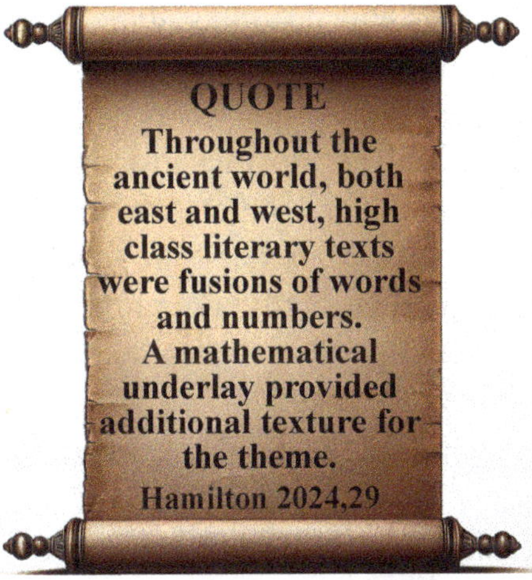
QUOTE
Throughout the ancient world, both east and west, high class literary texts were fusions of words and numbers.
A mathematical underlay provided additional texture for the theme.
Hamilton 2024,29

In the mind of the author then, it is clear that both God the Father and Jesus, equally, have this quality, which we are calling timeless. This means that they live, and move, and have their being, outside of earthly time. This is because they were there before Creation of the world, and before time began, and they will still be there when it all comes to an end. In the meantime, they continue to be present and are unchanging, for it is only within the system of time, that there is change and decay.

Likewise, they, along with this timeless attribute, are present throughout the book. There may only be a few overt references to this notion of timelessness, but, nonetheless, as topics do, and as prosodies do, this divine characteristic pervades the whole book.

This has two important implications for our interpretation of the message of this book. Both the things which Jesus accomplished on the earth, as the Lamb of God, and also everything which He said, whether it was before, during, or after His incarnation, are timeless, just as He is timeless.

So, for example, He died just once while on the earth, which event, including His resurrection, took three days of earthly time. However, its effects are timeless. This means that it is possible for anyone to benefit from the spiritual redemption which took place at that moment in history. So it is that some people who lived and died before Jesus came, will be in the colossal company of God's people in Heaven, as will be many of those who were alive at the time of Christ.

By the same token, anyone who has lived during the 2000 years since then, can also benefit from that blessing, and aspire to be in that company. All this is no problem for God, who is outside time, and for most of us who understand these things already, it is not a problem either. These timeless blessings are available to anyone, regardless of the moment of earthly time, within which they find, or found, themselves.

But the point is this: if this is true for this particular thing which Jesus accomplished, then it is true for everything which He has done, and for everything, which is said and done by Him in this book. In this book we observe Jesus opening the seals on God's special scroll. Whether He went through this process just once or several times we do not know, but the effects of what He accomplished must, of necessity, be timeless. That is to say that their effects must be relevant to, and operative for anyone, regardless of when exactly that person lived on the earth.

Likewise, through John's eyes, we see Him riding His white horse, with His companions following on behind. Did He do this just once or many times? We do not know and it does not matter. The effects, and the implications arising from the fact that He rides on a white horse are timeless, and relevant to all of us, regardless of our place in the earthly timeline. If we could open our eyes to see into Heaven as John did, then we would be able to see Jesus, and He would still be riding His white horse.

So then, let's consider one more example which is really important for an adequate interpretation of the message of this book. In the book, the dragon, Satan, is thrown out of Heaven, and is put into a pit just once. In this case it was a contingent event. That is to say, that it was dependent on what Jesus did, for this act could only be accomplished after Jesus had accomplished His complete victory on the Cross. This has already happened once, so it does not need to happen again, sometime in the future.

In addition, the effects of this event must be timeless. That is to say that they must be operative, and effective, for all the time which has passed since then. If this were not the case, then the members of the Church of Jesus could not aspire to be overcomers, and could not be victorious over their adversary, as they need to be. If Jesus is timeless, what He accomplished, and all the effects of what He accomplished, must also be timeless. They must, of necessity, be available to, and relevant for, anyone who comes along afterwards, and puts their confidence in the promises (which are also timeless) to be found in this book.

That is what we mean by timeless. Everything in this book is for anyone who reads the words and puts their confidence in them. To interpret the message in any other way, which excludes anyone, from any generation, from the benefits and the effects, of all that is recounted in it, is not reasonable, and needs to be avoided. This is because it is not taking account of all the data and therefore, is inadequate.

7.4.7 The Written Word

Everything about this book, is that it is a written document, from the very first letter, through to the last full stop. In addition, many things are said about words and the fact that they should be written down. There is a reference under the sub-topic of the Career of the Church, about the importance of the testimony about Jesus, which is, of course, composed of words. More was said in the immediately preceding section about the fact that Jesus' words are timeless, just as He is timeless.

In the Greek it is *logos*, which is the word for 'a word', which we are mostly concerned about, and this occurs 12 times. These are all positive uses of the word, used in the context of recounting the testimony, either about Jesus (19:13), or of the Church. There is one element of uncertainty in 17:17, where 'word' occurs in our English Bibles, but it is used here in a different context. In this case it refers to God's word, but it is a word which is very specifically related to the negative concept and context of judgment, and man's rebellion against God.

Further research reveals that this is a textual variant and represents uncertainty in the transmission of the text. In the Nestlé version of the Greek, it is transmitted as *logos*, but in the Textus Receptus another Greek word is used, namely, *rhéma*. This word *rhéma,* would seem to be a more appropriate usage for the context in 17:17, where a very specific word of God is implied, which is directed towards a particular situation. *Logos*, on the other hand is more general in nature, and can be applied to any broad situation. Consequently, this occurrence of 'word' in 17:17, is not included in the list of 12 occurrences.

As we trace this thread through the book, it brings three particularly significant pieces of information to our attention as follows:

- One of Jesus' names is *The Word of God*, and this is applied to Him in the context of His complete victory, as described in 19:13. This is in direct parallel in the context, with the picture that His words are like a sharp sword emanating from His mouth. Not only are His words bound to be timeless, but they are also a weapon to be used against His, and our, spiritual adversaries, at any time or place.
- This testimony about Jesus is also the testimony of His followers. Consequently, one of the ways in which they can overcome their adversaries is by the *word* of their testimony, as described in 12:11.

- The words about Jesus, and given by Jesus, as written in this book, are the ruler by which people are, and will be, measured. So it is important to *keep* these words (1:3, 3:8 etc.), for our ultimate destiny depends on this. This same measure is the one which will define whether a follower loved their King enough to even give up their lives for Him. So it is that the ones who suffered a martyr's death, did so because they kept these words right to the end, and refused to deny them, even under the threat of death, as indicated in 6:9 and 20:4.

Now let's look at the verb 'to write' which is represented in the Greek by various forms of *grapho.* Counting all the forms of 'write' and 'written', there are 27 occurrences spread throughout the book. Almost without exception, they are positive words, written for the encouragement, or for the warning (22:18), of the Church. There are 3 exceptions, which are negative and which are all identical. These are references to those who are *not* written in the Lamb's book of life, and these can be found at 13:8, 17:8 and 20:15. So even this triplet of negatives, communicates an important message which should not be overlooked.

It just so happens that the number 27 is another very interesting symbolic number. Upon reflection it can be seen that it is a combination of 17 and 10. As we have already seen in our previous discussion of the Career of the Church, number 17 is its number, and represents their testimony of complete victory. So this is the same number 17, but this time underlined, and bolded, by the addition of a further number 10, which speaks a second time of the *word* of our testimony. Another way of interpreting the number 27 is by observing that it is the same as 9 x 3, which is another way of symbolizing the ultimate in divine perfection.

Because of all these intricately interwoven connections, it is commonly understood that the number 27 particularly represents the preaching of the Good News, which the Father wants to make known to us. This Good News, or Gospel, is the same as the revelation about what Jesus has accomplished on our behalf, and for our benefit. This is quite remarkable because the preaching of the *eternal* gospel is a feature of Revelation, for it is described in 14:6. As we all know, preaching the gospel requires words, but the word for 'a word' is not used in this context. So it is only because of this number symbolism that this similar word has been included in our discussion here, and this turns out to be very important.

This is because we are specifically told in this verse that the words of this gospel are 'eternal', or timeless, which confirms what we have been trying to explain by other means in the previous paragraphs. Then secondly, the 'written words' which we have discussed previously, were for the benefit of, or about, the Church. But on this occasion we are specifically told that God's intention is that the words of His good news should go out and be heard by all the inhabitants of the earth, in every nation, tribe and people.

Not only that, but thirdly, since time immemorial, humans have always thought that testimonies which are particularly important, should be written down in order to ensure their preservation, and accurate transmission, to succeeding generations. This situation is no exception. The words contained in this book, as we are reminded many times, are so important that they must be written down, and then carefully 'kept' by anyone and everyone who makes the effort to read them, or listen to them being read. Since these words are timeless, this basic truth is still applicable today.

7.4.8 A Summary of the Sub-Topics

I think that it is fair to say that, as I have consulted very many commentaries on Revelation over the years, I do not recall that a single one of them has ever made any reference to the sub-topics of the book. It is only rarely that they make any allusion to the topic as such, but the sub-topics themselves, are passed over in silence, as if they are not there. Yet, the author took the trouble to clearly lay out these seven sub-topics for all to see, as soon as he had finished his very first introductory words about the topic itself.

As we have seen throughout our brief summary of these sub-topics in the discussion in the preceding paragraphs, these elements of the discourse are not brief asides, which have no relevance to the message of the book and make no impact on the reader. On the contrary, they are intricately and tightly woven together, with all sorts of hidden mysteries contained within them. Due to the tight, semantic network which they create together, they contribute a great deal of pertinent information to the book, in support of the thematic material discussed in Chapter 4. Consequently, if all references to them were removed, or ignored, as is often the case, then the texture of the book would be greatly diminished.

As a reminder then, these are the semantic domains which the sub-topics expand upon:

- **John's Personal Example**
  As a recognized leader in the Church of his era and as a prophetic spokesman for God, he not only speaks by his words, but also speaks by his example. Everything, therefore, which he contributes by word or deed, contributes to the volitional import of the book, by providing a motivational example for anyone else who will later read it.

- **The Blessings**
  This sub-topic covers all the blessings and promises, whether they are explicit or implicit: the promises which God offers to all those who will forsake everything to follow the Lamb wherever He goes.
- **The Church's Career**
  This is a vast topic in its own right and covers anything, and everything, which is of concern to the Church. All this needs to be fully taken into account.
- **Worship**
  This is also a vast topic, which is not surprising, since it is the most central activity in Heaven. Consequently, it would appear to be a practice which the Church needs to cultivate to the full. There are many exhortations as regards worship, and many practical examples as to how to do it.
- **Jesus is Coming Again**
  This sub-topic is only briefly mentioned, but, nonetheless, pervades the whole book. The point being made is that Jesus is coming again, soon. Since no one knows exactly when, and neither does any one know under exactly what conditions, this information provides a very powerful motivating force which colors everything else.
- **Jesus is Timeless**
  This also is a sub-topic which is only very briefly mentioned, but it clearly reminds us that there is an eternal dimension to everything, including our normal earthly experience. Death is a fact of life for everyone, and there are no repeats, and no second chances. So what then? This book spells out exactly what the issues are. Namely, that from an eternal, heavenly perspective, there are only ever two groups of people on the earth, and only two destinations when we each, in turn, pass from the temporal to the timeless realm. Keep on reading and you will find out about those basic mysteries: how to get it right and end up in paradise on the one hand, or the doom and gloom awaiting those who are remiss about, or who reject, the eternally good, Good News.
- **The Written Word**
  There are no excuses. Everything important has been written down, preserved and passed on. Then, in later generations, it was translated into all the languages imaginable, and transported to every part of the globe. Nothing which has been done to destroy it has succeeded, and the result today is that God's Word to us is still a best seller.

CHAPTER 7b

The Proof of the Analysis: The Harmony of the Macro Structure and the Micro Structure

7.5 The Internal Organization of Cycle 1: The Seven Letters 1:9-3:22

As previously explained in the introduction to this chapter, the proof of the macro-analysis is in the micro analysis of the units in the mid and lower levels of the hierarchy. This is because it is as the micro analysis harmonizes with, and thereby confirms, the macro analysis, that the latter is established as being reliable and useful.

In this section then, we will be taking a closer look at Cycle 1. This Cycle is important because it contains the biggest single contribution to the volitional import aspect of the discourse. In addition, it also provides the single biggest component concerning the sub-topic of the career of the Church.

7.5.1 The Setting

This cycle is composed of a setting (1:9-20) and a body composed of seven letters (2:1-3:22). The setting is a simple ABA' structure as follows:

A. Setting for the Introductory Vision 1:9-11
  B. The Introductory Vision of the Risen Christ 1:12-16
A' Conclusion for the Introductory Vision 1:17-20

A and A' are in parallel because they are both part of the Narrative Framework and include the active participation of John. Both include speeches by the risen Christ, of which the principal component is an instruction to write (1:10 and 19). By contrast section B is limited to a description of what John saw, and includes no action or speech apart from the introductory action 'and I turned' in 1:12. This verb is interpreted as being in parallel with 'I was' (twice) in 1:9-10, and 'and... I fell' in 1:17, thereby indicating the beginning of each sub-unit (ABA').

This interpretation provides one possible explanation why the unusual, and therefore prominent, independent first person singular pronoun 'I' occurs at 1:9. Its presence draws attention to the use of the first person pronoun used with reference to John, and thereby initiates a structural pattern repeated in verses 12 and 17, which delineates the structural framework of the whole section. This interpretation does not annul the fact that 'I' in verse 9 is also in parallel with the same word in verse 8, thereby creating a connection backwards with what precedes as well as creating a link forwards with what follows.

This is because a single feature may, concurrently, have functions at different levels of the organizational hierarchy.

The senders are, of course, described in the setting to the cycle and an element of the description of Jesus reoccurs in most of the letters. However, in the case of Laodicea, the allusion refers back to 1:5 and anticipates 19:11, and in the case of Philadelphia, one reference, holy and true, anticipates 6:10, while the other reference to the key of David, has no direct corollary in the whole book. The nearest possible parallel is, nonetheless, at 1:18, which refers to the keys of death and hell.

7.5.2 The Body of the Cycle 2:1-3:22

The body of the cycle is composed of seven autonomous units which are the letters to the seven churches referred to in the setting at 1:11. The overall organization is that of a list, since there is no overt linguistic or logical connection between the seven letters which would suggest that there is a linear development throughout the seven sub-units. Since this is the case, it is not possible to argue that the seventh letter is acting in some way as a conclusion to the whole set and is, therefore, more naturally prominent than the others.

Some commentators have suggested that the seven letters relate to each other in a chiastic arrangement. Since the central letter to Thyatira in 2:18-29 is the longest and has the greatest concentration of key elements, this, for the moment, seems to be the best analysis. On this basis then, it can be proposed that this central sub-unit of the chiasm is the most prominent part of the body of this cycle, and this issue will be developed further in the following sections.

7.5.3 The Structure of the Letters

Each of the seven letters is composed of some or all of the following constituent parts:

1. A formal epistolary introduction
(This includes an order to write and the addressees)
2. Identification of the sender
(beginning: 'the one who says these things..')
3. A statement of the sender's knowledge of the situation
(beginning: 'I know')
4. An amplification of 3, in the form of a commendation.
5. An amplification of 3, in the form of a reproach.
6. A central exhortation (marked by imperatives)
7. A warning or an invitation
8. A generic exhortation ('he who has an ear...')
9. A promise for the overcomers
(beginning: 'to the one overcoming' or 'the one overcoming')

Semantically a warning and an invitation, especially of the kind found in these letters, are almost identical. Both invite a choice. In the case of a warning, the negative consequences of the choice are clearly in view, although implicit is the fact that if the warning is heeded, positive consequences will ensue. The invitation views the same situation from the opposite point of view: the positive benefits of the choice are in view, but implicit is the fact that negative consequences will ensue if the invitation is not accepted.

The letter to Philadelphia is slightly different in that a warning about a coming test is issued in 3:10b but, immediately prior to that, the church is assured that it will be kept during the test. It is also different because this warning comes before the central exhortation in 3:11, instead of after it. But, included in the promise to be protected, is the commendation that they already had endured through previous tests. Given that the following exhortation is also about enduring, or holding fast (3:11), the total effect of the sentence is to provide an implicit invitation to keep on persevering in the face of the next test, which will be for everybody, and not just for them. Elements of both warning and invitation can, therefore, be discerned here, even if they are considerably attenuated by their placement in this particular, rather ambiguous, context. Nonetheless, for the sake of simplicity, the analysis which is presented below, is that there is no overt invitation, or warning, specifically directed to the church at Philadelphia.

The nine constituents, listed above, form internal groupings thereby creating a three-part overall structure as follows:

A. Constituents 1 and 2 create a setting or introduction
B. Constituents 3-7 form the body of the letter
A' Constituents 8 and 9 provide a conclusion

The setting has a fixed order of constituents while the order of the two constituent parts of the conclusion is reversed for the last four letters. The body, which contains the main part of the message to each of the churches, has the most structural variations. The body begins with the verb 'I know'. The sections immediately following 'I know' are usually closely connected to it, however, in this analysis it was considered preferable to distinguish all the semantic categories, thereby distinguishing the commendations from the reproaches, since these so clearly occur. Nonetheless, the close connection with what precedes, is indicated by tagging constituents 4. and 5. with the label 'amplification'.

Three of the reproaches (2:4,14 and 20) and three of the commendations (2:6,9b and 3:4) begin with 'but'. At 2:3 and 2:13, what can be interpreted as the commendation occurs in a new sentence with an independent verb (at 2:19 it is the same, except that the verb is an elided verb 'to be'). Another reason for treating them as separate constituents is that they can occur in different places in the structure and are not always directly attached to the 'I know' constituent. Thus, for example, in the letter to Ephesus there are two separate commendations occurring at 2:3 and 6, and in the letter to Sardis the commendation occurs in the seventh position at 3:4 after the warning.

As regards constituents 8 and 9, two primary reasons for treating them together as the conclusion, are firstly, because they always function together, even if the order can be reversed, and they are never separated by any other constituent. Then, secondly, because they have a similar, and therefore parallel, structure, in that they both begin with a verbal noun composed of an article and a present participle.

7.5.4 The Variations in the Structure of the Letters

The order of the constituents as presented above, was established on the basis of the first letter to Ephesus, and the order of the third letter to Pergamum, which is the most complete and least disturbed by special features. The order of the constituents in each of the letters is as follows:

Chart 52.
The Internal Organization of the Seven Letters

Letters 1-7	Setting	Body	Conclusion	Reference
Ephesus	1. 2.	3. 4a. 5. 6. 7. 4b	8. 9.	2 :1-7
Smyrna	1. 2.	3a. 4. 3b. # 6. (7a.7b)	8. 9.	2:8-11
Pergamum	1. 2.	3. 4. 5. 6. 7.	8. 9.	2:12-17
Thyatira	1. 2.	3. 4. 5. 7. 6.	9. 8.	2:18-29
Sardis	1. 2.	3. 5. 6. 7. 4.	9. 8.	3:1-6
Philadelphia	1. 2.	3. 4. # 6. #	9. 8.	3:7-13
Laodicea	1. 2.	3. # 5. 6. 7.	9. 8.	3:14-22

NOTES FOR CHART 52.

1. When a particular constituent either occurs twice (as in the case of Ephesus) or is split in two by an intervening constituent (as in the case of Smyrna), the two occurrences of the constituent are indicated by the letters 'a' and 'b'.
2. In the letter to Smyrna 3:10b and 10c could be interpreted as a warning followed by an invitation. This possible interpretation is included in parentheses as 7a and 7b.
3. The references for the divisions are as follows:

Ephesus: 2:1a,1b,2,3,4,5a,5b,6,7a,7b;
Smyrna: 2:8a,8b,9a,9b,9c,10a,(10b,10c),11a,11b;
Pergamum: 2:12a,12b,13a,13b,14-5,16a,16b,17a,17b;
Thyatira: 2:18a,18b, 19a,19b,20-1,22-3,24-5,26-8,29;
Sardis: 3:1a,1b,1c,1d,2-3a,3b,4,5,6;
Philadelphia: 3:7a,7b,8a,8b-10, (3:11a is interpreted as a book level prosody and not as one of the letter constituents), 11b,12,13;
Laodicea: 3:14a,14b,15,16-8,19,20,21,22,23.

Perusal of the above list indicates that the changes in the ordering of the constituents are not random, but fall into two main categories. Firstly, the order of the two concluding units 8 and 9 are reversed from the fourth letter to Thyatira onwards. The effect of this change is to bring the generic exhortation ('He who has ears...'), which draws attention to all the instructions contained in the letters, to the attention of the reader more quickly and unexpectedly in this fourth letter to Thyatira. This contributes an element of special prominence to the letter to Thyatira.

Secondly, all the other variations are limited to the body of the letters. The variations revealed by the list are the fact that particular constituents may be missing entirely (indicated by #), or may occur in a different position. This latter variation, with one exception, is limited to the commendation (Constituent 4). The exception is again in the letter to Thyatira, where the warning (Constituent 7, 2:22-3) occurs before the main exhortation (Constituent 6) because it is a continuation of the reproach (Constituent 5, 2:20-1).

A further variation, which the list does not show, but which helps to explain some of the changes in order, is that certain constituents in some of the letters are particularly long and contain more information than their counterparts. This variation seems to particularly affect Constituent 6, which is the central exhortation. Possible reasons for these variations will become clearer in the following discussion.

7.5.4 Volitional Import and Natural and Special Prominence

One of the most important generalizations which can be made about the letters is that, with the exception of the first constituent, which is a formal introduction, all of the constituents combine to create a volitional import text. Consequently, they have the characteristics which are typical of volitional import, or hortatory, text.

- Constituent 2 of each letter, which links back to the setting of the cycle as a whole, provides a validation of the person who is issuing the evaluations and the exhortations.
- Constituent 3 provides support for this validation process since it reveals the fact that the sender of the letters is speaking, not only from a position of inherent authority, but also on the basis of incisive awareness of the situation in each place. This also serves as a motivator, because right from the beginning the recipients know that Christ is aware of even their hidden faults, so that there is no point in arguing or justifying themselves in any way.
- Constituent 6, which contains the primary exhortation, is the only obligatory component of a volitional import message and is, therefore, the most naturally prominent constituent.

- Constituent 8 is also an exhortation, but a more general one, which supports and underlines the importance of all the more detailed exhortations.

The other constituents provide a range of both positive and contrasting negative reinforcement.

- Constituent 4 is the commendation and
- Constituent 5 is the reproach, and so these two constituents provide positive and negative motivation on the basis of what has already been accomplished. This serves as a springboard for a future response to the following exhortations, since these indicate how the addressees can continue on in an appropriate way, and so obtain further commendations. They also indicate how to avoid what is inappropriate, and thus any further reproaches.
- Constituent 7, being either a warning or an invitation (only the letter to Smyrna contains what may be interpreted as both a warning and an invitation 2:10b), provides negative or positive reinforcement, as the case may be. It does this by indicating the negative or positive consequences, which are contingent on the response of the addressees to the instructions received.

The fact that Cycle 1 is totally composed of volitional import text sets the tone for the whole book, since it is the first, and therefore introductory, part of the body of the book as a whole. Although it is not overtly stated, it is clearly implicit from this starting point, that the author's overall purpose in all that he says, is to influence the behavior of his addressees. Since the volitional text is the furthest one can go down the purposive chain, this kind of text is the most important for the author's purpose, and it is this primary purpose which provides the context for the cycles which follow.

As noted above, most of the letters have some variations in the order of the constituents, and also some differences in the extent to which certain constituents are developed. Since all the letters are otherwise so similar in structure, these variations are interpreted as indicators of special prominence at the level of the individual letters. It can be noted therefore, that for the letter to Ephesus, the commendation would seem to be particularly prominent. This is because it is longer than most and contains considerable detail. It also has several reasons for being approved and a repetition of the key word 'endurance' (2:2-3). In addition, another commendation occurs later in 2:6.

For the letter to Smyrna, it is Constituent 7 which is the most developed (2:10b-c). It is marked by 'behold', and, implicitly at least, contains both a warning concerning their next test, and also an invitation to remain faithful which, in turn, contains an inherent extra promise.

Pergamum's letter conforms the most to the standard format and has no noticeable variations and no occurrence of 'behold'. The only special feature which it has, is the presence of *dé* 'but' at 2:16. In this context, this is interpreted as a contrastive feature which, along with the phrase 'I am coming quickly', does contribute a heightened prominence to the following warning. This would seem to be the only part which is specially prominent.

INFORMATION

The functor *dé* 'but' occurs so rarely in Revelation that it can be considered to be a prominence marker wherever it occurs. It is interpreted as such for the letters to Ephesus (2:5), Pergamum (2:16) and Thyatira (2:24). The warning to the church at Sardis (3:3) is marked by 'therefore' rather than by *dé* 'but'. This usage of 'therefore' is also interpreted as a prominence marker, firstly, by analogy with the usage in the Ephesian and Pergamum letters, secondly, because of its rarity in Revelation, and thirdly, because it occurs twice in two consecutive sentences, thereby forming a doublet.

The letter to Thyatira has several prominence markers as will be discussed in more detail in the following section.

In the letter to Sardis, the commendation is displaced and the reproach is very short. The net effect is that the central exhortation (3:2-3) comes more rapidly than usual to the reader's attention. In addition, this exhortation is particularly developed, and contains five imperatives intertwined with an extra element of reproach (3:2b).

It is the promises in the letter to Philadelphia which are specially prominent. The commendation (3:8c) is bracketed by three extra promises, two of which are marked by 'behold' (3:8b, 9a-b and 10), and the usual promise constituent (number 9) is particularly long (3:12). This is reinforced by the fact that there is no reproach and no warning or invitation. It is as if the promises in their case are unconditional.

By contrast, Laodicea's special prominence highlights the element of invitation/warning in association with the reproach. The reproach 3:15b-18 is particularly developed, but most of this development consists of an extra warning ('I am about to vomit you...' 3:16) and invitation ('I counsel you...' 3:18a) which build on the reproach but lead the readers towards a positive solution. The normal invitation constituent (number 7 at 3:20) is not particularly long, but is marked by 'behold'.

This is reinforced by the fact that there is no commendation. In addition, the extra information contained in the central exhortation (3:19), speaks to this same issue, in that Jesus makes it clear that rebuke and chastening are for those whom He loves.

Review of the above features indicates that, apart from the introductory statement beginning ‘I know’ (Constituent 3), and the general exhortation (Constituent 8), all the constituents in the body and the conclusion of the letters are made specially prominent in one or other of the letters. This indicates that the organization reflects a certain systematization. The net result is that in the course of the seven letters all the constituents, which contain significant hortatory implications, are emphasized at one point or another in the cycle. Consequently, the readers are left with the overall impression that each of the hortatory aspects of Christ’s messages to them should be taken seriously.

7.5.5 The Natural and Special Prominence of the Letters Cycle Viewed as a Whole

Since the letters are organized in the form of a simple list with no obvious linear connection between them, it is impossible to say that one of them is more naturally prominent than any other. At this level, each of them is important, and for any particular church concerned, the one addressed to them personally, would be the most important for them. The fact that each of the primary hortatory constituents is marked in turn as specially prominent, as described above, reinforces this view that the author, at one level at least, intended that each of the parts of his exhortation should be taken seriously. This is true internally for each of the letters, but it would also seem to be true for each of the letters as a unit in a series.

Since the most naturally prominent part of each letter is the central exhortation (Constituent 6), the only other way of determining the prominent part of the cycle as a whole, is to take account of all of these exhortations in some kind of aggregate or summarized form. The first of the two primary exhortations which summarize all the others is the command, ‘Repent’. This particular exhortation is also implicit in the commands ‘remember from where you have fallen’ and ‘(Go back and) do the same works as before’ 2:5.

The second most significant exhortation is the one which urges the readers to ‘persevere’. This latter concept is communicated by many different verbal forms, such as ‘hold fast’ 2:25, ‘watch (out)’ 3:2, ‘enduring’, ‘(keep on) remembering’ 3:3a, ‘keeping’ 3:3b, and ‘be faithful’ 2:10. It is also implicit in the exhortation to ‘not fear’, in the face of suffering in 2:10. These same words and concepts also occur in constituents other than the central exhortation constituent.

Overall the word ‘repent’ occurs with various degrees of repetition as follows:

- twice in Letter 1,
- once in Letter 3,
- three times in Letter 4, and
- once each in Letters 5 and 6.

The concept of endurance, or remaining faithful, occurs as follows:

- four times in Letter 1,
- once in Letter 2,
- three times in Letters 3, 4 and 5, and
- four times in Letter 6.

In addition, the concept is also implicit in all the letters in the reference to the overcomer in Constituent 9.

Upon reflection it can be seen that these two concepts have similar hortatory implications. 'Repent' implies that a person has already fallen into sin, but now needs to turn back to their previous state and avoid the negative consequences, which will otherwise come upon them. The concept inherent in 'perseverance' implies that a person is confronted with the possibility of falling, but needs to remain firm in the face of that danger, once again with the aim of avoiding the inherent negative consequences.

The word/concept 'repent' in its positive form only occurs in Cycle 1 and is, therefore, considered to be a particular characteristic of this cycle and, consequently, one of the unique contributions which it makes to the book as a whole. It occurs eight times in the seven letters 2:5(x2),16,21(x2),22; 3:3,19. It also occurs four times elsewhere (9:20,21 and 16:9,11) with reference to those who did not repent.

By contrast, the word/concept 'perseverance/endurance' occurs in many other places throughout the book (e.g. 13:10) and is, therefore, considered to be a book-level theme, in the sense that it is not limited to one particular cycle.

It is considered therefore, that these two concepts together, form the most naturally prominent part of the seven letters taken together as a series. Further study of these concepts as they occur in the central exhortation of each letter, also leads to a clearer understanding of the special prominence of the cycle. When they are aligned in order to facilitate comparison, the following pattern emerges, as can be seen in Chart 53 below.

The letters are so similar in form and content that there is no dispute that they are in parallel to one another, in general structural terms. In addition, there is considerable semantic and surface structure parallelism, the most obvious examples of which, are already contained in the chart.

As can be seen in the chart, there is a definite alternating pattern of the two main concepts under discussion. In addition to that pattern, the regular occurrence of the specific imperative 'Repent', creates another complementary, clear-cut alternation, with consequent parallelism, between the sub-units. As a result, therefore, positing a chiasm for the entire set of letters, becomes a distinct possibility.

Chart 53.
The Chiastic Organization of the Letters Cycle

A. Ephesus: Remember, **Repent !** and do (again) your first works. 2:5
B. Smyrna: Do not fear, be faithful **(hold on)** in order to get your crown 2:10
C. Pergamum: **Repent !** (2:16)
D. Thyatira: Hold on to what you have until I come. 2:25
C' Sardis: Remember what you received and keep it, and **Repent !** 3:3
B' Philadelphia: **Hold on** to what you have in order to keep your crown. 3:11
A' Laodicea: Be hot (again) and **Repent !** 3:19

Furthermore, the accompanying commands for Ephesus and Laodicea, 'Do (again) your first works', and 'Be (again) hot', are saying the same thing in direct, and metaphorical, language respectively, which means that they are particularly in parallel to each other. Between them, these two letters, with the occurrence of the verb 'to repent' and its accompanying verb 'to do' or 'to become', also create a parallel, abb'a' pattern, namely: a. repent, b. do first works : b' become hot again, a' repent.

Ephesus contains a warning about a possible removal of their lamp stand which means that they would no longer be able to see. Laodicea contains an invitation to buy eye medicine so that they can see again. Pergamum and Sardis both contain a warning about Christ 'coming' to them in judgment, with a sword (2:16) and as a thief (3:3) respectively. This element also puts them in parallel with the Ephesus letter, which has a similar reference to Christ coming in judgment in 2:5.

Both Pergamum and Sardis make reference to a white object in the promise to the overcomers. It is a white stone in 2:17, and white garments in 3:5. This supports the notion that these two pairs of letters are specifically in parallel, as well as participating in an alternating pattern based on the word 'repent'.

In addition, the Smyrna and Philadelphia letters are in specific parallelism with each other, because they are the only ones which refer to a crown (2:10 and 3:11) and both refer to imminent suffering. In the one case, the Christians have to pass through it patiently, and in the other they will be protected, as per 2:10 and 3:10.

When all this evidence is combined, then an ABCDC'B'A' chiasm becomes definitely plausible. This means that the letter to Thyatira

(2:18- 29), being at the center of the chiasm, is the most specially prominent of all the letters.

Closer examination of this letter confirms this proposal, because it has the largest concentration of special prominence features of all the letters, as indicated below:

- This letter is the longest.
- Constituent 7, the warning, is fronted one position, thereby coming to the readers' attention more rapidly than usual (2:22-23).
- This feature mitigates the naturally prominent exhortation which now follows (2:24- 25).
- It has a triple repetition of the verb 'to repent' (2:21 x 2, and 23), which are in addition to the central exhortation, which is focused on the exhortation to persevere.
- This central exhortation is marked by the presence of *dé* 'but'.
- It has a double repetition of the verb 'to throw', both of which are dynamic and unusual metaphorical usages (2:22 and 24).
- The first of these occurrences is marked by 'behold'.
- It has the hyperbolic phrase 'I will kill with death' (2:23), which is the most unusually graphic idiom in the whole cycle, possibly even in the whole book.
- It contains the striking occurrence of the title for Jesus, 'the Son of God', which is the only place in the book where it occurs.
- It has a unique extra reference to 'all the churches' (2:23).
- It has a four-fold repetition of the verb 'to give' (2:21,23,26,28).
- It has the longest promise to the overcomers, which is also made more prominent by being fronted, since this is the first place where Constituents 8 and 9 change positions.

INFORMATION

Length in and of itself is not a mark of prominence. Whatever stands out as different in its context is prominent, and so the length feature falls into this category for the seven letters. This is confirmed by the observation that the second longest letter (to Philadelphia) which occurs in Longacre's post-peak position (op.cit. 1983a,22), is likely to be the second highest point of prominence in the cycle. This proposal is supported by the fact that this letter has a very long promise (Constituent 9) and has three occurrences of 'behold'.

So it can be seen then, that there are many features which make this letter, as a whole, different from the other letters, thereby marking it out as more prominent than the others.

Internally, however, the letter's own characteristics, which display the greatest amount of development, and the greatest concentration of prominence features, draw particular attention to Constituents 5 and 7. These are the reproach and the warning constituents, and, in this case, they are brought together in one paragraph in 2:20-23. The purpose of this combination of reproach and warning is to underscore the importance of repentance.

After a brief pause provided by the extra introductory material and a switch of focus, indicated by *dé* 'but' 2:24, the call to repent is followed by the naturally prominent central exhortation, which emphasizes the need to persevere in 2:25. There is also a striking parallelism between the two sections, marked by 'behold', which highlights the fact that they are designed to work together.

In 2:22, speaking of Jezebel, Christ says: 'Behold, I am throwing her onto a bed, and the ones committing adultery with her (I am throwing) into great affliction, unless they repent of what she has done (literally: 'her works')'. Then in 2:24 he continues his speech by saying 'But I say to the rest of you at Thyatira who (implicitly) have not followed her... I am not throwing on you an extra burden, unless (it is) that you hold fast to what you have until I come'. This then continues on with the promise to the overcomers (2:26) which is addressed to those who 'keep my (Christ's) works until the end'.

This means that the letter to Thyatira is the only one which devotes a whole section to each of these two exhortations, thereby giving approximately equal weight to each. In this way, the two principal exhortations of the entire cycle, are brought together in the same unit at the center of the chiasm.

7.5.6 An Overview of the Message of the Letters Cycle

The analysis described above has made it possible to locate the most important parts of the total message which is contained in the first cycle, composed of the letters to the seven churches. These parts are the central exhortations of each letter, which are the most naturally prominent part of each, and the parts which are marked for special prominence. The information contained in these passages combined together in summary form is presented in Chart 53 above. The primary imperatives of the central exhortation are in bold face for ease of reference, and equivalent concepts are in brackets.

Chart 54 presents the material in Cycle 1 which is prominent in one way or another. It is an illustration of the fact that a careful study of linguistic prominence is not only useful but is, in fact, essential, for discovering what the main message of a text is, according to the intention of the author. Accurate interpretation can only take place once the main message has been established on the basis of objective evidence. This objective evidence is data which can be located in the text, and which is interpreted using a consistent set of criteria, which can be used and tested by others.

Chart 54.

An Overview of the Message of the Letters Cycle

A. Ephesus: Your perseverance is commendable. But remember from where you have fallen. **Repent,** and return to your first works which were works of love. But if not I will remove your lamp stand (your source of light and life).

B. Smyrna: **Persevere** in face of the coming test. If you **persevere** even in the face of death, I will give you the crown of life.

C. Pergamum: Repent! But if not I am coming soon, and will fight (bring death) with my sword (like a warrior or judge).

D. Thyatira: Jezebel must **repent** of her works! But since she will **not repent** I am throwing her into a bed (test), and will kill her children with death. But as for you, I throw on you no other burden except that you should **persevere** (by continuing to do my works) until I come. All the churches should take note of this.

C' Sardis: Watch out and restore the things (your works) which are dying. Remember what you received before, and keep on (persevering) and **repent.** (But) if not I will come like a thief (to destroy/kill).

B' Philadelphia: I give you all you need for life and protection from the coming great test. I am coming soon, so **persevere** in what you have, in order to keep your crown (of life).

('life' is used as a conceptual resume of the promises of hope and of vindication given in vv.8-9 and 12)

A' Laodicea: I rebuke the people I love, so **repent** and be hot (ardent as you were at first). If you will **repent** I will come in and provide all that you need for life.

The chart as it stands particularly highlights the parallel organization, which is a direct result of the repetition of a similar structural organization in each letter. It also demonstrates, by its chiastic form, how that the cycle, as a whole, is not just a monotonous list, but also has its own peak of special interest, just as most well-formed discourses do. It also provides a basis for comparing and contrasting the different elements, which are in parallel to each other, and which, in turn, can lead to an understanding of linear thematic developments which are not at first apparent.

So, for example, in sections A, C. and C' Christ says 'I am coming' or 'I will come', but in section A' He has come and is present at the door. In B. the faithful are promised protection as they go through their test, but in B' they are assured that they will be spared the test entirely. Meanwhile, in D., the unrepentant are tested to the point of death. In A. the loss of the source of life (the lamp stand) is threatened, and as a result the implied house would be full of darkness, while in A' the offer of on-going life is a present reality as the risen Christ proposes to come through the door into their house. In B., future life is promised, while in B', the hope of life is a present assurance.

In short, the structural interweaving at the micro level, is both subtle and systematic. Nonetheless, it harmonizes, both structurally and semantically, with the macro structure. It is possible to study it in as much detail as is desired, but it will withstand the scrutiny. This is because, whether at the cycle level, the sub-unit level, or the lower levels, it is not random, but is consistent with the author's overall communicative purpose. All the details support this overall purpose in some way or another, and all contribute to the total impact of his message. Each of the structural strands which have been described in the above discussion, can be pursued wherever they may lead, and each of them will reveal a part of the rich tapestry of the total message.

7.5.7 Conclusion

In addition to the harmony at the micro level, the first cycle harmonizes with, and thereby provides support for, three major elements of the macro structure.

Firstly, the volitional nature of its message is unmistakable. This harmonizes with other volitional import material elsewhere in the book. This hortatory material occurs primarily in the Prologue and in the Epilogue, but also, in more scattered form, in other parts of the book.

Secondly, in terms of the number of types of units, the first cycle also confirms what has been observed for other parts of the book. It was proposed above, that each letter is composed of a maximum possible number of nine constituents, most of which are obligatory, and some of which are optional. This internal structure of the letters is in harmony with the structural organization of other parts of the book, for the book itself is composed of nine principal parts, namely, the Prologue, the seven cycles, and the Epilogue. In addition, the dominant structural pattern for the cycles themselves, is also an organization with nine principal parts, most of which are obligatory, and one of which is optional. Thus it is that most of the cycles are composed of a setting, a body with seven principal parts, and an optional interlude.

Thirdly, this cycle contains two levels of exhortation. There are the specific exhortations to repent and persevere for example, and there is also the more general exhortation, 'He who has ears to hear...', which urges the reader to live out the specific exhortations. This is also a feature of the book as a whole, which has both these kinds of exhortation. The specific ones occur in the body of the book, and the more general ones occur in the Prologue and the Epilogue.

7.6 The Contribution of Cycle 1 to the Informational Flow of the Book

In the previous section we concentrated almost entirely on the contribution which Cycle 1 makes to the volitional import thrust of the book. This is because an exploration of the natural, and the special prominence of the cycle led down this path. As important as this is, this cycle does, nonetheless, accomplish more than that, for it also makes a significant contribution to the informational flow of the book and this should not be overlooked.

7.6.1 The Contribution to the Development of the Topic

As has been explained previously, the topic of the book, in specific terms, is the person of Jesus, the Messiah. Regardless of any other considerations, He is important, wherever He occurs as a participant, because of who He is, and also because He is the topic of the book. However, since He is the topic, He can be an active participant without this fact being clearly stated all the time.

This is the case for the Letters Cycle. It is possible to get so much caught up with the career of the Church as it is developed in this cycle, that it can be forgotten that Jesus is, nonetheless, the master of ceremonies. He is the one who is dictating each and every one of the letters. As was highlighted in the discussion about Him in Chapter 6.8.2, He is the Commander in Chief of the Church, and so He talks to them in the seven letters from that position of authority.

This very general statement was made in Chapter 6, but now in this section we will give a brief review of how that works out, and is exemplified, at the lower, more detailed levels.

Jesus' Kingly Attributes

Jesus is not overtly named in any of the letters, for His presence is taken for granted, because He was introduced in the Prologue, and it was stated there that He was in the process of sending a letter, or letters, to the churches. However, His participation is re-activated each time, by a repetition of one or more of His personal characteristics. These usually recall the description of Jesus as King, which is given in considerable detail, in the Prologue, and in the setting to this cycle.

These are as follows:

- ➢ The One holding the seven stars in His right hand and who walks among the seven lamp stands 2:1

- The One who is the first and the last, who died, but is alive again 2:8
- The One who has the two-edged sword 2:12
- The One who is the Son of God, who has eyes like flames of fire, and feet like burnished bronze 2:18. Note that the occurrence of 'the Son of God' is new information and is not a repetition, and this is in the letter to Thyatira, which is the most prominent letter.
- The One having the seven Spirits of God and the seven stars 3:1. Note that the seven Spirits of God are mentioned in 1:4, but the statement that Jesus 'has' them, is new information.
- The One who is Holy and True, who has the key of David to open and shut doors unopposed 3:7. This is all new information.
- The One who is the Amen, the faithful and true witness, the Chief of God's creation 3:14. This is also new information except for the faithful witness.

Jesus' Kingly Actions

When these attributes are linked to the things which Jesus is described as doing, then further insights can be deduced. So, for example, He has the seven Spirits of God, and so it is not surprising that He knows everything about what is going on, and this fact is stated in each letter, sometimes more than once as in 2:23.

He is the one who has the double-edged sword. This means that He has the authority to decide. This could mean a decision regarding what is not up to His standard, which implies reproof (2:14), or even final judgment (2:22-23). It could also mean a positive decision of commendation and reward as in 2:10, for example, in all the promises to the overcomers, and in 2:23 once again.

He is the Son of God, the Eternal One, and the one who paid the price by giving His life before being raised again. This means that He clearly has the right, and the authority, to tell them what they should be doing, and what they should not be doing, as has been evident in the discussion of the exhortations presented in the previous sections.

These are all attributes and actions characteristic of a Commander in Chief. Consequently, it can be seen that what was stated, at first, in general terms on the basis of a study of the macro structure, is confirmed in meticulous detail, as one looks at the intricacies of the micro structure.

7.6.2 The Contribution to the Sub-Topic of the Career of the Church

Having said all that, Jesus is not alone, for He has companions, and in this cycle, it is clear that those companions are the members of the various local churches. As a consequence, because He is a King, they also can aspire to be kings and to rule and reign with Him. The seed thought for this thread was sown right at the beginning in 1:6. However, this idea did not get picked up previously because, at the time, it was just a detail, embedded in the sub-topic of worship as described in 7.4.4 above.

Interestingly, when this seed thought about the Church being made kings and priests for God, is repeated, almost word for word in 5:10, this information is also embedded into a context of worship. Of course, being a priest implies serving God in worship, as well as serving God in shepherding His people (cf. 2:27), as the priests did in the Old Testament.

> **QUOTE**
> **Humans exercise royal rule.**
> **Gentry 2008,23**

But in any case, this verse also adds the extra information that they will specifically reign on, or over, the earth, which is the same jurisdiction as for Jesus. It is also totally in line with the very important coda, which occurs right at the end of the body of the book, at 22:5c, which also appears in the following list.

The verb 'to reign' occurs specifically in the book seven times. If the two references cited above about the Church being made kings (or literally 'a kingdom'), are included, that makes a total of nine references to this concept of reigning.

The seven specific references are as follows:

- ➢ Those purchased by the blood of the Lamb will reign on the earth 5:10 (as above)
- ➢ Two references to the reign of Jesus, proclaimed at the time of the seventh trumpet 11:15,17
- ➢ A reference to God's reign proclaimed in a context of worship in the last interlude 19:6
- ➢ Two references to those who die for Jesus, saying that they will reign with Him 20:4,6
- ➢ The final coda to the whole book referring to the eternal reign of the people of God 22:5c

Another word which supports the concept of reigning as a king, is the word 'crown'. This word occurs eight time in the whole book, but only twice referring to the members of the churches on the earth, as indicated in 2:10 and 3:11. In these verses it shows that Jesus is the one who has the right to award crowns, or to decide if they should be taken away again, which adds to the list of His kingly actions. In 2:10 it is specifically described as the crown of life, but regardless of that, a crown implies kingly authority, even if it can be used in a variety of contexts. So, for example, in 4:10, the 24 elders throw their crowns down before God's throne, as an act of worship.

So, from these brief allusions then, it can be deduced that all the members of the churches can aspire to receive the crown of life, and thereby to receive all the rights, privileges and responsibilities which go with it. Maybe they can even aspire to wear crowns like the elders when they get to glory as well. In any case, even though the word 'crown' is used in different contexts in the book, the one thing in common is that the crown always represents an authority of some sort, which enables the wearer to also act with authority, in whichever jurisdiction they happen to be placed.

The Church's Kingly Attributes

In the previous sections it was observed that the most important parts of the Letters Cycle are the instructions or the exhortations given by the Commander in Chief to His followers, that is, to the members of the churches. However, that is not all that can be said, for, naturally enough, these letters have other things to communicate, which maybe of secondary importance, but which still have, nonetheless, a significant level of importance. These secondary issues are important because they serve to support and confirm the whole concept of reigning.

The particular concept in view here, is the concept of overcoming. This is the part of each letter which is second in importance. This is because it is always part of the conclusion to the letters, regardless of whether it comes in ninth or eighth position, and is, therefore, in the position of highest natural prominence.

Secondly, it is because it is specifically repeated seven times, once in each letter, and thirdly because, it is conceptually synonymous with the concepts of kings and of reigning. The point about reigning is that somebody or other may resist your authority, in which case, the rightful king has to exert his authority and overcome the opposition. This is accomplished by one means or another, as appropriate to the principles of his kingdom. This issue, and this necessary implication of kingship, is a universal of human experience, and is a constant theme within Revelation itself.

This issue is so important that Jesus addresses it specifically each time. Technically, the words to the overcomers are expressed as promises, but they could also be interpreted as mitigated, or disguised, exhortations. This is because these utterances could be interpreted as saying; 'You should be an overcomer, and I want you to be an overcomer, and if you learn to be an overcomer, you will receive this reward'.

In the following list will be found the concepts which are linked to being an overcomer. This is because they are the promises attached to the implied exhortation to work at becoming an overcomer:

- They will be able to eat of the tree of life 2:7. This is similar to receiving the crown of life.
- They will be exempt from the second death 2:11.
- They will be able eat special food, known as the hidden manna 2:17.
- They will receive a white stone which bears a new, unique name for them 2:17.
- They will have authority over the nations and will shepherd them with a rod of iron 2:26-27
- They will receive the morning star 2:28
- They will receive white clothes 3:5
- They will not run the risk of having their names removed from the book of life 3:5
- They will be spoken for by Jesus before God 3:5
- They will be (like) a permanent pillar in God's temple 3:12
- Jesus will write on them God's name, the name of the New Jerusalem, and His own new name 3:12
- They will sit on the kingly throne with Jesus; this is the destiny for overcomers because it was Jesus' own destiny, who was also an overcomer 3:21

It is noteworthy that there are twelve individual items in this list, and the verb 'to overcome' also occurs twelve times in the book. It happens that the number twelve, by coincidence of course, is the number which symbolizes, the most complete, or the most perfect form of government which is possible.

The Church's Kingly Actions

Some of the promises included in the above list are difficult for us to comprehend completely, for they obviously refer to timeless, spiritual conditions or qualities, and not to the finite, temporal ones which we are used to. Nonetheless, we can reasonably deduce that several of them are to do with obtaining eternal life, and others are to do with our eternal identity, purpose and value, while others refer to what the overcomer can expect to accomplish in this life as well as on into eternity.

So we know from 19:8 that the white clothes represent the actions which an overcomer is enabled to accomplish, which please God, because they are in line with His righteousness. Then there are also two clear references to exercising Jesus' authority and so reigning with Him. In this case 12:11 tells us the methods by which the overcomers overcome those opposing them, and thus they establish their rule. These methods are:

- Using the authority of the blood of the Lamb,
- Declaring their own Testimony
- By being willing to give up their lives in service of the Lamb.

These are clearly not the physical methods used in the world's system, but are the methods which are appropriate and effective in the system of God's Kingdom. Nonetheless, this information is confirmed as accurate because Jesus Himself used the same methods while on the earth.

If there is any doubt about that, then we are given a practical example in the Trumpets Interlude in Chapter 11, where we have the example of the Two Witnesses. Being two witnesses, like the disciples who went out in twos, these two witnesses obviously are representative of the followers of Jesus, in other words, of the Church.

Their story clearly indicates that they operated with a supernatural authority, and not with a mere human authority. It indicates also that their primary method of operating was by the words, the testimony, which came from their mouths. Then ultimately, at the last battle, they were willing to give their lives for the cause of Christ. But it was not a defeat; it was their ultimate victory, for by this means they overcame the worst of their enemies, and were totally victorious. Then, from there, they moved on to eternal life and glory, with a new name and a new identity, in God's presence.

This is not an isolated example either, for other references to those who were unjustly killed because they were followers of the Lamb are to be found in 6:9-11 and 20:4. In this latter case, we are specifically told that these people were overcomers, because they had resisted the wiles of the devil while on the earth, and had possibly paid the ultimate price with their lives as well, if this reading is correct. Either way, they were definitely destined to be seated on thrones in order to reign with Jesus. Reigning with Christ then, is clearly one of the good works, or kingly actions, which the overcomers can, and do, get involved in, in the course of their career.

So, in section 7.4.3 above, it was seen in general terms, that becoming an overcomer was part of the Church's mandate and career. As we have looked at the information provided about the Church, and its calling and destiny, in the details of Cycle 1, then we have found that this is confirmed. This is another thread which appears in different places throughout the book.

7.7 The Internal Organization of Cycle 4: The Seven Signs 11:15-16:1

As previously explained in Chapter 6, the Signs Cycle is the most specially prominent of all the cycles and is, therefore, a pivotal point in the whole discourse. For this reason then, we will take a moment to look at it in a bit more detail, to see what other new things we can learn, and to confirm that the details coincide, and correspond, with what we have already learned from the overview picture of the macro structure.

The internal structure of each sub-unit of this cycle will be laid out again below, as a reminder, in order to facilitate this process.

The first thing to be noticed is right at the beginning, in the setting to the cycle, as demonstrated below. The specific items which are re-activated for the specific setting to this cycle are that Jesus, reigning from the throne of His Father, God Almighty, has taken up His authority to reign over the earth. This is all proclaimed and set in motion in a context of worship, as we have seen before. Notably, it is the worship which is the most important element and not the reigning.

7.7.1 The Setting 11:15-19

A. Introductory Event in Heaven 11:15a

  B. Direct Speech: Generic statement about the Reign of Christ 11:15b

    C. A response: Worship 11:16

  B' Direct Speech: Specific Statements about the Reign of God Almighty 11:17-18

A' Concluding Event in Heaven 11:19

This setting is clearly a direct continuation from what was set out in Cycle 1, as explained above. But also, more specifically, it arises out of the highly developed setting to Cycles 2-6 in Chapters 4 and 5, which is the starting point for all of these middle cycles.

It can be seen then, that the starting point for this cycle, and the source from which everything else flows, is that Jesus is King, and He, therefore, decides what is going to happen and what is not. It is from this base then, that the rest follows, and the rest is that the dragon is totally defeated and thrown down from his previous place of authority. As a result, he is obliged to call up two proxies, the two beasts, who are commissioned to do his dirty work for him.

So that explains that. Jesus is King and, therefore, the dragon and his minions can only do what they are permitted to do. No more and no less.

7.7.2 Sub-Unit 1 of The Body : Signs 1 and 2 12:1-18

A. Introduction of the first two personages (signs) and their first encounter. 12:1-6

B. War in Heaven and the dragon is thrown down to the earth. 12:7-9

B' Explanation of the significance of the dragon being thrown down. 12:10-12

A' Conclusion of the narrative: second encounter and denouement. 12:13-17b

Coda: Transition (tail-head link 'sea') to next sub-unit. 12:18

This unit is in the form of a symmetric structure, rather than a chiasm with its single sub-unit at the point of the arrow. This means that the prominence is flatter and less marked. This means, in turn, that the overall message is what is important, not just one part of it.

So, in this case, what is in focus and therefore important, is the defeat of the dragon, and the consequent, supernatural success of the woman and her Seed. This Seed, of course, was destined, from the beginning of time, to crush the serpentine dragon's head. Previously, the dragon had had access to Heaven and had an authority which was commensurate with that freedom of access. From this point in the story onwards, he is consigned to the earth and only permitted to operate in the earth realm, with the more limited authority which that implies. This sounds very similar to the report of him being consigned to a pit, as described in Chapter 20.

7.7.3 Sub-Unit 2 : Sign 3 13:1-10

The structure of the second sub-unit is as follows:

A. Description of the first beast emphasizing its great authority over people of the earth. It is 'as though it had been killed'. 13:1-3

B. Its Authority: it leads the inhabitants of the earth to false worship 13:4

B' Its Authority: it blasphemes God and the inhabitants of Heaven. 13:5-6

A' Resume concerning the use of its authority over people on the earth. These are the saints and those not written in the book of 'the Lamb who has been killed' 13:7-8

Coda: Exhortation directed at the reader. 13:9-10

This sub-unit has the same internal structure as the previous one. In fact, all the first four sub-units, that is, the first three sign units and the interlude, have the same structure. Two observations can be made arising from this. In the Letters Cycle, all the letters had a very similar internal structure and so they are in parallel to each other for that reason. But now, in the Signs Cycle, the internal organization of the signs sub-units uses quite a different system.

Nonetheless, all the sub-units use a similar, concentric system, which is not the linear system of the letters, and the structure of four of the seven sub-units are identical. So the observations are, that the cycles do not have the same internal structures, but these can be quite different. Yet, at the same time, they are all based on an underlying system of parallelism.

This sub-unit is all about the concept of authority. Authority is that intangible asset which gives its holder the right to make decisions, and to some extent impose its will, in a certain, specified domain. Appropriate authority is an essential ingredient for governing, without which it is impossible to be involved in the process of reigning.

The domain of authority in question is the earth. Ostensibly the beast received its authority from the dragon (13:2-4), who had indeed had authority over the earth for a long time. However, at the same time, we are told that its authority was limited by what someone, who is unnamed, permitted it to do. This is indicated by the repeated use of the phrase 'it was given to it' in 13:5,7a and 7b. Presumably this 'someone' is God Almighty, the Creator of the earth and the ultimate authority over everything and everyone.

The main point is that the dragon, having been thrown out of Heaven, does retain some authority over the earth, by means of this other spiritual being called, a beast. However, this authority is limited, and between them, they can only accomplish what 'is given to them' to accomplish.

7.7.4 Sub-Unit 3 : Sign 4 13:11-18

The structure of the third sub-unit is as follows:

A. Description of the second beast emphasizing its authority. 13:11-12a

B. Its Authority: it leads the inhabitants of the earth to false worship using signs v12b-13

B' Its Authority: one of these signs is a talking statue to be worshiped. 13:14-15

A' Resume concerning the use of its authority on the earth. 13:16-17

Coda: Exhortation directed at the reader. 13:18

This sub-unit describes a second beast which is similar to, and has the same authority and purpose, as the first one. This sub-unit picks up on, and develops, a subsidiary issue which was already referred to in the previous sub-unit. The issue is that of worship, which is an important sub-topic of the book as we have already seen. In these two sign units, it becomes clear that worship is an activity which falls into the domain and the purview of the earth-dwellers.

In this case, it is a false worship, which the beasts are consigned to stir up or elicit. Consequently, it is not directed towards those who are worthy of worship, either because they are the Creator of the earth, or the Redeemer of the earth-dwellers, as in Chapters 4 and 5, but it is directed towards a devious usurper of power, the dragon.

The timeless bottom-line question is this: 'Who will rule the world?'. The cosmic conflict is between God, the Creator, and thus the 'owner' of the world, and His Christ, on the one side, and the created cherub, who became an accuser and an adversary, on the other. This conflict and its outcome, was briefly summarized in sub-unit 1, above.

However, there is a third party involved in this conflict, who actually holds the balance of power, and these are the earth-dwellers, the members of the human race. The Creator, in His wisdom, delegated the authority to govern the earth to Adam and his descendants, and that decision has never been revoked. Consequently, it is the earth-dwellers who decide, who elect, if you like, the spiritual, ultimate source of power, who will be the actual, representative, government of their planet.

They decide this by choosing who they have confidence in, and who they will look to, to look after them and to provide for them. Having made this decision, they pledge their allegiance to this source of power, and they manifest that allegiance by their worship.

In these two sub-units this allegiance and worship is directed, inappropriately, towards the dragon, but, nonetheless, enough detail is provided which reveals how the system works.

7.7.5 Sub-Unit 4 : Interlude 14:1-5

The structure of the fourth sub-unit is as follows:

A. Description of the Lamb and His entourage of 144,000 people. 14:1

B. Worship: the sound of harps in Heaven 14:2

B' Worship: sound of new song before the Throne and the inhabitants of Heaven 14:3a

A' Those who sing the new song are the 144,000 only. 14:3b

Coda: Explanation concerning the identity of the 144,000. 14:4-5

(Note: This coda is particularly well developed and also has an abb'a' structure. See Appendix 4.1.4 for the detail.)

Next comes the interlude which is in direct contrast with what has gone before. The previous two sub-units presented, if you like, the viewpoint of those on the earth. They had the unfortunate predicament of having the dragon thrown down to co-habit with them, on the earth. He, in turn, had called up his two proxies to do his bidding, also on the earth. Their main task and goal was, by all means possible, to persuade the inhabitants of the earth to direct their allegiance and their worship towards the dragon, which they did.

By contrast, the interlude gives the viewpoint of Heaven, and of those aligned with Heaven. Here we see the Lamb standing on Mount Sion. Mountains in the Bible represent authority, which is what we have been talking about already in this cycle. The general knowledge of the readers would have informed them that, not only is this a mountain, but this is the one which represents the highest possible authority, that emanating from the throne room in Heaven. This is in direct contrast with the dragon. The last time we got a glimpse of him, he was down on the sea-shore. The sea-shore is not a mountain. It is the lowest place on terra firma that you can get, which goes to show that his authority is very minimal – the lowest possible – and is nothing compared to the Lamb's.

So the Lamb is standing – also a position of authority – and what do we hear and see? The answer is the same as before: the central activity going on is worship. This time it is the 144,000, who represent the people of God, who specifically are worshiping. If it was not clear before, then it becomes obvious here, that this group represent the redeemed people of God. This is because the key, new characteristic described, is that they have God's name written on their foreheads. We came across this before in Cycle 1, because one of the promises to the overcomers in 3:12, is that Jesus Himself would write God's name on them.

So it is only them. Only the redeemed, sealed (cf. 7:3), named, overcomers can sing this new song. By this means they are clearly supporting the Lamb in His position of authority, and by this means also, they are voting that He should reign where e're the sun's successive journeys run. As we said before, worship is crucial for authority, and it is by this means that the relevant authority is released to actually do the job of governing in practice. Even God Himself respects His own decrees, and so He limits Himself to only doing on the earth, whatever has been decreed and mandated by His people on the earth. This is why Jesus needs human companions, and why they follow Him wherever He goes, and participate in agreement with whatever He is doing.

So Jesus, the Lamb, does actually rule the world, despite all appearances to the contrary. This is not only because of God's decree who placed Him on Mount Sion, but also by the decision, the vote, and the support, of the descendants of Adam, who put their confidence in Him and committed their lives to Him.

As might be expected, these same concepts are continued, and developed further, in the next sub-unit.

7.7.6 Sub-Unit 5 : Sign 5 14:6-13

The structure of the fifth sub-unit is as follows:

A. The first angel and his speech to people on the earth: Fear God and Worship Him. 14:6-7

B. The second angel and his speech: Babylon is fallen. 14:8

A' The third angel and his speech: Condemnation on those who worship the beast. 14:9-11

Coda: Exhortation directed at the reader. 14:12-13

Including: A blessing which is part of the Narrative Framework and also a book level prominence feature.

This sub-unit is different in that it has a different internal structure. Its main part is composed of three speeches by three angels which, on the informational level, would all seem to be of equal weight and importance. They are all warnings preparing the way for the judgments which will fall and will be described in the following cycles.

The first one gives a final, definitive declaration concerning the issue of authority. As regards authority, we should fear God. It does not need to be explicitly stated, for it is obvious that He is the ultimate source of all power and authority, which is why we should give Him the glory. But in case it is not obvious, then we should fear Him because the time for His judgment has come, so we all need to look sharp, and take our precautions.

Then, in tandem with that, is a definitive statement about worship. We should worship God. Why? Because He is the Creator of all things. This includes the earth and the sea. These details are of interest because the two beasts came out of the earth and the sea. This means that they only came out of something which God created, so they too, are subject to His supreme authority.

These two declarations are directed specifically at all the inhabitants of the earth, not just at the Church. This means that everyone knows what they should do. God has spoken and made His will known, now it is up to each individual to make up his mind and decide for himself which side he is going to align himself with. It is in line with that decision that his eventual fate, or destiny, as the case may be, will be decided.

The second angel tells us that Babylon has fallen. This is in the aorist form of the verb, so it is described in general terms as an accomplished work. This, by implication, is because it has already been decided in Heaven, the price has been paid, and the essential work to accomplish this task has been completed. These implications were all set out in the setting of Chapters 4 and 5. This judgment on Babylon, implicitly, will also fall on those who have chosen to put themselves under her authority.

Since we are dealing with a chiastic structure here, then this section B. is marked for special prominence, and so is the most important of the three announcements. This is the first reference to Babylon in the book, and she/it is mentioned without any formal or polite introduction. This implies that Babylon, in and of itself, is not important in the overall scheme of things in this book. Nonetheless, this statement is marked as prominent because it announces her demise and destruction. This is another clarion call echoing down through the book, in preparation for what is to follow, that King Jesus is already victorious, and that Babylon is next on the list to be dealt with and demolished.

The third angel picks up this implication and makes it explicit. There is no doubt that all those people who chose to worship the beast, and thereby give him the right to reign over them, then they will share in his fate which, ultimately, is to be consigned to the lake of fire for ever.

7.7.7 Sub-Unit 6 : Sign 6 14:14-20

The structure of the sixth sub-unit is as follows:

A1. Description of one like a Son of Man who is ready to harvest. 14:14

B1. Another angel and his speech: Reap the (grain) harvest 14:15

A1' The harvesting action of the one like a Son of Man. 14:16

A2. Another angel goes out ready to harvest. 14:17

B2. Another angel and his speech: Reap the (wine) harvest 14:18

A2' The harvesting action of the angel (A2.) 14:19

Coda: Explanation, giving details of the aftermath of the harvest. 14:20

This sub-unit contains Sign 6. Consequently, in line with the sixth item in each of Cycles 2-6, this presents a particular view of the final judgment. This one is interesting both structurally and thematically in that it is composed of two almost identical components. Structurally, it is composed of two distinct parts, so it is a double unit. This is quite rare in Revelation, although it does happen elsewhere. But this one is unique because both parts are structurally identical.

This double structure highlights the double message, which is also unique in the book. In this case, we are told that the final 'judgment' is composed of two distinct parts, which are almost identical, but not quite. They both use the image of harvesting. The first one is the grain harvest, which is undertaken specifically by Jesus Himself, in His role as the Son of Man, or, in other words, in His role as representative of humanity, and therefore, as their Kinsman-Redeemer.

The text does not specifically tell us who the people are, who are concerned by the grain harvest. However, in the light of the culture at the time, and some of Jesus' words in the Gospels, we can deduce that these are the people of God. This is because grain is normally harvested to be placed in the owner's barn, where it is carefully stored, protected, and kept for a future positive use.

By contrast, the second harvest is the gathering of the grapes. This is not undertaken by Jesus but is delegated to angels. This time we are specifically told that it is a harvest which represents the final judgment, which will be the final manifestation of God's anger. This completes the picture of what will happen to those who choose to worship the beast, as previously evoked in the last part of Sign 5.

It is noteworthy that these sub-units, the interlude included, all end with a coda. This also is rare in the book as a whole, and it is also very rare that all the sub-units of a particular component of the discourse, would have a coda. However, it is possible that it was intentional to do this in this prominent central cycle, in order to sow the idea of coda in the minds of the readers at this stage in the process. The purpose of this would have been to prepare them to take notice of the very important coda, which they would find at the very end of the story, in 22:5c.

The codas have different functions. One function is to provide extra information, and so this just contributes to function of the cycle as a whole, which is to provide explanations about what is going on behind the scenes. Others of them provide extra hortatory material, and this will be discussed in more detail below.

7.7.8 Sub-Unit 7 : Sign 7 15:1-16:1.
This is also the Setting of the Bowls Cycle

The structure of the seventh sub-unit is as follows:

A. A Great and Wonderful Sign is seen in Heaven:
7 Angels with the 7 Last Plagues which will complete God's Anger 15:1-2

B. On the Glassy Sea: The Overcomers Stand and Sing Before God - Great and Wonderful are the Works of God Almighty, Who will not Fear and Glorify His Name? 15:3-4

A' The Sanctuary in Heaven Releases the 7 Angels who are given the Bowls of the Anger of God - The Sanctuary is so Filled with Smoke that no one can enter until the completion of the Seven Plagues. 15:5-8

Coda. Final Instructions to the 7 Angels. 16:1

Note: Some of the parallels between A and A' are conceptual and allusive rather than lexical. The 7 angels are generically designated as 'great and wonderful' in 15:1 (A) and their magnificence is specifically described in 15:6 (A'). The sea (A) and the sanctuary with the 4 living creatures (A') are elements of the throne-room setting.

As is the case with all the cycles from Cycle 2 to Cycle 5, this sub-unit is an overlap link with the next cycle. Technically, it is the conclusion to the Signs Cycle and contains the last sign, but, practically speaking, it contributes no new explanations, apart from moving us on, and getting us ready for what will happen in the Bowls Cycle.

7.7.9 The Prominence Features of the Signs Cycle

It was proposed in Chapter 6 that prominence features are like mountains which are noticeable, even from a distance, because they rise up above the valleys which surround them. Now we can go a little further, and say that not all mountains look the same. Some of them have a clear pointed peak, which rises even above the rest of the mountain, but some mountains have no peak and are more gently rounded.

This is the case with the Signs Cycle. We have said previously that the whole cycle is prominent at the book level, relative to the cycles which are on either side of it. But right now, we are in the process of studying just the Signs Cycle in its own right, and we can observe that it has no noticeable peak. Even though the sub-units are parallel to one another, there is no discernible concentric organization, and so there is no chiasm, with a prominent peak in the middle.

We have already noticed that the principle organization for the sub-units is an ABBA structure which has no prominent peak. This sets the tone for the whole cycle which, we are now proposing, has a flatter, more rounded, prominence profile, just like most of its sub-units. This means that the whole of the cycle is indeed prominent as we said before, but no one part of it is really more prominent than the rest. If there is indeed a sub-unit which is more prominent than the others, then it is hard to decide which one it is.

However, that does not mean to say that there are no prominence features at all embedded within this cycle, for there are several, which we will now review.

The Codas

Starting with the last first, we noted above that some of the codas contain exhortations directed at the reader. These are as follows:

- A series of rather enigmatic statements beginning with 'he who has an ear let him hear', and ending with 'Here is (something to challenge) the endurance and the faith of the saints'. In short it is an exhortation to persevere 13:9-10.
- Another enigmatic challenge beginning 'Here is…', to calculate the number of the beast. In short it is an exhortation to seek wisdom. 13:18
- The third 'Here is…' challenge to the people of God. This time it is clearly an exhortation to persevere, by keeping God's commands, and maintaining their faith in Jesus 14-12-13.

The Blessing 14:13

There is also a blessing attached to this last coda, which reinforces its exhortation to a certain degree.

The point about these exhortations, and the attached blessing, is that they are volitional import texts, and so they have a high level of prominence, as explained in Chapter 6. However in this case, the volitional import contained in the codas does not have any bearing on the content of their particular sub-unit. These codas are really operating at a higher level. Their function is to maintain the volitional import thread throughout the book, rather than to raise the level of prominence of the unit where they are attached. The same is true for the attached blessing in 14:13.

Deviation From Norms

Another possibility is that sub-unit 5, which contains Sign 5, is prominent because it is the first unit to break the established pattern, and so is in the form of an ABA' chiasm, instead of the previous ABB'A' system. A chiasm, of course has a peak which makes it prominent. In this case the peak is at 14:8, which contains the very forceful, repeated declaration that Babylon has fallen. There is no doubt that this verse is more prominent than any of its surroundings, for all the above reasons, but what is its true function?

Its function, once again, is a book level function, because, in the wider context beyond its own cycle, it is clearly announcing what is going to be the main topic of interest for the next two cycles. That topic is the destruction of Babylon, and the ensuing judgment of all who were intoxicated and deceived by her.

The Double Chiasm in Sub-Unit 6

The same can be said for the following unit, which is Sign 6, located in 14:14-20. This is a doublet, and a double chiasm at that. Jesus is a participant in this case, and we are given new information about who He is, and about what He is going to do. These are definitely prominence features, but once again we need to ask what their function is. In this case, they are bringing extra attention to bear on this sixth sign, but this is within a wider system, and not just specific to this cycle.

As mentioned above, all the central sixth sub-units refer to the final judgment, so they are working together as another book-level thread, and are not just operating within their specific cycle. The extra prominence here is probably operating in tandem with the declaration about Babylon, and is preparing the reader for the following cycles, which are going to be almost exclusively devoted to issues to do with the final judgment.

So the conclusion so far then, is that these are all definitely prominence features, which rise up above their surroundings, but that they are operating at the book level, and not just internally to the cycle. This conclusion, based on a study of the details, only serves to confirm what was posited in previous chapters on the basis of an analysis of the macro structure. That is, that this whole cycle is prominent in the context of the whole book, and as a consequence, it has many prominence features contributing to this overall prominence. But, at the same time, we can now see more clearly, that it is a rounded kind of mountain, which does not have any noticeable internal points of prominence.

The Interlude 14:1-5

That just leaves the interlude as another possible point of prominence. As we have explained in previous discussion, the interludes in Revelation are always more naturally prominent than the text all around them. This is because they are a deviation from the established norm, and interrupt the flow of discourse which had been running from the beginning of their cycle. As such they are an unexpected intrusion.

In the case of this particular interlude, there is a second element of unexpected intrusion to further boost its prominence. This is because this interlude has been fronted, and so it occurs between the fourth and fifth signs. This is sooner than would have been expected according to the system which had been previously established in the preceding cycles, when the interludes occurred between the sixth and seventh units in their cycle.

Another reason why all the interludes are more prominent than the surrounding material, is because they carry the Salvation Theme. The Salvation Theme is more prominent than the Judgment Theme for several reasons. It is because the positive wins out over the negative, light wins over darkness, life wins over death, and the grace of God wins over everything else. Furthermore, the effects of God's plan of salvation are timeless, and will never cease to exist, while His plan of judgment is only temporary and temporal. It only exists to deal with the problem of evil, and once that is done, judgment and everything associated with it will be finished, left behind, and forgotten – at least as far as God's people are concerned.

So then, if any sub-unit is a candidate to be considered the most important part of this cycle, then it is this interlude. Then, when you take a moment to look again at what it is explaining so that we may really understand what is going on, it just goes to confirm this proposal.

So in review then, in this interlude we are presented with a picture in words. It is like a snapshot taken out of our Heavenly Father's photograph album of timeless memories, and unforgettable people and events. In the picture we see the Lamb, in all His majesty and glory, having been raised from the grave, as the first-born from the dead. He is standing, resplendent in power, as a victorious king might pose for his portrait to be painted.

Then there is the situation and the background. He is standing on a mountain top, which is a dramatic and memorable place for any pictorial souvenir. But this is no ordinary mountain, this is Mount Sion, the mountain of God, the highest, and most important, high place in the universe.

Then there is the supporting cast, and this is no small group, for there are 144,000 of them, also resplendent in their magnificent robes of righteousness. We can imagine that they have crowns on their heads, because we are told elsewhere that they do have crowns. This is because they are co-rulers with the victorious King, and, if you have read to the end of the book, you know that this is correct. In any case, they definitely have the name of

God written on their foreheads, which means that they belong to Him, are protected by Him, and are precious to Him.

Yet, there is more, for I forgot to say that this is not just an old-fashioned, black and white, faded, old photograph. Amazing though it may seem, this is an up to the minute, twenty-first century, animated, personal, tik-tok type memory of a unique, never to be forgotten moment in my pilgrimage on this earth. There is the music also dubbed into the background, for if you listen carefully you can hear the music of Heaven wafting in through the pictures. The music of an untold number of harps making a simmering sound, like the ripples of flowing water, with an occasional royal rumble of thunder's drum-beat thrown in. The music then flows into song, an amazing, unique, first performance of a new song, which will never be forgotten, for it will be indelibly imprinted in your memory for all eternity.

This is what you find in this interlude. Arguably, it is the greatest of all the amazing revelations in this book. A brief insight into who Jesus really is, and who His companions are, and what their eternal place and purpose are destined to be.

Yes, it is all amazing and worth taking a moment to meditate on it all. Yet, to make this explanation fully clear, maybe we should still take the time to propose a coherent explanation as to who those 144,000 people really are. But before we do that, let's take a look at *where* they are.

A Memorable Motif

Another example of the tapestry metaphor with its intricacy and beauty, is to be found in the strategic central cycle. At the micro level, there is, once again, additional evidence which confirms the analysis presented, yet without contributing, in a direct sense, to the overt structure. It manifests itself in terms of a recurring motif. Consequently, it does not have the same weight of logic as some of the other evidence, but contributes, as it were, to the richness of the texture of the text. From this position embedded in the details of the discourse, it illustrates the beauty of the symmetry and patterning, which is to be found even in the smaller details - just as in a tapestry.

Signs 1 and 2 are specifically stated to be signs which 'were seen in heaven' (12:1 and 3). In the course of the story there is war in heaven and the dragon is thrown down from Heaven, where he had been standing, so that the earth becomes his domain of operation (12:7,9,12-18). In 12:18 he is specifically left 'standing on the sand of the sea'. This sentence has apparently caused debate for centuries, as is perhaps indicated by the textual variant, 'I stood' versus 'he stood'.

Unless it is contributing to some larger motif as is being proposed here, this clause has no compelling structural, semantic, grammatical or logical usefulness. Why then, was it included in the text? The earthly sea which is in view in Chapters 12 and 13 may also be intentionally in contrast to the heavenly sea first observed at 4:6, and which reoccurs in Sign 7 in 15:2. This is a different motif which could be explored separately. Since the dragon was also seen 'standing' in heaven prior to his downfall in 12:4, then presumably, he must have been standing on the shore of the heavenly sea at that point in his career.

The sea-shore, which is in view here, designates the boundary between two major earthly domains, namely the dry land and the sea, and situates the dragon at the crossroads between the two. From this situation the dragon's two helpers emerge, one from the sea and one from the earth (13:1 and 11). This triad then, clearly belong to the domain of the earth.

In contrast to this, the Lamb is also seen standing with his 144,000 followers in another situation. In this case he is 'standing' up on the solid rock of a mountain (in contrast to sand down by the sea), and the following context suggests that this Mount Sion is the heavenly one (14:1-3). Next, John sees an angel specifically flying in 'mid-heaven'. This reference to an angel flying in mid-heaven only occurs once in Revelation. A curious person would be justified in asking questions like these: Why should such a specific and unusual reference be made at all? If at all, why only once and why precisely at this point in the text? A complete analysis of a text needs at least to try and include reasonable answers to questions such as these.

So, the angel is half-way between earth and heaven, which are the two domains which are in view here, and they are being placed next to each other in order, presumably, to set up a contrast between them. From this vantage point the angel makes appeal to those who are 'sitting' on the earth (14:6). By any standards, this is an unusual use of the verb 'to sit'. This is especially true in the light of the context of 13:14, for example, where human beings are designated by the much more natural phrase, 'those who live on the earth'.

When something unusual like this happens, this is a deviation from the surrounding norms, which, in turn, contributes some extra prominence, either to the immediate, or to the broader, context. A possible explanation then, for such an unusual usage, is that it contributes intentionally to a motif contrasting 'stand' and 'sit' which has been woven into the pattern of the Signs Cycle, and this, in turn, contributes to the prominence of the cycle.

The last two signs are also colored by this motif. The last sign is once more in heaven where the overcomers are 'standing' before God (15:1-2) on the heavenly sea, and the penultimate one (14:14) depicts one like a man (i.e. one who, from external appearances, would seem to be an inhabitant of the earth) 'sitting' on a cloud. Whether the cloud is interpreted symbolically as being part of the heavenly domain, or literally, as half-way between heaven and earth, as in the case of the angel cited above, it does not really matter. The development of the motif continues and the contrast between his glorious seat, and the previous earthly seat, of his fellow 'men' (14:6) is clear. This contrast, is of course, directly parallel with the contrast between the dragon and the Lamb.

Chart 55.

The Sit/Stand Motif of the Signs Cycle

The Setting The 24 Elders are **sitting** on thrones around or on the glassy **sea** in **Heaven,** where voices declare that the **world (= Heaven** and **Earth** implied) has become Christ's to rule for ever, and He will destroy those destroying the **Earth** 11:15-19

Sign 1 A Woman was seen in **Heaven,** presumably in a **sitting** position 12:1-2

Sign 2 A dragon was seen **standing** before her in **Heaven** 12:3-6
The dragon was thrown down from **Heaven** onto the **Earth** and was last seen **standing** on the shore of the **earthly sea** 12:9 & 18

Sign 3 The first beast came up out of the **sea.** He was given authority over the **Earth** and those living on the **Earth** 13:1 & 7-8

Sign 4 The second beast came up out of the **Earth.** It deceived those living on the **Earth**, especially by making fire come down from **Heaven** to **Earth** 13:11 & 13-14

The Interlude The Lamb is **standing** on Mt. Sion in **Heaven,** along with those who had been purchased from the **Earth**. The music of harps and singing comes from **Heaven** 14:1-5

Sign 5 An Angel flies between **Heaven** and **Earth**, and preaches to those **sitting** on the **Earth,** saying they should fear God because He made **Heaven** and **Earth** 14:6-7

Sign 6 Someone like a man was **sitting** on a cloud (between **Heaven** and **Earth**) and He reaped the grain harvest of the **Earth.** Two angels from **Heaven** brought in the grape harvest from the **Earth** 14:14-20

Sign 7 In **Heaven** the 7 Bowl Angels prepared to pour out the bowls of God's anger on to the **Earth**, accompanied by the overcomers, the ones playing harps and singing a song, who were **standing** on the glassy **sea** in **Heaven** 15:1-16:2

It would appear then, that the thread of the motif, using the words 'standing' and 'sitting' as guides, takes the reader on an interesting journey, from heaven down to earth and back up to heaven. This movement is laid out for ease of reference in Chart 55.

It clearly starts out in the HQ of the universe, that is in the Throne Room of Heaven, where a very important decision is announced. Presumably at an earlier stage of his career, the dragon might also have been seen standing in this same place in Heaven. However, there is a mysterious woman who comes into the story and it is clear that her role is to give birth to an equally mysterious baby boy, who was born on the earth but was then taken back to Heaven.

Contingent on these events we hear that the dragon, having stood for this purpose in front of the woman, fails in his attempt to destroy the baby boy. As a result he is banished from Heaven completely, and ends up at the lowest point possible on the earth (i.e. at sea-level 12:18). Although he does his best to drum up support from both the sea and the earth, he is doomed to failure again (13:1-18).

This is because the Lamb is standing in glory in Heaven with His 144,000 followers (14:1). Those same followers obviously were originally among those who were 'sitting on the earth' in 14:6. However, they had learned how to get themselves bought back out of their situation on the earth, so that they could now stand in Heaven with the elders and the four living creatures (14:3-5).

The story transits, as it were, in mid-heaven, from which vantage point, the inhabitants of the earth, who, apparently, can belong to either the earthly or the heavenly domain, are summoned to cast their lot in with the denizens of Heaven (14:6-7). Otherwise, they will suffer the judgment which is bound to fall on them on the earth, as indicated in 14:9-11, which judgment is also, apparently, executed from mid-heaven as indicated in 14:14-16.

Despite all that nonetheless, the story ends back up in Heaven where the overcomers who follow the Lamb wherever He goes, are now seen standing proudly on the sea in Heaven in 15:2.

A literary motif, by its very nature, is a rather ephemeral linguistic phenomenon, whose presence can best be perceived rather than proved. Just like a single thread in a tapestry, it can be a viewed as an element of beauty in the texture of the material for those who can see it, or it can be viewed as an element with no particular value by those who cannot.

What is important for analytical purposes is that, by a remarkable coincidence, the motif of 'sit/stand', in association with the locations of Heaven, with its sea, the Earth, with its sea and mid-heaven, between Heaven and the Earth, is present in the setting, in each of the sign units, and in the interlude. If the motif is appreciated and its value accepted, it can be adduced as further secondary evidence that the presentation of seven signs plus an interlude, is an intentional, organizational schema which is objectively present in the text. In addition, an awareness of this motif helps justify the intentional presence of 'he stood' in 12:18, and the intentional use of the verb 'to sit' in 14:6.

The verbs 'to stand' and 'to sit' do also occur many times, spread evenly through the book, but no particularly noticeable patterns can be discerned. The most striking pattern is in the Signs Cycle itself, where 'to sit' occurs 3 times and 'to stand' occurs 4 times, which makes a total of 7 occurrences. When the Lamb is first introduced in 5:6, He is standing in Heaven, in company with the 24 elders who are sitting on their thrones. The last use of the verb 'to stand' is in 20:12, where the inhabitants of the earth are standing before the person who is sitting on the throne, awaiting their final judgment. These two somewhat isolated references connect this thread in the Signs Cycle to the beginning and the ending of the book.

The words for Heaven and Earth also occur very many times, spread evenly throughout the book. However, the only place where they co-occur with the frequency indicated in the chart above, is in the Signs Cycle. Apart from these brief remarks, more research would be required before any other statements about these words could be made, and concerning any other possible patterns of their use at the book level.

7.8 An Explanatory Word Concerning Symbolic Numbers

It has to be admitted that I did not expect to end up writing a book on the use of numbers in the Bible, but in practice it could hardly be avoided. There are so many numbers everywhere in Revelation, both overt numbers on the page, as well as more mysterious ones hidden within the folds of the textual structures, that it can hardly be argued that they are merely unintentional coincidences.

In order, therefore, for the analysis to be complete, and in order to make an attempt, at least, to account for all the data, for an analysis which does not account for all the data is inadequate, then something had to be done. As you may have noticed in reading the preceding pages, I have already started making reference to the most obvious of these numbers, but because this issue was not in focus, I have only made brief allusions to them, with minimal explanation.

Consequently, the goal of this next section is to take a brief moment to look at this issue of the numbers more closely. The goal is not to discuss every single example of the use of numbers in the book, for that would just about take another whole book, but to take into a little more consideration one or two examples which we have already found in our study so far, which also buttress an important theme. In addition, we will try and trace this thread through the whole Bible, which, it is to be hoped, will demonstrate clearly, why this subject should not be ignored, but should be integrated, as fully as a possible, into a study such as this one.

From a technical, linguistic point of view, it can be stated with some assurance that from the very beginning of time, when writing first began, letters and numbers have had an intricately entwined, symbiotic relationship. The reason for this is because right at the very beginning when letters first began to be used as abstract symbols in order to construct words, there were no separate symbols for numbers. Instead, each letter was assigned a numerical value and so could be used for arithmetic, and other mathematical uses as well as for writing.

INFORMATION

Dr. Miles Jones is one person who has done considerable research into the true beginnings of what has become our modern day alphabetical system of writing. Prior to the beginnings of this system, ancient civilizations used pictorial methods of writing or cuneiform. The traditional academic view is that the alphabet came to us through the Phoenicians. This may be partially correct in that they were a sea-faring people and were ideally suited for disseminating far and wide any new, useful inventions. However, did they actually invent the alphabet or did they just transmit it? There is no evidence available to indicate that they invented it. On the other hand, Dr. Jones has painstakingly accumulated remarkable archaeological evidence that the original form of our current western alphabet first appeared in northern Midian in the vicinity of Mont Sinai, at the time when the nascent nation of Israel was camped there for some time. In addition, the earliest form of the Hebrew alphabet uses those very same symbols. Dr. Jones' proposal is that the alphabet was a gift of God Himself, which He gave to them when He wrote their first laws on the tablets of stone. For more information regarding these remarkable proposals, please consult his books and web-site which are listed in the references.

This system of letters being used as numbers continued on at least until the time of the Romans. So, in other words, letters were used to represent numbers, but in addition, it has to be understood, that numbers could be used to communicate verbal messages as well. This is what we are talking about here, for we are saying that many, if not most, of the numbers, which occur in Revelation, are being used to communicate verbal messages and not just numerical messages. If this were not the case, then there would be no point at all for the author to take all that trouble to organize such intricate and lengthy systems, based around numbers, as the seven cycles are, for example.

So, let's go back to the beginning, back to the time when the three first authorities were set in the heavens, to the time when the first prophetic word about the woman's Seed, was given. At that time, we are told, God Almighty created the heavens and the earth. Right at that time, numbers first began to be used, and the pattern of 6 + 1, which equals 7, was established in the first week of Creation. The word 'week', of course, really only exists to represent a number, which serves to prove the point about symbiosis, which we are making here.

But that is not all. When God came to the pinnacle of creation, He started out by making just one 'Adam'. But when He stepped back to admire what He had made, and, of course, it was very good, He nonetheless, decided that it was not quite right, and made that momentous statement that it was not good for Adam to be alone, just one, or 'al(l)-one'. Consequently, the caring Father, hand made for him a hand-maid, who was called Eve. Together they made 'two', and so it was established that the best, basic, human team, which could work together in unity, was composed of two people.

This was not only the establishment of a social precedent, it was also the establishment of a legal precedent, because Adam and Eve together were mandated to agree and decide, and so to govern the earth. This legal precedent was later confirmed and set in stone, as it were, when it was officially stated that two witnesses were the minimum requirement to decide and establish the truth of a matter, as recorded in Deuteronomy 17:6. This same official statement also confirmed that the minimum for a human team could be '2', or '3'.

Prior to that, the first team of Adam and Eve, eventually, after some difficulties became a team of three with their son, Seth. This was a mirror image of the original team of three, who had discussed, decided and planned the whole of Creation.

So after Seth came along, some considerable time passed and then we come to the story of Noah. Once again, God decided to start over, but this time the new group, whose task was to launch a new beginning, was composed of not just two, but eight people. This is significant in its own way, because eight is composed of seven plus one, which symbolizes a new beginning, as was established in Adam's time, at the beginning of the second week.

Then more time passes and God, once again, starts a new chapter in history with one man, Abraham this time. But Abraham was not just one, alone, because he was two, along with Sarah. In due time, after many testing times, they became a team of three again, along with their son Isaac.

Isaac then started another new thing because he, in turn, produced 12 grandsons, and from them came the 12 tribes of Israel. Up until now God had worked with families, which are the basic, minimal social unit, but now He began working with whole tribes, which were the embryo of a whole nation. The number 12 from which this first nation to represent God on the earth found its source, is composed of the basic unit of 2 people plus 10, which is the number symbolizing law. This is because when you start operating at the nation level, with this many people, then you have to have an operating system; that is to say that you have to have laws.

This notion was systematized and officialized at Mount Sinai, when Israel first became a nation, in the true sense of the word, instead of just being a collection of 12 disparate tribes. So, it is not surprising that the first thing which God did, having rescued them from Egypt, was to give them His Law, through Moses, in order to regulate, and cement into place, their new-found national unity.

The purpose for all this was set out, prophetically once again, in the song of Moses and Miriam, as recorded in Exodus 15:17. Here it is stated that the people whom He had redeemed (15:13), would be established on the mountain, where God had His dwelling, with the purpose that God Himself would reign for ever and ever. In the course of this process, the people would face difficulties, but would learn to be overcomers, as foreseen in Exodus 15:13-16. It is obvious that this reign would be through this nation of redeemed people, otherwise there would have been no need for them to learn to be overcomers, nor even for them to be in the story at all. This had been true at the time of Adam, at the time of Noah, and has been true at all periods, timelessly, throughout history. Everyone has had to overcome difficulties as they walked with God, and established His government on the earth, as had been planned and intended from the beginning.

As mentioned before, a large number of people requires, of necessity, organization and laws. This is illustrated by the events recounted in Exodus 18. The initial system of government was two people, Moses and Aaron, supplemented later, by a third, Hur (17:10). In times of need, as in Exodus 17:5, the next step in establishing a governmental system was to draw on the elders. Obviously, these were the elders in terms of age, and were the patriarchs and the leaders of the families, clans and tribes. When this system was officialized, following Jethro's advice (himself a patriarch), these same elders and leaders, of necessity, had to be drawn from each of the 12 tribes. This basic system then continued on all through Israel's history as a nation.

Fast forward now to the time of Jesus. Like Moses, He had also come to earth, firstly to redeem a people for the Father, but also, and with them, to establish God's Kingdom, or His reign, in all its fullness, on the earth.

Like the people of Moses' time, they would have to learn to be overcomers in order to accomplish this task to its full extent. But notice the first thing which Jesus did in terms of official activity. He himself had to demonstrate that He was an overcomer, and therefore, knew how to reign. So it was that He was compelled by the Holy Spirit Himself, to go out and confront the devil on his own territory. There, He provoked a dry run in the desert, a prophetic preview of the cosmic victory, which He had come to accomplish once and for all time, over the age-old serpentine dragon.

Then the very next thing which He did, was to call out 12 disciples, who later became (after some difficulties) the 12 apostles, and they were to constitute the first team for service, and also the first government of this new phase of God's reign on the earth. This is made clear by what Jesus Himself said in Matthew 16, and also by how the disciples were used to organize the people when they came together in large numbers. Notice also that when the disciples were broken down into smaller teams, they went out two by two, and their task was to testify about, or to be witnesses for, Jesus, God's representative on the earth at that time.

So then, we have set out that historical background, which describes how certain numbers have resonated all through history with certain specific associations and symbolic meanings, with a purpose in view. The purpose is so that we can now much better appreciate the importance of the numbers which we have found reoccurring in Revelation.

Let's start then, at the beginning again, with the number two. The obvious use of the number two, is The 2 Witnesses. Once again we have the minimal social and legal team for operating in unity on the earth. This is clearly reminiscent of the first disciples, and must, therefore, represent all disciples of Jesus when broken down into the smallest, standard work team. They are specifically called witnesses, which tells us what their primary function is, and that is to speak and to testify about the one who sent them, and whom they represent.

If we look back in history now with this advantage of hind-sight, we can see that all the teams of two, who paved the way for today, did exactly the same thing. The task of each one was the same. It was to be in relationship with the Creator, to listen to His words of advice and of instruction, and then to speak those same words out into the world in which they lived in. Their task was to represent Him, and to do all that they could to see that His will was done on the earth, as it was in Heaven, and, by this means, to establish His Kingdom, His reign, in the here and now of their generation.

It is still the same today for those people who are timelessly represented in Revelation, by The Two Witnesses. We see in their own story that they caused ructions by their words, that they were overcomers, and by all that they did, whether in life or in death, they ruled on God's behalf, over their jurisdiction on the earth.

The next example in the book, is that of the 24 Elders. It is clear that they must be representative of many more people than that. So, who are these people? The word 'elder', of course, is rich with Old Testament connotations as we have seen in our brief historical review above. At that time, the minimum number of elders which was needed for a quorum, was 12, since they had to represent each of the 12 tribes. Twenty-four is 12 + 12, or 12 x 2. Whichever way that you calculate it, there is another 12 to be included and most commentators, as a matter of course, assume that these must be the 12 disciples.

So then, the 24 Elders represent God's people of the Old Testament period, plus the representatives of God's people of the New Testament period. They are, therefore, the representative government in Heaven, of all God's people. This group of people would include those, having died and come to the end of their time of living on the earth, who are now alive in Heaven, as well as those still living on the earth.

INFORMATION

Here is another way of looking at the number 12. It can be seen that it is composed of 6 + 6, or 6 x 2. The number 6 is the number for humanity as a whole. Here it is placed together twice, or multiplied by 2. Two is the basic human team working in unity. So when you place humanity as a whole, in a team, working together in unity, then, naturally enough, a large-scale government is the end result.

This proposal is later concretized in Chapter 21 where we are told that the gates of the New Jerusalem symbolically represent the 12 tribes once again. Not only do we have the repetition of the number 12 here, but we also know from history that the gates of a city were the places of government. The places where the elders sat to deliberate and decide, on behalf of the rest of the population. But that is not all, for the foundations of the great wall symbolically represent the 12 disciples of Jesus.

Clearly the foundations were contiguous with the gates, for the gates were built on the foundations, and would have been the precise place where the elders sat (there is the sit/stand motif again) for their parliament. Not only that, the government's first and foremost job, was to keep watch from the gates, and to act, as necessary, in order to protect the inhabitants. The walls of the city themselves obviously have this same function and purpose.

So here again, we see that the 12 tribes and the 12 disciples, as a group, are synonymous with one another, having the same primary governmental function and purpose.

This viewpoint is confirmed by the next passage to be reviewed, which is Chapter 7 of Revelation. This is the first interlude and is a double description of the people of God. The first part is thoroughly rooted in the Old Testament and portrays 12,000 people being taken from each of the 12 tribes of Israel. The number 12 is the number of government at the level of a nation or a kingdom. So that makes a full governmental quorum being taken from each of the tribes. Because of the history which we have reviewed, then this would seem to be only proper, that a symbolic representation of the government of Israel should be the foundational component for this new insight into the heavenly view of government. The number 1000 would normally be considered to be the largest number which is possible, and so we have here then, the ultimate government of the largest possible nation or kingdom. The number 1000 can also represent a number which is so big that it is, humanly speaking, impossible to count.

This matches well with what follows for the second part of this interlude is thought, by many, to represent the same group of people. This is a group of people which is so big that they cannot be counted – it is actually described as such on this occasion, and not just left to the implications of symbolism. These people are drawn from all the nations, as opposed to just Israel, and have clearly learned to be overcomers, having come through the great time of testing, or affliction. They are among the redeemed, because they have been clothed in white robes, which have been washed in the blood of the Lamb. They now serve God day and night with their worship, and, as we have seen before, worship is an activity and a theme, which is closely associated with, and entwined with the themes of government and authority.

This then brings us back to the Signs Cycle where this excursus about the numbers started. It is in the interlude of the Signs Cycle, which, we surmised, is the most prominent part of this cycle, that the 144,000 redeemed people reappear. Presumably, at this point the number 144,000 is used as a convenient, and memorable, symbol to represent all these people who were introduced to us in the very first interlude. They are clearly the people of God, whichever way you look at it. There are so many of them, it is impossible to count their exact number, and their identity and purpose in life is clearly rooted in the notion of government. They are the ultimate epitome of human government, since we are talking about 12 x 12, multiplied by 1000. They are the government of the Kingdom of God, along with the Lamb, of course, standing with Him at the pinnacle of the universe, and they will reign with Him for ever and ever, as confirmed by the final coda in 20:5c. In doing so, they give glory to God by their song and their worship.

However, before we close off this discussion of numbers, here is one more mathematical matrix to ponder. We have been discussing the details of the central Signs Cycle. This cycle is composed of a setting and seven sub-units, including the interlude. This makes a total of **8** units, which is reminiscent of Noah. Could it be that this cycle is describing a new beginning?

The setting is composed of 5 smaller units. Sub-units 1 to 4 are also composed of 5 smaller units. This makes 5 sub-units composed of 5 units, 5 being the number of grace, and together they make a total of **25** units.

Sub-unit 5 (14:6-13) is composed of 4 units which are similar to the ones in the previous sub-units, but, exceptionally, it also contains a blessing, which has been analyzed as a component of the Narrative Framework. So this means that it also has a total of **5** components. Sub-unit 6 has the perfect number, even though it is all about the final judgment, and so, it has **7** components. Finally, sub-unit 7 has just **4** components.

If we add all these numbers together: 8 + 25 + 5 + 7 + 4, this is what we get. The total is 49. In its turn, 49 = 7 x 7. All I have done is to present to you the data produced by the analysis. Is it a coincidence or another of those mysteries which is being revealed to us by the Living God Himself? I will leave it to you to decide.

7.9 The Internal Organization of Cycle 7: The Seven New Things Part 1.

Cycle 7 is the third cycle which is very prominent in the overall organization of Revelation. For this reason then, we will take a look at the details of its internal structure. The purpose will be to see what its particular characteristics are like, and to see how those details mesh with the organization of the macro structure, which has already been described.

This cycle follows the standard pattern for the book, and also for each of the cycles, in terms of its most simple, overall organization. Consequently, it is composed of three basic parts, a setting, a body and a conclusion. These parts are as follows:

1. The Setting 20:1-15
2. The Body 21:1-22:5
3. The Conclusion 22:6-7

Otherwise this cycle is quite distinctive in its organization compared to the other cycles. The primary reason for this is because it does not have a body composed of seven distinct sub-units. In addition, it is not organized according to a numbered, linear schema, which differentiates it from the Letters Cycle, as well as the Seals, Trumpets and Bowls cycles. In contrast to them, it is mainly organized using parallel patterns of various kinds.

In contrast to the Signs and Proclamations cycles, it does not have a noticeable key word, which facilitates the division into units, or which enables the analyst to easily trace the unifying theme, or motif.

The parallel patterns which are to be discerned, do contribute to the structural organization of the setting, but for the body of the cycle they do not. The many parallels which do exist in the body of the cycle, create an intricate pattern of interweaving ideas at the lower levels of the discourse.

So, even though these parallel structures did not contribute anything significant to the previous analysis of the macro structure, they do, nonetheless, reveal the remarkable intricacy and coherence of the details, as is demonstrated in Chart 55 below and in the following discussion.

7.9.1 The Setting 20:1-15

The structure of the setting is as displayed in the following chart.

Chart 56.

The Setting of Cycle 7 20:1-15

A. Satan's Imprisonment and Temporary Demise 20:1-3
  B. The Martyred Witnesses Sit to Judge 20:4-6
A' Satan's Release and Final Destiny 20:7-10
  B' The (Other) Dead Stand to be Judged 20:11-15

The repetitions which create the parallelism of this setting will be laid out in the following paragraphs. They involve noticeably the concepts of going or coming down, and the complementary concept of coming or going up. These ideas harmonize very well with the previous contrasts which were made between standing/sitting in Heaven or on the Earth. Not only that, but the same contrasts between sitting and standing also re-occur in this introductory unit for Cycle 7, as can be seen below.

Sub-Unit A. 20:1-3
An angel *comes down* from Heaven.
Satan is bound, and thrown *(down)* into the pit, no longer to deceive the nations for 1000 years. Afterwards he will be released *(comes back up)* for a short time.

Sub-Unit A' 20:7-10
Satan is released *(comes back up)* after the 1000 years and once more deceives the nations. The nations *go up* against the saints, but fire *comes down* out of Heaven and destroys them.

The devil who deceived them is thrown *(down)* into the lake of fire.

Sub-Unit B. 20:4-6
I saw thrones.
The witnesses who overcome the beast by the word of their testimony are *seated* on them. From this position they have the right to act as judges.
They live *(stand)* and reign with Christ, during the 1000 years.
(Two references in verses 4 and 6)
This is the first resurrection and the second death has no power over them.
The remainder of the dead do not live *(stand)* again until after the 1000 years.

Sub-Unit B' 20:11-15
I saw... a throne. Someone was *seated* on it.
The (remainder of) dead (now restored to life) *stand* before the throne, (because they did not benefit from the first resurrection).
They are judged by the books and their works.
Those not found in the book of life are thrown *(down)* into the lake of fire.
This is the second death.

The most prominent parts of this setting are the sub-units B. and B'. This is because the setting has a double linear structure. This means that the two conclusions are the most naturally prominent parts of the structure. As a consequence of this observation, it can be stated with confidence that it is the contrastive fate of the two groups of people in view, which is in focus, and which should, therefore, be given the most weight in any subsequent interpretation.

The two groups of people are those who benefit from the first resurrection, and those who do not. Included in the first group are the martyrs, that is to say the people who have preferred to give their lives for the Lamb rather than be unfaithful to Him. These are exactly the same kind of people who are portrayed by The Two Witnesses in Chapter 11.

The key thing about them, as will become clear in the detailed analysis of verse 4 below, is that they were overcomers. That is, they overcame the devil because they were no longer deceived by him, and so did not believe his lies anymore. As a consequence, they also overcame the two beasts, the devil's proxies, and refused to listen to them and to do what they demanded. This end result was all connected to a new life which they received, and which is called here, the first resurrection. Since they were in possession of this new life, they were qualified to participate in the ruling, reigning, and judgment processes along with the Lamb.

By contrast, all the other people in the world did not conduct themselves like this, and so they received a completely different fate. They continued to be deceived by the devil's proxies, and so did everything that the beasts required them to do. As a consequence, they did not fear God, and did not follow the Lamb everywhere, and certainly did not give their lives for him. Their fate was to miss the first resurrection. They were only raised to life again in order to face their final judgment before the Great White Throne, and then to be consigned to the lake of fire, which is the second death. It is important to note that everyone will end up in death together with those whom they followed in life. Those who chose to follow the Lamb will end up gloriously reigning with Him in life for ever. But, on the other hand, those who chose to follow the dragon will have the same fate as him. They will be ignominiously consigned to the lake of fire, to be consumed by the second death.

The corollary to all this, is that the story of what happened to the dragon, as recounted in sub-units A. and A', is only of very secondary importance, and so should not be paid too much time or attention.

7.9.2 The Details of the Structure of the Setting Sub-Units

In this section each sub-unit of the setting of Cycle 7 will be presented in more detail. These presentations will be followed by some comments concerning the contribution of each of them to the overall thrust, and message, of this introductory part of the cycle.

Sub-Unit A. Satan's Imprisonment and Temporary Demise 20:1-3

The structure of sub-unit A. is as follows:

A. An angel comes down from Heaven 20:1a

  B. He holds the key to the abyss and a great chain 20:1b

    C. He took hold of the dragon, the serpent, the devil, Satan 20:2a

    C' He bound him for 1000 years 20:2b

  B' He threw him into the abyss, and shut and sealed it 20:3a

A' In order that he may no longer deceive the nations, until the 1000 years are over 20:3b

Coda: Afterwards he will be released for a short time 20:3c

There is no peak of prominence in this sub-unit, arising out of the parallel structure, so it is the overall message which is important. This message is that the dragon has been bound and put in a pit for 1000 years, so that he can no longer deceive the nations. Arguably, this last point (A'), is the most prominent part of all, because it is the conclusion to a linear narrative, and tells us the ultimate *result* of what the angel came down from Heaven to accomplish.

It is noteworthy that the dragon is not even the topic of this sub-section, for the angel is. Consequently, the dragon has no linguistic importance in this part of his own story at all. This detail confirms what was already proposed in previous chapters, that the dragon is systematically downgraded by the author, in order to show that he is of very little importance in the overall scheme of things.

Sub-Unit B. The Overcomer Witnesses Sit to Judge 20:4-6

The structure of sub-unit B. is as follows:

A. I saw thrones and those seated on them have the authority to act as judges 20:4a

B. These are the ones who lost their life 20:4b

C. Because of their testimony for Jesus and the word of God 20:4b

C' Because they did not worship the beast, nor receive its mark on forehead or hand 20:4c

B' They are alive or, were living 20:4d

A' They reigned with Christ, during the 1000 years 20:4e

Coda: The remainder of the dead do not live again until after the 1000 years 20:5a
This is the first resurrection (so the second death has no power over them) 20:5b

The structure of this sub-unit is the same as the previous one and, being a concentric structure, but not a chiastic one, it has no peak of prominence. Once again the most likely point of prominence is section A' because it is the conclusion of a linear narrative. This means that the fact that the faithful people of God reign with Christ during the 1000 years, is the most important part of this story.

This insight is further confirmed by considering verse 4 from an alternative point of view. In this case the parameter used to follow the semantic thread is the parameter of generic, followed by specific, which is the principal semantic parameter used in Cycle 7. By looking at it from this perspective, this is what we can observe:

Sub-Unit B. The Overcomer Witnesses Sit to Judge 20:4-6
An Alternative Analysis

As indicated in previous discussion, in some cases it is possible to discern legitimate alternative analyses, which constructively organize the data into a coherent pattern but, which, nonetheless produce a slightly different perspective. In this particular case, it changes nothing with regard to the main message of the unit, but rather confirms that it is the kingly role of the Overcomer Witnesses which is in focus.

A. And I saw thrones, And they (people-generic) sat on them
And (authority to pronounce) judgment was given to them 20:4a

B. And these people were (specifically 1.) those killed because of their testimony about Jesus, and because of the Word of God 20:4b

C. And who (specifically 2.) did **not** worship the beast, **nor** its image, and did **not** receive its mark on their forehead, and **(nor)** on their hand 20:4c

B' And they lived (again or still) 20:4d

A' And they reigned (= pronounced judgment) with Christ (on thrones) 1000 years 20:4e

Coda: The rest of the dead did not live (again) until after the 1000 years 20:5a
This is the first resurrection 20:5b

In this case a prominent peak does emerge in sub-unit C. This confirms that the people who are in focus were overcomers. They absorbed all that the dragon could throw at them through his proxies, they refused to submit to them, and so they became overcomers for God and for the Lamb.

As we have said before, overcoming the enemy of our souls is part of, and a prerequisite for, what it means to sit on thrones and to reign as kings. But the point is, that this struggle, and this learning to be overcomers must have taken place during their lives on earth. This means, in turn, that the process of learning to reign with Christ, must also begin while His followers are still living in this present age on the earth.

The Blessing 20:6

Verse 6 is a unique element in the whole chapter, and therefore, needs some commentary. It is one of the seven blessings, which appear throughout the book, and is part of the volitional import schema. It is also unique among this set of seven, since it is the only one which says that the people concerned are both blessed and holy. Since it is a blessing, it is operating at the book level, and this is confirmed by the fact that it could be removed from its context, and it would make no difference to the overall message of this setting.

At the same time, however, it is very precisely adjusted to fit into its context. So, it can be observed then, that it not only provides a word of blessing, but also provides a word of information and confirmation, concerning the people who have been in focus in verse 4.

This integration is such that it is hard to know exactly where the blessing starts. It could start with the phrase 'This is the first resurrection' (v.5b), which clearly provides a connection with what has just gone before, but also introduces the blessing, which repeats this same phrase for emphasis within its first statement in verse 6a.

On balance, it was decided to assign this phrase to the coda of the preceding section, as shown in the analysis above. This is because it is clearly a concluding, explanatory statement, which sums up a key insight into what had been set out just before. Then, when this phrase is immediately repeated at the beginning of the blessing proper, a tail-head link is formed. This not only shows that the blessing is tightly connected to the preceding sub-unit, but also give us grounds for proposing that the blessing is, nonetheless, a separate sub-unit.

Whichever solution is preferred, viewed as an integral part of the sub-unit 20:4-6, or as a separate sub-unit, it is a component with a double function. It firstly provides a blessing, which is true, and relevant, whether it is read in its context or not. Then, secondly, it provides strong confirmatory support for the importance of the preceding sub-unit, especially with its repetition of, and emphasis on, the fact of reigning with Christ for the 1000 years.

Verse 6 then, with its unique and unexpected characteristics, raises a number of questions, and thereby causes some turbulence in this part of the discourse. Turbulence, as we have previously learned, is something which can be caused by prominence features. So this verse then, has been analyzed as a prominence feature. It provides prominence at the book level, because it provides motivational input to the volitional import schema, but it also focuses attention on this whole issue of the first resurrection and the second death, as the end of the book approaches.

However, it also makes the preceding sub-unit prominent in its context, because of the tight integration with it, which has already been noted. In particular, it singles out the whole notion of the people of God reigning with Christ as being of particular importance. It does this, not only by the marked repetition of this concept, but also by the affirmation of these particular characteristics of this reign. These are:

- The participants in this reign are holy, as well as blessed 20:6a
- The participants benefit from the first resurrection 20:6a
- They avoid the second death 20:6b
- They function as priests for God and Jesus (in the OT priests helped rule the nation) 20:6c
  (This makes a connection with the previous references to priests at 1:6 and 5:10, making 3 in all)
- They will reign with Him for the 1000 years 20:6d

It is interesting to note that the Signs Cycle also had a blessing inserted into its overall structure at 14:13. This blessing was also attached at the end of a coda, and also served to reinforce the message of the preceding sub-unit, as well as contributing to the book level thread of the blessings.

Sub-Unit A' Satan's Release and Final Destiny 20:7-10

The structure of sub-unit A' is as follows:

A. Satan is released after the 1000 years 20:7

B. He will go out to deceive the nations 20:8a

C. The nations who are at the four corners of the earth, that is, Gog and Magog, to assemble them for war, innumerable as the sand of the sea 20:8b-c

C' They *went up* over the land to encircle the saints' camp and the beloved city, but fire *came down* out of Heaven and destroyed them 20:9

B' The devil who deceived was thrown into the lake of fire with the 2 beasts 20:10a

A' They will be tormented day and night for ever 20:10b

The ABCC'B'A' structure is the same as the preceding sub-units so there is no prominent peak. The message is carried by the whole of the unit in equal proportions: the dragon and his minions are the for-ever losers and will end up in the lake of fire, with no way out. There is no coda this time. It is as if they are not even worthy of an extra coda. The saints, by contrast, had a coda and an extra, lengthy blessing tacked on the end of their sub-unit.

Sub-Unit B' The (Other) Dead Stand to be Judged 20:11-15

The structure of sub-unit B' is as follows:

A. I saw a great white throne 20:11a

B. Someone was sitting on it : **a.** Heaven and earth fled from before His face
b. No place was found for them 20:11b

A' The dead were standing before the throne, and the books were opened 20:12a

B' The Book of Life opened, the dead were judged by their works as written in the books 20:12b

A'' The dead were released from where they were held:
a. From the sea and
b. From death & Hades 20:13a

B'' The dead from there were judged according to their works 20:13b

A''' Death and Hades were thrown into the Lake of Fire, which is the second death 20:14

B''' Anyone not written in the Book of Life was thrown into the Lake of Fire 20:15

As can be seen, this sub-unit is composed of six A.B. (or a.b.) parallel units. This is different from all the preceding sub-units, but is the same linear pattern as was used for the macro structure of the whole setting, as indicated in Chart 56 above. The prominent points are, therefore, all the B. components. These texts describe the fate of the dead people who had not benefited from the first resurrection, which was described previously. Because they had not benefited from the first resurrection, they were not exempt from the second death. In this sub-unit we are specifically told that the Lake of Fire is the second death. This is one of the few places in the book where the structure is based on the number six, but this is totally in harmony with the content.

The most prominent B. component of all is the very last one, precisely because it is the last in a linear system, and also because it is a generic statement which encompasses all the previous more specific ones.

The decision as to who is consigned to the second death is taken on the basis of what is written in Heaven's record books. What is written there is the record of the works produced during the person's life-time on earth.

A Summary

In summary then, it can be seen that the internal organization of the setting to Cycle 7 is very systematic. There are variations, of course, as one would expect, but there is a lot of similarity and matching between the different sub-units and also, between the last sub-unit, in particular, and the macro structure of the whole setting.

It is also interesting to note that there are some similarities with Cycle 4. These are, in particular, the systematic use of codas, and the inclusion of a blessing as an extra prominence feature.

The most important part about the setting is that it focuses on people as being the point of interest. It informs us that from God's point of view, with His heavenly worldview, there are only two groups of people living on the earth, or now residing in the place of the dead. The key issue for Him, is whether they are followers of the Lamb, and have their names written, therefore, in the Lamb's book of life.

Such people automatically benefit from the first resurrection. As a consequence they live, that is to say that they are alive, and being alive, they live to serve the Lamb and to reign with Him. As a further consequence, the second death has no power over them. This means, in turn, that even if they die physically, for whatever reason, they still remain alive and continue to reign with the Lamb. In this particular part of the book, the reigning period is focused on the symbolic, temporal period of 1000 years, but elsewhere in the book, not least at 22:5c, the reigning period is timeless and is, therefore, for all eternity as well.

The fact that this reigning period includes the time while alive on the earth, is brought out by the fact that part of the reigning process is learning to be an overcomer, by defeating the dragon and his minions, just as Jesus had done while on earth. This can only be done while on earth and has to be done by resisting devious ploys, blandishments of all sorts, and even downright threats, by refusing to worship the dragon, or give him recognition of any kind. Part of this process is also preparing to face physical death with equanimity. For the followers of the Lamb, even death holds no fear for them any longer. If they give their lives as a consequence of following the Lamb wherever He goes, then that it is just another means of overcoming the dragon and sharing in Jesus' authoritative rule over him.

The other group of people are quite the opposite. They never figured out how to become followers of the Lamb, how to get their names written in His book of life, and how, therefore, to benefit from the first resurrection. Consequently, they easily fall prey to the dragon's beguiling bewitchments and so, whether they realize it or not, they spend their lives following him, worshiping him, and being led by him, and with him, down the broad path which leads to destruction.

The end of the story for them is that they cannot avoid the second death, and so they end up in the lake of fire, along with the dragon and his two beasts.

On the subject of the dragon, he is not the focus of interest in this setting, and therefore, in this cycle. The fact that he starts out the storyline should not deceive us, because this storyline is all about how it ends, and not about how it starts. It ends with the total defeat, and elimination, of the dragon, his two proxies, and all the people who put their faith in him and his lies. This all culminates in the total victory of the Lamb, along with all who put their faith in Him, and His promises.

As a consequence of all this, it is a big mistake to pay too much attention to the dragon, or give him any credit for anything. The point about this setting is that it establishes firmly, and for good, that the problem of evil has been finally, and fully, finished with. This is the necessary precursor for the body of the cycle which is to follow, which is also the conclusion of the book. Evil has ended, so this opens door to a full description of paradise, which is the place to be, from here on out and into eternity.

One final point, or coda, if you like, for those interested in these things, is as follows. The mathematics of this setting works out like this. The setting as a whole has 4 constituents. These four constituents, between them, have a total of 29 primary components (A.B.C. etc. + codas), including the blessing, counted as a separate unit. This makes a total of 33 (4+29) components in all. The number 33, symbolically represents a promise or promises. The number 30 represents the blood of Christ, and 3 is a 'perfect' number which also represents the resurrection. Hence, for 33 we have the promise of a glorious resurrection through the blood of Christ. This is a most appropriate summary of the message of this setting.

Furthermore, if you include the four lower level components (a.b. x2) which occur in 20:11b and 20:13a, that makes a total of 37 constituents. The number 37 symbolizes the Word of God. This extra insight provides us with a different summary of the message of this passage of Scripture. If the Word of God is in view, then it is as if this is God's final word on the history of the world. This word is firstly, that all evil will be dealt with and eliminated according to what has been done by the guilty parties.

Then secondly, the only ones left standing are those, who have learned to overcome that evil by the blood of the Lamb, and who will, therefore, continue to live and reign with Christ, not only for the 1000 years, but also for ever. As we saw above, 30 represents the blood of Christ, while 7 continues to be the perfect, complete number. So we see that it is the blood of

Christ which brings everything to perfect completion. On the one hand, He completely dealt with all evil, and on the other hand, He opened the door to the new birth, so that the overcomers could benefit from the first resurrection and so to live and reign with Him.

The number 37 is also composed of 20 + 17. From this viewpoint, we can say that the final word of God, and the completed mission of Christ are both summed up as redemption (20), which brings complete victory (17).

All these truth gems are wrapped up in the person of Jesus, and the mission which He has accomplished through His life on earth, His death, His resurrection and His ascension to God's glorious throne room.

7.10 The Use of the Words 'To Live' and 'Testimony' in 20:4

As has been said before, Revelation is a complex book with considerable intricacy involved in the interweaving of its various textual units. In this section we will take a look at two small details which have, nonetheless, provoked considerable discussion and disagreement among the commentators of bygone eras.

These details particularly concern 20:4 which, as we have seen, is a prominent element in the setting of Cycle 7. Our goal is to see if a careful study of the underlying linguistic organization of the text, as text, can help clarify the issues. If so, then it will enable us to follow through with an interpretation of the text, which is constrained by the author's line of thought, and does not do an injustice to what he was trying to accomplish.

The general principle underlying this discussion is that it is not appropriate to try and force a text to be what it is not. Neither is it appropriate to say explicitly, or assume implicitly, that such and so was the author's purpose, when it was not. Firstly, it needs to be understood that this book was not written as a manual of theology. It is not appropriate therefore, to try and answer precise theological questions, with reference to one or two words which happen to occur in the text. The book as whole, and Cycle 7 in particular, is impressionistic in nature, and portrays a view of reality as seen from Heaven's perspective. It does not, therefore, and cannot be made to, equate with and align itself with, a particular human system of theology.

The second point which most people find hard to appreciate, if they have ever thought about it at all, is that tenses from a linguistic point of view, are never absolute in nature. On the contrary, they are always relative, and dependent, to a greater or lesser extent, on their particular use in a particular context. This continues to be true even in modern European languages, but it was even more true back at the era of New Testament Greek, when life in general was far from being time oriented, as it is today. Then, prior to that, for the Hebrew language of that era, the whole issue of tenses has always been a moot point. So it is not appropriate for us today to impose on those older linguistic systems a more recently contrived grid, which tries to make the exact time when an event occurred, the holy grail of semantics, and of biblical interpretation.

7.10.1 The Use of the Verb 'To Live' in 19:20 and 20:4

The following discussion concerns one particular word, which is grammatically redundant in one place, and ambiguous in its immediate context in another place. Nonetheless, it has generated a major theological argument which appears to have no resolution. Examination of the underlying linguistic issues at the micro level, suggest, nonetheless, that these words were intentionally used, and this linguistic insight, if accepted, may provide a possible way forward in this theological debate.

In 19:20 it is stated that the beast and the false-prophet are thrown 'living', or 'alive' into the lake of fire. This is an unusual linguistic collocation which ought to provoke some reflection. In this context, this word is redundant because there is no need to state that they are 'living'. Furthermore, the word for 'alive' is fronted to the very beginning of the sentence, so that it is prominently made the topic of the following unit. This means that it is not there by accident, but by design, even though it seems to be redundant.

Since these two personages are assumed to be spiritual beings, then they presumably cannot be killed, as is the case for 'the rest' in 19:21. This means that they are automatically 'alive', albeit not in a physical sense of the word, but in a spiritual sense.

If they had been human beings, just to consider all the possibilities, then they must be 'dead' physically, since the overall context (cf. 20:10-15) indicates that the lake of fire is a post-death experience. But if they are going through a traumatic post-death situation they must be able to experience it (as is stated in 20:10), otherwise there would be no value in describing the experience to warn others. This means that they also are 'alive', since they have to be 'alive' to experience and to be conscious of the torment of being in a fire. Once again, one is forced to the conclusion that the word 'alive' must refer to being 'alive', and conscious, spiritually speaking, since they are otherwise physically dead, or 'not alive'.

This last comment reveals one of the linguistic strands of the problem. The verb 'to be alive', or, 'to live' is a stative verb and not an event verb. This means that it describes an existential state and not an action. The consequence is that time gets warped, as it were, with stative verbs. They are basically timeless because you either exist or you don't.

You can start existing or have your existence ended, but while you exist, you exist regardless of time. There was no time in the past when you did not exist and there will be no time in the future when you will not exist. You just exist, timelessly.

Furthermore, if we are talking about a spiritual being, which we are in this case, then the spirit world is not constrained by time, which is a feature of physical, earthly existence. If the spiritual world has any time at all, we do not know what it is like nor how it operates.

There is another existential problem in this same context. In the following verse, 19:21, it says that the rest, who are human beings, are killed by the sword which came out of the mouth of the rider on the horse. How can this be? People cannot be physically killed by anything coming from the mouth, since only words come from the mouth. They can do damage but cannot physically cause harm. The only real solution to these difficulties is to understand that these verses are describing spiritual realities, or states of existence, and not physical ones. The spiritual world is timeless so there is no time warp involved, and in the spiritual world also, words are powerful, they can cause harm, and they can therefore, also possibly 'kill' people, in some sense or other of the word.

This viewpoint, that we are dealing with spiritual issues and realities in this text, is not an enormous issue to overcome. It just requires a change of viewpoint and a decision to read the text from Heaven's spiritually based perspective, rather than from a human point of view. This is totally in line with all the rest of the book, which is explicitly stated to be a series of revelations, given by God from His heavenly viewpoint, as a spiritual being. It is unreasonable therefore, and inappropriate, to try and force an earthly, physical viewpoint on this particular passage, or any of the subsequent ones.

So, going back to our starting point with the word 'alive', or 'living' in 19:20. Why then is this detail included in the text, since there is no immediately apparent reason for this redundancy. It is possible that a contrast was intended with the following 'the rest were killed' but it has to be admitted that if the word 'living' is removed, the meaning of the section does not change and the contrast between the fate of the spiritual beings and 'the rest' is not lost.

However, one reason for this redundant usage may be the fact that these words were chosen to participate in a complex overlapping transition between two major units of text. This proposal is warranted because, even though the verb 'to live' occurs sporadically throughout Cycles 1-5, the last previous usage was at 16:3. After this, there is the occurrence in 19:20, followed, soon after, by two occurrences in 20:4 and 5. These last three occurrences, in close proximity to each other, create a tail-head link across the cycle boundary, which falls between 19:21 and 20:1.

Furthermore, as was noticed previously in 3.6.3, and in 5.4.4 above, such transitions may often signal concepts which will be important in the following unit. In this case, even though the verb is no longer used after its use in the transition, the cognate noun 'life' occurs six times in Cycle 7 and three more times in the Epilogue.

It can be seen then, from a linguistic point of view, that there are very good reasons why this particular verb, 'to live', was chosen to be included in this particular passage in 19:20. This is because it was to participate, in the first instance, in a structural plan to link Cycles 6 and 7 together. This extra information concerning the concept of life, only serves to confirm the tail-head link which was described at section 5.4.4 above, and in no way contradicts it.

INFORMATION

The verb 'to live' in various forms occurs 15 times in the whole book, with the last of these being in 20:4. The noun 'life' also occurs 15 times in the whole book, with 9 of these occurrences being after 20:4. All these occurrences are used in a positive sense with the implications of new life being attached to these uses of the word, in line with the main theme of Cycle 7. The number 15 symbolizes rest, which corresponds well with the ethos of this new life which is to be lived in the paradise of God. The sum of the two numbers makes 30. The symbolism of the number 30 is the Blood of Christ. The Blood of Christ is the first cause which produces this new life, which, in turn, leads to rest. Then there is another reference which is an anomaly, and that is the reference in 20:5. In the critical versions of the Greek text the verb here is the same as in 20:4. However, in the Textus Receptus, it is a different verb, which means 'to live again'. If this reference is also included in the count, the total is 31. This number symbolizes the concepts of being born, birth, or offspring. This corresponds with the notion that in order to be alive, one needs to be born. As one is born physically in order to be alive physically, so it is that one needs to be born again spiritually, in order to be alive spiritually, and in order to live for ever. This is the new life which is obtained by laying hold of the benefits of the blood of the Lamb, and thereby entering into God's rest.

This, in and of itself, is already a good reason for using these words in these exact places, but there is more to it than that. In addition to helping to mark the connection and the transition between the end of Cycle 6 and the beginning of Cycle 7, this precise word also serves as an advance signal, that the main goal of the following body of the cycle, is to describe what true 'life' is all about.

It is reasonable to suppose that the author's primary intention then, was to draw his readers' attention to the centrality of the theme of 'life' in a broad sense within the context of Cycle 7, rather than to provide a watertight theological definition of all that may have been implied by this term. Please see the Appendix following this chapter if a more detailed discussion of the technicalities of this theological debate, is required.

In conclusion then, the presence of 'living' in 19:20 and the two occurrences of 'to live' in 20:4-5 are linguistically coherent, in that they contribute to a complex tail-head link, which confirms a break between major sections of text, between 19:21 and 20:1. The break is major because this tail-head link draws attention to the major theme of the cycle beginning at 20:1 which is new life. This life is new because, by implication, it is a timeless kind of life, which will be lived out in a predominantly spiritual environment, untainted by evil. So it is not just a repeat of the physical, time-bound life, which was typical of human life on earth, as it was since the Fall, but is describing life at a new level, in a new dimension. It is the kind of life which Christ lived both before, as well as after His resurrection, and one which His followers can now also aspire to live, after their new birth, at which time their names are (presumably) inscribed in the Lamb's special book of life.

We have seen again then, in this discussion, that we need to have no fear in delving into the details of the organization of the book. It all bears scrutiny and the courageous analyst will come out of it as an overcomer. In this case, the detail of the micro level of analysis, which concerns the unusual use of the word 'living' in 19:20, and the ambiguous use of 'to live' in 20:4-5, contributes to, and confirms, the macro level analysis.

7.10.2 The Word 'Testimony' in 19:10

As has been mentioned before, the true beauty of something like a tapestry or a text like Revelation is discovered in its finest details: details which are perceptible to the human spirit but not necessarily provable in the true scientific sense of the word.

The last sentence of 19:10 contains such a detail. The sentence in question reads like this: 'The testimony about Jesus is the spirit of prophecy', but, like the word 'living' in 19:20, it could be considered to be redundant. This is because it is a sentence which could truly be taken to be extraneous in that it appears to have no connection at all to its context. Rich as it is in theological substance, it could theoretically appear anywhere in the book, or in the New Testament for that matter, and still 'fit' just as well as it does here. Except, that is, for a very important detail.

The key word is 'a testimony' and it just so happens that Cycle 6, within which this verse occurs, is composed of a series of testimonies. There are two types: the first six proclamations are, in effect, testimonies concerning Babylon and her fate. They are negative in content, and testify to the totality of Babylon's demise. In the interlude of the cycle (19:1-8) the testimonies are addressed to God, concern His just plans, especially His plans for the Lamb, and they are positive in nature. This means that, of the seven proclamations, six of them are testimonies, which, with the testimony in the interlude, makes a total of seven.

In 19:10, John receives some personal tuition and is informed that the prophet (i.e. he, himself) should concentrate on testimony which concerns itself with Jesus - either testimony that comes from Jesus or is about Jesus (cf. 1:2). This is relevant here, precisely because John has just been witnessing and meditating on a series of proclamations which are testimonies. So, this small detail harmonizes with, and confirms the general thrust of the analysis presented, that Cycle 6 is composed of a series of proclamations which, for the most part, are testimonies. Not only that, it adds an extra reference to the concept of testimony about Jesus, and so, makes a total of eight of them all together. This in turn harmonizes with the 7+1 principle, which is very noticeable in Cycle 7 which follows, and which was explained in Chapter 5.5.5 above.

This seemingly extraneous statement is important for another reason, in that it specifically supports what we have been saying about the topic of the book. We have been at pains to point out that this book is about Jesus, and that this is one of its primary purposes for existing. If this book is a prophecy, which is what it claims to be, then in order to be truly in the flow of the spirit of prophecy, then it must be a testimony about Jesus. Any interpretation which, intentionally, or unintentionally, gives the impression that the book is primarily about something else, then, according to this admonition to John, it also is not in the flow of the spirit of prophecy. He who has ears to hear, let him hear.

Having said all that, we have still not exhausted all the gems of insight which are to be found in this verse. The fact of the matter is that this word 'a testimony' does not occur just once in this verse. Because of this extra piece about the spirit of prophecy, which is tacked on the end, the word is used twice. As we have said many times before, when a word, or even a concept, is repeated, especially when it is repeated in quick succession, as in this case, then that means it is important. One of the primary reasons why an author intentionally repeats himself, is in order to draw the reader's, or listener's, attention to that particular word.

So if we accept that logic, then it stands to reason, that we should proceed to ask the question why the author would do that. The wider context of Chapter 19 does not otherwise talk about testimonies. It talks about reigning, and even about the up-coming wedding, and the sub-unit in which this word occurs, talks about worship – but not testimonies. The answer to this question lies a bit further on in the discourse, for we find it repeated again, at the beginning of the next cycle in 20:4. Yes, 20:4 again, that information packed verse, which we have come across before.

So, in review then, the word 'a testimony' occurs twice in quick succession, in 19:10, after a long gap, throughout which it was not used at all. It is used in a context where the author is no longer talking about testimonies as such, in any shape or form. Then, just a short time afterwards, it re-occurs near the beginning of the next cycle, after which it is not used again until the very end of the book. These then are all indicators that it is probably participating in a tail-head link.

Linguistically speaking it must be participating in the tail-head link between the end of Cycle 6 and the beginning of Cycle 7, thereby confirming again the existence of this link, which was described in detail previously. However, it is also continuing an important book-level thread, which began way back in Chapter 1, and will end in Chapter 22. This thread reminds us that this revelation is all about providing a testimony. This is specifically a description of what Jesus has accomplished, for the benefit of all who will listen to the words of this testimony.

Once again, this exploration of the smaller details of the book has not revealed any inconsistencies, or incoherent ramblings. On the contrary, it has demonstrated, that this book is a remarkably well constructed piece of artistry. A tapestry of words and concepts which any weaver could be proud of.

For more detailed discussion of smaller issues concerning the setting of Cycle 7, please consult the Appendix at the end of this chapter.

7.11 The Internal Organization of Cycle 7: The Seven New Things Part 2.

There turned out to be so much to say about the setting of this seventh cycle, that I had to divide the discussion of the whole of it into two distinct parts, so that we did not all get lost in the verbiage. So, as a reminder then, here is the structure of the whole cycle once again, and it is a three part linear structure.

1. The Setting 20:1-15

2. The Body 21:1-22:5

3. The Conclusion 22:6-7

We have dealt with the setting in some detail, in the preceding sections, and so now we will look at some of the intricacies of the internal organization of the rest of the cycle. Since it is somewhat complicated, we will try and advance step by step. There is so much amazing detail embedded in these parts of the book, that it creates quite a dilemma. On the one hand, the detail is so intricately, and harmoniously interwoven, that you want to take account of it and try to appreciate it. Yet, at the same time, there is so much of it, that it is hard to take it all in. So we will proceed slowly, but I encourage you to read and re-read, taking as much time as you need, to explore these wonders of the New Creation.

7.11.1 The Body of Cycle 7 – A General Overview

As can be seen in the following chart, the body of the cycle has a three part linear structure, which is very similar to the structure of the whole cycle. The differences are two-fold. The linear structure is not just a simple setting, body, conclusion, but is built upon the semantic relationship of Generic-Specific. This relationship creates enough repetition, and consequent parallelism, to warrant the use of the alphabetical labeling system instead of the numeric one. The second difference is that it has a coda at the end.

Chart 57.
The Structure of the Body of Cycle 7 as a Complete Unit

A. Generic Introduction 21:1-8
- **B.** Specific Development 1. 21:9-21
  - **C.** Specific Development 2. 21:22-22:5b
  - **Coda.** Summary 22:5c

The whole of the body of this cycle is taken up with revealing and describing the Seven New Things which are characteristic of the timeless, eternal destiny, which God has prepared for those who remain faithful to Jesus, the Lamb.

The generic introduction provides a general overview of this vision of the end goal of God's plan of salvation. It is followed by two specific descriptions of the two main components of the generic introduction. The first specific component describes the New Creation, which is composed of a New Heaven and a New Earth, which is, of course, a repetition of, and in parallel with, the Creation of the first heaven and the first earth, as described in Genesis 1. The second specific section describes a new city, within which God Himself will dwell with His redeemed people. This is the New Jerusalem.

As we move through these three components of the body, we find that the descriptions get more and more detailed and specific. As they do so, at the same time, the structures created to encapsulate those descriptions get increasingly complex, and finely tuned as well. Once again, the semantic structure seems to mirror, and illustrate, the content of the message, which is being communicated through the structure.

7.11.2 The Generic Introduction to the Body of Cycle 7 21:1-8

This Introduction mirrors the structure of the whole of the body of the cycle, but as we just mentioned in the preceding paragraph, it gets considerably more developed and more complex as we proceed. So, as can be seen in Chart 58, this introduction to the body, is composed of not just one ABC linear structure, but two of them, and then each part is followed by a coda.

However, this chart is still a somewhat simplified version of the real thing, in order not to overwhelm you with all the detail. For the sake of completeness, some of this detail will be provided in the following paragraphs, but if all this detail is not necessary for you, then please feel free to move on to the next sub-title.

Chart 58.

Component A. of the Body of Cycle 7 21:1-8

Generic Introduction to the Characteristics of the New Creation and the New Jerusalem

A. Generic Vision of the New Creation 21:1

B. Generic Vision of the New Jerusalem 21:2

C. Specific Descriptions of the New Creation: Including positive aspects and the absence of negative aspects 21:3-4b

Coda. Repetition of Summary Explanation Concerning Old Things which have been Removed 21:4c (cf.21:1)

A' Generic Statement Referring to Renewal 21:5

B' Generic Statement Referring to Completion 21:6a

C' Specific Descriptions of the New Creation: Including positive aspects and the absence of negative aspects 21:6b-8a

Coda. Repetition of Summary Explanation Concerning the Second Death 21:8b (cf.20:6,14)

As can be seen in the sub-headings in the chart, the whole structural system in the body of Cycle 7 is based on the interplay between generic descriptions of the new world which is in view, and specific descriptions of various parts of it. The most common feature, after that, is that, in line with the contrast between the setting of the cycle, and the body of the cycle, there is a constant contrastive, cross-over between positive descriptions, and descriptions of the *absence* of negative features. This can be seen in the sections **C.** and **C'** in the chart. This feature is the most marked in this introduction to the body, but also re-appears regularly throughout.

In previous discussion, these contrastive cross-overs between a fully positive viewpoint and a more negative viewpoint, have been described, in more technical terms, as a series of antitheses. Now that we are getting into the details, it can be stated clearly that the examples of this contrast between the positive, and the elimination of the negative, all contribute to the organizational features which are actually antitheses.

So it is then, that throughout the cycle there are many positive descriptions of what God has included in His plan for the New Creation and the New Jerusalem, but these are interlaced with descriptions of aspects of the old system, which will be removed and eliminated. This feature appears, and then reappears regularly throughout the cycle. In this introduction to the body of the cycle, the positive characteristics are listed in 21:3 and 21:6-7, and the negative elements which will be removed, are to be found in 21:4 and 21:8.

As we have been saying all through this book, a careful analyst needs to locate the parts of the text which are the most important for the communication of the author's message. This is why it is essential to carefully take note of the structure of a discourse. This is because this is the only way the analyst can objectively find the parts which are marked for prominence.

For ease of reference here is a list of the various prominence features which will be found throughout the body of the cycle:

- There are many references to God the Father in this passage, more than elsewhere in the book. Whenever God is mentioned it makes the whole context more prominent than it normally would be.
- The last sections of linear ABC, or AB structures, are naturally prominent.
- Generic statements are more naturally prominent than specific ones. This means that any **A.** or **A'** constituents, which are generic in nature, are also naturally prominent.
- There are several Direct Speeches scattered through the various constituents, and these are always prominent. This is even more true when the speech contains an imperative like 'Write!'.
- The codas also tend to be prominent because they are drawing particular attention to one small part of the overall discourse.

- In the Greek version of the text, the title 'the Alpha and the Omega' occurs. This is considered to be a book level prominence marker, at least for this version of the book, which is the basis of this study.

If you take the time to look at all these prominence features closely, you will find that all the eight sub-units of the introduction to the body of the cycle are, either naturally prominent, or marked for prominence in some way. What does this mean? It means that everything is important! Yes, we are subtly, but clearly, being informed that everything in the body of this cycle is important. That is quite something in and of itself, and something quite unusual in linguistic terms.

So then, this unusual feature brings with it a second noticeable consequence. Since everything is prominent, there is nothing which is more prominent than its neighbors. This means that there is no noticeable peak within the cycle, which you can point to, and say that this is the most important part of the message.

This study of the smaller details of the structure confirms what was deduced from our previous survey of the macro structure. At that time we pointed out that this cycle is very impressionistic, and general, in terms of its informational content. We also proposed at that time, that the most prominent points in the cycle are the two categorical direct speeches made by God Himself in 21:5 and 21:6. This still holds true. This is because when it is difficult to decide which particular point is the most important, as in this case, then whenever God is involved, that segment gets the highest ranking. If it is a direct speech, then that segment also gets a very high ranking.

In this case it is a doublet, accompanied by 'behold', both of which features increase the prominence ranking of the segment. In addition, the doublet is entwined with two other significant special prominence markers, namely the imperative 'Write!' in verse 5, and the reference to the Alpha and the Omega in verse 6. Consequently, we can state with confidence, that this study of the micro structure serves to confirm the proposals previously made about the prominence of this cycle.

God's first statement occurs in sub-unit **A'**, and it is about renewal. Inspection of the whole passage in view shows that most, if not all, of the promises made to the overcomers in Cycle 1 and in 7:15-17, re-occur in this cycle. In fact, in verse 7 it is explicitly stated that the good things which are being described, are for the benefit of the overcomers. These are all things which will be renewed, or made new, by God as part of this New Creation.

God's second statement is that what He has promised has already been done, so it is a statement about completion, and can be found in sub-unit **B'**. This statement about completion, itself completes a whole series of references to this concept, as can be found, for example, in 10:6-7, 11:15-18, 12:12, 15:1,8, 16:17-19, 17:17, 19:1-2. Most of these references refer to events, or accomplishments, which have already been completed, at the time of writing, at least from Heaven's point of view. The ones completed already were obviously completed through Jesus' death and resurrection. The rest will be completed at the time of His return. This, in turn, confirms the proposals made previously that this is the only time period which is clearly delineated in the book.

7.11.3 The Specific Development 1 of the Body of Cycle 7 21:9-21

The second part of the body of Cycle 7 is component **B.** of the overall structure and its internal structure is laid out in Chart 59.

Chart 59.

Component B. of the Body of Cycle 7 21:9-21

Specific Development 1: Detailed Description of the Characteristics of the New Jerusalem

A. Introduction by one of the Bowl Angels including repetition of a generic statement about the New Jerusalem 21:9-11a

B. Specific Description of the New Jerusalem in terms of a physical city 21:11b-21

This sub-unit B. has a very complex internal structure which will be laid out in the next chart.

On the surface, it looks as if it has a very simple set of components, with only two parts: an introduction **A.** and a second complementary component, section **B.** However, appearances can be deceiving, because the internal structure of section **B.** is very complex. As a consequence, it was decided to devote a whole chart to this section, which will be Chart 60, rather than to make Chart 59 complicated and difficult to read.

The issues of prominence are the same as for the whole of the body. Because it is a linear structure, sub-unit **B.** is naturally the most prominent. This is confirmed by the fact of its extra length and complexity. However, sub-unit **A.** is a generic statement, followed by a specific development. This means that on the basis of this semantic relationship, it is the most prominent sub-unit of the pair. The end result is that they are both prominent, for different reasons, as was the case for the introduction of the body, described above.

So let's now look at the internal workings of sub-unit **B.** Since this sub-unit is operating at a very low level of the hierarchy, we have purposely used a smaller font, and lower case letters for the parallel structure indicators.

This is to provide a visual reminder that this linguistic unit is operating at the micro level, rather than the macro level.

Chart 60.

The Internal Structure of the Specific Description of the New Jerusalem

Specific Description of the New Jerusalem in Terms of a Physical City 21:11b-21

a. Description of its glory v.11b (light, aura, valuable, jasper, crystal)
b. Description of the wall and gates vv.12-13
c. Description of the foundations **(generic)** v.14

d. Measurement and Evaluation vv.15-18
(Containing: a. Measuring City, and Gates/Wall **generic** v.15
b. Measuring City and Wall **specific** vv.16-17
a' Evaluating Wall and City **generic** v.18
Note repetition of 'gold' a-a', also jasper, pure, pure glass)

c' Description of the foundations **(specific)** vv.19-20
b' Description of the gates **(specific)** v.21a
a' Description of its (main) street v.21b
(lightness, aura, gold, pure, transparent glass)

As we look at this chart, there are a number of observations which we can make. The first is, that even though we are here operating very much at the micro level of analysis, there is no discordance, or difficulty. However big or small the semantic units may be, they are always organized into a coherent structure, which can be observed and described.

Secondly, we can observe that there is also agreement between the various parts of the structure. Please see Appendix A7.3.7 at the end of this chapter for more explanation about this principle of agreement. What this means in practice, is that all the various components are talking about the same thing in a harmonious and progressive way. The same concepts and words are repeated at different levels, using the same types of semantic relationships, and using the same types of structures, as in the larger units within which they are contained. Yet, at the same time, the accumulating descriptions move the reader forward progressively in his comprehension of what is being revealed, until it is as complete as a finite mind can handle.

So, let's start with the words and concepts first. In Chart 60 the primary repetitions are indicated in parentheses. These are words and concepts to do with lightness, transparency or whiteness, brightness, and beauty, to name but a few. These echo a very different image, but with similar connotations, which was used in 21:2. In this case, it is the first general description of the New Jerusalem, where she is described as being like a bride, who is beautifully dressed, and bedecked and bejeweled, in preparation to meet her husband. Then to complete the sequence, after this detailed description of the new city is finished, there is an ongoing reverberation of the same concepts in 21:22-27. This is where it is revealed that there is no physical sun and moon any more, because it is the glory of God and of the Lamb, which provide bright light, and a beautiful aura of illumination, for the city.

Next we can observe that the principal semantic relationship which is regularly used at all levels of this part of the discourse, is the generic-specific relationship. The whole cycle at the upper levels, is based around this relationship, as shown in Charts 57-58 above. But now at the micro level, it is the same relationship which predominates as can be seen in Charts 59-60.

Then finally, it is always the same kind of structures which are systematically used. Cycle 7 is a bit different from the previous cycles, in that there are more linear ABC structures than were used before. But, nonetheless, the system is still built around repetition and parallelism, as is the case for the whole book. Within the cycle, the macro structure is a double three part linear structure, as illustrated in Charts 57 and 58.

Then, in this section which is under consideration here, we find embedded in that three part, linear structure, a classic double chiasm. It is a clean, seven part chiasm, with a tidy gem of a three part chiasm nestled in its center. It is a structure which could easily have found itself a place in any other part of this book, and could have been the pride and joy of any well deserving Hebrew poet.

There is nothing discordant or out of place, to contradict or obstruct the flow of the author's descriptions of what he saw, and which he recorded for our benefit, even now, 2000 years later.

Finally, we cannot move on without making a brief mention of prominence once again. We have already stated that every component of the body of Cycle 7 is prominent in some way or another, and because of that, the issues and outcomes in Cycle 7 are not as predictable as in some other cycles. So here, in this case of the lengthy sub-unit 21:11b-21, we have a double chiasm, which obviously has a very notable prominent point at 21:15-18. Even though this is operating at the lower level of the discourse, and cannot be said to be particularly prominent at the level of the cycle, at the same time, it can hardly be passed over with no mention at all.

As we have said before, the whole of the body of Cycle 7 is prominent in some way. As a consequence, if one is going to try, nonetheless, to discern the peaks embedded within the mountain top, then one has to use other more refined criteria. The first one which we attempted above, was on the basis that, whatever God says in direct speech, is bound to be more important than anything else.

Now, in this case, it would seem to be structural criteria which can guide us. It is noticeable that in a book full of chiasms and concentric structures of all sorts, this whole cycle, even though it still has parallel structures, is organized in a linear fashion. Then in the middle of this series of linear patterns there is this large, complex, double chiasm, which is a classic seven part chiasm with a three part chiasm embedded. All these features combined create an obvious prominence feature. This is so obvious, once you see it, that I am very much inclined to propose that the point of this chiasm, which is 21:15-18, is the second most prominent point of the cycle.

However, when you go back to look at the verse, it is the kind of verse which most people, myself included, would skip over, because it seems to communicate nothing important, and what it does say about the measure of a man, being the measure of an angel, is extremely enigmatic. So, in cases like this, we need to do our due diligence. To accomplish this we need to ask whether the analysis is truly pointing to a prominent point (bearing in mind, as we have said, that it is not in line to be the most prominent point of all) in the cycle, or whether there is a some mismatch or other incongruity here.

So let's start with first reactions. If you hit an unexpected obstacle and don't know quite how to proceed, then first reactions are a good place to start. When I went back to re-read these verses and saw that it was all about measuring and mathematics, the first thought that jumped into my mind was this quotation from 2 Timothy 2:19, which says 'The Lord knows those who belong to Him'.

But when I went back to look at that verse in more precise detail, I was quite taken aback to see that the whole verse reads like this:

> However, the foundation of God stands firmly in place, with this inscription stamped upon it: 'The Lord *really knows* those who belong to Him', and, 'Let everyone who names the name of the Lord, keep well away from evil'.
> (2 Timothy 2:19. The emphasis is implicit in the Greek.)

The first question which arises is what the firm foundation refers to, for Paul does not specifically explain this reference. However, from within a biblical context the only two possibilities would be the foundation of the Temple of God, or the foundation of the City of God. This would be the same city which Abraham saw from afar, and the one which we can now see in more detail in Revelation 21. This is intriguing, because the two verses in Revelation which flank the ones which we are studying, describe these very foundations of the City of God.

Furthermore, it is even more intriguing to see that the whole context in the letter to Timothy could easily fit somewhere in Revelation, because it re-iterates some of the exact same themes. For example Paul refers to the following topics:

- He, personally, like John, is in a situation of suffering due to persecution, v.9.
- He is having to persevere and endure hardship, like the Christians in Asia Minor, v.10.
- He refers to Christ's resurrection, as happens throughout Revelation, v.8
- He states that Christians are considered to have died with Christ and also to have been raised with Christ to a new life, as re-occurs in Revelation 20, v.11.
- He states that the overcomers – those who endure hardship – will also reign with Christ, v.12. He uses the future tense but note that it is specifically in condition-consequence clauses introduced by 'if'. See Appendix A7.3.10 below concerning the blessing of 20:6.
- He implies that the foundation in verse 19 refers to 'a great house' which contains gold and silver vessels v.20. This could easily refer to the New Jerusalem, which is characterized by gold and precious metals and stones, and which is God's house, where He will live together with His people.
- In the light of the above, his final exhortation is that Timothy, like everybody who names the name (testifies about, or, is a witness for) of the Lord, should remove all evil from their life v.19b.

It is to be granted that these are only oblique references to Revelation, but there are definitely some correspondences. Therefore, if we accept the principle that Scripture is illuminated by Scripture, then these comparisons are worth considering.

So, now to consider the content of 21:15-18 itself, we can note the following points:

- It is all about measuring the city.
- The measuring is done with a golden rod: this symbol speaks volumes.

- The measuring is done by an angel, which suggests strongly that this continues to be a spiritual activity seen by John in his vision. The spiritual nature of the measuring is also implied by 'the measure of an angel' in verse 17.
- At the same time, verse 17 also tells us that the measurements are given in terms of the measurement of a man. This presumably means that the spiritual concepts are being communicated in human terms so that, to some extent, we can understand them. This use of human words to transmit heavenly ideas is explained in more detail in Appendix A7.3.9 below. This enigmatic mixing of the spiritual with the human, reminds us that these measurements are intended to be interpreted symbolically.
- The city is a perfect cube. This matches exactly the shape of God's first permanent house on earth, which was the Holy of Holies in the Temple, which was also a cube.
- However, the size of it is so huge (approximately 2,200 kilometers cube), that this cannot possibly be a physical city in the terms which are relevant to the current 'old' heaven and earth.
- Likewise the wall is so small (+/-65m), compared to the height of the city, that it has no physical usefulness.
- It would seem then, that the description is either that of a spiritual city, for which we do not have an appropriate grid to comprehend it, or that the description is symbolic and must be interpreted in that manner.
- The main information which we are given are the numbers, which we can, at least, understand.

So, the numbers then, are the 12,000 stadia for the size of the cube, which incorporates the city, 12, which is the number of the gates, and 144 cubits which is the height of the wall. The basic number in view is 12, which is the number which symbolizes government. As we have seen previously, the first government for the nation of Israel was based on the number 12, just as the 12 gates have the names of the tribes of Israel inscribed on them as well. In Heaven John saw the 24 Elders, now we have a city based on the number 12. This must, at least by implication, indicate that it is a city of rulership. Since it is so big, and so perfect, it must be the City of the Great King, from where He rules the universe.

As is explained in more detail in Appendix A7.3.9, the number 1000 is a human number which is very big, to the point of being humanly uncountable. So any number or concept symbolically attached to 1000, is the largest possible example of that particular category. So in this case, this is the largest, and most important, center of government which has ever existed.

The number 144 is also a multiple of 12, being 12 x 12, and, therefore, another governmental number. The number is obviously reminiscent of the 144,000 people in Chapter 7, who were also associated with the 12 tribes, and, at the same time also, with an uncountable number of people. It is just a small step of the imagination then, to envisage this huge crowd of people, as represented by the 144,000, comfortably co-habiting in this huge, glorious city which is also totally based on the number 12.

This is because it is all about the people. 1 Peter 2:5 tells us that it is the people of God who are the 'living' stones (same word for 'living' as in 20:4) used by God to build Himself both a home (cf. 21:3) and a priesthood (cf. 20:6). These are the same stones with which the city is built as described in 21:19-21, but not only that, it is obvious on reflection, that no city is built to stand empty. A city does not exist for itself, but to provide a tabernacle, a resting place for people, for people who have journeyed long, and labored hard.

So when we get to this pinpoint of prominence, at the center of the chiasm in 21:15-18, what can we observe ? We observe that God measures His city and records for us its basic dimensions. We observe that He has a plan, just as we have seen all through the book, and that He is meticulous in His planning, measuring, and preparing, one of His ultimate goals, which is this city. But it is all about the people. This is why we can quite appropriately say here, that the Lord knows those who belong to Him. Just as He knows everything about every stone of the city, so He knows everything about each individual person, who will be part of that city, both as a living stone and as a citizen.

What we learn from these verses is that He is preparing everything with care. A city where we can be at rest and benefit from many wonderful provisions, as described in the surrounding verses, but also with a 144 cubit (65m) high wall, which is an obvious symbol of safety and protection. For those who had been harassed and hounded even to death, this is not an insignificant symbol.

But that is not all, for the whole city is based on the number 12, the number of government. Even the gates and the foundation stones are grouped by 12. Twelve gates to represent the 12 tribes of Israel (21:12), and 12 foundation stones to represent the 12 apostles of the Lamb (21:14). All this together, means that the people who will live here, descendants of Israel along with the spiritual descendants of the apostles, will live to rule and reign for ever, together with Christ, the King of kings and the Lord of lords. For this is what we are told in the final coda of the book in 22:5c. Since this coda brings to our attention what is possibly the most important thread in this cycle, and in the whole book, then it may well qualify as being the third most prominent of all the prominent points in Cycle 7.

INFORMATION

Here is another piece of information about the numbers embedded in this text. The double chiasm in 21:15-18, which we are talking about here, is composed of a chiasm of 7 parts plus a chiasm of 3 parts, 'living' within it. These two together make up a structure composed of 10 parts. As we have seen before, 10 is the number of a testimony. This beautiful, perfectly dimensioned city, plus the people living within it, will be an eternal testimony to God's grace, and Jesus' redemptive accomplishments.

Once again, we can see that no matter how much we explore the finer details of the book, we find that everything is meticulously planned. All the smaller parts fit harmoniously in their place, and make their particular contribution to the overall message. Furthermore, an analysis of this nature brings to your attention smaller segments of the text, like 21:15-18, which might otherwise have been overlooked. This attention to detail, in turn, leads to deeper, richer insights. It makes possible the discovery of the hidden gems of the text, which have been placed carefully where they will only be found by the enterprising explorer.

7.11.4 The Specific Development 2 of the Body of Cycle 7 21:22-22:5b

This is the final part, C., of the three part body of Cycle 7. In this case, it is no longer a linear structure as the previous constituents were, but is formulated in a symmetric ABB'A' pattern, as laid out in Chart 61.

Chart 61.

Component C. of the Body of Cycle 7 21:22-22:5b

Specific Development 2: Detailed Description of Characteristics of the New Creation which are Associated with the New Jerusalem 21:22-22:5b

A. Specific Explanation About the Sanctuary of God and the Lamb and About the Glory of God which illuminates the City 21:22-23

B. Specific Explanation Concerning the Role of the Nations 21:24-27

B' Specific Explanation concerning the Healing of the Nations 22:1-3a

A' Specific Explanation About the Throne of God and the Lamb and About (the Glory of) God which illuminates His People 22:3b-5b

As a consequence, there is no noticeable prominent peak. As remarked previously, the prominence profile continues to be flat. God is constantly present and being referred to in this segment of text which makes the whole of it prominent relative to the previous cycles, but the internal profile of the cycle remains flat.

The key information which is provided in this part of the body of the cycle is firstly about the glory of God, which is present in the city. This is the source of light and illumination. It is also presumably the source of the translucent aura which seems to emanate from everywhere, including from the stones themselves.

The second key piece of information is about the nations. They too will find a place in the city of God, and will find not only rest and protection like everyone else, but healing as well.

Apart from the symmetric structure illustrated above, the other key feature of the organization of this section of the body, is the intertwining of the positive aspects of the New Creation, and the absence of the negative aspects of the old creation. This continues the thread of the antitheses. There is quite a bit of detail in these specific passages, so for ease of reference this information will be presented in Chart 62.

The labels 'Positive' and 'Negative' have been used in the interests of optics rather than for their accuracy of description. What we have here is a series of antitheses, which is one of the features of Cycle 7 as mentioned above. In this cycle there are a lot of contrasts between the new features which God has prepared in His New Creation, confirmed and complemented by opposite features which are no longer present.

So it was necessary in the setting to the cycle, that the dragon and all evil had to be dealt with and eliminated first, in order to make way for the new world which was to come. In the same way, this basic antithesis is continued on in the body of the cycle, as various details of the new order are highlighted one against the other.

As a consequence, some of the items labeled as 'Negative' for visual convenience in the chart, are not negative in a bad sense, but are features of the old order which have been superseded and, therefore, are no longer needed. This is the case, for example, for the reference to the temple in 21:22, and to the sun and moon in 21:23, which were not negative features of the old world, but have, nonetheless, been replaced by something better.

The purpose of these labels then, is to enable us to easily see, and follow the movement of this interweaving of these different antitheses. As can be seen, the effect is systematic and harmonious, and is not at all random or disjointed.

So it is that, the overall pattern begins with some negative features, interwoven with some positive ones. Then as we progress through the sub-unit, the pattern changes so that there are more positive features, interwoven with just a few negative ones. Then, at the end, we have nothing but a series of positives with no references to anything negative at all, to spoil the party. That is how the whole book ends, as we have seen before, because they all lived happily ever after.

Chart 62.

The Internal Structures of Component C. of Cycle 7

The Organization of the Positive Statements and Negative Statements

A. Specific Explanation Concerning the Sanctuary of God 21:22-23

a. **Negative:** There is no temple in the city v.22a

b. **Positive**: God and the Lamb are personally present in place of the temple v.22b

a' **Negative:** The city no longer has the sun or the moon for light v.23a

b' **Positive:** The glory of God illuminates the city v.23b

Coda. Positive: The Lamb is its lamp v.23c

B. Specific Explanation Concerning the Role of the Nations 21:24-27

a. **Positive:** The nations and their kings walk in this light and bring their glory in v.24

b. **Negative:** The gates are never shut because there is no night there v.25

a' **Positive:** The glory and honor of the nations will be brought into the city v.26

b' **Negative:** Nothing based on evil, corruption or lies allowed into the city v.27a

Coda. Positive: Only those who are written in the Lamb's Book of Life will be allowed into the city v.27b

B' Specific Explanation Concerning the Healing of the Nations 22:1-3a

a. **Positive:** The river of water of life flows from the throne of God and the Lamb v.1

b. **Positive:** The tree of life is there with 12 fruits v.2a

c. **Positive:** The leaves of the tree are for healing the nations v.2b

Coda. Negative: There is no curse there any more v.3a

A' Specific Explanation About the Throne of God and the Lamb and About (the Glory of) God which illuminates His People 22:3b-5b

a. **Positive:** The throne of God and the Lamb will be there v.3b

b. **Positive:** The Lamb's servants will be there and able to see Him face to face v.3c-4a

c. **Positive:** His name will be on their foreheads v.4b

Coda. Positive: They will reign for ever and ever v.5c.

(The coda for section A' is, at the same time, a coda to the whole cycle. Consequently, it is treated as a separate unit, and appears again below.)

It turns out that there are five negative, or insufficient, items which have been removed as a demonstration of God's grace. Then, by contrast, there are more than double that number of positive new features, which are presented by the author by this means. Internally to the Component C. of the body, which is under review here, and integral to its own autonomous organization, there are exactly twelve positive features which are described. Yes, it's that number 12 again.

That only leaves one remaining proposition to account for, which is the final coda. Perusal of the chart above shows that codas are systematically used throughout this last component of the body. See also Charts 57 and 58 for more codas in the body of Cycle 7. This is reminiscent of the Signs Cycle, which also had a lot of codas and was also another prominent cycle in the book. This pattern confirms that the final coda is not out of place. It is not there just for analytical convenience, but it is there because the author clearly had a system and the coda is part of the system. This is now confirmed by the fact that it is an extra one, following after a complete series of 12. Codas are always separate from the unit to which they are attached. But, as well as pointing back to something in the preceding context, they can also have the function of starting off a new series. This is exactly what happens here.

7.11.5 The Coda of the Body of Cycle 7 22:5c

This coda contains a final summary statement and explanation concerning the people of God. Although it is possible to analyze it as a coda, which is simply attached to the end of Component C. of the body of Cycle 7, as indicated above, it is actually a book level feature, which brings the whole body of the book to a close. This feature has already been discussed at length in Chapter 5.5.5.

Suffice it to say here, that this study of the lower levels of the discourse have only confirmed what was proposed in Chapter 5, that this short sentence 'and they will reign for ever and ever', is indeed functionally and semantically a coda to the whole book. Functionally, it has a double function, like many other constituents of the book, in that it is both a coda to the body of Cycle 7, and also a coda to the body of the book.

Semantically it also has a double function. Its content about reigning points back to the specific double references to God's people reigning with Christ in 20:4 and 6. It also underscores all the number 12s in Cycle 7 confirming that reigning and governing is indeed the most important of all the threads in this cycle. But, at the same time it is a coda, which is also an eighth and a fiftieth and so it starts a new era, resplendent with new beginnings. By means of the future tense in the verb it points the reader towards the future. The future is unseen from that vantage point, we have to take it on faith that it will be very good, because of God's promises to that effect. Yet, out of all the good new things, the ultimate privilege and destiny reserved for the followers of the Lamb is to rule and reign with Him over the new universe for ever. This is one of the most crucial messages of the book of Revelation. It is timeless in nature and something which believers in Jesus the Messiah can aspire to in any generation.

APPENDIX 7

A Brief Review of the Literature Concerning Cycle 1 and Cycle 7

With Particular Reference to the Theological Debate over Chapter 20:4-5

PREFACE

This Appendix has been placed here to provide extra technical information relating to the analysis of the Cycles 1 and 7 for those who wish to explore these matters further. There is no need to read this Appendix if this extra information is not required, for the technical information already given in the main text is sufficient for the general purpose of understanding the structural organization of the book. The Appendix just broadens out what has already been explained and makes more specific what has been contributed by the commentators who have gone before.

It is Chapter 20 of Revelation in particular, which has sparked the most debate and disagreement between biblical commentators representing different schools of thought.

As we have been at pains to point out in the course of this study, a discourse of this nature is first and foremost a linguistic artifact. This means that it should be studied first of all from a linguistic point of view, before any other kind analysis is attempted. The evidence would suggest that this has not been done adequately in the past. This lack of methodological discipline, right there, may account for some of the disagreements.

An attempt will be made therefore, in the following discussion, to clarify some of the underlying linguistic issues and discrepancies. The aim in doing that, is to shed some light on what the author was really trying to say, and to accomplish. If all concerned are willing to listen to what the author is saying, maybe we can then come to agreement on his basic message and leave our disagreements behind us.

APPENDIX 7
A Brief Review of the Literature Concerning Cycles 1 and 7

A7.1 Introduction

So many commentaries of various kinds and quality have been written on the book of Revelation, that it would be an impossible task to take account of them all. For a full list of those which were consulted in the course of preparing the research for this book, please see the bibliographies in Schooling 2004. The purpose here then, is not to give a complete review of everything which has ever been said. The purpose here is to give a brief review of certain specific points, in order to make some practical recommendations for the readers of the twenty-first century.

The main point in question, is that linguistics in general is a modern, twentieth century discipline, which biblical scholars of an earlier era did not have access to. That means in particular, that the production of serious, and helpful, linguistics-based studies of books like Revelation is still very much in its infancy.

Consequently, when we observe in the following paragraphs, that these commentators did not perceive many of the linguistic structures, around which the book is constructed, that is not intended to be a criticism as such. In point of fact, many commentators have made many astute observations about the book, for which they should be given due credit, but at the same time, through no direct fault of their own, they were not able to get a grasp of the whole picture.

The purpose here, then is to recommend that the modern reader handle these earlier comments and view-points with care, and with a certain spirit of respectful dissatisfaction. This is because, even though many comments may be pertinent and helpful, the overall result will still be inadequate to the extent that their analysis does not take account of all the data. In some cases, this may have no serious consequences, but in other cases it may be worthwhile to do some more research, and listen to other points of view, in order to avoid being guided down an unhelpful path.

A7.2 Some Comments on Cycle 1. – The 7 Letters

There is no question that the Letters Cycle is the most clearly delineated cycle of them all. As a consequence, it has been studied in detail, and preached and commented on, more than any other part of the book, apart, that is, from Chapter 20 which will be reviewed below.

A7.2.1 References to the Structure of the Cycle and to Internal Structures of the Letters

Naturally enough, since it is so obvious, all commentators recognize that there are seven letters. However, for most of them, their concern for the structural organization stops there. It is only a minority of them who have any understanding that the structure plays a part in communicating the overall message.

So, for those who do make some reference to the structure of this cycle, then, it is understandable that they have realized that the repetition of the number seven in the book is significant, and have tried to take this symbolism seriously. Having said that, not everyone by any means, pays any serious attention to the structure of each letter, even though that is not too difficult to discern.

Nonetheless, quite a few have done so, with the result that, some of them specifically listed seven internal components for each letter, in line with the numeric arrangement of the seven letters themselves. For example, Wilcock 1975,37 does this, as does Hendriksen 1940,59. Morris 1987,58 and Beale 1999,225, dimly discern the nine points listed at 7.5.3 above although they are collapsed into seven more complex points. Some, like Ladd 1972,36 and Hayford 1995,478, considerably oversimplify the issues. Ladd overlooks the all important exhortation, and Hayford only presents an analysis of the body of the letters. Mounce 1977,84 condenses them all into six components and also overlooks the central exhortation. Beale 1999,223-8 provides a wide range of references to other authors and their views on this matter.

So, even though there are some insights present, the main issues still remain under the radar. In actual fact, the internal structures of the letters are composed of nine constituents, and this is in line with the organization of the book as a whole, and not in line with the system based on seven. This is not an anomaly, because all of Cycles 1-6 have nine possible constituents, with the interlude being optional.

The above proposals, therefore, are missing a major insight into the structure of the book as a whole, and so are leading the unwary reader down an incorrect path.

A7.2.2 References to the Content of the Letters and to Prominence

So, in the above best case scenarios, a limited insight into the structural organization is brought to light, but the result is only a partial picture. It is as if an artist had covered not even three-quarters of his canvas with paint, but had left the rest blank. The result is inadequate and unsatisfactory at best, or inadequate and misleading at worst.

As already explained, even though some commentators discerned some of the internal structure, for quite a number of them, they actually overlooked the most important component of all, which is the central command or exhortation. If you do not even see this component, then it is not at all possible to talk about what is the most important part. Unfortunately, without some knowledge of linguistics and semantics, biblical commentators do not even seem to have a mental grid for such things. As you read the commentaries, you get the impression that every part of a particular passage has about the same value, and level of importance, as every other part.

So, to take Mounce 1977,83-130 as a representative example, in nearly fifty pages of discussion of the Letters Cycle, he only mentions repentance in passing twice, a brief reference to holding fast what they received, and no reference to the concept of perseverance or endurance at all. Then, as a contrastive example, Collins 1984,113 notices that 'emphasis is repeatedly placed on the quality of endurance or steadfastness'. But at the same time she overlooks the dominance of the concept of repentance in the Letters Cycle.

As far as I am aware, at the time of this writing, nobody was aware of the chiastic structure of the whole cycle. Consequently, nobody was able to discern that the letter to Thyatira is the most important of all the letters. Similarly, those who discuss the structure usually recognize that there are variations in the organization, but no attempt is made to try and explain the significance of those variations.

So it can be seen then, that the commentators cannot be relied on to provide complete and accurate information with regard to what is going on in the text. Many important pieces of information are missing, because nothing is said about them at all, and some things which are said are inaccurate and are, therefore, misleading.

A7.3 Some Comments on Cycle 7 – The 7 New Things

Chapter 20 of Revelation has become quite well-known for being a hot-bed of theological discussion, debate and disagreement. For the moment, the fact that there is so much, sometimes, even virulent, disagreement over a basic understanding of an important part of Scripture, shows that there is something lacking in our system. There must be an important piece of the puzzle missing which makes it impossible for a true and sensible consensus to be built up. At the risk of venturing unnecessarily into a minefield, I feel, nonetheless, duty-bound to make some contribution to this discussion.

The reason for this is that, in my opinion, if we are to make any progress at all, in coming to agreement, then the only sensible, and mutually respectful, way forward, is to agree to review our brief from the beginning. The starting point is that we really need to work through the linguistic underpinnings in a thorough manner, before going any further.

This task is further complicated by the fact that there is not just one point of disagreement, but there are several. The first one is the issue of what it really means for the dragon to be put in the pit. When does this happen? What is the true first cause, and is it a new event in a linear sequence, or is it in parallel, and therefore a repetition in another form, of the events recounted in Chapter 12? Is it symbolic, spiritual, or literal?

Then there is the 1000 year period. Is this symbolic or literal? When does it begin and when does it end? Is this also in linear sequence, or parallel with the same concept expressed differently in another part of the book?

What is the status of the people referred to in the chapter. Are they alive or are they dead? If they are alive, can they die in the 1000 year period? If they die what happens to them? Where are the thrones, and are they literal or symbolic? Can the beast still bother the people during this period? And so the list goes on.

This knotty problem is very real and, for some, has been a real blockage which prevents them from appreciating this book at all. This is so much the case, that whole books have been written to try and constructively confront this problem. So, for example, Newton 2009 has done just that, in order to try and defuse some of the mines, and clear a way through the wreckage left by our theological debates, so that ordinary people can reclaim the message of this book, and not have to write it off for ever.

To be realistic, it would take another whole book to thoroughly review all these issues, but let's just make an attempt with one issue in order to see what comes out the other end. The one which we will intentionally tackle here, is the issue revolving around the verb 'to live' in 20:4. This is because we have already provided an extensive review of this issue in section 7.10.1 above. The aim here is to go a bit further, and provide more detailed insights into the linguistic issues which are fueling this debate. Our hope is that as you, the reader, see these issues more clearly, this may equip you to make your own decisions on some of these issues, based on a better understanding of some of the underlying issues, which complicate matters behind the scenes.

A7.3.1 A Review of the Issues At Stake

According to Mounce 1977,356 then, this is a crucial issue, for he explains and buttresses his viewpoint of 20:4 in this way:

> These martyrs are said to live and reign with Christ for a thousand years. How one interprets this simple statement reveals his

position on the millennial question. Ladd 1972,265, correctly observes that the crux of the entire exegetical problem is the meaning of "they came to life again".

Proponents of the futurist viewpoint on eschatology, like Mounce, insist that this must refer to a physical coming to life or a bodily resurrection. The main reason for this, they argue, is that it must be identical in meaning to the use of the same verb in 20:5, where the physical resurrection interpretation is universally accepted (see Beale 1999,1003). So, in the light of this assumption, he goes on to say:

> If "they lived" in verse 4 means a spiritual resurrection to new life in Christ, then we are faced with the problem of discovering in the context some persuasive reason to interpret the same verb differently within one concise unit. No such reason can be found.

This is a very categorical statement, and a good rule of thumb is to doubt, and to double check, such categorical declarations, until you are sure that they are well founded on reliable data. As a matter of fact, there is not just one, but several, reasons why this statement is not justified, and, therefore, not a reliable guide to our interpretation of the verse.

A7.3.2 What the Author May and May not Do

One of the basic assumptions of linguistic analysis is that the data is the data. This means that we respect the author's right to say what he wants to say, in whatever manner he sees fit. The reader, or the analyst, does not have some divine right to say that an author cannot do things like this, or that he must always do things like that.

So, in this case then, it is a spurious argument even before we start, to say that the author cannot use a certain verb in one way in one verse, and then use it in a different way in the next. This is especially true at a distance in time of 2000 years, and with vast differences in cultural and social traditions, which affect our expectations, and our worldview.

It is the author's job to present his discourse in whatever way he sees fit, and it is the analyst's job to take the data as it stands, and try and understand what the author was trying to accomplish. If, at first, he does not understand, then he needs to do some more work to try and adapt himself to the author's point of view. At this distance in time, none of us can say for sure what the acceptable and normal literary traditions of that previous era were exactly. Consequently, we need to proceed with caution and humility, and be open to new ideas and different traditions.

There is, nonetheless, one condition which needs to be appended to this basic statement. If an author clearly does deviate from the known or expected norms, then, if at all possible, the analyst needs to propose a reason why he may have done so. To that extent Dr. Mounce, quoted above, is right about having a good reason for what we propose. This is a double edged sword. He needs a good reason for being categorical in his position, and anyone who wishes to counter it must also have some good reasons. Our purpose in these paragraphs is to provide a number of possible reasons for our viewpoint.

A7.3.3 What the Author Did, in Fact, Do

Unfortunately for him, Mounce rather rashly said that no such reason can be found to warrant two different uses of the same word in the same context. However, it so happens that our author did use the same word twice with different meanings, right in this same context.

In 20:4 it says that the martyrs both lived and reigned for the 1000 years. In this case both verbs are in the aorist form, and this is usually taken to imply a past tense. This is a significant matter in itself, which we will discuss more fully below. But for the moment, let's just take note of the presence of the verb 'to reign'. However, just a few lines later in 20:6, we are told that these same people *will* reign with Christ for the 1000 years, and this is now expressed in the future tense. So one minute it seems to be a past tense, and the next it is in the future tense. Obviously, we can deduce from this data, that the author can play around with words, as it suits him, and Mounce's argument is seriously called into question.

However, that is not all, because there are several examples, within the context of the whole book, where John uses words in unusual ways, without any apology or explanation. Two of these examples we have already studied in some detail in sections 7.7.9 and 7.10.1 above. The first one is the use of the verb 'to sit' to describe the situation of the inhabitants of the earth in 14:6. Yet, in the same context, John several times refers to the same situation using another more normal verb.

The other example brings us back again to the verb 'to live' as it is used in 19:20. In this case, since it refers to a spiritual being, it cannot possibly be alluding to a bodily resurrection, and is, therefore, in contradiction once again, with the received interpretation of the same word in 20:5.

Our conclusion has to be that Mounce, and the others like him, have bitten off more than they can chew in making such a bold claim. Even if we still do not understand the nuances of what is happening in 20:4-5, we can, nonetheless, state with some confidence that John was certainly capable of using words in unusual, and thought-provoking, ways. This did not seem to be a problem for him. In the case of these last two examples, we did discover a probable reason why he chose to express himself in those particular ways.

A modern day analyst may have to bend his mind a bit, and make the effort to adapt his worldview to accommodate the kind of literary architecture which was in vogue back then. But if we make the effort to do that, and that is our job, then the explanations which we found, are very reasonable and plausible. If that was the case for those examples, then we can assume that, if we hunt carefully enough, we will also be able to find a reasonable explanation for the double use of the verb 'to live' in 20:4-5 as well.

A7.3.4 Variety is the Spice of 'Life'

Unlike John, I am going to be very pedantic, and say outright that I have chosen this sub-title on purpose to make a point. This is a title which includes some metaphorical symbolism, for we are not talking here about literal, physical spices. It is also an intentional play on words, using the word 'life' as the focal point, precisely because we are in the process of talking about 'life', in its various forms, and the ancillary verb 'to live'.

The point which I making here, is that every language in every era, has the capacity for metaphorical symbolism and for plays on words. Not only that, as every serious writer, poet and song composer knows, human beings love such ingenious, and mind-bending, verbal intricacies. Just as people love spice on their food, so they love spice in their conversations, and in the books which they read. One of the best forms of spice, in this case, is variety.

So, in John's day then, any writer worth his salt (there we go again) would have spiced up his rhetoric, both to please his readers and also to keep them reading. This is a no-brainer (there we go again, are you hooked yet?) that John would have used as many tricks of the writer's trade, and as much variety as he could muster, in order to accomplish his task, and, let's not forget, his task was a hortatory one, so he was really motivated to get through to his readers.

Furthermore, in his day and age, the literary architecture which was popular, and which he chose to use, was the style based on repetition and parallelism. The thing is, if you decide to use that style, then you purposely want to say the same things more than once. Yet, at the same time you do not want to make each repetition identical, for that would be boring and take the fun out of it for the reader. So, one of the great skills needed for a writer like him, was to find all sorts of variety in his use of words, so that he could say the same thing more than once, but never in exactly the same way.

So then, I think that I have made my point. It is totally predictable, and to be expected, that John is likely to use the same words, with different nuances, and intentionally crafted word plays in his discourse, and he can do this in a variety of ways and for a variety of reasons. By the same token therefore, it is extremely pedantic, to the point of being unreasonable, to make a theological point dependent, as if balanced on the head of a pin, on the specious argument that a writer must never use the same word twice with slightly different meanings. That is, if he did actually use the word 'to live', with two different meanings.

A7.3.5 What is the Real Meaning of 'to Live'?

In support of his contention that the verb 'to live' in 20:4 must refer to a bodily resurrection, Mounce makes appeal to other uses of the verb in Revelation. According to him (op.cit., 356) 'the verb is found…in but two other places: in 2:8 of Christ… and in 13:14 of the beast', and these examples for him, by implication at least, prove his point. However, closer scrutiny of the evidence, demonstrates that this argument is seriously flawed, to the point of being self-contradictory.

Let's take the last one first. The beast who supposedly came alive again is, by all accounts, a spiritual being and cannot, therefore, be a beneficiary of a bodily resurrection. This is because it would have had no physical body in the first place. In the parallel passage in 13:3, it merely says that its wound was healed, and not that it came alive again, so this example of variety creates uncertainty about the facts of the matter. The context of 13:14 says that these two beasts work on the basis of deception, so their testimony can hardly be taken as reliable. The most that we can say with confidence is that, if it did come alive again in some way, then it had to be a spiritual kind of life which is in view, and not a bodily one. So this is not relevant to establishing the meaning of the word in 20:4.

Now, the example of Jesus is more relevant and more convincing, but it is not a straight-forward comparison either. Most would agree that when Jesus was alive on the earth, He was fully human and was, therefore, a spirit being living in a physical body. We also agree that He physically died and was laid in a tomb for three days. There is no disagreement either, that He was bodily raised from the dead by a supernatural intervention of God the Father. To all intents and purposes, it was the same body because it still showed the nail prints and the wound in his side.

Yet, at the same time, the Gospels clearly tell us that there was something different about His 'livingness' after His resurrection. The indicators are not sufficiently clear to precisely prove anything, but they are clear enough to sow doubt into any categorical statements about the matter.

What we know for sure is that Jesus, after His resurrection, had an extra dimension added to His physical life, and that is, He could not die again. He had defeated death, and so, death no longer had any hold on Him, so He could never die again. In other words, His physical, temporal, life had become a life which was now eternal, or timeless, and the second death had no claim on His life.

We can only suppose that this was accomplished by adding something from the spiritual world, by means of the Holy Spirit, to make this possible. In very general terms, we talk about His resurrected body as being a glorified body. We do this in order to talk about this new element of His 'livingness', and in order to make a distinction between the kind of life He had after the resurrection, as compared to before.

However, there is a much more serious flaw in Mounce's reasoning than that. He openly claims that there are only two other uses of the verb 'to live' in Revelation, apart from the two uses in 20:4-5. Yet, a quick check in a concordance will demonstrate that this claim is patently false, as follows:

- The verb 'to live' in various forms occurs 15 times in the book.
- The cognate noun 'life' occurs 15 times as well.
- The 4 living creatures are literally 'the living ones', or, 'things' and occur 18 times.

This makes a total of nearly fifty uses of this root, which is a very long way from the four uses which Mounce quoted. To put it very simply, and very politely, he has not at all taken account of all the data, and so any interpretation which he projects from his very limited data, is bound to be inadequate.

So what does the data tell us? Firstly, the majority of the occurrences refer to God the Father, so, in the first instance, the kind of life which we are talking about, is His kind of life, and that is spiritual, eternal and definitely not linked to a physical body. The second category is Jesus Himself, but Jesus is God as well as being man, and so, therefore, shares the same quality of life as the Father, and this would have been particularly true after His resurrection.

The word is also applied to the various beasts referred to in the book, as well as the four living creatures. However, these are all spiritual beings, as we have said before, and so they have no physical body which could be made to live again, unlike humans.

Finally, there is one other very intriguing reference where this word is applied to humans. This is in 3:1 where Jesus is talking to the Christians at Sardis. As far as I know, these people were human beings, who were still alive at the time, and had not yet died, physically speaking. Yet Jesus says of them: 'You have the appearance of being alive, but yet you are dead!'.

How can this be? This is really an example of playing around with words, but yet, that is what He said.

In other words, these people, who were physically alive, were not as alive as they should have been, and Jesus could see the difference between the two. He was obviously so disappointed with their lack of life, that He wrote them off as being dead! So how do we resolve this dilemma? The only solution is to accept that there are different kinds of life, but there is only one word available to talk about it. So that means that we have to work harder to discern the true meaning of any given usage.

The conclusion which we deduce from this review of all the available data, is that the kind of life which is being referenced in 20:4-5, has to be God's kind of life, and not a kind of life which is limited to the human, natural, bodily realm. It has to be a kind of life which is supernatural, spiritual and timeless. In addition, we can notice from the reference in 3:1, that people can be alive physically, and also have the extra dimension of eternal, spiritual life, or not, as the case may be.

This last point is confirmed by considering a counter example, which you should always do if you are going to take account of all the data. In 12:11, for example, there is another reference to 'a life', where it says that the people of God 'overcame him (the accuser)… because they did not love their *life* unto death'. In this case, this reference clearly refers to Christians, but the life being referred to here, is their physical, bodily life, because this is the life they are going to lose if they pursue their combat against evil to the bitter end.

However, a different word is used here in the Greek. It is *psuché* which, as we can understand, refers to soulish life, rather than spiritual life. Another place where it is used is in 8:9, where it refers to the life of the creatures in the sea. Since the text says that the creatures died, it is clear that this kind of life is temporary and temporal, and, therefore, can be ended. All the uses of *psuché* in the book refer to people, or creatures, which have a physical body and can die.

From these examples we can deduce quite readily, that the other word used, which is *zaö*, which has nearly fifty uses, as cited above, is not this kind of life at all. This is because, by definition, it must be a spiritual, eternal, non-temporal kind of life, which cannot be ended by physical death.

From there we can come back to *zoë,* which is the noun for 'a life', which is cognate with *zaö* 'to live'. This word is used together with other nouns which give us various phrases, the most striking of which, is the Lamb's Book of life. This remarkable book obviously contains the names of the people who have this kind of *zoë* life, which we are talking about. The other uses, with sample references, are:

- The Tree of life 2:7
- The Crown of life 2:10
- The Spirit of life from God 11:11
- The Water of life 21:6

As you can see, all these examples refer to the same spiritual, eternal, God-given life, which is the concept which we are trying to understand. There are no contradictions, and no counter examples left to be accounted for. The only contradiction which becomes apparent, is that this study of a broad sweep of the data, contradicts the position which Mounce championed, on the basis of a very limited selection of data.

A7.3.6 Textual Variants

When dealing with an ancient text like this one, another part of the data which needs to be considered is the fact that there are textual variants. This indicates immediately that there is some doubt about which was the original word used, and which was a mistake, or even a later intentional change. Whatever the exact cause of the change may have been, the fact that there is more than one version of the text, indicates to us who read it 2000 years later, that, even back then, there was some uncertainty or ambiguity about the reading. Since this is the case, it is wise not make a major theological point depend on such ambiguity and uncertainty. Rather than expending our valor in tilting at windmills, and then being made to look foolish, it is more sensible to proceed cautiously and examine what the variants are, and explore why they may have happened.

In the case of Revelation, there are now two places to look for possible variants. The first is in the various versions of the Greek text, and the other is in the Hebrew version of the book. It is only very recently that it has come back to our attention that there are Hebrew versions of Revelation, and that one of the Hebrew versions may, in fact, have been the original. If this is the case, then the original version ought surely to carry more weight in our interpretive decisions, than any subsequent translation. So, thanks to those people who have done all the work to make those Hebrew versions available to us, it is now possible to clarify interpretation issues like this one, with reference to the Hebrew. For more information on this topic, please consult the discussion in the final chapter, and below, and also the references to the Hebrew Revelation at the end of this book.

If we take the Greek first, then we find that, in the background, things were not as straightforward as commentators like Mounce, would have us believe. Their whole argument depends on the fact that it is exactly the same verb 'to live' which is used in both 20:4 and 20:5. However, in the Textus Receptus a different word is actually used in verse 5, which means 'to live again'. Whatever the cause for this difference, it definitely implies that somewhere along the line, somebody felt that there was an ambiguity here, which required clarifying. Be that as it may, this piece of data destroys the futurist's argument based on these verses, because it is distinctly possible that there are two different verbs in play here, and, therefore, it is not a problem that there should be two different meanings in the same context as well.

Proponents of eschatological positions other than the futurist position, have always argued that the verb 'to live' in 20:4, refers to a spiritual coming to life, and not necessarily a physical one. This would seem to be the case, when all the data is considered. In any case, if two different words were used originally, then there is no case to answer, and there is no need for there to be any further disagreement over the usage and meanings of these two verbs. From here on then, this deadlock can be unlocked, if we choose to do so, because there appears indeed to be considerable objective data available, which can at least mitigate, if not completely override, this difference in opinion.

A7.3.7 The Focal Point of Each of the Verbs

It has always been a problem for commentators and linguists alike to appropriately explain the meanings of verbs. This is particularly true for ancient languages like New Testament Greek or Old Testament Hebrew, but the issue is still with us today. One of the main reasons for this is because verbal meanings are primarily differentiated with reference to what is called Tense and Aspect. The Tense part is easy to understand because it refers to the time when an event or an action occurred. Most readers, most of the time, need to know when, in chronological time, the events, which he is reading about took place. Aspect, on the other hand, has to do with other *aspects* of the event or action, other than its situation in time.

The problem is that most people do not understand the difference between the two, and this confusion is perpetuated by the on-going misuse of these labels. So, for example, one regularly hears about the Imperfect Tense, or the Perfect Tense, and most of us probably learned that in school. However, these are unhelpful misnomers. This is because the words 'imperfect', and 'perfect' are labels for *aspects* of the verb, indicating whether the action or event is complete, or 'perfect', or incomplete, and, therefore, 'imperfect'. In and of themselves, these labels have nothing to do with the timing of the event. The timing has to be deduced from the context. This becomes very important to understand in decorticating issues like this present one.

So the point here is, that in 20:4-6 there are thirteen verbs, all functioning together, in order to tell us what John saw, and what he understood by what he saw.

Here is the list for ease of reference:

- 20:4a People *seated* on thrones, and authority to judge (reign) was *given* to them – Aorist Aspect
- 20:4b The souls of the ones *having been beheaded* – Perfect Aspect, implies past completion
- 20:4c They did not *worship* the beast, nor *receive* its mark – Aorist Aspect
- 20:4d They *live* and *reign* along with Christ for the 1000 year period – Aorist Aspect
- 20:5a The rest of the dead do not *live* until the 1000 years are *finished* – Aorist Aspect
- 20:5b This (is) the first resurrection – No verb, but present tense of the verb 'to be' implied
- 20:6a **Blessed** are they who *have* a part in the first resurrection – Present Tense
- 20:6b The second death *has* no authority over them – Present Tense
- 20:6c They *will be* priests for God and of Christ – Future Tense
- 20:6d They *will reign* with Him for the 1000 years – Future Tense

In 20:4 it is the same people being talked about, with a description of a certain number of their characteristics, so that they can be identified. All the verbs, except one, are in the aorist form. This is an aspect, not a tense. This aspect indicates that it is the event, or the action, itself, which is in focus, and should, therefore, be the center of attention. Some people say that it is the action, or event, as a total unit, which is in view. Their mistake is to then go on to say that it must be a completed action and is, therefore, in the past. This is not correct, for no tense is indicated by the form of the verb.

It is like saying in English, that 'the sky is blue'. This is a stative verb, and, as we mentioned in the main text above, statives generally do not have any tense attached to them either, because they are always true, or timeless, to use a different concept. But I give this as an example because this is easier to understand than with an event verb.

So if we now apply this timeless idea to some of the other verbs, what is the result.

- *They sit on thrones*. In this form, this is also a stative verb, for it describes their 'state'. There is no indicator in the verb of when this state started or when it will end, it just *is* a true state of affairs, and that is all.

- *They reign with Christ,* likewise, has no indicator in the verb of when this state, or process, started or when it will end. It is a fact, and that is all that is said.
- *They live… with Christ.* This is the same as the above two examples. There is no indicator in the verb of when this state started or when it will end, it just is a true state of affairs and that is all.

Next, after verse 4, there is a comparison with some other people in 20:5a. The description of these people is also in the aorist aspect form, for they are being treated and described in exactly the same way as the people in verse 4. These statements are made in a general, timeless way, with the event, or the state, indicated in the verb being in focus, and with no particular time-frame being implied by the verbs themselves. It should also be noted that for the verb 'to live', it does not mean 'to live again'. 'Again', is an extra word and concept which the translators have inserted here, either because they felt it did not make sense otherwise, or because it did not fit their theology.

The sentence in 20:5b which says, 'This is the first resurrection', is like a title, or explanatory summary, and has no verb at all. We have to use our brains here and see that this title does not apply to verse 5a, which has been put in here for explanatory convenience. The title obviously refers to verse 4 and provides a new piece of information about the people described in that verse.

The advantage of working on a complex text like this from a linguistics view point, is that the underlying theoretical framework will provide, if it is a well-founded theory, basic principles which provide guidelines and predict probabilities. In this case, I am going to invoke the principle of agreement. That is the principle which predicts that words, and concepts operating in the same semantic field, and in the same purposive domain, will be in agreement with one another. That is, they will say the same thing, have connotations which are in harmony, and will move the discourse down the same, coherent, logical track. In layman's terms, they will not contradict each other, or violate the norms of comprehensible communication.

The reason for talking about this is because of the presence of verse 4b about the souls of those who had been beheaded. This is an anomaly because it violates the principle of agreement, and so should alert the analyst to realize that there is a problem here, which needs to be scrutinized with care. It is an anomaly on the grammatical level first of all, because the verb is in the perfect aspect instead of the aorist. This is obviously a different aspect, and so is not in agreement with the other verbs in its context.

But, in addition, the perfect aspect has very much stronger implications of a past, completed, action or event, and so creates a clash, in terms of the focal point and the timing of the event.

This clause also creates an anomaly on the conceptual level. The whole purpose of the flow of the verse is to explain who the people are, who are sitting on the thrones. The list starts off with a categorical, perfect aspect statement, that these people are already dead. So that, in itself, already raises the question as to why they should be sitting on thrones, if they are dead, and this undercurrent of an anomaly has, in fact, helped fuel the theological disagreements mentioned previously. Then, having stated that these people are dead, the author subsequently goes on, with no explanation, to continue his list with various things which these people did, and did not do, while they were still alive. Why then, would he put his list in this non-chronological, and illogical order? By doing this, he has created conceptual turbulence at best, or a conceptual contradiction at worst.

If you have been following what I have explained previously about prominence, you may be sharp enough to counter the thought process in the preceding paragraph, by saying that this is a deviation from norms, which creates turbulence, so, therefore, this must be a prominence feature. This is a very good point, but like every good point, it needs to be tested against the data. Turbulence is often caused by prominence features, but it will also be caused by an outright anomaly, so which is it?

I have come across analyses which are theoretically sound, but they create turbulence, nonetheless. In one case, the analyst freely admitted that the point which had come out as prominent, did not make sense in the context, for it was basically in contradiction with the overall thrust of the passage in question. He had found unexpected turbulence and, in a case like that he needed to stop and review his analysis. When I did that for him, after the fact, I found the error in the analysis, and when it was adjusted accordingly, the prominent point which came out as a result, was fully in agreement with the flow of the text. So this is what we need to do here, and search for the real cause of the turbulence.

As you look at the whole unit of discourse, which is 20:4-6, this clause has nothing in favor of it being prominent. The main reason for this is because there is something else which is obviously prominent. This is the statement that these people lived and reigned with Christ for 1000 years. The reasons for this are as follows :

- The topic is the word 'thrones', which is fronted for prominence. This indicates that the main point is going to be something related to thrones.

- The clause about reigning is in agreement with the topic, previously established.
- It is also the conclusion of a linear, list-like, narrative, which makes it naturally prominent.
- It is made more prominent by a coda-like comment or summary which is 20:5b.
- It is made even more prominent, by being followed by a lengthy blessing which repeats the basic statement about living and reigning with Christ. The apparently extraneous statement about the second death is another way of saying that these people are alive, and supernaturally so.

Since this part of the text is so obviously prominent, then the clause about the beheaded people cannot possibly be prominent. Even though it sticks out above its context, it can now be seen that it sticks out like a sore thumb, and not because it harmoniously contributes a prominent point to the flow of this mini discourse.

In short then, our provisional conclusion about this clause, on the basis of the evidence examined so far, is that this lack of conceptual and grammatical agreement is an anomaly. For the moment, we do not know why it is an anomaly, and if we are going to fully resolve this issue, then we will have to look elsewhere for the answer. But before we do that, let's complete our review of the data and tidy up the remaining loose ends.

A7.3.8 What is the Timing of these Events?

In the previous discussion we only talked about the aspect of the verbs and left the concept of tense, or timing, to one side. The aim in talking about these characteristics of verbs separately, is to try and keep them distinct in our thinking and not confuse them. So, as regards the tense side of things, as we stated above, there is no tense element inherent in the verbs in 20:4 and 5.

There is a perfect aspect verb in verse 4 but this is, first and foremost, an aspect and not a tense. The time elements which can be derived from it are only implications, even though, in this case, the implications are strong. In any case, as we have noted, the presence of this phrase is an anomaly. By contrast, verse 6 has two present tense verbs and two future tense verbs, and we will deal with those in a moment, in the next sub-section.

Even though there is no tense inherent in the verbs of 20:4, there is, nonetheless, a strong time element provided by the phrase concerning the 1000 years. This is obviously a time reference which is repeated several times in the context, and tells us, in this case, that the people we are considering, live and reign with Christ, at some time or another within the 1000 year period. In the case of 20:5a, we are told that the people concerned will live, or live again, *after* the 1000 year period has ended. It is clear then, that there is a time reference here, but the chronology still remains totally unclear, until we have successfully established when, exactly, the 1000 year period occurs in relation to the human calendars which we are used to.

This is another knotty problem, which has remained without a real resolution for centuries. The commentators and scholars have agreed to disagree on the matter (more or less), and the people on the ground tend not to think about it too much, and try not to lose friends in arguing about it. So then, is there a constructive way forward, or is it a hopeless case? I believe that there is a way forward, providing that all parties are prepared to do some work, and make some concessions if needs be, in the interest of discovering the truth of the matter.

It is the desire, above all, to get as near to the truth as we can with our finite minds, which can unite us around a consensus, instead of dividing us. This may be possible if are willing to accept a common starting point. This then, is a proposal for a starting point which can be modified if it is found to be truly inadequate in some way.

- Let's be positive and agree to agree, instead of agreeing to disagree.
- Let's be respectful and permit the author to be the arbitrator of our doubts and uncertainties through the linguistic data which he has provided for us.
- Let's be willing to adapt our worldview to his, and to refrain from imposing on him perceptions and ideas which may have been foreign to his view of life.
- Let's agree to invoke the age-old principle of letting the Scriptures influence the interpretation of the Scripture in question. This would specifically include letting the Gospel of John, by the same author, influence our interpretation of Revelation.

Evidence from within the text

From within the text we can deduce the following time elements. The starting point for those who live and reign must be within the 1000 years, it cannot be before it, or after it, but must be within its confines. The conditions for receiving, or having this life, as described in verse 4c, are that these people are, in effect, overcomers. That is to say, they learned and chose to resist the beast and thwart his power over them, and so by default, they remained faithful to their testimony for Jesus. These things must have happened during their life on earth, and either precede the coming to life, and reigning, or must be concurrent with it. As we have said before, overcoming obstacles and enemies is part of reigning, so it seems likely that this description is as much a fruit of their reigning, as it is an antecedent.

We have already suggested that 20:4b, about the beheaded people, is anomalous. But if it is not, a proposal has to be made as to why all the other verbs are not also in the perfect tense. Since the beheaded people are dead, and this is seen as a perfect, completed event, then why are the things which they did before dying, not also seen as completed events? Logically, the fact that they had not worshiped the beast etc., was the condition of, and the reason why, they then lost their heads.

The new, or different, kind of life, which is in view in 20:4d, is specifically called the first resurrection. This means that if we can pinpoint the time when the first resurrection takes place, then we can also pinpoint the time when the reigning begins. This, in turn, will help to define the parameters of the 1000 years.

Evidence from within the context of Chapter 20

Just like the rest of the book, the vast majority of references to personages or events in Chapter 20 are spiritual references. The whole perspective is a heavenly perspective with a spiritual worldview, because everything which John sees is either within Heaven itself, or looking out and down from Heaven's point of view.

So, here are a few examples to confirm this statement.

- 20:1-2 An angel and the dragon; both are spiritual beings.
- 20:1-3 The abyss, the key and the chain must all be spiritual items in order to incarcerate a spiritual being.
- 20:4 The beast is spiritual and so must everything that is associated with it.
- 20:4-5 God and Jesus are in Heaven. Jesus is now glorified and in Heaven, in a spiritual location.
- 20:4 and 11 These thrones are in Heaven and so are spiritual in nature.
- 20:11-15 These events are specifically not on the physical earth and concern people who are physically dead, but are nonetheless still alive in the spiritual realm.

The only apparent exception is 'the nations' in 20:8. However, this is very ambiguous. The word is generic and could just refer to people, and the whole context is spiritual, so the people concerned must be people as they are viewed, and are able to be active, in the spiritual realm.

On this basis, since the whole of the context is spiritual, then the 1000 years must also be interpreted from a heavenly, spiritual point of view. For those who want to take it literally, then the onus is on them to demonstrate persuasively why an exception should be made in this case.

Evidence from the wider context of the book as a whole and the NT

The book as a whole, only gives two time references which can be related to our calendar. In 1:18 there is a very specific reference to the fact that Jesus had died, and had been raised again from the dead. This is all past history, but, by implication, it is in the recent past when John had the vision. In any case, John is still alive, and the whole book must have been written soon after Jesus lived and died. Then, in Chapter 5 He is clearly in Heaven, so His time on earth is finished and He is back in Heaven, but He is already reigning from there. He is in a spiritual location, reigning from there over a spiritual kingdom, using spiritual methods. These spiritual methods are primarily His words which He speaks, as symbolized by the sword which comes from his mouth.

The other fixed point is that the book tells us, already from 1:7 onwards, that He is coming again at some time in the future. The implications of that verse is that this coming again will be when He comes in judgment, and this is confirmed by verses like 20:11-12. Meanwhile, it is clear from all the rest of the book that, while in Heaven, He is not just sitting idly by, but is actively reigning by implementing and facilitating God's plan of judgment and salvation. So, clearly then, He is reigning from the time of His ascension onwards, and since it is an eternal kingdom, over which He presides, this reign will never end. It will go on to His second coming, and when that time period is finished, it will continue on for ever. So this earthly time period, is the only one which is clearly evoked in the book, and there is no other one.

Since Jesus is reigning during this time period, is it possible for the people of God to be also reigning with Him at the same time? The answer is 'Yes'. The passage under study, 20:4, indicates that the condition for reigning with Christ, is firstly to be 'alive'. From here now we can go on to deduce that this must mean that they are alive in a spiritual sense, similar to the way in which Jesus is alive, so that they can also reign with Him, in the same way, over a spiritual kingdom. This process, or event, of coming alive, is so specific that it is called the first resurrection. This means that there must also be a second resurrection.

In order to be alive, and to be qualified to be a true member of a kingdom, one normally needs to be born into it. Born to be alive, but born also to a true citizen of the kingdom. This is precisely what Jesus said to Nicodemus in the Gospel of John, Chapter 3. If one wishes to enter the Kingdom of God one has to be born again – not physically by the flesh, but spiritually, by the Spirit of God. This event is what provides the spiritual life which qualifies one to enter this kingdom. Once someone has, therefore, entered God's Kingdom, by believing in Jesus and, therefore, by participating by faith in His death and resurrection, then that person is alive, and ready and able to reign with Him.

All this is explained over and over in other parts of the New Testament. Ephesians is just one good example. So, in Ephesians 2:4-7 it specifically says that God made us alive with Christ. This is the same verb 'to live' as in Revelation 20:4. The only difference is that the prefix 'with' is added on the front, to make it abundantly clear that we are raised with Christ, and in an identical fashion as Him. This then makes it possible, being clothed in this spiritual life, to be seated in the heavenly places with Him, from where we can reign along with Him.

Logically then, being born again of the Spirit of God, is the same as being raised from the dead, spiritually speaking, by faith in Jesus' resurrection. This then logically, is the first resurrection. This new birth into a new life, qualifies a person to reign with Christ in the heavenly places, even though he is still living in his physical body on the earth. John, and the two witnesses give us examples of how this works out in practice. The insights into the lives of the people in the churches in Cycle 1 also give us insights into this process. Then, in addition, the interludes give insights as to how this works out from a spiritual, heavenly point of view. The whole book is impregnated with this message. The people of God are beneficiaries of a new life, provided by Jesus, which enables them to become overcomers, and to reign in life as well as in death, with Christ.

The two witnesses eventually died physically, as did John. But this now holds no fear for them, for after that, they were called up to Heaven to live there directly with the risen Christ, where, we can safely assume, they will continue to reign with Him as part of the innumerable cloud of witnesses. Then after that, Jesus is coming back to earth again, not only to judge but also to bring His rewards. At this point Revelation 20 takes up the story for us again, for it is clear in 20:12-15, that everyone who has ever lived and died, will be raised to life again at that point. So this must be the second resurrection. As 20:5 tells us, those who have not benefited from the first resurrection, that is, have not been born again, will only be resurrected at this point to be consigned to the second death. By contrast, the believers in Jesus no longer fear either this second resurrection, or the second death, for they will live and reign with Him for ever (22:5c).

In the light of all this evidence then, it is becoming increasingly clear that there is only one time period into which the 1000 years can fit. That is the time between Jesus' death, resurrection and ascension, and His coming a second a time to judge the dead and send them to the lake of fire, which is the second death, and to reward is faithful followers. During this time, and only during this time, is it possible to benefit from the first resurrection by being born again. From then on, the believer can sit in the heavenly places and reign with Christ, even though on the earth he may go through various trials and tribulations. This is necessary, because, as an apprentice ruler, he needs to learn to be an overcomer.

However, this time period has now lasted over 2000 years, so that means that the 1000 years in Revelation 20, cannot be a literal 1000 years. But this is not a problem.

A7.3.9 How Best to Interpret the 1000 Years

The first thing to be stated quite clearly is that, without a shadow of a doubt, a good ninety per cent or more of this book is composed of language which describes a spiritual world and spiritual beings. Even when it is talking about things which happen on the earth, it does so from a heavenly, or spiritual, point of view.

Consequently, most of the language in the book is symbolic, or metaphorical, in nature. This is because we do not know what language is used in Heaven, and we do not know what words are used to describe certain events and creatures, which only exist in that spiritual world. The only way to communicate at all, therefore, is to use earthly words which are similar in nature, but are being used as symbolic, picture language to communicate something else. This language, which is couched in our terms on the surface at least, gives us some idea of what is being said. But then it requires us also to do the work necessary to discern the point of comparison, so that we correctly understand the message.

Obviously this means that there is quite a bit of scope for misunderstandings and misinterpretations. Therefore, it is a wise person who proceeds cautiously, who refuses to jump categorically to instant conclusions, and who is willing to listen to advice. Some basic advice is that, since this is a text, then linguistic principles should be our starting point. The next one is that it is the author who has the right to tell us how we should interpret his discourse, and not the other way round. Thirdly, if he has made it clear that nearly all his message is couched in symbolic terms, then we should not contradict him, but should go with the flow.

This means in turn, that the 1000 years, which is the subject of our discussion here, must be interpreted as being symbolic. That is, what we read on the page is expressed in earthly terms, but this must, of necessity, be interpreted as expressing something other than a literal series of 1000 earthly, calendar years, based on the physical turning of the earth around its sun. To say that this one phrase, out of all the picture language in the book, should be interpreted physically and literally, is completely arbitrary, and anomalous. In point of fact, anything which is interpreted literally in this book should be fully supported by clear data by the proponents of such a point of view, which is the opposite to what is stated very categorically in many commentaries.

So, what is the symbolism of a number like 1000. The first thing to be said is that it is a human number. That means that it is finite, and normally would have a clear beginning, and a clear end. It is not a symbol of some ephemeral, eternal, timelessness. In this book, an ageless eternity, is expressed in other ways, and never by a human number.

Secondly, it is a very big number. In John's day, it was the biggest number that they could express in words, without repeating themselves. Some say that a big number like this is symbolically equivalent of the innumerable mass of people which John saw in some of his visions. Even though it is finite, and God, for example, would be able to count its beginning and its end, human beings would maybe have much more difficulty. For them it is a number which is so big, that you can only count it in very general terms, and not in detailed, specific terms. For us today, it would by like talking about a trillion.

Thirdly, its primary mathematical characteristic is that it is the equivalent of 10 times 10 times 10. This threefold repetition is one reason why this number is often interpreted as another symbol of divine completeness. The 1000 years represents the perfect number which God has ordained for the completion of His purposes. We have already proposed in the previous section, that the period indicated in this book, can only run from Christ's passion and ascension until His return. If now this time period is associated with 1000, then this indicates that it is the perfect, complete, time period for God to accomplish His purposes through the Body of Christ on earth. That is, through the Church of all the generations between these two points.

But there is more to it than that. As we have seen previously, 10 is the number for a testimony, or a witness. Jesus sent out His disciples to be witnesses for Him, who testify about what He has accomplished for everyone. As we have seen already, this talk about testimony and witness is a recurring thread in this book. It is the distinguishing hallmark for individual believers in Jesus, as well as for the corporate body of the Church.

The number 10, three times over then, is the perfect, complete testimony. As a consequence, during this complete time period which the Father has allotted to the Church, they are called to be faithful in their testimony for Jesus. Then, when all the generations have played their part, that combined testimony to the Lamb will be complete and perfect. God's will, will have been done, and His plan will have been fully accomplished. The Gospel of the Kingdom will have been preached throughout the earth, and then the end will come.

The symbolism of numbers is so rich, that probably more insights can be derived from this number 1000, in addition to the ones noted above. However, this summary will suffice to demonstrate that the proposal that 1000 should be interpreted symbolically, is fully in harmony with the rest of the message of the book. Not only that, but in this review of the various numbers I have tried to be consistent. I have taken the position that the numbers must be symbolic unless there is a very good reason to suppose that this is not the case. In each case where I have addressed the issue in some detail, I have tried to give reasonable explanations as to why the proposed scenario is viable and justifiable.

By contrast, the commentators can often be quite inconsistent and loose with their argumentation. So, for example, Mounce 1977,380 just categorically states that 'the numbers are symbolic' in Revelation 21:15-18, and this includes, of course, the number 12,000. But in dealing with the number 1000 in 20:4-5, he plays it safe and tries to sit on the fence. He covers himself (op. cit. 354-359) by quoting different viewpoints on the interpretation of the number. But it is clear in context that he wants to interpret it literally, without doing the work to support this position based on data from within the text itself. The argumentation he does provides is basically speculation and then at the end of it all, he finishes off by saying 'In short, John taught a literal millennium, but its essential meaning may be realized in something other than a temporal fulfillment' (op. cit.359).

He does not exactly say where John actually taught a literal millennium. Then, if anyone can explain to me what is meant by the second half of his statement, I would be glad to know. For me, at best, it is incomprehensible, and at worst, it contradicts what is said in the first part. What do you think?

For myself, I think that those who would wish to interpret literally the numbers in Revelation, including the 1000 years, then they are the ones, who need to search in the book to see where there is any evidence to support such a proposal.

A7.3.10 The Blessing of 20:6

In order to take account of all the data, brief mention needs to be made of the blessing in 20:6, before we move on. From the macro structure point of view, it is actually functioning at the book level as part the blessings sub-topic. Yet, at the same time, it is tightly integrated into the context where it is located, and clearly forms a conclusion, both grammatical and semantic to the sub-unit 20:4-6.

This verse is composed of a series of three doublets. The first is that it is stated that the beneficiaries of this blessing are both blessed, and considered to be holy. This combination of blessed and holy is unusual and only occurs here.

The second doublet is a repeated reference to the first resurrection, but this time it is contrastively linked with the second death. As John writes to his readers the first resurrection is apparently a present reality, and not just a future promise. The purpose of the repetition here is to emphasize the benefits of taking up the option of the first resurrection. One of its benefits is that the second death already, in the present, has no authority over them. This is a great blessing because it means that one's eternal destiny is settled, and the beneficiary no longer needs to live in fear of death, or of anything for that matter.

The third doublet is the promise that the people in view in this verse, will be priests of, or for, God, and will reign with Christ for the 1000 years. These last two verbs are in the future tense, but this does not automatically mean that it is an absolute future tense. That is to say that the time in view is not future for every reader, and is not implying that these promises of being priests and reigning, will only be fulfilled, at the end of time when Christ returns. If that were the case there would be very little value in Jesus making these grand promises to people of John's time. They were people who were suffering and struggling under the whiplash of persecution and the prospect of a premature death. To receive a promise that they will be set free from the fear of death in maybe about 2000 years time, would not have been of much encouragement to them.

To think, or talk like that, is missing the linguistic point of the future verbs in this context. The basic point is that, linguistically speaking, this verse is a promise. The promise is intended to encourage and motivate people who, in their daily lives, were having to refuse the pressure to worship the beast and its image. The penalty for this resistance was death, and so it was a dire situation.

From a meaning point of view, a promise is a condition-consequence semantic relationship. In other words, Jesus, through John, is saying that *if* you fulfill the conditions to be an overcomer, then you will, as an automatic consequence, be blessed by being authorized to be priests for God and to reign with Christ. This happens straight away after the conditions have been fulfilled, and not at some far distant future time.

The future tense of the verb is relative to, and contingent on, the condition being fulfilled. Before the condition is fulfilled, the blessing remains future for that person. But once the condition is fulfilled, the blessing becomes a present reality for that person.

Consequently, this blessing happened for the people of John's era, in their own lifetime, so it is not still a future promise for them, but is already past history. So it has been, and will be, for any other generation of reader. If they decide to listen to Jesus' words and do them, as he explained in Cycle 1, then they will learn how to be overcomers. As a consequence, they will then automatically be inducted into the royal priesthood, and be authorized to serve as priests and kings with Christ, who reigns from the heavenly places.

The reference to the priests in this verse is an echo of another doublet which occurred right at the beginning of this story in 1:6, which tells us that the people who have been set free from their sins will be made kings and priests for God. In the Old Testament era, priests fully participated in the government of the nation, from the time of their institution until AD 70. So, in this context, priests and kings are basically synonymous, for their functions were very similar and were complementary to each other.

The repetition of this concept of reigning right at the end of the sub-unit confirms that this is the main point which this sub-unit is making. The destiny of the people of God, especially the overcomers among them, is to rule and reign with Christ for the 1000 year period on the earth, and then for ever. For obvious reasons, this is a very great responsibility, but also a very great blessing

A7.3.11 A Consideration of the Data Available in the Hebrew Version of Revelation

The advantage which we have now which previous generations did not have, and that is that we now have access to a Hebrew version of Revelation. It is distinctly possible that this is the original version of the book, and that the Greek version is a translation. In any case, this is another version of the book, and this means that wherever there are textual variants, then care needs to be taken not to force issues of theological interpretation, which may not be warranted.

Here then is a translation of the Hebrew version of 20:4, line by line, based on Baca 2024,319.

Line 1:

And I saw thrones,
/ and they (people) sitting upon them /
and to them he gave authority to judge

Commentary:
This is a three part sentence structured as a series of parallels, all linked by 'and'. This is a very typical Hebrew discourse style. By this means the general topic of the whole unit is established, which is 'thrones', because it comes first. Then afterwards, the details about the thrones are established, and this provides a setting for the whole mini discourse.

The next important topic is the people. However, this is very generic because it does not specifically say 'the people', for this is implied. What is provided is a pre-posed pronoun marked as 'they', and 'to them', in the translation above. This pronoun comes first and is preceded by the prefix which is translated as 'and'. The fact that it comes first, indicates that it is the topic. If the prefix 'and' were to be interpreted as a topic marker, as is distinctly possible, then this is another way in which the author tells the reader what the next, or on-going, topic is going to be. In modern grammatical terms, it could be said that these pronouns are demonstrative pronouns, for they clearly point out who, or what, the author is talking about. The whole book in Hebrew starts out with a demonstrative pronoun of this nature, and this is so, because its function is to establish the topic, by pointing to it, like a signpost.

The verb 'to judge' is a very general word which means at root 'to decide'. It is a governmental term rather than a judicial term, because deciding is the basic function of all aspects of government. It is important to remember that when Israel was first established as a nation, the first people to be authorized to 'judge' or to 'decide' on behalf of the nation, were the elders (cf. the 24 Elders in Heaven). Afterwards, this function was passed to, or shared with, the priests. They were the judges, and deciders, for the nation, long before there were kings, and they continued on in this function, even when there were kings later on.

Line 2:

These (are the ones) believing and testifying about Jesus / and these (are the ones) who did not take the sign of the beast upon their foreheads, / and they did not pray to him or to his idol.

Commentary:
This is another three part sentence. Please notice the agreement and the systematic parallelism inherent in this organization.

There is no 'and' at the beginning of the sentence. This indicates that it is a new unit and not a continuation of the previous one. This absence of an overt connection also indicates that it is a new sub-topic which begins here. Previously the topic was 'the thrones', but now it is the people sitting on the thrones, who are in view.

Each of the three sub-units is introduced by a pronoun or by a demonstrative pronoun, which continues on the same pattern as established in the previous sentence. The people concerned are consistently referred to by this means, and they are not otherwise specified in the subject category of the sentence. The people are only specified and described by the information contained in the verb and by what comes after the verb.

Line 3:

And these (are the ones who) live
/ and they rule with Jesus /
for a thousand years.

Commentary:

This is another three part sentence, just like the previous ones. It begins with 'and' and so is a continuation of the previous sentence and continues to describe the people on the thrones. The grammatical organization is the same as before, with the subject being indicated by a demonstrative pronoun.

Concluding Comment:

The most important thing to notice is that the whole sentence concerning the souls who have been beheaded, is completely missing. This item of information is just not present in the Hebrew version. The logical deduction therefore, is that the Greek version is a translation of the Hebrew and that this sentence was added in by the translator. Now that we have looked at the Hebrew, we can see how well it is organized, with three sets of three parallels, which are all in agreement in terms of the kind of verb used and the way the subjects are indicated.

The other, intruding sentence clearly does not match that pattern at all and completely disrupts it. The subject is indicated by 'the souls', instead of by a demonstrative. The verb is in the passive, with a perfect aspect and implied past tense, which is not the case for any of the other verbs. This sentence is also introduced by 'and' in the Greek, which it should not be, and finally, its inclusion would make line 2 a unit with four sub-units instead of three. The changes and differences are far too numerous to be just unfortunate blips on the radar.

We can deduce from these anomalies then, that the translator was a mother-tongue speaker of Greek (which would be logical) and was not, therefore, in tune with the Hebraic way of organizing sentences and paragraphs. This explains why this sentence sticks out like a sore thumb and is, in fact, an anomaly, which is the conclusion which we had come to previously, just based on general linguistic principles, and without having consulted the Hebrew version.

This insight into what has been going on behind the scenes is extremely important, because it makes certain interpretations of this text completely untenable. Otherwise, if someone wishes to still maintain those particular interpretations, then they will need to provide persuasive arguments as to why such an anomaly should be retained and used for establishing significant theological positions.

The fact of the matter is that this passage does not describe what happens to certain Christians based on their manner of death at all. It is no longer possible to push the implications of this passage into the future so that they only apply to a certain elite group. The text as it has come down to us through the Hebrew version, shows that the privilege of living and reigning with Jesus is open to all Christians, and it is open to them while they are still living on the earth. The only conditions are, that they be spiritually alive, and that they have learned to be overcomers, having refused to follow the dragon and its proxies, and have remained faithful to Jesus in the process. Just like the Two Witnesses.

A7.4 Concluding Recommendations

We started out this Appendix by engaging in a discussion with biblical commentators of previous generations, because there were some things which they had made claims about, which needed clarification and even correction. However, my first recommendation, nonetheless, is that we should give credit where credit is due, and to acknowledge with appreciation, all the work which previous commentators have done to provide for us many important insights into this complex book. It is only possible for us in our generation to make further progress in our study of this book, because we can take for granted the pioneering work of the previous generations. To that extent then, we are able to stand on their shoulders and to see the road ahead more clearly than they could, and this needs to be acknowledged.

Having said that, it also needs to be said that the possibility of studying the Scriptures based on sound linguistic principles is a recent innovation. This innovation is a reality and needs to influence our thought processes and our research methodologies in two contrastive ways. Firstly, looking to the past, we can accept that previous generations of scholars did not have access to these linguistic tools, as they had not yet been discovered and described. So it is not their fault that they did not know certain things, but, at the same time, it has to be admitted that they did not take account of very basic, well-known principles of language, and did not provide information about them.

So, for example, it is very rare to find any detailed description of what the topic of a book like Revelation is, and it is basically impossible to find any coherent account of the concept of prominence (i.e. what parts of a text are more important relative to other parts) and its practical implications. So, in the past then, some important issues and notions were passed over in silence. It is important to understand this and not to expect commentaries to provide any relevant information on these matters, which were either unknown at the time when the books were written, or were traditionally not considered worthy of comment. It is recommended then, that commentaries be read with the caveat that they are not complete, and will not provide any information at all on certain important subjects.

In addition to that, we have given examples above, that commentators sometimes do not take account of all the data, even though that data was available at the time. It is obviously not possible to state why this kind of thing happens, but it can, nonetheless, be stated that it does happen. So the next recommendation, is to be wary of any categorical statements and to take out your concordance, for example, and check for yourself, to see if all the data has been properly accounted for.

However, as of this writing, those linguistic principles and hypotheses have indeed been described and explained in some detail. This has been one of the purposes of this book, to show how modern linguistic theories can help us make positive progress in resolving previously unresolved issues. From there, if we can agree to agree, then it definitely becomes feasible to construct a more solid consensus around the issues which provoke differences of opinion and of interpretation. Even more information can be found in the publications listed in the references at the end of this book.

This means that looking to the future, anyone who wishes to make any comments on a book like Revelation must, of necessity, take account of these more recent linguistic insights. So the final recommendation is that, any discourse should be treated first and foremost as the linguistic artifact which it is. This means making an accurate assessment of the linguistic data which is in the book for all to see. Then from that assessment, doing everything possible to account for all the important information which is relevant to getting a complete and accurate understanding of the book.

A7.5 A Postscript re the Use of Numbers

I have confessed quite freely that I have only recently found out about the Hebrew version of the book of Revelation, and even more recently about the pervasive use of numbers in ancient writings. My knowledge of these things is limited, not to mention the space available in this book, so this is not the time or place for me to explain either of these topics in any great detail.

As regards the numbers, I was forced to confront this issue purely for practical reasons. This was because there were so many numbers in Revelation, being used in so many different ways, that, in order merely to do justice to the data, I felt an obligation to make some mention of them. So, I did some experiments for myself, and they all, without exception, produced some thought-provoking results.

I have shared the results of these investigations in the main text and the appendix above, so that anyone may feel free to evaluate them and to pursue the matter further, if so desired. It so happens that other people have done more research than I have on this issue. According to them, writing books based around a system of numbers, was common practice 2000 years ago. This practice was only lost to us, living in a westernized culture, about 600 years ago, which is relatively recent compared to the history of this practice.

Consequently, I would recommend the books by Anne Hamilton who has done considerable research into this issue and has even proved that it can be done, by doing it herself. You will find a number of her books listed in the references at the end of this one, and in those books she also cites other people who have done other kinds of research into this topic. One of the reasons, she says, why numbers occur everywhere in literature, is because they also occur everywhere in the created universe. If they appear in God's Creation, then it is not unreasonable that they should also appear in human creations as well. But that is another huge topic, far too big for me to get into, so, if that interests you, please feel free to consult her books.

WRESTLING WITH WORLDVIEWS (2)

I don't know how you see things, and whether you take much time to reflect on why you do what you do, the way that you do. Some call it introspection, and most of us have imbibed the notion that such a thing, or, too much of such a thing, can be bad for our health. But working on a book such as this seems to have a way of making you consider the deeper, and maybe more important, issues of life.

For myself, as I have observed my own reactions and ways of interacting with a text like this one, I have noticed a number of habits and preferences, which I observe also in most of the commentaries which I have consulted. I like straight lines. I look for time-lines and story-lines, anything in fact which will make me feel that I am going somewhere and making progress – if possible towards a clear goal. I like things to be tidy and contiguous like links of a chain. For this reason, I automatically start looking for divisions to see how I can divide the text up into neat individualistic bits. Then I like to get them lined up in an orderly fashion, like soldiers in a row, with no gaps or inconsistencies.

I am time orientated, to such an extent that the minute is often my master rather than my servant. I am also a planner and love to look forward into the future to try and discern *what* is going to happen next, or even way down in the future. Please do not ask me to go back on myself, or constantly walk around the same circuit.

As you can see already, I find repetition irritating. When re-reading various versions of this book, I have caught myself several times removing or changing, what I consider to be an inappropriate repetition, even to the point of eliminating whole sentences.

I find discontinuity disconcerting. Why is it that the author suddenly breaks the flow of his thought and talks about something else? Furthermore, why on earth does he not explain to us what he is doing as he proceeds? When this happens I lose the pleasure and comfort of feeling that I am going somewhere, and I become disorientated and lose my bearings. Most of us react to this discomfort by trying to eliminate the source of the discomfort by pretending that it is not there, or that it is a mistake of some sort.

All this happens because of my training, my traditions and my preferences, some of which may be purely personal, but many of which are cultural, and common to most people from my cultural background. It has to do with worldview and assumptions. These, in turn, shape my perspective and my expectations, regardless of what I am doing. From those beginnings, in our earliest days we accumulate a set of experiences and decisions, which shape the way we see and do life, and so, therefore, the way in which we react to whatever we may read, see, hear or otherwise experience in the future.

However, can I assume that the Hebrew people living 2000 years ago had the same training, experiences and preferences? Of course not. We have to have the perspicacity to admit that this sort of self-centered assumption is most unlikely to be true. None of us can go back in time to get first-hand experience of that long distant culture. Nonetheless, we do have the record of the Scriptures and, from them, we can deduce with a reasonable degree of accuracy, what the worldview of the time was probably like.

All these kinds of things, which we are talking about here, are learned by experience. The experiences are melded into traditions, and traditions are expressed, and passed on from generation to generation, in oral lore and written books. So it is that from their discourses we can tell that, it was just not a problem to them, that things were not in straight lines, not necessarily in chronological order, and that almost contradictory notions could be talked about one after the other, with no other explanation.

I came to understand that I am the one who has to adapt, or run the risk of misunderstanding the intended message. But if I am willing to make that effort, then it can be guaranteed that I will get much closer to the truth of the matter. This is important for me personally, and for those who may read this book. If we are really concerned about truth, then we owe it to ourselves to make that effort.

This soliloquy is 777 words long.

CHAPTER 8

The End, But Also A New Beginning: The Hebrew Characteristics of Revelation and their Implications

The previous chapter brought to a close the discussion of the linguistic analysis of the discourse structure of Revelation. Very appropriately the chapter number was seven, because the work was finished, the description of the book was complete, and it seemed as if nothing more needed to be added. However, the subject of discussion is the Word of God, which continues to be living and powerful, and is intended to communicate truth and so to inspire hope, courage and perseverance to all who read it. It needs to be imbibed and lived out, and not just studied as an academic exercise, which may inspire the mind but leave the soul unmoved. So, in order to go beyond the intellectual pursuit of truth, this chapter is being included in the process of our discussion.

> **QUOTE**
> **The meaning of the biblical texts is not only to be found in the words themselves, but often in the way the biblical authors and editors structure these words.**
> **Levinson 2020,271**

The goal is to open up some new avenues of understanding, and a new season of wisdom. This will be accomplished as some of the implications of the data in the previous seven chapters are reviewed, and explored, with a different, but complementary, perspective in mind. Obviously, the structure of a book such as this, interesting as that may be, is only a means to an end. The real end in view is to grasp the message conveyed by the organization of the words, sentences and paragraphs on the page. The message which we need to grasp, is the same message which was intended, when first written, to influence the first readers' thoughts, choices, and actions, as well as to inform their minds.

With this goal in view then, in the following pages some of the most important points about the organization of the book will be reviewed once again. But this time it will be with the purpose of demonstrating how this understanding of the structure needs also to influence, and if needs be, to modify, the way the message is perceived, interpreted, and put into practice, by those of us reading it today.

This is a modern day example of the 7 + 1 Principle, which is a principle, deeply rooted in the Scriptures, and which will be described in more detail below, along with other characteristics of Hebrew discourses.

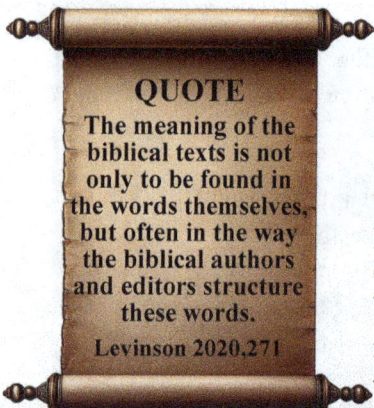

8.1 Revelation in Review
A Guide to its Hebrew Discourse Structure

Human language is so complex, and so finely tuned, that it is possible to communicate clearly using a variety methods and systems of organization. Nonetheless, in spite of the range of possible choices, the cultural context, including the worldview of the writers and readers/listeners, may cause some systems to be more popular and widely used than others. Research has shown that different cultures may have quite distinct preferences on this subject, with the result that those preferred structures will be a lot more common than other kinds of structures, within the context of the given culture. Kaplan 1966, provides a considerable amount of information on this topic.

Research into the organization of the books of the Old Testament has shown that there were definite preferences in the culture of that era, with the result that certain structures and systems of organization occur very frequently and can be documented. See, for example, other publications by the author to be found in the references and also Dorsey 1999. In some cases these preferences, such as the ubiquitous nature of repetition and parallelism, may be explicable by the fact that the culture at the time, was basically an oral culture, with literacy being limited to a very small percentage of the population, and books being very rare. This is confirmed by the fact that these same characteristics are also still common today in basically oral cultures, as well as in oral genres of communication, such as jokes, or oral story-telling, and even in face-to-face teaching. Other characteristics, such as the penchant for the number seven, is more likely to be due to the specific religious culture and beliefs of the Hebrew people.

When the research previously described in this book was first undertaken, it was based on the Greek version of the book. Nonetheless, even though it was written in another language, it was most noticeable that the structure was very Hebraic in nature, both in the larger structures of the discourse, but also even in some of the finer details of the sentences and the relationships between individual words.

So it was then, that it was literally a great revelation to discover at a later date that this book was quite probably written in Hebrew at the outset, and that the Greek version was a translation. The linguistic evidence which is available so far, strongly supports the contention that the so-called Cochin, or Cambridge Hebrew manuscript could be the original.

It then became totally explicable why this book was so dominated by Hebrew structures and discourse 'idioms' if we may call them that. Apparently, a Hebrew wrote it originally in Hebrew, to be read aloud to a

Hebrew audience. So he would obviously do that in a way which they would appreciate, and with a methodology which would best communicate his message to them.

INFORMATION

There are several versions of the Hebrew Revelation available, but it is not being claimed here that they are all originals, for some of them are clearly translations back from the Greek version. The first version to be produced for English readers was by Van Rensberg on the website www.hebrewgospels.com then in book form in 2024. Another version of the same manuscript is Baca 2024, which is particularly useful, since it provides an interlinear translation of the Hebrew, and also a translation of the Aramaic version of Revelation. Both of these translations are of the Cochin/Cambridge manuscript, which is reputedly the original. Jones 2019/2021 provides fascinating insights into the history of the Hebrew versions of NT books in general. More information about the Hebrew Revelation may be found on his website www.writingofgod.com Unfortunately, his version of Revelation is based on several different manuscripts, which may not all be originals. So, for example, the phrase 'the Alpha and the Omega' does not occur at all in the Cochin/Cambridge manuscript. The Hebrew versions which reproduce this as 'the Aleph and the Tau' are likely to be translations back from the Greek, and so are not originals. This reference to 'the Aleph and the Tau' is fascinating, but is probably not the original version. The original Hebrew version simply provides a straight-forward reference to God as 'the Beginning and the End', and 'the First and the Last' which are allusions to Old Testament descriptions of God, as well as direct quotations, such as are found in Ecclesiastes 3:11, or Isaiah 41:26, 44:6 and 48:12-16.

For those of us today who now wish to read and understand this same book, whether in Hebrew still, or translated into another language, it goes without saying that one has to do some extra work to decipher, de-code, and then digest, the Hebraic structures, which were used to communicate the overall message of the book. It is important then to permit this total translation process to influence our understanding, and interpretation, of the message of the book, instead of imposing western (Greek-based) preferences and worldviews on the text.

To facilitate this process a list will be provided in the following paragraphs of the primary characteristics of Hebrew discourse organization. Each item will be accompanied by some brief explanatory notes and one or two examples from the Old Testament, and a brief review of examples from Revelation, to accommodate those readers who may not have ventured into all the technical detail provided in the previous chapters. The goal here is only to open a door onto a new way of interpreting this timeless message, and not to provide a full commentary on the book, for such a project will have to be left for another time and place.

It is to be noted that these characteristics are not necessarily exclusive to Hebrew, for many of them can be found exemplified in other languages and cultures, for language is a universal phenomenon of human experience. Nonetheless, they are characteristics which are so common in both the Hebrew Revelation, and the Old Testament Scriptures, that they can be considered typical of Hebrew literature of that period of history at least.

8.1.1 Repetition

All Hebrew literature is characterized by the systematic repetition of sounds, words, phrases, and whole linguistic units of various kinds and sizes. This is very different from the western system, which we are probably the most familiar with. Although our system does in fact have some repetition, for the most part it is considered to be bad style, and is kept to a minimum.

However, for the Hebrews, the opposite is the case and they seemed to delight in creating a whole, interwoven fabric of repetition of different kinds. Many of the characteristics listed below are forms of repetition.

These repetitions may be exact repetitions, for such a phenomenon is not excluded. However, the majority of repetitions are not exactly identical repetitions, but will take up the same idea and repeat it in a similar or contrastive manner. The possible variations are endless and limited only by the author's imagination.

8.1.2 Parallelism

Once you repeat a concept a second time, you have created a parallel. If you go back on yourself to repeat something and thus create a parallel, you cannot possibly proceed in a straight line. Such a process, by definition, becomes almost impossible. This does not mean that there is no linear progression in a Hebrew discourse at all, because there is. But the point is that these linear structures are not so common and not so important in the Hebraic system.

The western, linear based system can be likened to a chain composed of a series of distinct units, which are attached to each other and follow each other sequentially, as exemplified by the chapters and paragraphs in this book. Following on from Greek philosophy and the Greek worldview, the individual unit in the system is what is important. For the Hebrews, relationships are much more important, and so, by means of the parallels and repetitions, the author can weave an intricate network of relationships between the different parts of his discourse. These relationships, as in the real world of human relationships, are almost never binary (as in the chain system) but are dense and multiplex in nature.

A minimal parallel consists of two components. Such structures have always been called doublets and they form the foundation of books like Psalms and Proverbs. Doublets such as these, at the lexical and sentence level are fairly uncommon in Revelation, but they do occur in two particular situations. They occur when they form an *inclusio,* which is the situation where the same word or phrase occurs at, or near, the beginning of a particular semantic unit, and also at, or near, the end of the same unit.

They also occur in what we have called Tail-Head links. This is when the same, or similar, words or phrases occur at, or near, the end of a semantic unit and then again, straight afterwards at, or near, the beginning of the following unit. Examples of these two kinds of doublet in Revelation can be found in various places in the preceding chapters.

INFORMATION

The linguistic doublet being based on the number 2 is particularly significant for a number of reasons. This is firstly because it benefits from the law of first mention. This is because it is the very first complex linguistic structure which is created on the basis of repetition, as explained in the main text. It is also the very first example of repetition, and of a lexical doublet, in the Bible, for we have an example in Genesis 1:1, where we are told that the first thing which God did for this universe was to create the Heavens and the Earth.

In that same context, He also created Adam and Eve as the first, and most basic, unit of human society, as previously explained in Chapter 7.8. But not only that, in so doing He also inaugurated the concept of 'covenant', which, by its very nature, is constructed on the number 2, and, therefore, is automatically symbolized by the number 2. In Genesis 4:1 in the Hebrew it says that Adam 'knew' his wife. In English this concept is considerably downplayed, if not papered over, for in Hebrew the word is very rich and implies the fact that the two became one, which is the essence of a covenantal relationship. Thus the covenant of marriage was created. But more than that, in the light of Genesis 2-4, it was clearly intended for there to be a covenantal relationship between God and the first humans as well. The proof of this is that a series of covenants formed the basis of God's relationship with humanity from then onwards, until it culminated in the New Covenant, of the New Testament.

For more insight into this topic please see P. Gentry 2008, and Hamilton 2015.

Revelation, however, is particularly characterized by double units operating at the middle levels of the linguistic hierarchy. These are composed of a doublets of very similar, yet distinct, units at the level of the paragraph and above. These units tend to be quite different in terms of content and structure. Yet, at the same time they are placed right next to each other with no other grammatical or semantic linkage. They usually would be the same type of unit (e.g. both being interlude material), and would be clearly functioning together to accomplish the same principal semantic purpose. Two examples of this phenomenon are the double vision in the first interlude (Chapter 7), and the double, book level, interlude in Chapters 10 and 11.

In theory, there is no limit to the maximum number of parallels. In practice, units with ten or more parallel constituents have been found, but it would be very unusual to find more than fifteen parallels in one unit.

8.1.3 Symmetric and Chiastic Structures

Once an author has decided to use repetition as the basis for the organization of his discourse, he can create a multiplicity of different patterns by organizing the constituent parallels in different combinations, and with different numbers of constituents.

Some structures are created with an even number of constituents and are usually called symmetric or concentric structures. However, in general, systems with an odd number of constituents are the most common, with three, five and seven being the most common number of constituents, and these are usually called chiasms.

Because of the odd number of constituents there will always be one unit standing alone in the middle which in turn creates an arrow-head type point to the whole unit. From a Hebraic perspective the chiasm shares the same symbolism as the menorah. These are the ones which are, strictly speaking, the true chiasms, because of their pointed, asymmetric shape, or their candelabra shape if you prefer. This is particularly true of a chiasm with seven constituents which has exactly the same number of constituents as a biblical menorah. Thus it is probably no coincidence that the seven part chiasm is the most common.

The whole of The Song of Solomon is composed of a chiasm of seven constituent parts. The Minor Prophets as a group form an eleven part chiasm. See Schooling 2017 and 2024b, for more details. These are just two of the very many examples to be found in the Old Testament.

As far as Revelation goes, the total book is a chiasm composed of nine parts. The main body of the book (excluding the Prologue and the Epilogue) is a chiasm composed of seven parts. The Seven Letters also form a chiasm as a group. These chiasms can be seen diagrammatically in the charts previously provided in Chapter 7 of this book, and in many other charts which are scattered throughout the preceding chapters.

8.1.4 The Three-Fold Parallelism Of Sentence Structure

Another interesting feature of Hebrew discourses is that they have a certain cadence, which contributes a measured rhythm to the flow of language. This is not a metrical rhythm as may be found in western style poetry, where the number of syllables, for example, can be counted with accuracy. The cadence is more related to the flow of the semantic structure of an utterance, rather than the flow of the surface structure words.

This cadence is created by the fact that the majority of Hebrew sentences are systematically constructed with three parts. This is a consistent feature of the Hebrew version of Revelation and a brief survey of several different genres, suggest that it is systematic in Old Testament Hebrew discourses as well. By contrast, a brief survey of modern discourses written in English, indicates that a regular three-fold pattern is not at all a characteristic of such literature. Perusal of this book will demonstrate that fact.

Here are two examples in order to make this concept more tangible. In reading these examples, it must be remembered that in Hebrew the verb (which has its own built in pronoun) comes first, and then is followed by the subject, when it is a noun.

In the Old Testament Genesis 1:1 is constructed like this:

In the beginning
/ He created, God, the heavens /
and (He created) the earth.

Revelation 1:1 in Hebrew goes like this, with two sets of three:

These are the mysteries
/ He gave, God, concerning Jesus the Messiah /
/ to show to His servants what would happen soon. /
/ And He sent them /
/ by the hand of His messenger /
to His servant John.

There are some exceptions to this general rule which serve to confirm the basic principle, because the exceptions which have been found so far, seem to have a specific reason for existing. For example, when there is direct speech, the introduction to the speech may have just one or two parts, but the speech itself will be divided into sequences with the usual three parts. Other introductory type phrases may well only be composed of one or two parts in a manner analogous to the direct speech formulas. By contrast, concluding or summary statements have just two constituents to create a shorter, more dramatic utterance. It can be predicted that whenever the three part pattern is not adhered to, then one is likely to find a special feature, such as prominence, occurring.

In order to understand why such a characteristic exists, it is necessary to go back to the beginning and understand how written discourses were transmitted 2000 years ago. As has been explained before, back in those days, there was no punctuation and no white spaces in those early manuscripts. As a consequence of this basic fact, there were no sentences or paragraphs which could be visually seen on the page either. This phenomenon can be seen quite graphically in the facsimiles of the manuscripts which are reproduced for us all to see in Baca 2024. The culture at the time was an oral culture, and the manuscripts existed in order to preserve important oral discourses, so that they could be read aloud again on future occasions.

So the reason for the organization of the writing was to harmonize with, and to facilitate, the transmission of a message which would be spoken out loud.

INFORMATION

The topic of the oral transmission of discourses is a big one and so we can do no more than allude to it here. However, it has been treated extensively by many authors. A fairly recent contribution was made by Garcìa Ureña 2014, which is of particular interest here, because she specifically talks about orality as it is manifested in the book of Revelation. She points out that Revelation is somewhat unusual in that it was specifically written down from the beginning of the transmission process, but that, at the same time, it was always intended to be read aloud to listeners, as if it was an oral discourse.

In her case she recognizes 'the intonation unit as the basis for spoken speech' op. cit.,314. For her this is a semantic unit because the intonation implies a certain minimal level of meaning. This is because she is viewing the communication process from the listener's perspective. Thus, the term 'an intonation unit' is appropriate because it contains 'the amount of active information that the person is capable of perceiving consciously in a moment' (ibid.,314).

It is also very interesting, and confirmatory of my own observations, that the examples which she gives of Rev.12:9, and Rev.20:2, show that complete semantic units are often, if not usually, comprised of three intonation units.

For myself, I have used the term 'breath group' to talk about the same phenomenon. This is because I am looking at it from the author/narrator's point of view, where emission of the message is in focus. Consequently, it is more appropriate to use a more fundamental linguistic term, which expresses a more basic physiological constraint, and which encompasses a broader view of language, regardless of whether semantic coloring is perceptibly present or not. As she, herself, sums up this interesting topic: 'Recognizing the presence of the oral style in the Book of Revelation leads to a reconsidering of the author's style and an appreciation of his literary technique' (ibid.,313).

This is quite unlike our modern books which are written in order to be read silently, and with no need to call upon our lungs for their cooperation. So it is then, that when an orator, or a reader, is speaking aloud, there is a basic law of nature which he has to contend with. That law is that most people, even with a normal pair of lungs, can only speak for a few seconds, and then they have to pause to take a breath.

In phonetics this is called a breath group and is the most basic and fundamental constituent of any, and of all, spoken languages. If you observe this phenomenon, you will notice that a speaker can usually manage three or four breath groups in a row, sometimes more, but then he has to take a slightly longer pause before carrying on with the next part of his message. It seems likely that the optimal number of breath groups in one go is three. This primary grouping of three breath groups (+/- 1 or 2) creates a larger constituent with a longer pause at the end, and this larger grouping, in turn, corresponds with what we now know to be a grammatical sentence.

This rhythmic patterning would not only help the orator not to get out of breath, but it would also help the listeners to follow the flow of the discourse. The regular cadence would lead them smoothly along the pathway of the speaker's thoughts, just as if they were cruising gently down a river. But the changes in the regular flow would also alert them to the fact that something different was happening in the communication process.

It is possible that all oral discourses are like that, but more research would be needed to confirm that hypothesis. However, we can say with some confidence that Hebrew of 2000 years ago was like that, with the written form mirroring in significant ways the spoken form of the language.

More examples of these triplets can be found in Appendix A7.3.11.

8.1.5 The Use of Numbers

Hebraic discourses are also characterized by their frequent use of numbers. This occurs in two ways. Firstly, actual cardinal numbers are regularly used. So, for example, in Rev.17:1 we are told that there are *seven* angels and *seven* bowls, and a bit later on, in verse 7, the woman who is being described is seen sitting on a beast with *seven* heads (which symbolize *seven* hills v.9) and *ten* horns.

The second way in which numbers are important is the fact that certain linguistic features occur a specific number of times, either in their context or in the whole book. We have noted already above, that chiasms are formed by using a specific number of constituents. In the following paragraphs other examples will be given illustrating the same principle. Overall, the number seven is by far the most commonly used number and this is clearly a reflection of the Hebrews' religious context and worldview.

This is, of course, the characteristic number for the book of Revelation and is used in a multitude of ways at various levels of the discourse hierarchy.

As far as an example from the Old Testament goes, Patrick 2005, has helpfully pointed out that the book of Job is structured around the number four. So for example, there are fourfold structures in the Prologue, the Epilogue and the introduction of Elihu. Job has four 'friends', he owns four categories of livestock, lived to be 140 and saw his descendants to the fourth generation. For a book which is as complex and culturally obscure for a modern reader, this numerical insight is like a shaft of light into the inner workings of this book, just as it would have been a semantic template for its original readers and hearers.

It is said, even today, that when a Jew speaks to someone else and says something once, that is normal. However, if he says it twice, then he is indicating that what he said is important. But, if he says it *three* times, then he is *shouting* at you !

This is an example of where the use of number symbolism and the use of repetition combine in a symbiotic relationship. This intermingling of apparently different concepts, and disparate means of expression, creates a level of meaning which is deeper, richer, and more intricate, than just a straightforward, logical use of words.

8.1.6 Word Chains, Word Plays and Puns

It is a universal that human beings delight to play around with words, both to entertain as well as to instruct. The Hebrews were no different, and even in serious contexts, they seem to have gone to great lengths to exploit the multi-media capacities of their language to the maximum. They are fortunate in that Hebrew is a root based language and so that means that there are many more possibilities available to them for word plays and puns. And they seem to have made the most of it.

So for example, Solomon's best song begins with this salvo, which being literally translated would come out in English as : "Kiss me with the kisses of your kisser !" (Song of Solomon 1:2) That is quite a mouthful (please excuse the pun !!) even for the opening, ear-catching blast of a love-song, where liberties might be more forgivable.

So, in the above example, all the three principal words are derived from the same root and, as a result, they look similar, sound similar and have very similar or related meanings. A similar short word-chain occurs in Revelation 18:20 in the Hebrew version, which says that God has **avenged** their **vengeance** against her. In Greek the chain **judged/judgment** is used.

All these references are obviously examples of repetition. In the case of the Song of Solomon example, it is a three-fold repetition in the space of one very short sentence. To a westerner that would seem like overkill and rather poor taste, but Solomon (and those who voted for this song) must have thought that it was prize-winning style. So, from the very beginning of this song then, repetition is employed as a basic methodology. In this case it was repetition at the word level, which, in turn, immediately created a word chain based on a very emotive and dynamic concept: that of kissing. If you stop and think about it, this strategy is quite effective, because it should stop any sleepy listener in his tracks, and set him up for what is to follow afterwards. But in addition, because of the semantic difference between the concept of 'a kiss' or of 'kissing' on the one hand, and 'mouth' on the other, a pun is also created. All that in one short sentence.

Another example of a pun occurs in the book of Micah. His name appears in the first sentence of the book, which is just normal practice for introducing a prophet. But his name in Hebrew has a meaning and it means 'Who is like God'. Then at the end of his discourse the concluding unit begins with the question 'Who is like God ?' (Mic.7:18). By any standard this would seem to be a very striking and appropriate opening and closing bracket (*inclusio*) for the whole discourse.

Revelation is also replete with word chains of various lengths which occur at different levels of the discourse hierarchy. Most of them are not contiguous, as in the Song of Solomon example, but occur at various points throughout the book. Their primary purpose is to provide cohesion for the discourse – they are part of the multiplex, relational network described above. But the whole series can also be studied as a unit. This is because together, they will usually elucidate a major theme of the book, or a sub-theme of some kind, depending on the level of the discourse at which they are functioning.

So, for example in Revelation, at the upper level of the discourse, the seven principal cycles create a word chain revolving mainly (but not exclusively) around the number *seven*. This number, of course, is symbolic of perfection or completion, and functions as a very significant prosody for the whole book. In this way, the extra message is communicated that the message of the whole book is, in some senses, perfect, or complete. There are at least 49 occurrences of this word and possibly 50 with variants.

At the lower levels, there are very many word chains as well, each with their own function and purpose. Examples of those relating to Jesus, as the topic and hero of the book, and to Satan, as the anti-hero, may be found at the end of Chapter 7.7 and in Chart 54. Another important word chain is the chain based on the word for 'sign', and a chart and explanation concerning this word chain can be found in Chapter 6.3.3, Chart 44.

8.1.7 Disjunctive Progression of Themes

When an author writes a book he will usually have more than one thing to say about the topic of his book. The important things which he divulges about his topic are called themes. Confronted with the need to develop his themes the author only has two choices. He can either fully develop one theme, and then, when that is finished, develop the next theme and so on, or he can intersperse them in some way or another. The first method would create a linear chain-like structure with no going back on oneself and no repetition, whereas the second method lends itself to many different kinds of structure.

However, as mentioned previously, if an author decides to organize his discourse by means of repetition and parallels, it is impossible for him to develop his themes in a linear fashion. This is because to create repetitions and parallels one must, of necessity, go back on oneself in a somewhat circular fashion, in order to say the same thing more than once in different forms, and in different places in the text.

When coherent aspects of a text are broken up into pieces and scattered through a discourse, with different material in between, this is called a disjunctive organization. The word chains which were described above are an example of this phenomenon at the lexical level. The words (or roots) relate to each other because they are identical to each other, or are synonymous, but they occur at various places in the discourse with many very different words in between.

The same thing can happen with larger chunks of text which are carrying information about the author's themes. In the case of Revelation, the author has two main themes which he develops throughout the book. These have been called the Judgment and Salvation Themes. So in perusing this book it can be seen that the Judgment Theme is developed in great detail, mainly in the body of Cycles 2 to 6. Please consult the charts in Chapter 7 to find the references. However, John does not say all that he has to say about judgment in one go. As you look at the detail, it can be seen that he repeats many of his ideas, and his motifs many times over, as has been seen with the chiasms and word chains described above.

But in addition to that, he develops the Salvation Theme at the same time by inserting portions of text which relate to this theme right in the middle of the general flow of the development of the Judgment Theme. This process, naturally enough, creates considerable disjunctivity, which is very disconcerting to those analysts and commentators who are looking for the straight lines of chronological or logical development, which we are used to in Greek-based culture.

So it is then, that it is not difficult to locate these different portions of text within the flow of Cycles 2 to 6. In the analysis which has been presented in the preceding chapters, these texts have been called Interludes. There are four main ones which are very similar in style, genre and content, and they have many parallels which link them together. They can and should be studied together, as they all contribute to the Salvation Theme. But there is also a fifth one, if we count the interlude contained within the Narrative Framework (see below), which number, as we said before, is symbolic of grace, which is very appropriate for the theme of salvation.

This phenomenon can only be fully appreciated if the book is looked at from a cyclic, and more fluid, Hebraic point of view. This perspective helps to bring about a better understanding of how repetition and parallels function, and work together, to create a particular kind of system. This kind of system is disjunctive certainly, but it nonetheless communicates a message in a comprehensive and comprehensible way. To overlook the interludes, or to consign them to parentheses, is to demonstrate a complete disregard for their importance, and likewise, for the other portions of text, which do not follow each other smoothly, in a logical or chronological order.

When dealing with a Hebrew style discourse, it is essential to come to terms with the disjunctive nature of the author's plan, and learn how to fully appreciate, and benefit from, all the tricks of his trade, and the intricacies of his art. If we do not, we could run the risk of missing the point completely.

8.1.8 Tail-Head Links

A Tail-Head link is a term which has been coined in certain branches of linguistics to denote a particular feature, which is very common in Hebraic literature of all genres. It is once again a feature derived from the concepts of repetition and parallelism – as we have been constantly repeating. In short, a feature, whether it be a word, a phrase or a grammatical construction will appear at the end of one linguistic unit, and it will then be repeated at the beginning of the next unit, even if the two occurrences are separated by a lengthy portion of text.

To immediately give an example from Revelation we can look at Revelation12:18 and 13:1. The dragon has been the sub-topic of the previous section and at the end of his story we are told that he stood on the shore of the *sea.* Then, as the next story starts in 13:1, we are told that the beast in question came up out of the *sea.* The word *sea* here is creating a tail-head link. Linguists use this phenomenon to decide where a break between units actually occurs. This is why most English translations now make a break in the text between 13:1 and 13:2, since they do not realize that the first reference is at the end of the previous unit and should be referenced as 12:18.

Although it is important to know where one constituent ends and the next one begins, and this feature can be legitimately used for that purpose, nonetheless it is still important to not miss the point. This feature is, in reality, marking a *link* between two units. What is important for the Hebrew mindset and system is to mark and show the connections: the connectivity of the discourse and its warp and woof of *relationships.* This is contrary to the Greek-based worldview, which concentrates on division and distinguishing individual units one from another. See also section 8.1.12 below.

Now for the hard part. The example given above of a Tail-Head link is only based on a single word, and is easy to locate once you know what you are looking for. However, in Revelation a large number of rather unusual Tail-Head links occur which involve units which are at least one paragraph in size. The whole unit is functioning as the Tail-Head link marker, not just one or two words.

These paragraph size Tail-Head links are the overlap links which have been described in detail in the previous chapters. What is quite amazing is that this feature is so intentionally planned and put in place, that there are, once again, seven of them, of similar size and import, in the whole of the book running from the Prologue right through to the Epilogue. There is also an eighth overlap link but it is operating at a different level of the structural hierarchy, which has been labeled the Narrative Framework. For more detailed commentary on the Narrative Framework, please see the next section which follows.

In this discussion of the Tail-Head links it is clear how much the author is determined to ensure that his discourse is fully and comprehensively *joined together.* In the case of the overlap links in particular, he has made it impossible for readers or commentators to prize apart the units concerned, and create a division between large, and very high level constituents of the discourse. This feature has created problems for western commentators for many centuries, and these problems have not previously been fully resolved.

Once again, to really appreciate and fully understand a book like Revelation, it is important to put aside one's own worldview bias, whatever it may be, and consciously look at it through the lens of the author's worldview, which, in this case, is a Hebraic one.

8.1.9 The Narrative Framework

Everyone likes a good story and the Hebrews are no exception for they seem to have a predilection for stories, parables and imagery of all kinds. Even their language itself has a reputation for being very concrete and rooted in the physical world. So it is then, that world-wide, narrative is the most common form of expression, and this would seem to be because, regardless of the content of a discourse, any kind of content is communicated best if it is expressed in the narrative form, that is, as a story.

So with this in mind then, it needs to be understood that there are many kinds of narratives and that a narrative can have different purposes, which may not be at all the goal of simply telling a story. This can be true to such an extent that a discourse may have the superficial *appearance* of being a narrative, without being a true narrative at all.

In order to overcome this problem and to facilitate discussion about it, linguists have coined the term Narrative Framework. Robert Longacre was one of the pioneers in the field of Hebrew discourse features and he did a lot of work to show that many books in the Old Testament have a distinctive Narrative Framework, even though the purpose of the whole discourse is not to just tell a story. This is particularly true of prophetic discourses, which are usually expository or hortatory in nature, but nonetheless may have clear narrative components. See for example, his articles and bibliographies in Bergen 1994. According to García Ureña 2014,322, a narrator's intrusion into his own discourse for various reasons, is also a feature which is characteristic of oral discourses in general.

Thus, for example, The Song of Solomon tells a story in order to teach a moral or a spiritual lesson. Hosea includes part of his personal story in his prophecy as does Jonah, of course, and many other prophets. So this is very relevant to Revelation, which is also a prophetic book fully in the flow of the Old Testament prophets, and which also has a distinctive narrative flavor, as it incorporates John's personal story into the total discourse.

It is important to state this clearly, therefore, so that it may be properly understood, that Revelation is not a true narrative whose purpose is just to tell a story, but that, nonetheless, it does have a Narrative Framework. The Narrative Framework in Revelation as described in the previous chapters was found quite independently of Longacre, which therefore serves to confirm his hypotheses. Where the Narrative Framework appears in the surface structure is shown in the charts previously cited.

The Narrative Framework does not serve to carry the author's principal message, but rather it serves as a kind of scaffolding which keeps the various discourse genres together in a coherent whole. At the same time, it also provides the extra reader interest inherent in a story, especially one which gives direct access to the author, as happens in this case.

The practical outworking of this clarification means that the book as a whole, is not organized according to a chronological time-line. If a book is a true narrative then it is likely to be organized chronologically, but this is not the case for Revelation. A Narrative Framework may also have a timeline, but this can only have secondary importance for the book as a whole, since the book as a whole is not a narrative, and will, therefore, be structured according to other criteria as was discussed in Chapter 2.

The true purpose of this book is hortatory in nature, as has been explained previously in Chapter 6, but there are also a considerable number of expository passages which elucidate the exhortations, and reinforce their moral effectiveness. To complicate matters further, most of these expository passages are formulated in a narrative style, with quite dramatic stories to drive the point home. Since the goal of the book is hortatory in nature, its principal structure will not be chronological. Its structure will be entirely dependent on the author's choice, and his choice was to organize it according to a series of parallel structures, which can best be described as cycles.

As a result then, it has to be admitted that Revelation is a complex book. Therefore, in order to do it justice, we need to translate and interpret it carefully. We need to always be willing, with due humility, to be ready to discover new treasures and glean new insights into what John was at pains to share with us.

8.1.10 Prominence and Volitional Import

Every writer will, of necessity, make a distinction in his discourse between parts of his discourse which are, for him, more important for the transmission of his message than others. This is a universal, and, as a result, authors for centuries have used their creativity to find numerous ways of indicating to their readers/listeners what they should be really paying attention to. At the same time, they will also indicate what parts of their discourse are secondary, and should not, therefore, be assigned an undue level of importance.

All these issues were discussed in Chapter 6 above, including the fact that the Hebrews have a specialty in this domain because they very often organize their discourses with repetition and parallelism, and are skilled in producing chiasms. The reason for reviewing this is because chiasms always have a point of prominence. But if you do not uncover the chiasms, then you cannot locate the points of prominence, which are crucial to unlocking a correct understanding of what the author wanted to communicate.

So, in the case of Revelation, since the whole book is organized in the form of a chiasm, then one of the principal prominent points in the book will be in the middle, which coincides with Cycle 4, the Signs Cycle. However, this is not the only point of prominence, because there are other chiasms with their point of prominence, and there are other methods which John uses to indicate complementary points of prominence.

Another way of indicating a prominent point is to use markers which can loosely be called signposts. These are portions of text which seem to have no useful purpose in the general flow of the author's message. They are of the sort that could be removed from the text and it would make no difference to the content of the message. Revelation has quite a number of these, approximately eleven in fact. As a result, commentators have always had great difficulty in accounting for these parts of the book and explaining their purpose, with the consequence that there is a plethora of opinions on these matters and very little consensus.

A recent study on Hosea (Schooling 2024a) uncovered one of those unique, and inexplicable verses, which commentators cannot account for, which is to be found in 9:14 of the book. The best and really, the only explanation, was that it is functioning as a book level prominence feature, or signpost, as is being described here.

The same basic principles are at work through all the prominence features as was explained in Chapter 6 above. They build suspense and reader anticipation as the book works towards a climax. Then, as it proceeds towards its closure, they continue to point out to the reader those elements of the text which the author considers important, and which he wants them to remember, even after the reading of the book has been completed.

There is also another way by which the author can indicate what is important in his message. This is by the so-called imports which he uses in his discourse. There are several of these, but the one which carries the most emotional weight with the reader, is the volitional import. It is called volitional because, by means of his message, the author is endeavoring to influence the readers' volition, or decision-making capacity.

In general and global terms, hortatory genre discourses are probably not very common. However, in the Bible they are predominant because the Bible is a book whose purpose is to not only inform, but also to persuade the reader. As a consequence, exhortations, or even outright commands, are very common, not least in the Hebrew Old Testament Scriptures. So the volitional import is the most important of all the imports, because with this influencing goal in view, the author is going as far down the purposive chain as it is possible to go.

Consequently, in locating and digesting the most important parts of a book like Revelation it is necessary to take note of the volitional import material where this occurs, for this is the ultimate purpose towards which the book inexorably moves.

8.1.11 Topics and Settings

This is a delicate issue. This is because everything that one hears or reads has a topic, a topic being whatever it is that a message is about. As a consequence, we are all so used to discerning what the topic of a message is (or so we think), that we do it automatically, without consciously processing the information which an author, or messenger, provides for us.

The proof is to be found in the commentaries that exist on this famous book. You can pick as many as you wish but you will be very fortunate to find two or three, if any of them, which take the time to carefully define the topic of the book as a whole.

So the point is, that all of us have a worldview, and that worldview defines our assumptions, and our assumptions influence every message which our mind processes. This means that if we do not make a conscious effort to put those assumptions aside, and try hard to imbibe the assumptions and worldview of the author, then we run the very great risk of imposing our own assumptions and worldview on the book. This procedure is doing it an injustice, and is likely to lead us down the wrong path.

It is the author's task to tell us what the topic of his book is, and in the vast majority of cases he will do so. But if we do not listen to what he says about his topic, then we will just be making assumptions and those assumptions may well be incorrect.

The notion of the topic of Revelation was presented in Chapter 4. But it was briefly done, only based on the opening words of the book. Nonetheless, this is where you would expect the topic to be laid out. In the Greek version, the topic is *a revelation* concerning Jesus (the) Christ. In Hebrew the topic is *the mysteries* or the secrets (*ha-sodot* in Hebrew) concerning Jesus the Messiah.

We can know these things because topics are laid out by the author in introductions or settings, which introduce, or set the scene for, what is to follow. In most cases, we would assume that there is one major setting at the beginning of the book, and that is it, for the rest of the journey.

However, for Revelation, that is not the case. All discourses have a setting of some kind even if it is very brief, but believe it or not, Revelation does not just have one setting but it actually has nine of them! The number nine being, of course, another important symbolic number in the Hebrew system, and 'coincidentally' matches the number of major components in the book. This is only trumped by the 7 x 7 formation which is the numerical insignia of the whole book, as has been discussed previously.

So what does this repetition of so many settings imply? Here are a few possibilities :

- Repetition of an item always means that it is important. To repeat something nine times is very unusual, and possibly the only example of a nine-fold repetition at the lower levels of the book. Nine represents the ultimate in divine completeness being composed of 3 times 3.
- A setting is designed to keep us focused on the topic at hand. Repetition of so many settings suggests that it was important for the author to constantly remind his reader/listeners of his topic, and to ensure that they kept focused on it and did not wander off the path.
- All the settings basically only repeat one message, and that is that Jesus, the Messiah, is the topic of the book. He is what John is talking about, and He is what he wants his readers to fix their attention upon.
- The only other thing of importance, which is repeated regularly throughout this series, is that the action of the book takes place in the throne room of Heaven, and as a result of what happens there. This, in turn, demonstrates quite clearly that Jesus is functioning as a ruling king in the highest place of authority in the universe. A partial exception is the setting for Cycle 7, but that is a complication which cannot be dealt with here.
- More information than this is provided in the setting at the beginning of the book, and the second largest one at the beginning of the set of cycles from Cycle 2 to Cycle 6 (4:1-5:14), but we will not take the space to develop those points here.

To state the obvious then, in conclusion, whether we are translating, commenting on, or just reading this important book, it behooves us to intentionally pay attention to the setting material provided by the author. This, in turn, must be allowed to influence our thinking and assumptions to such an extent, that our native worldview is displaced, and replaced, by one which is synchronized with that of the authors.

8.1.12 Cohesion Predominates over Unit Division

One of the fundamental difficulties that commentators have had in the past with this book is to agree where some of the units end, and the next one begins. As I have personally wrestled with this issue myself, over many years, I have finally come to the conclusion that there are deep-rooted issues of perspective and expectation, which are at stake here. These are difficult issues to explain and to adjust to, and this, in turn, may explain why there has been such difficulty, and slow progress, in developing consensus on these issues. So, let's see if we can try harder and proceed further.

The reason for the difficulty is because the adjustments which need to be made, do not fall into the domain of normal methodological practice. It is not as simple as just looking for components of the text, like Narrative Framework components, or prominence features, which we had not been looking out for before. But this adaptation involves visceral elements of the analyst's own person-hood, which are much more difficult to come to terms with, and even more difficult to consciously change.

Perspective and evaluation are skills which arise out of our attitudes and preferences, which in turn are influenced, ever so subtly, but also ever so strongly, by our worldview. When I began to face this issue honestly, and make an effort to think, and see, things differently, I also began to make progress in understanding the objective linguistic problems which had been dogging my steps.

So with those proposals in mind, let's go back to the text of Revelation and try to look at it with a greater degree of objectivity. If you search and count you will not find many overt markers which clearly, and exclusively, mark a division between units. This may be because the author was not concerned to clearly mark the divisions, because it was not of primary importance to him.

On the other hand, there are so many markers of cohesion everywhere you look, that it is very difficult to miss them. Here are just two examples. There are the overlap links. In all my experience of different languages, of different eras, I have never come across a connection between units which is so tightly glued together.

Then there are the settings. Why are there so many, and what is their purpose? Closer inspection reveals that the settings of the cycles are not designed to start something new, like a new unit. They do not semantically, or even lexically, connect back to, or proceed from, the unit which immediately precedes, as we would expect in our system of doing things. Instead they connect back over a long stretch of intervening text to their source setting. Once this is observed, it can be seen that the cycles mirror the season-based year. Each cycle is a complete cycle. It has its beginning, middle and end. And then what happens? The answer is (and this would have been obvious to a Hebrew with a season-based worldview) you go back to the beginning and start another cycle with its own beginning, middle and end. Yet, this second cycle is not identical in all its detail with the previous cycle, just as this current year is not identical in all its events and experiences, to the previous year.

So, for example, all the settings of Cycles 2-6 refer back to, and so connect back to, the long setting for the whole of the series which is to be found in Chapters 4 and 5. Then, in the case of Cycle 7, its setting stretches back even further and connects back to its matching bracket, which is the setting of Cycle 1. In this way a whole network of relationships are created (along with all the other cohesion features), which harmoniously weave together all the various parts of the discourse, which are not all the same and do not have identical functions.

The more you study these relationships and connections, the more you can see that it is not a random, hope-for-the-best kind of system. On the contrary, the intricate, interwoven harmony is so amazing, that the result is like a tapestry. Nobody can say that a tapestry is random or uninteresting. On the contrary, a creation of this nature is a beautiful product, and is satisfying to both the eye and to the soul.

The irony of all this is that, if you take the time to understand and appreciate the cohesion which is woven into this tapestry-like discourse, you will end up by finding out exactly where the divisions between all the units actually occur. This is because when you look at a finished tapestry as a whole, from a top-down viewpoint, then you can easily see the shapes of the people or the animals, which the weaver has woven into his work of art.

All this is to explain why it is being proposed here, that when studying Hebrew discourses, it is important from the outset, to get our mind around a new but fundamental concept. That concept is that Cohesion predominates over Unit Division. If we are able to take this step of faith, and, in this way to allow our mind-set to be modified, then we may be able to see the text from a different point of view. From this new vantage point we may be enabled to perceive some things which we could never see before.

8.1.13 The 7 + 1 Principle

This is a principle which is deeply rooted in Scripture, and has a profound significance. It all began at the beginning when God created the heavens and the earth in six days, and then rested on the seventh. However, the story did not stop there, for it is legitimate to ask what happened next. The answer is that, on the eighth day, which is the same as seven-days-plus-one, a new season, or a new era began, for on that day Adam and Eve began to fulfill their mandate, and to live out their destiny. This has been going on ever since, in an accumulation of cycles, as the regular sequences of days have gone by, followed by the cycles of the weeks, and the months, and the seasons.

Fast forward to the middle of the story, and we find that God came to the earth in the form of Jesus, and lived as a man for the normal span of a man's life. He did what He came to do, and declared from the cross that all was finished. Then, on the seventh day He was found to be resting in the grave, with the season of His life on earth completed. But again, that was not the end of the story, because on the first day of the week after the previous seven, He was found to be alive again, and in the process of inaugurating yet another new season, which was a whole new era.

So this is a book which is also structured according to a series of seven; seven of them in this case. However, closer observation reveals that in most cases the seventh unit is not just a seventh which brings to an end the preceding unit, but it is also a new beginning for it functions also as the first unit (7 + 1)which starts out the next unit. These are the overlap links which have been previously discussed.

As the end of the book is reached, and the end of the story seems to lie before us, it is to be observed that the book of Revelation does not bring us to a clear ending, but rather to a new beginning. The vista which opens out before us at that point in the book, includes the picture of a new Heaven and a new Earth, along with a new City, complete with gardens fit for a king. Everything is foreseen as continuing on into eternity, with the people who have the privilege of living there, ruling and reigning for ever, together with their King.

You would have thought that when the book reaches the end of the seven sevens, when it seems as if everything has been said and done, and all is completed, that that would be the end of the matter. But, in reality, it terminates with a most profound message: that that is not the end of the story at all. On the contrary, when we reach that end, we discover that it leads into a new beginning: a new season or era, which will have no end because it is called eternity. This extraordinary concept is, nonetheless, illustrated by the structure of this book, which, if you can see it, has no end in the usual sense of the word.

It is not surprising therefore, that this principle is alluded to in other parts of Scripture as well. This is particularly true of Hosea. In his case, the main purpose of writing his book was to show that, even when a person, or a nation, has come to the end of everything, and there is nothing else left to hope for, then there is still hope. This is because the God of all grace, surprised His people with the revelation that He was determined to start a new era all over again. This was true even though the previous one had to be consigned to the ash heap. The 7+1 principle also occurs in Micah. See Schooling 2024a and 2024b.

8.1.13 + 1 Conclusion

The purpose of this brief overview of Hebrew discourse features has been to try and demonstrate first-hand, that there is a lot about the organization of the book of Revelation, which has not previously been clearly passed on from generation to generation. It is a system which is different to the one which is generally acceptable in the western world, since it is representative of a very different culture and worldview. It is interesting to note in passing that it was composed of thirteen components. This was not done intentionally, but 'happened' quite naturally. This would seem to be an unfortunate number to end with, although there were, nonetheless, thirteen tribes of Israel when Manasseh and Ephraim's names replaced that of Joseph.

However, that very neatly paved the way for this part of our discussion. This last section is only present to serve as a conclusion, or a coda, that is, as a '+ 1' unit, as a means of summing everything up. Consequently, this last part creates a fourteenth constituent which appropriately symbolizes not only a complex level of completeness, but also a new beginning at the same time.

So, not only is the Hebrew system different, but the organization is so integrated with the message that, of necessity, it informs, influences, and shapes the message. It is not so much that the medium *is* the message, but that the medium is so artfully integrated with the message, that the two cannot be separated. Any attempt to separate them is likely to distort, if not destroy, the essence of the message.

This is because the Hebrews did not have white spaces, punctuation, bolding, or italics to show the reader where units ended, or where new topics began, and so many other things which are now taken for granted. In that era the author had to reveal the flow of his thoughts by linguistic features which were embedded inside the text. This is advantageous to us because we have access to almost all the features, which the original readers had access to. But the disadvantage is that the analyst has to make the effort to learn the system, and to learn to 'read' those features, as well as the words on the page.

So, how then can progress be made from this point onwards in integrating these linguistic based, and discourse orientated, observations? From there, how can we use these insights derived from linguistics in order to obtain a better understanding of the message of this book?

8.2 Revelation in Review
A Guide to the Hebrew Education System

The Hebrews, like anyone else for that matter, had two basic parts to their education system, the method of teaching, and the method of learning. In all that will be explained in the following paragraphs, it is to be freely admitted from the outset, that no system of education is completely homogenous with no exceptions.

So, what we will be describing is what was considered to be normal most of the time for the Hebrews. That is to say, that from among the different methodologies available to any human beings, they systematically preferred certain ones most of the time. By the same token, in our day and age, there are also certain methods which, generally speaking, are used most of the time. But, at the same time, some teachers do organize themselves differently, some of the time. So let's bear in mind that we are talking about generalities and preferences, and not immutable laws.

8.2.1 The Method of Teaching

The Hebrew method of teaching revolved mainly around these four principles.

- It was based on relationships. That is, the teacher and the students knew each other well, usually in more contexts than just in the classroom.
- It was based on personal example. That is, the teacher would live out, and demonstrate by the example of his life, the principles taught in the classroom.
- It was based on a system of questions and corresponding answers. That is, by means of his questions the teacher aimed to get the student to learn as much as he could by himself. The student was also taught to ask questions himself.
- It was iterative in nature. That is, repetition was fully employed in the process of teaching, with lessons being taught more than once if necessary, until the students had assimilated all that they needed to learn.

In the modern, western methods of education, the lecture system as used in universities, and in many schools, is considered to be the best system. It is certainly the most common. This is probably because it is the most economically viable system. This is because by this means, the most amount of information can be transferred to the largest number of people, in the shortest amount of time, for the least cost. The professor just walks into the room, gives his lecture and then walks out again.

There is no need for him to be known by the students in any other role, or for him to be in any kind of personal relationship with them. In this system, it is the teacher who is the key person in the process, not the student. Even though he is the key person, he does not have to have any personal commitment to what he is teaching at all. He does not have to care if the students are learning well or not, and he does not have to demonstrate by his life a confirmation, or an example of what he has taught.

This would not have been the case at all in the Hebrew system. For a start, education began in the home, and was overseen by a parent or a family member. In any case, the student was the key person in the process, and everything revolved around whether he was making good progress in the learning process, or not. For the Hebrews the goal was to transmit wisdom, which implies life skills and knowing how to do something, and how to practically accomplish a given task. Whereas for the Greeks, and the westerners who have followed them, the goal is simply to pass on facts and information, and that is the end of the matter. When practical skills are the goal, then the personal example of the teacher is an important part of the process, as a complement to the transmission of information.

A system of question and answers, and a consequent, inter-active process of learning by experimentation and self-discovery, takes time. Any system which repeats an idea, or a stage in the process, more than once, also takes time. This is good for the student, and good for learning the lessons well, as all of us would probably agree, but these are not good methods when economy of time, effort and money are in view.

However, on brief reflection, it can be seen that these are the methods of teaching which are commonly found in the Bible as a whole, and in Revelation in particular. So it is that these methods are exemplified by Jesus in the Gospels, and it will come as no surprise, therefore, that we observe that He used the same methods in Revelation. The only difference is that He does not do so much teaching directly, but He accomplishes it through an intermediary, namely His follower, the prophet John.

So, in the first instance, when John was writing his letter, he was writing to instruct and to exhort people whom he knew well, and with whom he had an established relationship. We who come along behind, two thousand years later, have to remember that we are listening in on somebody else's personal conversation, and not to an impersonal lecture. The goal of the book, as we have said many time over, is not just to transmit information, but to impart life-style values, and life-changing principles; not just to inform, but to direct destiny-shaping decisions.

As a result, in the course of this process, we have John's own example as he learns new things through his visions, and grows strong in his calling as a disciple, and as a prophetic witness. The example is there, as it should be for any reliable Hebrew teacher, so that those following behind can see for themselves, how it works out in practice in another person's life. This underscores the importance of the double interlude in Chapters 10 and 11, where we have portrayed John's own personal example of perseverance, as well as the symbolic example of the two witnesses.

The repetition in Revelation is so self-evident, it hardly needs mentioning again, but, nonetheless, it is there, and confirms for us, if such is needed, that this methodology was deeply embedded in the Hebraic worldview, and in their educational principles and practice. In the same way, the method of learning by question and answer occurs in the book as well. Presumably this practice also happens in Heaven, as well as among the Hebrews, because it is exemplified in John's own encounter with one of the elders in 7:13.

8.2.2 The Method of Learning

According to Jewish tradition, their method of learning also had four parts to it. It could be described as a ladder with four rungs, which leads to Heaven. The student had to start on the bottom rung, and then he stayed there until he had mastered its principles, and only then could he move up to the next level. It took many years to reach the top level, and only the great teachers of the Torah ever attained these heights because, at that level, one could claim to understand, and explain, the mysteries which came from God Himself. See Roth 2024,9 quoting Hillel the Elder for example.

The four levels, starting from the lowest level, are as follows:

- Firstly there is ***pshat.*** This Hebrew word refers to the plain, or normal meaning of a word. In linguistic terms, we would say that this is the referential meaning of the words in question. That is, what they refer to, with reference to the physical world around us, which can be seen and heard, touched and felt.
- The second level is ***remez***. This word refers to the deeper meanings which can be hidden in a word. This could be just a hint of an idea which is not expressed overtly. In technical terms today, we would call this the implications contained in a word. However, the possibilities are very far ranging. It includes the possibility that a word may have multiple meanings. This was very common in Hebrew which is a root based language. This means that a given root may have multiple forms, all of which

would carry different nuances of meaning. *Remez* also includes all possibilities of metaphorical and symbolic meanings of various kinds, including numbers, which for them were part of the alphabet in any case. Analogies, comparisons explicit or implicit, parables, illustrations, examples given in the form of embedded narratives and so on. The possibilities in this category are almost endless.

- Then there is the level of ***drash***. This is where the repetitions in the text are taken into account. At this level, the (mi-)*drash* student has to develop an analytical mind which enables him firstly, to find all the different references, or even implied allusions (*remez*), to the word, or concept, which he is studying. From there he has to learn to make comparisons, develop hypotheses, make connections, draw conclusions, and go much deeper in his studies than in the previous levels.

- Finally, there is the top level, which is the level of ***sod***. The most basic meaning of this word is, a secret, or a mystery, but, as with most Hebrew words, it actually has a range of more precise meanings, which all, nonetheless, revolve around this basic meaning. They all have to do with something which is known only to a few, and which is at first, kept secret.

DEFINITION

A Mystery

A Mystery is a crucial piece of information about some one or some thing which is intentionally kept hidden by those who created the secret, and thereby, created the mystery. Other people know that this information exists, but, because it is kept secret, they do not know what that information is. This is why it is a mystery. A mystery creates in people a strong desire to discover the content of the secret behind the mystery. In most cases, the intention is for the secret to be revealed at the right time. At that moment in time, or in history, the mystery is no longer a true mystery, because anyone who cares to investigate the matter, can find out what the mystery is.

Since it is a secret and only known to a few, then for the rest of the population it is, therefore, a mystery. However, and this is crucial to an understanding of this word, the secret can be made known under the right circumstances, to the right people. This is the big motivation in Hebrew education. If you work hard and equip yourself in the appropriate ways, then you can rise to the *sod* level, and become qualified to have the mysteries of life revealed to you, and, for the Hebrew student, those mysteries come from God Himself. This helps explain why Paul said in 1 Corinthians 1:20, that Jews seek signs. Signs, in and of themselves, are mysteries, but they also point the way to understanding mysteries.

- The PRDS acronym. In typical Hebrew fashion, they took the basic ingredients of the first letters of these four words, turned them into an acronym, and created something more out of the basic ingredients. The four consonants PRDS create the word ***pardes,*** which means 'a garden' or, more commonly, 'paradise'! So, the hidden meaning of these four words, taken together, is that by climbing this ladder, one can reach paradise, the garden of God!

8.2.3 The Lessons to be Learned

This summary of the Hebrew view of learning is not at all anodyne, but is highly relevant to this subject which we are exploring together. It complements and supports what we have been learning in two ways. Believe it or not, this concept of education, and of language in particular, supports the linguistic analysis which has been presented in the preceding chapters. Secondly, it supports the notion that God has a plan, which idea we have been drawing out of this book from the beginning.

So then, firstly, let's remind ourselves that this philosophy of education goes back several millennia, yet, at the same time, it is remarkably modern. These insights into life and language are ancient, yet they remain timeless, because they captured the essence of what is true about education.

In brief, education is the process whereby information known to one generation is transmitted to the next generation. The important spin-off of a good education is that good students learn to think for themselves. This means that they can take the principles which they have learned in school, and then apply them to new fields of study and, by this means, discover new things which were not known by the previous generations. This is the story of life and of civilization. In moving from the old to the new, from known information to completely new information, new ideas are created and new things are invented. By this means, the younger generations bringing to light things which were only mysteries to the forefathers, life has expanded, and civilization has progressed from one stage of technology to the next.

However, information is transmitted by the means of language. So this means that any study, in any discipline, has to be accomplished through the medium of language. As we review the summary above, it can be seen that the Hebrews understood that language, and, therefore, learning, operated at different levels. Each level can be studied one at a time in order to learn, but in order to fully benefit from that knowledge, then, sooner or later, all the levels need to be integrated so that they work together, all at the same time.

It is no use staying at the ***pshat*** level for ever, because if you do, you will be considered to be an ignorant primary school student. On the contrary, the goal of their education system was that you pass through all the levels, and then become competent in using all that you have learned at each level, all together, in a creative and coherent fashion.

By contrast to the above, the discipline of linguistics is a very modern development in the study of language. Yet, what is remarkable, is that by applying modern methods to the study of how language is used, then identical results have been produced. When this kind of thing happens, especially at such a great distance of time and cultural expression, then it leads you to believe that there is some truth here which is being uncovered. It is as if we come to realize that they, and we, have been investigating the same proverbial elephant. Using different methods in a different time and place certainly, but discovering the same truths.

So it is then that one of the tenets of this study is that language is organized according to a hierarchy, which means, in turn, that it is composed of different levels. These can be studied separately in order to understand them, but, in the end, language functions as an optimal means of communication when all the levels are integrated, and work together harmoniously.

So, in Revelation, for example the bottom level of the message of the book is the referential level, or, in Hebraic terms, the ***pshat*** level. Consequently, the starting point is that we have a story about a man named John, who was living at the time on an island in the Mediterranean, called Patmos. During his sojourn there, he had some visions – call them dreams if you wish, to be more down-to-earth about it – and he was so excited about them, that he wrote a letter to tell his friends in Ephesus, and elsewhere, about them. This is all referential information, not symbolic or metaphorical, and some of it can still be physically verified today.

All of this referential material was encapsulated and set out for review in what we have called the Narrative Framework. This then, in other terms, is the basic infrastructure of the book which anchors it in the real, referential world, with which we are all very familiar. The repeated phrases, ‘and I saw’, ‘and I saw’, ‘and I saw’ now really begin to make sense, for they form the basic, solid ***pshat*** foundation, upon which the rest of the book is constructed. But the story does not stop there, for if it did, it would be very uninteresting and there would be no reason to record it for posterity. After the referential foundation has been laid, then comes the content. Since the content of the story concerns otherworldly visions, it is not surprising that there are a lot of pictures, symbols, metaphors and signs of all kinds to be found throughout the book.

So, for example, there is a reference to a person who is called the Lamb, and at one point He is seen standing on a place called Mount Sion. There is a double metaphor here. How can a person be called a Lamb? Well, to understand that mystery you need to read the rest of the book, but for our purposes here, John is clearly not talking about a woolly, referential lamb, which you might find in a farmyard. No, and so to grapple with the true meaning of this message we have to learn to cope with the ***remez*** level of the text, the level of implications, allusions and analogies.

Then, there is Mount Sion. Most people realize that there is no point going to look for a geographical location in our natural world, in order to get a glimpse of this Lamb. That would serve no useful purpose at all. This is because the image of a mountain, or a high place, is metaphorical, and symbolic of a high place of authority from which a powerful person may rule over what lies below him.

The simplest definition of the word ***remez*** is 'a hint'. We have also discovered hints in Revelation. A very good example of this are the brief allusions to the wedding of the Lamb. The references are there, but they do little more than hint at the reality which it is referring to. To a westerner it is unthinkable that such an important event should be passed over, with basically no meaningful description or explanation. That is not the way we do it, for such important topics should be laid out with great clarity, and with great attention to detail.

However, for the Hebrews this was not the case. It is still true in some cultures today that it is not appropriate to come out and say important truths in a bare-faced, hard-nosed fashion. No, for them, important and delicate things like a wedding need to be treated with discretion, even a little modesty, and so they would only be hinted at. In their system, it was not the teacher's job to do all the work, and lay everything out for all to see. It was the student's job to pick up the hints, and to discover for himself the truths which lay behind the veiled manner of speaking.

So, with this different perspective incorporated into our tool-kit, it can now be seen that this kind of approach to transmitting information is a valid approach, even if it is different to the normal western way of doing things. We can now see that what was an intuition before, what was barely a hint of an idea, is being confirmed.

In different places in the study presented in the previous chapters, we have proposed that just because a topic gets less air time, it does not mean that it is less important in the author's eyes. We are now beginning to see more clearly that it is quite the opposite in fact. Topics which get fewer words attributed to them are, by all accounts, more important than the topics which are laid out in graphic detail.

This insight is relevant to such topics as the Lamb's wedding, as just mentioned, but it is also relevant to our appreciation of the interludes, and of the related Salvation Theme.

The next level of study and research is the ***drash*** level. This is the level of analysis in general, and the elucidation of the structural organization in particular, which leads to insight, explanation, and interpretation. In the case of Revelation, the analysis of the repetitions and the structural clues laid out in the text, led to positing of the Prologue, the Epilogue, and the seven cycles. The interludes and the prominence features were also discovered in the course of pursuing this line of thought. This, in turn, led to the discovery of various threads, which were somewhat hidden, as per the previous point, like the governmental thread.

Finally, as a result of all that work, it began to become clear that there was yet another level at work, even above the book level, which was in view during the ***drash*** process. In most books, this would probably not have happened, but for Revelation it did happen, because, after all, it is a biblical book and for that reason is rather unusual.

However, the point is, that just in trying to accomplish a linguistic analysis of the book, it was not possible to explain everything. It was not possible to explain everything, and to harmonize some of the seeming contradictions, without assuming a higher level of thought, activity and authority. It was only as this higher level of significance and understanding was increasingly assumed, that all the pieces of the puzzle could be put together in a meaningful way.

It is only now, with hindsight, that I have come to realize that I had hit the ***sod*** level, without even knowing that such a thing existed! But the result of this process, intuitive though it was at the time, was that, of necessity, I began to talk about God's plan, even though that actual word did not occur in the book at all – at least not in the Greek version. If you care to look back over the first six chapters, you will see that that is the case, and I only learned about the word *sod* much later on, long after the first version of this research was completed.

So then, we have reached the ***sod*** level, which is the highest possible level of learning and understanding. Since this word is obviously very rich in meaning, and pregnant with possibilities, let's move on into the second main part of this particular discussion. As indicated at the outset, the aim here is to try and explain why the book of Revelation is all about God's plan for the world, and what its relationship is with this mysterious word *sod.*

Secondly then, the word *sod* is a very rich word with multiple related meanings. In all languages, but particularly in Hebrew, a word is not just a word and that's it. A word is like a door which leads into another space, and that space may be large or small, depending on the precise word which is in view. Then, having passed through the door, that space behind it may turn out to be a corridor, which leads in all sorts of surprising directions.

So, at its simplest, and most basic, level the Hebrew word *sod* means 'a secret'. But from there the mystery unfolds, because a single word like this derives its more precise meanings from the contexts in which it is most normally used. In this case, the most crucial piece of extra information which needs to be added to the mix, is that a secret cannot exist in a vacuum. A secret can only exist if somebody knows what the secret is and, therefore, for that person, or that group of people, it is not a secret. Contradictory? No, just mysterious, and needing a bit of reflection to figure it all out.

So with this extra information included in the equation, the next question to ask (notice the question and answer method), is who are the most likely people to be in a position to have, and to hold for themselves alone, secrets of any great significance? The answer to this question takes us in two directions (remember the idea of one or more corridors?), so we will deal with them one at a time.

The most obvious answer to this question for people living at the time of the ancient Hebrews, if not so much for us today, is that the gods would be a likely group of people to have secrets, which humans knew nothing about. The second category would be the people close to the gods, that is the human leaders and rulers at the highest levels of nation, state or empire.

Starting in chiastic order, with the last one first, what commonplace word might be used to describe the things which human leaders talk about, to which nobody else is privy? The answer is that they might talk about how to get richer, how to successfully invade a neighboring territory, or how to keep the peasants from revolting. But whatever the content of the discussion actually was, or how ever the debate process unfolded, or how ever it was recorded and transmitted to others, the essence of it all was that it was secret, and that nobody else should know about it.

As a result of this human activity and use of language, the word *sod* was coined to denote first of all the content of these secret discussions and decisions. Then, in turn, by association, it came to designate the word 'counsel', which is the official name for words, which emanate from an august body like a government of some kind. In addition, it also came to apply to the assembly, or the group of people, who deliberated on such important matters, and so it came to mean 'a council' as well. It is interesting to note that these two words also come from the same root in English as well, which makes the point that these words are related, and demonstrate for us how different meanings are developed from the same root.

So then, the council and the councilors are fully aware of the content of these discussions behind closed doors, but because this information is kept secret, the rest of the population know nothing about it. They know that discussions take place, and that decisions are made, but it all remains a mystery to them, because these are secrets belonging to the high places of power. Only those who are suitably qualified, and 'in the know', can access the secret councils and counsels.

All these things which we have explained, were true on the human level, and continue to be true today, not only in any type of governmental assembly, but also in the domains of science and technology. Those who have studied hard and qualified themselves, become 'in the know' experts, who are capable of discussing, and making decisions, about arcane subjects which remain a mystery to the rest of the population.

So, having established the above human precedent, it is a small step to make the point that God also has His own council. In fact, of course, it was really He who invented such a system, and the human examples are only dim reflections and copies of that Heavenly Council. This was very important to the Hebrews, because God, the God of Creation and Covenant, was central to all their thinking and doing. Therefore, for them the goal of their education system was to study to become qualified to become privy to the secrets – the *sodot* – which were elaborated in the Council of Heaven. The only people who could do that, were those who had studied to show themselves approved over many years. These were men of God who were recognized to be prophets. Only they could claim to have had access to God's Council, and to be qualified to bring the understanding of the mysteries of that place back to the rest of the population.

This whole set of concepts was so important, that the Hebrews had several different words for an assembly of this nature, and for the words, or proposals, which were produced by them. One of these words is *sod*, as we have seen, which very specifically could mean, both an assembled council, and the proposals or counsels, which emanated from it, and this can be seen in the Old Testament in Psalm 25:14 (note also how the parallelism of this verse connects God's secrets with His covenant), and 55:14. Then the same word is used with negative connotations in Psalm 64:2 and 83:3. Additionally, it occurs in Proverbs 3:32, Jeremiah 23:18 & 22, and Amos 3:7, all of which indicate that God will (only) share His secret counsels with approved people, particularly His prophets.

This is all very relevant to Revelation, because this is the only book in the Bible which provides a detailed description of God's Council, and of how it operates. Most of this information is contained in Chapters 4 and 5, which describe God's Throne Room. This is, of course, the place where the Heavenly Council meets and deliberates. However, John, being a recognized prophet, was qualified to enter that august chamber, participate in the deliberations, and bring a report of them back to earth.

We have taken the time to explain all this background information, in order to bring us to a final, but very important conclusion. When a council of the stature of God's council deliberates and decides, these are not just isolated, random decisions which are produced. In such situations, complex matters have to be dealt with, and the decisions which are handed down, are handed down in batches, containing a whole series of related articles. These, in turn, have to be integrated, harmonized, and executed in a coordinated fashion, in order to produce the desired result.

But, in normal, human language we have a word for a series of related decisions and proposals, which are intended to function together to produce one major, significant result. We call such a set of decisions, a plan. It is for these reasons then, that the Hebrew word *sod* can also mean a plan. This is part and parcel of the message of this book of mysteries.

God has a plan, and what the book reveals to us is that, in simple terms, God's plan can be seen as a double edged sword. On the one hand, He has a plan to justly deal with the problem of evil, once and for all. Then, on the other hand, He also has a plan to offer salvation and eternal life to those who will receive it. Both of these aspects of the plan are designed to work together to produce one end result. That result is blessing, protection, provision, and a future of eternal prosperity, for His people – those who are faithful followers of the Lamb.

This is such an important point that we have been talking about this all through the preceding chapters. Consequently, we will also continue talking about it some more, before we finish this present chapter.

8.3 An Appeal for an Adjustment in Our Worldview

The main purpose of this final chapter, is to bring this book to a close, but, at the same time, to intentionally leave the reader looking out into the future, and possibly asking the question, 'What comes next?'.

A conclusion usually has an element which looks backwards and tries to answer questions like 'Where have we come from?', 'What has the journey been like?', and, 'What have we learned in the process?'. In this case, one of the surprising, but striking, discoveries to emerge from this study of the structure of Revelation, has been the discovery of its Hebraic roots and characteristics.

But looking forward to the future, what implications do this discovery have for our future study and exegesis of this book?

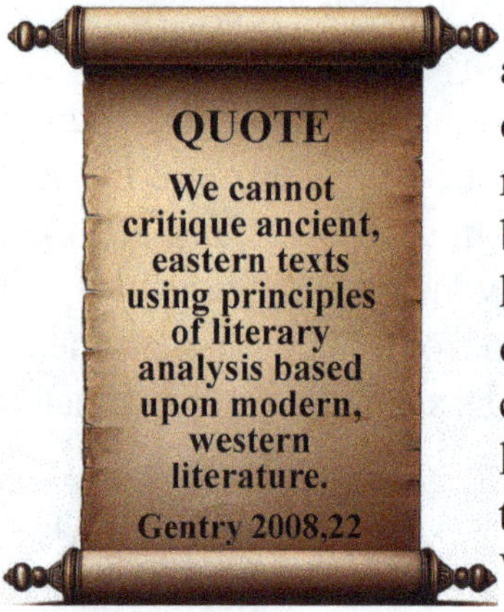
QUOTE
We cannot critique ancient, eastern texts using principles of literary analysis based upon modern, western literature.
Gentry 2008,22

One of the difficulties with traditional approaches to Revelation is that, despite centuries of study and debate, we seem to be no nearer arriving at a consensus, but there seems to be as much division and diversity, as there ever has been. Hardly anybody seems to be building on the foundation of others, in order to bring us closer to each other, and there seems to be very little 'scientific' research which puts hypotheses to the test, and discards those found wanting. What we get is a constant flow of opinions, and we are left with the impression that we just need to pick the one which suits us the best, with no consideration for the truth of the matter.

So what can be done then, to constructively build a meaningful consensus on the true meaning and purpose of this book? Here are a few suggestions to try and provoke some reflection and positive response to this issue.

Firstly, I believe that a positive, and non-threatening way forward, is for all parties to be willing to re-assess their worldview. Everyone has a worldview, and most people are unaware of this fact, and, of those who do have some awareness, most would be hard pressed to accurately and honestly describe it. We need to become aware of it, and be honest about its implications, and also about the assumptions which it feeds into us, and which we take for granted.

Secondly, we need to be willing to honestly assess the worldview of the author of this book. Although more could be said on this subject, nonetheless considerable data has been presented in this book to demonstrate that the authors of Revelation had a very different worldview, compared to those of us who are now deeply embedded in a 21st century culture.

Not to put too fine a point on it, it is Hebraic in nature and very different to our modern, western, Greek-based worldview. Once we have accepted that it is different, then we need to decide to be willing to investigate it, and try to understand their point of view, and their preferences.

Thirdly, we need to be determined in our decision that we, the readers, are the ones who must change our point of view, in order to interact appropriately with the author's perspective and preferences. Under no circumstances should we impose our assumptions and preferences on his message, whether consciously or unconsciously.

So then, we need to develop an idea of what categories of thinking and perception need to be worked on, in order to do justice to what the author has provided us with. This is a big subject of discussion, but here are a few preliminary ideas which will perhaps provoke further reflection and research.

It would appear that the Hebrews were much more holistic in their thinking: more concrete and less abstract, image based and relationship based, rather than reason or logic based. They tended to see the big picture first, and working down from there, rather than the minute detail and then working up from that. It is clear that they were not obsessed with individual prowess and personal satisfaction, but their stories and their lives were focused on families and communities. Relationships, and communal harmony were more important than self-aggrandizement and competition.

They obviously did not live their lives to the minute as we tend to do. Nor even to the hour, for such things were not even measurable for most people. They lived by the sun and the seasons, which flowed into each other with no discernible break between them. As they looked into the future as they probably did, they could foresee with confidence that the next day would dawn after the night, and that the same seasons would repeat themselves in about 360 or so days time.

In other words, time would inexorably move forward in predictable cycles without having to worry about the details. All the same, their focus was not on the future but rather their preoccupation was to live in the present, and to enjoy it to the full. Their principal question would have been one of practical wisdom : *How* should we then live ?

The repetitious cycles of the seasons would have been comforting to them and not an irritation. From the texts which they have left behind, their love of repetition, in all its various shapes and sizes, has been clearly displayed as their preferred method of recording history, accumulated wisdom, and theology.

For more insights into the differences between the Hebraic worldview and our modern Greek-based worldview, please feel free to consult the articles and books by Benthien, Boris, Denton and Hamilton in the references at the end of this book. For a more technical, but very systematic, overview of a biblical worldview, please see Gentry and Wellum.

So, how then can progress be made from this point onwards in integrating these linguistic-based, and discourse-orientated, observations into a better understanding of the message of this book?

8.4 A Proposed Interpretive Framework Based on A Hebrew Worldview

Another way in which we can make progress in benefiting from what we have learned so far, and using this to construct a more comprehensive consensus, is if we are willing to review our interpretive framework. It should go without saying that we can only make progress in our pursuit of truth, if new insights are integrated into our methodology as they appear. If new insights and new technologies are rejected wholesale without being tested, then we will make as much progress as the proverbial ostrich, with its head stuck in the sand.

So, in this next section, a preliminary attempt will be made to propose a way forward. This will be accomplished by suggesting practical ways in which some of the previously described insights may be constructively applied to our approach to Revelation from here onwards, as we look towards the future. The discourse characteristics listed above, in tandem with the underlying worldview principles which they embody, will be used to propose a set of perspectives. These perspectives, in turn, can be used to influence future more detailed commentary on the book and its message.

8.4.1 A Review of Hermeneutical Approaches

Historically speaking there have been two main hermeneutic approaches to Revelation both of which relate to time. These are, firstly, the preterist approach which considers that the book was primarily written to, and for, the benefit of the Christians of the first century.

> **DEFINITION**
>
> ***Preterist***
>
> The system of interpretation which presupposes that the Biblical prophecies of Revelation refer to historical events which have already taken place.

This, of course, is true, but the preterists give the impression of stopping there, and the conclusion which is left with the more casual reader, is that most of what is explained and foretold, has already been accomplished, primarily in the period around AD 70. On the other hand, there is the futurist approach, which, as the name suggests, considers that the book is primarily about the future. According to them, most of what is explained and foretold in the book, especially from Chapter 4 onwards, will only be accomplished in the period prior to the second coming of Christ. Apart from the seven letters perhaps, what is written in the book, therefore, is only of real value to those people who will live at the time just prior to Christ's return.

INFORMATION

There is a third western interpretive framework which is known as the amillenial position. This, as the name suggests, is characterized by the fact that it does not foresee a literal 1000 year millennium. In modern day evangelicalism it is arguably the least well known, and the least 'popular' position. It has never succeeded in building bridges between the two other opposing positions and therefore, has not contributed to any consensus building either. This is why I have not included it in the discussion above. It has some very good points included within it, some of which will be reflected in the discussion below. However, I personally feel that the name assigned to it is a misnomer, which is outmoded and rather unhelpful. I feel instead, that it is time to move on, building on what has gone before certainly, but proposing middle ground solutions. Solutions which will take us forward in a positive direction, and, hopefully, with good will all round, enable us to come to greater agreement on these matters.

It can be easily seen that, as they stand, these two approaches are mutually exclusive, being separated now by nearly two thousand years. Yet, the irony is that there is an element of truth in both positions, because it is fair to say that the message of this book was indeed relevant and helpful to the Christians of the first century, to whom it was first addressed. But at the same time, it is also reasonable to suppose, that this same book will be relevant and helpful to those who will be living at the time of Christ's return, even though that will be at least two thousand years later.

However, even though these viewpoints contain an element of truth, they have not, unfortunately, been very helpful in leading us into all the truth which this book contains. In addition, because these two viewpoints are obviously in opposition to each other, they have also engendered a lot of division and disagreement within the Body of Christ down through the ages.

One of the reasons for this dichotomy is because both sides assume from start to finish, that the main aim of the book is to predict future events; future, that is from the stand-point of the author, so this statement applies to both the above interpretive positions. Both these perspectives are asking questions like 'When did (or will) these events happen?' and 'In what order did (or will) these events take place?'

However, as we have seen in the course of this study, that is not the main purpose of the book. The main purpose of the book is volitional in nature, that is to say, that its purpose is to influence the readers' behavior in the present, even as they are reading. It is answering the questions which a person from a Hebrew culture might ask, namely, '*How* should we then live, in the here and now?'. Another practical question which it also answers is this one: 'How can we best relate to the King of kings, who now rules the earth from God's throne in Heaven?'.

The latter two questions are practical and relational, rather than being logical and chronological. The first two above are searching for a theoretical timeline and a historical road map, whereas the last two are searching for a personal relationship, and a line of conduct which will guide those listening and obeying, safely through the trials and tribulations of life. The first two questions, of necessity, can only be answered at a particular time in history, but the second two are relevant at all periods of history.

> **QUOTE**
> **What we are trying to do is to wrestle with some of the differences among us to attain a greater unity as we sit under the truth of God's Word.**
> **Gentry and Wellum 2012/2018,17**

The reason for this is because these two western theological viewpoints assume that there is something linearly chronological, about this book. Consequently, they assume that it is appropriate for a linear, time-based grid to be imposed on it, in order to best explain it. As has been indicated already, the book of Revelation is not organized according to a western style time based system. It has a Narrative Framework, which is time-based, but the book, as a whole, is not time based in this sense. In the light of the remarks which have been made above about the differences in worldviews between east and west, it may be time to pause and reconsider our presuppositions. Is it really true that Revelation projects a linear, and time based, view of reality, or is it really a product of a cyclic, practical, relationship-based culture?

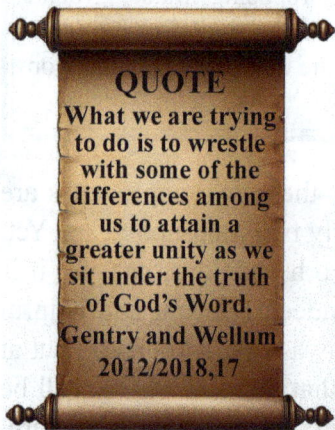

If time is to be used as a grid at all, then it is the Hebraic season-based view of time which is cyclic and repetitive, which would be more helpful and more productive. Unfortunately, the time-based systems which have held sway until now, started out from the beginning on the wrong premise. Experience has shown that it has not produced consensus, but has rather promoted division into mutually exclusive camps.

However, rather than throw everything out in a radical, pedantic fashion, maybe it is possible to give credit where credit is due, and build upon the thoughts of those who have gone before. As mentioned above, the two main approaches, do contain an element of truth, but those two elements do not seem, for the moment, to join together to make a coherent whole. So is it possible to recognize those two truths rather than discarding them, and then to build a bridge between them so that a larger, more unified, view of the message of this book can emerge?

8.4.2 An Alternative Approach

Once again, to give credit where credit is due, other commentators have tried to do this, although it would seem that they have not been fully successful in providing a complete and coherent overview of the book, nor have they succeeded in generating a preponderance of support for their view point. One of these people was William Hendriksen 1940, who was possibly a pioneer in this regard. He certainly believed that Revelation was written for, and was relevant to, the Christians of the first century. But at the same time he had a strong conviction that it also had an abiding importance for all Christians.

One of the points which seems to get completely overlooked when these issues are discussed, is that Revelation from the beginning, has been accepted as part of the canon of Scripture. Normally speaking, Christians read the Scriptures as the Word of God, and assume therefore, that they are capable of inspiring and informing every generation of reader. So it is then, that by far the majority of Christians believe that the Bible still speaks today, just as it has been speaking to every generation previously for thousands of years.

Most churches everywhere, regardless of their views on eschatology, are likely to preach on the letters to the seven churches in Revelation, and maybe even Chapters 21 and 22. This is because apparently, they believe that the assumption that God's Word is living and powerful and speaks to us all, applies even to those chapters of the book. Yet, at the same time most churches also tend to treat Chapters 4 to 20 with suspicion and, in practice, do not preach on them at all – unless it is by a specially qualified 'expert' – insinuating thereby, that those chapters are neither directly relevant to, nor comprehensible for, every type of Christian.

So then, it is important to be honest about these discrepancies in thinking and practice, and to be more zealous in championing the integrity of the Scriptures, as well as safeguarding our own integrity in these matters. The solution towards which Hendriksen pointed the way, is to re-establish the principle that all of God's Word has to be relevant and applicable to every generation of Christians, in some way or another. So the question which needs to be answered is whether this can be accomplished in the case of Revelation, and whether it can be done without violating the integrity of Scripture, or even our own integrity.

INFORMATION

Kenneth Gentry 1992/2021 has provided us with a magisterial work, which lays out, in great detail, the various aspects of the preterist approach to eschatology in general, and the book of Revelation in particular. For, myself, I am quite sympathetic to this approach, but as a relative new-comer to the topic, I think that I could be forgiven for assuming that this approach consigns almost everything in Revelation to the past. The obvious implication of this impression is that, it has nothing much to say to anyone like me, who may read it today. When challenged on this, the preterists deny this charge, but they do not at all defend this viewpoint with the same vigor, as they do to promote their fulfilled in-the-remote-past interpretation of John's visions. So in Gentry's book, for example, I only managed to find (op.cit.,167-68) a very brief passage, which says that Revelation has not, thereby, been rendered irrelevant for modern readers. But that is all. There is basically no information in the book on this issue, and no help for readers who want to know how these visions are, in fact, relevant to them today. I tried looking to find out what he might say about the interludes, which do give an insight into how God's people are seen from heaven's viewpoint. But to no avail. The index, unfortunately, was incorrect, and the one reference to 7:14 (ibid.,398) which I found, just homes in on the reference to 'the great tribulation', which occurs in that interlude. My plea, and my proposal, therefore, is that we may agree to agree, on what we agree on. The preterist and the futurist (and the amillenial, idealistic) positions have all been laid out in multiple books. So, as a positive way forward, could we not now agree to spend more time in explaining in practical detail how we should then live, in the here and now, in the light of all that is revealed to us in this important book?

It will be proposed in the following discussion that it can be done, but not without cost. The first price to pay is to be willing to honestly listen to the author and to discern carefully what he actually said, and how he actually said it. The second price to pay is that it may be necessary to have the humility to change our mind, and point of view, because integrity requires that the author should be allowed to have the final say on everything. He should not be forced to conform to an external, foreign mind-set, and worldview. It is being suggested here then, that integrity and honesty are the issues at stake, and, in order to maintain those qualities in good condition, it is a small price to pay if some inadequate belief systems need to be modified and made more God-honoring.

8.4.3 The Proposed Alternative Terminology

In line then, with the intention of building on what has gone before rather than discarding it wholesale, it is being proposed here to promote the wider use of a different term. It is not a completely new term but it is not widely used so far either. Its double advantage is that it is also rooted in the concept of time, but, hopefully, may have less emotion attached to it.

The purpose of this new term will not be to replace the previous terms but to build a bridge between them. This will serve the purpose of confirming the insights which they contribute to our understanding on the one hand, but also with the goal of making the message of Revelation relevant to all generations, and particularly to the current generation.

The term which is in view is the word ***'timeless'***, and it is, of course, noticeable, that I have intentionally sprinkled this word quite liberally throughout the preceding chapters. There are a number of reasons for this choice of word, which will be explained in the paragraphs which follow.

Firstly, this is being written with the assumption, and the conviction, that it is God's Word which is the subject of discussion, and not simply human words. The God of the Bible is timeless. That is to say that, one of His most basic qualities is that He is eternal. In other words, He is outside time, He created time and is its master, but He himself is not subject to it, or bound by it in any way.

Secondly, it is very interesting to note that He also chose to communicate with us, in by far the majority of cases, in the Hebrew language. Hebrew is a language which is verb based. So the verb normally comes first in the sentence, and thereby comes immediately to the attention of the hearer or reader. Linguistically speaking, the verb is dominant and carries more semantic weight or value than the nouns. However, Hebrew verbs, important as they are in the overall system, have a particular characteristic, which may be unique in all the languages which have ever existed. Unlike most, if not all of the languages with which we may be familiar, Hebrew verbs, as used in the Old Testament at least, are not overtly marked for time. That is, they do not have any tenses directly marked, but the timing of the event in view is left to the reader or hearer to discern.

One recent source has explained it like this :

> Earlier forms of the Hebrew language did not have strictly defined past, present, or future tenses, but merely perfective and imperfective aspects, with past, present, or future connotation depending on context. (Modern Hebrew Verbs, Wikipedia.)

This is such a perplexing phenomenon that, even after many decades of debate, there is no clear agreement on how this tense-less language should best be interpreted or explained. However, one thing is clear, for the first users of Hebrew at least, indicating the timing of an event was far less important than stating that the event, as an event, had eventuated or was about to eventuate. This is consonant with the Hebraic worldview which is much more concerned with *what* the event or action was, *who* was the actor, and *how* it happened, and then only to a much lesser extent with *when* it happened, or *how long* it took. See, for example, Boris 2020, and Denton 2020, for complementary discussion of some of these issues.

The underlying logic is not difficult to discern. Since the God of the Bible is timeless, it is not difficult to accept, in principle, that He might speak in a language which is timeless. The reason for this is because any message which He is communicating from His timeless world, is also timeless. That is to say, that it could have been relevant, and lived out, some time in the past. By the same token, since it is timeless, it would still be relevant, and could still be lived out, in the present, or again, at any time in the future.

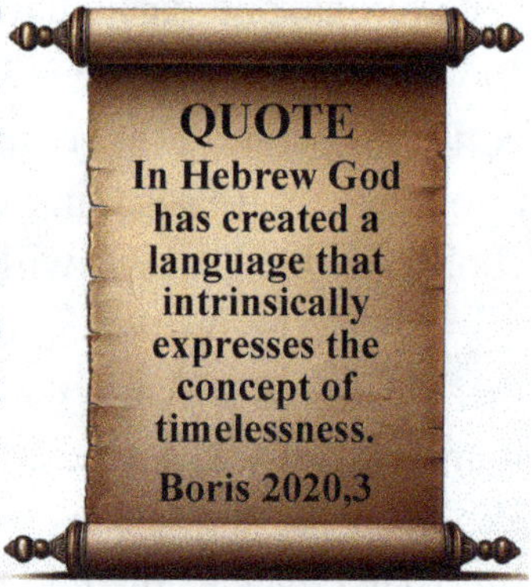

QUOTE
In Hebrew God has created a language that intrinsically expresses the concept of timelessness.
Boris 2020,3

Boris 2020, develops this point at some length. He sees a connection between the Eternal God, whose personal name Yahweh, identifies Him as the one who is eternal, or timeless, and the language in which He chose to record His words and His ways, which is also tense-less, or timeless. It is a provocative idea, which not everyone may find to their liking, but I will leave it up to you, the reader, to explore that idea further, and make up your own mind, as you see fit.

This concept is not as difficult as all that to master, because Jews and Christians of all ages for millennia, have read and studied God's Word with that mind-set. It is obvious that the Bible, whether it be the Old Testament, or the New Testament, is always read and studied for its wisdom, insight, and practical instruction, in the reader's present situation, whenever that may have been in history. As has been mentioned above, at least some parts of Revelation itself, have also been treated in the same way, for as long as can be remembered. Consequently, all that needs to be done is to change our mind-set and expectations, and read the whole of the book with the expectation that it contains and reveals truths which are timeless. As such, they are relevant and applicable to every generation of reader.

The advantage of the analysis of the book which has been described in the previous chapters, is that it not only shows how to do that, but it also reveals that that is what the author intended from the beginning. The following paragraphs will attempt to show the way.

8.5 Discovering the Timeless Nature of Revelation's Message

This discussion is not intended to be a complete commentary on the book, but a summary of how the structure needs to impact our interpretation of the message. The aim is to provide food for thought on this important matter. It will be topical and cyclical in nature rather than a linear, verse by verse parsing of the text. In alignment with the Hebrew worldview, the aim is to give a broad sense of the texture and the tone of the book. Once these have been imbibed, they can be used subsequently to influence all our on-going reading, and study, of the details of God's secret mysteries.

8.5.1 The Seven Cycles – The Seasons of Life

The single most evident characteristic of the structural analysis of Revelation which has been presented in the preceding chapters, is that this book is composed of cycles, and is not organized in any kind of noteworthy linear fashion. This conclusion is the result of following the author's lead where he sets out clearly his structural template in the first nine chapters, but also of being aware that the Hebrews lived according to the cycles of the seasons.

In fact, if it is looked at dispassionately, regardless of one's cultural background, it is obvious that everything is cyclic in the physical world. Straight lines are nowhere to be found in nature, but everything in Creation is constructed with curves and contours. Likewise, when considering human history, the same basic sets of events can be observed to happen in re-occurring cycles, rather than in random unpredictability.

So it was for the Hebrews, whose view of history was based on the Old Testament, for they could hardly have seen it in any other way. This is because the Old Testament, in its turn, is predominantly cyclic in nature, even as it recounts the history of the world, and of a nation, over a period of several thousand years. Evidence for this is the fact that Old Testament history progresses by means of a series of very similar covenants. Covenants which God made with a number of different people spread over that long period of time.

This conclusion also confirms what has been discerned by previous commentators, for many of them had dimly discerned the cyclic nature of the book, without being able to fully delineate all seven of the cycles. If there was any consensus at all being built up in previous decades, then this was the primary one. However, once the pattern is seen and explored to the fullest extent, the evidence which is present in the book can hardly be denied. So the point has been reached now where this hypothesis needs to be more widely accepted, and used to constrain our on-going interpretation and understanding of John's message.

Otherwise, a better hypothesis and explanation of the data needs to be set out, which is thoroughly buttressed by convincing evidence.

Just to be clear, the whole book is composed of nine parts but it is the seven cycles, which comprise the body of the book, which are particularly in view here. This is because the number seven is the classic case of a number which represents a complete set. This implies that even though the message of Revelation progresses in a cyclic manner, it is, nonetheless, a complete unit. That is, it provides all the information and explanation which is required for a good understanding, and does not leave out anything important. Since it is a complete unit, then the only interpretation which is legitimate, is one which takes account of everything which the author has to say. This precludes the possibility of dividing the book up into smaller parts, and then saying that one part is relevant for one period in time, and that other parts are only relevant at some other time period.

QUOTE

One can only show that one's metanarrative is correct when it encompasses more data than other competing metanarratives and has better explanatory power in dealing with the details.

Gentry & Wellum 2012/2018,17

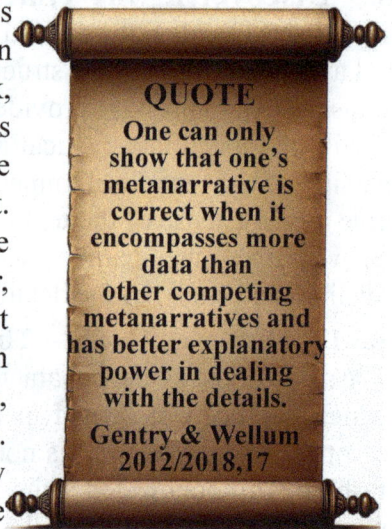

The point about cycles is that they clearly imply timelessness. The truths contained in them are always true, and the events described or implied, can occur, and re-occur, as many times as are needed, and at any period of time, as appropriate. To repeat once again, cycles imply the timelessness of a view of time, based on the seasonal cycles. So it is that, many years ago, my grand-father experienced about eighty seasonal cycles in his life-time. That is, he lived through a winter followed by a spring, and then by a summer, and then by a fall and so on. Each season was different from the previous ones, but it was the same cycle of seasons, with the in-built predictability which that implies. In the same manner, I am now living out my set of seasonal cycles. Obviously, they are not identical in every respect to those of my grand-father, but they are recognizably the same set of seasons, along with the features which characterize each season. So it will be in the future, for the generations yet to come.

This is what is meant by saying that Revelation is timeless.

Cycle 1, containing the seven letters therefore, can be taken as a concrete example of the principle being enunciated here. This is especially true, for most commentators already accept that ultimately, this part of the book is addressed to the church throughout the ages.

Looked at as a whole, for the Hebrews were very holistic in their outlook on life, it is self-evident that in this cycle the risen Christ, in His role as the Head, and the Lord, of the church, is giving His people instructions. These instructions are practical and concrete. They are telling the recipients how they should then live, even though the people themselves were imperfect, and the circumstances, within which they lived, were difficult.

In modern terms, it might be said that this is a hand-book on discipleship. If such a hand-book were to be constructed in our day, the process would be divided up into bits, or units, and then set out one unit at a time, and only once for each unit, in step by step logical order. It would be abstract, impersonal and unit based, like links on a chain, just as is done in our culture.

But Jesus does not do this. He provides a hand-book which is culturally appropriate. Firstly, it is personal and relational, addressed to each of the seven churches in turn, so that each one gets some personal attention. But there are seven of them, which clearly has a symbolic nature and implies completeness, so it is both seven individual churches in turn, but also all the churches, all at the same time, which are in view. Then it is concrete, practical instruction that can be lived out, and is not composed of abstract and theoretical hypotheses, which leave room for argument or misunderstanding.

But the main point is that the seven letters are most obviously constructed to be similar and, therefore, to be read in parallel to each other. It is like a Christian experience divided into seven seasons, for it can hardly be read in any other way. Since the complete set of instructions are destined to be read by the church of all the ages, then Christians living in any era can find in this handbook, words of encouragement, words of warning and, above all, instructions about *how* they should live out their walk with Christ.

In other words, they are timeless, and this is how the majority of Christians from that day until this, have understood and benefited from this first cycle in the book. Each of us may live in a different historical season, but the way to live out our walk with God will be informed by the same principles in each season, whenever that may happen to be. People in all periods of history have the same access to the Timeless God and His truth.

8.5.2 The Narrative Framework – The Time-Frames of the Book

The Narrative Framework is the only part of the book which is constrained by notions of earthly time. This is because it charts for us the process by which John received and recounted the visions and revelations, which he then passed on to us. However, the time-frame within which a vision is received, and the time-frame of the content of that vision are two completely different things, and therefore must be kept separate. They must, of necessity, be interpreted separately and not be conflated either intentionally or by oversight. If anyone wishes to view this point differently they then they must, of necessity, buttress their perspective with convincing arguments, and data drawn from the book itself.

The time frame of each these two aspects of the book, is determined by the referential world within which it is rooted. Each referential world that exists or is created, operates according to its own notion of time, or of timelessness, as the case may be, and these differences have to be appropriately accounted for.

So the Narrative Framework, as it first appears in the Prologue, is connected to two referential worlds at once. John is clearly situated on Patmos which is in the earthly realm, but the point of this introduction to the book is that the Risen Christ, who now obviously belongs in the heavenly realm, comes to visit him. As a consequence, the two worlds meet. So which time-frame is operative? In these opening verses, as John adjusts to this encounter, it would seem as if it is still the earthly time-frame which is operative. This is especially so, since he is already preparing his words to explain all that he was experiencing to the churches, to whom he is going to send his report.

However, once Christ starts speaking to the seven churches, it is clear that it is He who dominates the narrative. It is also clear that He is speaking from his heavenly position and perspective. As was explained above with regard to the seven letters, it is not difficult to perceive that all He had to say to them was timeless. His words were, and still are, eternally true and relevant, and constantly applicable to every cycle of human experience as lived out on the earth.

These kinds of concepts, and this kind of talk, are difficult for people to handle who have had any concept of a heavenly, timeless realm erased from their worldview. But for the Hebrews in general, and especially for the Christians of that first era who were Hebrews themselves, or more closely connected to that culture than we are today, this would not have been a problem at all. This is because the Hebrews already had a top-down view of life and reality. They believed in the supernatural, and realized that it was ubiquitous and influenced everything. Then, in particular, their view of the earthly realm was reflective of God's view, because their whole culture was permeated with, and influenced by, their Old Testament based belief system.

However, when the Narrative Framework next comes to the fore in Chapter 4, the referential world changes. Here it is explained quite clearly, that John is no longer seeing and experiencing things from his normal earthly stand-point. Instead, he is quite specifically transported to the heavenly realm. From then on, until the end of the book, he is located in a timeless world and describes everything, even the things which he observes apparently happening on the earth, from that timeless point of view.

This is irrefutable evidence that the author has specifically informed the reader of this important change of referential world, and it, therefore, has to be taken into account in an intentional and logical manner. The conclusion that is being drawn here is that, on this basis alone, it must be accepted that the message which John is at pains to communicate, must, at root at least, be timeless in nature. It is up to the reader then to decide how it actually works out in practice, within the constraints of his particular time-based era. This is nothing new for Scriptural discourses, but continues a long-standing and very venerable tradition.

The reason for saying this, is because the Hebrews themselves were fully accustomed to living and interacting with a timeless world. As explained just a few paragraphs previously in section 8.5.1, their own language was timeless, so that they were fully accustomed to applying the needed time-frame to the situation in view, according to the context of the communication. So, in making this proposal for Revelation, it is only recognizing its Hebraic roots, and continuing on in the same tradition with which its first readers would have been fully familiar. It seems clear then, that for anyone who still wishes to impose an external Greek-based time-frame on the book, the onus is on them to defend their decision, and to produce a linguistics-based hypothesis which establishes the validity of their proposal.

8.5.3 The Importance of Cohesion: God's Plan of Judgment for His Enemies

As has been mentioned several times previously, cohesion in a discourse appears to have been far more important to the Hebrews, than the ability to clearly perceive the joints between the building blocks of the message. This is because they had a top-down view of reality which perceived, first and foremost, the broad scheme of things in a holistic manner. As a result, they tended to relegate perception of, and thus consideration of, the smaller building blocks of life to secondary positions in their order of priorities.

The Overlap Links

This element of cohesion is made obvious in Revelation by the presence of the overlap links, which serve as the linkage between Cycles 2 through to 6. In this case, this is not just an isolated example of one particular feature surrounded by many other different ones, but of a whole series of identical features working together in a series. The result is the creation of one very big unit of text, Chapter 4:1 through to Chapter 19:21. This linguistic phenomenon which is objectively present in the text, clearly puts constraints on the reader.

Despite the fact that there are many repetitions and parallels in this block of text, and different sections which can be discerned, like the seven seals and the seven trumpets, it still has to be considered firstly, as a single coherent part of the discourse. This means that it is not consistent with the author's purpose to divide it as a priority into many smaller, individual units. To follow the author's lead, therefore, and to understand what he was trying to say, it is necessary, first of all, to try and discern what the thrust of that single coherent message might be.

The Development of the Judgment Theme

In terms of quantity, there is no question that the primary thematic material in this section concerns God's judgment upon evil in the earth, and, on this matter, all commentators are agreed. Once this obvious point is made, an immediate question which arises is this: is it not a fact that God has always been concerned about evil, on an on-going basis, and, is it not also a fact that He has been dealing with it in judgment all through recorded history? The Bible is full of such re-assurances that God does not just let evil run rampant, regardless of its effects on humanity, but that He watches over it, limits it, restrains it, and at times eradicates it. So it was in the time of Noah, at the time of Moses, at the time of Mordecai, and many other times in between. So is this not then, an example of a cyclic, timeless, aspect of both human history on the one hand, but also of an aspect of God's relationship to what goes on on the earth?

So then how does this cyclic component of human experience play out in Revelation, and what instruction on this subject can we draw from the book's message? The answer to this question will be derived from reviewing the contribution made by the smaller components of this stretch of text, as they work together in a series, to create a unified, holistic message. For ease of reference a summary of the content of each cycle is provided in Chart 63.

These cycles inform us that when God acts in judgment, this plays out on the earth in a variety of ways. It could be by war, through famine, by means of an earthquake, and, of course, whenever death occurs, by whatever means. These active components of judgment are repeated several times in the course of these five cycles in different contexts. This suggests right there that God's actions in judgment are not once and for all, at a given point in time, but are constantly repeated throughout the course of history.

Chart 63.
The Contribution of Cycles 2-6 to the Development of the Judgment Theme

Cycle	Ref.	Earthly Reference	Point of Comparison	Sub-Title
2	5:1-8:6*	The Seven Seals	Opening to Reveal	Revelation of Judgment
3	8:1-11:19*	The Seven Trumpets	Sounding to Warn	Warning of Judgment
4	11:15-16:1*	The Seven Signs	Pointing to Enlighten	Explanation of Judgment
5	15:1-16:21*	The Seven Bowls	Poured Out to Complete	Consummation of Judgment
6	16:17-19:21	The Seven Proclamations	Shouted Out to Confirm	Certainty of Judgment

(* an asterisk indicates that an overlap link connects the units so marked with the unit which follows)

Since it is clear from history in general, and from the biblical record in particular, that God's judgments are repetitive and regular, why should it be any different just for the book of Revelation? Why relegate God's judgment to the past, or consign it arbitrarily to the future? That seems to be just a bit too convenient for people living in the present. The simple answer turns out to be the obvious one: God's concern with evil and judgment are timeless in His world, which means that they can play out at any time, and in any way, on the earth according to His plans and purposes.

In practice then, whenever there is a war, or an earthquake for example, these events, according to Revelation invite those who witness them, to consider them as examples of God's activity in judgment. They are not just random events happening by chance, as the Greek worldview would have us believe. The Hebrew worldview interprets everything as being sacred rather than secular, and, therefore, it is God at work in the context of His relationship with the people He created. From the perspective of their worldview, such events are not merely the result of an abstract, impersonal force of nature randomly impacting the inhabitants of the earth.

The Interludes and the Salvation Theme

But the God we are talking about has indicated that His mercy will always triumph over His judgment. It is noticeable that this part of Revelation which is in view here is composed of five components, which have been called interludes. Five is the number of grace so that, even in the context of judgment, there would appear to be a revelation of grace. On the one hand, judgment is unfortunately necessary, because evil is so evil, and cannot be tolerated in the long term. But, on the other hand, God never acts in judgment without first warning about what He is going to do, explaining the reasons and giving everyone a chance to repent. This is what we see here, just as can be seen in all the Old Testament prophecies as well. In addition, when God liberates His people from the tyranny of evil, He is also showing great grace and kindness to them, in and through the very acts of judgment, which may take place around them.

So then, to see it all through the eyes of the mysteries which are being revealed in this book, this is the scenario which is portrayed. An act of judgment may occur at any time. To some who are witnesses of these events, it may be the first time that they have experienced this, or, it maybe that the penny suddenly drops for the first time. They suddenly understand and it is **revealed** to them that judgment is real and that God is serious about it. This is the first step: the seal has been opened and they suddenly get it!

For another person in the same circumstances, all this may not be a new idea for them, but because they have never done anything about what they had previously understood, they perceive the judgment event as a trumpet blast. All of a sudden the **warning** gets through. The trumpet has sounded, and they take notice and run for cover. This is the second step in the process.

Another way in which a judgment event can speak to us is that it can promote our understanding of what is happening. As a person reflects on the events, which may be dramatic and traumatic, going on around them, they may suddenly perceive them as **signs** which point to, and reveal, the hidden causes behind those events. The signs reveal that these are not just human events happening by chance, but that there is an invisible scenario playing out in the heavens, which are the real things which need to be understood and taken into account.

The real war is a cosmic war between good and evil, and, more specifically, between the risen Christ and the dragon. This is why the message of this book is so important, because it clues us in as to what is really going on. It makes us realize that the stakes are enormously high, and that, therefore, we need to take steps to ensure that we are on the winning side. Fortunately, we can do that because we know how it all ends, and that Christ has already won the crucial battle, and so if we listen to what He has to say to the churches, we can make sure that we are counted among His faithful followers. This is the third step in the process.

The Final Judgment

The judgment events which have been enumerated so far in Cycles 2 to 4 are, for the most part, partial in nature and not of eternal significance. However, in amongst them all, because it is being assumed here that they actually happen on a regular basis, some of them are final and terminal. In other words, in the course of any judgment event it may be that some people lose their lives, and have come to the end of their opportunities to choose for themselves what will happen to them. In other words, **the bowl** of God's anger has been poured out on them and so, for them, they went to meet the Judge of all mankind and they experienced their final judgment from which there is no return and no recourse.

It should be obvious, but in case it is not, this kind of final judgment is only for those who have done evil, and have consistently refused to repent and to turn back to God in search of reconciliation. God only brings final judgment on people as a last resort measure, for while there is life there is always hope. But in the longer term, this book makes it clear that God will not permit evil to continue for ever, and so He has a plan to deal with it, and to remove it from our experience for ever. In the meantime, He is extending grace to all concerned, by revealing, forewarning and explaining about His plan of judgment, but also about His plan of salvation. The bowls then, are the next stage: step four.

The Testimony of the Witnesses

Then there is one more stage in the process. In some cases the final judgment falls on some people, but it is clear that there are also those who survive the judgment event, and live to be witnesses of it. Cycle 6 then describes people who are aware of the enormity of what has happened, and so they weep and wail and lament, and talk about what they have observed, with loud announcements, or, **proclamations.**

The people portrayed in these vignettes would seem to be former colleagues, and co-workers, in worldly affairs with those who have gone on before them. These are the ones, apparently, who proclaim to all who will listen, what has happened to the various evil structures of human society. Their woeful proclamations just serve to communicate that God's plan of judgment is certain, and is sure to happen sooner or later for everyone.

But the fact that there are human witnesses at all to these 'final' judgment events imply quite clearly that such events are only final in a relative, or cyclic, sense of the word, and are not final, in the absolute sense of the word. This is because these events are not a final judgment which deals with everybody, and leaves no survivors, but, the whole point is, there are some survivors who live to tell us what happened.

This, in turn, reinforces the notion of 'final' judgments for some, happening on a regular basis throughout history, and these will continue, presumably, until the final, final one takes place at the end of history. After that, there will be no more survivors, and no more such judgment events. This final, final judgment is foreseen, right at the end of everything else on this earth as it is right now, as described in 20:11-15.

But for the redeemed of God's people, the followers of the Lamb, it is a different story. They can rejoice because they see that God has both protected them, and also avenged them with vengeance. However, this positive view of the judgment events is not portrayed in the context of the development of the Judgment Theme, but is described in the thread which describes the salvation elements of God's plan. So the proclamations of those who have witnessed the severity and enormity of God's judgments, remind everybody that the wrath to come is certain, and there is no way to escape it.

However, the way in which the people of God respond to all this, is different, as described in the components of the book which elucidate the contrasting and hope filled Salvation Theme.

8.5.4 The Function of Disjunctivity: God's Plan of Salvation for His People

The theme which develops God's plan of salvation actually begins in the Prologue, and runs right through the book to the Epilogue. However, in order to focus, and to make the point about this theme, we will just consider how it is presented in Cycles 2-6, where it contrasts best with the Judgment Theme previously described.

For ease of reference, a summary of the components of the Salvation Theme in Cycles 2-6, is provided in the list which follows. This summary also contains a list of the benefits which the people of God obtain, through this plan of salvation. It is of interest to note that there are seven of them, for, as has been noted before, the use of numbers is very typical in Hebrew discourses, and various numbers have been noted previously, and will continue to be noted throughout this discussion.

1) Introduction To Cycles 2-6, 4:1-5:14 : The Lamb Reigns

- The Lamb who had Died is Alive and is in a Place of Honor and Authority in Heaven.
- He Alone is Worthy to Execute God's Plans of Judgment and Salvation for the Earth
- He has Already Purchased God's People from the Earth by His Blood
- His Purpose for them is that they Reign with Him on the Earth

The **PEOPLE** who are in View:

They are the ones purchased by the Blood of the Lamb.

2) Interlude 1 : Cycle 2, 7:1-17 : The Lamb Protects and Provides
Earth's Viewpoint :

Protection for all God's people on the Earth from judgments events on the earth.

Heaven's Viewpoint :

God's People includes ALL nations, not just Israel.

They are characterized by :

Peace, Purity, Praise, Presence, Protection, Participation, Provision.

The People's **IDENTITY :**

They are from All the Nations.

The Double Conjoined Interlude Part 1

3) The Interlude of the Narrative Framework, 10:1-11:2 :
Persevere in Testifying

Part 1 of the Message :

No more delay, the mysteries of God will be accomplished.

Part 2 of the Message :

The prophet's calling may have delays and difficulties but it will be accomplished.

The People's **CALLING:**

To Persevere at All Costs.

The Double Conjoined Interlude Part 2

4) Interlude 2 : Being the Interlude of Cycle 3, 11:1-13 :
Persevere, even Through Death

Part 1 of the Message :

The Earthly Vendetta of the People of God (the Two Witnesses).

Part 2 of the Message :

The Heavenly Vindication of the People of God (the Two Witnesses).

The People's **MINISTRY – To Persevere in being Witnesses for the Lamb.**

5) Interlude 3 Cycle 4, 14:1-5 :
A New People are in Heaven with a New Song & New Mandate

The People's **PURPOSE:**

To Worship and Follow the Lamb Wherever He Goes.

6) Interlude 4 : Cycle 6 19:1-8 The Song Comes to a Crescendo

because God has Crushed Satan under His Feet and
liberated His People from the Corruption of the Earth, and
because He has Celebrated the Marriage of the Lamb and
has Crowned His Bride with Glory and Honor.

The People's **DESTINY:**

To Become the Bride of the Lamb

7) Conclusion To Cycles 2-6 19:11-21: The Lamb is Victorious

He Rides and Rules in Majestic Triumph Along with His Purified People
He Reigns on the Earth Along With His People
He Oversees the Judgment of God
He Destroys All His Enemies

The People's **POSITION:**

To Accompany and Assist the Lamb as He Reigns Over the Earth

The Judgment Theme which was discussed in the preceding paragraphs has been easily identified by generations of readers and students, because it takes up so much space in the book, and is graphically portrayed by the series of seven seals, trumpets and bowls etc. However, it has often been overlooked that there is also a Salvation Theme running through the book, which is less obvious to the casual observer but is, actually, at least as important as the Judgment Theme, and maybe more so.

It is less obvious because it takes up less space, but also because it is broken up into smaller blocks of text, which have no direct grammatical connection between them. They are linked purely because of the repetition of identical sub-topics, concepts, and words, which produces a series of parallels. These parallels can be overlooked on the basis of a cursory reading of the book, because they are separated by large stretches of text which are different. However, once the phenomenon of parallelism is noticed, the thematic relationship between these portions of text becomes obvious, as the list above illustrates.

This textual arrangement is an example of what is being called in this section of discussion, the principle of disjunctivity. This is the process whereby information is processed and presented by blocks of text, which are disconnected at a physical level from one another. This phenomenon is probably an outflow of the Hebraic worldview which takes a large-scale, holistic view of reality, preferring to process larger blocks of information first, rather than the smaller sub-units. Their view of life would lead them to view and evaluate a building in terms of its rooms and its functions, rather than in terms of the size and color of the bricks. Their view of a tapestry would have been to focus on admiring the total, overall image, which was its reason for being created in the first place. There seems little doubt that they would have considered it laughable to focus on the back side, to admire the intricacies of the weaver's work.

In addition, in the era when this book was written, juxta-positioning of blocks of text with different themes, without any overt connection was considered normal and even good style. For the Hebrews in particular, this kind of ambiguity, which may create a seeming contradiction in the mind of the reader, was not an issue, for they welcomed change, and were not phased by apparent contradictions. Life was like that, so a description of life as contained in a book, could be like that as well.

In fact, this phenomenon has not completely disappeared with the passage of time. Many books today written in languages of the western world still do the same thing. The only difference is that we have developed the convention that topics can be changed abruptly, and without warning, if it is at the beginning of a chapter. So it is then, that in reading a book, the reader may turn the page and find the beginning of a new chapter. But immediately, he knows that this is not only the start of a new chapter, but that it may also signal the start of a new topic or theme, or the continuation of previous topic which has been in abeyance for a while.

So this set of interludes – we will call all the components of this set, 'interludes', for the sake of economy and convenience – actually begins in the introduction to Cycles 2-6. Here the risen Christ is formally introduced once again, but this time in his persona of the Lamb who had died, but is alive again. The main action is that He takes the scroll, and begins to open the seals which reveal the judgments of God. Nonetheless, we are also specifically told that He has *already* **purchased** people from all nations back for God, so that they can reign with Him on the earth (5:9-10). This is clearly past history and so then, these two key points become assumptions which underlay everything else which is stated about the Salvation Theme, from that point onwards. The rest of the interludes then continue to develop and add more information to this scenario.

Perusing the list above it can be seen that all these blocks of text clearly develop the same theme. As a consequence, there is considerable repetition and parallelism, so that the reader knows that he is hearing about the same people, and the same set of actions. Yet, at the same time, there is not a sufficient number of unique groupings of similar concepts to warrant positing a chiasm, or any kind of concentric structure for the whole group. So, in this case, the system of parallels does not indicate which part of this set is the most prominent, and, therefore, the most important.

To uncover that information it is necessary to look elsewhere. As a reminder, something is likely to be prominent if it is unusual in any way, and especially with regard to its context, or any other units in its set. On this basis then, it can be stated with some confidence that the unusual grouping of two interludes, which are tightly joined together like Siamese twins, must be marked for prominence. The interludes in question are the Narrative Framework Interlude and the Interlude for Cycle 3, Numbers 3) and 4) in the list above.

Everything about this sub-set of two interludes is based on the number two. Everything about it is in twos, and this is also true of other parts of the whole set of seven interludes. This kind of arrangement is quite unusual for Revelation and it may even be a unique phenomenon for this book. So there are the two interludes to start with, which are both obviously interludes in their context,

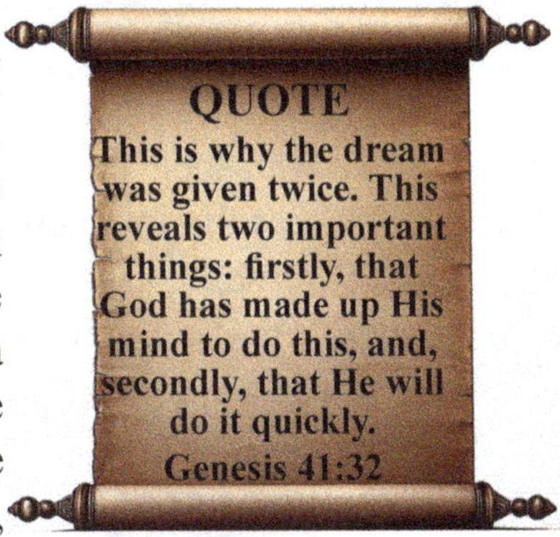
QUOTE
This is why the dream was given twice. This reveals two important things: firstly, that God has made up His mind to do this, and, secondly, that He will do it quickly.
Genesis 41:32

but are actually functioning at different levels of the linguistic hierarchy, even though their content is similar. Each interlude then divides easily into two complementary parts, and the content of each interlude develops two complementary aspects of the overall Salvation Theme.

The first of these interludes, in its first part, makes a strong statement that God's purposes will definitely be accomplished. This sentence is at the center of a chiasm in its context, which makes it prominent. In addition, the key word translated 'the mysteries', *ha sodot* in Hebrew, is also at the center of a chiastic word-chain with five components in the Hebrew version of Revelation, which makes this short statement very prominent in the book as a whole. This sentence is also directly intertwined with references to the seventh trumpet, which, in its turn, is another book level prominence marker.

These two interludes together describe the **Ministry** of God's people as represented in this vignette by His servants the prophets. We can notice that there are specifically **two** witnesses because God's servants tended to operate in teams of two, as exemplified by the disciples and then the apostles, or in the Old Testament by Elijah and Elisha. Then, in addition, as God's servants work together in their ministry in cooperation with God, to speak out His Word, and so to help bring to accomplishment God's mysteries, we find that there are two sets of two distinct aspects to their ministry.

Firstly, there is an earthly aspect, because clearly these prophetic witnesses, who represent all the people of God, work out their ministry on the earth. In the first of these interludes, the prophetic ministry is represented by John himself, since this interlude is part of the narrative about John. In his case we know that he was physically in Patmos, and in this encounter he is told that he will continue to have a prophetic ministry on the earth for a time, which is yet still future. But, at the same time, it must not be forgotten that he is in the spirit in Heaven and he is actively participating as well, in what is going on in Heaven. So he has a double ministry, in Heaven but also on the earth, at the same time, as it were, and in parallel to one another, not one after the other in two distinct and consecutive phases.

Then, in the second interlude of the pair, the story of the two witnesses is similar. The first aspect of their ministry is on the earth, but it does not stop there, but in their case their ministry also continues on in Heaven as well. Notice that the instruction given to them at the turning point in their ministry is 'Come Up Here !' (11:12), which is exactly the same as what John was told in 4:1. Even though in their case their ministry, superficially at least, seems to start on the earth and then end up in heaven, this is not the whole story. In actual fact, while they are on the earth, their ministry is totally permeated, and characterized, by heavenly actions and interventions.

They had a heavenly, supernatural ministry, just like Elijah and Moses, while still operating on the earth. It is in this way that they cooperated with God, to help bring about the revelation and the accomplishment of God's secret mysteries, and His signs upon the earth.

Then, for the second set of characteristics of their ministry, we can observe these features. Sometimes their ministry seems to be blocked and ineffective. Even though they are not subject at all to God's activity to judge and destroy evil, which is clearly stated or implied in other places in these interludes, but, nonetheless, God's people are not exempt from difficulties and suffering. These experiences may be summed up variously as trials, tribulations, testings, corrections and even persecution, but not judgment, as they are no longer subject to God's anger, but are protected from it. However, the second aspect in this sub-set is that, despite all the trials and tribulations which they may have to go through, they learn to persevere, they will always come out victorious in the end, and their ministry will effectively accomplish the purposes which God set for them.

So, in John's case, in the Narrative Interlude, at one point he is told to stop writing what he had heard, but then later he is shown that he will indeed continue to prophesy again, and is straight away given another prophetic task to perform. In the case of the two witnesses, their ministry on earth ends in death and apparent defeat, just like the Lamb's, but like Him, they also rise again as unstoppable overcomers.

So, this is the most important aspect of the whole of the information set out in the central, Salvation Theme network of texts. This part of the message is only overshadowed but what happens right at the end of the book in Cycle 7, since that conclusion is also a prominent part of the book and brings the Salvation Theme to completion.

For the rest of the interludes their message contributes the following elements. Firstly, in the interlude of Cycle 2 the **Identity** of these people is established. God's people are intimately connected in some way with the twelve tribes of Israel and have issued forth from this source. As such, being God's covenant people they are sealed, and are protected from all ensuing judgments. But, at the same time, they are also drawn from all the nations of the earth. This is another example of one harmonious whole composed of **two** almost contradictory components at the same time.

The identity of these people is characterized by seven particular blessings or hall-marks. These are **Peace, Purity, Praise**, as they stand in God's **Presence**. Then from that standpoint, they also enjoy His **Protection**, the privilege of **Participation** in the activities of Heaven, and the **Provision** of all their needs.

The interlude of Cycle 4 reveals these people's **Purpose** which is also a **Privilege.** They stand before God, and sing a new song, which only they are allowed to sing, which describes their ultimate heavenly purpose. But they also follow the Lamb wherever He goes, because they were **purchased** by Him. Obviously, they must be accompanying Him, and cooperating with Him, in His ruling activities. Implicitly, this must be as much on the earth, as in Heaven, because we have already been told that they are to reign with Him on the earth.

Then, in the interlude of Cycle 6, the song comes to a crescendo, and reveals to us their final **Destiny**. Their ruling and reigning ministry with the Lamb is so successful, that all of God's, and their, enemies have been totally destroyed and removed from the scene. So that is one major blessing: the removal of all evil, which is followed and completed by a second. In that happy state, the blood-bought people of God discover that, through their trials and tribulations, they have been transformed into a beautiful bride, who is now ready for her wedding.

Then, finally, in the conclusion to Cycles 2-6 the most important elements of the introduction and of the intervening interludes are summarized in one final, glorious statement, well worthy of a conclusion such as this. But, nonetheless, it is to be noted in this dramatic, conclusive summary, that the activity in view is still activity based on the earth. It is not referring to the new heavens and the new earth of Cycle 7. This is because it tells us that the Lamb is still in the process of striking down the nations with the sword of His word. This is necessary because these nations are, presumably, still in rebellion against Him. Then in the next sentence, it says that He rules them with a rod of iron and is preparing to tread out the grapes of wrath. All this, with the saints still following Him wherever He goes.

These events cannot be happening in Heaven and so they must be happening on the earth. They cannot be happening in the context of the New Creation, so they must be happening still in the Old Creation, prior to the second coming of the reigning and victorious King.

So this final statement, along with everything else described in these interludes about God's plan of salvation, reveal that this activity of ruling and reigning takes place in the here and now. It seems clear that this is the calling of every generation of purchased and purified saints, to be active with the Lamb in curbing and castigating evil while they are still on the earth. They are still on the earth with all its woes and imperfections, but that does not prevent them from tasting and enjoying the glories of Heaven at the same time. This experience is timeless and for all.

The interludes are like windows into the timeless world of Heaven. By looking through these windows we see life in the spiritual world as God sees it. There are the 24 Elders and the 4 Living Creatures, but we also see God's people as He sees them. They are dressed in their white robes and are singing praise to Him, but they are also following the Lamb wherever He goes. In doing so they are witnesses for Him, and may sometimes suffer as He did, but in the same manner they will be totally victorious as He was, and timelessly, still is. They have died with the Lamb, and that is sufficient for them to be raised to new life, in order to rule and reign with Him on the earth, and for ever. This all happens by faith certainly, but it happens, nonetheless.

There is no reason in the text to insist that the people seen in the interludes must have died physically first, in order to be seen in Heaven. This viewpoint, ubiquitous though it may be, is really derived from an unaligned worldview, which cannot see things from Heaven's perspective. The evidence in the text strongly suggests that all these things, which are described in the list of interludes above, are happening timelessly, all the time. The implicit invitation is there to all believers in Jesus, at any generation of earthly time, to receive these blessings by faith and to fully enter into them, just as John did, in order to show us the way. The command, or invitation, still rings out across the millennia: 'Come Up Here !'.

So, let's say this again, a second time, to make the point clear. If anyone has been raised to newness of (spiritual) life by faith in the Blood of the Lamb, then that automatically qualifies that person to also rule and reign on the earth along with the Lamb. God is no respecter of persons. This blessing and privilege is not reserved just for a special, elite group of persons, but is for any of the Blood-Bought people of God. It is for any of them, timelessly, regardless of when they lived, or where they lived, and so it will be for ever.

8.5.5 Prominence – Discerning What is What

Quite a bit has been said about prominence already in the preceding chapters and also in the preceding paragraphs. This is not surprising, since what is prominent semantically speaking, is by definition, important for the communication of the message. It is self-evident, that important matters tend to get repeated more than less important matters. In this section we will briefly review the relevance of the most prominent points of the book as a whole, for a correct understanding of the overall message.

Cycle 4, the Signs Cycle is the specially prominent part of the book as a whole. In this cycle the dragon is formally introduced for the first time. Previously he was only alluded to in passing in Cycle 1, without being properly introduced. He was treated as old information back there, which is basically saying the same as saying that he is 'old hat', in modern parlance.

However, even in Cycle 4, he is only presented very briefly, and, basically, the only information worthy of note, which is given, is his identity as being the same personage as Satan or the devil. After that, the main point of introducing him at all was to inform us that he is a loser, and has already lost the war. Consequently, he has been driven out of Heaven, and has been hurled to the earth. This happened because God and His Christ are in charge, and because God's people have been given the power to overcome him in whatever confrontations may subsequently take place. After that we only hear about his proxies who are obviously less important than him.

How is this story to be understood and why is it important? The Hebrews were well acquainted with signs, for this cycle is composed of seven signs. Their Scriptures are full of them, and the testimony of the New Testament is that they went after signs far more than the Greeks. Signs, pictures or parables. They are all talking about the same thing. They are objects, or personages, in this particular case, which are described in human, even physical, terms so that the reader can imagine them and obtain some kind of understanding. Yet, it should go without saying, since they are signs, that what can be perceived in the sign itself is not what is important. What is important is that they represent, and point to, objects, or beings, which exist in the spiritual world. But since these things are spiritual in nature, they are, therefore, invisible to human eyes, and consequently, somewhat difficult for earth-bound humans to understand.

This is why signs and pictures are necessary in order to talk about them at all, for you cannot talk about things which you have never seen, and for which you have no words to accurately describe them. Jesus taught in parables, using human language and pictures to convey spiritual truth for this same reason. This basic linguistic insight needs to be accepted at face value, and as a consequence, it has to be accepted that there may well be things which we still will not understand about the spiritual world, even after we have digested the parable to the best of our ability. The Hebrews did not seem to worry about these things, and we, as modern day readers looking over their shoulder, as it were, need to copy their example. The same is true for all the imagery which occurs throughout the whole book and not just in this cycle.

Nonetheless, even if it is necessary to use parables, or signs, because of what the author is trying to talk about, the basic truth which is in view, can be grasped. This truth which is being revealed and explained in this cycle, is that there is a spiritual world which exists beyond the limits of our human, earthly realm. In this spiritual realm, there is a cosmic war going on, but we can know who wins. Jesus, the Lamb, who is also a Lion, has already won, and so He is ruling both in Heaven and on the earth.

The fact that this war is going on, explains why there is still trouble and tribulation on the earth and, in particular, why God's people face persecution. History proves to us that this has happened in every generation from Pentecost to the present day. This is a reality of human existence, and is certainly not something that only happens at certain periods of history. But to help us in this task of overcoming evil, the rest of the cycle outlines the dragon's tactics, which do not change regardless of the passage of earthly time. In addition, we are told how we, as God's people, can always overcome our adversary, and this does not change with the passage of time either.

This is one of the most important parts of this book, and a significant reason as to why it was written. However, it is not the only one, because Cycle 7, being the conclusion of the whole book which tells us how it all ends, is also important. In that cycle we learn that all evil is eventually eradicated and removed, with the last enemy, Death, being consigned to oblivion as well. Once this has been accomplished, there will be a New Creation and a new life in the Paradise of God, where His people will live with Him for ever.

8.5.6 The Function and Message of Chapter 20: All's Well that Ends Well

From a linguistic point of view, the most important thing to understand about Chapter 20 of Revelation is that it is the setting of the final cycle, Cycle 7. This has been discussed in detail in previous chapters, so we will do no more here than summarize the most important points concerning this matter. In the list of interludes provided in section 8.5.4 above, we were reminded that Chapter 19 brought the whole of Cycles 2-6 to a closure. Chapter 19 is a conclusion so, therefore, Chapter 20 must be a new beginning and, since all the cycles have a setting in first position, then Chapter 20 must be a setting. To interpret it in any other way an analyst must, of necessity, come up with a better and more convincing analysis of the whole book.

Secondly, it can be noticed that the author carefully joined together Cycles 2 to 6. It is as if he papered over the joints between them by means of the overlap links previously discussed. We are obliged to conclude that he did this to emphasize the importance of the cohesion that he saw in this series of cycles, and to down-play the separations which do, nonetheless, exist between the different components of the series. However, when we get to the connection between Cycle 6 and Cycle 7, there is no overlap link, just as there is no overlap between Cycle 1 and Cycle 2 at the beginning of the series. This makes it quite clear that Cycle 1, along with Cycle 7 were supposed to be seen as set off from the middle set of five, and therefore different. Different that is, from the set of five, but similar to each other.

This linguistic phenomenon demonstrates that Chapter 20 begins a new Cycle, which is not a continuation of the previous one, and that, therefore, it must be the setting of the next cycle in order to match all the other cycles. Not only that, it becomes obvious, when viewed from within the system set up by the author himself, that the setting of Cycle 7 is also most likely to be in parallel in some way with the setting of Cycle 1.

Settings, linguistically speaking, are not important parts of the discourse and so they cannot, and do not, carry much weight as regards the information they contain. Settings contain just minimal information, sufficient to set the scene and to set the tone for what is to come afterwards. Their greatest value is that they introduce the participants and the topic and, by the same token, give an indicator of the value and importance of those items. It is a mistake, therefore, to try and derive a complex teaching or to establish an important theological point based on material which only occurs in a setting. In this case, it is the last setting in the book, and, therefore, the one which has the least importance among all the many settings in the book.

Because of the parallel cyclic structure of the whole book, Cycle 7 is parallel to Cycle 1, and together, they function as a matching pair, being the introduction to the body of the book and its conclusion. Not only is there this natural, functional parallelism, but there is also parallelism of both form and content. In this case it is a contrastive parallelism rather than a synonymous parallelism, which is unusual, if not unique, for the book as a whole. This is not surprising because Cycle 7 stands out as different from the other cycles in a number of ways, and these differences all confirm and contribute to its prominence as the conclusion of the book.

A contrastive parallel, as the label indicates, is one which provides a contrast to what has gone before. In this way it complements and completes a discourse by rounding it out, and providing the additional points of view about the topic, which had not been previously included in the discussion.

So in the case of the main information provided by these two cycles, they are both mainly about the church. In the first cycle, the church is seen from an earthly view point. It is the church which is still physically on the earth, which is in view. Even though the people in it have already been redeemed and incorporated into God's family, and definitely have some good points, yet, at the same time, it seems as if most of the space is taken up with commenting on, and correcting its imperfections and flaws.

In Cycle 7 the church is no longer in its earthly state, but is now in the New Creation and the New Jerusalem. They are now in their glorious state, in which the imperfections and flaws of earthly life will no longer haunt them, because all such things, including disease and death, have been eliminated for ever.

Now for the settings. Jesus actually gets introduced three times, in the Prologue, in the setting to Cycle 1 and again in Chapter 4. So He gets a lot of airtime, and many impressive details are provided about who He is, and what He has accomplished. It is all positive. In the setting to Cycle 1 alone, seven verses are dedicated to describing Him. A summary of the information given is provided in Chart 64.

Chart 64.
A Comparison of the Settings of Cycle 1 and Cycle 7

Cycle 1 : Jesus 1:4-20	Cycle 7 : Satan 20:1-10
Hero	Villain
Victorious	Defeated
Enthroned in Heaven	Consigned to a Pit
Has eternal power and glory	Characterized by ignominy
Free to act as He wishes	Bound
Eternal ruler of the kings of the earth	The lake of fire is his destiny
Loves people and freed them	Hates people and seeks to destroy them
His glory is described at length	He is not described at all
He is like a Lamb, who died but is alive	He is like a dragon who was alive but can be considered dead because defeated
Jesus redeemed His people to be kings and priests	The dragon makes war on them and seems to defeat them but in fact they rule over him

(The reference to the Lamb is taken from Ch. 4 but Cycle 1 refers to His death and resurrection in any case)

However, the case of the dragon is quite different. He does not appear at all in the settings at the beginning of the book. This is unusual, since arguably, he should be considered as the second most important protagonist in the book, being the foil to the hero, which is Jesus. The fact that he is passed over in silence is immediately an indicator that he is being intentionally downgraded in importance.

Then in Cycle 4, near the middle of the book, he is finally formally introduced, but this is not even in the setting which is the normal place for such introductions, and so once again he is down graded as this indicates that he is not even the topic of the cycle. The setting in this case is a dramatic description of a very noisy proclamation in Heaven concerning the Lamb's victory and authority. This is the true overriding topic of the cycle. So when the dragon is finally introduced, in about third position, it is only to immediately announce his defeat and failure to impress.

So now that we consider the setting to Cycle 7 what do we find? The dragon is not formally introduced here, since this was done in Chapter 12, and now he is 'old' information and he is not the topic at all of the following cycle. The topic of the cycle is something like: 'the completion of God's plan of judgment and of salvation'. So what is the purpose then of the dragon being in this setting in Chapter 20? Settings can have various purposes and sometimes they provide a summary in order to set the scene for what is to follow on afterwards.

If we look back at the setting at the beginning of the book, Jesus dominates it, both in the Prologue and in the setting to Cycle 1. Even though it is quite lengthy, it is, nonetheless, a summary. It is a summary of who He is, what He has accomplished, and the scope of His influence on the history of the world. In other words, it is a summary of His career. Between the two of them it is a complete summary running, in His case, from the beginning of time, then with special emphasis on what He accomplished by His death and resurrection, right through to the end of time, where eternity begins. So it is a summary which is enormous in scope, and which sets the scene for the whole book. This summary about Jesus is completed by a briefer summary of the career of the people of God. This is summed up in one sentence which says that He has (past tense) made (them) to be kings and priests to serve His God and Father (1:6). Everything else which follows in the book must be understood in the light of this back-drop.

This then, helps us make sense of the setting of Cycle 7, which is its matching bracket. It can be seen then, that apart from introducing the topic of the cycle it does not introduce anything else because it is, after all, the last cycle in the book. But for the rest it is a summary. Firstly, it is a summary of the dragon's career. This is reasonable and is to be expected because it is true that he is the protagonist, the villain if you like, whose dramatic role is to stand as a contrasting counter-point to Jesus. So then, the summary of his career is placed in the setting of Cycle 7, in parallel, and in contrast to, the career of Jesus which dominates the setting of Cycle 1.

On examining this more closely it can be seen that his career is divided into two parts. The first part describes an interim period in his career. In this period he is only bound as a temporary measure. This would be like putting an arrested person in hand-cuffs to restrain them while they awaited their trial and transfer to a more secure location. This period is a period which is defined in terms of human time, that is, it is limited to 'a thousand years' (20:2). Then in a second stage, with the time period having ended, he is released from his interim restraint order, in order to be definitively dealt with by being put in an eternal, high-security prison (20:10).

Even though the dragon is presumably a spiritual being, his origins are not referred to, for unlike Jesus he is not important enough to have those origins clearly referenced. So the starting point of his career is his defeat, which is described in some detail in Chapter 12:3-9. It is only at the end of this passage, in verse 9, that a very brief allusion is made to his first appearance in earthly history in the Garden of Eden. Following that very brief introduction, the story of his earthly career is brought to closure by the report of his consequent partial incarceration in Chapter 20, which must have happened as a consequence of Christ's victory on the cross as is made plain by the context of the book as a whole.

Let's note in passing that in 12:9 his career is described in one word, in that he sought to 'deceive' the nations of the earth. This puts fully into context the single fact which is stated in the summary in 20:3, that he could *no longer deceive* the nations. From there it spans the rest of time, and terminates at the end of time and the beginning of eternity in 20:10, the same as the summary of Christ's career.

It was noted previously in Chapter 5 that the body of Cycle 7 is constructed around a series of antitheses. However, antitheses are not clearly apparent in the setting of the cycle when this is considered in isolation. But, nonetheless, what can be observed now at this point in the discussion, is that the setting of Cycle 7 does contain some significant antitheses because it is in an antithetical relationship to the combined setting of the Prologue and the setting to Cycle 1 as was demonstrated in Chart 64.

However, that is not all because, just as at the beginning of the book, there is included as well, a summary of the career of the church. This time it is the church victorious, which is seen in its role of reigning along with the risen Christ. As such, it is empowered to defeat the devil at every turn, even if it involves suffering and death, just as is illustrated by the two witnesses. According to the beginning of the book, this reigning period is already a past tense accomplishment. In other words, the starting point was from the time when it became possible to be among those who had been bought back for God, by the blood of the Lamb. If this is correct, then the only possible time period which would match the symbolic '1000 years' is the period from Christ's ascension, when His victorious work was fully completed and He could sit down, until His second coming, when clearly He will wrap every thing up, and there will be no more time.

It goes without saying that the 1000 years is a big theological issue. The goal here is not to fully resolve that issue which would take up far too much space, but just to show what the implications of this present study are. A good understanding of the contribution which the structure of Revelation makes to our understanding of its message, leads us down this logical path.

The devil is a loser, who was defeated at the cross. Inevitably his power must have been diminished at that point, and not just at some time in the future. By the same token, the church was bought and purified as from the Cross onwards. Consequently, they share in Christ's reign from that point in history onward, whether they are still physically on earth or are continuing to reign from Heaven. The only difference is that in Heaven they have been promoted to higher positions of authority than before. I will leave the readers free to pursue those thoughts further if they wish.

However, people counter this reasoning by asking why there is still so much evil in the world if the devil is bound and in a pit already. This is a good question, but the answer is fairly simple and has two parts. Firstly, those of us with a western mind-set need constantly to make the effort to realize that all through Revelation the language being used is primarily symbolic or parabolic. The author is trying to describe spiritual beings and spiritual things, but, of necessity, he is using human language, which normally describes physical things. By this means it is possible to get a good idea of the essential part of the message but, at the same time, it is not possible to grasp all the details. Like the Hebrews, we have to learn to be content with this linguistic ambivalence.

So then, the devil is a spiritual being and the chain and the pit, therefore, must also refer to spiritual things. The essence of the message is that he has been temporarily and partially restrained. The next stage is to listen carefully to exactly what the author tells us, because he most likely will tell us what we need to know, but he has no need to tell us what we do not need to know. What he tells us is that this restraining process has the effect of preventing the devil from 'deceiving the nations anymore' (20:3). This statement, in itself is clear, but it turns out to be very significant because the term 'to deceive' is repeated in various places throughout the book.

In fact, it forms a seven part word-chain, as laid out in Chart 65, which makes it extremely significant, although this fact is, unfortunately, lost in most English translations. All these occurrences refer to the devil deceiving the nations, either himself or through his proxies. In 12:9 (the first reference) this deception is the one significant thing which is said about him, and the concept is repeated again in 20:10, which is the last reference, and again, it is the only thing said about him as he is consigned to the lake of fire.

So the question then arises as to whether the devil deceives the nations in current world history or not. The answer is that he does not, or at least he does not deceive like he used to.

In the Old Testament period, apart from a few individual exceptions, the nations as a whole did not know the living God, they did not serve Him and could not be counted as members of His family. At Pentecost all that changed. On that very day 3000 people came into God's Kingdom and many were from the nations. From that time on, the good news spread like wildfire, with the people of the nations coming into the Kingdom of God by the thousands.

Chart 65.
The Word Chain Based on the Verb 'To Deceive'

A. The devil, Satan, who **deceives** the whole earth, was thrown down 12:9

B. And it (the beast) **deceives** the inhabitants of the earth 13:14

C. (Babylon's) sorcery **deceived** all the nations 18:23

D. The beast and the false prophet who did the signs, who **deceived** the ones who followed and worshiped the beast were seized and thrown into the lake of fire 19:20

C' In order that Satan should no longer **deceive** the nations 20:3

B' Satan will go out (again) to **deceive** the nations to the four corners of the earth 20:8

A' The devil, who **deceived** them, will be thrown into the lake of fire 2 20:10

This has continued until today to such an extent that it is probably safe to say that all the nations are now well represented in God's Kingdom. So it is clear that the devil has lost his power to deceive them. The text does not at all say that all evil is eliminated at the same time. On the contrary, it tells us quite clearly that bad things will continue to happen – even to God's people – right until the very end, when all evil is removed and the devil himself is eliminated for ever.

In summary then, of a fairly complex argument, here are the main points that need to be considered concerning Chapter 20.

- It is a setting to the final cycle, Cycle 7. As such, it sets the scene for what is to follow by explaining how God has a plan to restrain evil so that it can no longer deceive people, and then to completely eliminate it for ever. This is a necessary prerequisite for the establishment of the New Creation, in which evil of all kinds, including sickness and death, will have no more place. Since it is a setting, it is not designed to carry the weight of a major theological argument in and of itself, but can only be legitimately used to *set the scene* for a major theological exposition.
- It is in parallel to the setting of Cycle 1. As such, Satan is clearly unfavorably compared with Jesus. He is, therefore, portrayed as a defeated foe, who only has limited power now, and will eventually have none at all.

- The key points in time provided by the book itself are the time of the Passion of Christ and His subsequent ascension, which is the primary beginning point for charting the career of Jesus, of Satan and of the Church. The end point is the end of time as we know it, which is where the book ends, and where Satan's career also ends. However, it is not the end for Jesus, nor for the overcoming church, because subsequent to this end, there will be a new beginning, and the Church will continue on for ever as the Bride of the Lamb.
- The two main protagonists are timeless, being spiritual beings who exist and operate outside time. Nonetheless, their actions have an impact on earth, which is encased in time, and this earthly time period is set out by the author as indicated in the preceding paragraph. The '1000 years' must be symbolic in nature, since human words (and time-frame) are being used to describe a situation which is at root timeless. To do otherwise is to make it an anomaly in its immediate context as well as in the whole book. It has to harmonize with the time frame which is established more clearly elsewhere in the book.
- Jesus can, and does, relate to the world at every generation, at any point in history, from the starting point indicated above. People can believe in Him and be ransomed by His blood for God, at any point in history, and there are no exceptions to this. Likewise the dragon, even though limited in his ability to act, can still act and impact history – mainly through his proxies – at any point in time. He is not at all limited in that respect.
- The career of the Church is also globally summarized in this setting. It adds nothing very new (as would be expected) apart from some nuances and clarifications, but repeats various characteristics previously described. It thereby performs its parallel function as would be expected of a conclusion in a cycle-based book. In particular, the purpose of the people of God is to be kings and priests for God which is in parallel to the first reference to them at the beginning of the book (1:6). Their career is characterized by persecution and even death, but in and through all that, they are victorious rulers. This is in direct parallel with the story of the Two Witnesses in 11:1-14. They remained true to their allegiance to Christ and refused allegiance to the dragon. This is in direct parallel to what is envisioned for them in the content of the Seven Letters. The fact that they can, and do, operate in the heavenly realm as well as in the earthly realm, was prefigured previously in the interludes.
- So then, the description of them in Chapter 20, is also a summary of their career in a global sense, and not a new stage in their career. This career spans the time from which it was possible to become a blood-bought child of God, i.e. after the death and resurrection of the Lamb. It continues on until the

> end of human time, when evil will be removed and all will be glory from then on. This means that it is the global, universal church which is in view, because what is described is timeless. That is to say, any person living on the earth during that time period can participate in this life-style of they so wish. These possibilities have to be open to Christians of every generation, and cannot, therefore, be arbitrarily assigned to only one particular generation.

So it can be seen from this brief discussion, that the structure of the book as a whole constrains and directs our understanding and interpretation of Chapter 20 of the book, in a certain direction. If we are going to be honest about this, and are going to treat the author with the respect which he deserves, then these factors must of necessity be taken into account.

It is the author's job to tell us what he means to say, both by the words on the page and also by the way in which he has organized those words into paragraphs and cycles. By the same token, it is the reader's job to listen carefully to all that he has said, and derive the book's message from that alone, and not from preconceived ideas imposed on the book from the outside, two thousand years later. Once again, the readers need to decide what they are going to do with those remarks.

8.5.7 The Hortatory Purpose – Keeping the Main Point the Main Point

The main objective here is to remind us that the main purpose of the book as a whole, is to be read as an extended exhortation to the people of God. Through the visions and words which John received, the Risen Christ is at great pains to make sure that everyone who reads the book has a good understanding of what is going on. He deals squarely and clearly with everything: the good, the bad and the ugly, and nothing important is overlooked.

So then, He tells us all about the bad stuff: where it came from, and who is behind it all. But He also tells how God plans to deal with all that once and for all, along with all the people who have chosen to go that way in life.

But He also tells us about the good stuff: how His death has made new beginnings possible for those who so choose. It is now possible, for the first time in history, for all people to escape the devil's deception. This means that everyone has the possibility to belong to God, to be free to do good things themselves, and to no longer do what is devilish and destructive.

Then there is the ugly stuff: so He does not hide the fact that His people may still suffer and even be martyred, but in doing so He also reassures them that they will come out winners in the end. The devil is still active on the earth by different means, but the bottom line is that God's people, as they follow the Lamb wherever He goes, will always be the ultimate rulers of the earth realm.

As people read all this, it is intended that they make their own decisions. Decisions to refuse evil, and to receive the good, to choose life and so avoid death, especially the second death.

This means that the whole book, and not just parts of it, must be available to, and relevant to, every generation of people living on the earth. It is not set out as an instruction manual, for it is much more intricate and interesting than that. This means that even though the overall message, the tone of the book, is really quite clear, the reader is left, nonetheless, with some work to do. Really and truly the best exhortations, or stories with an important moral, are like that. So the crucial parts of the book are the 'how to' parts, which do not occur just in one place but are woven through the whole texture of this text. Sometimes with direct instructions, but more often woven into the fabric of someone else's story, or of a parable of some kind.

If such a book is going to have any value at all to accomplish its hortatory purpose, which is to influence people's volition, or decision-making machinery, then it must be accessible. It must be accessible to all generations of people, from Pentecost until the Parousia. Otherwise, there is no point at all in it having been written, preserved at great cost, and translated multiple times into hundreds of languages, so that the nations can read it for themselves.

That is what we mean by saying that the message of this book is timeless. Its whole texture and tone is that it is timeless and, therefore, of eternal value to people of all eras. Everyone has the right and privilege to scour all its pages and to appropriate all its truths for themselves.

INFORMATION

The word in Hebrew for 'a mystery' is *sod*, or *sod-ot* in the plural. This is what Hebrew scholar, Andrew Roth has to say about it:

The word *sod* has a power and majesty to it that is unique to Hebrew, and the Aramaic term *araza* and Greek *apokalupsis* are pale substitutes for it by comparison.

Roth 2024, 9

8.6 Discovering the Mysterious Nature of Revelation's Message

We are getting to the end of our journey. The macro structure of this amazing book, as it has been preserved in Greek, has been analyzed and described to the fullest extent that is possible, with the resources which are currently available. We have also taken an exploratory trip down into the lower levels of the structure, in order to demonstrate that everything fits together and is in harmony. All along the way, we have tried to unpackage the meaning of the text to make it as accessible to everybody as possible.

8.6.1 The Discovery of the Mystery Hebrew Version of Revelation

But there is one more thing which we need to do before bringing our journey to a close, one more revelation to bring to your attention. In the course of the work accomplished to prepare this book, an extra, unexpected discovery was made, and we have made brief references to this discovery in the course of the preceding chapters. This discovery was that a version of Revelation existed in Hebrew which had never been translated into English, and so remained inaccessible to modern day readers.

This particular version is the one which was found in the nineteenth century in Cochin, in south-west India, in a synagogue of the, so-called, Black Jews. This was taken to England by Claudius Buchanan, and eventually ended up in the library of Cambridge University. Since 2024 it has been made available in English and the most useful version can be found in Baca 2024. Other versions can be found in the references under Jones and Van Rensberg.

Kadavumbhagam Ernakulam Malabar Jewish Synagogue in Cochin India

So, one might ask, why did this manuscript end up in India? Nobody really knows, of course, but an educated guess can be made. History informs us that the Hebrews had colonies all along the western coast of India for centuries prior to the time of Jesus, and these continued in existence right until the twentieth century, when the remaining people of Hebrew descent migrated back to Israel. These colonies primarily served as trading posts, but in times of adversity, they also became obvious places of refuge and self-imposed exile. This happened several times in Israel's history, and it is for the same reason, that there were also large colonies of Jews in Spain, right up until the

Middle Ages. So one of those times when a place of refuge was needed was, of course, at the time of the destruction of Jerusalem by the Romans, in AD 70.

In the case of the colony at Cochin, one of these events was recorded for posterity in the best way they knew how, and that was by a painting of the arrival of Jews in Cochin seeking refuge. Whenever it was they arrived, the Jews would have brought with them their precious possessions, including their sacred scrolls.

Receiving Jews in Cochin, India

Naturally enough, some of those arriving in AD 70, may have been Jews who believed in Jesus as their Messiah. Consequently, they would almost certainly also have brought copies of what are now the New Testament Scriptures, including the book of Revelation.

As various people looked into this, it was realized that a number of different versions of the Hebrew Revelation existed which were not all the same, and many of them seemed clearly to be translations of the Greek version. However, the Cochin version, cited above, has a number of linguistic features, which strongly suggest that it was the original version, and that the Greek version was translated from the Hebrew. See Van Rensberg 2022 for more details on this matter.

8.6.2 The Discovery of the Mystery Word Chain

As would be expected, there are some differences between this Hebrew version and the Greek version. The most important of these have been explored in Van Rensberg 2022,17-61. For myself, I made mention of the absence of the title 'the Alpha and the Omega' in the information box in section 8.1, and the absence of 'the souls of those who have been beheaded' in 20:4, in Appendix A7.3.11. But I have saved the best for last.

It is fortunate, or perhaps we should say that it is a divine overruling, but there are no differences which cause any really major theological problems. The ones which I mentioned above, might well disturb some people's sacred cows, but perhaps a little worldview re-alignment may help to smooth over the difficulty. But, there is, nonetheless, one difference which caused a shiver to go down my spine, when I first came across it.

The most intriguing, or shall we say, the most mysterious, difference between the Hebrew and the Greek occurs right in the first word, of the first sentence of the book. In the Greek it starts out *apokalupsis...,* which means 'a revelation'. In the Hebrew it starts out as *ele ha' sodot...,* which means 'this (is) the mysteries'. Both then go on to say that the revelation, or the mysteries, are about Jesus and were given by God to John.

This difference is intriguing for several reasons. The first is that these first words introduce for us the topic of the book, as has been explained several times previously. This change means, therefore, that our perspective of the topic has to change. Fortunately, the two words have some similarities so that the difference is not enormous, but at the same time, they are definitely not the same word.

> **QUOTE**
>
> **No non-Hebrew reader would fully comprehend the whole point of (the aforementioned word *sod*) ...a wider Gentile audience...would very much be drawn into a "revelation" instead, (but) without a true appreciation of the original Hebrew meaning.**
>
> **Roth 2024,9**

Greek actually has a word for mysteries, and this word is used four times elsewhere in Revelation, so then, why was it not also used here in 1:1? This question actually reveals a linguistic anomaly in the Greek version of Revelation. Given that it is so totally Hebraic in nature, it is extremely unusual that this key word 'a revelation', which occurs as the first word of the book, only occurs once in the book, and is never repeated. This would certainly not be normal style at that period, even for a writer in Greek.

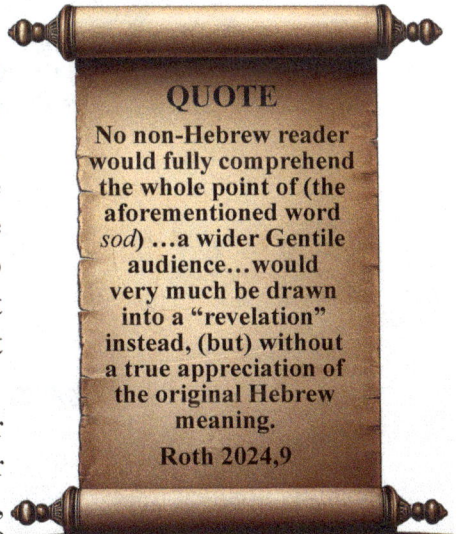

As we have seen before, linguistic anomalies of this nature are resolved when the Hebrew version is consulted. Hebrew has several words for 'a revelation', but to my knowledge none of them are used in the book. So, we are in the process of observing that the writer of the Hebrew used the word for ‘mysteries’, or ‘secret counsels’, not only here in this position of door-keeper to the whole book, but also four other times in the book.

Yes, that is right, the four places where the Greek uses ‘mysteries’, the Hebrew word is also ‘mysteries’. The difference which we are explaining here, is the fact that the Hebrew also has this word in first position as well.

This makes a total of five occurrences of the word in the book, which is a very appropriate symbolic number, which gives us another intriguing word-chain to explore. This is laid out in detail in Chart 66.

Chart 66.
The Word Chain based on the word ‘Mystery’ in the Hebrew Version

A. These are the **mysteries** concerning Jesus the Messiah 1:1

B. The **mystery** of the seven stars: these are the seven angel messengers 1:20

C. The blowing of the trumpets by the seven angels will accomplish all the **mysteries** of God which He announced to His servants the prophets 10:7

B' On her head was written a name, a secret, a **mystery**: Babylon the Great... 17:5

A' I want to tell you the secret, the **mystery**, of the woman 17:7

(The English translations are based on the Hebrew text rather than the Greek text.)

Just looking at it superficially in English, the arrangement in the form of a chiasm is not strikingly obvious, except that the central sub-unit C is a very important part of the book, as we have seen previously, and contains a very strong, direct speech. These features make it very prominent in its original context and make it, therefore, an obvious candidate to be found at the center of a chiasm. In addition, it is different from, and longer than, the other sub-units, in the context of the word chain. So these kinds of clues can stimulate further research, which can yield fruitful results.

In looking into it further, we can see that the first two sub-units are about Jesus, both of which are very near the beginning of the book. In contrast to that, the last two are about Babylon, which is the last negative protagonist to appear, very near the end of the book.

In addition, in the finer detail, there is some repetition of the same words, and repetition of some similar sounds, which creates assonance based on the sibilants *'s'* and *'sh'*, as follows.

- In 1:1 in Hebrew it begins *ha'sodot... l'yeshu ha'mashiach* 'the mysteries concerning Jesus the Messiah'. It also has the word for an angel in close proximity.
- In 17:7 you will find the words *ha'sod m'ha'isha* 'the mystery concerning the woman', with an angel also in very close proximity. Then, in addition, the name Jesus (*Yeshua*) reoccurs just in the preceding sentence, once again in close proximity to *ha'isha* 'the woman'.
- In 1:1 the name of God appears immediately before Jesus' name, and whenever His name appears, that is important. But it is written and pronounced, *ha'shem*, which means 'The Name', and provides another *sh-* sound, to add to the assonance. In this case, it is written with an abbreviation, since it represents God's name, but it makes no difference to the pronunciation.
- In 17:5 the word *ha'shem* reoccurs, the only difference being that it is written out in full, because it means 'the name', referring to the woman. The full phrase is *ha'shem shel ha'sod* 'the name of the mystery', which uses the word *ha'sod* again, plus an extra sibilant sound.

This data shows that there is quite a bit of repetition at the word and sound level, to warrant the positing of a series of parallels, which links these different verses, even though they are widely separated in the discourse. But that is not all, because, as you push on further, there are a number of conceptual parallels as well.

- In 1:1 the mysteries concern Jesus, the Messiah, whose name means 'savior' and whose title means 'anointed'. In becoming a savior, He made a way to God. He became the door, or the gate, to God, and was known as the Prince of Peace.
- In 17:7 the mystery is about Babylon. At the very beginning this name probably meant 'the gate of god', or 'of the gods' (Young n.d.,66). In other words, all the early cities were built on hills because these high places were considered to be the best way to get close to, and to make peace with, the gods. However, this system was a failure and the name, Babylon, later came to mean the place of chaos and confusion. Like Jesus, she was clothed in a purple robe, but her name was associated with all sorts of abominations and unclean things – quite the opposite of what is associated with someone who is anointed. Instead of providing salvation for the people, she preyed on them, and sought to destroy them.

This is another contrastive comparison between Jesus and an evil protagonist, just as in Chapter 20.

- In 1:20 the mystery is about the seven stars. The mystery is that these stars are, or represent, angels or heavenly messengers. From the beginning of time, the stars were seen as spiritual powers and rulers, or representatives, messengers or agents of such rulers. In this case, the stars are angels who are the messengers, whose task it is, to serve the Church and to bring helpful and edifying messages from Heaven to them.
- In 17:5 Babylon is portrayed as an authority, just as stars are. But she was a lower authority representing other spiritual powers more senior than herself, just as stars, or angels, were. In the wider context of 17:9, it is said that she is seated on seven hills. These, as mentioned above already, represent places of authority which connect with the spiritual high places. The purpose, in the case of Babylon, is to ensnare and enslave the people of the earth in the name of the evil spiritual powers, which she represents.
- The stars, or angels, represent a spiritual system which connects Heaven with the earth. These seven representative messengers, bring messages of hope, wisdom and salvation to the people on the earth, notably the people in the church. The angels are part of a wider system of angels whose task is to bring about God's plans for good for His people.
- Babylon represents also a system which connects the evil spiritual forces of darkness with the earth. There are no stars associated with her, but instead she is said to be a place where demons live (18:2). Through her messages of seduction and enticement, along with false promises and vain illusions, she deceives the people of the earth on behalf of the dragon and his proxies. The result for those who listen is fear, hopelessness, and stupidity, and the end result is that they go to their doom, under the judgment of God, and end up in the lake of fire, with all the other agents of that evil system.

This is an implicit comparison of two groups of people and two systems of world government. On the one hand, Jesus is King and He rules from Heaven over His people, the Church, using angels as intermediaries. Together they rule the earth, and will do so for ever. Babylon is the name for the opposing, evil world system controlled by the dragon, who is also a spiritual being, operating in the spiritual realm, through spiritual intermediaries. By deceiving and using the people who obey him and his beastly representatives, he tries to rule the world. But he fails, he always fails, and will end up in the lake of fire.

It can be seen then, on the basis of the data provided, that this word chain also forms a discernible pattern. It sets up a dramatic contrast between Jesus and Babylon, to form a matching pair with the contrast between Jesus and the dragon. These word chains form, as it were, gold threads in the book, which draw our attention to certain facets of the book, which would not be otherwise noticed. This one, in particular, would not have been found without the discovery of the Cochin Hebrew Revelation.

INFORMATION

The set of comparisons inherent in the chiasm in Chart 66 above are somewhat more ephemeral and conceptual than some of the others which we have studied previously. As a consequence, they have to be explained more carefully, but once this is done, it can be seen that the similarities are present, and so the concept of parallelism between the disparate texts is also present. For the Hebrews, with their view of the world, this was not a problem. They were very flexible and had good imaginations and seemed to take delight in creating, and then sniffing out, all sorts of seemingly impossible comparisons. This was facilitated by the fact that their language has a limited vocabulary and is absolutely crammed full of images and pictures of all sorts. At the same time, it was a system of numbers as well. Anne Hamilton 2023 and 2024 (et al.), has done us a great service by exploring and discovering, against all the odds, many of these hidden comparisons which exist in the Scriptures, the Hebrew based ones especially. My favorite one is the similarity between a sandal and a fish. When she was first challenged to consider the similarities between these two words and concepts, she was convinced that there could not be any connection between them. But much time and scrutiny later, she became convinced that there was indeed a connection between these items, and that she was not just imagining it. These connections turned out to be numerous. They were impressionistic, theological, numerical, cultural, religious, legal and cartographical, and maybe there are more which are yet to be discovered. See Hamilton 2023,187-203 for more detail on the connections between footwear and fish.

However, the most important thread is the central one, which tells us, in no uncertain terms that, all of God's mysteries will be accomplished. These mysteries are His secret counsels which He has held in His plan from since the dawn of time, but now is the time to reveal them. The good news is that we have the privilege of living in the era during which these mysteries have been revealed and are, therefore, accessible to us. That is not to say that these mysteries are easy to grasp, for they embody spiritual truths which have to be understood in spiritual terms, that is, in God's terms. But we are being told here that not only will these mysteries be revealed, but they will be accomplished as well.

So, the process may require us to shelve some of our preconceived ideas, and it may require a shift in our worldview, but all these things are possible if we are willing to follow the instructions on the box, that is, to repent, and to persevere. If we are willing to do that, then we will find that these mysteries will lead us to freedom, hope, faith, new life, victorious living, increased authority and eternal glory. It is the best way to find, and to bring to fruition, our final, most fulfilling destiny.

Let's explore the content of some of those mysteries, before we close out this book.

8.6.3 The Discovery of the Mystery Sub-Topics in the Prologue

> The Apostle Paul tells us this: **there is a hidden mystery**, conceived before time began, and hidden for all time until now, which has been revealed for the benefit of all the nations. God has planned it, so that those who know Christ, and are known by Him, can now hope to embrace and experience this glorious mystery.
>
> He goes on to say: I want you to know how much I fight for you, so that in your innermost being you may be caught up to rest in the Father's arms, and be inextricably entwined in the timeless texture of God's love. For, it is only from this position, that you will discern and receive for yourselves, the enormous riches of wisdom and knowledge which adorn God's great mystery. This mystery which had been hidden since all ages in the annals of Heaven but has now been revealed to you. **God's mystery is Christ.**

(An Expanded Translation of Colossians 1:26-27 and 2:1-3.)

We have been preparing the way for this moment for a long time, because we have explained the notion of a topic on several occasions previously. In the course of that previous discussion we have seen that, in the Greek version, the topic of the book is 'a revelation' given by God. Then, in due course we observed that this revelation is all about Jesus, and that it is about Him, and was given through Him.

However, now that we have access to the Hebrew version, that definition of the topic needs to be slightly revised. This is because the Hebrew version tells us that the topic of the book, is ***'the mysteries'*** (plural), which God gave, ultimately to John, to give to the churches. If God gave them then He must have known beforehand what they were, for these secret counsels obviously came from Him, which reinforces the notion that He had a plan, and that this book is all about the outworking of that plan. The other difference which we can notice is that the word 'revelation' in the Greek, is an abstract concept, which is very resonant with Greek thinking and the Greek way of talking about things. It is not a word that is provocative in any way. It is very general, vague and theoretical, and carries no imagery or content with it. It is a neutral word and not very inspiring.

On the other hand, the word 'mystery' is very much in line with the way the Hebrews thought and talked since, as we have seen in previous discussion, it was the focus and goal of their education system. This was so much the case, that they were world renowned for being very interested in mysteries, which means that they must have talked about such things a lot. Regardless of that, the words 'mystery', or 'secret', for any one, even for a child, is a very vibrant, dynamic word. Even though, by the very nature of the word, it has no specific content, it evokes an immediate interest and a burning desire to know what that mystery, or that secret, might be. The whole point of a mystery is that there must be something fascinating near at hand, which we will want to find out about.

Chart 67.
The Five Mysteries About Jesus in the Prologue

1. The Faithful Witness who Revealed God to Us 1:5
2. The First-Born from the Dead who Saved Us 1:5
3. The Ruler of the Kings of the Earth 1:5
4. The One who Loved Us and Freed us by His Blood 1:5
5. He Made Us to Be Kings and Priests for God 1:6

But apart from that, the rest of the definition does not change because those mysteries must, of necessity, be about Jesus, since Jesus is the topical thread which runs all through the book from the first verse right through to the last verse. So the interest for us then, is to look at the book again through the new lens of the word *sod,* 'a secret mystery' and see what new riches that can reveal to us about Jesus, who is the center of interest for everything.

The first place to look is at the beginning, where the sub-topics are laid out as, previously discussed in Chapter 7.4 above. In this case, we are reviewing what John told us about Jesus in the Prologue, and looking to see what mysteries about Him are being revealed.

The characteristics attributed to Jesus which occur in those introductory verses, when John specifically starts presenting the content of his message, from 1:4 through to 1:6, are set out in Chart 67.

Jesus, the Faithful Witness

This title is clearly referring, in summary form, to the time when Jesus was alive on the earth. It is clear that, in the author's mind, this aspect of His earthly ministry was the most important of all of them. This is already a bit of a mystery, before we even start, because it would be very unusual to find a human book which summed up Christ's ministry in this way, attributing its most important accomplishment to that of being a faithful witness.

So what does it mean to be a faithful witness? A witness is someone who talks about, and, you could say, does publicity for, someone, or something else. The complementary word used in Revelation is that the witness *testifies* about that other person. We know from the Gospels that Jesus came to earth to reveal the Father. He did this in three ways. He talked constantly about the Kingdom of God. In doing so He talked about the Father's position of reigning over the affairs of the earth, and of His plan for redeeming humanity.

Secondly, He demonstrated the Father's ruling power over all aspects of Creation, and His compassionate love for people, by the signs and wonders which He performed. Then thirdly, by His death and resurrection, He concretely exhibited the purposeful determination of the Father to remove Satan from the power equation, and to fully and finally, redeem a people for Himself. A people who would live with Him in a relationship of love for ever. He was faithful in accomplishing that assignment, and saw it through to the end, when He could rightfully say 'It is finished!'.

So, we are proposing here then, that this mission to be a faithful witness for the Father is the first mystery about Jesus which this book reveals. We can argue that it is the most important of them all, because it is a generic summary of everything which He did, and which He continues to do. It is not surprising therefore, that this thread about being a faithful witness occurs regularly throughout the book. Not only do we find out throughout the book specific insights as to what it means for Jesus to be a faithful witness, but in addition, we see how John himself, and the churches, were also called to imitate this example, and to be faithful witnesses in their turn.

Jesus, The First-Born from the Dead

This mystery obviously refers to the mystery of Jesus' resurrection. He went willingly, and by His own choice, down into death, even though He did not deserve it, and did not need to. In doing so He was faithful to the Father's assignment. But the great secret, which had been hidden from human eyes from the beginning of time, then was revealed.

In theory, death had a grip on every human born since the time when Adam and Eve betrayed their first covenant with the Father, and made a new one with the dragon. This is why death is called humanity's last enemy, because it is the greatest, the most all-encompassing enemy, and is awaiting every single one of us at our last moment of earthly existence. It is the last enemy to be faced and, as such, the last one to be dealt with.

But there was a secret plan held in reserve for such an eventuality. If a man lived perfectly on the earth, without breaking his covenant with the Creator, and was then unjustly put to death, then death would not be allowed to hold him. Then, in breaking that death grip, death's grip on the whole of humanity would, in turn, be removed. God's righteous laws would be respected by this process, but the curse introduced in the Garden of Eden would be reversed at the same time.

That is an amazing mystery which fooled everyone, including the most powerful of all the lesser spiritual powers. It was the master plan, and the check-mate move, which changed the course of history for everyone, timelessly, from the beginning of time, until the end of time.

This is a mystery to do with reigning. It is about who has the authority to decide what happens on the earth. In this case, it has been decided that death no longer has the last word about anyone or anything, but Jesus does.

Jesus, The Ruler of the Kings of the Earth

This is another mystery to do with reigning. We have said it before, and it is worth saying again: the whole story of human history is about who rules the world. The Creator's plan and choice was that humans should rule the world. But, unfortunately, those first representative humans chose, using their God-given free-will, to give that authority over to the dragon. Since that time, he ruled over the world, still through humans, because he could not change that basic law of the universe. But, nonetheless, he made sure to use humans who worshiped and obeyed him, instead of their Creator.

The system which he installed to accomplish this is called Babylon, and by this means he ruled the earth using the human kings of the earth. However, things changed when the Faithful Witness came on the scene.

As we have already seen, when Jesus conquered death, He also conquered the entire network of evil which enslaved humanity. So it is then, that the heavenly realms rejoiced when the seventh trumpet sounded (11:15-17). This was the moment when it was proclaimed loud and clear, that the Lamb, who had been killed and raised to life, had taken up His great power to reign, and would reign over the earth for ever.

Just to spell it out, so that we do not miss the enormity of these events. In the same context (10:7), we are told that God's great mystery will be accomplished upon the signal of the seventh trumpet. This is it. The Lamb is now the ruler of the earth. All is now clear. The mystery has both been accomplished and has also been revealed.

Then, to complete the story, it is proclaimed in advance in 14:8, that the whole evil infrastructure, called Babylon, has fallen, and its destruction is described in 16:19, along with the fall of the cities of the nations under its control. This detail is important because it is from their cities and citadels, that the human kings exercise their rule over the nations. They no longer rule as they did before, because the Jesus, the Faithful Witness has become the Ruler of the kings of the earth.

Nowhere in Revelation, or elsewhere in the Scriptures, are we given a time frame, in earthly terms, of exactly when this moment of truth took place, when Jesus took over the authority to rule over the earth. It could actually have happened right at the moment of His resurrection. However, from what we know, it is most likely to have happened at the time of His ascension or soon after.

Jesus, The One who Loved Us and Freed us by His Blood

This mystery has to do with redemption, and is the one which, perhaps, expresses to the greatest degree, the Father's heart of compassion towards humanity. It clearly refers to Christ's death on the cross. This is because it is by His death, as represented by His blood, that people can be freed from death's clutches, and re-established in a correct, covenantal relationship with their Creator.

This mystery is the one which was the most frequently hinted at in the Old Testament, and portrayed therein, by various images and symbols. Nonetheless, how it would all work out in practice, still remained a mystery until Jesus appeared to complete His mission. Obviously, if the powers-that-be had understood God's secret plan, then they would never have nailed Jesus to the cross. Fortunately for us, the secret was kept intact until after the fact, when it could then be revealed and talked about without constraint.

This mystery matches the second one above, because they are the only two which specifically, and directly, refer to Jesus' death and resurrection. The first one focuses on the reigning part of the doublet, and this one focuses on the redemption part of the doublet.

Jesus, Who Made Us to Be Kings and Priests for God

This mystery is similar to the first one listed above. This is because it combines allusions to both reigning and redemption. Since priests historically shared the task of ruling the people, along with the kings, these two functions are clearly governmental functions. So, what this mystery reveals to us is that Jesus' purpose in accomplishing His mission was to redeem humanity, so that they could be restored to their rightful place in human history. God's intended function for them was to serve God as priests, and to reign over the earth as kings. So now, because of what Jesus had accomplished, this could actually happen, just as had been decided at the dawn of time.

Chart 68.
The Five Mysteries About Jesus Viewed As a Chiasm

A. The Faithful Witness who Revealed God to Us 1:5

B. The First-Born from the Dead who Saved Us 1:5

C. The Ruler of the Kings of the Earth 1:5

B' The One who Loved Us and Freed us by His Blood 1:5

A' The One who Made Us to Be Kings and Priests for God 1:6

The first mystery in this list is that Jesus is the Faithful Witness. His task was to serve God by representing Him according to the plan. This plan was that He should demonstrate God's power by ruling over the various domains of the earth. He was also destined to represent and reveal God's love by redeeming mankind.

Once the people had been freed by His blood, then they were also qualified to become faithful witnesses, in their turn, as mentioned previously. But under the category of this mystery, it becomes plain that that mission of being a witness, was intentionally accomplished by continuing a ministry towards God as priests, for the benefit of the people. Then in parallel, the witnesses were also destined to create a connection between God and the earth-realm, by functioning as kings.

In conclusion it is reasonable to suppose that this list of Jesus' various accomplishments creates a five part chiasm. Since each description is very short, there is not much scope for the parallels to be based on individual words. Consequently, the chiasm, which is set out in Chart 68, can only be posited on the basis of the underlying concepts. My seasoned opinion is that such a set of connections would have been quite acceptable to the Hebrews. But I leave it to the reader to make up their own mind on the matter, since it is an interesting embellishment to this discussion, but is not essential for its validity.

The evidence for the parallelism is briefly given in the discussion above. The most important observation arising is that the center of the chiasm states that Jesus has been established in the highest possible position of human government. He is the King of kings, and now rules over all the kings of the earth. This extra vignette continues to confirm that the theme of government, particularly the question of who rules the earth, is a dominant theme in Revelation.

The Apostle Paul apparently received special insight into these mysteries concerning Jesus. Here is a summary of what he had to say about this in Ephesians 1:19, 3:3-4,9, 5:32 and 6:19. He is quite clear and matter-of-fact about it all.

God has taken great delight in preparing and bringing to light this long range plan. The mystery of it, but now revealed to us, is that everything both in Heaven and on Earth, will be brought to completion, and will be accomplished, in, through, by, for, and because of, who Jesus Christ is, and what He has accomplished.

This mystery was not known in previous generations but was only revealed in the spirit to His prophets. But now, the stewardship of this mystery has been entrusted to us, the apostles, for the benefit of you, the nations.

Our task is to steward this mystery so that it is plainly seen and understood by the spiritual rulers in the heavenly places. This is accomplished when all that Christ has accomplished, is seen to be demonstrated, and lived out, in front of them, by the Church. Part of this mystery is that Christ and the Church are so united and joined together in this task, that they can be considered to be like a husband with His wife.

Let us pray for boldness, then, so that we may steward and proclaim this mystery, as we ought to.

8.6.4 The Discovery of the Mysteries About Jesus in the Rest of the Book

Once we realized that Revelation was probably originally written in Hebrew, it is, in any case, very Hebraic in nature, and once we realized that the original key word was ‘a mystery’, rather than ‘a revelation’, then that changed a lot of things. As we have seen in the previous paragraphs, this new information produced a complete, five-part chiastic word chain, which was not available to explore previously. Then it led us to review the sub-topics listed in the

Prologue, in the light of this new information, and that produced another intriguing chiasm to investigate.

But the exploration process should not stop there. Now that we know that mysteries concerning Jesus are a crucial part of the book, then it gives us every reason to look for more mysteries about Jesus in other parts of the book as well. Knowing what we now know about the characteristics of Hebrew discourses, then we can envisage that this information will not be found in a discrete block somewhere. The different parts of it are likely to be found, seemingly scattered throughout the book, like an expanded word chain. However, on closer study, it is quite probable that this semantic thread will be arranged in an intentionally intricate pattern of some kind. Let's see what we can find.

As we can see in Chart 69, there are, once again, seven items (+ 1) in the thread, and we do not have to look far to find the first part of it.

Chart 69.
The Seven Mysteries About Jesus in the Book

1. The Mystery that Jesus is Coming Again 1:7 and 22:12
2. The Mystery of the Seven Stars and the Seven Lampstands 1:20
3. The Mystery of the Lion Who Is A Lamb 5:5-6
4. The Mystery of the One Who Fits the Bill 5:7-14
5. The Mystery of the Vulnerable New-Born Baby 12:1-6
6. The Mystery of the Conquering King 19:11-21
7. The Mystery of the Bridegroom 19:7-9 and 21:1-2, 9-10
8. = 7 + 1 The Mystery that, like God, Jesus is Eternal 1:8 & 22:13

The Mystery that Jesus is Coming Again 1:7 and 22:12

The five mysteries which were listed in Charts 67 and 68 were described together above, because they form a homogenous set. They are all descriptions directly ascribed to Jesus, and all occur together in one sentence. The sentence then ends with an emphatic 'Amen!'. Even though the immediately following verse (1:7) is also a description of Jesus, it clearly starts a new linguistic unit, with its own characteristics. In addition, unlike the other mysteries in this thread, it has another very clear echo, right at the end of the book, which is in an almost identical context, as will be noted below. Consequently, it is being analyzed here, as the starting point of the next set of mysteries, and not as the completion of the previous set.

This mystery then, is the very unusual notion that a person who has lived on the earth, and then has died, having finished his race, could come back to life again. Then, not only that, but that he could re-appear in bodily form on the earth once again. But this is what is being claimed for Jesus. Furthermore, this verse is linguistically mysterious as well, because there are several ambiguities, which make interpretation a challenge.

Once again, it has to be said that we cannot take the task of interpreting Scripture lightly. It is not appropriate to impose our ideas on what the author says. By the same token, it is not sufficient to arbitrarily take one side of an ambiguity as the truth of the matter, while completely ignoring the other side of it. As we have said before, the best linguistic approach is to treat both sides of an ambiguity with respect, and to try and find ways to give credence to both of them.

It is basically a worldview problem again. People with Greek-based worldviews usually see things in black and white. For them, an ambiguity has to be forced into an either/or solution. However the Hebrews were much more flexible than that. They enjoyed mysteries and would rather explore the both/and solution. They savored the fact that some things are hidden and unclear, and have to be discerned in order to be appreciated. They relished the process of perceiving how two, seemingly contradictory notions, could be harmonized in order to reveal a truth deeper than the sum of the two parts. So, let's start at the beginning. The text says 'Behold (a prominence feature), he comes with the clouds'. In context, this must refer to Jesus, who is the nearest previous antecedent.

Everyone agrees that the reference to the clouds is a reference to Daniel 7:13. Not everyone agrees on the interpretation of this enigmatic vision, but it is undeniable that the description which follows these words at least, are very reminiscent of how we have been describing Jesus in the last few pages. There is also no doubt that Jesus was described as 'coming to', or 'approaching', the Father on the clouds, at the time of His ascension in Acts 1:9-11.

So the topic of the verse is Jesus – it is about Him – and the semantic focus of the sentence is 'he comes'. This is because it is the verb, which is placed in its normal position at the beginning of the sentence, and is marked for prominence by 'behold'. Right there, it is impossible to state, as some do, that this verse is about judgment. The notion of judgment is not directly present in the verse, and what is alluded to by the reference to weeping, may not be a reference to judgment events at all.

Everyone agrees that the reference here to those who are weeping is a fulfillment of Zechariah 12:10-14. However, if you look at the source text, and its context, it is not talking about judgment at all. The catalyst to the weeping is that God pours out on the people a spirit of grace and heart-felt turning to Him in prayer. The whole purpose and tenor of the text, is that God is working out His plan of salvation and forgiveness, and not His plan of judgment. In support of that, have a good look at Zechariah 12:7-8 and 13:1, which are the preceding and following contexts.

The weeping, as for a child who died too soon, is much more akin to a sorrow and grief due to a premature loss. It speaks positively of regret and remorse, and therefore is very close to repentance. But it does not at all imply weeping due to the fear of an impending judgment which is about to fall on them. This means that our automatic assumptions about judgment, which is due to previous teaching, which does not carefully parse the ambiguities and nuances of meaning, need to be held in check, and possibly revised.

Next, in the Greek, it says that '*every* eye will see Him', just as it says that '*all* the tribes or families of the earth/land will weep'. These two words clearly imply a global event and not just a local event. However, to complicate matters, the Hebrew (because in this chapter we are trying to take into account what is preserved for us in the Hebrew version) does not have 'every eye', but says very plainly that 'those who pierced Him will see Him'. So is it a global event, or is it one which will only be experienced by those who pierced Him, that is, the nation of Israel? Answer: it is ambiguous, because it seems to be saying both things, at the same time!

So, let's go a bit further. The fact that those who pierced Him are among those who will see Him coming again, is not really a problem, because they can be in the Israel category, and they can also fit into the global category, just as easily. However, the phrase translated literally from the Greek as 'the tribes of the earth', creates a double problem of ambiguity.

In the Greek the first word used in this phrase is the normal word for 'tribes', and this word would quite naturally evoke the concept of the tribes of Israel, for example. However, in the Hebrew, it does not use the normal word for 'tribes', but it uses the normal word for 'families', which is different. At the same time, the second noun in the phrase can be translated 'the land', which would imply, in a biblical context, 'the land' of Israel. But, at the same time, the same word can also be translated 'the earth'. This is true both in the Greek, as well as in the Hebrew.

So, between the Greek and Hebrew versions, sometimes using the same basic word, and sometimes using a different word, we end up with a serving of semantic soup. When Jesus comes again, He could be seen by 'all the tribes of the land', including those who pierced Him, or He could be seen by 'all the families of the earth', which would also include those who pierced Him. The first version would imply that it was a local event, only implicating the nation of Israel, while the second version implies that it is a global event, implicating the whole world. So, which is it?

The answer is that we do not know!! There is definite ambiguity, so we need to accept that, and proceed with care, and, in particular, to be careful not to be dogmatic about our interpretations. This means that we cannot make an important theological point depend on our interpretation of a verse like this one.

Since the first part of the verse is clear, the most basic piece of information in the verse is that, when Jesus comes, it will be visible and that everyone will mourn over this event, either in remorse or in repentance. It is not very likely, therefore, that this could refer to a local event only implicating Israel. If it had happened like this in the past, then surely there would be some historical record of such a major, visible event, and, as far as anyone knows, there is no such record. In addition, if that had happened, then clearly Jesus then went back to Heaven, and life carried on as before. Such a scenario does not cohere at all with the rest of Scripture and with the rest of Revelation.

INFORMATION

To complicate matters there are underlying textual variants in 1:8. For those interested in such matters they are as follows. The phrases are given in abbreviated form but are given in the same order in which they appear in the various versions. The forms of 22:13 are also given for comparison.

1:8		**22:13**
First/Last, Beginning/End, He who Is/Was	**Hebrew**	First/Last, Beginning/End
Alpha/Omega, Beginning/End, Is/Was	**T.R.**	Alpha/Omega, Beginning/End, First/Last
Alpha/Omega, He who Is/Was…	**M.T.**	Alpha/Omega, First/Last, Beginning/End
Alpha/Omega, He who Is/Was	**C.T.**	Alpha/Omega, First/Last, Beginning/End

T.R. = Textus Receptus Greek Version. **M.T.** = Majority Text in Greek. **C.T.** = The Critical Text of both the Bible Societies Greek version and the Nestlé-Aland Gk version. Fortunately, these differences do not change the overall thrust and meaning of the verse.

In the case of Revelation's internal data, it needs to be pointed out also, that this verse is the first part of a doublet, which creates an *inclusio*, and so it needs to be read in the light of its matching pair, which is 22:12. In this second part of the doublet, the reference to Jesus' coming is not identical, but, nonetheless, both verses are immediately followed by the reference to the Alpha and the Omega, in the Greek, and to the Beginning and the End, in both the Greek and the Hebrew. So, when the total context is taken into account, these two verses are clearly in parallel with each other, and are not parallel, in the same way, with any other verse.

The extra, new information which is provided in 22:12 is that, when Jesus comes again, He will bring His rewards with Him, and it will be the time when He then renders to each person according to what they have done, while living on the earth. The Hebrew version just uses a verb for 'reward', and not a noun followed by a synonymous verb, but the meaning is the same: 'to reward', or 'to repay', good or bad, as the case may be.

The first point to be made then, is that the word 'reward' is a positive word, and clearly implies positive recognition of those who have served Him faithfully. This supports the proposal made a few paragraphs previously, that some of the weeping which will occur upon Christ's return, may be weeping due to repentance, and, in this case, it may even be tears of joy and relief.

Secondly, this does not preclude the possibility of judgment, for the 'reward' for those who have resisted and disobeyed Him, can also include punitive retribution. But, the point is, in either case, this must happen at the end of time, when Jesus returns definitively to wrap things up. This can only be true if it is a global event encompassing all the families of the earth, and cannot be a local event only concerning Israel. Having said that, the inherent ambiguities do not at all exclude the possibility of Jesus 'coming' at other times in history, to bring retribution on those who deserved it, as clearly happened in AD 70. He says as much Himself in Cycle 1, so there is enough wriggle room to include various possibilities within the broad sweep of the generic universal, end-time event, which is in view here.

So, it can be seen then, that this mystery concerning Jesus is quite mysterious, because it has taken a lot of space to explain all the possibilities and all the innuendos. But it is necessary to do this, because if we do not make an attempt to take account of all the data, then our analysis, and its concomitant interpretation of the text, may well be inadequate and misleading.

So having done all that work, we can now state with confidence that one of the mysteries which are definitely revealed in this book, is that Jesus is definitely coming back again in a visible manner. Not only that, but at that time also, there will be a universal prize-giving – some for good, and some for not so good. Let us all listen to what the Spirit is saying to the churches.

The Mystery of the Seven Stars and the Seven Lamp Stands 1:20

This is certainly a very enigmatic description of Jesus, which is very brief and only adorned with the scantiest of explanations. However, as we look at the details closely, we can see that this is another doublet, where there are two different pictures provided, but which, nonetheless, communicate a complementary and consistent message.

In section 8.6.2 above, we have already mentioned the seven stars in some detail, and these are angels, who represent spiritual, or heavenly, authorities. They are messengers, or Heaven-sent agents, who connect the heavenly realm with the earth realm. Yet, Jesus is seen as holding them in the palm of His hand. This means that He is closely connected with them, and it clearly implies that He controls them, and so, as their Master, He also calls them when needed, and sends them on missions. But in this case, these particular angels have a particular assignment to the churches, so that means that their main task, is to take messages, and to make connections, between Jesus and the churches.

The other part of this doublet of images is traditionally represented by a candlestick in English. However, it was really and truly a lamp stand upon which oil was burned. This is confirmed by the Hebrew version, which uses the well-known Hebrew word for lamp stand, which is a *menorah*. This specific word, immediately establishes a clear connection with the menorah which was a central feature of the Israelite Temple and all its religious ritual. So there is continuity implied here, but continuity with a difference. In the Temple there was one central menorah, but now there are seven, for apparently each of the seven churches has its own menorah, just as it has its own angel messenger.

Traditionally, based on the Greek version, we have been given to understand that the lamp stands represent the churches. So, as we imagine this scene, it looks as if Jesus is standing surrounded by the seven lamp stands, as if He was standing in the middle of a grove of trees. Or, to make it more dynamic, because the text does not actually specify what Jesus is doing, maybe we could say that He is walking in a garden, as if in among its trees. This reminds us of another Old Testament antecedent, because it recalls how God walked with Adam in their garden at the beginning of time. This is certainly not unreasonable.

However, the Hebrew version highlights a different detail, which does not negate what has just been described, but makes it more dynamic than ever. In the Hebrew version, it does not say that the lamp stands represent the churches, but it says that the seven menorahs represent seven elders. So this means that Jesus is standing, or walking, whichever you prefer, in amongst seven people, which clearly implies relationship, intimacy and conversation. This is now getting quite dramatic and life-like, and no longer something which is stiff and starchy, abstract, and soul-less.

With this perspective in view, we can make a new connection between the stars and the lamp stands, which was not possible before, based on the Greek version alone. We have said before that stars are heavenly authorities, or representatives of such authorities. Now we can point out that elders are also authorities, but they are based on the earth, representing earthly families or communities.

So, having done all that work to literally flesh out the picture of Jesus which is given in this verse, we can now discern with more clarity what this mystery is all about. The picture we have is Jesus, in His bodily form doing two things at once. On the one hand, He lightly balances seven stars in His glorious grip. However, as you look more closely, the stars morph into seven glittering and glowing figures which move, which dance, if you like, as if they are alive. Yes, that is right, they are living angels. They are not dancing on the head of a pin this time, but dancing with joyful anticipation, on and around the palm of their Master's hand, ready to be launched off into an assignment at a moment's notice.

But, on the other hand (please forgive the pun!), He is also walking and talking together with a group of wise, experienced men, who nod with understanding as they, in turn, commune with joyful anticipation, with their Master. They too are ready to be launched off into their next assignment at a moment's notice. How exciting is that?

The mystery is that Jesus is at the center of all this activity. He is the meeting point, the touchstone, and the hinge between Heaven and Earth. He is very closely associated with all that goes on in Heaven, and directs its activity. Yet, at the same time, He is also closely associated with what goes on, on the earth, especially as regards, His Body, the Church. In this double, pictorial embodiment of this mystery, Jesus is seen as masterfully involved in the angelic activity which goes on in the Heavenly realm. Yet, at the same time, He is seen to be entwined in an intimate, personal relationship with His human followers on the earth. There is nobody else quite like this.

The Mystery of the Lion Who Is A Lamb 5:5-6

The next mystery concerning Jesus is to be found in the Setting to Cycles 2-6, in Chapters 4 and 5 of Revelation. This setting describes what is going on in the Heavenly throne-room, and John is witness to this scene.

In the course of his observations, and of his conversation with those around him, John is told that someone called 'the Lion of the Tribe of Judah' is there to save the day. This Lion is also known as 'the Root of David', which in itself is a mystery for this implies that He was the very first of David's antecedents, but at the same time His claim to fame is that He is also issued from the tribe of Judah, as David was. Nonetheless, both titles connect him intimately with King David of the Old Testament, and a study of David's story will also help us understand what this mysterious Lion is really like.

However, the great mystery of this second double image, is that when John turns to look for this lion, what He sees, to his astonishment, is a lamb. But it was not any kind of lamb, for it was one which looked as if it had been sacrificially killed, and yet it was standing there as alive as ever. The extra details about this lamb which are often overlooked, is that it had seven horns, which represent perfect, if not divine, authority. In addition to that, it had seven eyes, which indicate how perfectly well it can see everything, for these eyes represent the seven spirits of God, no less, which were referred to previously in the Prologue at 1:4.

This particular mystery has been quite well fore-shadowed in the Old Testament. Consequently, we know about sacrificial lambs and why they were necessary. We also know a lot about lions, who are reputed for being the kings of the jungle, and, as mentioned above, the connection with King David does a great deal to flesh out what this particular king is like. He is a mighty conqueror, and highly successful in all his campaigns.

In short then, there is one person in view, and that is Jesus, but He has two primary personas, or two primary functions. The first is that He has a redemptive function, and so, by the shedding of His blood at Calvary, like the sacrificial lambs which prepared the way for Him, He paid the price for all humanity to be redeemed for God.

But then, at the same time, and by the same event, He earned the right to reign. This is because He faced down and defeated, all the powers of darkness, including death itself. By so doing, He successfully set in motion the greatest military mission in the history of the world, and accomplished the greatest victory of any conquering commander, who ever embarked on any previous campaign to set people free from tyranny. This one is a mighty mystery indeed, for this is the Lamb, who accomplished more than all the lambs in history ever did, and this is the King who out-kings all the lions, and all the human kings, who have ever existed as well.

The Mystery of the One Who Fits the Bill 5:7-14

This mystery is intimately linked with the previous one and is to be found in the same part of the book. This mystery is to do with worthiness, to use an old-fashioned term, or you could say, in more modern terms, it has to do with who is qualified to undertake a certain task.

When John was transported to Heaven in Chapter 4, he was taken to witness a crashing crescendo of praise, but also a celestial crisis. Books, or scrolls, seem to be quite important in Heaven, because it appears that everything which is decided and done, is written down and recorded for posterity. But the protocols would also seem to be quite strict, such that everybody has their place, but they must also stay in their place and do what they are supposed to do, without impinging on the freedoms and functions of others.

So in this case, John tells us, there was a scroll which had been written, presumably way in the distant past, which had some instructions which were due to be put into action when the time was right. So the time was right, and this was being announced in Chapter 5, so that all could hear. Evidently, this was a very important event, like the opening of a will, for example, and we may dare assume that John had been summoned to the throne room himself, precisely for this purpose. Perhaps a living human was needed both as a witness, and also as a prophet to take the news back to earth, so that everyone could now know about this mystery.

But the contents of this scroll were so particular and, presumably, so important, that it was not for just any one to open it, but it had to be the right person, the one who was suitably qualified to do so. So here we are then, with everybody assembled in the HQ of the universe for this momentous event, when the crisis occurred. Nobody was found anywhere in heaven or earth, or even under the earth to add to the suspense, who was qualified to step forward and open the scroll, and to look into it in order to read it. For us, it would be like coming together for a wedding and the bride was not there, or assembling for a coronation, but only to find that the crown prince had taken flight to parts unknown.

However, the crisis was averted because it turned out that Jesus was the mystery figure, the only person in the whole universe who was qualified to open the seals of this scroll. He was qualified precisely because He had earned the right to be the Lamb, who was also a Lion, as described in the previous paragraphs. So now we also know what this mystery is. There is someone who fits the bill, the only person qualified to show us the way back to God, by the path of redemption, and the only one qualified to reign, because He has already defeated all of our enemies. His name is Jesus.

The Mystery of the Vulnerable New-Born Baby 12:1-6

In Chapter 12 we come across another mystery. There we find a mother who gives birth to a son, right in the face of a huge and horrible dragon, who is positioned so as to destroy this vulnerable baby, even before he has barely opened his eyes for the first time. Even though there are three participants in this vignette of a story, yet, the flow of the narrative tells us that it is this baby who is the most important part of the story.

So there are several mysteries here all rolled into one. Firstly, it is all about signs, and the participants are neither introduced, nor identified. For the mother, we have to figure her identity out from the symbols provided, and this we did earlier. We deduced at that time that the most likely identity was that she is the mysterious, unknown, and unnamed woman who will produce a head-crushing 'seed'. The dragon is only identified after this story of the baby is finished, and the baby is not identified at all. So everything is very mysterious.

Secondly, what we are told about the baby is that, even though he is barely born, yet he is to lead the nations like a shepherd, but also with a rod of iron. The verb in the Hebrew clearly implies both the action of leading, or even driving, and the presence of a shepherd. Furthermore, the Hebrew verb is a present participle which suggests that even as he is born, the baby is already leading the nations. This is another mystery. How can a new-born baby lead, or rule over, the nations, and why would a shepherd need a rod of iron in order to look after his flock?

Thirdly, this baby has no earthly father in the story, which would seem to be rather unusual, since a child's identity is usually dependent on knowing who his father is. Yet, even though he would seem to be an orphan, from a human point of view, nonetheless, when his life is in danger, God steps in to rescue him. Even though it is not stated clearly, it is almost as if God treats him with the same care as He would His own son.

If this were all the information we were given about this child, then it would be impossible to decipher the meaning of these signs, and the mystery would remain impenetrable. However, every text has a context, and so we have the context of Revelation, and of the whole Bible, which enables us to delve into the depths of this mystery. Genesis 3:14-15 tells us about the circumstances of the baby's birth of a mother, with no earthly father, and of his relationship to the dragon. The Gospels leave us in no doubt that there was a person whose birth fulfilled this mysterious prophecy in a remarkable way. There was baby who was born as a victorious world ruler, victorious even over the fiercest spiritual ruler of them all.

Then, Revelation itself, tells us that this remarkable person came in order to defeat the dragon, and thereby to take back the authority to rule over the nations. It also gives us enough information to know that, if they needed a bit of pressure to whip them into shape, then He would not be averse to using a rod of iron. Who is this remarkable person? His name is Jesus. When He is brought into the picture, then all these mysteries become clear.

The Mystery of the Conquering King 19:11-21

So we move on to the next mystery, which is that of the rider on the white horse. Once again, as in most of the previous mysteries in this list, the main protagonist is not directly identified. It would hardly be a mystery otherwise. Nonetheless, the writer gives us some clues – seven of them to be exact –

which enable us to put the pieces together. So this person on the white horse has the following characteristics.

- He is called Faithful and True
- He judges and wages war with righteousness (reigning)
- His eyes are like the flames of a fire (personal characteristic)
    - **He is a supreme king because He is crowned with many crowns**
- He has a mysterious name, unique to Himself (personal characteristic)
- He is clothed in a robe which has been dipped in blood (redemption)
- He is called the Word of God

If you look closely you can see that it creates a chiasm. This, in turn, means that the central item is the most important. This characteristic indicates that He is a supreme ruler, which confirms once again that the predominant thread in the whole book concerns ruling and reigning. As if that was not enough, when the set of seven characteristics is completed, there is a clear new beginning at verse 14, since there is a new grammatical subject, which introduces a new sub-topic and new participants. These are the armies of Heaven, who follow the King wherever He goes, just as the redeemed from the earth followed the Lamb wherever He goes, as recorded in 14:4. But this brief switch in the topic, only serves to introduce another five characteristics of this mysterious King, as follows:

- He is followed by the armies of Heaven kitted out in fine white robes
- He has a sword issuing from His mouth in order to strike down the nations
    - **He shepherds/leads them with a rod of iron**
- He rightly rebukes them with the fierceness of God's anger, because they tortured the earth (this is a translation of the Hebrew where there is no reference to a wine press)
- The name written on His clothes is King of kings and Lord of lords (there is no reference to his thigh in the Hebrew)

Once again, the central component of a probable chiasm has to do with ruling and reigning. In addition, the total number of characteristics in these two lists is 12, which is the number which symbolizes government. There are a remarkable number of truth gems hidden within these mysteries.

So, as we have seen before, since many of these clues are repeated elsewhere in the book, we can accumulate enough insight to perceive that this mysterious person is Jesus.

The Mystery of the Bridegroom 19:7-9 and 21:1-2, 9-10

This is another mystery, among all the other mysteries. Even though we are searching for mysteries concerning Jesus, He is not obviously, and directly, present in these texts. It is as if He is still hiding, or waiting, in the wings. In addition, even though we have put the word 'Bridegroom' in the sub-title, there is no reference to a bridegroom in these texts either. This is the thing with mysteries, they are not obvious at first glance, otherwise they would not be mysteries. By definition, they require some work on the part of the reader, who needs to know how to read the signs, follow the trails, and make the connections, in order to derive that deep satisfaction which comes from finally solving the mystery.

In this case, we have a preview of the mystery in the first text, and a double confirmation in the second. So this repetition indicates to us that this is information which is important, and needs to be noticed, even though it is not directly in focus in these passages.

The actual information which we are given, is that there is a bride who has made herself ready for her wedding, and the actual marriage is referred to. So, in the course of that revelation of crucial information, we are told that it is the bride of the Lamb who is in view, and that the marriage is the marriage of the Lamb. So we know that much, and from there we have to refer back to the mystery of the Lamb to confirm that it is, indeed, Jesus, who is the royal Bridegroom.

No more than that is said about the heavenly Bridegroom. If we want to know more about the bride, then we have to study the career of the church, which has been done elsewhere in this book.

8.6.5 A Review of the Seven Mysteries About Jesus

As has been said many times before in the course of this study, Revelation is a very complex book. It is not surprising, therefore, that this smaller study of the mysteries about Jesus, turns out to be quite complicated as well. For that reason, I have decided to divide it up into smaller parts to make it easier for all of us, so that we may best assimilate what is important for us to learn from these mysteries.

So far then, we have seen that here are two sets of mysteries, which are specifically linked to Jesus. The first, was a set of five, which we considered to be in the form of a chiasm, as indicated in Chart 67 above. The second set, which we have just looked at, is a set of seven more mysteries, which makes a total of twelve. So our purpose here, before proceeding any further, is to see if this second set is also in the form as a chiasm. I believe that it is, as indicated in Chart 70.

The evidence for positing this set of parallels is as follows below.

Chart 70.
The Seven Mysteries About Jesus Reviewed as a Chiasm

A. The Mystery that Jesus is Coming Again 1:7 and 22:12
- **B.** The Mystery of the Seven Stars and the Seven Lamp Stands 1:20
  - **C.** The Mystery of the Lion Who Is A Lamb 5:5-6
    - **D.** The Mystery of the One Who Fits the Bill 5:7-14
  - **C'** The Mystery of the Vulnerable New-Born Baby 12:1-6
- **B'** The Mystery of the Conquering King 19:11-21

A' The Mystery of the Bridegroom 19:7-9 and 21:1-2, 9-10

The Evidence for the A./A' Parallel

The first mystery is that Jesus is coming again. Even though the first reference to this event is right at the beginning of the book and of this list, it is, nonetheless, projecting our attention right to the end of history. His coming again obviously occurs right at the end of everything else.

When He comes again, one of His main purposes will be to claim His bride. This is the focus of the last mystery, so this establishes a clear conceptual parallelism between A. and A'.

The Evidence for the B./B' Parallel

The focus of the second mystery is that Jesus operates in two domains at once, as a leader and as a ruler. He relates to the spiritual world, as represented by the angels, yet at the same time He relates to the earth realm. In particular, He relates to His body, and future bride, the Church as represented by the seven elders. So this mystery has to do with Jesus interacting with two realms at once, and accomplishing two tasks at the same time.

This intertwining of two realms and two tasks at the same time, also occurs in section B'. In this case Jesus is seen as the Conquering King and, as such, His focus is on His enemies who are listed in 19:17-21. There are both humans and spiritual beings in this list, which shows that He deals with both domains at once.

However, as well as being a Conquering King, he is also a Commander in Chief, for He does not go into battle alone, or even just with angels. He goes into battle with His followers, who are dressed in the same fine linen as the bride (19:8 and 19:14). So, this piece of information shows that these people are clearly the redeemed members of the Church. Jesus, therefore, obviously relates to these people in the same way as He related to the elders, as He walked among the lamp stands with them in 1:20.

The Evidence for the C./C' Parallel

This set of parallels also involves the intertwining of two different things at once, just like the previous set. In mystery C we have the picture of a person who is both a lion and a lamb, all at the same time. These two images are completely contradictory, as far as human experience and logic is concerned. But that is the point of the mystery. Even though the intertwining of these two opposite concepts seems illogical to us, nonetheless, that is the reality of who Jesus is. He is both a Lion and a Lamb, all at the same time.

It is exactly the same with the mystery which is set out in section C'. In this case, the first part of the central image introduced to us, is that of a vulnerable, helpless new born-baby. But He is not just any normal baby, but is born right into the jaws of a dragon, which could hardly be a more vulnerable and dangerous place to be. Yet, at the same time, this baby is seen as a world ruler even from the moment of birth. He is a ruler who has a shepherd's heart apparently, and yet is not at all disinclined to use a rod of iron in His ruling, if needs be.

This seems to be remarkably similar to the image of the Lion and the Lamb. The Lion is the ferocious, implacable king of the jungle. Yet the Lamb, obviously, would seem to be as caring, and as gentle, as any genuine shepherd would be.

Finally, we can notice that Jesus in His persona of the Lion who is a Lamb, resides in the presence of God, who is seated on His throne in Heaven. Likewise, from the very start, this baby is also seen as living with the Father right near, or even sitting upon His throne.

The Importance of the Central Mystery (D.)

Once again, when you delve into these mysteries, it is not the detail which is lacking. There is plenty of evidence to establish a chiastic pattern. This means, in turn, that the central mystery, D., is the most important mystery of the set. As was mentioned briefly above already, the importance of the mystery in Chapter 5, is that Jesus is identified as a unique person in the universe. As a result of what He accomplished as the sacrificial Lamb of God, He has respect, kudos, and position, add whatever you like to this list, like no other person in the universe. His position is right at the top of the ladder, which is obviously a position of supreme authority, like no-one else, except God, the Father, Himself.

As a consequence of all these factors, we can safely deduce that the opening of the scroll, which is also described in Chapter 5, was not some insignificant and minor affair. Even though the details of the contents are never divulged, it is clear that it has to do with ruling and reigning. Not just over Israel as an individual nation, but over the whole world. Not just for a period of earthly time, but timelessly, for ever.

8.6.6 The Mystery of Timelessness

For those of you who have a penchant for picking up details, you may have noticed that Chart 69 had an eighth item in the original list, which we have not yet dealt with. So, now is the time. When there is an eighth item which has clear connections with a neighboring set of seven, and yet it does not quite fit neatly into that set, then you have a situation where the 7 + 1 principle may resolve the analytical conundrum. The 7 + 1 principle was previously explained in section 8.1.13 above, and is a characteristic of the Hebraic worldview and, for this reason, can also occur in their discourses.

We have here, then, another case in point. The very first of the seven mysteries discussed above, had embedded in it, an analytical problem which we left to one side in order to progress slowly, with a view to rendering the complexities inherent in the text, as simple as possible.

The first mystery is to be found in 1:7 and has to do with the notion that Jesus, who has meantime ascended to Heaven after His stint on earth, but is, nonetheless, due to come back again. This is an element of this mystery, which we passed over very briefly, in the previous discussion. But the point is, how can someone who is reputed to be a genuine human being do this? From our point of view, it is mysterious to the point of being impossible. Human beings normally do not die, or disappear from the earth, and then come back and re-appear again on the earth at some later date. Apart from a couple of very isolated instances recorded in the Bible, including the example of Jesus Himself, this kind of thing just does not happen.

So, what can we do to try and resolve this logical anomaly and make it more comprehensible? One answer is to look at the context and to see if we can find any clues to help us.

So it is then, that this verse is followed by the first reference to the Alpha and the Omega, in the Greek, and to the Beginning and the End, in both the Greek and the Hebrew. As we have said before, the Alpha and the Omega only occurs in the Greek, but the Hebrew, nonetheless, also has a synonymous triplet: the First and the Last, the Beginning and the End, and He who Is, who Was and Is to Come. This conjunction of the concept of Jesus coming again, and of the reference to the one who is the First and the Last, re-occurs in 22:12-13, which means, in turn, that this feature is not an isolated case in 1:7-8, but is part of a larger pattern. As a reminder about these differences between the Greek versions and the Hebrew version, please see the Information box in section 8.6.4 above.

However, upon closer inspection of 1:8, we see that there is some linguistic turbulence here. This is due to the fact that verses 7 and 8 have different topics, and yet are placed next to each other with no overt grammatical or semantic connection between them. This means that they have been put together, but do not belong together in any immediate, logical sense of the word.

Nonetheless, this is normal style at the time, at least for the Hebrews. When two different things are placed together with no connection and no explanation, the message is that the author intends the reader to understand that they do, nonetheless, belong together in some way. Yet, at the same time, he is being purposefully a bit mysterious, and is also saying to the reader that he must do some work, and figure out for himself what the intended connection is.

The big example of this technique in the book is the whole issue of the interludes which was discussed in Chapter 4 above. What is happening here, is the same thing, but just on a smaller scale. In Revelation 1:6, the main topic of discussion is Jesus, with a large section about Him being in 1:5-7, which just precedes verse 8. In the rest of the chapter, after John formally introduces himself in 1:9-10, it is once again, all about Jesus. But the anomaly which creates the turbulence, is that right in the middle of all this, we have this powerful verse which is all about God the Father.

So, is it an anomaly or not? Well no, it is not an anomaly because nothing about God the Father, who is the Almighty, can be considered to be an anomaly. Then, from a linguistic point of view, we can notice that God the Father actually gets a triple mention in this chapter. These are to be found in 1:1, 1:4 and now in 1:8. So a threefold mention of God in a short space like this one, is very appropriate for Him, and is a clear indicator that this is an intentional pattern being created by the author, and is not random forgetfulness, or some other evidence of human febrility. In addition, the reference in 1:4 is identical to 1:8 with a reference to the one Who Is, Who Was, and Is to Come, so this creates an obvious connection between the two verses. This repetition reinforces the notion that there is an intentional pattern which is being created here.

If we can accept then, that there is an intentional pattern here, but that the author has left it to us to discern what the intended message is, then the next step is to observe what the pattern is, first of all. Then, from there, we need to do our best to deduce what the message is.

So going back to the beginning again, to pick up where we left off, the primary aspect of the mystery element of the notion that Jesus is due to come again, is the hint that He is timeless. The verse does not say it overtly, but the hint is there if this idea is to make any sense to us at all. In other words, human beings, normally speaking, cannot come and go from this earth as they please. We are basically living in a box constrained by time and space. No one can get out of that box, and get back in again, for, once we are released from that box at the end of our life, then apart from the exceptions mentioned above, no one comes back again.

So what this means for Jesus is that He is an exception to the normal rule. This means that He must have the capacity to live outside the box of time and space most of the time, and yet He also has the capacity to enter the box of our world when it suits Him. The only other important person who lives outside of our time and space is God Himself, and even though that is still something of a mystery, it is probably something which we can conceive of more easily.

But that is the point of what is happening here. John talks about Jesus coming again, and this is the first time that he does so. In talking in this way, he hints at the mystery of it, that for this to be possible, He must, in some way or another, live a timeless existence. In order to help us along this path of understanding John prepares the way with a reference to timelessness in 1:4. Then immediately after the reference to the coming again, he reminds us about God the Father. He reminds us that He is the Almighty, so that means that He can do anything which He wants to do, and, above all, that He is eternally existent. Unlike us, He is the One who exists, currently in the present. In addition to that, He existed previously in the past, and He is the one we will be constantly moving towards, as we move into the future, because He is already there, existing timelessly.

All those things are true, but from a linguistic point of view, this threesome is just a manner of speaking, or an idiom. It would be possible to talk about God's timelessness in different ways, but this kind of idiom in three parts, is very typical of the way the Hebrews liked to express themselves. The fact of the matter is that this method of expressing oneself is not just unique to them, for it also occurs in other languages as well. So, for example, in English we can say that some one or something is 'here, there, and everywhere', which is a colorful, and forceful, way of saying that something seems to be all over the place. In talking about something which is eternal, or timeless, we might easily say that it goes on 'for ever, and ever, and ever'.

So, the point about this expression as regards God's timelessness, is that it is a dramatic, and, you could say, all-encompassing, way of saying that He has always existed, without any respect for our notion of time.

So this juxtaposition of Jesus' coming again and God's timelessness is only a hint to point us down a certain path of exploration, but we cannot say, just on the basis of these two verses, that Jesus is definitely characterized by timelessness. This is why this mystery of timelessness could not be included directly in the list of seven mysteries about Jesus which we are currently studying. It is definitely alluded to, as we are in the process of explaining, but it is an adjunct to the set, and not a full member. This is why we are invoking the 7 + 1 principle in order to explain the turbulence which this unusual conjunction of concepts is creating. Nonetheless, the mystery of Jesus' timelessness is not just a fanciful idea, because it is present in the book as a whole. But, in order to find it, we need to press on and read the rest of message.

So the complete thread in the book which speaks of Jesus coming again in a definitive way at the end of the world, has three parts. So this makes another triplet, which harmonizes with the triplet which refers to God the Father in Chapter 1. The first of the three is 1:7, which we have just looked at. The next one is in 22:7, but all it says is that He is coming quickly, or soon.

INFORMATION

The phrase 'I am coming quickly', also occurs at 3:11. However this occurrence is ambiguous and it is not at all clear that it is referring to Christ's final, bodily, visible return. This is why it is not included in the list of the three occurrences referring to Jesus' final return. In its context 3:11 is more likely to be referring to a non-visible 'coming', with short term, limited goals in view. This would be similar to the use of 'come' in 2:5. However, the interest of this occurrence of this phrase is that it creates a another triplet of an identical phrase, 'I am coming quickly' which occurs, therefore, at 3:11, 22:7 and 22:12. This goes to show, once again, that Revelation is very deftly woven together, with threads going in all directions, and connecting all sorts of disparate parts. Yet, as you investigate these details it is amazing how systematic it usually is. These threads which do have a significance at the book level, usually occur in sets of two, three, five or seven. A few sets have four components, but I have yet to find one with six parts, unless it is referring to a negative concept.

Semantically it would seem that the purpose of this reference is to create the triplet, but also to re-introduce the notion of Christ's return, after a long silence on the matter, in order to prepare the way for the last reference which is in 22:12. This reference also repeats the word for 'quickly' which links it back to 22:7. Then it also tells us that He is coming with His rewards, which harmonizes with all the other things which will happen at the end, and which are described in the surrounding context in Cycle 7.

But, and this is the big but, verse 12 is followed by verse 13, which is very clearly in parallel with 1:8, which we discussed in the preceding paragraphs. But the big difference between 1:8 and 22:13, is that the first one clearly referred to God the Father, but this last one is clearly referring to Jesus. Although the exact parallelism has been lost in the Greek, it is, nonetheless, retained in the Hebrew version. In this version, in both 1:8 and 22:13, the Hebrew includes the two epithets which tell us that God, or Jesus, as the case may be, is the First and the Last, and the Beginning and the End, as well as the reference to the One who Is, who Was and Is to Come, in 1:8. Even with these textual variants, the concept of timelessness is still present in both texts, even in the Greek. Please see the information box in section 8.6.4 above, for a reminder of the details and the references for the differences between the Greek and Hebrew versions.

So, the deduction which can now be made, is that the author intends us to see Jesus as being very similar, if not identical, to God the Father in this respect. He is, therefore, timeless, because He was at the beginning, and will also be at the end. By the implication of association, He is, He was and He will continue to be existent, just like the Father. He is timeless.

Just to confirm the intentionality of this thread, it too forms a triplet. So there are three references to the One who Is, who Was, and who Is to Come. All three refer to the Father in 1:4, 1:8, and then again in 4:8. But there are also two echoes of the same concept in 1:18 and 2:8, in an allusive, but synonymous form. These two echoes are clearly, and specifically, referring to Jesus. In both these verses He says of Himself that He was dead, which means that He Was, or Had Been, otherwise he could not die, and that He will continue to be alive for ever and ever (and ever), which is the same as saying that He Is to Come.

Then, for good measure in 2:8, it also says that He is living, which means, in other words that He Is, and also, in the same breath, it says that He is the First and the Last. So, if we take all these conceptual parallels as a set, then there are five of them in total, three referring to the Father and two referring to Jesus.

When all these details are taken into consideration, then the deduction becomes concretized. It is unmistakable now, that by the power of association, John has not only made it clear that God the Father, the Almighty, is timeless, just as the Hebrews always believed, but that Jesus, the Messiah, the Christ, the Lion who is the Lamb, is also timeless, just as the Father is. There is no difference between them, because the same concepts are applied to them by the means of using the same set of words to refer to them both, even if it is in different places in the book.

Much to the frustration of many western thinkers whose worldview expects a clear, logical, systematically connected argument, to make a statement like this believable, John did not express his thoughts on this matter using that methodology. He used a methodology derived from a Hebraic worldview. He treats mysteries with the respect which is their due and does not undress them, so to speak. Instead with the reverence due to the subject matter, and to the people concerned, he gives hints on the matter, and points the reader down a certain path, and that is all that he does. For him, and so it should be for us too, a mystery, in the end, is still a mystery.

It is for those who approach the mystery with the same reverential awe, who will know how to follow the trail, and make the connections which are indicated. If we do this, we will be able to perceive the truth of the matter with our spirit, rather than have it all logically figured out with our minds. By their very nature, there are some things about mysteries which can never be logically figured out, and so, if we want to appreciate them at all, then we have to be content with that.

So then, we have taken the time to try and explain the method of communication which John has used, thereby we have explored the path which he has laid out for us, but without riding roughshod over the mystery itself. The end result is that we have another double, intertwined mystery, much as some of the other mysteries have been. The double mystery is firstly that, even though Jesus lived on the earth 2000 years ago now, and has long since been gone again, yet, He is coming again. But at the same time we are shown that He exists outside the world of time that we are encased in. Just like God the Father He is timeless. The logic of this connection is that, in order to come back again in the way envisaged, then He must, of necessity, be exempt from the normal constraints of time.

This means, in turn, that all the mysteries about Him which we have been exploring must also be timeless. Then, as a consequence of that, as well as the mysteries, all the things which we are told about Him in this book, are also timeless. So, it is not possible to remove some of them from consideration by arguing that they were, or will be, only applicable at a certain point of time. It is true that this book was relevant and applicable when it was first written, just as it will still be relevant and applicable at the time when Jesus comes back again. In the meantime, the good news for those of us who may be reading these words in the present day, is that all these words continue to be eternally relevant, and meaningful for us today. They can be appropriated by anyone who cares to exercise their faith and receive them for themselves.

This is what we mean when we say that the message of this book is timeless.

8.7 Conclusion: the End but a New Beginning

In the first version of this study, there were seven chapters. At the time, this seemed to be entirely appropriate for a study of the structure of this book which is so full of sevens. However, in the course of time, as this second edition was conceived and brought to birth, it turns out that it has eight chapters. Nonetheless, this is still entirely appropriate because we have reached the end of our journey of exploration, yet, at the same time, we must evoke the concept of a new beginning before reaching the end of the last page.

So the number seven still has its place. In Chapter 7 we reached the end of the analysis of the semantic structure of the book. This remains the same, and is a complete set of reflections and explanations, which can stand alone. Yet, with the same, new information was discovered which was very important, and needed to be incorporated into the whole, and yet, it by no means fit neatly into the previous set of seven chapters. So the solution was to add one chapter to the seven thereby making eight, and, as is inherent in the 7 + 1 principle, the eighth component ushers us into a new beginning.

This, once again, and doubtless by a divine overruling, happens to harmonize well with the organization of the book of Revelation itself, and creates one of those threesomes which we have been talking about a lot in this chapter. The first part of the triplet is the fact that the book itself ends with an example of the 7 + 1 principle. Since it is a book level feature it was a very unusual and expansive example of this principle, for it was an example of 49 constituents (= 7 x 7), plus one, as was described in Chapter 5 above. So this is how the whole book of Revelation ends: it is the end of the story of Creation and of life on this earth as it is currently. But at the end of everything, we discover a new beginning. It is an amazing and wonderful new beginning which looks out timelessly into eternity, and encompasses a New Heaven and a New Earth.

At this point I need to explain what the extra information was which provoked this eighth chapter. It was the realization, at the end of the study of the Greek text, that the whole of Revelation is very Hebraic in nature. This insight was confirmed when, at an even later date, it came to light that there actually was a Hebrew version of Revelation, which had all the hallmarks of being the original version. As a consequence of this discovery, we were led to explore the mysteries contained in the book.

As we studied those mysteries, we found that we were forced to posit the 7 + 1 principle again, in order to incorporate a good explanation of all the data which was available. So this is the second member of the set, which we just finished talking about a few paragraphs ago.

This then, in turn, brings us back to the subject of this book which also has an ending based on the 7 + 1 principle. So the 7 + 1 principle, the principle of an ending which leads into a new beginning, has come to the surface as a very important component, not only of Revelation itself, but also of this book, which has been written with the goal of shedding some more light on the mysteries contained in God's Word, but preserved for our benefit and enjoyment. I invite you to keep that thought in mind as we wend our way to the end of this conclusion.

So in this eighth chapter, we started out again into our new beginning with an exploration of something new, which was the Hebrew version of Revelation. To begin with, we gave a good overview of the characteristics of a Hebrew discourse, as exemplified by this book, but also with the some examples from the Old Testament.

The most important difference between the Greek and Hebrew versions led us to review the topic of the book, which led, in turn, to explore the mysteries about Jesus which are hidden away within its pages. This is a good example of how new information, and new beginnings, can lead us unexpectedly into a more profound discovery of truth than had been possible in the old system. For it is safe to say that without the insight into the concept of a mystery provided by the Hebrew version, we would never have explored in depth the thread of mysteries in the book. Yet, this process undoubtedly led us to new insights into who Jesus is, and, since He is the topic of the book, this is extremely important. Without the catalyst of the Hebrew version, these hidden gems of truth may have continued to stay hidden for a very long time, if not for ever.

But now the onus is upon us, the readers, for, when all is said and done, it must never be forgotten that the most important part of the book of Revelation overall, is the fact that it is an extended exhortation. Its purpose for existing is to urge the people of God to change their thinking and to change their ways, for this is what repentance means. It is very often the case that when we encounter new ideas on the road of life, then that experience forces us to re-evaluate what we have previously believed to be true, and how we, therefore, have lived out our life, up until then.

This book has purposefully brought us all to a point of closure, which is, at the same time, a vantage point from which we can look out in to the future and envisage new beginnings. In the course of this chapter we have been proposing three possible ways in which we may want to try and change our point of view, in order to be open to receive more of God's life-giving truth, which restores, invigorates and challenges us to move on.

As we have been studying this book, we have had to come to terms with the fact that it is not written according to a style and methodology which we are used to in the western world with its Greek-based culture. Western culture has a preference for straight lines, clear explanations and logically structured arguments. If you look for such things in Revelation, then you will not find them in any significant measure. This misunderstanding has been a stumbling block, which has prevented generations of Bible students from truly appreciating the profundity of its message.

We have been at pains to point out, therefore, that in order to truly come to terms with this book, then we have to be willing to modify our worldview, and to see this book for what it really is. It is clearly a Hebraic book, with a penchant for circles and cycles, for allusions and associations, for parallels and purposefully discontinuous threads. It is most akin to a tapestry with a texture that is subtly sewn together, to form intricate patterns which blend together, rather than being strictly separated. As such, it is not an example of classical architecture, constructed with straight lines, corners and geometrical shapes.

So now that we have come this far and completed a study of the Hebraic organization of the book, and become acquainted with the preferred systems and structures, then a new beginning is possible. It is possible now to go back over the book with these concepts in mind, approaching it with deference to a different worldview. If we are willing to do this, then the possibilities of understanding its purpose, and discerning its subtleties, are considerably expanded.

However, if we do decide to do this, it will not be without its consequences, because a different understanding of this book's message may well have an impact on our previously held theological ideas, especially about the end times, but more than that as well. I know that for myself, one of the first results of completing this research, was that I not only had to adjust my worldview, but also my theological perceptions. However, I do not consider at all that this was a bad thing. On the contrary, I am grateful for the experience and have no regrets. If one is a true seeker after truth, then it stands to reason that, when we discover new truths, then it is to our advantage if misconceived ideas are corrected, and if downright untruth is replaced by the pristine light from Heaven's throne room itself. I trust that if this happens to you as well, that you will take it in your stride, and move on to the beginning of a new season in your life, and in your growth to maturity.

Thirdly, and finally, our theology ought not to be a sterile theory, which has no practical value. Our theology is shorthand for talking about our knowledge about God and His ways. His instruction to us through this book is that we learn about repentance and perseverance, and become capable of living those instructions out in real life. We mentioned repentance before, and the fact that it implies a change of heart and mind. This may mean a change in worldview and theological perspective, but once those steps are in place, then the second instruction comes into play. This instruction is to persevere in doing, and living out, what is right in His sight.

This book serves to confirm what we have probably learned previously from the Gospels. For God the Father the most important person, and the most important in ingredient for all of life and godliness, is a knowledge of Jesus, His Son. We should listen to Him. We have learned, even in this chapter, that there is a lot about Him which are mysteries. But biblical mysteries, especially if approached with a Hebraic mindset, are not designed to stay secretly hidden away out of sight for ever. On the contrary, another of the main purposes of this book has been to bring revelation to us, to bring us into a deeper understanding of these mysteries about Jesus, which have now been set out so that we can all see them and have access to the truths hidden in them.

So this is the most important new beginning of them all. Let's not just close this book and put it back on the shelf, but let's make a decision to persevere, to press on from here and embrace, with great anticipation, a new season of life: a season of exploring, exploiting and expropriating all that we can learn from the mysteries about Jesus.

We have the assurance that the one who holds the seven stars in His right hand, and who walks with ease in and out of the seven menorahs, is still timelessly the same today, as He has been for ever. We all have the invitation and opportunity to follow the Lamb wherever He goes, if we so choose. Following Him will entail all sorts of opportunities and possibilities. He may take us to the top of Mount Sion, or He may lead us into battle against those who would destroy the earth and lead the inhabitants of the earth into death and decay. But, whatever it may be, we can be sure of coming through it all victoriously.

We shall be victorious because the Lamb of God has become the ruler of the world, and nothing can prevent Him from accomplishing God's purposes for the whole universe. The message of this book is not that He will rule and reign over the earth at some distant time in the future, but that He is doing it right now, ever since His ascension to the Father's right hand.

Consequently, if we also decide to follow Him wherever He goes, then, we too, can learn to be overcomers and to rule and reign over the circumstances of our lives with Him, and come out victorious.

So, as we reach the end of this journey together, the possibility of a new beginning lies before us all. The choice is open to each one of us. We can seize the opportunity, if we wish, to decide to become an overcomer by following the Lamb wherever He may lead us, and then to learn to rule and reign over the challenges of life, along with Him. I have done my best to take you down the same purposive chain as John did in Revelation, but now it is up to each person who has come this far to make their own choice.

For the Lord God will make His light shine on them,
and they will reign for ever and ever.
(Revelation 22:5c)

REFERENCES

ABBREVIATIONS

AUSS	Andrews University Seminary Studies, Andrews University Press, Berrien Springs MI.
CBQ	The Catholic Biblical Quarterly
CUP	The Cambridge University Press
EQ	The Evangelical Quarterly
ET	The Expository Times
Int	Interpretation
IVP	The Inter-Varsity Press
JBL	The Journal of Biblical Literature
JETS	The Journal of the Evangelical Theological Society
JOTT	The Journal of Translation and Textlinguistics, The Summer Institute of Linguistics, Dallas.
JP	Jerusalem Perspective, Jerusalem Perspective Publishing, Jerusalem.
JSNT	The Journal for the Study of the New Testament
JSOT	The Journal for the Study of the Old Testament
NIGTC	The New International Greek Testament Commentary
NOL	Notes on Linguistics, The Summer Institute of Linguistics, Dallas.
NOT	Notes on Translation, The Summer Institute of Linguistics, Dallas.
NovT	Novum Testamentum
OPTAT	Occasional Papers in Translation and Textlinguistics, The Summer Institute of Linguistics, Dallas.
OUP	The Oxford University Press
SIL	The Summer Institute of Linguistics
START	Selected Technical Articles Related to Translation, The Summer Institute of Linguistics, Dallas.
TBT-TP	The Bible Translator - Technical Papers, The United Bible Societies, New York.

Allo, E.B. (1933) *Saint Jean: L'Apocalypse.* (Paris: J. Gabalda et Cie).

Alter, Robert (1981) *The Art of Biblical Narrative* (New York: Basic Books).

Alter, Robert (1985) *The Art of Biblical Poetry* (New York: Basic Books).

Alter, Robert and Frank Kermode eds. (1987) *The Literary Guide to the Bible* (Cambridge Mass: Belknap Press of Harvard University Press).

Aune, David E. (1987) *The New Testament in its Literary Environment* (Cambridge: James Clark and Co).

Aune, David E. (1998a) *Word Biblical Commentary Vol 52b, Revelation 6-16* (Nashville: Thomas Nelson).

Aune, David E. (1998b) *Word Biblical Commentary Vol 52c, Revelation 17-22* (Nashville: Thomas Nelson).

Baca, Janice F. (2024) *The Scroll of Mysteries: Cochin Hebrew Revelation* Second Edition. A translation into English of the Hebrew Version of Revelation, based on the Cambridge Manuscript Oo.1.16.2, found in Cochin India. *https://www.academia.edu/119756514/The_Scroll_of_Mysteries_Cochin_Hebrew_Revelation*

Bailey, Kenneth E. (1983) *Poet and Peasant/Through Peasant Eyes.* Combined Edition (Grand Rapids: Eerdmans).

Baldwin, Joyce G. (1972) *Haggai, Zechariah and Malachi: An Introduction and Commentary* (Leicester/Downer's Grove: IVP).

Bandy, Alan S. (2009) 'The Layers of the Apocalypse: An Integrative Approach to Revelation's Macrostructure', *Journal for the Study of the New Testament 31.469.* Also on www.academia.edu

Barr, David L. (1984) 'The Apocalypse as a Symbolic Transformation of the World: A Literary Analysis', *Int 38.1:* 39-50.

Bauckham, Richard (1977) 'The Eschatological Earthquake in the Apocalypse of John', *NovT 19:* 224-33.

Bauckham, Richard (1993) *The Climax of Prophecy, Studies on the Book of Revelation* (Edinburgh: T&T Clark).

Beale, G.K. (1992) 'The Interpretive Problem of Revelation 1:19', *NovT 34.4*: 360-87.

Beale, G.K. (1998) *John's Use of the Old Testament in Revelation* (Sheffield: Sheffield Academic Press).

Beale, G.K. (1999) *The Book of Revelation: A Commentary on the Greek Text (NIGTC)* (Grand Rapids: Eerdmans/Carlisle: Paternoster).

Beekman, John and John Callow (1974) *Translating the Word of God* (Grand Rapids: Zondervan).

Beekman, John, John C. Callow and Michael F. Kopesec (1981) *The Semantic Structure of Written Communication,* Fifth Revision. Reprinted in 2017 and 2022 (Dallas: SIL).

Benthien, George W. (2013) *The Hebrew Language and Way of Thinking* https://www.academia.edu/92312156/The_Hebrew_Language_and_Way_of_Thinking

Bergen, Robert D. (1987) 'Text as a Guide to Authorial Intention: An Introduction to Discourse Criticism', *JETS 30.3:*327-36.

Bergen, Robert D. ed. (1994) *Biblical Hebrew and Discourse Linguistics* (Dallas: SIL/Winona Lake: Eisenbrauns).

Bergli, Agot (2023) *Text Analysis with an Eye to Artistic Patterning,* SIL e-Books 83, www.sil.org/resources/publications/entry/96718 (Dallas: SIL)

Black, David Alan, Katherine Barnwell and Stephen Levinsohn eds. (1992) *Linguistics and New Testament Interpretation: Essays on Discourse Analysis.* (Nashville: Broadman Press)

Bliese, Loren F. (1993) 'Chiastic and Homogenous Metrical Structures Enhanced by Word Patterns in Obadiah', *JOTT 6.3:* 210-27.

Blomberg, Craig L. (1989) 'The Structure of 2 Corinthians 1-7', *CTR 4:* 3-20.

Boring, M. Eugene (1989) *Revelation: Interpretation. A Bible Commentary for Teaching and Preaching* (Louisville: John Knox Press)

Boris, David (2020) *Hebrew Tenses: Language of an Eternal Being – No Past, Present and Future.* www.davidboris.wordpress.com/biblical-languages/ accessed 11/2024.

Bowman, J.W. (1962) 'The Book of Revelation'. In *Interpreters' Dictionary of the Bible* (ed. G.A.Buttrick; New York: Abingdon) Vol.4:58-71.

Bowman, J.W. (1968) *The First Christian Drama* (Philadelphia: Westminster. Previously published by Westminster as *The Drama of the Book of Revelation* 1955).

Breck, John (1987) 'Biblical Chiasmus: Exploring Structure for Meaning', *Biblical Theology Bulletin 17:* 70-4.

Brewer, William F. (1985) 'The Story Schema: Universal and Culture-specific Properties', in *Literacy, Language and Learning: The Nature and Consequences of Reading and Writing,* (David R. Olson, Nancy Torrance and Angela Hildyard eds.; Cambridge: CUP) 167-94.

Bringhurst, Robert (2002) *The Elements of Typographical Style* (Vancouver BC: Hartley and Marks). Quoted on etymonline.com under 'text', accessed July 2024.

Brogden, Chip (2020) *The Book of Revelation (Volume 1)* (Independent Publisher)

Brogden, Chip (2022) *The Book of Revelation (Volume 2)* (Independent Publisher)

Brown, Gillian and George Yule (1983) *Discourse Analysis* (Cambridge: CUP).

Callow, Kathleen (1974) *Discourse Considerations in Translating the Word of God* (Grand Rapids: Zondervan).

Callow, Kathleen (1998) *Man and Message: A Guide to Meaning-Based Text Analysis* (Lanham NY: University Press of America/Dallas: SIL).

Callow, Kathleen and John C. Callow (1992) 'Text as Purposive Communication: A Meaning- Based Analysis', in Mann and Thompson eds. (1992) 5-37.

Ceresko, Anthony R. (1976) 'The Chiastic Word Pattern in Hebrew', *CBQ 38:* 303-11.

Charles, R.H. (1920) *A Critical and Exegetical Commentary on the Revelation of St. John* (Edinburgh: T&T Clark).

Clouse, Robert G. ed. (1977) *The Meaning of the Millenium: Four Views* (Leicester/Downer's Grove: IVP).

Collins, Adela Yarbro (1976) *The Combat Myth in the Book of Revelation* (Ann Arbor: Edwards Brothers).

Collins, Adela Yarbro (1984) *Crisis and Cartharsis: The Power of the Apocalypse* (Philadelphia: Westminster).

Collins, John J. (1979) 'Introduction: Towards the Morphology of a Genre', *Semeia 14:* 1-20.

Cotterell, Peter and Max Turner (1989) *Linguistics and Biblical Interpretation.* (Downers Grove: IVP).

Davis, John J. (1968) *Biblical Numerology: A Basic Study of the Use of Numbers in the Bible* (Grand Rapids: Baker).

Dawson, David Allan (1994) *Text-Linguistics and Biblical Hebrew.* JSOT Supplement Series 177. (Sheffield: Sheffield Academic Press).

Denton, Clifford (2020) *Comparing Greek and Hebrew Worldviews,* Teaching Articles, Article 6/6. https://www.prophecytoday.uk/study/teaching-articles/item/1735

Dooley, Robert A. and Stephen H. Levinsohn (2001) *Analyzing Discourse: A Manual of Basic Concepts.* (Dallas:SIL). A revised version (2023) now available.

Dorsey, David A. (1988) 'Lamentations: Communicating Meaning through Structure', *Evangelical Journal 6:* 83-90.

Dorsey, David A. (1992) 'Literary Architecture and Aural Structuring Techniques in Amos', *Biblica 73:* 305-30.

Dorsey, David A. (1999) *The Literary Structure of the Old Testament: A Commentary on Genesis-Malachi.* (Grand Rapids: Baker).

Erickson, Millard J. (1977) *Contemporary Options in Eschatology* (Grand Rapids: Baker).

Fiorenza, E. Schüssler (1976) 'The Book of Revelation', in *Interpreters' Dictionary of the Bible Supplementary Volume* (ed. K.Crim; New York: Abingdon)

Fiorenza, E. Schüssler (1977) 'Composition and Structure of the Book of Revelation', *CBQ 39.3:* 344-66.

Ford, Boris (1982) *Medieval Literature: Chaucer and the Alliterative Tradition Vol.1.* Part 1 of the New Pelican Guide to English Literature (Harmondsworth UK/New York: Penguin Books).

Ford, J. Massyngberde (1975) *Revelation, Introduction, Translation and Commentary. The Anchor Bible* (Garden City NY: Doubleday & Co.).

Ford, J. Massyngberde (1987) 'The Structure and Meaning of Revelation 16', *ET 98.11:* 327-31.

Frankovic, Joseph (1995) 'The Power of Parables', *JP 48:* 10-5.

Garcìa Ureña, Lourdes (2014) 'The Book of Revelation: A Written Text Towards the Oral Performance', in *Between Orality and Literacy: Communication and Adaptation in Antiquity. Orality and Literacy in the Ancient World.* (Ruth Scodel, ed., Leiden: Brill NV). Vol. 10:309-330 https://www.academia.edu/20085659/The_Book_of_Revelation_A_Written_Text_Towards_the_Oral_Performance Accessed March 2025.

Gentry, Kenneth L. Jnr. (2021) *He Shall Have Dominion: A Postmillennial Eschatology,* Third Edition (Chesnee SC: Victorious Hope Publishing).

Gentry, Peter J. (2008) Kingdom Through Covenant: Humanity as the Divine Image, *Southern Baptist Journal of Theology* 16-42. https://www.academia.edu/1161802/Kingdom_Through_Covenant_Humanity_as_the_Divine_Image accessed November 2024.

Gentry Peter J. and Stephen J. Wellum (2018) *Kingdom Through Covenant: A Biblical Theological Understanding of the Covenants,* Second Edition (Wheaton IL: Crossway).

Giblin, Charles Homer (1991) *The Book of Revelation: The Open Book of Prophecy* (Collegeville: The Liturgical Press).

Grenz, S.J. (1992) *The Millenial Maze* (Leicester/Downer's Grove: IVP).

Grimes, Joseph E. (1975) *The Thread of Discourse* (New York: Mouton (1984)).

Hall, Mark Seaborn (2002) 'The Hook Interlocking Structure of Revelation: The Most Important Verses in the Book and How They May Unify its Structure', *NovT 44:*278-296

Hamilton, Anne (2015) *God's Pageantry: The Threshold Guardians and the Covenant Defender* (Corinda Qld: Armour Books)

Hamilton, Anne (2023) *The Elijah Tapestry: Mystery, Majesty and Mathematics in John's Gospel #1* (Corinda Qld: Armour Books)

Hamilton, Anne (2024) *The Summoning of Time: Mystery, Majesty and Mathematics in John's Gospel #2* (Corinda Qld: Armour Books)

Harvey, John D. (1998) *Listening to the Text: Oral Patterning in Paul's Letters* (Grand Rapids: Baker/Leicester: IVP).

Hayford, Jack W. ed. (1991) *The Spirit-Filled Life Bible,* (Nashville: Thomas Nelson)

Hayford, Jack W. ed. (1995) *Hayford's Bible Handbook* (Nashville: Thomas Nelson).

Hebrew Revelation. See Baca (2024), Van Rensberg J. and M. (2024), and Jones (2021).

Hebrew Verbs. (2025): *Modern Hebrew Verbs.* https://en.wikipedia.org/wiki/Modern_Hebrew_verbs. Accessed April 2025.

Heckert, Jacob K. (1996) *Discourse Function of Conjoiners in the Pastoral Epistles* (Dallas: SIL).

Heimerdinger, Jean-Marc (1999) *Topic, Focus and Foreground in Ancient Hebrew Narratives.* JSOT Supplement Series 295 (Sheffield: Sheffield Academic Press).

Hendriksen, William (1940) *More than Conquerors: An Interpretation of the Book of Revelation* (London: Tyndale Press reprinted 1969).

Hodges, Zane C. and Arthur L. Farstad eds. (1985) *The Greek New Testament According to the Majority Text,* Second Edition (New York: Nelson).

Johnson, Alan (1981) 'Revelation', in *The Expositor's Bible Commentary Vol.12* (ed. Frank E. Gabelein; Grand Rapids: Zondervan) 399-603.

Jones, Miles (2021) *Sons of Zion versus Sons of Greece. Volume 1: The Survival of the Hebrew Gospels and the Messianic Church,* Second Edition (Kerrville TX: Benai Emunah Institute). See also www.writingofgod.com .

Kaplan, Robert B. (1966) 'Cultural Thought Patterns in Inter-Cultural Education', *Language Learning 16:* 1-20.

Kline, Meredith (1996) 'Har-Megedon: The End of the Millenium', *JETS 39.2:* 207-22.

Kuen, Alfred (1997) *L'Apocalypse: Introduction au Nouveau Testament Vol.4* (St Légier: Emmaus)

Kuykendall, Michael (2017) 'The Twelve Visions of John: Another Attempt at Structuring the Book of Revelation', *JETS 60.3:* 533-555.

Labov, William (1972) 'Language in the Inner City: Studies in Black English Vernacular', *Conduct and Communication 3:* 354-96.

Labov, William, and Joshua Waletzky (1967) 'Narrative Analysis: Oral Versions of Personal Experience', in *Essays on the Verbal and Visual Arts :* (June Helms ed.; Seattle: University of Washington Press) 12-44.

Ladd, George Eldon (1972) *A Commentary on the Revelation of John* (Grand Rapids: Eerdmans).

Lambrecht, J. (1980) 'A Structuration of Revelation 4:1-22:5', in *L'Apocalypse Johannique et l'Apocalyptique dans le Nouveau Testament* (J. Lambrecht ed.; Louvain: Leuven University Press) 78-104.

Larson, Mildred L. (1984) *Meaning-Based Translation: A Guide to Cross-Language Equivalence* (New York: University Press of America).

Lenski, R.C.H. (1943) *The Interpretation of St. John's Revelation* (Columbus: The Wartburg Press).

Levinsohn, Stephen H. (1992) *Discourse Features of New Testament Greek. A Coursebook.* Second Edition, revised (2024) (Dallas: SIL).

Levinsohn, Stephen (2020) 'Galatians', in Scacewater ed. (2020) 298-330.

Levinsohn, Stephen H. (2023a) *Self-Instruction Materials on Narrative Discourse Analysis* (Dallas: SIL).

Levinsohn, Stephen H. (2023b) *Self-Instruction Materials on Non-Narrative Discourse Analysis* (Dallas: SIL).

Levinson, Bernard (2020), 'The Significance of Chiasm as a Structuring Device in the Hebrew Bible', *Word and World 40:3*, 271–80.

Lewis, Arthur H. (1980) *The Dark Side of the Millennium: The Problem of Evil in Rev.20:1-10* (Grand Rapids: Baker).

Lewis, C. S. (1950) *The Lion, the Witch and the Wardrobe.* Puffin Edition 1959 (Harmondsworth: Penguin Books) .

Lewis, C. S. (1956) *The Last Battle* (London: Bodley Head). Lions Edition 1980 (London: Collins).

Longacre, Robert E. (1976) *An Anatomy of Speech Notions* (Lisse: Peter de Ridder Press).

Longacre, Robert E. (1980) 'An Apparatus for the Identification of Paragraph Types', *NOL 15:* 5-22.

Longacre, Robert E. (1983a) *The Grammar of Discourse.* (New York: Plenum Press).

Longacre, Robert E. (1983b) 'Exhortation and Mitigation in 1 John', *START 9:* 3-44.

Longacre, Robert E. (1985) 'Discourse Peak as a Zone of Turbulence', in Wirth ed. (1985) 83-98.

Longacre, Robert E. (1992) 'The Discourse Strategy of an Appeals Letter', in Mann and Thompson eds. (1992) 109-30.

Longacre, Robert E. (1999) 'A Top-Down, Template-Driven Narrative Analysis, Illustrated by Application to Mark's Gospel', in Porter and Reed eds. (1999) 140-68.

Longacre, Robert E. (2003) *Holistic Textlinguistics* SIL Electronic Working Papers 2003-004, www.sil.org/resources/publications/entry/7834 (Dallas: SIL).

Longacre, Robert (2020) 'Mark', in Scacewater ed. (2020) 63-90.

Longacre, Robert E. and Shin Ja J. Hwang (1994) 'A Textlinguistic Approach to the Biblical Narrative of Jonah', in Bergen ed. (1994) 336-58.

Longacre, Robert E. and Shin Ja J. Hwang (2012) *Holistic Discourse Analysis,* Second edition, (Dallas: SIL).

Longenecker, Bruce W. (2001) ' "Linked Like a Chain": Rev.22.6-9 in Light of an Ancient Transition Technique', *New Testament Studies 47:*105-17.

Loenertz, R.J. (1947) *The Apocalypse of St. John.* Translated by H.J. Carpenter (London: Sheed and Ward).

Lohmeyer, Ernst (1926) *Die Offenbarung des Johannes* (Tübingen: JCB Mohr).

Louw, Johannes (1973) 'Discourse Analysis and the Greek New Testament', *TBT-TP 24.1:* 101- 18.

Lund, Nils W. (1970) *Chiasmus in the New Testament: A Study in the Form and Function of Chiastic Structure* (Peabody Mass.: Hendrickson Publishers). Originally published as *Chiasmus in the New Testament: A Study in Formgeschichte* (1942) (Chapel Hill: University of North Carolina Press).

Manabe, Takashi (1984) 'Authorial Intent and Intents of Participants in a Narrative Text', *START 1.* Special Edition 3-35.

Mann, William C., Christian M. I .M. Mattheissen and Sandra A. Thompson (1992) 'Rhetorical Structure Theory and Text Analysis', in Mann and Thompson eds. (1992) 39-79.

Mann, William C. and Sandra A. Thompson eds. (1992) *Discourse Description: Diverse Linguistic Analyses of a Fund-Raising Text* (Amsterdam/Philadelphia: John Benjamins Publishing).

Maycock, A.L. (n.d.) *The Apocalypse* (Dacre Press).

McGinn, Bernard (1987) 'Revelation', in Alter and Kermode eds. (1987) 523-41.

McLean, John A. (1991) 'The Structure of the Book of Revelation and its Implications for the Pre-Wrath Rapture, Part 1', *Michigan Theological Journal 2.2*: 138-167.

McLean, John A. (1992) 'The Structure of the Book of Revelation and its Implications for the Pre-Wrath Rapture, Part 2', *Michigan Theological Journal 3.1*: 5-40.

Metzger, Bruce M. (1993) *Breaking the Code: Understanding the Book of Revelation* (Nashville: Abingdon).

Michaels, J. Ramsey (1991) 'Revelation 1:19 and the Narrative Voices of the Apocalypse' *New Testament Studies 37:*604-20.

Miller, George A. (1956) 'The Magical Number Seven, Plus or Minus Two', *The Psychological Review 63.2:* 81-97.

Moffat, James (n.d.) 'The Revelation of St. John the Divine', in *The Expositor's Greek Testament Vol. 5* (W. Robertson Nicoll ed.; Grand Rapids: Eerdmans) 279-494.

Morales, Erwin T. (2007) *Discourse Analysis of the Book of Revelation,* MA Thesis Biola University https://www.academia.edu/32897002/Discourse_Analysis_of_the_Book_of_Revelation_Whole_Thesis Accessed April 2025.

Morey, Earl Wesley (1991) 'The Revelation of Jesus Christ', in *The Spirit-Filled Life Bible,* (Jack W.Hayford ed.; Nashville: Thomas Nelson) 1925-58.

Morris, Leon (1969) *The Book of Revelation; An Introduction and Commentary.* Second Edition 1987 (Leicester: IVP/Grand Rapids: Eerdmans).

Morris, Leon (1972) *Apocalyptic* (Leicester/Downer's Grove: IVP).

Motyer, Alec (1993) *The Prophecy of Isaiah* (Leicester: IVP).

Mounce, Robert H. (1977) *The Book of Revelation.* (The New International Commentary on the New Testament; ed. F.F.Bruce; Grand Rapids: Eerdmans).

Neeley, Linda Lloyd (1987) 'A Discourse Analysis of Hebrews', *OPTAT 1.3-4:* 1-146.

Nestle, Eberhard and Erwin, Barbara and Kurt Aland, Johannes Karavidopoulos, Carlo M. Martini and Bruce M. Metzger eds. (1993) *Novum Testamentum Graece.* 27th Edition, 8th Corrected Version 2001 (Stuttgart: Deutsche Bibelgesellschaft).

Newton, Jon K. (2009) *Revelation Reclaimed: The Use and Misuse of the Apocalypse* (Milton Keynes: Paternoster).

Nida, Eugene A. (1984) *Signs, Sense and Translation* (Cape Town: Bible Society of South Africa).

Palmer, F.R. (1970) *Prosodic Analysis* (Oxford/New York: OUP).

Parunak, H. van Dyke (1981) 'Oral Typesetting: Some Uses of Biblical Structure', *Biblica 62:*153-68.

Parunak, H. van Dyke (1983a) 'Transitional Techniques in the Bible', *JBL 102.4:* 525-48.

Parunak, H. van Dyke (1983b) 'Some Axioms for Literary Architecture', *Semitics 8:*1-16.

Parunak, H. van Dyke (1992) 'Dimensions of Discourse Structure: A Multidimensional Analysis of the Components and Transitions of Paul's Epistle to the Galatians', in Black et al. eds. (1992) 207-39.

Patrick, James E. (2005) 'The Four-fold Structure of Job: Variations on a Theme', *Vetus Testamentum 55.2:* 185-206. https://www.academia.edu/12805235/The_Fourfold_Structure_of_Job_Variations_on_a_Theme accessed November 2024.

Pattemore, Stephen (2020) 'Revelation', in Scacewater ed. (2020) 713-744

Patton, Matthew H. and Frederic Clarke Putnam (2019) *Basics of Hebrew Discourse: A Guide to Working with Hebrew Prose and Poetry,* (Miles V. Van Pelt ed.; Grand Rapids: Zondervan).

Persson, Andrew (2016) *A Semantic and Structural Analysis of Revelation* (Dallas: SIL).

Pike, Eunice V. (1967) 'Skewing of the Lexical and Grammatical Hierarchy as it Affects Translation', *NOT 23.2:* 1-7.

Pike, Kenneth L. (1959) 'Language as Particle, Wave and Field', *The Texas Quarterly 2.2:* 37-54. Reprinted in *Kenneth L. Pike: Selected Writings,* ed. Ruth M. Brend (1972) (The Hague: Mouton) 129-43.

Pike, Kenneth L. and Eunice G. Pike (1982) *Grammatical Analysis* (Dallas: SIL/University of Texas at Arlington).

Porter, Stanley E. (1995) 'Discourse Analysis and New Testament Studies', in Porter and Carson eds. (1995) 14-35.

Porter, Stanley E. and D.A. Carson eds. (1995) *Discourse Analysis and Other Topics in Biblical Greek.* JSNT Supplement Series 113 (Sheffield: Sheffield Academic Press).

Porter, Stanley E. and Jeffrey T. Reed eds. (1999) *Discourse Analysis and the New Testament: Approaches and Results.* JSNT Supplement Series 170 Studies in New Testament Greek 4 (Sheffield: Sheffield Academic Press).

Reed, Jeffery T. (1993) 'Discourse Features in New Testament Letters', *JOTT 6.3:* 228-52.

Reed, Jeffery T. (1995) 'Identifying Theme in the New Testament: Insights from Discourse Analysis', in Porter and Carson eds. (1995) 75-101.

Reed, Jeffery T. (1996) 'Discourse Analysis as New Testament Hermeneutic: A Retrospective and Prospective Appraisal', *JETS 39.2:* 223-40.

Roth, Andrew Gabriel (2024) *Mystery at Travancore: Has the Original Hebrew Renewed Covenant Finally Been Found?* https://www.academia.edu/120168046/Mystery_at_Travancore Accessed December 2024.

Ryken, Leland (1974) *The Literature of the Bible* (Grand Rapids: Zondervan).

Ryken, Leland (1993) 'Revelation', in Ryken and Longman eds. (1993) 458-69.

Ryken, Leland and Tremper Longman eds. (1993) *A Complete Literary Guide to the Bible* (Grand Rapids: Zondervan).

Ryrie, Charles C. (1996) *Revelation,* Everyman's Bible Commentary (Chicago: Moody Press).

Sandford, John and Paula (1977) *The Elijah Task* (Tulsa:Victory House).

Scacewater, Todd A. ed. (2020) *Discourse Analysis of the New Testament Writings* (Dallas: Fontes Press)

Schooling, Stephen J. (1985) 'More on Matthew's Brackets: A Study of the Function of Time References in Matthew's Gospel' *START 13:* 14-27.

Schooling, Stephen J. (1990) *Language Maintenance in Melanesia: Sociolinguistics and Social Networks in New Caledonia,* Publications in Linguistics 91 (Dallas: SIL).

Schooling, Stephen J. (1992) 'The Phonology of Yuanga: A Language of New Caledonia', in *Papers in Austronesian Linguistics No.2.* Pacific Linguistics Series A.82. ed. M.D. Ross. (Canberra: Australian National University) 97-146.

Schooling, Stephen J. (2004) *The Structure of Revelation: A Discourse Analysis Perspective*. A dissertation submitted in accordance with the requirements for the degree of Doctor of Philosophy, from Trinity College, Bristol, validated by the University of Bristol. Available in two parts, Chapters 1-7 and Appendices, https://doi.org/10.5281/zenodo.14346115 and https://www.academia.edu/126201297/The_Structure_of_the_Book_of_Revelation_A_Discourse_Analysis_Perspective_by_Stephen_J_Schooling and https://www.academia.edu/121806000/The_Structure_of_the_Book_of_Revelation_Part_2_Appendices_and_Bibliographies.

Schooling, Stephen (2017) *Can You See? A Study of the Song of Solomon,* (Rothwell: MCM). https://www.academia.edu/126078347/Can_You_See_A_Study_of_The_Song_of_Solomon.

Schooling, Stephen J. (2024a) *God Calls His Unfaithful People Back to their First Love: A Discourse Analysis Study of the Book of Hosea.* https://www.academia.edu/128054142/God_Calls_His_Unfaithful_People_Back_to_their_First_Love_A_Discourse_Analysis_Study_of_The_Book_of_Hosea.

Schooling, Stephen J. (2024b) *Micah's Surprising Role and Message: A Discourse Analysis Study of the 12 Minor Prophets,* being a translation from the French, with additions and improvements, of an article 'La Place de Michée Dans le Contexte des Douze Petits Prophètes' originally published in the *European Journal of Theology VII.1*:25-36 (1998). Now re-published and available on https://biblicalstudies.org.uk and https://www.academia.edu/128054336/Micah_s_Surprising_Role_and_Message_A_Discourse_Analysis_of_the_12_Minor_Prophets.

Schooling, Stephen J. (2025) *The Function of Connectives in NT Greek at the Higher Levels of Discourse: With Special Reference to the Book of Revelation* www.academia.edu.

Sherman, Grace E. and John C. Tuggy (1994) *A Semantic and Structural Analysis of the Johannine Epistles* (Dallas: SIL).

Smith, Christopher R. (1990a) 'The Portrayal of the Church as the New Israel in the Names and Order of the Tribes in Revelation 7:5-8', *JSNT 39:* 111-18.

Smith, Christopher R. (1990b) 'Revelation 1:19: An Eschatologically Escalated Prophetic Convention', *JETS 33.4:* 461-66.

Smith, Christopher R. (1994) 'The Structure of the Book of Revelation in the Light of Apocalyptic Literary Conventions', *NovT 36.4:* 373-93.

Snyder, Barbara W. (1991) *Combat Myth in the Apocalypse: The Liturgy of the Day of the Lord and the Dedication of the Heavenly Temple,* Ph.D dissertation, Graduate Theological Union and University of California, Berkeley.

Spinks, Leroy C. (1978) 'A Critical Examination of J. W. Bowman's Proposed Structure of the Revelation', *EQ 50.4:* 211-22.

Sternberg, Meir (1985) *The Poetics of Biblical Narrative: Ideological Literature and the Drama of Reading* (Bloomington: Indiana University Press).

Strand, Kenneth A. (1979) *Interpreting the Book of Revelation.* Second Edition (Ann Arbor: Ann Arbor Publishers).

Strand, Kenneth A. (1987) 'The Eight Basic Visions in the Book of Revelation', *AUSS 25.1:*107-21.

Tenney, Merrill C. (1953) *New Testament Survey.* Revised Edition 1985. (Grand Rapids: Eerdmans/ Leicester: IVP).

Terry, Ralph Bruce (1992) 'Some Aspects of the Discourse Structure of James', *JOTT 5.2:* 106- 25.

Terry, Ralph Bruce (1995) *A Discourse Analysis of 1 Corinthians.* Publications in Linguistics 120 (Dallas: SIL/University of Texas at Arlington).

Textus Receptus (n.d.) *The Textus Receptus Version of the Greek New Testament* www.logosapostolic.org/bibles/textus_receptus.

Thomas, Robert L. (1992) *Revelation 1-7: An Exegetical Commentary Vol.1* (Chicago: Moody Press).

Thomas, Robert L. (1995) *Revelation 8-22: An Exegetical Commentary Vol.2* (Chicago: Moody Press).

Thompson, Leonard L. (1990) *The Book of Revelation: Apocalypse and Empire* (Oxford/New York: OUP).

Vallowe, Ed. F. (1984) *Biblical Mathematics: Keys to Scripture Numerics* (Forest Park GA: E.F.V. Evangelistic Association).

Van Otterloo, Roger (1988) 'Towards an Understanding of "Lo" and "Behold", Functions of *idou* and *idé* in the Greek New Testament', *OPTAT 2.1:* 34-64.

Van Rensberg Justin J. (2022) *Ele Ha Sodot: The Hebrew Revelation,* pdf file downloaded from www.hebrewgospels.com/revelation July 2023.

Van Rensberg Justin J. and Michael J. Van Rensberg (2024) *The Hebrew Revelation, James and Jude* www.hebrewgospels.com/books (Queensland, Australia: The Van Rensberg Family).

Welch, John W. ed. (1981) *Chiasmus in Antiquity: Structure, Analyses, Exegesis* (Hildesheim: Gerstenberg Verlag).

Wendland, Ernst R. (1985) 'Linear and Concentric Patterns in Malachi', *TBT-TP 36.1:*108-121.

Wendland, Ernst R. (1990) '7x7(x7): A Structural and Thematic Outline of John's Apocalypse', *OPTAT 4.4:* 371-87.

Wendland, Ernst R. (1992) 'A Tale of Two Debtors: On the Interaction of Text, Co-Text and Context in a New Testament Dramatic Narrative', in Black et al. eds. (1992) 101-43.

Wendland, Ernst R. (1998) *Analyzing the Psalms* (Dallas: SIL/Winona Lake: Eisenbrauns).

Wendland, Ernst R. (2014) 'The Hermeneutical Significance of Literary Structure in Revelation', *Neotestamentica 48.2:*447-475. Downloaded November 2024 from www.academia.edu under the title 'Unfolding Sevenfold Revelations: A Literary-Structural Overview of the Apocalypse'.

White, R. Fowler (1994) 'Making Sense of Revelation 20:1-10, Harold Hoehner versus Recapitulation', *JETS 37.4:* 539-51.

Wilcock, Michael (1975) *I Saw Heaven Opened: The Message of Revelation* (Leicester/ Downer's Grove: IVP).

Wirth, Jessica ed. (1985) *Beyond the Sentence: Discourse and Sententiel Form* (Ann Arbor: Karoma Publishers).

Young, Robert (n.d.) *Analytical Concordance to the Bible* (New York: Funk and Wagnell).

OTHER BOOKS BY THE SAME AUTHOR
Still In The Planning Stage

The Seven Mysteries of the Book of Revelation
A Dynamic English Translation of the Hebrew
Version of Revelation
(With Study Aids)

Revelation For Today
365 Meditations Based on the Hebrew Version
of the Book of Revelation

Exploring Hebrew Poetry
A Discourse Analysis of the Song of Songs and Lamentations

Exploring the Hebrew Prophets
A Discourse Analysis of the Minor Prophets

If you would like to keep informed regarding the progress being made on these projects, please feel free to follow me on academia.edu, in which case you should receive updates automatically. Otherwise, check into my home page from time to time.
Any questions or comments are welcome.

Total 742 pages
700 = 7 x 10 x 10 = A Most Complete Testimony
42 = Jesus' First Coming and also His Second Coming

www.ingramcontent.com/pod-product-compliance
Lightning Source LLC
Chambersburg PA
CBHW050218270326
41914CB00003BA/473